495

WORDSW
OF WOR

*General Editor:*

# THE LIVES OF THE NOBLE
# GRECIANS AND ROMANS

# Plutarch
# The Lives of the Noble Grecians and Romans

❖

*Translated by Thomas North*

*Selected, and with an Introduction,*
*by Judith Mossman*

WORDSWORTH CLASSICS
OF WORLD LITERATURE

This edition published 1998 by Wordsworth Editions Limited
Cumberland House, Crib Street, Ware, Hertfordshire SG12 9ET

ISBN I 85326 794 5

Typeset by Antony Gray

Printed and bound in Great Britain by
Mackays of Chatham, Chatham, Kent

# CONTENTS

# INTRODUCTION

## 1 Plutarch and his *Lives*

Here we have a man, sitting in his little Boeotian village, who
has neither a title nor a profession. He is a Roman citizen and
an honorary citizen of Athens, but that does not mean much:
many people are both. But this man does not even want to
become a somebody. He is well-off, but not one of those rich
people who pay for popularity and honours. Yet in his hospit-
able house one does not only meet Greeks from all over the
province of Achaea, but people also come from distant places,
even though Chaeronea is never on anyone's way; and there
come not merely many Romans who have retired to Greece
(including consulars), but also high officials who are passing
through, even the great Governor from Corinth. In such a case
the entertainment becomes as much a burden as an honour, as
it was for ourselves in former days, when the generals on
manoeuvre billeted at an estate. Yet the visitors might miss
their host, because he may be on the way to inspect the
cleaning of the streets of the little town, for he never regards
any municipal office as too lowly for his person. Why should
these people come, except for the man and his personality?
And the only place they can find him is his home.[1]

This was the picture the great German scholar Wilamowitz
drew of the life of Plutarch. Its charm and interest lie partly in the

---

1 U. von Wilamowitz-Moellendorff, 'Plutarch als Biograph', in *Reden und
Vorträge*, 2. 4, Berlin 1926, 247–79, tr. J. Kerkhecker in B. Scardigli (ed.),
*Essays on Plutarch's Lives*, Oxford 1995, 47–74, esp. 52–3.

fact that Wilamowitz clearly saw Plutarch as an earlier version of the Prussian *Junker*, or country squire, that he was by birth himself. Plutarch throughout the ages has been refashioned in the image of those who read him. He has had particular appeal to the general reader, who warms to the agreeable *persona* Plutarch's writings create and thrills to his story-telling skills without fretting too much about historical accuracy; but scholars have enjoyed him too. Wilamowitz expresses important things about Plutarch well: his unambitious yet conscientious approach to local politics, his hospitality, the variety and number of his friends, both Greek and Roman, his love of his wife and family, and his devotion to philosophy and learning. Any account of Plutarch's life makes it sound very pleasant: scholarship, improving travel, family life, local business, a life both useful and beautiful. Plutarch is very good at setting up a vision of himself as someone one would like to have to dinner.

Wilamowitz was wrong about one thing, though: Chaeronea, where Plutarch was born in about 45 AD, is very much on the way both from northern to southern Greece and from east to west; and it is midway between Delphi and Athens. It is the natural place to defend southern Greece once invaders from the north have passed the narrows of Thermopylae. Hence this little town was the scene of two big battles: in 338 BC Greek liberty perished there when Philip of Macedon defeated the combined forces of Athens and Thebes; and in 86 BC Sulla defeated Archelaus, the general of Mithridates, and consolidated Roman power in Greece once and for all. Chaeronea suffered badly from this latter conflict, and was only saved from total destruction by two interventions by Lucullus: this is one reason why Plutarch wrote a biography of him. During the Roman civil wars, Chaeronea also suffered from the presence of Antony's army in Greece: all the citizens of Chaeronea, including Plutarch's great-grandfather, were forced to carry grain for the troops down to the Corinthian gulf, hurried along with whips by Antony's men. Only Antony's defeat at Actium saved them; shortly after the battle Octavian (later the emperor Augustus) sailed into Athens and distributed grain to all the local cities, including Chaeronea. So Plutarch grew up in the shadow of the great stone lion which still stands in commemoration of the gallant end of classical Greek autonomy; at the same time, he and his family had had every reason to appreciate the peace and consequent prosperity which generations of stable Roman imperial rule had brought.

Plutarch probably visited Rome at least twice, once in the reign of Vespasian, some time between 70 and 79, and once in the early 90s under Domitian. He had received the honour of Roman citizenship, probably through the good offices of L. Mestrius Florus, a friend of Vespasian's; Plutarch's Roman name was L. Mestrius Plutarchus. He had many Roman friends, some of them, as Wilamowitz says, very important men indeed. The *Parallel Lives*, and several of Plutarch's other writings, are dedicated to Q. Sosius Senecio, a man of the highest eminence, twice *consul ordinarius* (ie consul for the first portion of the year, the most honourable spell) under Trajan. Throughout Plutarch's *oeuvre* one can discern several competing attitudes to Rome, the prevailing one being great admiration and gratitude to her; but there are also passages which seem more competitive, more concerned to demonstrate something Plutarch perhaps thought the Romans ought to have known already: namely, that Greece had been as great as, and in some ways greater than, Rome. This was perhaps an inescapable conclusion for one who was a devotee of philosophy all his life: Romans, as the poet Vergil and the orator Cicero admitted in very different ways, can't really do philosophy. And philosophy for Plutarch was not just an academic discipline: it was a means of attaining both personal happiness and worldly success, of meeting both triumph and disaster with courage and integrity.

How better, then, to explain the benefits of Greek culture and the glories of her political past to the Romans who were so indisputably now the masters of the world than by a series of related biographies, the *Parallel Lives*? It should be emphasised that in cultural matters Plutarch was not in general preaching to the unconverted: the Roman love-affair with Greek culture was a long-standing one. But, as Donald Russell has pointed out, 'one of the leading themes of the *Parallel Lives* was to demonstrate to the Romans that the greatness of Greece had been political greatness, and that [Greek education] was a road [to good government]. We may think of Plutarch as answering the petulant prejudices of a Juvenal (3.60ff.), and pointing out that not all [Greeklings] were

X    THE LIVES OF THE NOBLE GRECIANS AND ROMANS

tightrope walkers.'[2] Modern analogies are risky; but one might compare Plutarch with a late twentieth century European trying to convince the American public that Europe is not just an endearing theme park with poor plumbing.

Sure enough, again and again in the *Lives*, Plutarch illustrates the importance of *paideia* (education) on the Greek model to his Roman heroes and their Greek counterparts. But he does so in a way which seeks to break down cultural barriers, not reinforce them, and which seeks to improve all his readers, Greek and Roman, not denigrate them or triumph over them. It may be much easier to be a great man if you have *paideia*, and lack of it may often cripple an otherwise fine character and allow great talents to go to waste;[3] but it is not an end in itself. Though proud of his Greekness, steeped in the achievements of Classical Greece, and a learned lover of Classical Greek literature, Plutarch was more a moralist than a propagandist.

Moralism pervades all his writings, both the *Lives* and the amazingly diverse corpus of other writings which in modern times has been known as the *Moral Essays* (*Moralia*). Some of his subjects, like Marius, he regards as moral examples of what not to do or resemble, as he specifically says: but in all the *Lives* the sympathetic power of his characterisations transcends simplistic moralism as well as nationality. The beauty of conveying moral messages through a series of biographies is that the complexity of the moral world can be expressed through the biographical treatment of the individual; Plutarch succeeds in making his central characters complicated and emotionally engaging even when he disapproves of them himself and fully expects us to do so too. In this he surpasses all earlier biography and often attains the emotional heights of tragedy, to which he often directly alludes and which he sometimes uses in very subtle ways.

Take for example the pair *Demetrius* and *Antony*. Plutarch says at

---

2  D. A. Russell, 'On Reading Plutarch's *Lives*', *Greece and Rome* 13 (1966), 139–54, repr. in Scardigli 1995, 75–94, esp. 78. The phrases in square brackets are in Greek and Latin in the original.

2  D. A. Russell, 'On Reading Plutarch's *Lives*', *Greece and Rome* 13 (1966), 139–54, repr. in Scardigli 1995, 75–94, esp. 78. The phrases in square brackets are in Greek and Latin in the original.

3  So S. C. R. Swain in an important essay, 'Hellenic Culture and the Roman Heroes of Plutarch', *Journal of Hellenic Studies* 110 (1990), 126–45, repr. Scardigli 1995, 229–64.

the start of the pair that these two subjects are definitely examples of How Not To Do It: from the tone of this opening and from the comparison of the two figures one might have expected a rather self-righteous litany of tabloid vices. But by adopting tragic imagery in the first *Life*, and in the second adding to that imagery tragic insight and grandeur, Plutarch enriches his subjects and makes them powerfully moving. Demetrius, faced with certain defeat by Pyrrhus, runs away. Not a noble action, but Plutarch gives it grandeur by describing it like this:

> So he went into his tent, and cast a black cloak about his face, instead of his rich and stately cloak he was wont to wear: not like unto a king, but like a common player when the play is done, and then secretly stole away.

Demetrius' funeral is surrounded by 'tragical pomp', and the *Life* ends:

> Now that the Macedonian hath played his part, give the Roman also leave to come upon the stage.

Antony is a more developed character than Demetrius, one of Plutarch's masterpieces; and the *Life* is also illuminated by the characterisation of Cleopatra, whose story is continued beyond the death of Antony in a unique manner. The tragic imagery continues. The Alexandrians say:

> that Antonius showed them a comical face, to wit, a merry countenance: and the Romans a tragical face, to say, a grim look.

But the tragedy in this *Life* runs deeper than the imagery; it consists in the portrait of a basically admirable and likeable person struggling against fate and his baser side and in the end losing everything; and also in the character of Cleopatra, who genuinely loves the man she destroys.[4]

Tragedy looms over other *Lives*, too: it is counterpointed with epic to characterise Alexander and Pyrrhus,[5] and brought to life in

4  See C. B. R. Pelling, *Plutarch: Life of Antony* (ed.), Cambridge 1988.
5  See J. M. Mossman, 'Tragedy and Epic in Plutarch's Alexander', *Journal of Hellenic Studies* 108 (1988), 83–93, repr. Scardigli 1995, 209–28

a hideous way at the end of *Crassus*, where the head of the dead Roman general becomes an obscene prop in the celebrations at the Parthian court:

> The same night Crassus' head was brought, the tables being all taken up, Jason a common player of interludes (born in the city of Tralles) came before the kings, and recited a place of the tragedy of the *Bacchantes* of Euripides, telling of the misfortune of Agave, who struck off [her] son's head. And as every man took great pleasure to hear him, Sillaces coming into the hall, after his humble duty first done to the king, delivered him Crassus' head before them all. The Parthians seeing that, fell a-clapping of their hands, and made an outcry of joy. The gentlemen ushers by the king's commandment, did set Sillaces at the table. Jason casting off his apparel representing Pentheus' person, gave it to another player to put on him, and counterfeiting the Bacchantes possessed with fury, began to rehearse these verses, with a gesture, tune, and voice of a man mad, and beside himself:
>
>> Behold, we from the forest bring a stag now newly slain,
>> A worthy booty and reward beseeming well our pain.
>
> This marvellously pleased the company: and specially singing these verses afterwards, where the Chorus both asked, and answered himself:
>
>> Who struck this stag?
>> None else but I thereof may brag.
>
> Pomaxathres hearing them dispute about the matter, being set at the table with others, rose straight, and went and took the head himself, to whom of right it belonged to say those words, and not unto the player that spoke them. King Hyrodes liked this sport marvellously, and rewarded Pomaxathres according to the manner of the country in such a case: and to Jason he also gave a talent. Such was the success of Crassus' enterprise and voyage, much like unto the end of a tragedy.

This scene shows Plutarch at his best. It is a vividly dramatic picture with very disturbing undertones. The actor on one level is pretending to be mad, and yet there is a strong suggestion that anyone who could play this scene under these terribly realistic circumstances must really be mad, or be about to become so. The original context of the drama is terrible enough: Agave has torn her son to pieces while maddened by Dionysus and appears carrying his head, which she believes to be that of a lion; but the Parthians who applaud this performance know the head is that of Crassus, and applaud anyway, and with enthusiasm. The climax comes when the audience enter the play, and the man who killed Crassus, Pomaxathres, asserts his achievement, destroying the fiction. The horrible reality thus imposes itself over the original drama. Plutarch goes on to report the death of king Hyrodes at the hands of his own son. In that this parricide is a happening from the world of tragedy which intrudes into real life, a satisfying reciprocity is created, which answers the earlier intrusion of non-fiction into fiction.[6]

This is one of Plutarch's artistic climaxes. There is no space to do justice to how cleverly he builds up to these high points. But it should be said that he does not only produce purple patches: he structures his *Lives* very carefully to produce complex characters and exciting scenes. In doing so he has to manipulate the very varied pieces of evidence he uses in order to create his effects. His willingness to change the order of events according to his artistic purpose has led to frustration among historians, and eventually to the decline of his reputation as a writer. But that is to treat him as a historian. As he says himself, he isn't one (though he is by no means without historical sophistication). He is writing biography, not history. Many supposed vices of his writing can be seen as virtues when this passage from the beginning of the *Alexander* is taken into account:

> My intent is not to write history, but only lives. For, the noblest deeds do not always show men's virtues and vices, but oftentimes a light occasion, a word, or some sport maketh men's natural dispositions and manners appear more plain, than the famous battles won, wherein are slain ten thousand men, or the great armies, or cities won by siege or assault. For like as painters or drawers of pictures, which make no account of

6  D. Braund, 'Dionysiac Tragedy in Plutarch, *Crassus*', *Classical Quarterly* 43 (1993), 468–74.

other parts of the body, do take the resemblances of the face and favour of the countenance, in the which consisteth the judgment of their manners and disposition, even so, they must give us leave to seek out the signs and tokens of the mind only, and thereby show the life of either of them [Alexander and Caesar], referring you unto others to write the wars, battles and other great things they did.

If we judge him on his own terms, we can see that he succeeds brilliantly.

## 2   New *Lives*: Amyot and North

Plutarch died, full of years and honours, around AD 120. His fame survived him: he was a popular and respected author in later antiquity and beloved of the scholars of Byzantium, by whom he was preserved. When Greek manuscripts began to return to the west in the fifteenth century, Plutarch was among them, and his works were eagerly translated into Latin, the *Lives* being particularly popular. The first printed edition of the *Lives* in Latin, by various translators, appeared in 1470 in Rome. Many others followed. Later the *Moral Essays* attracted extremely distinguished translators, notably Erasmus, who found Plutarch's style difficult, but very congenial for its variety and for the breadth of the learning Plutarch displays. Vernacular translations of both the *Lives* and the *Moral Essays* into all the major European languages began to be made alongside the Latin versions for the less scholarly public in the early sixteenth century. It is worth considering that this translating activity, at least at its highest level, was being carried on within a complex theoretical framework first developed by Erasmus, and most clearly enunciated by Du Bellay. Both repudiated word for word translation in favour of translating the real sense of a text, and both insisted that the finished product of translation should be seen as a new work in its own right.[7] In that

7   See T. Cave, *The Cornucopian Text: Problems of Writing in the French Renaissance*, Oxford 1979, ch. 2.

context it becomes less inexplicable that an Englishman should want to translate a French translation of a Greek text, probably without ever referring to the original Greek, and yet should have his work highly, and justly, admired in his own day and after.

Plutarch might have had a good deal in common with Thomas North; Jacques Amyot had a career which he might have enjoyed making into a slightly disapproving *Life*. Amyot was born in 1513 at Melun of poor but honest parentage, and studied in Paris, waiting on his richer contemporaries to pay for his studies and reading by firelight because he could not afford candles. Eventually, however, he came to the attention of Marguerite of Navarre and became a Professor at the University of Bourges. At this time he began translating the Greek novels, and then turned to the *Lives* at the instigation of François I, becoming Abbot of Bellozane at about the same time (1546). Royal patronage continued: Amyot was an envoy of Henri II at the Council of Trent, and in 1554 was appointed tutor to the royal princes. He published his version of the *Lives* in 1559, just before becoming Grand Almoner of France, and in 1570 he was given the bishopric of Auxerre. But he fell foul of the Catholic League because he supported Henri III after the murder of the Duc de Guise; his diocese refused to accept his authority. In 1591 he lost his post as Grand Almoner, and he died in 1593 under a cloud.

North's career was less spectacular, rather more like Plutarch's own. He was the second son of Edward, Lord North (the first Baron, Lord Lieutenant of Cambridgeshire and the Isle of Ely). Born about 1535, he was probably educated at Peterhouse, Cambridge. He was supposed to become a lawyer, and entered Lincoln's Inn, but he seems to have preferred writing, and gave up the law. He was described by Lord Leicester in a letter to Lord Burghley as 'a very honest gentleman, and hath many good things in him, which are drowned only by poverty'. In 1574 he joined his brother Roger, who was now Lord North, on an embassy to Henri III; it was presumably on this occasion that he came across Amyot's *Lives*.

He was already an accomplished translator, having produced versions of a Spanish adaptation of the *Meditations* of Marcus Aurelius and a work called *The Morall Philosophie of Doni*, which was translated from the Italian. His *Lives* were first published in

1579, with subsequent editions in 1595 and 1603. In 1588 North commanded a force of three hundred men of Ely during the invasion scare; in 1591 he was knighted. He became a Justice of the Peace in the following year; in 1601 he received a pension of £40 from the Queen, to whom his work was dedicated. He probably died in 1603. He was, according to his great-nephew, 'a man of courage'.

Why did each undertake his translation? The answers are apparent from their respective prefaces, and are not untypical. Like many Renaissance scholars, they argue for the claims of their text by saying that they are both attractive and morally useful. And moral utility can be practically useful, too; even if the morality is pagan, Christians, being inherently better people, can profit all the more from it. So North writes in his dedication to Elizabeth I:

> For, most gracious Sovereign, though this book be no book for your Majesty's self, who are meeter to be the chief story, than a student therein, and can better understand it in Greek, than any man can make it English [she translated *On Curiosity* herself in 1598]: yet I hope the common sort of your subjects, shall not only profit themselves hereby, but also be animated to the better service of your Majesty. For among all the profane books, that are in reputation at this day, there is none (your Highness best knows) that teacheth so much honour, love, obedience, reverence, zeal, and devotion to Princes, as these *Lives* of Plutarch do. How many examples shall your subjects read here, of several persons, and whole armies, of noble and base, of young and old, that both by sea and land, at home and abroad, have strained their wits, not regarded their states, ventured their persons, cast away their lives, not only for the honour and safety, but also for the pleasure of their Princes? Then well may the Readers think, if they have done this for heathen Kings, what should we do for Christian Princes? If they have done this without hope of heaven, what should we do that look for immortality? And so adding the encouragement of these examples, to the forwardness of their own dispositions: what service is there in war, what honour in peace, which they will not be ready to do, for their worthy Queen?

And Amyot had written in his Preface (translated by North):

> The reading of books which bring but a vain and unprofitable pleasure to the Reader, is justly misliked of wise and grave men. Again, the reading of such as do only bring profit, and make the Reader to be in love therewith, and do not ease the pain of the reading by some pleasantness in the same: do seem somewhat harsh to diverse delicate wits, that cannot tarry long upon them. But such books as yield pleasure and profit, and do both delight and teach, have all that a man can desire why they should be universally liked and allowed of all sorts of men. . .

The aim of both translators, then, was to produce a text that would both delight *and* instruct, and, particularly in the case of Amyot, to convey something of the essence of the original:

> Nevertheless if it so fortune that men find not the speech of this translation so flowing, as they have found some other of mine, that are abroad in mens' hands: I beseech the readers to consider, that the office of a fit translator, consisteth not only in the faithful expressing of his author's meaning, but also in a certain resembling and shadowing out of the form of his style and the manner of his speaking. . .

That said, Amyot and North both tend to alter Plutarch's style, often breaking up his periods, adding details and explanations, and imbuing Plutarch with a distinctively Renaissance feeling.[8] As was argued earlier, this was entirely proper in the context of Renaissance translation theory: these changes are not 'inaccuracies', they are legitimate interpretations. The licence they take is probably greater than most modern translators would take (though any translation would have to break down some of Plutarch's periods); but then the result is considerably more vigorous and vivid, and in that sense can fairly be said to convey more of the essence and spirit of the original than a crib. Here are two deaths of Alcibiades:

> The men who were sent to kill him did not dare to enter his house, but surrounded it and set it on fire. When Alcibiades

8  This has been brilliantly demonstrated by D. A. Russell, *Plutarch*, London 1973, 143–58.

discovered this, he collected most of the clothes and bedding in the house and threw them on the fire. Then he wrapped his cloak round his left arm, and with the sword in his right dashed through the flames untouched before his clothes could catch alight, and scattered the barbarians, who fled at the sight of him. None of them stood their ground nor attempted to close with him, but kept out of reach and shot at him with javelins and arrows. So Alcibiades fell, and when the barbarians had gone, Timandra took up his body, covered it, and wrapped it in her own clothes and gave it as sumptuous and honourable burial as she could provide.[9]

Those that were sent to kill him, durst not enter the house where he was, but set it afire round about. Alcibiades spying the fire, got such apparel and hangings as he had, and threw it on the fire, *thinking to have put it out*: and so casting his cloak about his left arm, took his naked sword in his other hand, and ran out of the house, himself not once touched with fire, *saving his clothes were a little singed*. *These murderers* so soon as they spied him, drew back, and stood asunder, and durst not one of them come near him, to stand and fight with him: but afar off, they bestowed *so many* arrows and darts of him, *that they killed him there*. Now when they had left him, Timandra went and took his body which she wrapped up *in the best linen she had*, and buried him as honourably as she could possible, with such things as she had, *and could get together*.[10]

The first is a fair approximation of the Greek; the second changes, or elaborates on, the Greek in the places italicised. The changes were all made by Amyot except one. The addition 'thinking to have put it out' is a fair assumption about Alcibiades' purpose, but is really made necessary because Amyot has decided to translate the Greek word for 'before' as 'except' ('saving that'). The difference which results is that Plutarch's Alcibiades makes no attempt to put out the fire, but simply buys enough time to make

9 Plutarch, *Life of Alcibiades* ch. 39, tr. I. Scott-Kilvert, Harmondsworth 1965.
10 North's version of the same passage.

his rush, whereas Amyot's, and North's, tries to extinguish the flames and rushes out only when he fails. One could argue that that scenario was actually more exciting. But in any case, there are many other ways in which it is North's translation which best conveys Plutarch's whole conception of the death of the flawed but magnificent Alcibiades. 'Naked sword' is much better, and actually closer to the Greek than simply 'sword'. 'These murderers', a change both from Amyot and from the Greek, where they are called simply 'the barbarians' is a lovely, and typically Northian, touch of partisanship, which is present in the Greek, though less openly expressed. 'To stand and fight with him' has a much more suitably martial and heroic ring to it than the flat 'to close with him' (the Greek means literally 'to come to his hands'). Alcibiades in Plutarch, as in the first passage, 'fell'; but to capture the lapidary effect of Plutarch's phrasing in English (or French) it is really necessary to turn the sentence round as North (and Amyot) have done and say 'they killed him there'. 'In the best linen she had' slightly obscures the fact that in the original these were her own clothes: a detail which looks back to Alcibiades' dream before he dies and which emphasises his transgressive qualities; but North's version is legitimate and brings out a pathos which is genuinely in the Greek as well. Adding 'and could get together' is another way of intensifying the pathos in Plutarch's account: the once proud Alcibiades is dependent on the good offices of a prostitute for his last rites, and she does her best for him from her limited resources. Again, it is an expansion, but it is a permissible one, and the end result is a good deal more exciting, and a good deal more musical, than the straightforward version of the first passage.

These qualities of passion, excitement, vigour and accuracy in the Renaissance sense ensured that North's *Lives* went into several editions: the second in 1595, the third in 1603, and the fourth in 1610–12. There was thus every reason, and every opportunity, for Shakespeare to read the *Lives*, as North was a popular author and so (in Latin) was Plutarch.

## 3  *Lives* On Stage: Plutarch and Shakespeare

It is well known that North's translation of Plutarch is the major
source for *Julius Caesar, Antony and Cleopatra, Coriolanus,* and *Timon
of Athens,* and it has been argued that his influence can be seen in
the non-Roman plays, too.[11] This is not really surprising: we have
already discussed Plutarch's dramatic qualities and his affinity with
tragedy. It is also interesting that, whereas ancient tragedy uses no
extended metaphors from the stage, Plutarch uses many, as we have
seen; and so does Shakespeare. Then, too, much of Plutarch's more
profound affinity with tragedy stems from his interest in the great-
spirited characters who are a prerequisite for tragedy. Shakespeare
was never slow to spot potential, and there is plenty of it in
Plutarch. Take *Antony and Cleopatra,*[12] a play where there are in fact
fewer verbal echoes from North than in *Coriolanus,* say, but on the
whole a greater correspondence between the play and the *Life* in
terms of overall ideas. There is one very large exception to that,
namely the character of Cleopatra, who for most of the play is not
the enigmatic but consistent schemer who imperceptibly falls in
love with her victim, as in Plutarch, but a far more mercurial
and paradoxical creation. The last scene serves to illustrate how
Shakespeare skilfully adapts Plutarch's scenic structure to his own
purposes, while retaining a good deal of the original where it is
apparent that it simply doesn't need changing.

So, because it is more suitable for his changeable Cleopatra and
because it works better in theatrical terms, rather than have one
great lament over the tomb, as Plutarch does, he brings out
Cleopatra's emotions in defeat in dialogue with her women, both
immediately after Antony's death and in the monument in the
final scene; and he presents on stage what in Plutarch is left
enigmatic: Cleopatra's decision to kill herself, the arrival of the
snakes in the basket, and the suicide itself, all of which in Plutarch
we see, as it were, from the Roman point of view – that is, we only

11 J. M. Mossman, '*Henry V* and Plutarch's *Alexander*', *Shakespeare Quarterly*
   45.1 (Spring 1994), 57–73.
12 The following discussion is heavily indebted to C. B. R. Pelling (ed.)
   *Plutarch: Life of Antony,* Cambridge 1988, 37–45.

discover her death when it is too late and have to reconstruct how it happened. But the last tableau, and the exchange between Charmian and the guard, are straight from North:

> One of the soldiers seeing her, angrily said unto her: 'Is that well done, Charmion?' 'Very well,' said she again, 'and meet for a princess descended from the race of so many noble kings.'

> 1ST GUARD: What work is here! – Charmian, is this well done?
> CHARMIAN: It is well done, and fitting for a princess descended of so many royal kings. Ah, soldier!

Pelling sums up well: 'What came first for Shakespeare was a peculiarly sensitive and thoughtful reading of the *Life*. What he did with Plutarch was remarkable: but scarcely less remarkable was what he learned from Plutarch about his story's dramatic potential, and the frequency with which he decided that Plutarch's own leading themes and ideas, when turned in his own way, would do very well.'[13]

## 4 Afterlife

Since Shakespeare was such a thoughtful reader of Plutarch, perhaps it is not surprising that it should be he who makes the most graceful expression of the common ground which Plutarch succeeds in making between his subjects and his readers in all times and in all places, in a speech of Fluellen (*Henry V*, IV, 7):

> I think it is in Macedon where Alexander is porn. I tell you, captain, if you look in the maps of the 'orld, I warrant you sall find, in the comparisons between Macedon and Monmouth, that the situations, look you, is both alike. There is a river in Macedon, and there is also moreover a river at Monmouth: it is called Wye at Monmouth; but it is out of my prains what is the name of the other river; but 'tis all one, 'tis alike as my fingers is to my fingers, and there is salmons in both. If you mark Alexander's life well, Harry of Monmouth's life is come after it indifferent well; for there is figures in all things.

13 Pelling 1988, 45.

That is Plutarch's great gift, as it is Shakespeare's: to make anyone reading him feel some emotional kinship with his heroes, however remote they may be in time and condition. That is what made the *Lives* so susceptible to dramatisation, and why both Napoleon and Wellington took them with them on campaign, and why General Gordon recommended them to his officers. And that is why they continue to compel and excite readers today. Let North have the last word:

> There is no profane study better than Plutarch. All other learning is private, fitter for universities than cities, fuller of contemplation than experience, more commendable in the students themselves, than profitable unto others. Whereas stories are fit for every place, reach to all persons, serve for all times, teach the living, revive the dead, so far excelling all other books, as it is better to see learning in noble men's lives, than to read it in philosophers' writings . . . And so I wish you all the profit of the book. Fare ye well.

JUDITH MOSSMAN
*Trinity College, Dublin*

# FURTHER READING

D. A. Russell, *Plutarch*, London 1973

C. P. Jones, *Plutarch and Rome*, Oxford 1971

B. Scardigli (ed), *Essays on Plutarch's Lives*, Oxford 1995

C. B. R. Pelling (ed), *Plutarch: Life of Antony*, Cambridge 1988

W. Shakespeare, *Coriolanus, Julius Caesar, Antony and Cleopatra*

T. J. B. Spencer, *Shakespeare's Plutarch*, Harmondsworth 1964

M. A. McGrail (ed), *Shakespeare's Plutarch* [Poetica 48],
    Tokyo 1997

# NOTE ON THE TEXT

The text reprinted in this edition is that of the edition of George Wyndham, in the Tudor Translation series edited by W. E. Henley, published in London in 1895 by David Nutt. The spelling and punctuation have been slightly modernised. It should be noted that North, like all sixteenth-century authors, does not aim at consistency in his spelling or punctuation, or in his use of capital letters, and some of these inconsistencies have been retained. His transliterations of Classical names are also variable and do not always correspond with the standard modern versions (which are themselves often arbitrary and inconsistent). In most cases it did not seem desirable to alter the original spelling of names, as to do so would often have changed the rhythm of North's prose and would have given a false impression of his practice: therefore a list has been appended of names whose spelling in North is idiosyncratic, and a more modern equivalent given for each.

# THESEUS
# ROMULUS

## Life of Theseus

1 Like as historiographers describing the world (friend Sossius Senecio) do of purpose refer to the uttermost parts of their maps the far distant regions whereof they be ignorant, with this note: these countries are by means of sands and droughts unnavigable, rude, full of venomous beasts, Scythian ice, and frozen seas. Even so may I (which in comparing noble men's lives have already gone so far into antiquity, as the true and certain history could lead me) of the rest, being things past all proof or challenge, very well say: that beyond this time all is full of suspicion and doubt, being delivered us by poets and tragedy makers, sometimes without truth and likelihood, and always without certainty. Howbeit, having heretofore set forth the lives of Lycurgus (which established the laws of the Lacedaemonians) and of King Numa Pompilius, methought I might go a little further to the life of Romulus, since I was come so near him. But considering myself as the poet Aeschilus did:

> What champion may with such a man compare?
> Or who (think I) shall be against him set?
> Who is so bold? Or who is he that dare
> Defend his force, in such encounter met?

In the end I resolved to match him which did set up the noble and famous city of Athens, with him which founded the glorious and invincible city of Rome. Wherein I would wish that the inventions of poets, and the traditions of fabulous antiquity, would suffer themselves to be purged and reduced to the form of a true and historical report: but when they square too much from likelihood, and cannot be made credible, the readers will of courtesy take in good part that which I could with most probability write of such antiquities.

2    Now surely methinks that Theseus in many things was much like unto Romulus. For being both begotten by stealth, and out of lawful matrimony, both were reputed to be borne of the seed of the gods.

Both valiant were, as all the world doth know.

Both joined valiancy with government. The one of them built Rome, and the other, by gathering into one dispersed people, erected the city of Athens: two of the most noble cities of the world. The one and the other were ravishers of women: and neither the one nor the other could avoid the mischief of quarrel and contention with their friends, nor the reproach of staining themselves with the blood of their nearest kinsmen. Moreover, they say that both the one and the other in the end did get the hate and ill will of their citizens: at the least if we will believe that report of Theseus, which carrieth greatest show of truth.

3    Theseus of his father's side was descended of the right lineage of Erictheus the great, and of the first inhabitants which occupied the country of Attica, the which since were called Autocthones, as much to say, as born of themselves. For there is no memory, or other mention made, that they came out of any other country than that. And of his mother's side he came of Pelops, who was in his time the mightiest king of all the country of Peloponnesus, not so much for his goods and riches, as for the number of children which he had. For his daughters which were many in number, he bestowed on the greatest lords of all the country: his sons also, which likewise were many, he dispersed into divers cities and free towns, finding means to make them governors and heads of the same. Pitheus, grandfather to Theseus on the mother's side, was one of his sons, and founded the little city of Troezen, and was reputed to be one of the wisest men of his time. But the knowledge and wisdom, which only carried estimation at that time, consisted altogether in grave sentences and moral sayings. As those are which won the poet Hesiodus such fame for his book entitled, *The Works and Days*: in the which is read even at this present, this goodly sentence, which they father upon Pitheus:

Thou shalt perform thy promise and thy pay
To hired men, and that without delay.

And this doth Aristotle the philosopher himself testify: and the poet
Euripides also, calling Hippolytus the scholar of the holy Pitheus,
doth sufficiently declare of what estimation he was. But Aegeus
desiring (as they say) to know how he might have children, went
unto the city of Delphes to the oracle of Apollo: where by Apollo's
nun that notable prophecy was given him for an answer. The which
did forbid him to touch or know any woman, until he was returned
again to Athens. And because the words of this prophecy were
somewhat dark and hard, he took his way by the city of Troezen, to
tell it unto Pitheus. The words of the prophecy were these:

> O thou which art a gem of perfect grace,
>   Pluck not the tap out of thy trusty tun:
> Before thou do, return unto thy place,
>   In Athens town, from whence thy race doth run.

Pitheus understanding the meaning persuaded him, or rather
cunningly by some devise deceived him in such sort, that he made
him to lie with his daughter called Aethra. Aegeus after he had
accompanied with her, knowing that she was Pitheus' daughter
with whom he had lain, and doubting that he had got her with
child, left her a sword and a pair of shoes, the which he hid under
a great hollow stone, the hollowness whereof served just to
receive those things which he laid under it; and made no living
creature privy to it but her alone, straightly charging her, that if
she happened to have a son, when he were come to man's state,
and of strength to remove the stone, and to take those things from
under it which he left there: that she should then send him unto
him by those tokens, as secretly as she could, that nobody else
might know of it. For he did greatly fear the children of one called
Pallas, the which lay in wait and spial by all the means they could
to kill him, only of despite because he had no children, they being
fifty brethren, and all begotten of one father. This done, he
departed from her.

4   And Aethra within few months after was delivered of a goodly
son, the which from that time was called Theseus: and as some say,
so called because of the tokens of knowledge his father had laid
under the stone. Yet some others write, that it was afterwards at
Athens when his father knew him, and avowed him for his son.
But in the meantime, during his infancy and childhood, he was

brought up in the house of his grandfather Pitheus, under the government and teaching of one called Connidas, his schoolmaster: in honour of whom the Athenians to this day do sacrifice a wether, the day before the great feast of Theseus, having more reason to honour the memory of this governor, than of a Silanion and of a Parrhasius, to whom they do honour also, because they painted and cast moulds of the images of Theseus.

5   Now there was a custom at that time in Greece, that the young men after their infancy and growth to man's state, went unto the city of Delphes, to offer part of their hairs in the temple of Apollo. Theseus also went thither as other did: and some say that the place where the ceremony of this offering was made, has ever since kept the old name, (and yet continueth) Theseia. Howbeit he did not shave his head but before only, as Homer sayeth, like the fashion of the Abantes in old time: and this manner of shaving of hairs was called for his sake, Theseida. And as concerning the Abantes, in truth they were the very first that shaved themselves after this fashion: nevertheless they learned it not of the Arabians as it was thought of some, neither did they it after the imitation of the Missians. But because they were warlike and valiant men, which did join near unto their enemy in battle, and above all men of the world were skilfullest in fight hand to hand, and would keep their ground: as the poet Archilochus witnesseth in these verses:

> They use no slings in foughten fields to have,
>   Nor bended bows, but swords and trenchant blades.
> For when fierce Mars beginneth for to rave,
>   In bloody field, then every man invades
> His fiercest foe, and fighteth hand to hand.
>   Then do they deeds, right cruel to recount.
> For in this wise, the brave and warlike band
>   Do show their force which come from Negrepont.

The cause why they were thus shaven before, was, for that their enemies should not have the vantage to take them by the hairs of the head while they were fighting. And for this selfsame consideration, Alexander the Great commanded his captains to cause all the Macedonians to shave their beards: because it is the easiest hold (and readiest for the hand) a man can have of his enemy in fighting, to hold him fast by the same.

6    But to return to Theseus. Aethra his mother had ever unto that time kept it secret from him, who was his true father. And Pitheus also had given it out abroad, that he was begotten of Neptune, because the Troezenians have this god in great veneration, and do worship him as patron and protector of their city, making offerings to him of their first fruits: and they have for the mark and stamp of their money, the three-picked mace, which is the sign of Neptune, called his Trident. But after he was come to the prime and lustiness of his youth, and that with the strength of his body he showed a great courage, joined with a natural wisdom, and staidness of wit: then his mother brought him to the place where this great hollow stone lay, and telling him truly the order of his birth, and by whom he was begotten, made him to take his father's tokens of knowledge, which he had hidden there, and gave him counsel to go by sea to Athens unto him. Theseus easily lifted up the stone, and took his father's tokens from under it: howbeit he answered plainly, that he would not go by sea, notwithstanding that it was a great deal the safer way, and that his mother and grandfather both had instantly entreated him, because the way by land from Troezen to Athens was very dangerous, all the ways being beset by robbers and murderers. For the world at that time brought forth men, which for strongness in their arms, for swiftness of feet, and for a general strength of the whole body, did far pass the common force of others, and were never weary for any labour or travail they took in hand. But for all this, they never employed these gifts of nature to any honest or profitable thing, but rather delighted villainously to hurt and wrong others: as if all the fruit and profit of their extraordinary strength had consisted in cruelty and violence only, and to be able to keep others under and in subjection, and to force, destroy, and spoil all that came to their hands. Thinking that the more part of those which think it a shame to do ill, and commend justice, equity, and humanity, do it of faint cowardly hearts, because they dare not wrong others, for fear they should receive wrong themselves: and therefore, that they which by might could have vantage over others, had nothing to do with such quiet qualities. Now Hercules, travelling abroad in the world, drove away many of those wicked thievish murderers, and some of them he slew and put to death, other as he passed through those places where they kept, did hide themselves for fear of him, and gave

place: in so much as Hercules, perceiving they were well tamed and brought low, made no further reckoning to pursue them any more. But after that by fortune he had slain Iphitus with his own hands, and that he was passed over the seas into the country of Lydia, where he served Queen Omphale a long time, condemning himself unto that voluntary pain, for the murder he had committed, all the realm of Lydia during his abode there, remained in great peace and security from such kind of people. Howbeit in Greece, and all thereabouts, these old mischiefs began again to renew, growing hotter and violenter than before: because there was no man that punished them, nor that durst take upon him to destroy them. By which occasion, the way to go from Peloponnesus to Athens by land was very perilous. And therefore Pitheus declaring unto Theseus, what manner of thieves there were that lay in the way, and the outrages and villainies they did to all travellers and wayfaring men, sought the rather to persuade him thereby to take his voyage along the seas. Howbeit in mine opinion, the fame and glory of Hercules' noble deeds had long before secretly set his heart on fire, so that he made reckoning of none other but of him, and lovingly hearkened unto those which would seem to describe him what manner of man he was, but chiefly unto those which had seen him, and been in his company, when he had said or done anything worthy of memory. For then he did manifestly open himself, that he felt the like passion in his heart, which Themistocles long time afterwards endured, when he said that the victory and triumph of Miltiades would not let him sleep. For even so, the wonderful admiration which Theseus had of Hercules' courage, made him in the night that he never dreamed but of his noble acts and doings, and in the day time, pricked forwards with emulation and envy of his glory, he determined with himself one day to do the like, and the rather, because they were near kinsmen, being cousins removed by the mother's side.

7    For Aethra was the daughter of Pitheus, and Alcmena (the mother of Hercules) was the daughter of Lysidices, the which was half sister to Pitheus, both children of Pelops and of his wife Hippodamia. So he thought he should be utterly shamed and disgraced, that Hercules travelling through the world in that sort, did seek out those wicked thieves to rid both sea and land of them:

and that he, far otherwise, should fly occasion that might be offered him, to fight with them that he should meet on his way. Moreover, he was of opinion he should greatly shame and dishonour him, whom fame and common bruit of people reported to be his father, if in shunning occasion to fight, he should convey himself by sea, and should carry to his true father also a pair of shoes (to make him known of him) and a sword not yet bathed in blood. Where he should rather seek cause, by manifest token of his worthy deeds, to make known to the world, of what noble blood he came, and from whence he was descended. With this determination, Theseus holdeth on his purposed journey, with intent to hurt no man, yet to defend himself, and to be revenged of those which would take upon them to assault him.

8   The first therefore whom he slew within the territories of the city of Epidaurum, was a robber called Periphetes. This robber used for his ordinary weapon to carry a club, and for that cause he was commonly surnamed Corynetes, that is to say, a club carrier. So he first struck at Theseus to make him stand: but Theseus fought so lustily with him, that he killed him. Whereof he was so glad, and chiefly for that he had won his club, that ever after he carried it himself about with him, as Hercules did the lion's skin. And like as this spoil of the lion did witness the greatness of the beast which Hercules had slain: even so Theseus went all about, showing that this club which he had got out of another's hands, was in his own hands invincible. And so going on further, in the straights of Peloponnesus he killed another, called Sinnis surnamed Pityo-camtes, that is to say, a wreather or bower of pine apple trees: whom he put to death in that self cruel manner that Sinnis had slain many other travellers before. Not that he had experience thereof, by any former practice or exercise: but only to show that clean strength could do more than either art or exercise. This Sinnis had a goodly fair daughter called Perigouna, which fled away, when she saw her father slain: whom he followed and sought all about. But she had hidden herself in a grove full of certain kinds of wild pricking rushes called Stoebe, and wild sparage, which she simply like a child entreated to hide her, as if they had heard and had sense to understand her: promising them with an oath, that if they saved her from being found, she would never cut them down, nor burn

them. But Theseus finding her, called her, and swore by his faith he would use her gently, and do her no hurt, nor displeasure at all. Upon which promise she came out of the bush, and lay with him, by whom she was conceived of a goodly boy, which was called Menalippus. Afterwards Theseus married her unto one Deioneus, the son of Euritus the Oechalian. Of this Menalippus, the son of Theseus, came Ioxus: the which with Ornytus brought men into the country of Caria, where he built the city of Ioxides. And hereof cometh that old ancient ceremony, observed yet unto this day by those of Ioxides, never to burn the briars of wild sparage, nor the Stoebe, but they have them in some honour and reverence.

9    Touching the wild savage sow of Crommyon, otherwise surnamed Phaea, that is to say, overgrown with age: she was not a beast to be made light account of, but was very fierce, and terrible to kill. Theseus notwithstanding tarried for her, and killed her in his journey, to the end it should not appear to the world, that all the valiant deeds he did, were done by compulsion, and of necessity: adding thereto his opinion also, that a valiant man should not only fight with men, to defend himself from the wicked: but that he should be the first to assault and slay wild hurtful beasts. Nevertheless others have written, that this Phaea was a woman robber, a murderer, and naught of her body, which spoiled those that passed by the place called Crommyonia, where she dwelt: and that she was surnamed a sow, for her beastly brutish behaviour, and wicked life, for the which in the end she was also slain by Theseus.

10    After her he killed Sciron, entering into the territories of Megara, because he robbed all travellers by the way, as the common report goeth: or as others say, for that of a cruel, wicked, and savage pleasure, he put forth his feet to those that passed by the sea side, and compelled them to wash them. And then when they thought to stoop to do it, he still spurned them with his feet, till he thrust them headlong into the sea: so Theseus threw him headlong down the rocks. Howbeit the writers of Megara impugning this common report, and desirous (as Simonides sayeth) to overthrow it that had continued by prescription of time: did maintain that this Sciron was never any robber, nor wicked person, but rather a pursuer and punisher of the wicked and a friend and a kinsman of the most honest and justest men of Greece. For there is no man but

will confess, that Aeacus was the most virtuous man among the Grecians in his time, and that Cychreus the Salaminian is honoured and reverenced as a god at Athens: and there is no man also but knoweth, that Peleus and Telamon were men of singular virtue. Now it is certain, that this Sciron was the son-in-law of Cychreus, father-in-law of Aeacus, and grandfather of Peleus and of Telamon, the which two were the children of Endeida, the daughter of the said Sciron, and of his wife Chariclo. Also it is not very likely, that so many good men would have had affinity with so naughty and wicked a man: in taking of him, and giving him that, which men love best of all things in the world. And therefore the historiographers say, that it was not the first time, when Theseus went unto Athens, that he killed Sciron: but that it was many days after, when he took the city of Eleusin, which the Megarians held at that time, where he deceived the governor of the city called Diocles, and there he slew Sciron. And these be the objections the Megarians alleged touching this matter.

11 He slew also Cercyon the Arcadian, in the city of Eleusin, wrestling with him. And going a little further, he slew Damastes, otherwise surnamed Procrustes, in the city of Hermionia: and that by stretching on him out, to make him even with the length and measure of his beds, as he was wont to do unto strangers that passed by. Theseus did that after the imitation of Hercules, who punished tyrants with the selfsame pain and torment, which they had made others suffer. For even so did Hercules sacrifice Busiris. So he stifled Antheus in wrestling. So he put Cycnus to death, fighting with him man to man. So he broke Termerus' head, from whom this proverb of Termerus' evil came, which continueth yet unto this day: for this Termerus did use to put them to death in this sort whom he met: to jolle his head against theirs. Thus proceeded Theseus after this self manner, punishing the wicked in like sort, justly compelling them to abide the same pain and torments, which they before had unjustly made others abide.

12 And so he held on his journey until he came to the river of Cephisus, where certain persons of the house of the Phytalides were the first which went to meet him, to honour him, and at his request they purified him according to the ceremonies used at that time: and afterwards having made a sacrifice of propitiation unto

their gods, they made him great cheer in their houses: and this was the first notable entertainment he found in all his journey. It is supposed he arrived in the city of Athens, the eight day of the month of June, which then they called Cronius. He found the commonwealth turmoiled with seditions, factions, and divisions, and particularly the house of Aegeus in very ill terms also, because that Medea (being banished out of the city of Corinth) was come to dwell in Athens, and remained with Aegeus, whom she had promised by virtue of certain medicines to make him to get children. But when she heard tell that Theseus was come, before that the good King Aegeus (who was now become old, suspicious, and afraid of sedition, by reason of the great factions within the city at that time) knew what he was, she persuaded him to poison him at a feast which they would make him as a stranger that passed by. Theseus failed not to go to this prepared feast whereunto he was bidden, but yet thought it not good to disclose himself. And the rather to give Aegeus occasion and mean to know him, when they brought the meat to the board, he drew out his sword, as though he would have cut withal, and showed it unto him. Aegeus seeing it, knew it straight, and forthwith overthrew the cup with poison which was prepared for him: and after he had enquired of him, and asked things, he embraced him as his son. Afterwards in the common assembly of the inhabitants of the city, he declared, how he avowed him for his son. Then all the people received him with exceeding joy, for the renown of his valiantness and manhood. And some say, that when Aegeus overthrew the cup, the poison which was in it, fell in that place where there is at this present a certain compass enclosed all about within the temple, which is called Delphinium. For even there in that place, in the old time, stood the house of Aegeus: in witness whereof, they call yet at this present time the image of Mercury (which is on the side of the temple looking towards the rising of the sun) the Mercury gate of Aegeus.

13   But the Pallantides, which before stood always in hope to recover the realm of Athens, at the least after Aegeus' death, because he had no children: when they saw that Theseus was known, and openly declared for his son and heir, and successor to the realm, they were not able any longer to bear it, seeing that

not only Aegeus (who was but the adopted son of Pandion, and nothing at all of the blood royal of the Erictheides) had usurped the kingdom over them, but that Theseus also should enjoy it after his death. Whereupon they determined to make war with them both, and dividing themselves into two parts, the one came openly in arms with their father, marching directly towards the city: the other lay close in ambush in the village Gargettus, meaning to give charge upon them in two places at one instant. Now they brought with them an herald born in the town of Agnus, called Leos, who bewrayed unto Theseus the secret and devise of all their enterprise. Theseus upon this intelligence went forth, and did set on those that lay in ambush, and put them all to the sword. The other which were in Pallas' company understanding thereof, did break and disperse themselves incontinently. And this is the cause (as some say) why those of Pallena do never make affinity nor marriage with those of Agnus at this day. And that in their town when any proclamation is made, they never speak these words which are cried everywhere else through out the whole country of Attica, *Acouete Leos*, (which is as much to say, as 'Hearken, O people') they do so extremely hate this word *Leos*, for that it was the herald's name which wrought them that treason.

14   This done, Theseus who would not live idly at home and do nothing, but desirous there withal to gratify the people, went his way to fight with the bull of Marathon, the which did great mischiefs to the inhabitants of the country of Tetrapolis. And having taken him alive, brought him through the city of Athens to be seen of all the inhabitants. Afterwards he did sacrifice him unto Apollo Delphias. Now concerning Hecale, who was reported to have lodged him, and to have given him good entertainment, it is not altogether untrue. For in the old time, those towns and villages thereabouts did assemble together, and made a common sacrifice which they called Hecalesion, in the honour of Jupiter Hecalian, where they honoured this old woman, calling her by a diminutive name, Hecalena: because that when she received Theseus into her house, being then but very young, she made much of him, and called him by many pretty made names, as old folks are wont to call young children. And forasmuch as she had made a vow to Jupiter to make him a solemn sacrifice, if Theseus returned safe from the

enterprise he went about, and that she died before his return: in recompense of the good cheer she had made him, she had that honour done unto her by Theseus' commandment, as Philochorus hath written of it.

15    Shortly after this exploit, there came certain of King Minos' ambassadors out of Creta, to ask tribute, being now the third time it was demanded, which the Athenians paid for this cause. Androgeus, the eldest son of King Minos, was slain by treason within the country of Attica: for which cause Minos pursuing the revenge of his death, made very hot and sharp wars upon the Athenians, and did them great hurt. But besides all this, the gods did sharply punish and scourge all the country, as well with barrenness and famine, as also with plague and other mischiefs, even to the drying up of their rivers. The Athenians perceiving these sore troubles and plagues, ran to the oracle of Apollo, who answered them that they should appease Minos: and when they had made their peace with him, that then the wrath of the gods would cease against them, and their troubles should have an end. Whereupon the Athenians sent immediately unto him, and entreated him for peace: which he granted them, with condition that they should be bound to send him yearly into Creta, seven young boys, and as many young girls. Now thus far, all the historiographers do very well agree: but in the rest not. And they which seem furthest off from the truth, do declare, that when these young boys were delivered in Creta, they caused them to be devoured by the Minotaur within the labyrinth: or else that they were shut within this labyrinth, wandering up and down, and could find no place to get out, until such time as they died, even famished for hunger. And this Minotaur, as Euripides the poet sayeth, was

> A corps combined, which monstrous might be deemed:
> A boy, a bull, both man and beast it seemed.

16    But Philochorus writeth, that the Cretans do not confess that, but say that this labyrinth was a jail or prison, in the which they had no other hurt, saving that they which were kept there under lock and key could not fly nor start away: and that Minos had, in the memory of his son Androgeus, instituted games and plays of prize, where he gave unto them that won the victory, those young children of Athens, the which in the meantime notwithstanding

were carefully kept and looked unto in the prison of the labyrinth: and that at the first games that were kept, one of the king's captains called Taurus, who was in best credit with his master, won the prize. This Taurus was a churlish and naughty natured man of condition, and very hard and cruel to these children of Athens. And to verify the same, the philosopher Aristotle himself, speaking of the commonwealth of the Bottieians, declareth very well, that he never thought that Minos did at any time cause the children of Athens to be put to death: but sayeth, that they poorly toiled in Creta even to crooked age, earning their living by true and painful service. For it is written, that the Cretans (to satisfy an old vow of theirs which they had made of ancient time) sent sometimes the first born of their children unto Apollo in the city of Delphes: and that amongst them they also mingled those which were descended of the ancient prisoners of Athens, and they went with them. But because they could not live there, they directed their journey first into Italy, where for a time they remained in the realm of Puglia, and afterwards from thence went into the confines of Thracia, where they had this name of Bottieians. In memory whereof, the daughters of the Bottieians in a solemn sacrifice they make, do use to sing the foot of this song: 'Let us to Athens go'. But thereby we may see how perilous a thing it is, to fall in displeasure and enmity with a city which can speak well, and where learning and eloquence doth flourish. For ever since that time, Minos was always blazed and disgraced throughout all the theatres of Athens. The testimony of Hesiodus, who calleth him the most worthy king, doth nothing help him at all, nor the praise of Homer, who nameth him Jupiter's familiar friend: because the tragical poets got the upper hand in disgracing him, notwithstanding all these. And upon their stages where all the tragedies were played, they still gave forth many ill-favoured words, and foul speeches of him: as against a man that had been most cruel and unnatural. Yet most men think, that Minos was the king which established the laws: and Radamanthus the judge and preserver of them, who caused the same also to be kept and observed.

17 The time now being come about for payment of the third tribute, when they came to compel the fathers which had children not yet married, to give them to be put forth to take their chance

and lot, the citizens of Athens began to murmur against Aegeus, alleging for their griefs, that he who only was the cause of all this evil, was only alone exempted from this grief. And that to bring the government of the realm to fall into the hands of a stranger his bastard, he cared not though they were bereft of all their natural children, and were unnaturally compelled to leave and forsake them. These just sorrows and complaints of the fathers, whose children were taken from them, did pierce the heart of Theseus, who willing to yield to reason, and to run the selfsame fortune as the citizens did, willingly offered himself to be sent thither, without regard taking to his hap or adventure. For which, the citizens greatly esteemed of his courage and honourable disposition, and dearly loved him for the good affection, he seemed to bear unto the commonalty. But Aegeus having used many reasons and persuasions, to cause him to turn, and stay from his purpose, and perceiving in the end there was no remedy but he would go: he then drew lots for the children which should go with him. Hellanicus notwithstanding doth write, that they were not those of the city which drew lots for the children they should send, but that Minos himself went thither in person and did choose them, as he chose Theseus the first, upon conditions agreed between them: that is to wit, that the Athenians should furnish them with a ship, and that the children should ship and embark with him, carrying no weapons of war: and that after the death of the Minotaur, this tribute should cease. Now before that time, there was never any hope of return, nor of safety of their children: therefore the Athenians always sent a ship to convey their children with a black sail, in token of assured loss. Nevertheless Theseus putting his father in good hope of him, being of a good courage, and promising boldly that he would set upon this Minotaur, Aegeus gave unto the master of the ship a white sail, commanding him that at his return he should put out the white sail if his son had escaped; if not, that then he should set up the black sail, to show him afar off his unlucky and unfortunate chance. Simonides notwithstanding doth say, that this sail which Aegeus gave to the master, was not white, but red, dyed in grain, and of the colour of scarlet: and that he gave it him to signify afar off, their delivery and safety. This master was called Phereclus Amarsiadas, as Simonides sayeth. But Philochorus writeth, that Scirus the Salaminian gave to Theseus a master called

Nausitheus, and another mariner to tackle the sails, who was called Phaeas: because the Athenians at that time were not greatly practised to the sea. And this did Scirus, for that one of the children on whom the lot fell was his nephew: and thus much the chapels do testify, which Theseus built afterwards in honour of Nausitheus, and of Phaeas, in the village of Phalerus, joining to the temple of Scirus. And it is said moreover, that the feast which they call Cybernesia, that is to say, the feast of Patrons of the ships, is celebrated in honour of them

18   Now after the lots were drawn, Theseus taking with him the children allotted for the tribute, went from the palace to the temple called Delphinion, to offer up to Apollo for him and for them, an offering of supplication which they call Hiceteria: which was an olive bough hallowed, wreathed about with white wool. After he had made his prayer, he went down to the sea side to embark, the sixth day of the month of March: on which day at this present time they do send their young girls to the same temple of Delphinion, there to make their prayers and petitions to the gods. But some say, that the oracle of Apollo in the city of Delphes had answered him, that he should take Venus for his guide, and that he should call upon her to conduct him in his voyage: for which cause he did sacrifice a goat unto her upon the sea side, which was found suddenly turned into a ram; and that therefore they surnamed this goddess Epitragia, as one would say, the goddess of the ram.

19   Furthermore, after he was arrived in Creta, he slew there the Minotaur (as the most part of ancient authors do write) by the means and help of Ariadne: who being fallen in fancy with him, did give him a clue of thread, by the help whereof she taught him, how he might easily wind out of the turnings and cranks of the Labyrinth. And they say, that having killed this Minotaur, he returned back again the same way he went, bringing with him those other young children of Athens, whom with Ariadne also he carried afterwards away. Pherecides sayeth moreover, that he broke the keels or bottoms of all the ships of Creta, because they should not suddenly set out after them. And Demon writeth, that Taurus (the captain of Minos) was killed in a fight by Theseus, even in the very haven mouth as they were ready to ship away, and hoist up sail. Yet Philochorus reporteth, that King Minos having set up the games, as

he was wont to do yearly in the honour and memory of his son, everyone began to envy captain Taurus, because they ever looked that he should carry away the game and victory, as he had done other years before: over and that, his authority got him much ill will and envy, because he was proud and stately, and had in suspicion that he was great with Queen Pasiphäe. Wherefore when Theseus required he might encounter with Taurus, Minos easily granted it. And being a solemn custom in Creta that the women should be present, to see these open sports and sights, Ariadne being at these games amongst the rest, fell further in love with Theseus, seeing him so goodly a person, so strong, and invincible in wrestling, that he far exceeded all that wrestled there that day. King Minos was so glad that he had taken away the honour from captain Taurus, that he sent him home frank and free into his country, rendering to him all the other prisoners of Athens: and for his sake, clearly released and forgave the city of Athens the tribute, which they should have paid him yearly. Howbeit Clidemus searching out the beginning of these things to the utmost, reciteth them very particularly, and after another sort. For he sayeth, about that time there was a general restraint through out all Greece, restraining all manner of people to bear sail in any vessel or bottom, wherein there were above five persons, except only Jason, who was chosen captain of the great ship Argus, and had commission to sail everywhere, to chase and drive away rovers and pirates, and to scour the seas throughout. About this time, Daedalus being fled from Creta to Athens in a little bark, Minos contrary to this restraint would needs follow him with a fleet of divers vessels with oars, who being by force of weather driven to the coast of Sicily, fortuned to die there. Afterwards his son Deucalion, being marvellously offended with the Athenians, sent to summon them to deliver Daedalus unto him, or else he would put the children to death, which were delivered to his father for hostages. But Theseus excused himself, and said he could not forsake Daedalus, considering he was his near kinsman, being his cousin germane, for he was the son of Merope, the daughter of Erichtheus. Howbeit by and by he caused many vessels secretly to be made, part of them within Attica self in the village of Thymetades, far from any highways: and part of them in the city of Troezen, by the sufferance of Pitheus his grandfather, to the end his purpose should be kept the secretlier. Afterwards when all his ships were ready, and rigged out, he took sea before the Cretans had any knowledge of it: in so much as when they saw them afar off, they did take them for the barks of their friends. Theseus landed without resistance, and took the haven. Then having Daedalus and other banished Cretans for guides, he entered the city self of Gnosus, where he slew Deucalion in a fight before the gates of the labyrinth, with all his guard and officers about him. By this means the kingdom of Creta fell by inheritance into the hands of his sister Ariadne. Theseus made league with her, and carried away the young children of Athens, which were kept as hostages, and concluded peace and amity between the Athenians and the Cretans: who promised, and swore, they would never make wars against them.

20 They report many other things also touching this matter, and specially of Ariadne, but there is no truth nor certainty in it. For some say, that Ariadne hung herself for sorrow, when she saw that Theseus had cast her off. Other write, that she was transported by mariners into the Isle of Naxos, where she was married unto Oenarus, the priest of Bacchus: and they think that Theseus left her, because he was in love with another, as by these verses should appear.

> Aegles the Nymph was loved of Theseus,
> Which was the daughter of Panopeus.

Hereas the Megarian sayeth, that these two verses in old time were among the verses of the poet Hesiodus, howbeit Pisistratus took them away: as he did in like manner add these other here in the description of the hells in Homer, to gratify the Athenians.

> Bold Theseus, and Pirithous stout,
>     Descended both from god's immortal race,
> Triumphing still, this weary world about
>     In feats of arms, and many a comely grace.

Other hold opinion, that Ariadne had two children by Theseus: the one of them was named Oenopion, and the other Staphylus. Thus amongst others the poet Ion writeth it, who was born in the Isle of Chio, and speaking of his city, he sayeth thus:

> Oenopion which was the son of worthy Theseus
>     Did cause men build this stately town which
>                     now triumpheth thus.

Now what things are found seemly in poets' fables, there is none but doth in manner sing them. But one Paenon born in the city of Amathunta, reciteth this clean after another sort, and contrary to all other: saying, that Theseus by tempest was driven with the Isle of Cyprus, having with him Ariadne, which was great with child, and so sore sea sick, that she was not able to abide it. In so much as he was forced to put her a land, and himself afterwards returning aboard hoping to save his ship against the storm, was forthwith compelled to luff into the sea. The women of the country did courteously receive and entreat Ariadne: and to comfort her again (for she was marvellously out of heart, to see she was thus forsaken), they counterfeited letters, as if Theseus had written them to her. And when her groaning time was come, and she to be laid, they did their best by all possible means to save her: but she died notwithstanding in labour, and could never be delivered. So she was honourably buried by the ladies of Cyprus. Theseus not long after returned thither again, who took her death marvellous heavily, and left money with the inhabitants of the country, to sacrifice unto her yearly: and for memory of her, he caused two little images to be molten, the one of copper, and the other of silver, which he dedicated unto her. This sacrifice is done the second day of September, on which they do yet observe this ceremony: they do lay a young child upon a bed, which pitifully cries and laments, as women travailing with child. They say also, that the Amathusians do yet call the grove where her tomb is set up, the wood of Venus Ariadne. And yet there are of the Naxians, that report this otherwise: saying, there were two Minoes, and two Ariadnes, whereof the one was married to Bacchus in the Isle of Naxos, of whom Staphylus was born: and the other the youngest, was ravished and carried away by Theseus, who afterwards forsook her, and she came into the Isle of Naxos with her nurse, called Corcyna, whose grave they do show yet to this day. This second Ariadne died there also, but she had no such honour done to her after her death, as to the first was given. For they celebrate the feast of the first with all joy and mirth: where the sacrifices done in memory of the second, be mingled with mourning and sorrow.

21 Theseus then departing from the Isle of Creta, arrived in the Isle of Delos, where he did sacrifice in the temple of Apollo, and gave there a little image of Venus, the which he had got of Ariadne. Then with the other young boys that he had delivered, he danced a kind of dance, which the Delians keep to this day, as they say: in which there are many turns and returns, much after the turnings of the labyrinth. And the Delians call this manner of dance the crane, as Dicaearcus sayeth. And Theseus danced it first about the altar, which is called Ceraton, that is to say, hornstaff: because it is made and builded of horns only, all on the left hand well and curiously set together without any other binding. It is said also that he made a game in this Isle of Delos, in which at the first was given to him that overcame, a branch of palm for reward of victory.

22 But when they drew near the coast of Attica, they were so joyful, he and his master, that they forgot to set up their white sail, by which they should have given knowledge of their health and safety to Aegeus. Who seeing the black sail afar off, being out of all hope evermore to see his son again, took such a grief at his heart, that he threw himself headlong from the top of a cliff, and killed himself. So soon as Theseus was arrived at the port named Phalerus, he performed the sacrifices which he had vowed to the gods at his departure: and sent an herald of his before unto the city, to carry news of his safe arrival. The herald found many of the city mourning the death of King Aegeus. Many other received him with great joy, as may be supposed. They would have crowned him also with a garland of flowers, for that he had brought so good tidings, that the children of the city were returned in safety. The herald was content to take the garland, yet would he not in any wise put it on his head, but did wind it about his herald's rod he bore in his hand, and so returns forthwith to the sea, where Theseus made his sacrifices. Who perceiving they were not yet done, did refuse to enter into the temple, and stayed without for troubling of the sacrifices. Afterwards all ceremonies finished, he went in and told him the news of his father's death. Then he and his company mourning for sorrow, hasted with speed towards the city. And this is the cause, why to this day, at the feast called Oscophoria (as who would say at the feast of boughs) the herald has not his head but his rod only crowned with flowers, and why the

assistants also after the sacrifice done, do make such cries and exclamations: *Ele, leuf, iou, iou*: whereof the first is the cry and voice they commonly use one to another to make haste, or else it is the foot of some song of triumph: and the other is the cry and voice of men as it were in fear and trouble. After he had ended the obsequies and funerals for his father, he performed also his sacrifices unto Apollo, which he had vowed the seventh day of the month of October, on which they arrived at their return into the city of Athens. Even so the custom which they use at this day, to seethe all manner of pulse, comes of this: that those which then returned with Theseus, did seethe in a great brass pot all the remain of their provision, and therewith made good cheer together. Even in such sort as this, came up the custom to carry a branch of olive, wreathed about with wool, which they call Iresione: because at that time they carried boughs of supplication, as we have told ye before. About which they hang all sorts of fruits: for then barrenness did cease, as the verses they sang afterwards did witness.

> Bring him good bread, that is of savoury taste,
>   With pleasant figs, and drops of dulcet mell,
> Then supple oil, his body for to baste,
>   And pure good wine, to make him sleep full well.

Howbeit there are some which will say, that these verses were made for the Heraclides, that is to say, those that descended from Hercules: which flying for their safety and succour unto the Athenians, were entertained and much made of by them for a time. But the most part hold opinion, they were made upon the occasion aforesaid.

23    The vessel in which Theseus went and returned, was a galliot of thirty oars, which the Athenians kept until the time of Demetrius the Phalerian, always taking away the old pieces of wood that were rotten, and ever renewing them with new in their places. So that ever since, in the disputations of the philosophers, touching things that increase, to wit, whether they remain always one, or else they be made others: this galliot was always brought in for an example of doubt. For some maintained, that it was still one vessel: others to the contrary defended it was not so. And they hold opinion also, that the feast of boughs which is celebrated at Athens at this time, was then first of all instituted by Theseus. It is said moreover, that

he did not carry all the wenches upon whom the lots did fall, but chose two fair young boys, whose faces were sweet and delicate as maidens be, that otherwise were hardy, and quick spirited. But he made them so oft bathe themselves in hot baths, and keep them in from the heat of the sun, and so many times to wash, anoint, and rub themselves with oils which serve to supple and smooth their skins, to keep fresh and fair their colour, to make yellow and bright their hairs: and withal did teach them so to counterfeit their speech, countenance and fashion of young maids, that they seemed to be like them, rather than young boys. For there was no manner of difference to be perceived outwardly, and he mingled them with the girls, without the knowledge of any man. Afterwards when he was returned, he made a procession, in which both he and the other young boys were apparelled then as they be now, which carry boughs on the day of the feast in their hands. They carry them in the honour of Bacchus and Ariadne, following the fable that is told of them: or rather because they returned home just at the time and season, when they gather the fruit of those trees. There are women which they call Deipnophores, that is to say, supper carriers, which are assistants to the sacrifice done that day, in representing the mothers of those upon whom the lots did fall, because they in like sort brought them both meat and drink. There they tell tales, for so did their mothers tattle to their children, to comfort and encourage them. All these particularities were written by Demon the histori-ographer. There was moreover a place chosen out to build him a temple in, and he himself ordained, that those houses which had paid tribute before unto the king of Creta, should now yearly thenceforth become contributories towards the charges of a solemn sacrifice, which should be done in the honour of him: and he did assign the order and administration of the same, unto the house of the Phytalides, in recompense of the courtesy which they showed him when he arrived.

24 Furthermore, after the death of his father Aegeus, he under-took a marvellous great enterprise. For he brought all the inhabitants of the whole province of Attica, to be within the city of Athens, and made them all one corporation, which were before dispersed into divers villages, and by reason thereof were very hard to be assembled together, when occasion was offered to establish

any order concerning the common state. Many times also they were at variance together, and by the ears, making wars one upon another. But Theseus took the pains to go from village to village, and from family to family, to let them understand the reasons why they should consent unto it. So he found the poor people and private men ready to obey and follow his will: but the rich, and such as had authority in every village, all against it. Nevertheless he won them, promising that it should be a commonwealth, and not subject to the power of any sole prince, but rather a popular state in which he would only reserve to himself the charge of the wars, and the preservation of the laws: for the rest, he was content that every citizen in all and for all should bear a like sway and authority. So there were some that willingly granted thereto. Other who had no liking thereof, yielded notwithstanding for fear of his displeasure and power which then was very great. So they thought it better to consent with goodwill unto that he required, than to tarry his forcible compulsion. Then he caused all the places where justice was ministered, and all their halls of assembly to be overthrown and pulled down. He removed straight all judges and officers, and built a town house and a council hall in the place where the city now stands, which the Athenians call Asty; but he called the whole corporation of them, Athens. Afterwards he instituted the great feast and common sacrifice for all of the country of Attica, which they call Panathenaea. Then he ordained another feast also upon the sixteenth day of the month of June, for all strangers which should come to dwell in Athens, which is called Metoecia and is kept even to this day. That done, he gave over his regal power according to his promise, and began to set up an estate or policy of a commonwealth, beginning first with the service of the gods. To know the good success of his enterprise, he sent at the very beginning to the oracle of Apollo in Delphes, to enquire of the fortune of this city: from whence this answer was brought unto him:

> O thou which art the son of Aegeus,
>> Begot by him on Pitheus' daughter dear.
> The mighty Jove, my father glorious,
>> By his decree, hath said there shall appear
> A fatal end of every city here.
>> Which end he will, shall also come adown,
> Within the walls of this thy stately town.

> Therefore show thou a valiant constant mind,
>   And let no care nor carke thy heart displease.
> For like unto a bladder blowen with wind
>   Thou shalt be tossed upon the surging seas.
> Yet let no dint of dolours thee disease.
>   For why? Thou shalt nor perish nor decay,
> Nor be o'ercome, nor yet be cast away.

It is found written also that Sibylla afterwards gave out such a like oracle over the city of Athens.

> The bladder blown may fleet upon the flood,
>   But cannot sink, nor stick in filthy mud.

25 Moreover, because he would further yet augment his people, and enlarge his city, he enticed many to come and dwell there, by offering them the selfsame freedom and privileges, which the natural born citizens had. So that many judge, that these words which are in use at this day in Athens, when any open proclamation is made, 'All people, Come ye hither', be the selfsame which Theseus then caused to be proclaimed, when he in that sort did gather a people together of all nations. Yet for all that, he suffered not the great multitude that came thither tag and rag, to be without distinction of degrees and orders. For he first divided the noblemen from husbandmen and artificers, appointing the noblemen as judges and magistrates to judge upon matters of religion, and touching the service of the gods: and of them also he did choose rulers, to bear civil office in the common weal, to determine the law, and to tell all holy and divine things. By this means he made the noblemen and the two other estates equal in voice. And as the noblemen did pass the other in honour, even so the artificers exceeded them in number, and the husbandmen them in profit. Now that Theseus was the first who of all others yielded to have a common weal or popular estate (as Aristotle sayeth) and did give over his regal power: Homer self seemeth to testify it, in numbering the ships which were in the Grecians' army before the city of Troia. For amongst all the Grecians, he only calleth the Athenians people. Moreover Theseus coined money, which he marked with the stamp of an ox, in memory of the bull of Marathon, or of Taurus the captain of Minos, or else to provoke his citizens to give themselves to labour. They say also that of this money they

were since called Hecatomboeon, and Decaboeon, which signifieth worth a hundred oxen, and worth ten oxen. Furthermore having joined all the territory of the city of Megara unto the country of Attica, he caused that notable four square pillar to be set up for their confines within the straight of Peloponnesus, and engraved thereupon this superscription, that declares the separation of both the countries which confine there together. The superscription is this.

> Where Titan doth begin his beams for to display,
>     Even that way stands Ionia, in fertile wise alway:
> And where again he goeth adown to take his rest,
>     There stands Peloponnesus land, for there I count it west.

It was he also which made the games called Isthmia, after the imitation of Hercules, to the end that as the Grecians did celebrate the feast, of games called Olympia, in the honour of Jupiter, by Hercules ordinance: so, that they should also celebrate the games called Isthmia, by his order and institution, in the honour of Neptune. For those that were done in the straits in the honour of Melicerta, were done in the night, and had rather form of sacrifice or of a mystery, than of games and open feast. Yet some will say, that these games of Isthmia were instituted in the honour and memory of Sciron, and that Theseus ordained them in satisfaction of his death: because he was his cousin germane, being the son of Canethus, and of Heniocha the daughter of Pitheus. Other say that it was Sinnis and not Sciron, and that for him Theseus made these games, and not for the memory of the other. Howsoever it was, he specially willed the Corinthians, that they should give unto those that came from Athens to see their games of Isthmia, so much place to sit down before them (in the most honourable part of the feast place) as the sail of their ship should cover, in the which they came from Athens: thus do Hellanicus and Andron Halicarnasseus write hereof.

26    Touching the voyage he made by the sea Major, Philochorus and some other hold opinion, that he went thither with Hercules against the Amazons: and that to honour his valiantness, Hercules gave him Antiopa the Amazon. But the more part of the other historiographers, namely Hellanicus, Pherecides, and Herodotus, do write, that Theseus went thither alone, after Hercules' voyage,

and that he took this Amazon prisoner, which is likeliest to be true. For we do not find that any other who went this journey with him, had taken any Amazon prisoner besides himself. Bion also the historiographer, this notwithstanding sayeth, that he brought her away by deceit and stealth. For the Amazons (sayeth he) naturally loving men, did not flee at all when they saw them land in their country, but sent them presents, and that Theseus enticed her to come into his ship, who brought him a present: and so soon as she was aboard, he hoist his sail, and so carried her away. Another historiographer Menecrates, who wrote the history of the city of Nicea, in the country of Bythinia, sayeth: that Theseus having this Amazon Antiopa with him, remained a certain time upon those coasts, and amongst others he had in his company three younger brethren of Athens, Euneus, Thoas, and Solois. This last, Solois, was marvellously in love with Antiopa, and never bewrayed it to any of his other companions, saving unto one with whom he was most familiar, and whom he trusted best: so that he reported this matter unto Antiopa. But she utterly rejected his suit, though otherwise she handled it wisely and courteously, and did not complain to Theseus of him. Howbeit the young man despairing to enjoy his love, took it so inwardly, that desperately he leapt into the river, and drowned himself. Which when Theseus understood, and the cause also that brought him to this desperation and end, he was very sorry, and angry also. Whereupon he remembered a certain oracle of Pythia, by whom he was commanded to build a city in that place in a strange country, where he should be most sorry, and that he should leave some that were about him at that time, to govern the same. For this cause therefore he built a city in that place, which he named Pythopolis, because he had built it only by the commandment of the Nun Pythia. He called the river in the which the young man was drowned, Solois, in memory of him: and left his two brethren for his deputies and as governors of this new city, with another gentleman of Athens, called Hermus. Hereof it cometh, that at this day the Pythopolitans call a certain place of their city, Hermus' house. But they fail in the accent, by putting it upon the last syllable: for in pronouncing it so, Hermus signifieth Mercury. By this means they do transfer the honour due to the memory of Hermus, unto the god Mercury.

27    Now hear what was the occasion of the wars of the Amazons, which methinks was not a matter of small moment, nor an enterprise of a woman. For they had not placed their camp within the very city of Athens, nor had not fought in the very place itself (called Pnyce) adjoining to the temple of the Muses, if they had not first conquered or subdued all the country thereabouts: neither had they all come at the first, so valiantly to assail the city of Athens. Now, whether they came by land from so far a country, or that they passed over an arm of the sea, which is called Bosphorus Cimmericus, being frozen as Hellanicus sayeth: it is hardly to be credited. But that they camped within the precinct of the very city itself, the names of the places which continue yet to this present day do witness it, and the graves also of the women which died there. But so it is, that both armies lay a great time one in the face of the other, ere they came to battle. Howbeit at the length Theseus having first made sacrifice unto Fear the goddess, according to the counsel of a prophecy he had received, he gave them battle in the month of August, on the same day, in the which the Athenians do even at this present solemnise the feast which they call Boedromia. But Clidemus the historiographer, desirous particularly to write all the circumstances of this encounter, sayeth that the left point of their battle bent towards the place which they call Amazonion: and that the right point marched by the side of Chrysa, even to the place which is called Pnyce, upon which, the Athenians coming towards the temple of the Muses, did first give their charge. And for proof that this is true, the graves of the women which died in this first encounter, are found yet in the great street which goeth towards the gate Piraica, near unto the chapel of the little god Chalcodus. And the Athenians (sayeth he) were in this place repulsed by the Amazons, even to the place where the images of Eumenides are, that is to say, of the Furies. But on the other side also, the Athenians coming towards the quarters of Palladium, Ardettus, and Lucium, drove back their right point even to within their camp, and slew a great number of them. Afterwards, at the end of four months, peace was taken between them by means of one of the women called Hyppolita. For this historiographer calleth the Amazon which Theseus married, Hyppolita, and not Antiopa. Nevertheless, some say that she was slain (fighting on Theseus' side) with a dart, by another called

Molpadia. In memory whereof, the pillar which is joining to the
temple of the Olympian ground, was set up in her honour. We are
not to marvel, if the history of things so ancient be found so
diversely written. For there are also that write, that Queen
Antiopa sent those secretly which were hurt then into the city of
Calcide, where some of them recovered, and were healed: and
others also died, which were buried near to the place called
Amazonion.

Howsoever it was, it is most certain that this war was ended by
agreement. For a place adjoining to the temple of Theseus, doth
bear record of it, being called Orcomosium: because the peace was
there by solemn oath concluded. And the sacrifice also doth truly
verify it, which they have made to the Amazons before the feast of
Theseus, long time out of mind. They of Megara also do show a
tomb of the Amazons in their city, which is as they go from the
market place to the place they call Rhus: where they find an ancient
tomb, cut in fashion and form of a lozenge. They say that there
died others of the Amazons also, near unto the city of Chaeronea,
which were buried all along the little brook passing by the same,
which in the old time (in mine opinion) was called Thermodon,
and is now named Haemon, as we have in other places written in
the life of Demosthenes. And it seemeth also, that they did not pass
through Thessalie without fighting: for there are seen yet of their
tombs all about the city of Scotusa, hard by the rocks, which be
called the dog's head.

28   And this is that which is worthy memory (in mine opinion)
touching the wars of these Amazons. How the poet telleth that the
Amazons made wars with Theseus to revenge the injury he did to
their Queen Antiopa, refusing her, to marry with Phaedra: and as
for the murder which he tells that Hercules did, that methinks is
altogether but devise of poets. It is very true, that after the death of
Antiopa, Theseus married Phaedra, having had before of Antiopa a
son called Hippolytus, or as the poet Pindarus writeth, Demophon.
And for that the historiographers do not in anything speak against
the tragical poets, in that which concerns the ill hap that chanced to
him in the persons of this his wife and of his son, we must needs
take it to be so, as we find it written in the tragedies.

29    And yet we find many other reports touching the marriages of Theseus, whose beginnings had no great good honest ground, neither fell out their ends very fortunate: and yet for all that they have made no tragedies of them, neither have they been played in the theatres. For we read that he took away Anaxo the Troezenian, and that after he had killed Sinnis and Cercyon, he took their daughters perforce: and that he did also marry Peribaea, the mother of Ajax, and afterwards Pherebaea, and Ioppa the daughter of Iphicles. And they blame him much also, for that he so lightly forsook his wife Ariadne, for the love of Aegles the daughter of Panopaeus, as we have recited before. Lastly, he took away Helen: which ravishment filled all the realm of Attica with wars, and finally was the very occasion that forced him to forsake his country, and brought him at the length to his end, as we will tell you hereafter. Albeit in his time other princes of Greece had done many goodly and notable exploits in the wars, yet Herodotus is of opinion, that Theseus was never in any one of them: saving that he was at the battle of the Lapithae against the Centauri. Others say to the contrary, that he was at the journey of Cholchide with Jason, and that he did help Meleager to kill the wild boar of Calydonia: from whence (as they say) this proverb came: 'Not without Theseus'. Meaning that such a thing was not done without great help of another. Howbeit it is certain that Theseus self did many acts, without aid of any man, and that for his valiantness this proverb came in use, which is spoken: 'This is another Theseus.' Also he did help Adrastus king of the Argives to recover the bodies of those that were slain in the battle before the city of Thebes. Howbeit it was not, as the poet Euripides sayeth, by force of arms, after he had overcome the Thebans in battle: but it was by composition. And thus the greatest number of the most ancient writers do declare it. Furthermore, Philochorus writeth, that this was the first treaty that ever was made to recover the dead bodies slain in battle: nevertheless we do read in the histories and gestes of Hercules, that he was the first that ever suffered his enemies to carry away their dead bodies, after they had been put to the sword. But whosoever he was, at this day in the village of Eleutheres, they do show the place where the people were buried, and where princes' tombs are seen about the city of Eleusin, which he made at the request of Adrastus. And for testimony hereof, the tragedy Aeschilus made of the Eleusinians,

where he causeth it to be spoken even thus to Theseus himself, doth clearly overthrow the petitioners in Euripides.

30    Touching the friendship betwixt Pirithous and him, it is said it began thus. The renown of his valiancy was marvellously blown abroad through all Greece, and Pirithous desirous to know it by experience, went even of purpose to invade his country, and brought away a certain booty of oxen of his taken out of the country of Marathon. Theseus being advertised thereof, armed straight, and went to the rescue. Pirithous hearing of his coming, fled not at all, but returned back suddenly to meet him. And so soon as they came to see one another, they both wondered at each other's beauty and courage, and so had they no desire to fight. But Pirithous reaching out his hand first to Theseus, said unto him. 'I make yourself judge of the damage you have sustained by my invasion, and with all my heart I will make such satisfaction, as it shall please you to assess it at.' Theseus then did not only release him of all the damages he had done, but also requested him he would become his friend, and brother in arms. Hereupon they were presently sworn brethren in the field: after which oath betwixt them, Pirithous married Deidamia, and sent to pray Theseus to come to his marriage, to visit his country, and to make merry with the Lapithae. He had bidden also the Centauri to the feast: who being drunk, committed many lewd parts, even to the forcing of women. Howbeit the Lapithae chastised them so well, that they slew some of them presently in the place, and drove the rest afterwards out of all the country by the help of Theseus, who armed himself, and fought on their side. Yet Herodotus writeth the matter somewhat contrary, saying that Theseus went not at all until the war was well begun: and that it was the first time that he saw Hercules, and spoke with him near unto the city of Trachina, when he was then quiet, having ended all his far voyages and greatest troubles. They report that this meeting together was full of great cheer, much kindness, and honourable entertainment between them, and how great courtesy was offered to each other. Nevertheless methinks we should give better credit to those writers that say they met many times together, and that Hercules was accepted and received into the brotherhood of the mysteries of Eleusin, by the means of the countenance and favour which Theseus showed unto

him: and that his purification also was thereby allowed of, who was
to be purged of necessity of all his ill deeds and cruelties, before he
could enter into the company of those holy mysteries.

31    Furthermore, Theseus was fifty years old when he took away
Helen and ravished her, which was very young, and not of age to
be married, as Hellanicus sayeth. By reason whereof, some seeking
to hide the ravishment of her as a heinous fact, do report it was not
he, but one Idas and Lynceus that carried her away, who left her in
his custody and keeping: and that Theseus would have kept her
from them, and would not have delivered her to her brethren
Castor and Pollux, which afterwards did demand her again of him.
Others again say it was her own father Tyndarus, who gave her
him to keep, for that he was afraid of Enarsphorus the son of
Hippocoon, who would have had her away by force. But that
which cometh nearest to the truth in this case, and which indeed
by many authors is testified, was in this sort. Theseus and Pirithous
went together to the city of Lacedaemon, where they took away
Helen (being yet very young) even as she was dancing in the
temple of Diana surnamed Orthia: and they fled for life. They of
Lacedaemon sent after her, but those that followed went no
further then the city of Tegea. Now when they were escaped out
of the country of Peloponnesus, they agreed to draw lots together,
which of them two should have her, with condition that whose
lot it were to have her, he should take her to his wife, and should
be bound also to help his companion to get him another. It was
Theseus' hap to light upon her, who carried her to the city of
Aphidnes, because she was yet too young to be married. Whither
he caused his mother to come to bring her up, and gave his friend
called Aphidnus the charge of them both, recommending her to
his good care, and to keep it so secretly, that nobody should know
what was become of her. Because he would do the like for
Pirithous (according to the agreement made betwixt them) he
went into Epirus with him to steal the daughter of Aidoneus, king
of the Molossians, who had surnamed his wife Proserpina, his
daughter Proserpina, and his dog Cerberus: with whom he made
them fight which came to ask his daughter in marriage, promising
to give her to him that should overcome his Cerberus. But the
king understanding that Pirithous was come, not to request his

daughter in marriage, but to steal her away, he took him prisoner with Theseus: and as for Pirithous, he caused him presently to be torn in pieces with his dog, and shut Theseus up in close prison.

32 In this meantime there was one at Athens called Menestheus, the son of Peteus: which Peteus was the son of Orneus, and Orneus was the son of Erictheus. This Menestheus was the first that began to flatter the people, and did seek to win the favour of the commonalty, by sweet enticing words: by which devise he stirred up the chiefest of the city against Theseus (who indeed long before began to be weary of him) by declaring unto them how Theseus had taken from them their royalties and seigniories, and had shut them up in such sort within the walls of a city, that he might the better keep them in subjection and obedience in all things, after his will. The poor inferior sort of people he did stir up also to rebellion, persuading them that it was no other than a dream of liberty which was promised them: and how contrariwise they were clearly dispossessed and thrown out of their own houses, of their temples, and from their natural places where they were born, to the end only that in lieu of many good and loving lords which they were wont to have before, they should now be compelled to serve one only head, and a strange lord. Even as Menestheus was very hot about this practice, the war of the Tyndarides fell out at that instant, which greatly furthered his pretence. For these Tyndarides (to wit the children of Tyndarus), Castor and Pollux, came down with a great army against the city of Athens: and some suspect sore that Menestheus was cause of their coming thither. Howbeit at the first entry they did no hurt at all in the country, but only demanded restitution of their sister. To whom the citizens made answer, that they knew not where she was left: and then the brethren began to make spoil, and offer war indeed. Howbeit there was one called Academus, who having knowledge (I cannot tell by what mean) that she was secretly hidden in the city of Aphidnes, revealed it unto them. By reason whereof the Tyndarides did always honour him very much, so long as he lived, and afterwards the Lacedaemonians, having often burnt and destroyed the whole country of Attica throughout, they would yet never touch the academy of Athens for Academus' sake. Yet Dicearchus sayeth, that in the army of the Tyndarides there were two Arcadians,

Echedemus and Marathus, and how of the name of one of them, it was then called the place of Echedemie, which since has been called Academia: and after the name of the other, there was a village called Marathon, because he willingly offered himself to be sacrificed before the battle, as obeying the order and command-ment of a prophecy. So they went and pitched their camp before the city of Aphidnes, and having won the battle, and taken the city by assault, they razed the place. They say that Alycus the son of Sciron was slain at this field, who was in the host of the Tyndarides, and that after his name, a certain quarter of the territory of Megara was called Alycus, in the which his body was buried. Howbeit Hereas writeth that Theseus self did kill him before Aphidnes: in witness whereof he alleges certain verses which speak of Alycus:

> While as he sought with all his might and main
>   (In thy defence, fair Helen) for to fight,
> In Aphidnes, upon the pleasant plain,
>   Bold Theseus to cruel death him dight.

Howbeit it is not likely to be true, that Theseus being there, the city of Aphidnes and his mother also were taken.

33   But when it was won, they of Athens began to quake for fear, and Menestheus counselled them to receive the Tyndarides into the city, and to make them good cheer, so they would make no wars but upon Theseus, which was the first that had done them the wrong and injury: and that to all other else they should show favour and goodwill. And so it fell out. For when the Tyndarides had all in their power to do as they listed, they demanded nothing else but that they might be received into their corporation, and not to be reckoned for strangers, no more then Hercules was: the which was granted the Tyndarides, and Aphidnus did adopt them for his children, as Pylius had adopted Hercules. Moreover they did honour them as if they had been gods, calling them Anaces, either because they ceased the wars, or for that they ordered themselves so well, that their whole army being lodged within the city, there was not any hurt or displeasure done to any person: but as it became those that have the charge of anything, they did carefully watch to preserve the good quiet thereof. All which this Greek word *Anacos* doth signify, whereof perchance it comes that they call the Kings Anactes. There are others also who hold

opinion that they were called Anaces, because of their stars which appeared in the air. For the Attican tongue sayeth *Anacas* and *Anecathen*, where the common people say *Ano* and *Anothen*, that is to say, above.

34   Nevertheless Aethra, Theseus' mother, was carried prisoner to Lacedaemon, and from thence to Troia with Helen, as some say: and as Homer himself doth witness in his verses, where he speaketh of the women that followed Helen.

> Aethra the daughter dear of Pitheus, aged sire,
>     And with her fair Clymene, she whose eyes most men desire.

Yet there are others who as well reject these two verses, and maintain they are not Homer's: as also they reprove all that is reported of Munychus. To wit, that Laodice being privately conceived of him by Demophon, he was brought up secretly by Aethra within Troia. But Hister the historian in his thirteenth of his histories of Attica, maketh a recital far contrary to other, saying that some hold opinion, that Paris Alexander was slain in battle by Achilles and Patroclus in the country of Thessalie, near to the river of Sperchius, and that his brother Hector took the city of Troezen, from whence he brought away Aethra: in which there is no manner of appearance or likelihood.

35   But Aedoneus king of the Molossians, feasting Hercules one day as he passed through his realm, descended by chance into talk of Theseus and of Pirithous, how they came to steal away his daughter secretly: and after told how they were also punished. Hercules was marvellous sorry to understand that one of them was now dead, and the other in danger to die, and thought with himself that to make his moan to Aedoneus, it would not help the matter: he besought him only that he would deliver Theseus for his sake. And he granted him. Thus Theseus being delivered of this captivity, returned to Athens, where his friends were not altogether kept under by his enemies: and at his return he did dedicate to Hercules all the temples, which the city had before caused to be built in his own honour. And where first of all they were called Thesea, he did now surname them all Herculea, excepting four, as Philochorus writeth. Now when he was arrived at Athens, he would immediately have commanded and ordered things as he was wont to do: but he found

himself troubled much with sedition, because those who had hated
him of long time, had added also to their old cankered hate a disdain
and contempt to fear him any more. And the common people now
were become so stubborn, that where before they would have done
all that they were commanded, and have spoken nothing to the
contrary: now they looked to be borne with, and flattered. Whereupon Theseus thought at the first to have used force, but he was
forced by the faction and contention of his enemies to let all alone,
and in the end, despairing he should ever bring his matters to pass to
his desire, he secretly sent away his children into the Isle of Euboea,
to Elphenor the son of Chalcodus. And himself, after he had made
many wishes and curses against the Athenians, in the village of
Gargettus, in a place which for that cause to this day is called
Araterion (that is to say, the place of cursings), he did take the seas,
and went into the Isle of Sciros, where he had goods, and thought
also to have found friends. Lycomedes reigned at that time, and was
king of the isle, unto whom Theseus made request for some land, as
intending to dwell there: albeit some say that he required him to
give him aid against the Athenians. Lycomedes, were it that he
doubted to entertain so great a personage, or that he did it to gratify
Menestheus, carried him up to the high rocks, feigning as though
he would from thence have showed him all his country round
about. But when he had him there, he threw him down headlong
from the top of the rocks to the bottom, and put him thus
unfortunately to death. Yet other write, that he fell down of himself
by an unfortunate chance, walking one day after supper as he was
wont to do. There was no man at that time that did follow or
pursue his death, but Menestheus quietly remained king of Athens:
and the children of Theseus, as private soldiers, followed Elphenor
in the wars of Troia. But after the death of Menestheus, who died in
the journey to Troie, Theseus' sons returned unto Athens, where
they recovered their state. Sithence, there were many occasions
which moved the Athenians to reverence and honour him as a
demigod. For in the battle of Marathon, many thought they saw his
shadow and image in arms, fighting against the barbarous people.

36    And after the wars of the Medes (the year wherein Phaedon
was governor of Athens) the nun Pithia answered the Athenians,
who had sent to the oracle of Apollo: that they should bring back

the bones of Theseus, and putting them in some honourable place, they should preserve and honour them devoutly. But it was a hard matter to find his grave: and if they had found it, yet had it been a harder thing to have brought his bones away, for the malice of those barbarous people which inhabited that isle: which were so wild and fierce, that none could trade or live with them. Notwithstanding Cimon having taken the island (as we have written in his life) and seeking his grave, perceived by good hap an eagle pecking with her beak, and scraping with her claws in a place of some pretty height. Straight it came into his mind (as by divine inspiration) to search and dig the place: where was found the tomb of a great body, with the head of a spear which was of brass, and a sword with it. All which things were brought to Athens by Cimon in the admiral galley. The Athenians received them with great joy, with processions and goodly sacrifices, as if Theseus himself had been alive, and had returned into the city again. At this day all these relics lay yet in the midst of the city, near to the place where the young men do use all their exercises of body. There is free liberty of access for all slaves and poor men (that are afflicted and pursued by any mightier than themselves), to pray and sacrifice in remembrance of Theseus: who while he lived was protector of the oppressed, and did courteously receive their requests and petitions that prayed to have aid of him. The greatest and most solemn sacrifice they do unto him, is on the eight day of October, in which he returned from Creta, with the other young children of Athens. Howbeit they do not leave to honour him every eight day of all other months, either because he arrived from Troezen at Athens the eight day of June, as Diodorus the cosmographer writeth: or for that they thought that number to be meetest for him, because the bruit ran he was begotten of Neptune. They do sacrifice also to Neptune, the eight day of every month, because the number of eight is the first cube made of even number, and the double of the first square: which doth represent a steadfastness immoveable, properly attributed to the might of Neptune, whom for this cause we surname Asphalius, and Gaeiochus, which by interpretation doth signify: the safe keeper, and the stayer of the earth.

THE END OF THESEUS' LIFE

# Life of Romulus

The historiographers do not agree in their writings, by whom, nor for what cause, the great name of the city of Rome (the glory whereof is blown abroad through all the world) was first given unto it. For some think that the Pelasgians, after they had overcome the greatest part of the world, and had inhabited and subdued many nations, in the end did stay themselves in that place where it was new builded: and for their great strength and power in arms, they gave the name of Rome unto the city, as signifying power in the Greek tongue. Other say, that after the taking and destruction of Troya, there were certain Troyans which saving themselves from the sword, took such vessels as they found at adventure in the haven, and were by winds put with the Thuscane shore, where they anchored near unto the river of Tyber. There their wives being so sore sea sick, that possibly they could not any more endure the boisterous surges of the seas, it happened one of them among the rest (the noblest and wisest of the company) called Roma, to counsel the other women of her companions to set their ships afire, which they did accordingly. Wherewith their husbands at the first were marvellously offended. But afterwards, being compelled of necessity to plant themselves near unto the city of Pallantium, they were appeased when they saw things prosper better then they hoped for, finding the soil there fertile, and the people their neighbours civil and gentle in entertaining them. Wherefore amongst other honours they did to requite this lady Roma, they called their city after her name, as from whom came the original cause of the building and foundation thereof. They say that from thence came this custom continuing yet to this day at Rome, that the women saluting their kinsfolks and husbands do kiss them in the mouth, for so did these Troyan ladies to please their husbands, and to win them again, after they had lost their favours, and procured their displeasures with burning of their ships.

2    Other say that Roma was the daughter of Italus, and of Lucaria, or else of Telephus the son of Hercules, and of the wife of Aeneas: other say of Ascanius, the son of Aeneas, who named the city after her name. Other hold opinion that it was Romanus (the son of Ulysses and of Circe) that first founded Rome: other will say that it was Romus the son of Emathion, whom Diomedes sent thither from Troya. Other write that it was one Romis a tyrant of the Latins, who drove the Thuscans out of those parts: which departing out of Thessaly went first of all into Lydia, and afterwards from Lydia into Italy. And furthermore, they who think that Romulus (as indeed it carrieth best likelihood) was he that gave the name to the city, do not agree about his ancestors. For some of them write, that he was the son of Aeneas and of Dexithea the daughter of Phorbus, and that he was brought into Italy of a little child with his brother Remus: and that at that time the river of Tyber being overflown, all other ships were cast away, saving the ship in which the two little boys were, which by great good hap came to a stay upon a very plain even ground on the bank; and because the children beyond all hope were saved by this means, therefore the place was afterwards called Roma. Other say that Roma the daughter of the first Troian lady was married unto Latinus the son of Telemachus, by whom she had Romulus. Other write, that it was Aemilia, the daughter of Aeneas and of Lavinia, which was got with child by the god Mars. Others tell a tale of Romulus' birth, nothing true nor likely. For it is said that there was sometime a king of Alba named Tarchetius, a very wicked and cruel man, in whose house through the permission of the gods appeared such a like vision: that there rose up in the hearth of his chimney the form and fashion of a man's privy member, which continued there many days. And they say, that at that time there was in Thuscane an oracle of Thetis, from whom they brought unto this wicked King Tarchetius such an answer: that he should cause his daughter yet unmarried to have carnal company with the strange thing, for she should bear a son that should be famous for his valiancy, for strength of body, and his happy success wherein he should exceed all men of his time. Tarchetius told this oracle unto one of his daughters, and willed her to entertain this strange thing: but she disdaining to do it, sent one of her waiting women to undertake the entertainment. But Tarchetius was so mad at this,

that he caused them both to be taken to put them to death:
howbeit the goddess Vesta appeared to him in his sleep in the
night, and charged him he should not do it. Whereupon he did
command them to make him a piece of cloth in the prison, with
promise that they should be married when they had finished it.
These poor maids toiled at it all the live long day, but in the night
there came other (by Tarchetius' commandment) that did undo all
they had done the day before. In the meantime, this waiting
woman that was got with child by this strange thing, was delivered
of two goodly boys or twins: whom Tarchetius gave unto one
Teratius, with express commandment he should cast them away.
This Teratius carried them unto the bank of the river: thither
came a she-wolf and gave them suck, and certain birds that
brought little crumbs and put them in their mouths, until a
swineherd perceiving them, and wondering at the sight, did
boldly go to the children, and took them away with him. These
infants being thus preserved, after they were come to man's state,
did set upon Tarchetius and slew him. One Promathion an Italian
writer, delivereth this story thus.

3   But the report that carrieth best credit of all, and is allowed of
by many writers, cometh from Diocles Peparethian (whom Fabius
Pictor followeth in many things), who was the first that put forth
this story among the Grecians, and specially the chiefest points of
it. Though this matter be somewhat diversely taken, yet in effect
the story is thus. The right line and blood of the kings of Alba
descended from Aeneas, by succession from the father to the son,
and the kingdom fell in the end between two brethren, Numitor
and Amulius. They agreed by lot to make division between them,
whereof the one to have the kingdom, and the other all the gold,
silver, ready money, goods, and jewels brought from Troia.
Numitor by his lot chose the realm for his portion: Amulius having
all the gold and treasure in his hands, did find himself thereby the
stronger, and so did easily take his realm from him. And fearing lest
his brother's daughter might have children which one day might
thrust him out again, he made her a nun of the goddess Vesta, there
to pass her days in virginity, and never to be married (some call her
Rhea, other Sylvia, and other Ilia): nevertheless not long after she
was found with child, against the rule and profession of the vestal

nuns. So nothing had saved her from present death, but the
petition of Antho the daughter of King Amulius, who entreated
her father for her life: yet notwithstanding she was straitly locked
up, that nobody could see her, nor speak with her, lest she should
be brought abed without Amulius' knowledge. In the end she was
delivered of two fair boys and marvellous great twins: which made
Amulius more afraid than before. So he commanded one of his
men to take the two children, and to throw them away and destroy
them. Some say that this servants name was Faustulus: other think
it was he that brought them up. But whosoever he was, he that had
the charge to throw them away, put them in a trough, and went
towards the river with intention to throw them in. Howbeit he
found it risen so high, and running so swiftly, that he durst not
come near the water's side, and so they being in the trough, he laid
them on the bank. In the meantime the river, swelling still, and
overflowing the bank, in such sort that it came under the trough,
did gently lift up the trough, and carried it unto a great plain, called
at this present Cermanum, and in the old time Germanum (as I
take it) because the Romans called the brothers of father and
mother, *germani*.

4   Now there was near unto this place a wild fig tree which
they called Ruminalis, of the name of Romulus as the most part
thought: or else because the beasts feeding there were wont to
come under the same in the extreme heat of the day, and there did
ruminate, that is, chew their cud in the shadow: or perhaps
because that the two children did suck the teat of the wolf, which
the ancient Latins call *ruma*, and they at this day do yet call the
goddess on whom they cry out to give their children suck,
Rumilia. And in their sacrifices to her they use no wine, but offer
up milk and water mingled with honey. To these two children
lying there in this sort, they write, there came a she-wolf and gave
them suck: and a hitwaw also which did help to nourish and keep
them. These two beasts are thought to be consecrated to the god
Mars, and the Latins do singularly honour and reverence the
hitwaw. This did much help to give credit to the words of the
mother, who affirmed she was conceived of those two children by
the god Mars. Howbeit some think she was deceived in her
opinion: for Amulius that had her maidenhead, went to her all

armed, and perforce did ravish her. Other hold opinion that the
name of the nurse which gave the two children suck with her
breasts, gave occasion to common report to err much in this tale,
by reason of the double signification thereof. For the Latins do call
with one self name she-wolves *lupas*, and women that give their
bodies to all comers: as this nurse the wife of Faustulus (that
brought these children home to her house) did use to do. By her
right name she was called Acca Laurentia, unto whom the Romans
do sacrifice yet unto this day: and the priest of Mars doth offer
unto her, in the month of April, the shedding of wine and milk
accustomed at burials, and the feast itself is called Larentia.

5   It is true that they honour also another Larentia, for like
occasion. The clerk or sexton of Hercules' temple, not knowing
one day how to drive away the time, as it should seem, of a certain
liveliness and boldness did desire the god Hercules to play at dice
with him, with condition that if he did win, Hercules should be
bound to send him some good fortune, and if it were his luck to
lose, then he promised Hercules he would provide him a very
good supper, and would besides bring him a fair gentlewoman to
lie withal. The conditions of the play thus rehearsed, the sexton
first cast the dice for Hercules, and afterwards for himself. It fell out
that Hercules won, and the sexton meaning good faith, and
thinking it very meet to perform the bargain that himself had
made, prepared a good supper, and hired this Laurentia the
courtesan, which was very fair, but as yet of no great fame to come
to it. Thus having feasted her within the temple, and prepared a
bed ready there, after supper he locked her into the temple, as if
Hercules should have come indeed and lain with her. And it is said
for truth, that Hercules came thither and commanded her in the
morning she should go into the market place, and salute the first
man she met, and keep him ever for her friend. Which thing she
performed, and the first man she met was called Tarrutius, a man of
great years, and one that had gathered together marvellous wealth
and riches. He had no children at all, neither was he ever married.
He fell acquainted with this Laurentia, and loved her so dearly that,
shortly after chancing to die, he made her heir of all he had:
whereof she disposed afterwards by her last will and testament, the
best and greatest part unto the people of Rome. Moreover it is

reported also, that she now being grown to be famous and of great honour (as thought to be the leman of a god) did vanish away suddenly in the selfsame place, where the first Laurentia was buried. The place at this day is called Velabrum: because the river being overflown, they were oftentimes compelled to pass by boat to go to the market place, and they called this manner of ferrying over, *velatura*. Other say, that those tumblers and common players, which showed sundry games and pastimes to win the favour of the people, were wont to cover that passage over with canvas cloths and veils, by which they go from the market place to the lists or show place where they run their horses, beginning their race even at the place: and they call a veil in their tongue, *velum*. This is the cause why the second Laurentia is honoured at Rome.

6    Faustulus, chief neatherd to Amulius, took up the two children and nobody knew it, as some say: or as other report (and likest to be true), with the privity and knowledge of Numitor, Amulius' brother, who secretly furnished them with money that brought up the two young children. It is said also they were both conveyed unto the city of the Gabians, where they were brought up at school, and taught all other honest things, which they use to teach the sons and children of good and noble men. Further they say they were named Remus and Romulus, because they were found sucking on the teats of a wolf. Now the beauty of their bodies did presently show, beholding only but their stature and manner of their countenances, of what nature and lineage they were: and as they grew in years, their manly courage increased marvellously, so as they became stout and hardy men, in so much as they were never troubled or astonished at any danger that was offered them. Howbeit it appeared plainly that Romulus had more wit and understanding than his brother Remus. For in all things wherein they were to deal with their neighbours, either concerning hunting, or the bounds and limits of their pastures, it was easily discerned in him, that he was born to command, and not to obey. For this cause they were both exceedingly beloved of their companions, and of those which were their inferiors. As for the king's herdmen, they passed not much for them, saying that they were even like themselves; and so seemed not to care a pin for their anger or displeasure, but wholly gave themselves to all gentlemanly

exercises and trades, thinking to live idly and at ease without travail, was neither comely nor convenient: but to exercise and harden their bodies with hunting, running, pursuing murderers and thieves, and to help those which were oppressed with wrong and violence, should be credit and commendation to them. By reason whereof, in very short time they grew to great fame and renown.

7 And it fell out by chance there rose some strife and variance between the herdmen of Amulius and the herdmen of Numitor: in so much as those that were Numitor's carried away by force some cattle of the others. The other side would not bear that, but pursued fast after, and beating them well-favouredly, they made them take their legs, and brought back again the greatest part of the cattle they had carried away with them. Whereat Numitor stormed marvellously, but yet his men seemed to make but little account of it, and proposing revenge, they gathered about them a good company of vagabonds (that had neither home, nor resting place) and certain fugitive bondmen which they enticed ill-favouredly, encouraging them to steal away from their masters. Thus one day whilst Romulus was busy about some sacrifice (being a devout man and religious, and well given to serve the gods, and to learn to divine and tell beforehand what things should happen and come to pass), it happened the herdmen of Numitor to meet Remus very slenderly accompanied: so they fell upon him suddenly, blows were dealt roundly on both sides, and men were hurt on either part. Howbeit Numitor's men in the end proved the stronger part, and did take Remus by force, and carried him straight before Numitor, alleging many complaints and matters against him. Numitor durst not punish him of his own authority, because he feared his brother Amulius, who was somewhat terrible: but went unto him, and earnestly besought him to do him justice, and not to suffer him, being his own brother, to receive such injury of his men. There was not a man in the city of Alba, but did greatly mislike the injury done to Numitor: and spoke it openly, that he was no person to be offered such a wrong. In so much as Amulius, moved herewith, did deliver Remus into his hands, to punish him as he thought good. Whereupon Numitor carried him home with him. But when he had him in his

house, he began to consider better of him, with admiration how goodly a young man he was, how in height and strength of body he passed all the rest of his people: and perceiving in his face an assured constancy, and bold steadfast courage that yielded not, nor was abashed for any danger he saw toward him, and hearing also the report of his acts and manhood to be answerable to that he saw (being chiefly moved in mine opinion by some secret inspiration of the gods, which ordain the depth of great matters), began partly by conjecture, and partly by chance, to take a conceit of him.

So he asked him what he was, and who was his father and mother, speaking to him in a more gentle wise, and with a friendlier countenance than before, to make him the bolder to answer, and be of better hope. Remus boldly answered him: 'Truly I will not hide the truth from thee, for thou seemest to me more worthy to be king, than thy brother Amulius. For thou enquirest, and hearest first before thou condemnest: and he condemneth before he examine or hear the parties. Until now, we thought we had been the children of two of the king's servants, to wit of Faustulus and of Laurentia: I say we, because my brother and I are two twins. But seeing we are now falsely accused unto thee, and by malicious surmised tales are wrongfully brought in danger of our lives, we intend to discover ourselves, and to declare strange things unto thee, whereof the present peril we stand now in, shall plainly prove the truth. Men say that we have been begotten miraculously, fostered and given suck more strangely, and in our tender years were fed by birds and wild beasts, to whom we were cast out as a prey. For a wolf gave us suck with her teats, and an hitwaw (they say) brought us little crumbs, and put them in our mouths, as we lay upon the bank by the river, where we were put in a trough that at this day remaineth whole, bound about with plates of copper, upon the which are some letters engraven half worn out, which peradventure one day will serve for some tokens of knowledge (unprofitable for our parents) when it shall be too late, and after we are dead and gone.' Numitor then comparing these words with the age the young man seemed to be of, and considering well his face, did not reject the hope of his imagination that smiled on him, but handled the matter so, that he found means to speak secretly with his daughter, notwithstanding at that time she was kept very straitly.

8    Faustulus in the meantime hearing that Remus was prisoner, and that the king had delivered him already into the hands of his brother Numitor to do justice, went to pray Romulus to help him, and told him then whose children they were: for before he had never opened it to them but in dark speeches, and glancingwise, and so much as sufficed to put them in some hope. So Faustulus taking the trough with him at that time, went unto Numitor in great haste, as marvellously afraid for the present danger he thought Remus in. The king's soldiers which warded at the gates of the city: began to gather some suspicion of Faustulus' manner of coming: and he made himself to be the more suspected, being questioned with about the cause of his repair thither, that he faltered in his words: besides, they espied his trough which he carried under his cloak. Now amongst the warders, there was by chance one that was the man to whom the children were committed to be cast away, and was present when they were left on the bank of the river to the mercy of fortune. This man knew the trough by and by, as well by the fashion, as by the letters graven upon it: who mistrusted straight that which was true indeed. So he did not neglect the thing, but went forthwith to the king to tell him the matter, and led Faustulus with him to have him confess the truth. Faustulus being in this perplexity, could not keep all close upon examination, but did utter out somewhat of the matter, and yet he told not all. For he plainly justified the children were alive: yet he said they were far from the city of Alba, where they kept beasts in the fields. And as for the trough, he was going to carry it to Ilia, because she had divers times prayed him to let her see and feel it: to the end she might be the more assured of her hope, who promised her that one day she should see her children again. So it chanced unto Amulius at that time, as it commonly doth unto those that are troubled and do anything in fear or anger, as a man amazed thereat, to send one presently (who in all other things was a very honest man, but a great friend of his brother Numitor's) to ask him if he had heard anything that his daughter's children were alive. This person being come to Numitor's house, found him ready to embrace Remus, who fell to be witness thereof, and of the good hap discovered unto Numitor: whereupon he persuaded him how to set upon his brother, and to dispatch the matter with speed. So from that time forwards, he took their part. On the

other side also the matter gave them no leisure to defer their enterprise, although they had been willing: for the whole case was somewhat blown abroad. So Romulus then got straight a power, and drew very near the city, and many of the citizens of Alba went out to join with him, who either feared or hated Amulius. Now Romulus' power which he brought (over and besides those citizens) was a good number of fighting men, and they were divided by hundreds, and every hundred had his captain who marched before his band, carrying little bundles of grass or of boughs tied to the end of their poles. The Latins call these bundles *manipulos*, whereof it cometh that yet at this day in an army of the Romans, the soldiers which are all under one ensign, are called *manipulares*. So Remus stirring up those that were within the city, and Romulus bringing in men from without, the tyrant Amulius fell in such fear and agony, that without providing anything for his safety, they came upon him suddenly in his palace, and slew him. Thus you hear how near Fabius Pictor and Diocles Peparethian do agree in reciting the story, who was the first in mine opinion that wrote the foundation of the city of Rome: howbeit there are that think they are all but fables and tales devised of pleasure. But methinks for all that, they are not altogether to be rejected or discredited, if we will consider fortune's strange effects upon times, and of the greatness also of the Roman empire, which had never achieved to her present possessed power and authority, if the gods had not from the beginning been workers of the same, and if there had not also been some strange cause, and wonderful foundation.

9   Amulius being now slain as before, and after that all things were appeased, and reduced to good order again, Remus and Romulus would not dwell in the city of Alba, being no lords thereof, nor also would be lords of it, so long as their grandfather by the mother's side was alive. Wherefore after they had restored him to his estate, and had done the honour and duty they ought unto their mother, they purposed to go and build a city in those places where they had been first brought up, for this was the honestest colour they could pretend for their departing from Alba. Peradventure they were enforced so to do whether they would or not, for the great number of banished men and fugitive slaves which were gathered together by them for their strength, who had been utterly lost and cast away,

if they had been once discharged by them. Therefore it was of necessity that they should dwell by themselves, separated in some place, to keep this number together and in some order. For it is true that the inhabitants of the city of Alba would not suffer such banished persons and runagates to be mingled amongst them, nor would receive them into their city to be free among them. All which appeareth sufficiently: first, because they took away women by force, and so not of insolency, but of necessity, when they found no man that would bestow any of them. It is manifest also they did greatly honour and make much of the women they had taken away before. Furthermore when their city began a little to be settled, they made a temple of refuge for all fugitives and afflicted persons, which they called the temple of the god Asylaeus, where there was sanctuary and safety for all sorts of people that repaired thither, and could get into the temple, for whom it was alleged they could not deliver any bondman to his master, nor debtor to his creditor, nor murderer to the justice that was fled thither for succour, because the oracle of Apollo the Delphian had expressly enjoined them to grant sanctuary to all those that would come thither for it. So by this means in short space their city flourished, and was replenished, where at the first foundation of it they say there was not above one thousand houses, as more at large hereafter shall be declared. When they came now to the building of their city, Romulus and Remus the two brethren fell suddenly at a strife together about the place where the city should be builded. For Romulus built Rome, which is called four square, and would needs it should remain in the place which he had chosen. Remus his brother chose another place very strong of situation, upon mount Aventine, which was called after his name Remonium, and now is called Rignarium. Notwithstanding, in the end they agreed between themselves this controversy should be decided by the flying of birds, which do give a happy divination of things to come. So being set in divers places by themselves to make observation, some say that there appeared unto Remus six, and to Romulus twelve, vultures. Others say that Remus truly saw six, and Romulus feigned from the beginning that he saw twice as many: but when Remus came to him, then there appeared twelve indeed unto Romulus, and this is the cause why the Romans at this day in their divinations and soothsayings of the flying of birds, do marvellously observe the flying of the vultures. It is true which the historiographer Herodorus Ponticus writeth: that Hercules rejoiced much when there appeared a vulture to him, being ready to begin any enterprise. For it is the fowl of the world that doth least hurt, and never marreth nor destroyeth anything that man doth sow, plant, or set: considering that she feedeth on carrion only, and doth never hurt nor kill any living thing. Also she doth not prey upon dead fowl, for the likeness that is between them: where the eagles, the dukes and the sakers do murder, kill, and eat those which are of their own kind. And yet as Aeschylus sayeth:

> Needs must that fowl accounted be most vile,
>   Most ravening, and full of filthy mind,
> Which doth himself continually defile,
>   By preying still upon his proper kind.

Moreover, other birds are always (as a man would say) before our eyes, and do daily show themselves unto us: where the vulture is a very rare bird, and hardly to be seen, and men do not easily find their eyries. Which has given some occasion to hold a false opinion, that the vultures are passagers, and come into these parts out of strange countries. The prognosticators also think, that such things which are not ordinary, and but seldom seen, be not natural, but miraculously sent by the gods to prognosticate something.

10    When Remus knew how his brother had mocked him, he was very angry with him. And when Romulus had cast a ditch, as it were for the wall about his city, Remus did not only scorn it, but hindered also his work, and in the end for a mockery leapt over his wall. To conclude, he did so much, that at the last he was slain there by Romulus' own hands as some say: or as others hold opinion, by the hands of one of his men which was called Celer. In this fight they slew Faustulus, and Plistinus also his brother, who had helped him to bring up Romulus. Howsoever the matter fell out, this Celer absented himself from Rome, and went into the country of Thuscane. And they say, that men which are quick, and ready upon a sudden, took their names ever after upon him, and were called Celeres. As amongst other, Quintus Metellus, after the death of his father, having in very few days made the people of Rome to see a combat of fencers (called Gladiators) fighting at the sharp, they surnamed him Celer, for that the Romans marvelled how he could prepare his things in so short a time.

11    Furthermore, Romulus, having now buried his brother, and his other two bringers up (called foster-fathers) in the place they call Remonia, began then to build and lay the foundation of his city, sending for men out of Thuscane, who did name and teach him particularly all the ceremonies he had to observe there, according to their laws and ordinances as a great holy mystery. And first of all they made a round ditch in the place called at this day Comitium, into which they did cast their chiefest and best things, which men use lawfully for good, and naturally as most necessary. After that they did throw also into it a little of the earth, from whence every man came, and mingled these all together. This ditch in their ceremonies is called the world, in Latin *mundus*, even the selfsame name the Latins call the universal. About this ditch they did trace the compass of the city they would build, even as one would draw a circle about a centre. This done, the founder of the city taketh a plough, to which he fastened a coulter or ploughshare of brass, and so yoked in the plough an ox and a cow; he himself holding the plough did make round about the compass of the city a deep furrow. Those which followed him, had the charge to throw the turfs of earth inward into the city, which the ploughshare raised up, and not to leave any of them turned outward. The furrow thus cast up was the whole compass of their wall, which they call in Latin p*omoerium*, by shortening of the syllables, for *post murum*: to wit, 'after wall'. But in the place where they determined to make a gate, they did take off the ploughshare, and draw the plough, with leaving a certain space of earth unbroken-up: whereupon the Romans think all the compass of their walls holy and sacred, except their gates. For if their gates had been hallowed and sanctified, they would have had a conscience through them to have brought in, or carried out of the city, anything necessary for the life of man, that had not been pure and clean.

12    Now they believe certainly, that this ceremony of the foundation of their city was made the one and twenty of April: because the Romans do yet keep that day holy day, and call it the feast of the nativity of their country. On which day they did not in old time sacrifice anything that had life, as esteeming that day (which was the nativity of their city) to be most meet to be kept clean and pure from being polluted or defiled with any blood. Notwith-

standing before Rome was builded, they had another feast called the shepherds or herdmen's holy day, which they did celebrate upon the same day, and called it Palilia. Now at this day the beginnings of the months with the Romans is clean contrary to the Grecians: yet for all this, they hold opinion for certainty that the day on which Romulus founded his city, was assuredly that which the Grecians call Triacada: that is to say, the thirty day. On which there was seen an eclipse of the moon, which they suppose was observed by the poet Antimachus (born in the city of Teos) in the thirteenth year of the sixth Olympiad. Likewise in the time of Marcus Varro (as a man learned, and one that had read as much of ancient stories as any Roman) there was a friend of his called Tarutius, a great philosopher and mathematician. Who being given to the calculation of astronomy for the delight of speculation only, wherein he was thought most excellent, it did fall out that Varro gave him this question, to search out what hour and day the nativity of Romulus was: who gathered it out by certain accidents, as they do in the resolutions of certain geometrical questions. For they say, that by the selfsame science, one may tell before of things to come, and to happen to a man in his life, knowing certainly the hour of his nativity: and how one may tell also the hour of his nativity, when by accidents they know what has happened to him all his life. Tarutius did the question that Varro gave him. And having thoroughly considered the adventures, deeds, and gestes of Romulus, how long he lived, and how he died: all which being gathered and conferred together, he did boldly judge for a certainty, that he was conceived in his mother's womb in the first year of the second Olympiad, the three and twenty day of the month which the Egyptians call Chaeac, and now is called December, about three of the clock in the morning, in which hour there was a whole eclipse of the sun; and that he was born into the world, the one and twentieth of the month of Thoth, which is the month of September, about the rising of the sun. And that Rome was begun by him on the ninth day of the month which the Egyptians call Pharmuthi, and answereth now to the month of April, between two and three of the clock in the morning. For they will say that a city hath his revolution and his time of continuance appointed, as well as the life of a man: and that they knew by the situation of the stars, the day of her beginning and foundation. These things and

such other like, peradventure will please the readers better for their
strangeness and curiosity, than offend or mislike them for their
falsehood.

13   Now after he had founded his city, he first and foremost did
divide in two companies, all those that were of age to carry armour.
In every one of these companies there were three thousand footmen, and three hundred horsemen: and they were called Legions,
because they were sorted of the chosen men that were picked out
amongst all the rest for to fight. The remain after these was called
Populus, which signifieth the people. After this, he made a hundred
counsellors of the best and honestest men of the city, which he
called patricians: and the whole company of them together he
called Senatus, as one would say, the council of the ancients. So
they were called patricians, as some will say, the council of the
fathers' lawful children, which few of the first inhabitants could
show. It may be, some will say this name was given them of
Patrocinium, as growing of the protection they had by the sanctuary of their city, which word they use at this day in the selfsame
signification: as one that followed Evander into Italy was called
Patron, because he was pitiful, and relieved the poor and little
children, and so got himself a name for his pity and humanity. But
methinks it were more like the truth to say, that Romulus did call
them so, because he thought the chiefest men should have a fatherly
care of the meaner sort: considering also it was to teach the meaner
sort that they should not fear the authority of the greater, nor envy
at their honours they had, but rather in all their causes should use
their favour and goodwill, by taking them as their fathers. For even
at this present, strangers call those of the senate, lords or captains:
but the natural Romans call them, Patres Conscripti, which is a
name of fatherhood and dignity without envy. It is true that at the
beginning they were only called Patres, but since, because they
were many joined unto the first, they have been named Patres
Conscripti, as a man should say, fathers of record together: which is
the honourablest name he could have devised to make a difference
betwixt the senators and the people. Furthermore, he made a
difference between the chiefer citizens and the baser people, by
calling the better sort Patroni, as much to say, as defenders: and the
meaner sort Clientes, as you would say, followers, or men pro-

tected. This did breed a marvellous great love and goodwill among them, making the one much beholding to the other, by many mutual courtesies and pleasures: for the patrons did help the clients to their right, defended their causes in judgment, did give unto them counsel, and did take all their matters in hand. The clients again interchangeably humbled themselves to their patrons, not only in outward honour and reverence towards them, but otherwise did help them with money to marry and advance their daughters, or else to pay their debts and credit, if they were poor or decayed. There was no law nor magistrate that could compel the patron to be a witness against his client: nor yet the client to witness against his patron. So they increased, and continued all other rights and offices of amity and friendship together, saving afterwards they thought it a great shame and reproach for the better and richer to take reward of the meaner and poor. And thus of this matter we have spoken sufficiently.

14    Moreover, four months after the foundation of the city was laid, Fabius writeth, there was a great ravishment of women. There are some which lay it upon Romulus, who being then of nature warlike, and given to prophecies and answers of the gods, foretold that his city should become very great and mighty, so as he raised it by wars, and increased it by arms: and he sought out this colour to do mischief, and to make war upon the Sabynes. To prove this true, some say he caused certain of their maids by force to be taken away, but not past thirty in number, as one that rather sought cause of wars, than did it for need of marriages: which methinks was not likely to be true, but rather I judge the contrary. For seeing his city was incontinently replenished with people of all sorts, whereof there were very few that had wives, and that they were men gathered out of all countries, and the most part of them poor and needy, so as their neighbours disdained them much, and did not look they would long dwell together, Romulus hoping by this violent taking of their maids and ravishing them, to have an entry into alliance with the Sabynes, and to entice them further to join with them in marriage, if they did gently entreat these wives they had got, enterprised this violent taking of their maids, and ravishing of them in such a sort. First he made it to be commonly bruited abroad in every place, that he had found the altar of a god

hidden in the ground, and he called the name of the god, Consus:
either because he was a god of counsel, whereupon the Romans at
this day in their tongue call *consilium*, which we call counsel; and
the chief magistrates of their city Consules, as we say counsellors.
Other say it was the altar of the god Neptune, surnamed the
patron of horses. For this altar is yet at this day within the great lists
of the city, and ever covered and hidden, but when they use the
running games of their horse race. Other say because counsel ever
must be kept close and secret, they had good reason to keep the
altar of this god Consus hidden in the ground. Now other write
when it was opened, Romulus made a sacrifice of wonderful joy,
and afterwards proclaimed it openly in divers places, that at such a
day there should be common plays in Rome, and a solemn feast
kept of the god Consus, where all that were disposed to come
should be welcome. Great numbers of people repaired thither
from all parts. He himself was set in the chiefest seat of the show
place, apparelled fair in purple, and accompanied with the chief of
his city about him. And there having purposed this ravishment
you have heard of, he had given the sign before: that the same
should begin, when he should rise up and fold a pleat of his gown,
and unfold the same again. Hereupon his men stood attending
with their swords: who so soon as they perceived the sign was
given, with their swords drawn in hand, and with great shouts and
cries ran violently on the maids and daughters of the Sabynes to
take them away and ravish them, and suffered the men to run
away, without doing them any hurt or violence. So some say,
there were but thirty ravished, after whose names were called the
thirty lineages of the people of Rome. Howbeit Valerius Antias
writeth, that there were five hundred and seven and twenty: and
Iuba, six hundred four score and three. In the which is singularly
to be noted for the commendation of Romulus, that he himself did
take then but only one of the maids, named Hersilia, that afterwards was the only cause and mediation of peace betwixt the
Sabynes and the Romans. Which argueth plainly, that it was not to
do the Sabynes any hurt, nor to satisfy any disordinate lust, that
they had so forcibly undertaken this ravishment: but to join two
peoples together, with the straitest bonds that could be between
men. This Hersilia, as some say, was married unto one Hostilius,
the noblest man at that time amongst the Romans: or as others

write, unto Romulus himself, which had two children by her. The first was a daughter, and her name was Prima, because she was the first: the other was a son, whom he named Aollius, because of the multitude of people he had assembled together in his city, and afterwards he was surnamed Abillius. Thus Zenodotus the Troezenian writeth, wherein notwithstanding there be divers that do contrary him.

15    Among those which ravished then the daughters of the Sabynes, it is said there were found certain mean men carrying away a marvellous passing fair one. These met by chance on the way certain of the chief of the city, who would have taken her by force from them, which they had done, but that they began to cry they carried her unto Talassius, who was a young man marvellously well beloved of everybody. Which when the others understood, they were exceeding glad, and they commended them: in so much as there were some which suddenly turned back again, and did accompany them for Talassius' sake, crying out aloud and often on his name. From whence the custom came, which to this day the Romans sing at their marriages, 'Talassius', like as the Grecians sing 'Hymeneus'. For it is said he was counted very happy that he met with this woman. But Sextius Sylla, a Carthaginian born, a man very wise and well learned, told me once it was the cry and sign which Romulus gave to his men, to begin the ravishment: whereupon those which carried them away went crying this word 'Talassius', and that from thence the custom has continued, that they sing it yet at their marriages. Nevertheless the most part of authors, specially Iuba, thinks it is a warning to remember the new-married women of their work, which is to spin, which the Grecians call 'talassia', the Italian words at that time being not mingled with the Greek. And if it be true the Romans used this term of 'talassia', as we of Greece do use, we might by conjecture yield another reason for it, which should carry a better likelihood and proof. For when the Sabynes after the battle had made peace with the Romans, they put in an article in favour of the women in the treaty, that they should not be bound to serve their husbands in any other work, but in spinning of wool. Ever since this custom hath grown, that those which give their daughters in marriage, and those who lead the bride, and such as are present at the wedding,

speak in sport to the new-married wife, laughing, 'Talassius': in
token that they do not lead the bride for any other work or service,
but to spin wool. Thereof this hath been the use to this day, that the
bride doth not of herself come over the threshold of her husband's
door, but she is hoist prettily into the house: because the Sabyne
women at that time were so lift up, and carried away by force.
They say also, that the manner of making the shed of the new-
wedded wives' hair, with the iron head of a javelin, came up then
likewise: this story being a manifest token that these first marriages
were made by force of arms, and as it were at the sword's point, as
we have written more at large in the book wherein we render and
show the causes of the Romans' fashions and customs. This
ravishment was put in execution about the eighteenth day of the
month then called Sextilis, and now named August: on which day
they yet celebrate the feast they call Consalia.

16  Now the Sabynes were good men of war, and had great
numbers of people, but they dwelt in villages, and not within
enclosed walls: being a thing fit for their noble courages that did
fear nothing, and as those who were descended from the
Lacedaemonians. Nevertheless, they seeing themselves bound and
tied to peace by pledges and hostages that were very near allied
unto them, and fearing their daughters should be ill entreated, sent
ambassadors to Romulus, by whom they made reasonable offers
and persuasions, that their daughters might be delivered unto
them again, without any force or violence, and then afterwards,
that he would cause them to be asked in marriage of their parents,
as both reason and law would require: to the end that with
goodwill and consent of all parties, both peoples might contract
amity and alliance together. Whereunto Romulus made answer,
he could not restore the maids which his people had taken away
and married: but most friendly he prayed the Sabynes to be
contented with their alliance. This answer being returned, and not
liked, whilst the princes and commonalty of the Sabynes were
occupied in consultation, and about the arming of themselves,
Acron king of the Ceninenses (a man exceeding courageous and
skilful in the wars, and one that from the beginning mistrusted the
overbold and stout enterprises that Romulus was likely to attempt,
considering the late ravishment of the Sabynes' daughters, and

how he was already greatly dreaded of his neighbours, and some-what untolerable, if he were not chastised and brought lower) first began to invade him with a puissant army, and to make hot and violent wars upon him. Romulus on the other side prepared also, and went forth to meet him. When they were come so near together that they might see one another, they sent defiance to each other, and prayed that they two might fight man-to-man amidst their armies, and neither of theirs to stir a foot. Both of them accepted of it, and Romulus making his prayer unto Jupiter, did promise, and made a vow that if he did give him the victory to overcome, he would offer up to him the armour of his enemy, which he did. For first he slew Acron in the field, and afterwards gave battle to his men, and overthrew them also. Lastly he took his city, where he did no hurt nor yet displeasure to any, saving that he did command them to pull down their houses, and destroy them, and to go dwell with him at Rome: where they should have the selfsame rights and privileges which the first inhabitants did enjoy. There was nothing more enlarged the city of Rome, than this manner of policy, to join always unto it those she had overcome and vanquished. Romulus now to discharge his vow, and in such sort that his offering might be acceptable to Jupiter, and pleasant to his citizens to behold, did cut down a goodly straight grown young oak, which he lighted on by good fortune, in the place where his camp did lie. The same he trimmed and did set forth after the manner of victory, hanging and tying all about it in fair order the armour and weapons of King Acron. Then he girding his gown to him, and putting upon his long bush of hair a garland of laurel, laid the young oak upon his right shoulder, and he first marched before towards his city, and sung a royal song of victory, all his army following him in arms unto the city in order of battle: where his citizens received him in all passing wise and triumph. This noble and stately entry ever since has given them minds in such sort, and in statelier wise, to make their triumph. The offering of this triumph was dedicated to Jupiter surnamed Feretrian: because the Latin word *ferire* signifieth to hurt and kill: and the prayer Romulus had made was, he might hurt and kill his enemy. Such spoils are called in Latin, *spolia opima*: therefore sayeth Varro, that *opes* signify riches. Howbeit methinks it were more likely to say, that they were so named of this word *opus*,

which betokeneth a deed, because he must needs be the chief of
the army, that hath slain with his own hands the general of his
enemies, and that must offer the spoils called *spolia opima*, as you
would say, his principal spoils and deeds. This never happened yet
but to three Roman captains only: of the which Romulus was the
first, who slew Acron, king of the Ceninenses. Cornelius Cossus
was the second, who killed Tolumnius, the general of the
Thuscans. Clodius Marcellus was the third, who slew Britomartus,
king of the Gauls, with his own hands. And for the two last,
Cossus and Marcellus, they made their entry into the city, carrying
their triumphs upon chariots triumphant: but Romulus did not so.
Therefore in this point Dionysius the historiographer has erred,
writing that Romulus did enter into Rome upon a chariot triumphant. For it was Tarquinius Priscus the son of Demaratus, who
first did set out triumphs in so stately and magnificent show.
Other hold opinion it was Valerius Publicola, who was the first
that ever entered upon triumphant chariot. Concerning Romulus,
his statues are yet to be seen in Rome, carrying his triumph afoot.

17 After this overthrow and taking of the Ceninenses, the
inhabitants of the cities of Fidena, Crustumerium, and Antemna,
rose altogether against the Romans, whiles the other Sabynes also
were a-preparing themselves. So they fought a battle, in which
they took the overthrow: and left their cities to the spoil of
Romulus, their lands to be given where he thought good, and
themselves to be carried to Rome. Romulus then did give their
lands among his citizens, except those lands which did belong to
the fathers of the maidens that they had taken away and ravished.
For he was contented that the fathers of them should keep still
their lands. By and by the other Sabynes stomaching thereat, did
choose them a general called Tatius, and so went with a puissant
army toward the city of Rome, whereunto to approach at that
time it was very hard, the castle or keep of their city being seated,
where at this day the Capitol standeth, within which there was a
great garrison, whereof Tarpeius was captain, and not his daughter
Tarpeia, as some will say, who set out Romulus as a fool. But
Tarpeia the captain's daughter, for the desire she had to have all
the gold bracelets which they did wear about their arms, sold the
fort to the Sabynes, and asked for reward of her treason, all they

did wear on their left arms. Tatius promised them unto her: and she opened them a gate in the night, by the which she did let all the Sabynes into the castle. Antigonus then was not alone, who said, he loved those which did betray, and hated them that had betrayed: nor yet Caesar Augustus, who told Rymitalces the Thracian, that he loved treason, but he hated traitors. And it is a common affection which we bear to wicked persons, whilst we stand in need of them: not unlike for all the world to those which have need of the gall and poison of venomous beasts. For when they find it, they are glad, and take it to serve their turn: but after their turn is served, and they have that they sought, they hate the cruelty of such beasts. So played Tatius at that time. For when he was got into the castle, he commanded the Sabynes (for performance of his promise he had made to Tarpeia) they should not stick to give her all they wear on their left arms, and to do as he did: who taking from his own arm first the bracelet which he ware, did cast it to her, and his target after. And so did all the rest in like sort, in so much as being borne down to the ground by the weight of bracelets and targets, she died as pressed to death under her burden. Nevertheless Tarpeius self was attainted, and condemned also of treason, by Romulus' order, as Iuba sayeth it is set forth by Sulpitius Galba. They that write now otherwise of Tarpeia, saying she was the daughter of Tatius, general of the Sabynes, and was forced by Romulus to lie with him, and how she was punished in this sort by her own father after her said treason committed: those I say, amongst whom Antigonus is one, are not to be credited. And the poet Simylus also doth dote most, who sayeth Tarpeia sold the Capitol not to the Sabynes, but to the king of Gauls, with whom she was in love: as in these verses doth appear.

> Tarpeia, that maid of foolish mind,
>     Which near unto the Capitol did dwell
> (In fervent flames of beastly love beblind,
>     Wherewith the king of Gauls did make her swell)
> Caused stately Rome surprised for to be
>     By enemies, as every man may see.
> And so through hope of his fidelity
>     Betrayed her sire, with all his family.

And a little after, in speaking of the manner of her death, he sayeth also:

Yet lo: the Gauls, those worthy men of might,
   Threw her not down into the waves of Po,
But from their arms, wherewith they wont to fight
   They cast their shields upon her body so,
That she suppressed with such an heavy weight
   (Ah woeful maid) to death was smothered straight.

18   This maiden therefore being buried in the same place, the whole hill was called afterwards Tarpeius after her name, which continued until Tarquinius the king did dedicate all the place to Jupiter: for then they carried her bones into some other place, and so it lost her name. Unless it be that rock of the Capitol, which at this present time they call Rupes Tarpeia, from the top whereof they were wont in old time to throw down headlong all wicked offenders. When the Sabynes now had got this hold, Romulus being exceeding wroth, sent them a defiance, and bade them battle if they durst. Tatius straight refused not, considering if by mischance they were distressed, they had a sure refuge to retire unto. The place between the two armies where the fight should be, was all round about environed with little hills, so as it was plain the fight could not be but sharp and dangerous, for the discommodiousness of the place where was neither ground for any to fly, nor yet any space for any long chase, it was of so small a compass. Now it fortuned by chance, the river of Tyber had overflown the banks a few days before, and there remained in it a deeper mud than men would have judged, because the ground was so plain, and was even where the great market place of Rome standeth at this day. They could discern nothing thereof by the eye, because the upper part of it was crusted, whereby it was the more ready for them to venture upon, and the worse to get out, for that it did sink underneath. So the Sabynes had gone upon it, had not Curtius danger seen, which by good fortune stayed them. He was one of the noblest and valiantest men of the Sabynes, who being mounted upon a courser, went on a good way before the army. This courser entering upon the crusted mud, and sinking withal, began to plunge and struggle in the mire: whereat Curtius proved a while with the spur to stir him, and get him out, but in the end seeing it would not be, he left his back, and saved himself. The same very place to this day is called after his name, Lacus Curtius. The Sabynes then escaping thus this danger, began

the battle. The fight did grow very cruel, and endured so a great while, the victory leaning no more to the one side than to the other. There died in a small space a great number of men, amongst whom Hostilius was one, who as they say was the husband of Hersilia, and grandfather to Hostilius that was king of Romans after Numa Pompilius. Afterwards there were (as we may think) many other encounters and battles between them: howbeit they make mention of the last above all the rest, wherein Romulus had so sore a blow on his head with a stone, that he was almost felled to the ground, in so much as he was driven to retire a little out of the battle. Upon which occasion the Romans gave back also, and drew towards mount Palatine, being driven out of the plain by force. Romulus began now to recover of the blow he had received, and so returned to give a new onset, and cried out all he might to his soldiers to tarry, and show their face again to their enemy. But for all his loud crying, they left no flying still for life, and there was not one that durst return again. Whereupon Romulus lifting up his hands straight to heaven, did most fervently pray unto Jupiter, that it would please him to stay the flying of his people, and not suffer the Romans' glory thus to fall to their utter destruction, but to repair it by his favour again. He had no sooner ended this prayer, but divers of his men that fled, began to be ashamed to fly before their king, and a sudden boldness came upon them, and their fear therewithal vanished away. The place they first stayed in was where as now is the temple of Jupiter Stator, which is as much to say, as Jupiter the stayer. Afterwards gathering themselves together again, they repulsed the Sabynes even to the place they call now Regia, and unto the temple of the goddess Vesta: where both the battles being prepared to give a new charge, there did fall out before them, a strange and an incredible thing to see, which stayed them they fought not.

19   For of the Sabyne women whom the Romans had ravished, some ran of the one side, other of the other side of the battles, with lamentations, cries, and shouts, stepping between their weapons, and among the slain bodies on the ground, in such sort that they seemed out of their wits, and carried as it were with some spirits. In this manner they went to find out their fathers and their husbands, some carrying their sucking babes in their arms, others having their hair loose about their eyes, and all of them calling,

now upon the Sabynes, now upon the Romans, with the gentlest
names that could be devised: which did melt the hearts of both
parties in such sort, that they gave back a little, and made them
place between both the battles. Then were the cries and lamentations of everyone plainly heard. There was not a man there but it
pitied him, as well to see them in that pitiful case as to hear the
lamentable words they spoke: adding to their most humble petitions and requests that could be any way imagined, passing wise
persuasions and reasons to induce them to a peace. 'For what
offence,' said they, 'or what displeasure have we done to you, that
we should deserve such an heap of evils, as we have already
suffered, and yet you make us bear? We were, as you know,
violently (and against all law) ravished by those whose now we
remain. But our fathers, our brethren, our mothers and friends
have left us with them so long, that process of time, and the straitest
bonds of the world, have tied us now so fast to them, whom
mortally before we hated, that we are constrained now to be
slighted thus, to see them fight, yea and to lament and die with
them, who before unjustly took us from you. For then you came
not to our rescue when we were virgins untouched, nor to recover
us from them when they wickedly assaulted us, poor souls: but
now ye come to take the wives from their husbands, and the
mothers from their little children. So as the help ye think to give us
now doth grieve us more, than the forsaking of us was sorrowful to
us then. Such is the love they have borne unto us, and such is the
kindness we bear again to them. Now, if ye did fight for any other
cause than for us, yet were it reason ye should let fall your arms for
our sakes (by whom you are made grandfathers and fathers-in-law,
cousins and brothers-in-law) even from those against whom you
now bend your force. But if all this war began for us, we heartily
beseech you then that you will receive us with your sons-in-law,
and your sons by them, and that you will restore unto us our
fathers, our brethren, our kinsfolks and friends, without spoiling us
of our husbands, of our children, and of our joys, and thereby make
us woeful captives and prisoners in our minds.' These requests and
persuasions by Hersilia and other the Sabyne women being heard,
both the armies stayed, and held everybody his hand, and straight
the two generals imparled together. During which parle they
brought their husbands and their children to their fathers and their

brethren. They brought meat and drink for them that would eat. They dressed up the wounds of those that were hurt. They carried them home with them to their houses. They showed them how they were mistresses there with their husbands. They made them see how greatly they were accounted of and esteemed: yea how with a wedlock love and reputation they were honoured. So in the end peace was concluded between them, wherein it was articled, that the Sabyne women which would remain with their husbands should tarry still, and be exempted from all work or service (as above recited) save only spinning of wool. And that the Sabynes and Romans should dwell together in the city, which should be called Roma, after Romulus' name: and the inhabitants should be called Quirites, after the name of the city of Tatius king of the Sabynes, and that they should reign and govern together by a common consent. The place where this peace was concluded, is called yet to this day Comitium: because that *coire*, in the Latin tongue, signifieth 'to assemble'.

20    So the city being augmented by the one half, they did choose of the Sabynes another hundred new patricians, unto the first hundred of the Romans that were chosen before. Then were the Legions made of six thousand footmen, and six hundred horsemen. After, they divided their inhabitants into three Tribes, whereof those that came of Romulus were called Ramnenses after his name; those that came of Tatius were called Tatienses after his name; and those that were of the third stock, were called Lucerenses, as from the Latin word *lucus*, called with us a grove in English, because thither great number of people of all sorts did gather, which afterwards were made citizens of Rome. The very word of *tribus* (which signifieth bands, wards, or hundreds) doth witness this beginning of Rome from wards, or hundreds. For hereupon the Romans call those at this day their tribunes, which are the chief heads of the people. But every one of these principal wards had afterwards ten other particular wards under them, which some think were called after the names of the thirty Sabyne women that were ravished: but that seemeth false, because many of them carry the names of the places they came from. Howbeit at that time many things were established and ordained in honour of women: as to give them place, the upper hand in meeting them, the upper

hand in streets; to speak no foul or dishonest word before them, no
man to unray himself, or show naked before them; that they should
not be called before criminal judges sitting upon homicides and
murderers; that their children should wear about their necks a kind
of a jewel called *bulla*, fashioned in manner like these water bubbles
that rise upon the water when it beginneth to rain: and that their
gowns should be garded with purple. Now the two kings did not
straight confer together so soon as any occasion of business was
offered them, but either of them did first counsel alone with his
hundred senators, and afterwards they did all assemble together.
Tatius dwelt in the place where now is the temple of Iuno Moneta:
Romulus in the place called at this present, the stairs of the fair
bank, then the descent of mount Palatine, as they go to the show
place or great lists, where they say was sometime the holy cornell
tree, whereof they make so great account. Romulus one day
desirous to prove his strength, threw (as it is said) a dart from
mount Aventine toward mount Palatine. The staff whereof was of
a cornell tree, and the iron of it entered so deep into the ground,
being a lusty fat soil, that no man could pull it out, although many
proved it, and did the best they could. The ground being very
good and fit to bring forth trees, did so nourish the end of this staff,
that it took root, and began to spread branches: so that in time it
became a fair great cornell tree, which the successors of Romulus
did enclose with a wall, and did keep and worship it as a very holy
thing. If by chance any went to see it, and found it looked not fresh
and green, but like a tree withered and dried away for lack of
moisture, he went away straight as one afraid, crying to all he met
(and they with him went crying still) in every place, 'water, water',
as it had been to have quenched a fire. Then ran they thither out of
all quarters with vessels of water, to water and moist the tree. In the
time of Caius Caesar, who caused the stairs about it to be repaired,
they say the labourers rasing the place, and digging about this
cornell tree, did by negligence hurt the roots of the same in such
sort, as afterwards it dried up altogether.

21  Now the Sabynes received the months after the manner of the
Romans, whereof we have written sufficiently in the life of Numa.
Romulus again used the Sabynes' shields, and both he and his
people changed the fashion of their armour and weapons they

used. For the Romans before did carry little shields after the fashion of the Argives. As for either of their holy days and sacrifices, they kept them both together, and did not take away any of them, which either the one or the other people observed before, but they added thereunto some other new. As that which they call Matronalia, which was instituted in honour of the women, because by their means peace was concluded. And that also of Carmentalia, in the honour of Carmenta, whom some suppose to be the goddess of fate or destiny, because she has rule and power over the nativities of men, by reason whereof the mothers call upon her often, and reverence her very much. Other say she was the wife of Evander the Arcadian, who being a prophetess inspired by the god Phoebus, gave the oracles in verse, whereupon she was surnamed Carmenta, because that *carmina* in Latin signify verses: for it is of certainty that her proper name was Nicostrata. Howbeit there are some which give another manner of derivation and interpretation of this word Carmenta, which is the likelier to be true: as if they would say, *carens mente*: which signifieth 'wanting wit', for the very fury that taketh them when they are inspired with the prophetic spirit. For in Latin *carere* betokeneth 'to lack' and *mens* signifieth 'wit'. As for the feast of Palilia, we have told of it before: but the feast of Lupercalia, considering the time of celebrating thereof, it seemeth it is ordained for a purification. For it is celebrated on the unfortunate days of the month of February, which are called the purging days. The days in the old time on which they did celebrate the same were called Februata. But the proper name of the feast is as much to say, as the feast of wolves. Wherefore it seemeth to be a feast of great antiquity, and instituted by the Arcadians which came in with Evander: albeit the name of wolves is as common to the females as the males, and so it might perhaps be called, by reason of the wolf that brought up Romulus. For we see those which run up and down the city that day, and they call Luperci, do begin their course in the very place where they say Romulus was cast out. Howbeit many things are done, whereof the original cause were hard now to be conjectured. For goats about a certain time of the year are killed; then they bring two young boys, noblemen's sons, whose foreheads they touch with the knife bebloodied with the blood of the goats that are sacrificed. By and by they dry their foreheads with wool dipped in milk. Then the young boys must laugh immediately after they have dried their foreheads. That done they cut the goats' skins, and make thongs of them, which they take in their hands, and run with them all about the city stark naked (saving they have a cloth before their secrets) and so they strike with these thongs all they meet in their way. The young wives do never shun them at all, but are well contented to be stricken with them, believing it helps them to be with child, and also to be easily delivered. There is another thing yet in this feast, that these Lupercians which run about the city, do also sacrifice a dog. Concerning this feast, the poet named Butas doth write somewhat in his elegies, where showing the occasion of the fond customs and ceremonies of the Romans, he doth say that Romulus after he had slain Amulius, did run straight with great joy to the very place where the wolf gave him and his brother suck; in memory of which running, he sayeth this feast of Lupercalia was celebrated: and that the noblemen's younger sons do run through the city, striking and laying on them which they meet in their way with their goat thongs, in token that Remus and Romulus ran from Alba unto that place, with their drawn swords in their hands. And that the touching of their forehead with a bloody knife is in remembrance of the danger they stood in at that time to have been slain. Last of all, the drying of their foreheads with wool dipped in milk, is in memory of the milk they sucked of the wolves. But Caius Acilius writeth, that Remus and Romulus before Rome was built, did happen to lose their beasts on a day, and after they had made certain prayers unto Faunus for the finding of them, they ran here and there stark naked as they went a-seeking of them, for fear they should have been troubled with overmuch heat and sweating. And this is the cause he sayeth, why the Lupercians do at this day run about naked. And if it be true they make this sacrifice for a purging, a man might say they might offer up a dog for that purpose, like as the Grecians in their sacrifices of purgation do use to carry out all their dogs. And in many places they do observe this ceremony, to drive out the dogs, which they call Periscylacismes. Otherwise, if it be of a thankfulness to the wolf that gave Romulus suck, and saved him from perishing, that the Romans do solemnise this feast: it is not impertinent they sacrifice a dog, because he is enemy to the wolves. Unless a man would say it was to punish this beast, which troubleth and letteth the Lupercians when they run.

22   Some say also it was Romulus who first instituted it a religion to keep holy fire, and that first ordained holy virgins, which are called Vestales: others do ascribe it to Numa Pompilius. Notwithstanding it is most certain otherwise, that Romulus was a very devout man, and greatly skilful in telling of things to come by the flying of birds: for which cause he did ordinarily carry the augur's crooked staff, called in Latin *lituus*. It is a rod crooked at the end, wherewith the augurs or soothsayers when they sit down to behold the flying of birds, do point out and mark the quarters of the heaven. They carefully kept it within the palace: howbeit it was lost in the time of wars with the Gauls, when the city of Rome was taken. Afterwards when these barbarous people were chased and driven out, it was found again (as it is said) all whole, within a great hill or heap of ashes, having no manner of hurt, where all things else about it had been consumed and marred with the fire. He is said to have made certain laws, among which there is one that seemeth somewhat hard, which is: that the man is suffered to put away his wife, and in some case to give her nothing; and like liberty is not given to the wife to put away her husband. As if she may be proved to have consented to the poisoning of her children, or to have counterfeited her husband's keys, or to have committed adultery. But if he put her away for any other cause, then the one half of the goods is adjudged to the wife, and the other half to the goddess Ceres: and he that putteth away his wife after this sort, is commanded further, to sacrifice to the gods of the earth. This also was notable in Romulus, who having ordained no pain nor punishment for parricides (that is for those that kill their parents) called yet all murder parricide, to show how detestable that murder was: and as for parricides, he thought it unpossible. And it seemed a great while, he had reason to think so, that such wickedness would never happen in the world. For in six hundred years together it was not known that any man in Rome committed such an offence: and the first parricide with them was Lucius Ostius, after the wars of Hannibal. But enough touching this matter.

23   Furthermore in the first year of the reign of Tatius, some of his kinsmen and friends met by chance on the way certain ambassadors, coming from the city of Laurentum unto Rome, whom they set upon, and meant to have robbed them. The

ambassadors resisting them, and not willing to deliver their money, they made no more ado, but slew them. This heinous deed being thus committed, Romulus was of opinion they should be executed openly in the highway for example. But Tatius deferred it still from day to day, and did always excuse the matter unto him, which was the only cause they fell out one with the other. For in all things else, they carried themselves as honestly as might be the one to the other, ruling and governing together, with a common consent and good accord. But the parents and kinsfolks of those who were murdered, when they saw they could have no justice because of Tatius, watched him one day as he sacrificed with Romulus, in the city of Lavinium, and stabbed him in, without offering Romulus any violence, but rather praised him for a good and righteous prince. Romulus caused the body of Tatius to be straight taken up, and buried him very honourably in mount Aventine, about the place now called Armilustrium. Further he never showed any countenance to revenge his death. There are some historiographers that write, that those of the city of Laurentum being afraid at this murder, did deliver forthwith to Romulus the murderers of the ambassadors. He notwithstanding did let them go again, saying one murder was requited by another. This gave some occasion of speech to think, he was glad he was rid of his companion: yet the Sabynes neither stirred nor rebelled for all this, but some of them were afraid of him for the great love they bore him, other for his power he was of, and other for the honour they gave him as a god, continuing still in duty and obedience towards him. Divers strangers also had Romulus' valiancy in great honour: as amongst other, those who then were called the ancient Latins, which sent ambassadors to him to make league and amity with him. He devised to take the city of Fidena which was near neighbour to Rome. Some say he took it upon a sudden, having sent before certain horsemen to break down the hooks and hinges with force, which the gates hang by: and himself came after the rest of his army, and stole upon them, before the city mistrusted anything. Other write that the Fidenates first invaded his country, and foraged unto the very suburbs of Rome, where they did great harm: and how Romulus laid an ambush in their way as they returned home, and slew a great number of them. When he took their city, he did not rase it, but made a colony of it (as a place to send the overincrease of Rome unto), whither he sent afterwards two thousand five hundred Romans to inhabit there: and it was on the thirteenth day of April, which the Romans call the Ides of the same month.

24    Not long after there rose such a great plague in Rome, that men died suddenly, and were not sick; the earth brought forth no fruit; brute beasts delivered no increase of their kind; there rained also drops of blood in Rome, as they say. In so much as besides the evils men felt in this extremity, they fell in a marvellous fear of the wrath of the gods. Afterwards perceiving the like happened to the inhabitants of Laurentum, then every man judged it was the very vengeance and heavy hand of the gods, who plagued and punished these two cities for the murder committed upon Tatius, and the ambassadors that were killed. Whereupon the murderers of both sides were apprehended, and executed: and these plagues by and by ceased both in the one and in the other city. Romulus besides did purify the cities with certain sacrifices that he devised, which they keep still at this day, at the gate called Ferentina. But before the plague ceased, the Camerines came to assault the Romans, and had overcome all the country, supposing they should not be able to withstand them, because they had been so sore troubled with the plague. Yet notwithstanding, Romulus set upon them with his army, and won the field of them, in which conflict there were slain about six thousand men. After the battle done, he took their city, and conveyed to Rome the one half of the inhabitants that remained. After this, he sent twice as many Romans as there were natural Camerians left at Camerine, to dwell there among them. This was done the first day of August: so great was the multitude of the inhabitants of Rome that had increased in sixteen years from the first foundation of the city. Among other spoils he got there, he carried away a chariot of brass with four horses, which he caused to be set up in the temple of Vulcan, and his own statue upon it, and victory crowning him with a garland triumphant.

25    His power being grown thus great, his weak neighbours did submit themselves unto him, being contented to live in peace by him. His stronger neighbours were afraid of him, and envied much his greatness, and did take it no good policy to suffer him thus to rise in the face of the world, and thought it meet speedily to daunt

his glory, and clip his wings. The first of the Thuscans that bent their power against him were the Veians, who had a great country, and dwelled in a strong and mighty city. To pick a quarrel to him, they sent to have redelivered to them the city of Fidena, which they said belonged unto them. This was thought not only unreasonable, but a thing worthy laughing at, considering that all the while the Fidenates were in war, and danger, the Thuscans never came to their aid, but had suffered them to be slain, and then came to demand their lands and tenements, when others had possession of them. Therefore Romulus having given them an answer full of mockery and derision, they divided their power into two armies, and sent the one against them of Fidena, and with the other they marched towards Rome. That which went against the city of Fidena, prevailed, and killed there two thousand Romans: the other was overthrown and discomfited by Romulus, in which there died eight thousand Veians. Afterwards, they met again somewhat near the city of the Fidenates, where they fought a battle: and all did confess, the chiefest exploit was done by Romulus' own hands that day, who showed all the skill and valiantness that was to be looked for in a worthy captain. It seemed that day, he far exceeded the common sort of men, in strength of body and feats of arms. Nevertheless that which some say, is hardly to be credited: and to be plain, is out of all compass of belief and possibility. For they write, there were fourteen thousand men slain at that battle, and that more then half of them were slain by Romulus' own hands: and the rather, for that every man judges it a vain brag and ostentation which the Messenians report of Aristomenes, who offered in sacrifice to the gods three hundred beasts of victory, as for so many Lacedaemonians himself had slain in the battle. Their army being thus broken, Romulus suffered them to fly who by swiftness could save themselves, and marched with all his power in good array towards their city. The citizens then considering their late great loss and overthrow, would not hazard the danger of withstanding him, but went out all together, and made their humble petition and suit for peace. All was granted them for a hundred years, save they should forgo their territory called Septemagium, that was the seventh part of their country, and yield to the Romans all their salt houses by the river's side, and deliver fifty of their chiefest citizens for their pledges. Romulus made his entry and triumph into Rome for them, the day of the Ides of October, which is the fifteenth day of the same month, leading in his triumph many prisoners taken in those wars: and among other, the general of the Veians, a very ancient man who fondly behaved himself in his charge, and showed by his doings, that his experience was far short for his years in the wars. And from thence it cometh, when they offer to the gods to give thanks for this victory, that even at this day, they bring to the capitol through the market place an old man apparelled in a purple robe, and with a jewel called *bulla* about his neck, which the gentlemen's young children wear about their necks: and a herald goeth hard by him, crying, 'Who buyeth who, the Sardianians?' Because they hold opinion the Thuscans are come of the Sardianians, and the very city of Veies standeth in the country of Thuscane.

26    This was the last war that Romulus had offered him: after which he could not beware of that which is wont to happen almost to all those, who by sudden prosperity and fortune's special favour are raised to high and great estate. For trusting to prosperity and good success of his acts, he began to grow more strange and stately, and to carry a sourer countenance than he was wont to do before: leaving to be after his old manner, a courteous and gracious prince, and gave himself in fashions to be somewhat like a tyrant, both for his apparel, and stately port and majesty that he carried. For he ware ever a coat of purple in grain, and upon that, a long robe of purple colour; and gave audience sitting in a wide chair of estate, having ever about him young men called Celeres, as we would say, flights for their swiftness and speed in executing of his commandments. Other there were that went before him, who carried as it were tipstaves in their hands, to make the people give room, and had leather thongs about their middle to bind fast straight, all the prince should command. Now in old time the Latins said *ligare* was 'to bind': but at this present they say *alligare*, from whence it comes that the ushers and sergeants are called Lictores. Howbeit methinks it were more likely to say, they had put to a *c*, and that before they were called Litores, without a *c*. For they be the very same which the Grecians call Liturgos, and be in English, ministers or officers: and at this day, *leitos*, or *leos*, in the Greek tongue signifieth the people.

27 Romulus now, after his grandfather Numitor was dead at the city of Alba, and that the realm by inheritance fell to him, to win the favour of the people there, turned the kingdom to a common weal, and every year did choose a new magistrate to minister justice to the Sabynes. This president taught the noblemen of Rome to seek and desire to have a free estate, where no subject should be at the commandment of a king alone, and where every man should command and obey as should be his course. Those which were called patricians in Rome, did meddle with nothing, but had only an honourable name and robe, and were called to council rather for a fashion, then to have their advice or counsel. For when they were assembled together, they did only hear the king's pleasure and commandment, but they might not speak one word, and so departed: having no other pre-eminence over the commonwealth, saving they were the first that did know what was done. All other things thereby did grieve them less. But when of his own mere authority, and as it were of himself, he would as pleased him bestow the conquered lands of his enemies to his soldiers, and restore again to the Veians their hostages as he did, therein plainly appeared, how great injury he did to the senate. Whereupon the senators were suspected afterwards that they killed him, when within few days after it was said, he vanished away so strangely, that no man ever knew what became of him. This was on the seventh day of the month now called July, which then was named *Quintilis*, leaving no manner of certainty else of his death that is known, save only of the day and the time when he vanished, as we have said before. For on that day, the Romans do at this present many things, in remembrance of the misfortune which happened to them then. It is not marvel, the certainty of his death was not known, seeing Scipio Africanus was found after supper dead in his house, and no man could tell, nor yet did know how he died. For some say that he fainted, and died suddenly being of weak complexion. Others say he poisoned himself: others think his enemies did get secretly in the night into his house, and smothered him in his bed. Yet they found his body laid on the ground, that everybody might at leisure consider, if they could find or conjecture the manner of his death. Howbeit Romulus vanished away suddenly, there was neither seen piece of his garments, nor yet was there found any part of his body. Therefore

some have thought that the whole senators fell upon him together in the temple of Vulcan, and how after they had cut him in pieces, everyone carried away a piece of him, folded close in the skirt of his robe. Other think also, this vanishing away was not in the temple of Vulcan, nor in the presence of the senators only: but they say that Romulus was at that time without the city, near the place called the goats' marsh, where he made an oration to the people, and that suddenly the weather changed, and overcast so terribly, as it is not to be told nor credited. For first, the sun was darkened as if it had been very night. This darkness was not in a calm or still, but there fell horrible thunders, boisterous winds, and flashing lightnings on every side, which made the people run away and scatter here and there, but the senators kept still close together. Afterwards when the lightning was past and gone, the day cleared up, and the element waxed fair as before. Then the people gathered together again, and sought for the king, asking what was become of him. But the noblemen would not suffer them to enquire any further after him, but counselled them to honour and reverence him as one taken up into heaven: and that thenceforth instead of a good king, he would be unto them a merciful and gracious god. The meaner sort of people (for the most part of them) took it well, and were very glad to hear thereof: and went their way worshipping Romulus in their hearts, with good hope they should prosper by him. Howbeit some seeking out the truth more eagerly did comber sore, and troubled the patricians: accusing them, that they abused the common people with vain and fond persuasions, whilst themselves in the meantime had murdered the king with their own hands.

28   While things were thus in hurly burly, some say there was one Julius Proculus, the noblest of all the patricians, being esteemed for a marvellous honest man, and known to have been very familiar with Romulus, and came with him from the city of Alba: that stepped forth before all the people, and affirmed (by the greatest and holiest oaths a man might swear) that he had met Romulus on the way, far greater and fairer than he had seen him ever before, and armed all in white armour, shining bright like fire: whereat being afraid in that sort to see him, he asked him yet: 'O king, why hast thou thus left and forsaken us, that are so falsely

accused and charged to our utter discredit and shame, by thy vanishing?' To whom Romulus gave this answer. 'Proculus, it hath pleased the gods from whom I came, that I should remain amongst men so long as I did: and now having built a city, which in glory and greatness of empire shall be the chiefest of the world, that I should return again to dwell with them, as before, in heaven. Therefore be of good comfort, and tell the Romans, that they exercising prowess and temperancy, shall be the mightiest and greatest people of the world. As for me, tell them I will henceforth be their god, protector and patron, and they shall call me Quirinus.' These words seemed credible to the Romans, as well for the honesty of the man that spoke them, as for the solemn oaths he made before them all. Yet I wot not how, some celestial motion or divine inspiration helped it much: for no man said a word against it. And so all suspicion and accusation laid aside, every man began to call upon Quirinus, to pray unto him, and to worship him. Truly this tale is much like the tales that the Grecians tell of Aristeas the Proconnesian, and of Cleomedes the Astypalaeian. For they say, that Aristeas died in a fuller's work house, and his friends coming to carry away his body, it fell out they could not tell what became of it: and at that instant there were some which came out of the fields, and affirmed they met and spoke with him, and how he kept his way towards the city of Crotona. It is said also that Cleomedes was more than a man naturally strong and great, and therewithal mad, and furious hasty. For after many desperate parts he had played, he came at the last on a day into a school house full of little children, the roof whereof was borne with one pillar, which he did hit with so terrible a blow of his fist, that he broke it in the midst, so as the whole roof fell and dashed the poor children in pieces. The people ran straight after him to take him. But he threw himself forthwith into a chest, and pulled the lid upon him. He held it so fast down, that many striving together all they could to open it, they were not able once to stir it. Whereupon they broke the chest all in pieces, but they found the man neither quick nor dead. Whereat they were marvellously amazed, and sent to Apollo Pythias, where the prophetess answered them in this verse:

Cleomedes the last of the demi-gods

The report goeth also that Alcmene's corse did vanish away, as they carried it to burial, and how instead thereof they found a stone laid in the bier. To conclude, men tell many other such wonders, that are far from any appearance of truth: only because they would make men to be as gods, and equal with them in power. It is true, that as to reprove and deny divine power, it were a lewd and wicked part: even so to compare earth and heaven together, it were a mere folly. Therefore we must let such fables go, being most certain that as Pindarus sayeth it is true.

> Each living corps must yield at last to death,
>     And every life must lease his vital breath,
>     The soul of man, that only lives on high,
>     And is an image of eternity.

For from heaven it came, and thither again it doth return, not with the body, but then soonest, when the soul is furthest off and separated from the body, and that she is kept holy, and is no more defiled with the flesh. It is that the philosopher Heraclitus meant, when he said: 'The dry light is the best soul which flieth out of the body, as lightning doth out of the cloud: but that which is joined with the body being full of corporal passions, is a gross vapour, dark and massive, and cannot flame, rise or shoot out like lightning.' We must not believe therefore, that the bodies of noble and virtuous men do go up together with their souls into heaven, against the order of nature. But this we are certainly to believe, that by the virtues of their souls (according to divine nature and justice) they do of men become saints, and of saints half gods, and of half gods, entire and perfect gods, after that they are perfectly (as it were by sacrifices of purgation) made clean and pure, being delivered from all pain and mortality, and not by any civil ordinance, but in truth and reason, they receive a most happy and glorious end.

29    Now touching Romulus' surname, which afterwards was called Quirinus, some say that it signifieth as much as warlike: other think he was so called because the Romans themselves were called Quirites. Other write, that men in old time did call the point of a spear, on the dart itself, *quiris*: by reason whereof the image of Iuno surnamed Quiritides, was set up with an iron spear, and the spear which was consecrated in the king's palace, was called Mars. Furthermore it is an use amongst men, to honour

them with a spear or dart, which have showed themselves valiant
in the wars: and that for this cause Romulus was surnamed
Quirinus, as who would say, god of the spears and wars. There was
since built a temple unto him, in the hill called Quirinus, and so
named of him. The day whereon he vanished, is called the flying
of the people, or otherwise the Nones of the goats. For on that
day, they go out of the city to do sacrifice in the place called the
Fen, or the goats' marsh: and the Romans call a goat, *capra*. As they
go thus together, they call with loud shouts and cries upon divers
Romans' names, as Marcus, Cneus and Gaius, in token of the
flying that was then: and that they called one another back again,
as they ran away in great fear and disorder. Howbeit other say, that
it is not done to show the running away, but to show their speed
and diligence, and refer it to the story. Now after the Gauls that
had taken Rome were expulsed by Camillus, the city was so
weakened, that they could scant recover their force and strength
again: wherefore many of the Latins joining together, went with a
great mighty army, under the conduct of Livius Posthumius, to
war against the Romans. This Posthumius brought his camp as
near the city of Rome as he could, and sent to the Romans by a
trumpet to let them understand, how the Latins were desirous by
new marriages, to restore their old ancient amity and kindred that
was near hand decayed between them: and therefore if the Romans would send them a convenient number of their daughters
and young widows to marry with them, they should have peace,
as they had before time with the Sabynes, upon the like occasion.
The Romans hereat were sore troubled, thinking that to deliver
their women in such sort was no better than to yield and submit
themselves to their enemies. But as they were thus perplexed, a
waiting maid called Philotis (or as others call her, Tutola) gave
them counsel to do neither the one nor the other, but to use a
policy with them, by means whereof they should escape the
danger of the wars, and should also not be tied nor bound by any
pledges. The devise was, they should send to the Latins herself,
and a certain number of their fairest bondmaids, trimmed up like
gentlewomen and the best citizen's daughters, and that in the
night she would lift them up a burning torch in the air, at which
sign they should come armed, and set upon their enemies as they
lay asleep. This was brought to pass: and the Latins thought verily

they had been the Romans' daughters. Philotis failed not in the night to lift up her sign, and to shelve them a burning torch in the top of a wild fig tree: and did hang certain coverlets and clothes behind it, that the enemies might not see the light, and the Romans contrariwise might discern it the better. Thereupon so soon as the Romans saw it they ran with all speed, calling one another by their names, and issued out of the gates of the city with great haste: and so took their enemies upon a sudden, and slew them. In memory of which victory, they do yet solemnise the feast called the Nones of the goats, because of the wild fig tree called in Latin *caprificus*. And they do feast the women without the city, under shadows made of the bough of fig trees. The waiting maids, they run up and down, and play here and there together. Afterwards they seem to fight, and throw stones one at another, as then they did when they helped the Romans in their fight. But few writers do avow this tale, because it is on the day time that they call so each other by, their names, and that they go to the place which they call the goats' marsh, as unto a sacrifice. It seemeth this agreeth better with the first history when they called one another by their names in the night, going against the Latins: unless peradventure these two things after many years happened upon one day. Furthermore, they say Romulus was taken out of the world when he was four and fifty years of age, and had reigned eight and thirty years by account.

## Comparison of Theseus with Romulus

Thus have we declared all things of Theseus and Romulus worthy memory. But to compare the one with the other, it appeareth first that Theseus of his own voluntary will, without compulsion of any (when he might with safety have reigned in the city of Troezen, and succeeded his grandfather in no small kingdom) did desire of himself, and rather sought means to aspire to great things: and that Romulus on the other side, to deliver himself from bondage and servitude that lay sore upon him, and to escape the threatened punishment which still did hang over his head, was certainly compelled (as Plato sayeth) to show himself hardy for fear: who seeing how extremely he was like to be handled, was of very force constrained to seek adventure, and hazard the enterprise of attaining high and great things. Moreover the chiefest act that ever he did was, when he slew one only tyrant of the city of Alba called Amulius: where Theseus in his journey only, as he travelled, gave his mind to greater enterprises, and slew Sciron, Sinnis, Procrustes, and Corynetes. And by ridding them out of the world, he delivered Greece of all those cruel tyrants, before any of those knew him whom he had delivered from them. Furthermore, he might have gone to Athens by sea, and never need to have travailed, or put himself in danger with these robbers, considering he never received hurt by any of them: whereas Romulus could not be in safety whilst Amulius lived. Hereupon it may be alleged, that Theseus unprovoked by any private wrong or hurt received, did set upon these detestable thieves and robbers: Remus and Romulus contrariwise, so long as the tyrant did them no harm, did suffer him to oppress and wrong all other. And if they allege these were noble deeds, and worthy memory: that Romulus was hurt fighting against the Sabynes, and that he slew King Acron with his own hands, and that he had overcome and subdued many of his enemies; then for Theseus on the other side may be objected, the battle of the

Centauri, the wars of the Amazons, the tribute due to the king of Creta: and how he ventured to go himself thither with the other young boys and wenches of Athens, as willingly offering himself to be devoured by a cruel beast, or else to be slain and sacrificed upon the tomb of Androgeus, or to become bondslave and tied in captivity to the vile service of cruel men and enemies, if by his courage and manhood he could not deliver himself. This was such an act of magnanimity, justice and glory, and briefly of so great virtue, that it is unpossible truly to be set out. Surely methinks the philosophers did not ill define love, when they said she was a servitor of the gods, to save young folks whom they thought meet to be preserved. For the love of Ariadne was in mine opinion the work of some god, and a mean purposely prepared for Theseus' safety. Therefore the woman is not to be reproached nor blamed for the love she bore Theseus, but rather it is much to be wondered at, that every man and woman in like wise did not love him. And if of herself she fell in love with him, I say (and not without cause) she afterwards deserved to be beloved of a god, as one that of her own nature loved valiantness and honour, and entertained men of singular value.

2    But both Theseus and Romulus being naturally given to rule and reign, neither the one nor the other kept the true form of a king, but both of them did degenerate alike: the one changing himself into a popular man, the other to a very tyrant. So that by sundry humours, they both fell into one mischief and error. For a prince above all things must keep his estate: which is no less preserved by doing nothing uncomely, as by doing all things honourably. But he that is more severe or remiss than he should be, remaineth now no more a king or a prince, but becometh a people pleaser, or a cruel tyrant: and so causeth his subjects to despise or hate him. Yet methinks the one is an error of too much pity and baseness, and the other of too much pride and cruelty.

3    But if we may not charge fortune with all mischances happening unto men, but that we ought to consider in them the diversities of manners and passions, seeing anger is unreasonable, and wrath rash and passionate: then can we not clear the one, nor excuse the other of extreme rage and passion, in the fact committed by the one against his brother, and by the other against his natural son.

Howbeit the occasion and beginning of anger doth much excuse Theseus, who, moved with the greatest cause that might be, was put into such choler and passion. But if Romulus' variance with his brother had proceeded of any matter of counsel, or cause of the common weal, there is none so simple to think, that his wisdom would so suddenly have set upon him. Whereas Theseus in contrary manner killed his son, provoked by those passions that few men can avoid: to wit, love, jealousy, and false report of his wife. Moreover Romulus' anger went to the effect, whereof the issue fell out very lamentable: Theseus' anger stretched no further, than to rough words, and old folks' curses in their heat. For it seems, cursed fortune, and nought else, was the cause of his son's only mishap, as forespoken and wished for somewhat by his father. These be the special things may be alleged for Theseus.

4 But for Romulus this was a noble thing in him. First his beginning being very low and mean, and his brother and he taken for bondmen, and the children of hogherds, before they were themselves all free, they set at liberty in manner all the Latins, winning at one instant many titles of glory and honour: as destroyers of their enemies, defenders of their parents, kings of nations, founders of new cities, and no overthrowers of the old; whereas Theseus of many habitations and houses made only one, and did overthrow and pluck down divers states, bearing the names of ancient kings, princes, and half gods of Attica. All these also did Romulus afterwards, and compelled his enemies whom he had overcome, to destroy their own houses, and to come and dwell with their conquerors. And in the beginning, he never changed nor increased any city that was built before, but built himself a new city out of the ground, getting all together, land, country, kingdom, kindred and marriages, without losing or killing any man: and to the contrary, rather he did good to many poor vagabonds, who had neither country, lands nor houses, and desired nothing else but to make a people amongst them, and to become citizens of some city. Also Romulus bent not himself to follow thieves and robbers, but subdued by force of arms many mighty and puissant people: he took cities, and triumphed over kings and princes which he had vanquished in battle.

5    And touching the murder of Remus, it is certainly not known of whose hands he died. The most part of authors do charge other with the death of him. But it is certain that Romulus delivered his mother from apparent death, and restored his grandfather to the royal throne of Aeneas, who before was deposed and brought from a king to servile obedience, without any regard of honour or dignity: to whom he did many more great pleasures and services. Besides he never offended him willingly, no not so much as ignorantly. Contrarily I think of Theseus, who failing by negligence to put out his white sail at his return, cannot be cleared of parricide, how eloquent an oration soever could be made for his excuse: yea though it were before the most favourable judges that could be. Wherefore an Athenian very well perceiving that it was an hard thing to excuse and defend so foul a fault, doth feign that the good old man Aegeus having news brought him that his son's ship was at hand, did run in so great haste to his castle, to see his son arrive afar off, that as he ran, his foot hit against something, and overthrew him: as though he had none of his people about him, or that never a man seeing him run so hastily to the sea side, did make haste to attend and wait upon him.

6    Furthermore, Theseus' faults touching women and ravishments, of the twain, had the less shadow and colour of honesty. Because Theseus did attempt it very often: for he stole away Ariadne, Antiope, and Anaxo the Troezenian. Again being steeped in years, and at later age, and past marriage, he stole away Helen in her minority, being nothing near to consent to marry. Then his taking of the daughters of the Troezenians, of the Lacedaemonians, and the Amazons (neither contracted to him, nor comparable to the birth and lineage of his own country which were at Athens, and descended of the noble race and progeny of Erichtheus and of Cecrops) did give men occasion to suspect that his womanishness was rather to satisfy lust, than of any great love. Romulus now in a contrary manner, when his people had taken eight hundred, or thereabouts, of the Sabyne women to ravish them, kept but only one for himself that was called Hersilia, as they say, and delivered the rest to his best and most honest citizens. Afterwards by the honour, love, and good entertainment that he caused them to have and receive of their husbands, he changed this violent force of ravish-

ment into a most perfect bond and league of amity: which did so knit and join in one these two nations, that it was the beginning of the great mutual love which grew afterwards betwixt those two people, and consequently of the joining of their powers together. Furthermore, time has given a good testimony of the love, reverence, constancy, kindness, and all matrimonial offices that he established by that means, betwixt man and wife. For in two hundred and thirty years afterwards, there was never man that durst forsake or put away his wife, nor the wife her husband. And as among the Grecians, the best learned men, and most curious observers of antiquities do know his name, that was the first murderer of his father or mother: even so all the Romans knew what he was, which first durst put away his wife. It was one called Spurius Carvilius, because his wife was barren and had no children. The effects also do agree with the testimony of the time. For the realm was common unto kings of both nations, and through the alliance of these marriages that began first of ravishments, both nations lived peaceably, and in equality, under one civil policy, and well governed common weal. The Athenians contrariwise, by Theseus' marriages, did get neither love nor kindred of any one person, but rather they procured wars, enmities, and the slaughter of their citizens, with the loss in the end of the city of Aphidnes: and yet very hardly, and by the mercy of their enemies (whom they honoured as gods) they escaped for him the danger which the Troians suffered afterwards, for the self act done by Alexander Paris. So it fell out at the last, that his mother was not only in danger, but even feelingly suffered like misery and captivity, which Hecuba did afterwards, when she was forsaken of her son: unless peradventure those things that they write of the imprisonment and captivity of Aethra be found false, and but fables; as for the fame and memory of Theseus were behoveful, that both it, and many other things also, were of no more truth nor likelihood. That which they write of Romulus' divinements, maketh great difference between him and Theseus. For Romulus in his birth was preserved by the marvellous favour of the gods: Theseus to the contrary, was begotten against the gods' wills, as appeared plainly by the answer of the oracle to Aegeus, that he should not meddle with any woman in strange and foreign country.

THE END OF ROMULUS' LIFE

ALCIBIADES
CORIOLANUS

# Life of Alcibiades

Alcibiades by his father's side was anciently descended of Eurysaces, that was the son of Ajax, and by his mother's side, of Alcmaeon: for his mother Dinomacha was the daughter of Megacles. His father Clinias having armed, and set forth a galley, at his own proper costs and charges, did win great honour in the battle by sea, that was fought along the coast of Artemisium, and he was slain afterwards in another battle fought at Coronea, against the Boeotians. His son Alcibiades' tutors were Pericles and Ariphron, Xanthippus' sons: who were also his near kinsmen. They say, and truly, that Socrates' goodwill and friendship did greatly further Alcibiades' honour. For it appeareth not, neither was it ever written, what were the names of the mothers of Nicias, of Demosthenes, of Lemachus, of Phormion, of Thrasibulus, and of Theramenes: all which were notable famous men in their time. And to the contrary, we find the nurse of Alcibiades, that she was a Lacedaemonian born, and was called Amicla, and that his schoolmaster was called Zopyrus: of the which, Antisthenes mentioneth the one, and Plato the other. Now for Alcibiades' beauty, it made no matter if we speak not of it, yet I will a little touch it by the way: for he was wonderful fair, being a child, a boy, and a man, and that at all times, which made him marvellous amiable, and beloved of every man. For where Euripides sayeth, that of all the fair times of the year, the autumn or latter season is the fairest: that commonly falleth not out true. And yet it proved true in Alcibiades, though in few other: for he was passing fair even to his latter time, and of good temperature of body. They write of him also, that his tongue was somewhat fat, and it did not become him ill, but gave him a certain natural pleasant grace in his talk: which Aristophanes mentioneth, mocking one Theorus that did counterfeit a lisping grace with his tongue.

This Alcibiades, with his fat lisping tongue,
  Into mine ears this trusty tale, and song full often sung.
Look upon Theolus (quoth he) lo there he bows,
  Behold his comely crow-bright face with fat and flatling blows.*
The son of Clinias would lisp it thus somewhiles,
  And sure he lispéd never a lie, but rightly hit his wiles.

And Archippus another poet also, mocking the son of Alcibiades,
sayeth thus:

Because he would be like his father every way,
  In his long trailing gown he would go jetting day by day.
And counterfeit his speech, his countenance and face:
  As though dame nature had him given therein a perfect grace.
To lisp and look aside, and hold his head awry,
  Even as his father looked and lisped, so would he prate and pry.

2    For his manners they altered and changed very oft with time,
which is not to be wondered at, seeing his marvellous great
prosperity, as also adversity that followed him afterwards. But of all
the great desires he had, and that by nature he was most inclined to,
was ambition, seeking to have the upper hand in all things, and to
be taken for the best person: as appeareth by certain of his deeds
and notable sayings in his youth, extant in writing. One day
wrestling with a companion of his, that handled him hardly, and
thereby was likely to have given him the fall, he got his fellow's
arm in his mouth, and bit so hard, as he would have eaten it off.
The other feeling him bite so hard, let go his hold straight, and said
unto him: 'What, Alcibiades, bitest thou like a woman?' 'No marry
do I not,' quoth he, 'but like a lion.' Another time being but a little
boy, he played at scales in the midst of the street with other of his
companions, and when his turn came about to throw, there came
a cart laden by chance that way: Alcibiades prayed the carter to stay
a while, until he had played out his game, because the scales were
set right in the highway where the cart should pass over. The carter
was a stubborn knave, and would not stay for any request the boy

* The equivocation of these two Greek words κορα and κολα, is hard to be
expressed in English, instead whereof I have set flatling blows, for flattering
brows, observing the grace of lisping, as near as I could, like to the Latin and
French translations, likewise Theolus for Theorus.

could make, but drove his horse on still, in so much as other boys gave back to let him go on: but Alcibiades fell flat to the ground before the cart, and bade the carter drive over an he durst. The carter being afraid, plucked back his horse to stay them: the neighbours flighted to see the danger, ran to the boy in all haste crying out. Afterwards when he was put to school to learn, he was very obedient to all his masters that taught him anything, saving that he disdained to learn to play of the flute or recorder: saying, that it was no gentlemanly quality. 'For,' said he, 'to play on the viol with a stick, doth not alter man's favour, nor disgraceth any gentleman: but otherwise, to play on the flute, his countenance altereth and changeth so often, that his familiar friends can scant know him. Moreover, the harp or viol doth not let him that playeth on them from speaking, or singing as he playeth: where he that playeth on the flute, holdeth his mouth so hard to it, that it taketh not only his words from him, but his voice. Therefore,' said he, 'let the children of the Thebans play on the flute, that cannot tell how to speak: as for us Athenians, we have (as our forefathers tell us) for protectors and patroness of our country, the goddess Pallas, and the god Apollo: of the which the one in old time (as it is said) broke the flute, and the other pulled his skin over his ears, that played upon the flute.' Thus Alcibiades alleging these reasons, partly in sport, and partly in good earnest, did not only himself leave to learn to play on the flute, but he turned his companions' minds also quite from it. For these words of Alcibiades, ran from boy to boy incontinently: that Alcibiades had reason to despise playing of the flute, and that he mocked all those that learned to play of it. So afterwards, it fell out at Athens, that teaching to play of the flute was put out of the number of honest and liberal exercises, and the flute itself was thought a vile instrument, and of no reputation.

3 Furthermore, in the accusations Antiphon wrote against Alcibiades, it is declared: that when he was a boy, he fled out of his tutor's house, into the house of Democrates one of his lovers, and how Ariphron one of his tutors thought to have made a beadle cry him through the city. But Pericles would not suffer him, saying that if he were dead, they should know it but one day sooner by crying of him; and if he were alive, that it would be such a shame

to him while he lived, that he had been better he had never been heard of again. The same Antiphon accuseth him further, that he had killed a servant of his that attended on him, in the wrestling place of Sibyrtius, with a blow of a staff. But there is no reason to credit his writing, who confesseth he speaketh all the ill he can of him, for the ill will he did bear him.

4    Now straight there were many great and rich men that made much of Alcibiades, and were glad to get his goodwill. But Socrates' love unto him had another end and cause, which witnessed that Alcibiades had a natural inclination to virtue. Who perceiving that virtue did appear in him, and was joined with the other beauty of his face and body, and fearing the corruption of riches, dignity and authority, and the great number of his companions, as well of the chiefest of the city, as of strangers, seeking to entice him by flattery, and by many other pleasures, he took upon him to protect him from them all, and not to suffer so goodly an imp to lose the hope of the good fruit of his youth. For fortune doth never so entangle nor snare a man without, with that which they commonly call riches, as to let and hinder him so, that philosophy should not take hold on him with her free, severe, and quick reasons. So Alcibiades was at the beginning assayed with all delights, and shut up as it were in their company that feasted him with all pleasures, only to turn him that he should not hearken to Socrates' words, who sought to bring him up at his charge, and to teach him. But Alcibiades notwithstanding, having a good natural wit, knew what Socrates was, and went to him, refusing the company of all his rich friends and their flatteries, and fell in a kind of familiar friendship with Socrates. Whom when he had heard speak, he noted his words very well, that they were no persuasions of a man seeking his dishonesty, but one that gave him good counsel, and went about to reform his faults and imperfections, and to pluck down the pride and presumption that was in him: then, as the common proverb sayeth,

> Like to the craven cock, he drooped down his wings,
>   Which cowardly doth run away, or from the pit out flings.

And did think with self, that all Socrates' love and following of young men, was indeed a thing sent from the gods, and ordained above for them whom they would have preserved, and put into the pathway of honour. Therefore he began to despise himself, and greatly to reverence Socrates, taking pleasure of his good using of him, and much embraced his virtue: so as he had (he wist not how) an image of love graven in his heart, or rather (as Plato sayeth) a mutual love, to wit, an holy and honest affection towards Socrates. Insomuch as all the world wondered at Alcibiades, to see him commonly at Socrates' board, to play, to wrestle, and to lodge in the wars with Socrates; and contrarily to chide his other well willers, who could not so much as have a good look at his hands, and besides became dangerous to some, as it is said he was unto Anytus, the son of Anthemion, being one of those that loved him well. Anytus making good cheer to certain strangers his friends that were come to see him, went and prayed Alcibiades to come and make merry with them: but he refused to go. For he went to make merry with certain of his companions at his own house, and after he had well taken in his cups, he went to Anytus' house to counterfeit the fool amongst them, and staying at the hall door, and seeing Anytus' table and cupboard full of plate of silver and gold, he commanded his servants to take away half of it, and carry it home to his house. But when he had thus taken his pleasure, he would come no nearer into the house, but went his way home. Anytus' friends and guests misliking this strange part of Alcibiades, said it was shamefully and boldly done so to abuse Anytus. 'Nay, gently done of him,' said Anytus: 'for he hath left us some, where he might have taken all.'

5   All others also that made much of him, he served after that sort. Saving a stranger that came to dwell in Athens: who being but a poor man as the voice went, sold all that he had, whereof he made about a hundred staters which he brought unto Alcibiades, and prayed him to take it at his hands. Alcibiades began to be merry, and being very glad to understand his goodwill towards him, took his honest offer, and prayed him to come to supper to him: so he welcomed him very heartily, and made him good cheer. When supper was done, he gave him his money again, and commanded him not to fail the next morning to meet him where the farms and lands of the city are wont to be let out to those that bid most, and charged him he should outbid all. The poor man would fain have excused himself, saying, the farms were too great for him to hire:

but Alcibiades threatened to whip him if he would not do it. For besides the desire he had to pleasure him, he bore a private grudge against the ordinary farmers of the city. The next morning the stranger was ready in the market place, where they did cry out the letting of their farms, and he raised one to a talent more, than all other did offer. The other farmers were as mad with him as they could be, that they all did set upon him, crying out: 'Let him put in surety straight,' supposing he could have found none. The stranger was marvellous blank thereat, and began to shrink back. Then cried Alcibiades out aloud to the officers that sat there to take the best offers: 'I will be his surety,' says he, 'put me in the book, for he is a friend of mine.' The farmers hearing him say so, were at their wits' end, and wist not what to do. For they being always accustomed to pay their yearly rent as it went before, by the help of the rest of the years that followed after: perceiving now that they should not be able to pay the arrearages of the rents due to the common weal, and seeing no other remedy, they prayed him to take a piece of money, and to leave the bargain. Then Alcibiades would in no wise he should take less than a talent, which they gave him willingly. So Alcibiades suffered the stranger then to depart, and made him gain by his devise.

6   Now Socrates' love which he bore him, though it had many mighty and great adversaries, yet it did stay much Alcibiades, sometime by his gentle nature, sometime by his grave counsel and advice: so as the reason thereof took deep root in him, and did so pierce his heart, that many times the tears ran down his cheeks. Another time also being carried away with the enticement of flatterers, that held up his humour with all pleasure and delights, he stole away from Socrates, and made him run after him to fetch him again, as if he had been a slave that had run away from his master's house: for Alcibiades stood in awe of no man but of Socrates only, and indeed he did reverence him, and did despise all other. And therefore Cleanthes was wont to say, that Alcibiades was held of Socrates by the ears: but that he gave his other lovers hold, which Socrates never sought for: for to say truly, Alcibiades was much given over to lust and pleasure. And peradventure it was that Thucydides meant of him, when he wrote that he was incontinent of body, and dissolute of life. Those that marred Alcibiades quite,

did still prick forward his ambition and desire of honour, and did put him in the head to thrust himself into great matters betimes, making him believe that if he did but once begin to show himself to deal in matters of state, he would not only blemish and deface all other governors, but far excel Pericles in authority and power among the Grecians. For like as iron by fire is made soft, to be wrought into any form, and by cold also doth shut and harden in again: even so Alcibiades being puffed up with vanity and opinion of himself, as oft as Socrates took him in hand, was made fast and firm again by his good persuasions, insomuch that when he saw his own fault and folly, and how far wide he had strayed from virtue, he became suddenly very humble and lowly again.

7   Now on a time when he was grown to man's state, he went into a grammar school, and asked the schoolmaster for one of Homer's books. The schoolmaster answered him, he had none of them: Alcibiades up with his fist, and gave him a good box on the ear, and went his way. Another grammarian told him on a time he had Homer which he had corrected. Alcibiades replied, 'Why, what meanst thou, to stand teaching little children their abc, when thou art able to correct Homer, and to teach young men, not boys?' Another time he came and knocked at Pericles' gate, desirous to speak with him: answer was made him, he was not at leisure now, for that he was busily occupied by himself, thinking on his reckonings he had to make with the Athenians. 'Why,' said he, going his way: 'it were better he were occupied thinking how to make no account at all.' Moreover, being but a young boy, he was at the journey of Potidaea, where he lay still with Socrates, who would never let him be from him in all battles and skirmishes he was in: among which there was one, very hot and bloody, where they both fought valiantly, and Alcibiades was hurt. But Socrates stepped before him, and did defend him so valiantly before them all, that he saved him and his weapon out of the enemies' hands. So the honour of this fight out of doubt, in equity and reason, was due unto Socrates: but yet the captains would fain have judged it on Alcibiades' side, because he was of a noble house. But Socrates, because he would increase his desire of honour, and would prick him forward to honest and commendable things, was the very first that witnessed Alcibiades had deserved it: and there-

fore prayed the captains to judge him the crown and complete armour. Afterwards, in the battle of Delion, the Athenians having received the overthrow, Socrates retired with a few others a-foot. Alcibiades being a-horseback, and overtaking him, would not go from him, but kept him company, and defended him against a troop of his enemies that followed him, and slew many of his company.

8    But that was a pretty while after, and before he gave a box of the ear unto Hipponicus, Callias' father, who was one of the greatest men of power in the city, being a nobleman born, and of great possessions: which was done upon a bravery and certain lustiness, as having laid a wager with his companions he would do it, and for no malice or quarrel that he bore the man. This light part was straight over all the city, and everyone that heard it, said it was lewdly done. But Alcibiades the next morning went to his house, and knocking at his gate was let in: so he stripping himself before him, delivered him his body to be whipped, and punished at his pleasure. Hipponicus pardoned him, and was friends with him, and gave him his daughter Hipparete afterwards in marriage. Howbeit some say, it was not Hipponicus that gave her to him: but Callias' son, with ten talents of gold with her. Afterwards at the birth of his first child he had by her, he asked ten talents more, saying they were promised him upon the contract, if his wife had children. But Callias, fearing lest this was an occasion sought of him to lay in wait to kill him for his goods, declared openly to the people, that he made him his heir general, if he died without heirs special of his body. This gentlewoman Hipparete, being an honest true wife to Alcibiades, misliking her husband did so much misuse her, as to entertain common light strumpets, as well citizens as strangers, she went abroad one day to her brothers' house, and told him of it. Alcibiades passed not for it, and made no further reckoning of the matter: but only bade his wife, if she would, present her cause of divorce before the judge. So she went thither herself, to sue the divorce between them, according to the law: but Alcibiades being there also, took her by the hand, and carried her through the market place home to his house, and no man durst meddle between them, to take her from him. And so she continued with him all the days of her life, which was not long after; for she died

when Alcibiades was in his journey he made to Ephesus. This force Alcibiades used, was not thought altogether unlawful, nor uncivil, because it seemeth that the law was grounded upon this cause: that the wife which would be divorced from her husband, should go herself openly before the judge to put up her complaint, to the end that by this means the husband might come to speak with his wife, and seek to stay her if he could.

9  Alcibiades had a marvellous fair great dog, that cost him three score and ten minas, and he cut off his tail that was his chief beauty. When his friends reproved him, and told him how every man blamed him for it, he fell a-laughing, and told them he had that he sought. 'For,' says he, 'I would have the Athenians rather prate upon that, than they should say worse of me.'

10  Moreover, it is said, the first time that Alcibiades spoke openly in the common weal, and began to deal in matters, was upon a gift of money he gave to the people, and not of any pretence, or former purpose he had to do it. One day as he came through the market place, hearing the people very loud, he asked what the matter was: they told him it was about money certain men had given to the people. Then Alcibiades went to them, and gave them money out of his own purse. The people were so glad at that, as they fell to shouting and clapping of their hands, in token of thankfulness: and himself was so glad for company, that he forgot a quail he had under his gown, which was so afraid of the noise, that she took her flight away. The people seeing the quail, made a greater noise than before, and many rose out of their places to run after her: so that in the end, it was taken up by a master of a ship called Antiochus, who brought him the quail again, and for that cause Alcibiades did love him ever after. Now albeit the nobility of his house, his goods, his worthiness, and the great number of his kinsmen and friends made his way open to take upon him government in the common weal, yet the only way he desired to win the favour of the common people by, was the grace of his eloquence. To prove he was eloquent, all the comical poets do testify it: and besides them, Demosthenes the prince of orators also doth say, in an oration he made against Midias, that Alcibiades above all other qualities he had, was most eloquent. And if we may believe Theophrastus, the greatest searcher of antiquities, and best historiographer above any

other philosopher; he hath written, that Alcibiades had as good a
wit to devise and consider what he would say, as any man that was
in his time. Howbeit sometimes studying what he should say, as
also to deliver good words, not having them very readily at his
tongue's end, he many times took breath by the way, and paused in
the midst of his tale, not speaking a word, until he had called it to
mind, that he would say.

11  His charge was great, and much spoken of also, for keeping of
running horses at games: not only because they were the best and
swiftest, but for the number of coaches he had besides. For never
private person, no nor any prince, that ever sent seven so well
appointed coaches, in all furniture, unto the games Olympical, as
he did: nor that at one course hath borne away the first, the
second, and the fourth prize, as Thucydides sayeth: or as Euripides
reporteth, the third. For in that game, he excelled all men in
honour and name that ever strived for victory therein. For
Euripides pronounced his praise, in a song he made of him, as
followeth:

> O son of Clinias, I will resound thy praise:
>   For thou art bold in martial deeds, and overcom'st always.
> Thy victories therewith do far exceed the rest
>   That ever were in Greece ygot, therefore I count them best.
> For at th'Olympic games, thou hast with chariots won,
>   The first prize, second, third and all, which there in race
>                                                           were run.
> With praise and little pain, thy head hath twice been crowned
>   With olive boughs for victory, and twice by trumpets sound
> The heralds have proclaimed thee victor by thy name,
>   Above all those which ran with thee, in hope to get the game.

12  Howbeit the good affection divers cities did bear him, contending which should gratify him best, did much increase his fame
and honour. For the Ephesians did set up a tent for him, very
sumptuously and richly furnished. Those of the city of Chio
furnished him with provender for his horse, and gave him muttons
besides, and other beasts to sacrifice withal. They of Lesbos also
sent him in wine and other provision for victuals, to help him to
defray the great charges he was at in keeping open house, and
feeding such a number of mouths daily. Yet the spite they did bear

him, or rather his breach of promise which he often made, with
this magnificence and state he showed, gave the people more cause
to speak of him than before. For they say there was one Diomedes
at Athens, a friend of Alcibiades, and no ill man, who desired once
in his life to win a game at the plays Olympical. This man being
informed that the Argives had a coach excellently furnished,
belonging to their common weal, and knowing that Alcibiades
could do very much in the city of Argos, because he had many
friends in the same, he came to entreat Alcibiades to buy this coach
for him. Alcibiades thereupon bought it, but kept it to himself, not
regarding Diomedes' request he had made. Diomedes seeing that
fell stark mad for anger, and called the gods and men to witnesses,
that Alcibiades did him open wrong: and it seemeth, that there
fell out suit in law upon the same. For Isocrates wrote an oration,
and drew a plea in defence of Alcibiades, being yet but a child,
touching a couple of horses: yet in this plea, his adversary was
called Tisias, and not Diomedes.

13 Furthermore, Alcibiades being yet but a young man, when he
came to practise and plead publicly, he put all other orators to
silence, but only two that were ever against him: the one was
Phaeax the son of Erasistratus, and the other Nicias, the son of
Niceratus. Of these two, Nicias was a man grown, and had won
the name and reputation of a good captain. And Phaeax began also
to come forward as he did, being of a good and honourable house:
but he lacked many things, and among other, eloquence specially.
For he could more properly talk and discourse among his friends
privately, than he had any good grace to open a matter openly
before the people. For he had, as Eupolis sayeth:

> Words enough, but no eloquence.

There is a certain oration extant in writing, against Alcibiades and
Phaeax, where among other accusations is brought in, how Alcibiades was ordinarily served in his house with gold and silver plate
that belonged to the common weal, and which were used to be
borne for state and magnificence, in solemn processions before
them, and how he used them as boldly, as if they had been his own.
Now there was one Hyperbolus in Athens at that time born in the
village of Perithoide: of whom Thucydides maketh mention, as of

a naughty wicked man, whose tongue was a fit instrument to deliver matter to all the comical poets of that time, to pour out all their taunts and mocks against men. Howbeit he was so impudent a person, and cared so little what men said of him, that he passed not though he were defamed, neither did anything grieve him, whatsoever they reported of him: which some do call boldness and courage, being no better indeed than plain impudence, extreme madness, and desperate folly. He would never please any man: and if the common people had any grudge to any nobleman or magistrate, whom they would any way accuse, Hyperbolus' wicked tongue was their instrument to utter their spite. Now the people (by Hyperbolus' procurement) being assembled, were ready to proceed to the banishment of *ostracismon* by most voices. The manner and custom of this kind of banishment was for a time to banish out of their city such a one, as seemed to have too great authority and credit in the city: and that was rather to satisfy their envy, than for to remedy their fear. And because it was manifest it would fall out to one of them three to be banished (to wit, Alcibiades, Nicias, or Phaeax) Alcibiades found means to join all their three factions in one, becoming friends one to another: and having conferred with Nicias about it, he made Hyperbolus self to be banished, who was the chief instrument to prepare the way of their banishment. Howbeit other say, he spoke not with Nicias about it, but with Phaeax, and joining his part with Phaeax, he caused Hyperbolus to be banished, who feared nothing less: for it was never seen before, that a man of mean countenance, and of small authority, fell into the hap of this banishment. As Plato the comical poet testifieth, speaking of Hyperbolus:

> Although for his deserts, this pain to him is due,
>     Or greater punishment prepared, the which might make
>                                                 him rue:
> Yet since he was by birth a person mean and base,
>     Such punishment therefore did seem (for him) too great
>                                                 of grace.
> Since *Ostracismon* was not made at first to be,
>     Nor yet devised as punishment, for such mean folk as he.

But of this matter, we have spoken more at large before: and now to return again to Alcibiades.

14 Nicias had great reputation among strangers, and his enemies grieved at it no less, than at the honour the citizens selves did unto him. For his house was the common inn for all Lacedaemonians when they came to Athens, and they ever lay with him: moreover he had very well entertained the Lacadaemon prisoners that were taken at the fort of Pyle. And afterwards, when peace was concluded between Lacedaemon and Athens, and their prisoners redelivered home again by Nicias' means only and procurement, they loved him more than ever they did before. This was blown abroad through Greece, that Pericles had kindled the wars amongst them, and Nicias quenched it: so some called this peace Nicium, as one would say, Nicias' work. But Alcibiades stomaching this, and envying Nicias' glory, determined to break the peace whatsoever came of it. Wherefore to compass this matter, knowing first of all that the Argives had no liking of the Lacedaemonians, but were their mortal enemies, and that they did but seek matter to fall out with them, he secretly put them in hope of peace and league with the Athenians. Moreover he did persuade them to it, both by letters and word of mouth, speaking with the magistrates, and such as had greatest authority and credit amongst the people: declaring unto them, that they should not fear the Lacedaemonians, nor yield to them at all, but to stick to the Athenians, who would soon repent them of the peace they had made, and break it with them. Afterwards when the Lacedaemonians had made league with the Boeotians, and had redelivered the city of Panactum to the Athenians, all defaced and spoiled, contrary to the league, Alcibiades perceiving how the people were much offended thereat, made them more earnest against them, and therewithal brought Nicias in disgrace with the people, and charged him with many matters of great likelihood. As at that time, when he was general, that he would never take any of the Lacedaemonians, when they were shut up within the Isle of Sphacteria, and much less distress them when he might: and moreover that when others had taken them prisoners by force, that he had found the means to deliver them, and send them home again, to gratify the Lacedaemonians. Furthermore, that being their friend, he did not his duty to dissuade the people from making of league offensive and defensive with the Boeotians and the Corinthians: and again also, if there were any people of Greece that had a desire to become friends and allies with the Athenians, that he did the best he could to let

them, if the Lacedaemonians had no liking of the matter. Now as
Nicias was thus in disgrace with the people, for the causes above
said, in the midst of this stir, ambassadors came by chance from
Lacedaemon to Athens, who at their coming gave very good words,
saying they had full power and commission to compound all controversies, under reasonable and equal conditions. The senate heard
them, and received them very courteously, and the people the next
day should assemble in council to give them audience: which
Alcibiades fearing much, he went to labour the ambassadors, and
spoke with them apart in this sort: 'What mean you, my lords of
Sparta: do ye not know that the senate has always accustomed to be
gracious and favourable unto those that sue unto them for any
matter, and that the people contrarily are of a proud nature, and
desirous to embrace all great matters? If therefore at the first sight, ye
do give them to understand that you are come hither with full
power to treat freely with them in all manner of causes, do you not
think that they make you stretch your authority far to grant them all
that they will demand. Therefore, my lords ambassadors, if you look
for indifferency at the Athenians' hands, and that they shall not press
you too far against your wills, to grant them anything of advantage,
I would wish you a little to cover your full commission, and in open
manner to propound certain articles, and reasonable capitulations of
peace, not acquainting them otherwise with your full power to
agree in all things: and for my part, I will assure you of my goodwill
in favour of the Lacedaemonians.' When he had told them this tale,
he gave them his faithful promise, and vowed as it were to perform
his word. Hereupon Alcibiades turned the ambassadors from the
trust they reposed in Nicias, and won them on his side: in so much
as they gave credit to no man but to him, wondering much at his
great wisdom and ready wit, and they thought him a rare and
notable man. The next morning the people were assembled to give
the ambassadors audience. They were sent for, and brought into the
market place. There Alcibiades gently asked them, what was the
cause of their coming. They answered that they were come to treat
of peace, but they had no power to determine anything. Then began
Alcibiades to be angry with them, as if they had done him wrong,
and not he any to them: calling them unfaithful, unconstant, and
fickle men, that were come neither to do nor say anything worth the
hearing. The senate also were offended with them, and the people

rated them very roughly: whereat Nicias was so ashamed and amazed withal, that he could not tell what to say, to see so sudden a change, knowing nothing of Alcibiades' malice and subtle practice with the ambassadors.

15 So the ambassadors of Lacedaemon were dispatched, without anything done, and Alcibiades chosen general: who presently brought the Argives, the Elians, and the Mantinians in league with the Athenians. Though no man did commend this practice of his, in working it after this sort, yet was it a marvellous thing of him to devise to put all Peloponnesus in arms, and to procure such a number of soldiers against the Lacedaemonians, as he did before the city of Mantinea, and to shift of the miseries of war and hazard of battle so far from Athens. Which if the Lacedaemonians did win, could not profit them much: and if they lost it, they could hardly save their city of Sparta. After this battle of Mantinea, the thousand men whom the city by an ancient order did keep continually in pay, as well in peace as in war, within the city of Argos, thinking now opportunity served them trimly, attempted to take the sovereign authority from the common people, and to make themselves lords of the city. And to bring this to pass, the Lacedaemonians coming in the meantime, did aid them in their purpose, and so did put down the government of the people: notwithstanding, immediately after the people took arms again, and became the stronger. Alcibiades coming thither even at that time did warrant them the victory, and to set up again the authority of the people. Then he persuaded them to make their walls longer to join their city to the sea, to the end they might more easily be aided by sea by the Athenians. He brought them also from Athens many carpenters, masons, stone hewers, and other workmen: and to conclude, he showed them by all the means and ways he could, that he did bear goodwill unto them, and thereby won himself no less favour particularly among them than generally he did good unto his country. He did persuade also the citizens of Patras to join their town to the sea, by making long walls, which they built out even to the cliffs of the sea. And when one said unto them, 'Alas poor people of Patras, what do ye mean? The Athenians will eat you out,' Alcibiades answered him, 'It may well be, but it shall be by little and little, beginning first at the feet: but the Lacedaemonians will devour you all at once, and

begin at the head.' Now although Alcibiades did make the city of Athens strong by sea, yet he did not leave to persuade the Athenians also, to make themselves strong by land. For he did put the young men oftentimes in mind of the oath they were made to swear in Agraulos, and did advise them to accomplish it indeed. Which was that they should take all corn fields, vines, and olive trees, to be the borders and confines of Attica, whereby they were taught to reckon all land theirs that was manured, and did bring forth fruit.

16    Yet with all these goodly deeds and fair words of Alcibiades, and with this great courage and quickness of understanding, he had many great faults and imperfections. For he was too dainty in his fare, wantonly given unto light women, riotous in banquets, vain and womanish in apparel: he ware ever a long purple gown that swept the market place as he walked up and down, it had such a train, and was too rich and costly for him to wear. And following these vain pleasures and delights, when he was in his galley, he caused the planks of the poop thereof to be cut and broken up, that he might lie the softer: for his bed was not laid upon the overlap, but lay upon girths strained over the hole, cut out and fastened to the sides, and he carried to the wars with him a gilded scutcheon, wherein he had no cognizance nor ordinary device of the Athenians, but only had the image of Cupid in it, holding lightning in his hand. The noblemen and best citizens of Athens perceiving this, they hated his fashions and conditions, and were much offended at him, and were afraid withal of his rashness and insolence: he did so condemn the laws and customs of their country, being manifest tokens of a man that aspired to be king, and would subvert and turn all over hand. And as for the goodwill of the common people towards him, the poet Aristophanes doth plainly express it in these words:

The people most desire, what most they hate to have:
And what their mind abhors, even that they seem to crave.

And in another place he said also, aggravating the suspicion they had of him:

For state or common weal, much better should it be
To keep within the country none such lions' looks as he.
But if they needs will keep a lion to their cost,
Then must they needs obey his will, for he will rule the roost.

For to say truly, his courtesies, his liberalities, and noble expenses to show the people so great pleasure and pastime as nothing could be more: the glorious memory of his ancestors, the grace of his eloquence, the beauty of his person, the strength and valiantness of his body, joined together with his wisdom and experience in martial affairs, were the very causes that made them to bear with him in all things, and that the Athenians did patiently endure all his light parts, and did cover his faults, with the best words and terms they could, calling them youthful, and gentlemen's sports. As when he kept Agartharchus the painter prisoner in his house by force, until he had painted all his walls within: and when he had done, did let him go, and rewarded him very honestly for his pains. Again when he gave a box of the ear to Taureas, who did pay the whole charges of a company of common players, in spite of him, to carry away the honour of the games. Also when he took away a young woman of Melia by his authority, that was taken among certain prisoners in the wars, and kept her for his concubine: by whom he had a child, which he caused to be brought up. Which they called a work of charity, albeit afterwards they burdened him, that he was the only cause of murdering of the poor Melians, saving the little children, because he had favoured and persuaded that unnatural and wicked decree, which another had propounded. Likewise where one Aristophon a painter, had painted a courtesan named Nemea, holding Alcibiades in her arms, and sitting in her lap, which all the people ran to see, and took great pleasure to behold it: the grave and ancient men were angry at these foolish parts, accounting them impudent things, and done against all civil modesty and temperance. Wherefore it seemed Archestratus' words were spoken to good purpose, when he said that Greece could not abide two Alcibiades at once. And on a day as he came from the council and assembly of the city, where he had made an excellent oration, to the great good liking and acceptation of all the hearers, and by means thereof had obtained the thing he desired, and was accompanied with a great train that followed him to his honour, Timon surnamed Misanthropus (as who would say, Loup-garou, or the manhater), meeting Alcibiades thus accompanied, did not pass by him, nor gave him way (as he was wont to do to all other men) but went straight to him, and took him by the hand, and said: 'O, thou dost well my son. I can thee thank, that thou goest on, and climbest up still: for if ever thou be in authority, woe be unto those that follow thee, for they are utterly undone.' When they had heard these words, those that stood by fell a-laughing: other reviled Timon, other again marked well his words, and thought of them many a time after, such sundry opinions they had of him for the unconstancy of his life, and waywardness of his nature and conditions.

17   Now for the taking of Sicily, the Athenians did marvellously covet it in Pericles' life, but yet they did not meddle withal, until after his death: and then they did it at the first under colour of friendship, as aiding those cities which were oppressed and spoiled by the Syracusans. This was in manner a plain bridge made, to pass afterwards a greater power and army thither. Howbeit the only procurer of the Athenians, and persuader of them, to send small companies thither no more, but to enter with a great army at once to conquer all the country together, was Alcibiades; who had so allured the people with his pleasant tongue, that upon his persuasion, they built castles in the air, and thought to do greater wonders, by winning only of Sicilia. For where others did set their minds upon the conquest of Sicily, being that they only hoped after, it was to Alcibiades but a beginning of further enterprises. And where Nicias commonly in all his persuasions did turn the Athenians from their purpose to make wars against the Syracusans, as being too great a matter for them to take the city of Syracusa, Alcibiades again had a further reach in his head, to go conquer Libya and Carthage, and that being conquered, to pass from thence into Italy, and so to Peloponnesus: so that Sicilia should serve but to furnish them with victuals, and to pay the soldiers for their conquests which he had imagined. Thus the young men were incontinently carried away with a marvellous hope and opinion of this journey, and gave good ear to old men's tales that told them wonders of the countries: insomuch as there was no other pastime nor exercise among the youth in their meetings, but companies of men to set round together, draw plates of Sicily, and describe the situation of Libya and Carthage. And yet they say, that neither Socrates the philosopher, nor Meton the astronomer, did ever hope to see any good success of this journey. For the one by the revealing of his familiar spirit, who told him all things to come, as

was thought, had no great opinion of it: and Meton, whether it was for the fear of the success of the journey he had by reason, or that he knew by divination of his art what would follow, he counterfeited the mad man, and holding a burning torch in his hand, made as though he would have set his house afire. Others say, that he did not counterfeit, but like a mad man indeed did set his house afire one night, and that the next morning betimes he went into the market place to pray the people, that in consideration of his great loss and his grievous calamity so late happened him, it would please them to discharge his son for going this voyage. So by this mad devise, he obtained his request of the people for his son, whom he abused much.

18    But Nicias against his will was chosen captain, to take charge of men in these wars: who misliked this journey, as well for his companion and associate in the charge of these wars, as for other misfortunes he foresaw therein. Howbeit the Athenians thought the war would fall out well, if they did not commit it wholly to Alcibiades' rashness and hardiness, but did join with him the wisdom of Nicias: and appointed Lamachus also for their third captain, whom they sent thither, though he were waxen now somewhat old, as one that had showed himself no less venturous and hardy in some battles, than Alcibiades himself. Now when they came to resolve of the number of soldiers, the furniture and order of these wars, Nicias sought crookedly to thwart this journey, and to break it off altogether: but Alcibiades withstood him, and got the better hand of him. There was an orator called Demostratus, who moved the people also that the captains whom they had chosen for these wars, might have full power and authority to levy men at their discretion, and to make such preparation as they thought good: whereunto the people condescended, and did authorise them. But when they were even ready to go their way, many signs of ill success lighted in the neck one of another: and amongst the rest this was one. That they were commanded to take ship, on the day of the celebration of the feast of Adonia, on the which the custom is, that women do set up in divers places of the city, in the midst of the streets, images, like to dead corpses which they carry to burial, and they represent the mourning and lamentations made at the funerals of the dead, with blubbering, and beating themselves, in token of

the sorrow the goddess Venus made, for the death of her friend
Adonis. Moreover, the Hermes (which are the images of Mercury,
and were wont to be set up in every lane and street) were found in
a night all hacked and hewed, and mangled specially in their faces:
but this put divers in great fear and trouble, yea even those that
made no account of such toys. Whereupon it was alleged that it
might be the Corinthians that did it, or procured that lewd act to be
done, favouring the Syracusans, who were their near kinsmen, and
had been the first founders of them, imagining upon this ill token,
it might be a cause to break off the enterprise, and to make the
people repent them, that they had taken this war in hand. Nevertheless, the people would not allow this excuse, neither hearken to
their words that said, they should not reckon of any such signs or
tokens, and that they were but some light-brained youths, that
being tippled, had played this shameful part in their bravery or for
sport. But for all these reasons, they took these signs very grievously, and were indeed not a little afraid, as thinking undoubtedly
that no man durst have been so bold to have done such an
abominable fact, but that there was some conspiracy in the matter.
Hereupon, they looked upon every suspicion and conjecture that
might be (how little or unlikely soever it were) and that very
severely: and both senate and people also met in council upon it,
very oft, and in a few days.

19  Now whilst they were busily searching out the matter,
Androcles a common counsellor, and orator in the commonwealth,
brought before the council certain slaves and strangers that dwelt in
Athens: who deposed that Alcibiades, and other of his friends and
companions, had hacked and mangled other images after that sort,
and in a mockery had counterfeited also in a banquet that he made,
the ceremonies of the holy mysteries, declaring these matters
particularly: how one Theodorus counterfeited the herald, that is
wont to make the proclamations, Polytion the torch bearer, and
Alcibiades the priest, who showeth the holy signs and mysteries:
and that his other companions were the assistants, as those that
make suit to be received into their religion and order, and into the
brotherhood of their holy mysteries, whom for this cause they call
Mystes. These very words are written in the accusation Thessalus
(Cimon's son) made against Alcibiades, charging him that he

had wickedly mocked the two goddesses, Ceres and Proserpina. Whereat the people being marvellously moved and offended, and the orator Androcles his mortal enemy aggravating and stirring them up the more against him, Alcibiades a little at the first began to be amazed at it. But afterwards, hearing that the mariners which were prepared for the voyage of Sicilia, and the soldiers also that were gathered, did bear him great goodwill, and specially how the aid, and that band that came from Argos and Mantinea (being a thousand footmen, well armed and appointed) did say openly, how it was for Alcibiades' sake they did take upon them so long a voyage beyond sea, and that if they went about to do him any hurt or wrong, they would presently return home again from whence they came: he began to be of a good courage again, and determined with this good favourable opportunity of time, to come before the council, to answer to all such articles and accusations as should be laid against him. Thereupon his enemies were a little cooled, fearing lest the people in this judgment would have showed him more favour, because they stood in need of him. Wherefore to prevent this danger, they had fed other orators who set a good face on the matter, as they had been Alcibiades' friends, and yet bore him no less goodwill, than the rankest enemies he had. These fine fellows rose up in open assembly, and said: it was no reason, that he that was now chosen one of the generals of so mighty and puissant an army (being ready to hoist sail, and the aid also of their allies and friends) should be driven to stay now, and to lose time and occasion of well doing, whilst they should go about to choose judges, and appoint him his hours and time of answer. Therefore, they said, it was fit he should take his journey betimes, and when wars were done, that he should present himself to require justice, and to purge himself of such matters as should be objected against him. But Alcibiades smelling straight their fetch, and perceiving the practice of his stay, stepped up, and declared how they did him great wrong, to make him depart with the charge of a general of so great an army, his mind being troubled with continual fear of so grievous curses, as he should leave upon him: and that he deserved death, if he could not purge and justify himself of all the unjust and surmised accusations against him. And if he had once cleared himself of all things, and had published his innocence, he should then have nothing in his head to trouble him, nor to think upon, but to go on lustily to fight with his enemies, and to cast behind him the danger of all his slanderous detractors.

20   But all this could not persuade them. And so he was presently commanded in the behalf of the people, to embark, and ship away his men. Thus he was compelled to take the seas with his other companions, having in their navy about a hundred and forty galleys, all having three oars to a bank: and five thousand one hundred footmen very well armed and appointed, and throwers with slings, archers, and other light armed men to the number of thirteen hundred, sufficiently furnished of all warlike and necessary munition. Now after they were arrived on the coast of Italy, they landed in the city of Rhegio: where, holding counsel in what sort they should direct these wars, it was resolved in the end that they should go straight unto Sicilia. This opinion was followed, although Nicias did contrary it, when Lamachus gave his consent thereunto: and at his first coming, he was the occasion of winning the city of Catana. But he never after did any exploit, for he was called home immediately by the Athenians, to come and answer certain accusations laid to his charge. For as we told you before, there was at the beginning certain light suspicions and accusations put up against him, by some slaves and strangers. But afterwards when he was gone, his enemies enforced them, and burdened him more cruelly, adding to his former fault, that he had broken the images of Mercury: and had committed sacrilege in counterfeiting in jest and mockery the holy ceremonies of the mysteries: and blew into the ears of the people, that both the one and the other proceeded of one set conspiracy, to change and alter the government of the state of the city. Upon these informations, the people took it in so ill part, that they committed all to prison, that were in any sort accused or suspected thereof, and would never let them come to their answer: and moreover did much repent them that they had not condemned Alcibiades, upon so great complaints and informations as were exhibited against him, while his offence was in question before them. And the fury and hatred of the people was such towards him, that if any of Alcibiades' friends and acquaintance came within their danger, they were the worse handled for his sake. Thucydides did not name his accusers, but some other do

name Dioclides and Teucer: amongst whom, Phrynicus the comical poet is one, who discovereth it in his verses, by bringing in one that speaks thus to the image of Mercury:

> My good friend Mercury, I pray thee take good heed,
> That thou fall not and break thy neck: for so thou mightst
> me breed
> Both danger and distrust, and though I guiltless be,
> Some Dioclides falsely might accuse and trouble me.

Mercury answereth:

> Take thou no thought for me; myself I shall well save,
> And will foresee full well therewith that Teucer (that
> false knave)
> Shall not the money get, which he by law hath won,
> For his promoter's bribing part and accusation.

And yet for all this, these tokens do show no certainty of anything. For one of them being asked, how he could know them by their faces in the night, that had broken and defaced these images, he answered, that he knew them well enough by the brightness of the moon. And hereby it appeareth plainly that he was perjured, because that the same night, on the which this fact was committed, there was a conjunction of the moon. This did a little trouble and stay men of judgment: howbeit the common sort of people, this notwithstanding, did not leave to be as sharp set to receive all accusations and informations, that were brought in against him, as ever they were before.

21 Now there was among the prisoners whose cause was hanging before them, the orator Andocides (whom Hellanicus the historiographer describeth to descend of the race of Ulysses) whom they took to be a man that hated the government of the common people, and bent altogether to favour the small number of the nobility. But one of the chiefest occasions why he was suspected to be one of them that had broken the images, was for that hard by his house there was a fair great image set up in old time, by the family or tribe of the Aegeides, and that alone amongst all the rest of so many famous images, was left whole and unbroken: whereupon it is called at this day, the Mercury of Andocides, and is so called generally of everybody, albeit the inscription showeth the con-

trary. Andocides being in prison, chanced to fall in acquaintance with one Timaeus, with whom he was more familiar then with all the rest, who was also prisoner with him for the self cause. This Timaeus was a man not so well known as he, but besides a wise man, and very hardy. He persuaded him, and put into his head, that he should accuse himself, and certain other with him; for taking the matter upon him, and confessing it, he should receive grace and pardon, according to the course and promise of the law. Where contrarily, if he should stand upon the courtesy of the judges' sentence, he might easily endanger himself: because judgments in such cases are uncertain to all people, and most to be doubted and feared toward the rich. And therefore he told him it were his best way, if he looked into the matter wisely, by lying to save his life, rather than to suffer death with shame, and to be condemned upon this false accusation. Also he said if he would have regard to the commonwealth, that it should in like case be wisely done of him, to put in danger a few of those (which stood doubtful whether in truth they were any of them or not) to save from the fury of the people, and terror of death, many honest men, who indeed were innocent of this lewd fact. Timaeus' words and persuasions wrought such effect with Andocides, that they made him yield unto them, and brought him to accuse himself, and certain other with him: by means whereof Alcibiades according to the law had his pardon. But all such as he named and accused, were every man put to death, saving such as saved themselves by running away. Furthermore, to shadow his accusation with some appearance of truth, Andocides among those that were accused, did accuse also certain of his own servants. Now though the people had no more occasion to occupy their busy heads about the breakers of these images, yet was not their malice thus appeased against Alcibiades, until they sent the galley called Salaminiana, commanding those they sent by a special commission to seek him out, in no case to attempt to take him by force, nor to lay hold on him by violence: but to use him with all the good words and courteous manner that they possibly could, and to will him only to appear in person before the people, to answer to certain accusations put up against him. If otherwise they should have used force, they feared much lest the army would have mutinied on his behalf within the country of their enemies, and that there would have grown some sedition amongst their soldiers. This might Alcibiades have easily done, if he had been disposed. For the soldiers were very sorry to see him depart, perceiving that the wars should be drawn out now in length, and be much prolonged under Nicias, seeing Alcibiades was taken from them, who was the only spur that pricked Nicias forward to do any service: and that Lamachus also, though he were a valiant man of his hands, yet he lacked honour and authority in the army, because he was but a mean man born, and poor besides.

22    Now Alcibiades for a farewell, disappointed the Athenians of winning the city of Messina: for they having intelligence by certain private persons within the city, that it would yield up into their hands, Alcibiades knowing them very well by their names, bewrayed them unto those that were the Syracusans' friends: whereupon all this practice was broken utterly. Afterwards when he came to the city of Thuries, so soon as he had landed, he went and hid himself incontinently in such sort, that such as sought for him, could not find him. Yet there was one that knew him where he was, and said: 'Why, how now Alcibiades, darest thou not trust the justice of thy country?' 'Yes very well,' quoth he, 'an it were in another matter: but my life standing upon it, I would not trust mine own mother, fearing lest negligently she should put in the black bean, where she should cast in the white.' For by the first, condemnation of death was signified: and by the other, pardon of life. But afterwards, hearing that the Athenians for malice had condemned him to death: 'Well,' quoth he, 'they shall know I am yet alive.' Now the manner of his accusation and indictment framed against him, was found written in this sort: 'Thessalus the son of Cimon, of the village of Laciades, hath accused, and doth accuse Alcibiades, the son of Clinias, of the village of Scambonides, to have offended against the goddesses, Ceres and Proserpina, counterfeiting in mockery their holy mysteries, and showing them to his familiar friends in his house, himself apparelled and arrayed in a long vestment or cope, like unto the vestment the priest weareth when he showeth these holy sacred mysteries: and naming himself the priest, Polytion the torch bearer, and Theodorus of the village of Phygea the verger, and the other lookers on, brethren, and fellow scorners with them, and all done in manifest contempt and

derision of holy ceremonies and mysteries of the Eumolpides, the
religious priests and ministers of the sacred temple of the city of
Eleusin.' So Alcibiades for his contempt and not appearing, was
condemned, and his goods confiscate. Besides this condemnation,
they decreed also, that all the religious priests and women should
ban and accurse him. But hereunto answered one of the nuns
called Theano, the daughter of Menon, of the village of Agraula,
saying: that she was professed religious, to pray and to bless, not to
curse and ban.

23   After this most grievous sentence and condemnation passed
against him, Alcibiades departed out of the city of Thuries, and
went into the country of Peloponnesus, where he continued a
good season in the city of Argos. But in the end fearing his
enemies, and having no hope to return again to his own country
with any safety, he sent unto Sparta to have safe conduct and
licence of the Lacedaemonians, that he might come and dwell in
their country, promising them he would do them more good
being now their friend, then he ever did them hurt, while he was
their enemy. The Lacedaemonians granted his request, and received him very willingly into their city: where even upon his first
coming, he did three things. The first was that the Lacedaemonians
by his persuasion and procurement, did determine speedily to send
aid to the Syracusans, whom they had long before delayed: and so
they sent Gylippus their captain to overthrow the Athenians' army,
which they had sent thither. The second thing he did for them, was
that he made them of Greece to begin war upon the Athenians.
The third, and greatest matter of importance, was that he did
counsel them to fortify the city of Decelea, which was within the
territories of Attica self: which consumed, and brought the power
of the Athenians lower, than any other thing whatsoever he could
have done. And if he were welcome, and well esteemed in Sparta,
for the service he did to the commonwealth, much more he won
the love and goodwills of private men, for that he lived after the
Laconian manner. So as they that saw his skin scraped to the flesh,
and saw him wash himself in cold water, and how he did eat brown
bread, and sup of their black broth, would have doubted (or to say
better, never have believed) that such a man had ever kept cook in
his house, nor that he ever had seen so much as a perfuming pan, or

had touched cloth of tissue made at Miletum. For among other qualities and properties he had (whereof he was full) this as they say was one whereby he most robbed men's hearts: that he could frame altogether with their manners and fashions of life, transforming himself more easily to all manner of shapes, than the chameleon. For it is reported, that the chameleon cannot take white colour: but Alcibiades could put upon him any manners, customs or fashions, of what nation soever, and could follow, exercise, and counterfeit them when he would, as well the good as the bad. For in Sparta, he was very painful, and in continual exercise: he lived sparingly with little, and led a straight life. In Ionia, to the contrary: there he lived daintily and superfluously, and gave himself to all mirth and pleasure. In Thracia, he drank ever, or was always a-horseback. If he came to Tissaphernes, lieutenant of the mighty king of Persia, he far exceeded the magnificence of Persia in pomp and sumptuousness. And these things notwithstanding, never altered his natural condition from one fashion to another, neither did his manners (to say truly) receive all sorts of changes. But because peradventure, if he had showed his natural disposition, he might in divers places where he came have offended those whose company he kept, he did with such a visor and cloak disguise himself, to fit their manners whom he companied with, by transforming himself into their natural countenance. As he that had seen him when he was at Sparta, to have looked upon the outward man, would have said as the common proverb sayeth:

It is not the son of Achilles, but Achilles' self:

Even so it is even he, whom Lycurgus brought up. But he that had inwardly seen his natural doings, and goodwill indeed lie naked before him, would have said contrarily, as they say commonly in another language:

This woman is no changeling.

For he entertained Queen Timaea, King Agis' wife of Sparta, so well in his absence, he being abroad in the wars, that he got her with child, and she herself denied it not. For she being brought a-bed of a son, who was named Leotychides, openly to the world called him by that name: but when she was amongst her familiars and very friends, she called him softly Alcibiades, she was so far in love with him. And Alcibiades jesting out the matter, said he had done it for no hurt, nor for any lust of flesh to satisfy his desire: but only to leave of his race, to reign amongst the Lacedaemonians. This matter was brought by divers unto King Agis' ears, who at the length believed it: but specially when he began to make a reckoning of the time, how long it was since he lay with his wife. For lying with his wife one night when there was a terrible earthquake, he ran out of his chamber for fear the house would fall on his head: so that it was ten months after ere he lay again with her. Whereupon, her son Leotychides being born at the end of ten months, he said he was none of his: and this was the cause that Leotychides did not succeed afterwards in the kingdom, because he was not of the blood royal.

24    After the utter overthrow of the Athenians in Sicilia, those of the Isles of Chio and Lesbos, with the Cyzicenians, did send all about a ten ambassadors to Sparta, to let the Lacedaemonians understand, they had goodwill to leave the Athenians, so they would send them aid to defend them. The Boeotians favoured those of Lesbos: Pharnabazus, the king of Persia's lieutenant, favoured the Cyzicenians. This notwithstanding, the Lacedaemonians were better affected to help those of Chio first, by the persuasion of Alcibiades, who took their matters in hand. And he took sea himself and went into Asia, where he almost turned the country of Ionia against the Athenians: and keeping always with the generals of the Lacedaemonians, he did much hurt the Athenians. Yet notwithstanding, King Agis did bear him ill will, partly for the injury he did him in dishonouring and defiling his wife, and partly also, for that he envied his glory: because the rumour ran about, that the most part of the goodly exploits of these wars did happen well, by Alcibiades' means. Other also of the greatest authority among the Spartans, that were most ambitious among them, began in their minds to be angry with Alcibiades, for the envy they bore him: who were of so great power, that they procured their governors to write their letters to their captains in the field, to kill him. Alcibiades hearing of this, did no whit desist to do all he could for the benefit of the Lacedaemonians: yet he had an eye behind him, flying all occasions to fall into their hands. So in the end, for more surety of his person, he went unto Tisaphernes,

one of the king of Persia's lieutenants, with whom he won
incontinently such credit, that he was the first and chiefest person
he had about him. For this barbarous man being no simple person,
but rather malicious and subtle of nature, and that loved fine and
crafty men, did wonder how he could so easily turn from one
manner of living to another, and also at his quick wit and understanding. Moreover, his company and manner to pass the time
away, was commonly marvellous full of mirth and pleasure, and he
had such pleasant comely devises with him, that no man was of so
sullen a nature, but he would make him merry, nor so churlish, but
he would make him gentle. So that both those that feared him, and
also envied him, they were yet glad to see him, and it did them
good to be in his company, and use talk with him. In so much as
this Tisaphernes (that otherwise was a churlish man, and naturally
hated the Grecians) did give himself so much unto Alcibiades'
flatteries, and they pleased him so well, that he himself did study to
flatter Alcibiades again, and make much of him. For he called
'Alcibiades' his fair house of pleasure, and goodly prospect: notwithstanding he had many goodly gardens, sweet springs, green
arbours and pleasant meadows, and those in all royal and magnificent manner.

25   Alcibiades despairing utterly to find any safety or friendship
among the Spartans, and fearing on the other side King Agis also,
he began to speak ill of them, and to disgrace all that they did, to
Tisaphernes. By this practice he stayed Tisaphernes from aiding
them so friendly as he might: moreover, he did not utterly destroy
the Athenians. For he persuaded him that he should furnish the
Lacedaemonians but with little money, to let them diminish and
consume by little and little: to the end that after one had troubled
and weakened the other, they both at the length should be the
easier for the king to overcome. This barbarous man did easily
consent to this devise. All the world then saw he loved Alcibiades,
and esteemed of him very much: in so much as he was sought to,
and regarded of all hands of the Grecians. Then were the Athenians
sorry, and repented them when they had received so great loss and
hurt, for that they had decreed so severely against Alcibiades, who
in like manner was very sorrowful, to see them brought to so hard
terms, fearing, if the city of Athens came to destruction, that he

himself should fall in the end into the hands of the Lacedaemonians, who maliced him to the death. Now about that time, all
the power of the Athenians were almost in the Isle of Samos, from
whence with their army by sea, they sought to suppress the rebels
that were up against them, and to keep all that which yet remained.
For they were yet prettily strong to resist their enemies, at the least
by sea: but they stood in great fear of the power of Tisaphernes,
and of the hundred and fifty galleys which were reported to be
coming out of the country of Phenicia, to the aid of their enemies,
which if they had come, the city of Athens had been utterly
spoiled, and forever without hope of recovery. The which
Alcibiades understanding, sent secretly unto the chiefest men that
were in the army of the Athenians at Samos, to give them hope he
would make Tisaphernes their friend: howbeit not of any desire he
had to gratify the people, nor that he trusted to the commonalty of
Athens, but only to the honourable and honest citizens, and that
conditionally so as they had the heart and courage to bridle a little
the over-licentiousness and insolence of the common people, and
that they would take upon them the authority to govern, and to
redress their state, and to preserve the city of Athens from final and
utter destruction. Upon this advertisement, all the heads and chief
men did give very good ear unto it: saving only Phrynichus, one of
the captains, and of the town of Dirades. Who mistrusting (that
was true indeed) that Alcibiades cared not which end went forward, nor who had the chief government of Athens, the nobility or
the commonalty, and did but seek all the devises and ways he
could, to return again if it might be possible, in any manner of sort,
and that he did but curry favour with the nobility, blaming and
accusing the people: he stood altogether against the motion,
whereupon Alcibiades' devise was not followed. And having now
showed himself open enemy to Alcibiades, he did secretly advertise
Astiochus then admiral to the Lacedaemonians, of Alcibiades'
practice, and warned him to take heed of him, and to lay him up
safe, as a double dealer, and one that had intelligence with both
sides: but he understood not how it was but one traitor to speak to
another. For this Astiochus was a follower of Tisaphernes for his
private commodity: and perceiving Alcibiades in such credit with
him, he did discover to Alcibiades all that Phrynichus had advertised him. Alcibiades straight sent men of purpose to Samos, unto

the captains there, to accuse Phrynichus of the treason he had revealed against them. Those of the council there, receiving this intelligence, were highly offended with Phrynichus. So, he seeing no better way to save himself for making of this fault, went about to make amends with committing a worse fault. Thereupon he sent again to Astiochus, complaining much he had disclosed him, and yet nevertheless he promised him, if he would keep his counsel, that he would deliver the whole fleet and army of the Athenians into his hands. Howbeit this treason of Phrynichus did the Athenians no hurt at all, by reason of Astiochus' counter treason: for he did let Alcibiades again understand what offer Phrynichus had made him. Phrynichus looking to be charged with this again, the second time before the council, by means of Alcibiades, did first advertise the chief of the army of the Athenians, that their enemies would come and set upon them, and where, and how: and gave them therefore warning to keep near their ships, to make a strong watch, and to fortify themselves with all speed, the which forthwith they did. And as they were about it, there came other letters from Alcibiades, by the which he did warn them again to take heed of Phrynichus, because he had practised again with their enemies, to deliver the whole army of Athens into their hands. But they gave no credit to his second letters: for they thought that he knowing the preparations and minds of the enemies, would serve his own turn with the false accusing of Phrynichus. Notwithstanding this, there was some falsehood in fellowship: for one Hermon, openly in the market place, stabbed Phrynichus in with a dagger, and killed him. The fact being pleaded in law, and thoroughly considered of, the dead body by the sentence of the people was condemned for a traitor, and Hermon the murderer, and his fellows, were crowned in recompense of their fact they had done to kill a traitor to the commonwealth.

26 Wherefore those that were Alcibiades' friends, being at that time the stronger, and greatest men of the council in the army at Samos, they sent one Pisander to Athens, to attempt to alter the government, and to encourage the noblemen to take upon them the authority, and to pluck it from the people: assuring them that Tisaphernes would give them aid to do it, by means of Alcibiades,

who would make him their friend. This was the colour and cloak
wherewith they served their turns, that did change the government
of Athens, and that brought it into the hands of a small number of
nobility: for they were in all but four hundred, and yet they called
themselves five thousand. But so soon as they felt themselves
strong, and that they had the whole authority of government
without contradiction in their hands, they made then no more
reckoning of Alcibiades, and so they made wars more coldly and
slackly than before. Partly because they mistrusted their citizens,
who found the change of government very strange, and partly also
because they were of opinion that the Lacedaemonians (who at all
times did most favour the government of nobility) would be better
inclined to make peace with them. Now the common people that
remained still in the city, stirred not, but were quiet against their
wills, for fear of danger, because there were many of them slain,
that boldly took upon them in open presence to resist these four
hundred. But those that were in the camp, in the Isle of Samos,
hearing these news, were so grievously offended that they resolved
to return incontinently again, unto the haven of Piraea. First of all,
they sent for Alcibiades, whom they chose their captain: then they
commanded him straightly to lead them against these tyrants, who
had usurped the liberty of the people of Athens. But nevertheless
he did not therein, as another would have done in this case, seeing
himself so suddenly crept again in favour with the common
people: for he did not think he should incontinently please and
gratify them in all things, though they had made him now their
general over all their ships and so great an army, being before but a
banished man, a vagabond, and a fugitive. But to the contrary, as it
became a general worthy of such a charge, he considered with
himself, that it was his part wisely to stay those, who would in a
rage and fury carelessly cast themselves away, and not suffer them
to do it. And truly Alcibiades was the cause of the preserving of the
city of Athens at that time from utter destruction. For if they had
suddenly (according to their determination) departed from Samos
to go to Athens, the enemies finding no man to let them, might
easily have won all the country of Ionia, of Hellespont, and of all
the other isles without stroke striking, whilst the Athenians were
busy fighting one against another in civil wars, and within the
compass of their own walls. This Alcibiades alone, and no other,

did prevent, not only by persuading the whole army, and declaring the inconvenience thereof, which would fall out upon their sudden departure: but also by entreating some particularly apart, and keeping a number back by very force. To bring this about, one Thrasibulus of the town of Stira, did help him much, who went through the army, and cried out upon them that were bent to enterprise this journey. For he had the biggest and loudest voice, as they say, of any man that was in all the city of Athens. This was a notable act, and a great piece of service done by Alcibiades: that he promised five hundred sail of the Phenicians (which the Lacedaemonians assuredly looked for, in their aid from the king of Persia) should not come at all, or else if they came, it should be in the favour of the Athenians. For he departed immediately, and went with great speed to Tisaphernes: whom he handled in such sort, that he brought not the ships that lay at road before the city of Aspenda, and so he broke promise with the Lacedaemonians. Therefore Alcibiades was marvellously blamed and accused, both of the one and the other side, to have altered Tisaphernes' mind, but chiefly of the Lacedaemonians, who said that he had persuaded this barbarous captain he should neither aid the one nor the other, but rather to suffer them one to devour and destroy each other. For it had been out of doubt, if this great fleet and navy of the King's had come to join their force with either party, that they had taken from the one of them, the seigniory and domination of the sea.

27  Shortly after, the four hundred noblemen that had usurped the authority and government of Athens, were utterly driven away and overthrown, by means of the friendly aid and assistance that Alcibiades' friends gave those that took the people's part. So the citizens were very well pleased with Alcibiades, in so much as they sent for him to return when he thought good. But he, judging with himself it would be no honour nor grace unto him to return without some well deserving, and before he had done some greater exploit, as only upon the people's favour and goodwill, whereas otherwise his return might be both glorious and triumphant, departed first from Samos with a small number of galleys, and went sailing up and down the Isles of Cos and of Gnidos. There he was advertised, that Mindarus, the admiral of the Lacedaemonians, was gone with all his fleet unto the strait of Hellespont, and that the

captains of the Athenians gave chase unto him. Thereupon he went also and sailed thither with speed, to aid the Athenians: and by very good fortune came with eighteen galleys even at the very instant, when they were both in the midst of their fight, with all their ships before the city of Abydos. The battle was cruelly fought between them from morning till night, both the one and the other having the better in one part of the battle, and the worst in another place. Now at the first discovery of Alcibiades' coming, both parts had indeed contrary imaginations of him. For the enemies took heart unto them, and the Athenians began to be afraid. But Alcibiades set up straight his flag in the top of the galley of his admiral, to show what he was. Wherewithal, he set upon the Peloponnesians that had the better, and had certain galleys of the Athenians in chase: whereupon the Peloponnesians gave over their chase, and fled. But Alcibiades followed them so lustily, that he ran divers of them aground, and broke their ships, and slew a great number of men that leapt into the sea, in hope to save themselves by swimming a-land. So notwithstanding that Pharnabazus was come thither to aid the Lacedaemonians, and did his best endeavour to save their galleys by the sea shore: yet the Athenians in the end won thirty galleys of their enemies, and saved all their own, and so did set up certain flags of triumph and victory. Alcibiades having now happily got this glorious victory, would needs go show himself in triumph unto Tisaphernes. So having prepared to present him with goodly rich presents, and appointed also a convenient train and number of sail meet for a general, he took his course directly to him. But he found not that entertainment he hoped for. For Tisaphernes standing in great hazard of displeasure, and fear of punishment at the king's hands, having long time before been defamed by the Lacedaemonians, who had complained of him, that he did not fulfil the king's commandment, thought that Alcibiades was arrived in very happy hour: whereupon he kept him prisoner in the city of Sardis, supposing the wrong he had done would by this means easily discharge, and purge him to the king.

28   Yet at the end of thirty days, Alcibiades by fortune got a horse, and stealing from his keepers, fled unto the city of Clazomenes: and this did more increase the suspicion they had of Tisaphernes, because they thought that underhand he had wrought his liberty.

Alcibiades took then sea again, and went to seek out the army of
the Athenians. Which when he had found, and heard news that
Mindarus and Pharnabazus were together in the city of Cizicum,
he made an oration to his soldiers, and declared unto them how it
was very requisite they should fight with their enemies, both by
sea and by land, and moreover that they should assault them
within their forts and castles, because otherwise they could have
no money to defray their charges. His oration ended, he made
them immediately hoist sail, and so to go lie at anchor in the Isle of
Proconesus: where he took order that they should keep in all the
pinnaces and brigantines among the ships of war, that the enemy
might have no manner of intelligence of his coming. The great
showers of rain also, with thunder and dark weather that fell out
suddenly upon it, did greatly further him in his attempt and
enterprise: in so much as not only his enemies, but the Athenians
that were there before, knew nothing of his coming. So some
made their reckoning, that they could do little or nothing all that
day: yet he made them suddenly embark, and hoist sail. They were
no sooner in the main sea, but they descried afar off the galleys of
their enemies, which lay at road before the haven of Cyzicum.
And fearing lest the great number of his fleet would make them
fly, and take land before he could come to them, he commanded
certain captains to stay behind, and to row softly after him, and
himself with forty galleys with him went towards the enemies to
provoke them to fight. The enemies supposing there had been no
more ships than those that were in sight, did set out presently
to fight with them. They were no sooner joined together, but
Alcibiades' ships that came behind, were also descried: the enemies
were so afraid thereat, that they cast about, and fled straight.
Alcibiades leaving his fleet, followed the chase with twenty of the
best galleys he had, and drove them a-land. Thereupon he landed
also, and pursued them so courageously at their heels, that he slew
a great number of them on the mainland, who thought by flying
to have saved themselves. Moreover, Mindarus and Pharnabazus,
being come out of the city to rescue their people, were overthrown both. He slew Mindarus in the field fighting valiantly: as
for Pharnabazus, he cowardly fled away. So the Athenians spoiled
the dead bodies (which were a great number) of a great deal of
armour and riches, and took besides all their enemies' ships. After

they took the city of Cizycum, Pharnabazus having left it. Then the Peloponnesians being slain, they had not only the possession of the whole country of Hellespont, which they kept: but they drove their enemies by force out of all parts of the sea. There were at that time certain letters intercepted, whereby a secretary gave advertisement unto the Ephori at Sparta, of the overthrow in this sort: 'All is lost, Mindarus is slain, our people die for hunger, and we know not what to do.'

29   Now the soldiers of Athens that had been at this journey and overthrow, grew to such a pride and reputation of themselves, that they would not, and disdained also to serve with the other soldiers that had been beaten many times, and went away with the worse. Where they to the contrary had never been overcome, as a little before it happened that the captain Thrasyllus had been overthrown by the city of Ephesus. And for this overthrow, the Ephesians had set up a triumph, and token of brass, to the utter shame and ignominy of the Athenians. For the which Alcibiades' soldiers did very much rebuke Thrasyllus' men, and did exceedingly extol their captain and themselves, and would neither encamp with them, neither have to do with them, nor yet keep them company, until such time as Pharnabazus came with a great army against them, as well of footmen as horsemen, when they ran a-foraging upon the Abydenians: and then Alcibiades went to the rescue of them, and gave Pharnabazus battle, and overthrew him once again, and did together with Thrasyllus chase him even until dark night. Then both Alcibiades' and Thrasyllus' soldiers did company together, one rejoicing with another: and so returned all with great joy into one camp. The next morning Alcibiades set up a triumph for the victory he had the day before, and then went to spoil and destroy Pharnabazus' country, where he was governor, and no man durst once come out to meet him. In this road there were taken prisoners certain priests and nuns of the country: but Alcibiades freely delivered them afterwards without ransom. And preparing to make wars against the Chalcedonians, who were revolted from the Athenians, and had received a garrison and governor of the Lacedaemonians into their city, he was advertised that they had brought in all their goods and chattels out of the fields, and had delivered them to the safe custody of the Bithynians,

who were their neighbours and friends. Hereupon he led his army into their borders, and sent a herald before to summon the Bithynians, to make amends for the wrong they had done the Athenians. The Bithynians fearing lest Alcibiades would set upon them, did straight deliver him the goods they had as afore in their custody, and moreover, made a league with the Athenians besides.

30    That done, he went and laid siege to the city of Chalcedon, the which he environed all about from the one side of the sea to the other. Pharnabazus came thither, thinking to have raised the siege. And Hippocrates, a captain of the Lacedaemonians, that was governor of the city, assembled all the force he was able to make within the same, and made a sally out also upon the Athenians at the very same time. Whereupon Alcibiades putting his men in order of battle, so as they might give a charge upon them both at one instant, he fought so valiantly, that he forced Pharnabazus to run his way with shame enough, and slew Hippocrates in the field, with a great number of his men. Then took he the seas again, to go towards the country of Hellespont, to get some money, where upon the sudden he did take the city of Selybrea, because he valiantly put himself in hazard before the time appointed him. For certain of his friends within, with whom he had secret practice, had given him a token, that when time served, they would show a burning torch in the air at midnight: but they were compelled to show this fire in the air before they were ready, for fear lest one of their confederacy would bewray the matter, who suddenly repented him. Now this torch burning in the air, was set up before Alcibiades was ready with his company. But he perceiving the sign set, took about thirty men with him in his company, and ran with them to the walls of the city, having commanded the rest of his army to follow him with all speed possible. The gate was opened to him, and to his thirty men: besides them there followed twenty other light armed men. Howbeit they were no sooner entered the city, but they heard the citizens armed come against them: so that there was no hope to escape, if he did tarry their coming. Nevertheless, considering that until that present time he was never overcome in battle, where he had taken charge, it grieved him very much to fly: wherefore it straight came in his head to make silence by sound of trumpet, and after silence made, he caused one of them that were about him to make proclamation

with a loud voice, that the Selybrianians should not take arms against the Athenians. This cooled them a little that would fain have been doing, because they supposed that all the army of the Athenians had been already in the city: the other on the contrary side, were very glad to talk of peace, without any further danger. And as they began to parle upon composition, the rest of Alcibiades' army was come on. Now he thinking indeed (which was true) that the Selybrianians sought nothing but peace, and fearing lest the Thracians which were many in number (and came with goodwill to serve him in that journey) would sack and spoil the city, he made them all to go out again: and so concluding peace with the chief of the Selybrianians, he did them no more hurt, upon their humble submission, but made them pay him a sum of money, and so leaving a garrison of the Athenians within the city, he departed thence.

31   Whilst Alcibiades was in treaty with the Selybrianians, the other Athenian captains that lay at the siege of Chalcedon made an agreement with Pharnabazus, that he should give them a sum of money, and give up the town into the Athenians' hands, to enjoy it as they had before. And with express condition also, that the Athenians should make no roads into Pharnabazus' dominions, to hurt or spoil any of his: and likewise should be bound to give good safe conduit unto the ambassadors of the Athenians, to go and come safe from time to time, to the king of Persia. The other captains being sworn to this peace, Pharnabazus conditioned also, that Alcibiades at his return should likewise be sworn to the peace and conditions thereof. But Alcibiades said, he would not be sworn at all, unless Pharnabazus were first sworn for his part. Thus when oaths were taken of either side, Alcibiades went also against those of Byzantium, who in like case had rebelled against the Athenians. At his first coming thither, he environed the city round about with a wall. Afterwards he practised with two secret friends of his, Anaxilaus and Lycurgus, and certain other within the city, who promised him to deliver it into his hands, so they might be assured he would do them no hurt. To colour this practice, he gave it out, that he must needs leave the siege, and depart with speed, for certain news that were come out of Ionia: and thereupon he embarked presently, and went out of the haven at noonday with all his ships, howbeit he returned again the same

night. And going a-land with the choicest and best armed men he
had, he approached the walls of the city, without any manner of
noise, having left order with them that remained in the ships, that
in the mean season they should row with all force into the haven,
with as great cries and shouts as might be, to fear and trouble the
enemies: partly to fear the Byzantines the more with their sudden
coming among them, and partly that his confederates within the
city might with better opportunity receive him and his company
into the town with the more assured safety, whilst every man ran to
the haven, to resist them that were upon the galleys. Nevertheless
they went not away unfought with. For those that lay in garrison
within the city, some of them Peloponnesians, other Boeotians,
and other Megarians, did so valiantly repulse them that came out of
their galleys, that they drove them to retire aboard again. Afterwards hearing how the Athenians were entered the city on the
other side, they put themselves in battle ray, and went to meet
them. The battle was terrible of both parts: but Alcibiades in the
end obtained victory, leading the right wing of his battle, and
Theramenes the left. The victory being gotten, he took 300 of his
enemies prisoners, who had escaped the fury of the battle. But after
the battle, there was not a Byzantine put to death, neither banished, nor his good confiscated: because it was capitulated by
Alcibiades with his confederates, that neither he, nor his, should
hurt any of the Byzantines either in person or goods, nor any way
should rifle them. And Anaxilaus being afterwards accused of
treason in Lacedaemon for this practice, he answered, and justified
himself in such sort, that they could not find he had committed the
fault laid unto his charge. For he said, that he was no Lacedaemonian, but a Byzantine: and that he saw not Lacedaemon in
danger, but Byzantium, which the enemies had compassed about
with a wall they had built, that it was impossible to bring anything into the city. Moreover he alleged, that they having very
small store of corn within the city (as was true indeed) the
Peloponnesians and Boeotians that lay there in garrison did eat it
up, while the poor Byzantines themselves, their wives and children, died for very hunger. Therefore it could not be said of him,
that he had betrayed his country, but rather that he had delivered it
from the miseries and calamities the wars brought upon it: wherein
he had followed the example of the honestest men of Lacedaemon,

who did acknowledge nothing honest and just, but that which was necessary and profitable for their country. The Lacedaemonians hearing his reasons he alleged for his purgation were ashamed to condemn him, and therefore they let him go.

32    Now Alcibiades desirous in the end to see his native country again (or to speak more truly, that his countrymen should see him) after he had so many times overthrown their enemies in battle: he hoist sail, and directed his course towards Athens, bringing with him all the galleys of the Athenians richly furnished, and decked all about with scutcheons and targets, and other armour and weapon gotten amongst the spoils of his enemies. Moreover, he brought with him many other ships, which he had won and broken in the wars, besides many ensigns and other ornaments: all which being counted together one with the other, made up the number of two hundred ships. Furthermore, where Duris Samian writeth (who challenges that he came of his house) that at his return one Chrysogonus, an excellent player of the flute (that had won certain of the Pythian games) did play such a note, that at the sound thereof the galley slaves would keep stroke with their oars, and that Callipides another excellent player of tragedies, playing the part of a comedy, did stir them to row, being in such players' garments as every master of such science useth commonly to wear, presenting himself in theatre or stage before the people to show his art; and that the admiral galley wherein himself was, entered the haven with a purple sail, as if some masque had come into a man's house after some great banquet made, neither Ephorus, nor Theopompus, nor Xenophon, make any mention of this at all. Furthermore, methinks it should not be true, that he returning from exile after so long a banishment, and having passed over such sorrows and calamities as he had sustained, would so proudly and presumptuously show himself unto the Athenians. But merely contrary, it is most certain that he returned in great fear and doubt. For when he was arrived in the haven of Piraea, he would not set foot a-land, before he first saw his nephew Euryptolemus, and divers other of his friends from the hatches of his ship, standing upon the sands in the haven mouth. Who were come thither to receive and welcome him, and told him that he might be bold to land, without fear of anything. He was no sooner landed, but all

the people ran out of every corner to see him, with so great love
and affection, that they took no heed of the other captains that
came with him, but clustered all to him only, and cried out for joy
to see him. Those that could come near him, did welcome and
embrace him: but all the people wholly followed him. And some
that came to him, put garlands of flowers upon his head: and those
that could not come near him, saw him afar off, and the old folks
did point him out to the younger sort. But this common joy was
mingled notwithstanding with tears and sorrow, when they came
to think upon their former misfortunes and calamities, and to
compare them with their present prosperity: weighing with themselves also how they had not lost Sicilia, nor their hope in all things
else had failed them, if they had delivered themselves and the
charge of their army into Alcibiades' hands, when they sent for
him to appear in person before them. Considering also how he
found the city of Athens in manner put from their signiory and
commandment on the sea, and on the other side how their force
by land was brought on to such extremity, that Athens scantly
could defend her suburbs, the city self being so divided and
turmoiled with civil dissension: yet he gathered together those
few, and small force that remained, and had now not only restored
Athens to her former power and sovereignty on the sea, but had
made her also a conqueror by land.

33   Now the decree for his repair home again, was passed before
by the people, at the instant request of Callias, the son of
Callaeschrus, who did prefer it: as he himself did testify in his
elegies, putting Alcibiades in remembrance of the good turn he had
done him, saying:

> I was the first that moved in open conference
>     The peoples voice to call thee home, when thou wert
>                                     banished hence.
> So was I eke the first, which thereto gave consent,
>     And therefore may I boldly say, by truth of such intent:
> I was the only mean, to call thee home again,
>     By such request so rightly made, to move the peoples vain.
> And this may serve for pledge, what friendship I thee bear:
>     Fast sealed with a faithful tongue, as plainly shall appear.

But notwithstanding, the people being assembled all in council,

Alcibiades came before them, and made an oration: wherein he first lamented all his mishaps, and found himself grieved a little with the wrongs they had offered him, yet he imputed all in the end to his cursed fortune, and some spiteful god that envied his glory and prosperity. Then he dilated at large the great hope their enemies had to have advantage of them: and therewithal persuaded the people to be of good courage, and afraid of nothing that was to come. And to conclude, the people crowned him with crowns of gold, and chose him general again of Athens, with sovereign power and authority both by land as by sea. And at that very instant it was decreed by the people, that he should be restored again to all his goods, and that the priests Eumolpides should absolve him of all their curses, and that the heralds should with open proclamation revoke the execrations and cursings they had thundered out against him before, by commandment of the people. Whereto they all agreed, and were very willing, saving Theodorus the bishop, who said: 'I did neither excommunicate him, nor curse him, if he hath done no hurt to the commonwealth.'

34  Now Alcibiades flourished in his chiefest prosperity, yet were there some notwithstanding that misliked very much the time of his landing, saying it was very unlucky and unfortunate. For the very day of his return and arrival, fell out by chance on the feast which they call Plynteria, as you would say, the washing day, which they celebrate in honour of Minerva: on the which day, the priests that they call Praxiergides do make certain secret and hidden sacrifices and ceremonies, being the five and twenty day of the month of September, and do take from the image of this goddess, all her raiment and jewels, and keep the image close covered over. Hereupon the Athenians do ascribe that day for a most unfortunate day, and are very circumspect to do any matter of importance on it. Moreover, it was commonly scanned abroad of everybody, that it seemed the goddess was not content, nor glad of Alcibiades' return: and that she did hide herself, because she would not see him, nor have him come near her. Notwithstanding all these toys and ceremonies, when Alcibiades found everything fall out well at his return, and as he would have wished it, he armed a hundred galleys presently, to return again to the wars. Howbeit he wisely regarded the time and solemnity of

celebration of these mysteries, and considerately stayed until they had finished all. And it fell out, that after the Lacedaemonians had taken and fortified the city of Decelea, within the territory of Attica, and that the enemies being the stronger in the field, did keep the way going from Athens to Eleusin, so as by no possible means they could make their solemn procession by land, with such honour and devotion as they were before accustomed to do: and thereby all the sacrifices, dances, and many other holy devout ceremonies they were wont to do by the way, in singing the holy song of Iacchus, came of very necessity to be left off, and clean laid aside. Then Alcibiades thought he should do a meritorious deed to the gods, and an acceptable to men, to bring the old ceremonies up again upon the said feast: and thereupon purposed to accompany the procession, and defend it by power, against all invasion and disturbance by the enemies. As one that foresaw one of those two things would come to pass: either that Agis king of the Lacedaemonians would not stir at all against the sacred ceremonies, and by this means should much imbase and diminish his reputation and glory, or if he did come out to the field, that he would make the battle very grateful to the gods, considering it should be in defence of their most holy feast and worship, and in the sight of his country, where the people should see and witness both his valiantness and also his courage. Alcibiades being fully resolved upon this procession, went and made the priests Eumolpides, their vergers, and other their ministers and officers of these mysteries, privy to his determination. Then he sent out scouts to watch on the side of the hills thereabouts, and to view the way of their perambulation. The next morning very early he sent out light horsemen also to scour the country. Then he made the priests, the professed, and all the ministers of religion, go in procession, together with those that followed the same: and he himself compassed them about with his army on every side, marching in battle ray, and very good order, and with great silence. This was an honourable and devout leading of an army, and such as if his greatest enemies would confess a truth, they could not but say, Alcibiades had as much showed the office of a high bishop, as of a noble soldier and good captain. So he ended this procession, returning to Athens in all safe order again, and not an enemy that durst once look out into the field to set upon him.

Now this did more increase the greatness of his mind, and therewith the people's good opinion of his sufficiency and wise conduction of an army: in so much as they thought him invinci-ble, having the sovereign power and authority of a general. Furthermore, he spoke so fair to the poor people, and meaner sort, that they chiefly wished and desired he would take upon him like a king: yea, and many went to him to persuade him in it, as though he should thereby withstand all envy, and drive away the laws and customs of trying of matters by the voices of the peoples and all such fond devises, as did destroy the state of the common weal. And furthermore, they said it was very needful that he alone should take upon him the whole rule and government of the city, that he might dispose all things according to his will, and not stand in fear of slanderous and wicked tongues.

35    Now, whether Alcibiades ever had any mind to usurp the kingdom, the matter is somewhat doubtful. But this is certain, the greatest men of the city, fearing lest indeed he meant some such thing, did hasten his departure as soon as they could possible, doing all other things according to his mind: and did assign him such associates in his charge of general, as he himself best liked. So in the end, he departed with a fleet of a hundred galleys, and first of all he fell with the Isle of Andros, where he overcame by fight the inhabitants of the said isle, and certain Lacedaemonians that were amongst them: but he took not the city, which was one of the first matters his enemies did accuse him for. For if ever man was overthrown and envied, for the estimation they had of his valour and sufficiency, truly Alcibiades was the man. For the notable and sundry services he had done won him such estimation of wisdom and valiantness, that where he slacked in any service whatsoever, he was presently suspected, judging the ill success not in that he could not, but for that he would not: and that where he undertook any enterprise, nothing could withstand or lie in his way. Hereupon the people persuading themselves, that immediately after his departure, they should hear that the Isle of Chio was taken, with all the country of Ionia, they were angry they could have no news so suddenly from him as they looked for. Moreover, they did not consider the lack of money he had, and specially making war with such enemies as were ever relieved with the great king of Persia's

aid, and that for necessity's sake he was sundry times driven to leave his camp, to seek money where he could get it to pay his soldiers, and to maintain his army. Now for testimony hereof, the last accusation that was against him, was only for this matter. Lysander being sent by the Lacedaemonians for admiral and general of their army by sea, used such policy with Cyrus, the king of Persia's brother, that he got into his hands a great sum of money: by means whereof he gave unto his mariners four obols a day for their wages, where before they were wont to have but three, and yet Alcibiades had much ado to furnish his with three only a day. For this cause, to get money, Alcibiades sailed into Caria. But in the meantime Antiochus, whom Alcibiades had left his lieutenant behind him, and had given him charge of all the ships in his absence, being a very skilful seaman, but otherwise a hasty harebrained fool, and of small capacity: he being expressly commanded by Alcibiades not to fight in any case, though the enemies offered him battle, was so foolish rash, and made so little reckoning of his strait commandment, that he armed his own galley, whereof himself was captain, and another besides, and went to the city of Ephesus, passing all along his enemies' galleys, reviling and offering villainy to those that stood upon the hatches of their galleys. Lysander being marvellously provoked by those words, went and encountered him at the first with a few ships. The other captains of the galleys of the Athenians, seeing Antiochus in danger, went to aid him, one after another. Then Lysander of his part also set out all his whole fleet against him, and in the end overcame them. Antiochus self was killed in the conflict, and many galleys and men were taken prisoners: wherefore Lysander set up shows of triumph in token of victory. Alcibiades hearing these ill-favoured news, returned presently with all possible speed to Samos: and when he came thither, he went with all the rest of his fleet to offer Lysander battle. But Lysander, quietly contenting himself with his first victory, went not out against him.

36 Now this victory was no sooner won, but one Thrasybulus the son of Thrason, Alcibiades' enemy, went incontinently from the camp, and got him to Athens, to accuse Alcibiades to the people: whom he informed how all went to wrack, and that he had lost many ships, for that he regarded not his charge, carelessly putting men in trust, whom he gave too great credit to, because

they were good fellows, and would drink drunk with him, and were full of mariners' mocks and knavish jests, such as they use commonly amongst themselves. And that he in the meantime took his pleasure abroad, here and there, scraping money together where he could come by it, keeping good cheer, and feasting of the Abydenian and Ionian courtesans, when the enemies' army was so near theirs as it was. Moreover, they laid to his charge, that he did fortify a castle in the country of Thracia, near unto the city of Bisanthe, for a place to retire himself unto, either because be could not, or rather that he would not, live any longer in his own country. Upon those accusations, the Athenians giving over credit to the report, did immediately choose new captains, and thereby declared their misliking. Alcibiades hearing of this, and fearing lest they would do him some worse harm, did leave straight the Athenians' camp, and gathering a certain number of strangers together, went of himself to make war upon certain free people of the Thracians, who were subject to no prince nor state: where he got a marvellous mass of money together, by means whereof he did assure the Grecians inhabiting those marches from all invasion of foreign enemies. Now Tydeus, Menander, and Adimanthus the Athenians' captains, being afterwards in a place commonly called the goat's river, with all the galleys the city of Athens had at that time upon that coast, used every morning commonly to go to the sea, to offer battle to Lysander, who rode at an anchor before the city of Lampsacus, with all the Lacedaemonians' army by sea, and commonly returned again to the place from whence they came, in very ill order, without either watch or ward, as men that were careless of their enemies. Alcibiades being on the land not far off, and finding their great fault and negligence, took his horse, and went to them, and told them that they lay on an ill shore, where there was no good road, nor town, and where they were driven to seek their victuals as far as to the city of Sestos, and that they suffered their mariners to leave their ships, and go a-land when they lay at anchor, straggling up and down the country as they would themselves, without regard that there lay a great army of their enemies before them, ready to be set out at their generals' commandment: and therefore he advised them to remove thence, and to go cast anchor before the city of Sestos.

37   Howbeit the captains would not be advised by him: and that which was worst of all, Tydeus, one of the captains, stoutly commanded him to get him away, as one that had nothing to do with the matter, and that other had charge of the army. Whereupon Alcibiades fearing they would purpose some treason against him, did depart presently from them. And as he went his way, he said to some of his friends which accompanied him out of the camp at his return, that if the captains of the Athenians had not been so round with him, he would have forced the Lacedaemonians to have come to the battle in despite of their beards, or else he would have driven them to forsake their ships. Some took this for a glorious brag: other thought he was like enough to have done it, because he could have brought from land a great number of Thracians, both archers and horsemen, with whom he might have given a charge upon the Lacedaemonians, and done great mischief unto their camp. But now, how wisely Alcibiades did foresee the faults he told the Athenians' captains of, their great misfortune and loss that followed incontinently did too plainly witness it to the world. For Lysander came so fiercely upon them on a sudden, that of all the ships they had in their whole fleet, only eight galleys were saved, with whom Conon fled: and the other being not much less than two hundred in number, were every one of them taken and carried away, with three thousand prisoners whom Lysander put to death. Shortly after, he took the city self of Athens, and razed their long walls even to the ground. After this great and notable victory, Alcibiades fearing sore the Lacedaemonians, who then without let or interruption of any, were only lords and princes by sea and by land, he went into the country of Bithynia, and caused great good to be brought after him, and took a marvellous sum of money with him, besides great riches he left also in the castles of Thracia, where he did remain before. Howbeit he lost much of his goods in Bithynia, which certain Thracians dwelling in that country had robbed him of, and taken from him. So he determined to repair forthwith unto King Artaxerxes, hoping that when the king had once proved him, he should find him a man of no less service, than he had found Themistocles before him: besides that the occasion of his going thither should be much juster than his was. For he did not go thither to make war against the city of Athens and his country, as

Themistocles did: but of a contrary intent, to make intercession to the king, that it would please him to aid them. Now, Alcibiades thinking he could use no better mean, than Pharnabazus' help only, to see him safely conducted to the king's court, he proposed his journey to him, into the country of Phrygia, where he abode a certain time to attend upon him, and was very honourably entertained and received of Pharnabazus.

38   All this while the Athenians found themselves desolate, and in miserable state to see their empire lost: but then much more, when Lysander had taken all their liberties, and did set thirty governors over their city. Now too late, after all was lost (where they might have recovered again, if they had been wise) they began together to bewail and lament their miseries and wretched state, looking back upon all their wilful faults and follies committed: among which, they did reckon their second time of falling out with Alcibiades, was their greatest fault. So they banished him only of malice and displeasure, not for any offence himself in person had committed against them, saving that his lieutenant in his absence had shamefully lost a few of their ships: and they themselves more shamefully had driven out of their city the noblest soldier and most skilful captain that they had. And yet they had some little poor hope left, that they were not altogether cast away, so long as Alcibiades lived, and had his health. For before, when he was a forsaken man, and led a banished life, yet he could not live idly, and do nothing. Wherefore now much more, said they to themselves, if there be any help at all, he will not suffer out of doubt the insolence and pride of the Lacedaemonians, nor yet abide the cruelties and outrages of these thirty tyrants. And surely the common people had some reason to have these thoughts in their heads, considering that the thirty governors themselves did what they could possibly to spy out Alcibiades' doings, and what he went about. In so much as Critias at the last declared to Lysander, that so long the Lacedaemonians might reckon themselves lords over all Greece, as they kept from the common people the rule and authority of the city of Athens. And further he added, that notwithstanding the people of Athens could well away to live like subjects under the government of a few, yet Alcibiades whilst he lived, would never suffer them so to be reigned over, but

would attempt by all devise he could to bring a change and innovation among them. Yet Lysander would not credit these persuasions, before special commandment was sent to him from the senate of Lacedaemon, upon his allegiance, that he should devise to kill Alcibiades by all means he could procure: either because in truth they feared the subtlety of his wit, and the greatness of his courage, to enterprise matters of great weight and danger, or else that they sought to gratify King Agis by it.

39 Lysander being thus straitly commanded, did send and practise incontinently with Pharnabazus to execute the fact: who gave his brother Magaeus, and his uncle Susamithres, commission to attempt the matter. Now was Alcibiades in a certain village of Phrygia, with a concubine of his called Timandra. So he thought he dreamed one night that be had put on his concubines' apparel, and how she dandling him in her arms, had dressed his head, frizzling his hair, and painted his face, as he had been a woman. Other say, that he thought Magaeus struck his head, and made his body to be burnt: and the voice goeth, this vision was but a little before his death. Those that were sent to kill him durst not enter the house where he was, but set it afire round about. Alcibiades spying the fire, got such apparel and hangings as he had, and threw it on the fire, thinking to have put it out: and so casting his cloak about his left arm, took his naked sword in his other hand, and ran out of the house, himself not once touched with fire, saving his clothes were a little singed. These murderers so soon as they spied him, drew back, and stood asunder, and durst not one of them come near him, to stand and fight with him: but afar off, they bestowed so many arrows and darts of him, that they killed him there. Now when they had left him, Timandra went and took his body which she wrapped up in the best linen she had, and buried him as honourably as she could possible, with such things as she had, and could get together. Some hold opinion that Lais, the only famous courtesan, which they say was of Corinth (though indeed she was born in a little town of Sicilia, called Hyccara, where she was taken) was his daughter. Notwithstanding, touching the death of Alcibiades, there are some that agree to all the rest I have written, saving that they say it was neither Pharnabazus nor Lysander, nor the Lacedaemonians, which caused him to be slain:

but that he keeping with him a young gentlewoman of a noble house, whom he had stolen away and enticed to folly, her brethren, to revenge this injury, went to set fire upon the house where he was, and that they killed him as we have told you, thinking to leap out of the fire.

### THE END OF ALCIBIADES' LIFE

## Life of Caius Martius Coriolanus

The house of the Martians at Rome was of the number of the patricians, out of the which hath sprung many noble personages: whereof Ancus Martius was one, King Numa's daughter's son, who was king of Rome after Tullus Hostilius. Of the same house were Publius and Quintus, who brought Rome their best water they had by conduits. Censorinus also came of that family, that was so surnamed, because the people had chosen him censor twice. Through whose persuasion they made a law, that no man from thenceforth might require or enjoy the censorship twice. Caius Martius, whose life we intend now to write, being left an orphan by his father, was brought up under his mother a widow, who taught us by experience, that orphanage bringeth many discommodities to a child, but doth not hinder him to become an honest man, and to excel in virtue above the common sort: as they are meanly born, wrongfully do complain, that it is the occasion of their casting away, for that no man in their youth taketh any care of them to see them well brought up, and taught that were meet. This man also is a good proof to confirm some men's opinions, that a rare and excellent wit untaught, doth bring forth many good and evil things together: like as a fat soil bringeth forth herbs and weeds, that lieth unmanured. For this Martius' natural wit and great heart did marvellously stir up his courage, to do and attempt notable acts. But on the other side for lack of education, he was so choleric and impatient, that he would yield to no living creature: which made him churlish, uncivil, and altogether unfit for any man's conversation. Yet men marvelling much at his constancy, that he was never overcome with pleasure, nor money, and how he would endure easily all manner of pains and travails; thereupon they well liked and commended his stoutness and temperancy. But for all that, they could not be acquainted with him, as one citizen useth to be with another in the city. His behaviour was so unpleasant to them, by reason of a certain insolent and stern manner he had, which because it was too lordly, was disliked. And to say truly, the greatest benefit that learning bringeth men unto, is this: that it teacheth men that be rude and rough of nature, by compass and rule of reason, to be civil and courteous, and to like better the mean state, than the higher. Now in those days, valiantness was honoured in Rome above all other virtues: which they called *virtus*, by the name of virtue self, as including in that general name, all other special virtues besides. So that *virtus* in the Latin, was as much as valiantness.

2   But Martius being more inclined to the wars than any other gentleman of his time, began from his childhood to give himself to handle weapons, and daily did exercise himself therein. And outward he esteemed armour to no purpose, unless one were naturally armed within. Moreover he did so exercise his body to hardness, and all kind of activity, that he was very swift in running, strong in wrestling, and mighty in gripping, so that no man could ever cast him. In so much as those that would try masteries with him for strength and nimbleness, would say when they were overcome, that all was by reason of his natural strength and hardness of ward, that never yielded to any pain or toil he took upon him.

3   The first time he went to the wars, being but a stripling, was when Tarquine surnamed the proud (that had been king of Rome, and was driven out for his pride, after many attempts made by sundry battles to come in again, wherein he was ever overcome) did come to Rome with all the aid of the Latins, and many other people of Italy: even as it were to set up his whole rest upon a battle by them, who with a great and mighty army had undertaken to put him into his kingdom again, not so much to pleasure him, as to overthrow the power of the Romans, whose greatness they both feared and envied. In this battle, wherein were many hot and sharp encounters of either party, Martius valiantly fought in the sight of the dictator, and a Roman soldier being thrown to the ground even hard by him, Martius straight bestrid him, and slew the enemy with his own hands that had before overthrown the Roman. Hereupon, after the battle was won, the dictator did not forget so noble an act, and therefore first of all he crowned Martius with a garland of

oaken boughs. For whosoever saveth the life a Roman, it is a manner among them, to honour him with such a garland. This was either because the law did this honour to the oak, in favour of the Arcadians, who by the oracle of Apollo were in very old time called eaters of acorns, or else because the soldiers might easily in every place come by oaken boughs: or lastly, because they thought it very necessary to give him that had saved a citizen's life, a crown of this tree to honour him, being properly dedicated unto Jupiter, the patron and protector of their cities, and thought amongst other wild trees to bring forth a profitable fruit, and of plants to be the strongest. Moreover, men at the first beginning did use acorns for their bread, and honey for their drink: and further, the oak did feed their beasts, and give them birds, by taking glue from the oaks, with the which they made birdlime to catch seely birds. They say that Castor and Pollux appeared in this battle, and how incontinently after the battle, men saw them in the market place at Rome, all their horses being on a white foam: and they were the first that brought news of the victory, even in the same place, where remaineth at this present a temple built in the honour of them near unto the fountain. And this is the cause, why the day of this victory (which was the fifteenth of July) is consecrated yet to this day unto Castor and Pollux.

4   Moreover it is daily seen, that honour and reputation lighting on young men before their time, and before they have no great courage by nature, the desire to win more dieth straight in them; which easily happeneth, the same having no deep root in them before. Where contrariwise, the first honour that valiant minds do come unto, doth quicken up their appetite, hasting them forward as with force of wind, to enterprise things of high deserving praise. For they esteem not to receive reward for service done, but rather take it for a remembrance and encouragement, to make them do better in time to come: and be ashamed also to cast their honour at their heels, not seeking to increase it still by like desert of worthy valiant deeds. This desire being bred in Martius, he strained still to pass himself in manliness: and being desirous to show a daily increase of his valiantness, his noble service did still advance his fame, bringing in spoils upon spoils from the enemy. Whereupon, the captains that came afterwards (for envy of them that went

before) did contend who should most honour him, and who should bear most honourable testimony of his valiantness. In so much the Romans having many wars and battles in those days, Coriolanus was at them all: and there was not a battle fought, from whence he returned not without some reward of honour. And as for other, the only respect that made them valiant, was they hoped to have honour: but touching Martius, the only thing that made him to love honour, was the joy he saw his mother did take of him. For he thought nothing made him so happy and honourable, as that his mother might always see him return with a crown upon his head, and that she might still embrace him with tears running down her cheeks for joy. Which desire they say Epaminondas did avow, and confess to have been in him: as to think himself a most happy and blessed man, that his father and mother in their lifetime had seen the victory he won in the plain of Leuctres. Now as for Epaminondas, he had this good hap, to have his father and mother living, to be partakers of his joy and prosperity. But Martius thinking all due to his mother, that had been also due to his father if he had lived, did not only content himself to rejoice and honour her, but at her desire took a wife also, by whom he had two children, and yet never left his mother's house therefore.

5    Now he being grown to great credit and authority in Rome for his valiantness, it fortuned there grew sedition in the city, because the senate did favour the rich against the people, who did complain of the sore oppression of usurers, of whom they borrowed money. For those that had little, were yet spoiled of that little they had by their creditors, for lack of ability to pay the usury: who offered their goods to be sold, to them that would give most. And such as had nothing left, their bodies were laid hold of, and they were made their bondmen, notwithstanding all the wounds and cuts they showed, which they had received in many battles, fighting for defence of their country and commonwealth: of the which, the last war they made was against the Sabynes, wherein they fought upon the promise the rich men had made them, that from thenceforth they would entreat them more gently, and also upon the word of Marcus Valerius chief of the senate, who by authority of the council, and in the behalf of the rich, said they should perform that they had promised. But after that they had faithfully served in this

last battle of all, where they overcame their enemies, seeing they
were never a whit the better, nor more gently entreated, and that
the senate would give no ear to them, but make as though they had
forgot their former promise, and suffered them to be made slaves
and bondmen to their creditors, and besides, to be turned out of all
that ever they had: they fell then even to flat rebellion and mutiny,
and to stir up dangerous tumults within the city. The Romans'
enemies hearing of this rebellion, did straight enter the territories
of Rome with a marvellous great power, spoiling and burning all as
they came. Whereupon the senate immediately made open proclamation by sound of trumpet, that all those which were of lawful
age to carry weapon, should come and enter their names into the
muster masters book, to go to the wars: but no man obeyed their
commandment. Whereupon their chief magistrates, and many of
the senate, began to be of divers opinions among themselves. For
some thought it was reason they should somewhat yield to the
poor people's request, and that they should a little qualify the
severity of the law. Other held hard against that opinion, and that
was Martius for one. For he alleged, that the creditors losing their
money they had lent, was not the worst thing that was thereby: but
that the lenity that was favoured, was a beginning of disobedience,
and that the proud attempt of the commonalty was to abolish law,
and to bring all to confusion. Therefore he said, if the senate were
wise, they should betimes prevent and quench this ill-favoured and
worse meant beginning.

6   The senate met many days in consultation about it: but in the
end they concluded nothing. The poor common people seeing no
redress, gathered themselves one day together, and one encouraging another, they all forsook the city, and encamped themselves
upon a hill, called at this day the holy hill, along the river of Tyber,
offering no creature any hurt or violence, or making any show of
actual rebellion: saving that they cried as they went up and down,
that the rich men had driven them out of the city, and that all Italy
through they should find air, water, and ground to bury them in.
Moreover, they said, to dwell at Rome was nothing else but to be
slain, or hurt with continual wars, and fighting for defence of the
rich men's goods. The senate being afraid of their departure, did
send unto them certain of the pleasantest old men, and the

most acceptable to the people among them. Of those, Menenius Agrippa was he who was sent for chief man of the message from the senate. He, after many good persuasions and gentle requests made to the people, on the behalf of the senate, knit up his oration in the end, with a notable tale, in this manner. That on a time all the members of man's body did rebel against the belly, complaining of it, that it only remained in the midst of the body, without doing anything, neither did bear any labour to the maintenance of the rest: whereas all other parts and members did labour painfully, and was very careful to satisfy the appetites and desires of the body. And so the belly, all this notwithstanding, laughed at their folly, and said: 'It is true, I first receive all meats that nourish man's body: but afterwards I send it again to the nourishment of other parts of the same.' 'Even so,' quoth he, 'O you, my masters, and citizens of Rome, the reason is alike between the senate and you. For matters being well digested, and their counsels thoroughly examined, touching the benefit of the commonwealth, the senators are cause of the common commodity that cometh unto every one of you.'

7   These persuasions pacified the people, conditionally, that the senate would grant there should be yearly chosen five magistrates, which they now call *Tribuni Plebis*, whose office should be to defend the poor people from violence and oppression. So Junius Brutus, and Sicinius Vellutus, were the first tribunes of the people that were chosen, who had only been the causers and procurers of this sedition. Hereupon the city being grown again to good quiet and unity, the people immediately went to the wars, showing that they had a goodwill to do better than ever they did, and to be very willing to obey the magistrates in that they would command, concerning the wars. Martius also, though it liked him nothing to see the greatness of the people thus increased, considering it was to the prejudice and imbasing of the nobility, and also saw that other noble patricians were troubled as well as himself, he did persuade the patricians, to show themselves no less forward and willing to fight for their country, than the common people were: and to let them know by their deeds and acts, that they did not so much pass the people in power and riches, as they did exceed them in true nobility and valiantness.

8 In the country of the Volsces, against whom the Romans made war at that time, there was a principal city and of most fame, that was called Corioles, before the which the consul Cominius did lay siege. Wherefore all the other Volsces fearing lest that city should be taken by assault, they came from all parts of the country to save it, intending to give the Romans battle before the city, and to give an onset on them in two several places. The consul Cominius understanding this, divided his army also in two parts, and taking the one part with himself, he marched towards them that were drawing to the city, out of the country: and the other part of his army he left in the camp with Titus Lartius (one of the valiantest men the Romans had at that time) to resist those that would make any sally out of the city upon them. So the Coriolans making small account of them that lay in camp before the city, made a sally out upon them, in the which at the first the Coriolans had the better, and drove the Romans back again into the trenches of their camp. But Martius being there at that time, running out of the camp with a few men with him, he slew the first enemies he met withal, and made the rest of them stay upon a sudden, crying out to the Romans that had turned their backs, and calling them again to fight with a loud voice. For he was even such another, as Cato would have a soldier and a captain to be: not only terrible, and fierce to lay about him, but to make the enemy afraid with the sound of his voice, and grimness of his countenance. Then there flocked about him immediately a great number of Romans: whereat the enemies were so afraid, that they gave back presently. But Martius not staying so, did chase and follow them to their own gates, that fled for life. And there, perceiving that the Romans retired back, for the great number of darts and arrows which flew about their ears from the walls of the city, and that there was not one man amongst them that durst venture himself to follow the flying enemies into the city, for that it was full of men of war, very well armed and appointed: he did encourage his fellows with words and deeds, crying out to them, that fortune had opened the gates of the city more for the followers than the flyers. But all this notwithstanding, few had the hearts to follow him. Howbeit Martius being in the throng among the enemies, thrust himself into the gates of the city, and entered the same among them that fled, without that any one of them durst at the first turn their face upon him, or else offer to

stay him. But he looking about him, and seeing he was entered the city with very few men to help him, and perceiving he was environed by his enemies that gathered round about to set upon him, did things then as it is written, wonderful and incredible, as well for the force of his hand, as also for the agility of his body: and with a wonderful courage and valiantness, he made a lane through the midst of them, and overthrew also those he laid at, that some he made run to the furthest part of the city, and other for fear he made yield themselves, and to let fall their weapons before him. By this means, Lartius that was gotten out, had some leisure to bring the Romans with more safety into the city.

9    The city being taken in this sort, the most part of the soldiers began incontinently to spoil, to carry away, and to look up the booty they had won. But Martius was marvellous angry with them, and cried out on them, that it was no time now to look after spoil, and to run straggling here and there to enrich themselves, whilst the other consul and their fellow citizens peradventure were fighting with their enemies: and how that leaving the spoil they should seek to wind themselves out of danger and peril. Howbeit, cry and say to them what he could, very few of them would hearken to him. Wherefore taking those that willingly offered themselves to follow him, he went out of the city, and took his way towards that part, where he understood the rest of the army was: exhorting and entreating them by the way that followed him, not to be fainthearted, and oft holding up his hands to heaven, he besought the gods to be so gracious and favourable unto him, that he might come in time to the battle, and in good hour to hazard his life in defence of his country men. Now the Romans when they were put in battle ray, and ready to take their targets on their arms, and to gird them upon their arming coats, had a custom to make their wills at that very instant, without any manner of writing, naming him only whom they would make their heir, in the presence of three or four witnesses. Martius came just to that reckoning, whilst the soldiers were a-doing after that sort, and that the enemies were approached so near, as one stood in view of the other. When they saw him at his first coming, all bloody, and in a sweat, and but with a few men following him, some thereupon began to be afraid. But soon after, when they saw him run with a

lively cheer to the consul and to take him by the hand, declaring how he had taken the city of Corioles, and that they saw the consul Cominius also kiss and embrace him, then there was not a man but took heart again to him, and began to be of a good courage, some hearing him report from point to point the happy success of this exploit, and other also conjecturing it by seeing their gestures afar off. Then they all began to call upon the consul to march forward, and to delay no longer, but to give charge upon the enemy. Martius asked him how the order of their enemies' battle was, and on which side they had placed their best fighting men. The consul made him answer, that he thought the bands which were in the forward of their battle, were those of the Antiates, whom they esteemed to be the warlikest men, and which for valiant courage would give no place to any of the host of their enemies. Then prayed Martius, to be set directly against them. The consul granted him, greatly praising his courage. Then Martius, when both armies came almost to join, advanced himself a good space before his company, and went so fiercely to give charge on the forward that came right against him, that they could stand no longer in his hands, he made such a lane through them, and opened a passage into the battle of the enemies. But the two wings of either side turned one to the other, to compass him in between them: which the consul Cominius perceiving, he sent thither straight of the best soldiers he had about him. So the battle was marvellous bloody about Martius, and in a very short space many were slain in the place. But in the end the Romans were so strong, that they distressed the enemies, and broke their array: and scattering them, made them fly. Then they prayed Martius that he would retire to the camp, because they saw he was able to do no more, he was already so wearied with the great pain he had taken, and so faint with the great wounds he had upon him. But Martius answered them, that it was not for conquerors to yield, nor to be faint-hearted: and thereupon began afresh to chase those that fled, until such time as the army of the enemies was utterly overthrown, and numbers of them slain, and taken prisoners.

10   The next morning betimes, Martius went to the consul, and the other Romans with him. There the consul Cominius going up to his chair of state, in the presence of the whole army, gave thanks

to the gods for so great, glorious, and prosperous a victory: then he spoke to Martius, whose valiantness he commended beyond the moon, both for that he himself saw him do with his eyes, as also for that Martius had reported unto him. So in the end he willed Martius, he should choose out of all the horses they had taken of their enemies, and of all the goods they had won (whereof there was great store) ten of every sort which he liked best, before any distribution should be made to others. Besides this great honourable offer he had made him, he gave him in testimony that he had won that day the price of prowess above all other, a goodly horse with a caparison, and all furniture to him: which the whole army beholding, did marvellously praise and commend. But Martius stepping forth, told the consul, he most thankfully accepted the gift of his horse, and was a glad man besides, that his service had deserved his general's commendation: and as for his other offer, which was rather a mercenary reward, than an honourable recompense, he would none of it, but was contented to have his equal part with other soldiers. 'Only, this grace,' said he, 'I crave, and beseech you to grant me. Among the Volsces there is an old friend and host of mine, an honest wealthy man, and now a prisoner, who living before in great wealth in his own country, liveth now a poor prisoner in the hands of his enemies: and yet notwithstanding all this his misery and misfortune, it would do me great pleasure if I could save him from this one danger: to keep him from being sold as a slave.' The soldiers hearing Martius' words, made a marvellous great shout among them: and they were more that wondered at his great contentation and abstinence, when they saw so little covetousness in him, than they were that highly praised and extolled his valiantness. For even they themselves, that did somewhat malice and envy his glory, to see him thus honoured, and passingly praised, did think him so much the more worthy of an honourable recompense for his valiant service, as the more carelessly he refused the great offer made him for his profit: and they esteemed more the virtue that was in him, that made him refuse such rewards, than that which made them to be offered him, as unto a worthy person. For it is far more commendable to use riches well, than to be valiant: and yet it is better not to desire them, than to use them well.

11 After this shout and noise of the assembly was somewhat appeased, the consul Cominius began to speak in this sort: 'We cannot compel Martius to take these gifts we offer him, if he will not receive them: but we will give him such a reward for the noble service he hath done, as he cannot refuse. Therefore we do order and decree, that henceforth he be called Coriolanus, unless his valiant acts have won him that name before our nomination.' And so ever since, he still bore the third name of Coriolanus. And thereby it appeareth, that the first name the Romans have, as Caius, was our Christian name now. The second, as Martius, was the name of the house and family they came of. The third was some addition given, either for some act or notable service, or for some mark on their face, or of some shape of their body, or else for some special virtue they had. Even so did the Grecians in old time give additions to princes, by reason of some notable act worthy memory. As when they have called some, Soter, and Callinicos: as much to say: Saviour, and Conqueror. Or else for some notable apparent mark on one's face, or on his body, they have called him Phiscon, and Grypos: as ye would say, Gorebelly, and Hook-nosed: or else for some virtue, as Euergetes, and Phyladelphos: to wit, a Benefactor, and Lover of his Brethren. Or otherwise for one's great felicity, as Eudaemon: as much to say, as Fortunate. For so was the second of the Battes surnamed. And some kings have had surnames of jest and mockery. As one of the Antigones that was called Doson, to say, the Giver: who was ever promising, and never giving. And one of the Ptolomees was called Lamyros: to say, Conceitive. The Romans use more than any other nation, to give names of mockery in this sort. As there was one Metellus surnamed Diadematus, the Banded, because he carried a band about his head of long time, by reason of a sore he had in his forehead. One other of his own family was called Celer, the Quick Fly, because a few days after the death of his father, he showed the people the cruel fight of fencers at unrebated swords, which they found wonderful for the shortness of time. Other had their sur-names derived of some accident of their birth. As to this day they call him Proculeius that is born, his father being in some far voyage: and him Posthumius, that is born after the death of his father. And when of two brethren twins, the one doth die, and the other surviveth, they call the survivor, Vopiscus. Sometimes also

they give surnames derived of some mark or misfortune of the body. As Sylla, to say, crooked-nosed: Niger, black: Rufus, red: Caecus, blind: Claudus, lame. They did wisely in this thing to accustom men to think, that neither the loss of their sight, nor other such misfortunes as may chance to men, are any shame or disgrace unto them, but the manner was to answer boldly to such names, as if they were called by their proper names. Howbeit these matters would be better amplified in other stories than this.

12   Now when this war was ended, the flatterers of the people began to stir up sedition again, without any new occasion, or just matter offered of complaint. For they did ground this second insurrection against the nobility and patricians upon the people's misery and misfortune, that could not but fall out, by reason of the former discord and sedition between them and the nobility. Because the most part of the arable land within the territory of Rome was become heathy and barren for lack of ploughing, for that they had no time nor mean to cause corn to be brought them out of other countries to sow, by reason of their wars which made the extreme dearth they had among them. Now those busy prattlers that sought the people's goodwill, by such flattering words, perceiving great scarcity of corn to be within the city, and though there had been plenty enough, yet the common people had no money to buy it, they spread abroad false tales and rumours against the nobility, that they in revenge of the people, had practised and procured the extreme dearth among them. Furthermore, in the midst of this stir, there came ambassadors to Rome from the city of Velitres, that offered up their city to the Romans, and prayed them they would send new inhabitants to replenish the same, because the plague had been so extreme among them, and had killed such a number of them, as there was not left alive the tenth person of the people that had been there before. So the wise men of Rome began to think, that the necessity of the Velitrians fell out in a most happy hour, and how by this occasion it was very meet in so great a scarcity of victuals, to disburden Rome of a great number of citizens: and by this means as well to take away this new sedition, and utterly to rid it out of the city, as also to clear the same of many mutinous and seditious persons, being the superfluous ill humours that grievously fed this disease. Hereupon the consuls pricked out

all those by a bill, whom they intended to send to Velitres, to go dwell there as in form of a colony: and they levied out of all the rest that remained in the city of Rome, a great number to go against the Volsces, hoping by the means of foreign war, to pacify their sedition at home. Moreover they imagined, when the poor with the rich, and the mean sort with the nobility, should by this devise be abroad in the wars, and in one camp, and in one service, and in one like danger, that then they would be more quiet and loving together.

13    But Sicinius and Brutus, two seditious tribunes, spoke against either of these devises, and cried out upon the noblemen, that under the gentle name of a colony, they would cloak and colour the most cruel and unnatural fact as might be: because they sent their poor citizens into a sore infected city and pestilent air, full of dead bodies unburied, and there also to dwell under the tuition of a strange god, that had so cruelly persecuted his people. 'This were,' said they, 'even as much, as if the senate should headlong cast down the people into a most bottomless pit. And are not yet contented to have famished some of the poor citizens heretofore to death, and to put others of them even to the mercy of the plague: but afresh, they have procured a voluntary war, to the end they would leave behind no kind of misery and ill, wherewith the poor silly people should not be plagued, and only because they are weary to serve the rich.' The common people being set on a broil and bravery with these words, would not appear when the consuls called their names by a bill, to prest them for the wars, neither would they be sent out to this new colony: in so much as the senate knew not well what to say or do in the matter. Martius then, who was now grown to great credit, and a stout man besides, and of great reputation with the noblest men of Rome, rose up, and openly spoke against these flattering tribunes. And for the replenishing of the city of Velitres he did compel those that were chosen to go thither, and to depart the city, upon great penalties to him that should disobey: but to the wars, the people by no means would be brought or constrained. So Martius taking his friends and followers with him, and such as he could by fair words entreat to go with him, did run certain forays into the dominion of the Antiates, where he met with great plenty of corn, and had a

marvellous great spoil, as well of cattle as of men he had taken prisoners, whom he brought away with him, and reserved nothing for himself. Afterwards having brought back again all his men that went out with him safe and sound to Rome, and every man rich and laden with spoil, then the hometarriers and housedoves that kept Rome still, began to repent them that it was not their hap to go with him, and so envied both them that had sped so well in this journey, and also of malice to Martius, they spited to see his credit and estimation increase still more and more, because they accounted him to be a great hinderer of the people.

14    Shortly after this, Martius stood for the consulship: and the common people favoured his suit, thinking it would be a shame to them to deny and refuse the chiefest nobleman of blood, and most worthy person of Rome, and specially him that had done so great service and good to the commonwealth. For the custom of Rome was at that time, that such as did sue for any office, should for certain days before be in the market place, only with a poor gown on their backs, and without any coat underneath, to pray the citizens to remember them at the day of election: which was thus devised, either to move the people the more, by requesting them in such mean apparel, or else because they might show them their wounds they had got in the wars in the service of the commonwealth, as manifest marks and testimony of their valiantness. Now it is not to be thought that the suitors went thus loose in a simple gown in the market place, without any coat under it, for fear and suspicion of the common people: for offices of dignity in the city were not then given by favour or corruption. It was but of late time, and long after this, that buying and selling fell out in election of officers, and that the voices of the electors were bought for money. But after corruption had once gotten way into the election of offices, it hath run from man to man, even to the very sentence of judges, and also among captains in the wars: so as in the end, that only turned commonwealths into kingdoms, by making arms subject to money. Therefore methinks he had reason that said: 'He that first made banquets, and gave money to the common people, was, the first that took away authority, and destroyed commonwealth.' But this pestilence crept in by little and little, and did secretly win ground still, continuing a long time in Rome, before it

was openly known and discovered. For no man can tell who was the first man that bought the people's voices for money, nor that corrupted the sentence of the judges. Howbeit at Athens some hold opinion that Anytus, the son of Anthemion, was the first man that fed the judges with money, about the end of the wars of Peloponnesus, being accused of treason for yielding up the fort of Pyle, at that time when the golden and unfoiled age remained yet whole in judgment at Rome.

15   Now Martius following this custom, showed many wounds and cuts upon his body, which he had received in seventeen years' service at the wars, and in many sundry battles, being ever the foremost man that did set out feet to fight. So that there was not a man among the people, but was ashamed of himself, to refuse so valiant a man: and one of them said to another, 'We must needs choose him consul, there is no remedy.' But when the day of election was come, and that Martius came to the market place with great pomp, accompanied with all the senate, and the whole nobility of the city about him, who sought to make him consul, with the greatest instance and entreaty they could, or ever attempted for any man or matter, then the love and goodwill of the common people turned straight to an hate and envy toward him, fearing to put this office of sovereign authority into his hands, being a man somewhat partial toward the nobility, and of great credit and authority amongst the patricians, and as one they might doubt would take away altogether the liberty from the people. Whereupon for these considerations, they refused Martius in the end, and made two other that were suitors, consuls. The senate being marvellously offended with the people, did account the shame of this refusal rather to redound to themselves, than to Martius: but Martius took it in far worse part than the senate, and was out of all patience. For he was a man too full of passion and choler, and too much given to over self-will and opinion, as one of a high mind and great courage, that lacked the gravity and affability that is got with judgment of learning and reason, which only is to be looked for in a governor of state: and that remembered not how wilfulness is the thing of the world, which a governor of a commonwealth for pleasing should shun, being that which Plato called solitariness. As in the end, all men that are wilfully given to

a self opinion and obstinate mind, and who will never yield to others' reason, but to their own, remain without company, and forsaken of all men. For a man that will live in the world, must needs have patience, which lusty bloods make but a mock at. So Martius being a stout man of nature, that never yielded in any respect, as one thinking that to overcome always, and to have the upper hand in all matters, was a token of magnanimity, and of no base and faint courage, which spits out anger from the most weak and passioned part of the heart, much like the matter of an impostume, went home to his house, full freighted with spite and malice against the people, being accompanied with all the lustiest young gentlemen, whose minds were nobly bent, as those that came of noble race, and commonly used for to follow and honour him. But then specially they flocked about him, and kept him company, to his much harm: for they did but kindle and inflame his choler more and more, being sorry with him for the injury the people offered him, because he was their captain and leader to the wars, that taught them all martial discipline, and stirred up in them a noble emulation of honour and valiantness, and yet without envy, praising them that deserved best.

16    In the mean season, there came great plenty of corn to Rome, that had been bought, part in Italy, and part was sent out of Sicily, as given by Gelon the tyrant of Syracusa: so that many stood in great hope, that the dearth of victuals being holpen, the civil dissension would also cease. The senate sat in council upon it immediately, the common people stood also about the palace where the council was kept, gaping what resolution would fall out: persuading themselves, that the corn they had bought should be sold good cheap, and that which was given, should be divided by the poll, without paying any penny: and the rather, because certain of the senators amongst them did so wish and persuade the same. But Martius standing up on his feet, did somewhat sharply take up those, who went about to gratify the people therein: and called them people-pleasers, and traitors to the nobility. Moreover he said they nourished against themselves the naughty seed and cockle of insolence and sedition, which had been sowed and scattered abroad amongst the people, whom they should have cut off, if they had been wise, and have prevented their greatness: and

not to their own destruction to have suffered the people to establish a magistrate for themselves of so great power and authority, as that man had, to whom they had granted it. Who was also to be feared, because he obtained what he would, and did nothing but what he listed, neither passed for any obedience to the consuls, but lived in all liberty, acknowledging no superior to command him, saving the only heads and authors of their faction, whom he called his magistrates. 'Therefore,' said he, 'they that gave counsel, and persuaded that the corn should be given out to the common people *gratis*, as they used to do in cities of Greece, where the people had more absolute power, did but only nourish their disobedience, which would break out in the end, to the utter ruin and overthrow of the whole state. For they will not think it is done in recompense of their service past, since they know well enough they have so oft refused to go to the wars, when they were commanded: neither for their mutinies when they went with us, whereby they have rebelled and forsaken their country: neither for their accusations which their flatterers have preferred unto them, and they have received, and made good against the senate: but they will rather judge we give and grant them this, as abasing ourselves, and standing in fear of them, and glad to flatter them every way. By this means, their disobedience will still grow worse and worse: and they will never leave to practise new sedition, and uproars. Therefore it were a great folly for us, methinks, to do it: yea, shall I say more? We should if we were wise, take from them their tribuneship, which most manifestly is the imbasing of the consulship, and the cause of the division of the city. The state whereof as it stands, is not now as it was wont to be, but becomes dismembered in two factions, which maintains always civil dissension and discord between us, and will never suffer us again to be united into one body.'

17 Martius dilating the matter with many suchlike reasons, won all the young men, and almost all the rich men to his opinion: in so much they rang it out, that he was the only man, and alone in the city, who stood out against the people, and never flattered them. There were only a few old men that spoke against him, fearing lest some mischief might fall out upon it, as indeed there followed no great good afterward. For the tribunes of the people, being present

at this consultation of the senate, when they saw that the opinion of Martius was confirmed with the more voices, they left the senate, and went down to the people, crying out for help, and that they would assemble to save their tribunes. Hereupon the people ran on head in tumult together, before whom the words that Martius spoke in the senate were openly reported: which the people so stomached, that even in that fury they were ready to fly upon the whole senate. But the tribunes laid all the fault and burden wholly upon Martius, and sent their sergeants forthwith to arrest him, presently to appear in person before the people, to answer the words he had spoken in the senate. Martius stoutly withstood these officers that came to arrest him. Then the tribunes in their own persons, accompanied with the aediles, went to fetch him by force, and so laid violent hands upon him. Howbeit the noble patricians gathering together about him, made the tribunes give back, and laid it sore upon the aediles: so for that time, the night parted them, and the tumult appeased. The next morning betimes, the consuls seeing the people in an uproar, running to the market place out of all parts of the city, they were afraid lest all the city would together by the ears: wherefore assembling the senate in all haste, they declared how it stood them upon, to appease the fury of the people with some gentle words, or grateful decrees in their favour: and moreover, like wise men they should consider, it was now no time to stand at defence and in contention, nor yet to fight for honour against the commonalty, they being fallen to so great an extremity, and offering such imminent danger. Wherefore they were to consider temperately of things, and to deliver some present and gentle pacification. The most part of the senators that were present at this council, thought this opinion best, and gave their consents unto it. Whereupon the consuls rising out of council, went to speak unto the people as gently as they could, and they did pacify their fury and anger, purging the senate of all the unjust accusations laid upon them, and used great modesty in persuading them, and also in reproving the faults they had committed. And as for the rest, that touched the sale of corn, they promised there should be no disliking offered them in the price.

18 So the most part of the people being pacified, and appearing so plainly by the great silence and still that was among them, as yielding to the consuls, and liking well of their words: the tribunes then of the people rose out of their seats, and said: forasmuch as the senate yielded unto reason, the people also for their part, as became them, did likewise give place unto them: but notwithstanding they would that Martius should come in person to answer to the articles they had devised. First, whether he had not solicited and procured the senate to change the present state of the common weal, and to take the sovereign authority out of the people's hands. Next, when he was sent for by authority of their officers, why he did contempt-uously resist and disobey. Lastly, seeing he had driven and beaten the aediles into the market place before all the world, if in doing this, he had not done as much as in him lay, to raise civil wars, and to set one citizen against another. All this was spoken to one of these two ends, either that Martius against his nature should be constrained to humble himself, and to abase his haughty and fierce mind: or else if he continued still in his stoutness, he should incur the people's displeasure and ill will so far, that he should never possibly win them again. Which they hoped would rather fall out so, than otherwise: as indeed they guessed unhappily, considering Martius' nature and disposition. So Martius came, and presented himself, to answer their accusations against him, and the people held their peace, and gave attentive ear, to hear what he would say. But where they thought to have heard very humble and lowly words come from him, he began not only to use his wonted boldness of speaking (which of itself was very rough and unpleasant, and did more aggravate his accusation than purge his innocence) but also gave himself in his words to thunder, and look therewithal so grimly, as though he made no reckoning of the matter. This stirred coals among the people, who were in wonder-ful fury at it, and their hate and malice grew so toward him, that they could hold no longer, bear, nor endure his bravery and careless boldness. Whereupon Sicinius, the cruellest and stoutest of the tribunes, after he had whispered a little with his companions, did openly pronounce in the face of all the people, Martius as condemned by the tribunes to die. Then presently he commanded the aediles to apprehend him, and carry him straight to the rock Tarpeian, and to cast him headlong down the same. When the

aediles came to lay hands upon Martius to do that they were commanded, divers of the people themselves thought it too cruel and violent a deed. The noblemen also being much troubled to see such force and rigour used, began to cry aloud, 'Help Martius': so those that laid hands of him being repulsed, they compassed him in round among themselves, and some of them holding up their hands to the people, besought them not to handle him thus cruelly. But neither their words, nor crying out could aught prevail, the tumult and hurly burly was so great, until such time as the tribunes' own friends and kinsmen weighing with themselves the impossibleness to convey Martius to execution, without great slaughter and murder of the nobility, did persuade and advise not to proceed in so violent and extraordinary a sort, as to put such a man to death, without lawful process in law, but that they should refer the sentence of his death to the free voice of the people. Then Sicinius bethinking himself a little, did ask the patricians, for what cause they took Martius out of the officers' hands that went to do execution. The patricians asked him again, why they would of themselves so cruelly and wickedly put to death so noble and valiant a Roman, as Martius was, and that without law or justice. 'Well,' then said Sicinius, 'if that be the matter, let there be no more quarrel or dissension against the people: for they do grant your demand, that his cause shall be heard according to the law.' Therefore said he to Martius, 'We do will and charge you to appear before the people, the third day of our next sitting and assembly here, to make your purgation for such articles as shall be objected against you, that by free voice the people may give sentence upon you as shall please them.'

19   The noblemen were glad then of the adjournment, and were much pleased they had got Martius out of this danger. In the mean space, before the third day of their next session came about, the same being kept every ninth day continually at Rome, whereupon they call it now in Latin, *nundinae*, there fell out war against the Antiates, which gave some hope to the nobility, that this adjournment would come to little effect, thinking that this war would hold them so long, as that the fury of the people against him would be well suaged or utterly forgotten, by reason of the trouble of the wars. But contrary to expectation, the peace was concluded pre-

sently with the Antiates, and the people returned again to Rome. Then the patricians assembled oftentimes together, to consult how they might stand to Martius, and keep the tribunes from occasion to cause the people to mutiny again, and rise against the nobility. And there Appius Clodius (one that was taken ever as an heavy enemy to the people) did avow and protest, that they would utterly abase the authority of the senate, and destroy the common weal, if they would suffer the common people to have authority by voices to give judgment against the nobility. On the other side again, the most ancient senators, and such as were given to favour the common people, said that when the people should see they had authority of life and death in their hands, they would not be so cruel and fierce, but gentle and civil. More also, that it was not for contempt of nobility or the senate, that they sought to have the authority of justice in their hands, as a pre-eminence and prerogative of honour: but because they feared that themselves should be condemned and hated of the nobility. So as they were persuaded, that so soon as they gave them authority to judge by voices, so soon would they leave all envy and malice to condemn any.

20 Martius seeing the senate in great doubt how to resolve, partly for the love and goodwill the nobility did bear him, and partly for the fear they stood in of the people. asked aloud of the tribunes, what matter they would burden him with. The tribunes answered him, that they would show how he did aspire to be king, and would prove that all his actions tended to usurp tyrannical power over Rome. Martius with that, rising up on his feet, said that thereupon he did willingly offer himself to the people, to be tried upon that accusation. And that if it were proved by him, he had so much as once thought of any such matter, that he would then refuse no kind of punishment they would offer him: 'conditionally,' quoth he, 'that you charge me with nothing else besides, and that ye do not also abuse the senate.' They promised they would not. Under these conditions the judgment was agreed upon, and the people assembled. And first of all the tribunes would in any case (whatsoever became of it) that the people would proceed to give their voices by tribes, and not by hundreds: for by this means the multitude of the poor needy people (and all such rabble as had nothing to lose, and had less regard of honesty before their eyes)

came to be of greater force (because their voices were numbered by the poll) than the noble honest citizens, whose persons and purse did dutifully serve the commonwealth in their wars. And then when the tribunes saw they could not prove he went about to make himself king, they began to broach afresh the former words that Martius had spoken in the senate, in hindering the distribution of the corn at mean price unto the common people, and persuading also to take the office of tribuneship from them. And for the third, they charged him anew, that he had not made the common distribution of the spoil he had got in the invading the territories of the Antiates: but had of his own authority divided it among them, who were with him in that journey. But this matter was most strange of all to Martius, looking least to have been burdened with that, as with any matter of offence. Whereupon being burdened on the sudden, and having no ready excuse to make even at that instant, he began to fall a-praising of the soldiers that had served with him in that journey. But those that were not with him, being the greater number, cried out so loud, and made such a noise, that he could not be heard. To conclude, when they came to tell the voices of the tribes, there were three voices odd, which condemned him to be banished for life. After declaration of the sentence, the people made such joy, as they never rejoiced more for any battle they had won upon their enemies, they were so brave and lively, and went home so jocundly from the assembly, for triumph of this sentence. The senate again in contrary manner were as sad and heavy, repenting themselves beyond measure, that they had not rather determined to have done and suffered anything whatsoever, before the common people should so arrogantly and outrageously have abused their authority. There needed no difference of garments, I warrant you, nor outward shows to know a plebeian from a patrician, for they were easily discerned by their looks. For he that was on the people's side, looked cheerily on the matter: but he that was sad, and hung down his head, he was sure of the noblemen's side.

21   Saving Martius alone, who neither in his countenance, nor in his gait, did ever show himself abashed, or once let fall his great courage: but he only of all other gentlemen that were angry at his fortune, did outwardly show no manner of passion, nor care at all

of himself. Not that he did patiently bear and temper his good hap, in respect of any reason he had, or by his quiet condition: but because he was so carried away with the vehemence of anger, and desire of revenge, that he had no sense nor feeling of the hard state he was in, which the common people judge not to be sorrow, although indeed it be the very same. For when sorrow (as you would say) is set afire, then it is converted into spite and malice, and driveth away for that time all faintness of heart and natural fear. And this is the cause why the choleric man is so altered, and mad in his actions, as a man set afire with a burning ague: for when a man's heart is troubled within, his pulse will beat marvellous strongly. Now that Martius was even in that taking, it appeared true soon after by his doings. For when he was come home to his house again, and had taken his leave of his mother and wife, finding them weeping, and shrieking out for sorrow, and had also comforted and persuaded them to be content with his chance, he went immediately to the gate of the city, accompanied with a great number of patricians that brought him thither, from whence he went on his way with three or four of his friends only, taking nothing with him, nor requesting anything of any man. So he remained a few days in the country at his houses, turmoiled with sundry sorts and kind of thoughts, such as the fire of his choler did stir up. In the end, seeing he could resolve no way to take a profitable or honourable course, but only was pricked forward still to be revenged of the Romans, he thought to raise up some great wars against them, by their nearest neighbours. Whereupon, he thought it his best way, first to stir up the Volsces against them, knowing they were yet able enough in strength and riches to encounter them, notwithstanding their former losses they had received not long before, and that their power was not so much impaired, as their malice and desire was increased, to be revenged of the Romans.

22 Now in the city of Antium, there was one called Tullus Aufidius, who for his riches, as also for his nobility and valiantness, was honoured among the Volsces as a king. Martius knew very well that Tullus did more malice and envy him, than he did all the Romans besides: because that many times in battles where they met, they were ever at the encounter one against another, like lusty

courageous youths, striving in all emulation of honour, and had encountered many times together. In so much as, besides the common quarrel between them, there was bred a marvellous private hate one against another. Yet notwithstanding, considering that Tullus Aufidius was a man of a great mind, and that he above all other of the Volsces most desired revenge of the Romans, for the injuries they had done unto them, he did an act that confirmed the true words of an ancient poet, who said:

> It is a thing full hard, man's anger to withstand,
>   If it be stiffly bent to take an enterprise in hand.
> For then most men will have the thing that they desire,
>   Although it cost their lives therefore, such force hath
>                                                     wicked ire.

And so did he. For he disguised himself in such array and attire, as he thought no man could ever have known him for the person he was, seeing him in that apparel he had upon his back: and as Homer said of Ulysses,

> So did he enter into the enemy's town.

23   It was even twilight when he entered the city of Antium, and many people met him in the streets, but no man knew him. So he went directly to Tullus Aufidius' house, and when he came thither, he got him up straight to the chimney hearth, and sat him down, and spoke not a word to any man, his face all muffled over. They of the house spying him, wondered what he should be, and yet they durst not bid him rise. For ill-favouredly muffled and disguised as he was, yet there appeared a certain majesty in his countenance, and in his silence: whereupon they went to Tullus who was at supper, to tell him of the strange disguising of this man. Tullus rose presently from the board, and coming towards him, asked him what he was, and wherefore he came. Then Martius unmuffled himself, and after he had paused awhile, making no answer, he said unto him: 'If thou knowest me not yet, Tullus, and seeing me, dost not perhaps believe me to be the man I am indeed, I must of necessity bewray myself to be that I am. I am Caius Martius, who hath done to thyself particularly, and to all the Volsces generally, great hurt and mischief, which I cannot deny for my surname of Coriolanus that I bear. For I never had other benefit nor recompense, of all the

true and painful service I have done, and the extreme dangers I have been in, but this only surname: a good memory and witness of the malice and displeasure thou shouldest bear me. Indeed the name only remaineth with me: for the rest, the envy and cruelty of the people of Rome have taken from me, by the sufferance of the dastardly nobility and magistrates, who have forsaken me, and let me be banished by the people. This extremity hath now driven me to come as a poor suitor, to take thy chimney hearth, not of any hope I have to save my life thereby. For if I had feared death, I would not have come hither to have put my life in hazard: but pricked forward with spite and desire I have to be revenged of them that thus have banished me, whom now I begin to be avenged on, putting my person between thy enemies. Wherefore, if thou hast any heart to be recked of the injuries thy enemies have done thee, speed thee now, and let my misery serve thy turn, and so use it, as my service may be a benefit to the Volsces: promising thee, that I will fight with better goodwill for all you, than ever I did when I was against you, knowing that they fight more valiantly who know the force of their enemy, than such as have never proved it. And if it be so that thou dare not, and that thou art weary to prove fortune any more, then am I also weary to live any longer. And it were no wisdom in thee, to save the life of him, who has been heretofore thy mortal enemy, and whose service now can nothing help nor pleasure thee.' Tullus hearing what he said, was a marvellous glad man, and taking him by the hand, he said unto him: 'Stand up, O Martius, and be of good cheer, for in proffering thyself unto us, thou dost us great honour: and by this means thou mayest hope also of greater things, at all the Volsces' hands.' So he feasted him for that time, and entertained him in the honourablest manner he could, talking with him in no other matters at that present: but within few days after, they fell to consultation together, in what sort they should begin their wars.

24 Now on the other side, the city of Rome was in marvellous uproar and discord, the nobility against the commonalty, and chiefly for Martius' condemnation and banishment. Moreover the priests, the soothsayers, and private men also, came and declared to the senate certain sights and wonders in the air, which they had seen, and were to be considered of: amongst the which, such a

vision happened. There was a citizen of Rome called Titus Latinus, a man of mean quality and condition, but otherwise an honest sober man, given to a quiet life, without superstition, and much less to vanity or lying. This man had a vision in his dream, in the which he thought that Jupiter appeared unto him, and commanded him to signify to the senate, that they had caused a very vile lewd dancer to go before the procession: and said, the first time this vision had appeared unto him, he made no reckoning of it: and coming again another time into his mind, he made not much more account of the matter than before. In the end, he saw one of his sons die, who had the best nature and condition of all his brethren: and suddenly he himself was so taken in all his limbs, that he became lame and impotent. Hereupon he told the whole circumstance of this vision before the senate, sitting upon his little couch or bed, whereon he was carried on men's arms: and he had no sooner reported this vision to the senate, but he presently felt his body and limbs restored again to their former strength and use. So raising up himself upon his couch, he got up on his feet at that instant, and walked home to his house, without help of any man. The senate being amazed at this matter, made diligent enquiry to understand the truth: and in the end they found there was such a thing. There was one that had delivered a bondman of his that had offended him, into the hands of other slaves and bondmen, and had commanded them to whip him up and down the market place, and afterwards to kill him: and as they had him in execution, whipping him cruelly, they did so martyr the poor wretch, that for the cruel smart and pain he felt, he turned and writhed his body, in strange and pitiful sort. The procession by chance came by even at the same time, and many that followed it, were heartily moved and offended with the sight, saying that this was no good sight to behold, nor meet to be met in procession time. But for all this, there was nothing done: saving they blamed and rebuked him, that punished his slave so cruelly. For the Romans at that time did use their bondmen very gently, because they themselves did labour with their own hands, and lived with them and among them: and therefore they did use them the more gently and familiarly. For the greatest punishment they gave a slave that had offended, was this. They made him carry a limmer on his shoulders that is fastened to the axletree of a coach, and compelled him to go up and down in that sort amongst all their neighbours. He that had once abidden this punishment, and was seen in that manner, was proclaimed and cried in every market town: so that no man would ever trust him after, and they called him Furcifer, because the Latins call the wood that runs into the axletree of the coach, *furca*, as much to say, as a fork.

25 Now when Latinus had made report to the senate of the vision that had happened to him, they were devising whom this unpleasant dancer should be, that went before the procession. Thereupon certain that stood by remembered the poor slave that was so cruelly whipped through the market place, whom they afterwards put to death: and the thing that made them remember it, was the strange and rare manner of his punishment. The priests hereupon were repaired unto for advice: they were wholly of opinion, that it was the whipping of the slave. So they caused the slaves' master to be punished, and began again a new procession, and all other shows and sights in honour of Jupiter. But hereby appeareth plainly, how King Numa did wisely ordain all other ceremonies concerning devotion to the gods, and specially this custom which he established, to bring the people to religion. For when the magistrates, bishops, priests, or other religious ministers go about any divine service, or matter of religion, an herald ever goeth before them, crying out aloud, '*Hoc age*': as to say, do this, or mind this. Hereby they are specially commanded, wholly to dispose themselves to serve God, leaving all other business and matters aside: knowing well enough, that whatsoever most men do, they do it as in a manner constrained unto it. But the Romans did ever use to begin again their sacrifices, processions, plays, and suchlike shows done in honour of the gods, not only upon such an occasion, but upon lighter causes than that. As when they went a procession through the city, and did carry the images of their gods, and such other like holy relics upon open hallowed coaches or chariots, called in Latin *thensae*: one of the coach horses that drew them stood still, and would draw no more, and because also the coachman took the reins of the bridle with the left hand, they ordained that the procession should be begun again anew. Of later time also, they did renew and begin a sacrifice thirty times one after another, because they thought still there fell out one fault or other in the same, so holy and devout were they to the gods.

26    Now Tullus and Martius had secret conference with the greatest personages of the city of Antium, declaring unto them, that now they had good time offered them to make war with the Romans, while they were in dissension one with another. They answered them, they were ashamed to break the league, considering that they were sworn to keep peace for two years. Howbeit shortly after, the Romans gave them great occasion to make war with them. For on a holy day, common plays being kept in Rome, upon some suspicion or false report, they made proclamation by sound of trumpet, that all the Volsces should avoid out of Rome before sunset. Some think this was a craft and deceit of Martius, who sent one to Rome to the consuls, to accuse the Volsces falsely, advertising them how they had made a conspiracy to set upon them, whilst they were busy in seeing these games, and also to set their city afire. This open proclamation made all the Volsces more offended with the Romans, than ever they were before: and Tullus aggravating the matter, did so inflame the Volsces against them, that in the end they sent their ambassadors to Rome, to summon them to deliver their lands and towns again, which they had taken from them in times past, or to look for present wars. The Romans hearing this, were marvellously nettled: and made no other answer but thus: 'If the Volsces be the first that begin war, the Romans will be the last that will end it.' Incontinently upon return of the Volsces' ambassadors, and delivery of the Romans' answer, Tullus caused an assembly general to be made of the Volsces, and concluded to make war upon the Romans. This done, Tullus did counsel them to take Martius into their service, and not to mistrust him for the remembrance of anything past, but boldly to trust him in any matter to come: for he would do them more service in fighting for them, than ever he did them displeasure in fighting against them.

27    So Martius was called forth, who spoke so excellently in the presence of them all, that he was thought no less eloquent in tongue, than warlike in show: and declared himself both expert in wars, and wise with valiantness. Thus he was joined in commission with Tullus as general of the Volsces, having absolute authority between them to follow and pursue the wars. But Martius fearing lest tract of time to bring this army together with all the munition

and furniture of the Volsces would rob him of the mean he had to execute his purpose and intent, left order with the rulers and chief of the city, to assemble the rest of their power and to prepare all necessary provision for the camp. Then he with the lightest soldiers he had, and that were willing to follow him, stole away upon the sudden, and marched with all speed, and entered the territories of Rome, before the Romans heard any news of his coming. In so much the Volsces found such spoil in the fields, as they had more than they could spend in their camp, and were weary to drive and carry away that they had. Howbeit the gain of the spoil and the hurt they did to the Romans in this invasion was the least part of his intent. For his chiefest purpose was, to increase still the malice and dissension between the nobility and the commonalty: and to draw that on, he was very careful to keep the noblemen's lands and goods safe from harm and burning, but spoiled all the whole country besides, and would suffer no man to take or hurt anything of the noblemen's. This made greater stir and broil between the nobility and people, than was before. For the noblemen fell out with the people, because they had so unjustly banished a man of so great valour and power. The people on the other side accused the nobility, how they had procured Martius to make these wars, to be revenged of them: because it pleased them to see their goods burnt and spoiled before their eyes, whilst themselves were well at ease, and did behold the people's losses and misfortunes, and knowing their own goods safe and out of danger: and how the war was not made against the noblemen, that had the enemy abroad to keep that they had in safety. Now Martius having done this first exploit (which made the Volsces bolder, and less fearful of the Romans) brought home all the army again, without loss of any man.

28 After their whole army (which was marvellous great, and very forward to service) was assembled in one camp, they agreed to leave part of it for garrison in the country about, and the other part should go on, and make the war upon the Romans. So Martius bade Tullus choose, and take which of the two charges he liked best. Tullus made him answer, he knew by experience that Martius was no less valiant than himself, and how he ever had better fortune and good hope in all battles, than himself had. Therefore he thought it best for him to have the leading of those that should make the wars

abroad: and himself would keep home, to provide for the safety of the cities and of his country, and to furnish the camp also of all necessary provision abroad. So Martius being stronger then before, went first of all unto the city of Circees, inhabited by the Romans, who willingly yielded themselves, and therefore had no hurt. From thence, he entered the country of the Latins, imagining the Romans would fight with him there to defend the Latins, who were their confederates, and had many times sent unto the Romans for their aid. But on the one side, the people of Rome were very ill willing to go, and on the other side, the consuls being upon their going out of their office, would not hazard themselves for so small a time: so that the ambassadors of the Latins returned home again, and did no good. Then Martius did besiege their cities, and having taken by force the towns of the Tolerinians, Vicanians, Pedanians, and the Bolanians, who made resistance, he sacked all their goods, and took them prisoners. Such as did yield themselves willingly unto him, he was as careful as possible might be to defend them from hurt: and because they should receive no damage by his will, he removed his camp as far from their confines as he could.

29    Afterwards, he took the city of Boles by assault, being about an hundred furlong from Rome, where he had a marvellous great spoil, and put every man to the sword that was able to carry weapon. The other Volsces that were appointed to remain in garrison for defence of their country, hearing this good news, would tarry no longer at home, but armed themselves, and ran to Martius' camp, saying they did acknowledge no other captain but him. Hereupon his fame ran through all Italy, and everyone praised him for a valiant captain, for that by change of one man for another, such and so strange events fell out in the state. In this while, all went still to wrack at Rome. For, to come into the field to fight with the enemy, they could not abide to hear of it, they were one so much against another, and full of seditious words, the nobility against the people and the people against the nobility. Until they had intelligence at the length that the enemies had laid siege to the city of Lavinium, in the which were all the temples and images of the gods their protectors, and from whence came first their ancient original, for that Aeneas at his first arrival into Italy did build that city. Then fell there out a marvellous sudden

change of mind among the people, and far more strange and contrary in the nobility. For the people thought good to repeal the condemnation and exile of Martius. The senate assembled upon it, would in no case yield to that. Who either did it of a self-will to be contrary to the people's desire: or because Martius should not return through the grace and favour of the people. Or else, because they were thoroughly angry and offended with him, that he would set upon the whole, being offended but by a few, and in his doings would show himself an open enemy besides unto his country: notwithstanding the most part of them took the wrong they had done him in marvellous ill part, and as if the injury had been done unto themselves. Report being made of the senate's resolution, the people found themselves in a strait: for they could authorise and confirm nothing by their voices, unless it had been first propounded and ordained by the senate.

30   But Martius hearing this stir about him, was in a greater rage with them than before: in so much as he raised his siege incontinently before the city of Lavinium, and going towards Rome, lodged his camp within forty furlong of the city, at the ditches called Cluiliae. His encamping so near Rome did put all the whole city in a wonderful fear: howbeit for the present time it appeased the sedition and dissension betwixt the nobility and the people. For there was no consul, senator, nor magistrate, that durst once contrary the opinion of the people, for the calling home again of Martius. When they saw the women in a marvellous fear, running up and down the city, the temples of the gods full of old people, weeping bitterly in their prayers to the gods, and finally, not a man either wise or hardy to provide for their safety: then they were all of opinion, that the people had reason to call home Martius again, to reconcile themselves to him, and that the senate on the contrary part, were in marvellous great fault to be angry and in choler with him, when it stood them upon rather to have gone out and entreated him. So they all agreed together to send ambassadors unto him, to let him understand how his countrymen did call him home again, and restored him to all his goods, and besought him to deliver them from this war. The ambassadors that were sent, were Martius' familiar friends and acquaintance, who looked at the least for a courteous welcome of him, as of their familiar friend and

kinsman. Howbeit they found nothing less. For at their coming, they were brought through the camp, to the place where he was set in his chair of state, with a marvellous and an unspeakable majesty, having the chiefest men of the Volsces about him: so he commanded them to declare openly the cause of their coming. Which they delivered in the most humble and lowly words they possibly could devise, and with all modest countenance and behaviour agreeable for the same. When they had done their message, for the injury they had done him, he answered them very hotly, and in great choler. But as general of the Volsces, he willed them to restore unto the Volsces, all their lands and cities they had taken from them in former wars: and moreover, that they should give them the like honour and freedom of Rome, as they had before given to the Latins. For otherwise they had no other mean to end this war, if they did not grant these honest and just conditions of peace. Thereupon he gave them thirty days' respite to make him answer. So the ambassadors returned straight to Rome, and Martius forthwith departed with his army out of the territories of the Romans.

31    This was, the first matter wherewith the Volsces (that most envied Martius' glory and authority) did charge Martius with. Among those, Tullus was chief: who though he had received no private injury or displeasure of Martius, yet the common fault and imperfection of man's nature wrought in him, and it grieved him to see his own reputation blemished, through Martius' great fame and honour, and so himself to be less esteemed of the Volsces, than he was before. This fell out the more, because every man honoured Martius, and thought he only could do all, and that all other governors and captains must be content with such credit and authority as he would please to countenance them with. From hence they derived all their first accusations and secret murmurings against Martius. For private captains conspiring against him, were very angry with him: and gave it out, that the removing of the camp was a manifest treason, not of the towns, nor forts, nor of arms, but of time and occasion, which was a loss of great importance, because it was that which in treason might both loose and bind all, and preserve the whole. Now Martius having given the Romans thirty days' respite for their answer, and specially because

the wars have not accustomed to make any great changes in less
space of time than that, he thought it good yet, not to lie asleep idle
all the while, but went and destroyed the lands of the enemy's
allies, and took seven cities of theirs well inhabited, and the
Romans durst not once put themselves into the field, to come to
their aid and help, they were so fainthearted, so mistrustful, and
loath besides to make wars. In so much as they properly resembled
the bodies paralytic, and loosed of their limbs and members: as
those which through the palsy have lost all their sense and feeling.
Wherefore, the time of peace expired, Martius being returned into
the dominions of the Romans again with all his army, they sent
another ambassador unto him, to pray peace, and the remove of
the Volsces out of their country: that afterwards they might with
better leisure fall to such agreements together, as should be thought
most meet and necessary. For the Romans were no men that would
ever yield for fear. But if he thought the Volsces had any ground to
demand reasonable articles and conditions, all that they would
reasonably ask should be granted unto by the Romans, who of
themselves would willingly yield to reason, conditionally, that they
did lay down arms. Martius to that answered: that as general of the
Volsces he would reply nothing unto it. But yet as a Roman
citizen, he would counsel them to let fall their pride, and to be
conformable to reason, if they were wise: and that they should
return again within three days, delivering up the articles agreed
upon, which he had first delivered them. Or otherwise, that he
would no more give them assurance or safe conduit to return again
into his camp, with such vain and frivolous messages.

32 When the ambassadors were returned to Rome, and had
reported Martius' answer to the senate, their city being in extreme
danger, and as it were in a terrible storm or tempest, they threw out
(as the common proverb says) their holy anchor. For then they
appointed all the bishops, priests, ministers of the gods, and keepers
of holy things, and all the augurs or soothsayers, which foreshow
things to come by observation of the flying of birds (which is an old
ancient kind of prophesying and divination amongst the Romans)
to go to Martius apparelled as when they do their sacrifices: and
first to entreat him to leave off war, and then that he would speak
to his countrymen, and conclude peace with the Volsces. Martius

suffered them to come into his camp, but yet he granted them
nothing the more, neither did he entertain them or speak more
courteously to them, than he did the first time that they came unto
him, saving only that he willed them to take the one of the two:
either to accept peace under the first conditions offered, or else to
receive war. When all this goodly rabble of superstition and priests
were returned, it was determined in council that none should go
out of the gates of the city, and that they should watch and ward
upon the walls, to repulse their enemies if they came to assault
them, referring themselves and all their hope to time, and fortune's
uncertain favour, not knowing otherwise how to remedy the
danger. Now all the city was full of tumult, fear, and marvellous
doubt what would happen: until at length there fell out such a like
matter, as Homer oftentimes said they would least have thought of.
For in great matters, that happen seldom, Homer sayeth, and crieth
out in this sort:

> The goddess Pallas she, with her fair glistering eyes,
>     Did put into his mind such thoughts, and made him so devise.

And in another place:

> But sure some god hath ta'en, out of the peoples' mind,
>     Both wit and understanding eke, and have therewith assigned
> Some other simple spirit, instead thereof to bide,
>     That so they might their doings all for lack of wit misguide.

And in another place:

> The people of themselves did either it consider,
>     Or else some god instructed them, and so they joined together.

Many reckon not of Homer, as referring matters unpossible, and
fables of no likelihood or truth, unto man's reason, free will, or
judgment: which indeed is not his meaning. But things true and
likely, he maketh to depend of our own free will and reason. For
he oft speaketh these words:

> I have thought it in my noble heart.

And in another place:

> Achilles angry was, and sorry for to hear
>     Him so to say, his heavy breast was fraught with pensive fear.

And again in another place:

> Bellerophon (she) could not move with her fair tongue,
>   So honest and so virtuous he was the rest among.

But in wondrous and extraordinary things, which are done by secret inspirations and motions, he doth not say that God taketh away from man his choice and freedom of will, but that he doth move it: neither that he doth work desire in us, but objecteth to our minds certain imaginations whereby we are led to desire, and thereby doth not make this our action forced, but openeth the way to our will, and addeth thereto courage, and hope of success. For, either we must say that the gods meddle not with the causes and beginnings of our actions: or else what other means have they to help and further men? It is apparent that they handle not our bodies, nor move not our feet and hands, when there is occasion to use them: but that part of our mind from which these motions proceed, is induced thereto, or carried away by such objects and reasons, as God offereth unto it.

33 Now the Roman ladies and gentlewomen did visit all the temples and gods of the same, to make their prayers unto them: but the greatest ladies (and more part of them) were continually about the altar of Jupiter Capitolin, among which troop by name, was Valeria, Publicola's own sister, the selfsame Publicola, who did such notable service to the Romans, both in peace and wars: and was dead also certain years before, as we have declared in his life. His sister Valeria was greatly honoured and reverenced among all the Romans: and did so modestly and wisely behave herself, that she did not shame nor dishonour the house she came of. So she suddenly fell into such a fancy, as we have rehearsed before, and had (by some god as I think) taken hold of a noble devise. Whereupon she rose, and the other ladies with her, and they all together went straight to the house of Volumnia, Martius' mother: and coming into her, found her and Martius' wife her daughter-in-law set together, and having her husband Martius' young children in her lap. Now all the train of these ladies sitting in a ring round about her, Valeria first began to speak in this sort unto her: 'We ladies are come to visit you ladies (my Lady Volumnia and Virgilia) by no direction from the senate, nor commandment of other magistrate: but through the inspiration (as I take it) of some god

above. Who having taken compassion and pity of our prayers, hath moved us to come unto you, to entreat you in a matter, as well beneficial for us, as also for the whole citizens in general: but to yourselves in especial (if it please you to credit me) and shall redound to our more fame and glory, than the daughters of the Sabynes obtained in former age, when they procured loving peace, instead of hateful war, between their fathers and their husbands. Come on good ladies, and let us go all together unto Martius, to entreat him to take pity upon us, and also to report the truth unto him, how much you are bound unto the citizens: who notwithstanding they have sustained great hurt and losses by him, yet they have not hitherto sought revenge upon your persons by any discourteous usage, neither ever conceived any such thought or intent against you, but do deliver ye safe into his hands, though thereby they look for no better grace or clemency from him.' When Valeria had spoken this unto them, all the other ladies together with one voice confirmed that she had said. Then Volumnia in this sort did answer her: 'My good ladies, we are partakers with you of the common misery and calamity of our country, and yet our grief exceedeth yours the more, by reason of our particular misfortune: to feel the loss of my son Martius' former valiancy and glory, and to see his person environed now with our enemies in arms, rather to see him forth coming and safe kept, than of any love to defend his person. But yet the greatest grief of our heaped mishaps is to see our poor country brought to such extremity, that all hope of the safety and preservation thereof, is now unfortunately cast upon us simple women: because we know not what account he will make of us, since he hath cast from him all care of his natural country and common weal, which heretofore he hath holden more dear and precious, than either his mother, wife, or children. Notwithstanding, if ye think we can do good, we will willingly do what you will have us: bring us to him I pray you. For if we cannot prevail, we may yet die at his feet, as humble suitors for the safety of our country.'

34    Her answer ended, she took her daughter-in-law, and Martius' children with her, and being accompanied with all the other Roman ladies, they went in troop together unto the Volsces' camp: whom when they saw, they of themselves did both pity and reverence her,

and there was not a man among them that once durst say a word
unto her. Now was Martius set then in his chair of state, with all the
honours of a general, and when he had spied the women coming
afar off, he marvelled what the matter meant: but afterwards knowing his wife which came foremost, he determined at the first to
persist in his obstinate and inflexible rancour. But overcome in the
end with natural affection, and being altogether altered to see them,
his heart would not serve him to tarry their coming to his chair, but
coming down in haste, he went to meet them, and first he kissed his
mother, and embraced her a pretty while, then his wife and little
children. And nature so wrought with him, that the tears fell from
his eyes, and he could not keep himself from making much of them,
but yielded to the affection of his blood, as if he had been violently
carried with the fury of a most swift running stream.

35 After he had thus lovingly received them, and perceiving that
his mother Volumnia would begin to speak to him, he called the
chiefest of the council of the Volsces to hear what she would say.
Then she spoke in this sort: 'If we held our peace, my son, and
determined not to speak, the state of our poor bodies, and present
sight of our raiment, would easily bewray to thee what life we have
led at home, since thy exile and abode abroad. But think now with
thyself, how much more unfortunately than all the women living
we are come hither, considering that the sight which should be
most pleasant to all other to behold, spiteful fortune hath made
most fearful to us: making myself to see my son, and my daughter
here her husband, besieging the walls of his native country. So as
that which is the only comfort to all other in their adversity and
misery, to pray unto the gods, and to call to them for aid, is the
only thing which plungeth us into most deep perplexity. For we
cannot (alas) together pray, both for victory for our country, and
for safety of thy life also: but a world of grievous curses, yea more
than any mortal enemy can heap upon us, are forcibly wrapped up
in our prayers. For the bitter sop of most hard choice is offered thy
wife and children, to forgo the one of the two: either to lose the
person of thyself, or the nurse of their native country. For myself,
my son, I am determined not to tarry, till fortune in my lifetime do
make an end of this war. For if I cannot persuade thee, rather to do
good unto both parties, than to overthrow and destroy the one,

preferring love and nature before the malice and calamity of wars, thou shalt see, my son, and trust unto it, thou shalt no sooner march forward to assault thy country, but thy foot shall tread upon thy mother's womb, that brought thee first into this world. And I may not defer to see the day, either that my son be led prisoner in triumph by his natural countrymen, or that he himself do triumph of them, and of his natural country. For if it were so, that my request tended to save thy country, in destroying the Volsces, I must confess, thou wouldst hardly and doubtfully resolve on that. For as to destroy thy natural country, it is altogether unmeet and unlawful: so were it not just, and less honourable, to betray those that put their trust in thee. But my only demand consisteth, to make equal delivery of all evils, which delivereth equal benefit and safety, both to the one and the other, but most honourable for the Volsces. For it shall appear, that having victory in their hands, they have of special favour granted us singular graces: peace and amity, albeit themselves have no less part of both, than we. Of which good, if so it came to pass, thyself is the only author, and so hast thou the only honour. But if it fail, and fall out contrary, thyself alone deservedly shall carry the shameful reproach and burden of either party. So, though the end of war be uncertain, yet this notwithstanding is most certain: that if it be thy chance to conquer, this benefit shalt thou reap of thy goodly conquest, to be chronicled the plague and destroyer of thy country. And if fortune also overthrow thee, then the world will say, that through desire to revenge thy private injuries, thou hast forever undone thy good friends, who did most lovingly and courteously receive thee.'

36  Martius gave good ear unto his mother's words, without interrupting her speech at all: and after she had said what she would, he held his peace a pretty while, and answered not a word. Hereupon she began again to speak unto him, and said: 'My son, why doest thou not answer me? Doest thou think it good altogether to give place unto thy choler and desire of revenge, and thinkest thou it not honesty for thee to grant thy mother's request, in so weighty a cause? Doest thou take it honourable for a nobleman to remember the wrongs and injuries done him: and doest not in like case think it an honest nobleman's part, to be thankful for the goodness that parents do show to their children, acknowledging the

duty and reverence they ought to bear unto them? No man living is more bound to show himself thankful in all parts and respects, than thyself, who so unnaturally showeth all ingratitude. Moreover, my son, thou hast sorely taken of thy country, exacting grievous payments upon them, in revenge of the injuries offered thee: besides, thou hast not hitherto showed thy poor mother any courtesy. And therefore, it is not only honest, but due unto me, that without compulsion I should obtain my so just and reasonable request of thee. But since by reason I cannot persuade thee to it, to what purpose do I defer my last hope?' And with these words, herself, his wife and children, fell down upon their knees before him. Martius seeing that, could refrain no longer, but went straight and lift her up, crying out: 'Oh mother, what have you done to me?' And holding her hard by the right hand, 'Oh mother,' said he, 'you have won a happy victory for your country, but mortal and unhappy for your son: for I see myself vanquished by you alone.' These words being spoken openly, he spoke a little apart with his mother and wife, and then let them return again to Rome, for so they did request him: and so remaining in camp that night, the next morning he dislodged, and marched homewards into the Volsces' country again, who were not all of one mind, nor all alike contented. For some misliked him, and that he had done. Other being well pleased that peace should be made, said that neither the one, nor the other, deserved blame nor reproach. Other, though they misliked that was done, did not think him an ill man for that he did, but said he was not to be blamed, though he yielded to such a forcible extremity. Howbeit no man contraried his departure, but all obeyed his commandment, more for respect of his worthiness and valiancy, than for fear of his authority.

37 Now the citizens of Rome plainly showed, in what fear and danger their city stood of this war, when they were delivered. For so soon as the watch upon the walls of the city perceived the Volsces' camp to remove, there was not a temple in the city but was presently set open, and full of men wearing garlands of flowers upon their heads, sacrificing to the gods, as they were wont to do upon the news of some great obtained victory. And this common joy was yet more manifestly showed, by the honourable courtesies the whole senate and people did bestow on their ladies. For they were all

thoroughly persuaded, and did certainly believe, that the ladies only were cause of the saving of the city, and delivering themselves from the instant danger of the war. Whereupon the senate ordained, that the magistrates to gratify and honour these ladies, should grant them all that they would require. And they only requested that they would build a temple of Fortune of the women, for the building whereof they offered themselves to defray the whole charge of the sacrifices, and other ceremonies belonging to the service of the gods. Nevertheless the senate, commending their goodwill and forwardness, ordained that the temple and image should be made at the common charge of the city. Notwithstanding that, the ladies gathered money among them, and made with the same a second image of Fortune, which the Romans say did speak as they offered her up in the temple, and did set her in her place: and they affirm, that she spoke these words: 'Ladies, ye have devoutly offered me up.'

38   Moreover, that she spoke that twice together, making us to believe things that never were, and are not to be credited. For to see images that seem to sweat or weep, or to put forth any humour red or bloody, it is not a thing unpossible. For wood and stone do commonly receive certain moisture, whereof is engendered an humour, which do yield of themselves, or do take of the air, many sorts and kinds of spots and colours: by which signs and tokens it is not amiss we think that the gods sometimes do warn men of things to come. And it is possible also, that these images and statues do sometimes put forth sounds, like unto sighs or mourning, when in the midst or bottom of the same, there is made some violent separation, or breaking asunder of things, blown or devised therein: but that a body which hath neither life nor soul should have any direct or exquisite word formed in it by express voice, that is altogether unpossible. For the soul nor god himself can distinctly speak without a body having necessary organs and instruments meet for the parts of the same, to form and utter distinct words. But where stories many times do force us to believe a thing reported to be true, by many grave testimonies, there we must say, that it is some passion contrary to our five natural senses, which being begotten in the imaginative part or understanding, draweth an opinion unto itself, even as we do in our sleeping. For many times we think we hear that we do not hear and we imagine we see

that we see not. Yet notwithstanding, such as are godly bent, and zealously given to think upon heavenly things, so as they can no way be drawn from believing that which is spoken of them, they have this reason to ground the foundation of their belief upon. That is, the omnipotence of god which is wonderful, and hath no manner of resemblance or likeliness of proportion unto ours, but is altogether contrary as touching our nature, our moving, our art, and our force: and therefore if he do anything unpossible to us, or do bring forth and devise things, without man's common reach and understanding, we must not therefore think it unpossible at all. For if in other things he is far contrary to us, much more in his works and secret operations, he far passeth all the rest: but the most part of god's doings, as Heraclitus sayeth, for lack of faith, are hidden and unknown unto us.

39  Now when Martius was returned again into the city of Antium from his voyage, Tullus, that hated and could no longer abide him for the fear he had of his authority, sought divers means to make him out of the way, thinking that if he let slip that present time, he should never recover the like and fit occasion again. Wherefore Tullus having procured many other of his confederacy, required Martius might be deposed from his estate, to render up account to the Volsces of his charge and government. Martius fearing to become a private man again under Tullus being general (whose authority was greater otherwise, than any other among all the Volsces) answered: he was willing to give up his charge, and would resign it into the hands of the lords of the Volsces, if they did all command him, as by all their commandment he received it. And moreover, that he would not refuse even at that present to give up an account unto the people, if they would tarry the hearing of it. The people hereupon called a common council, in which assembly there were certain orators appointed, that stirred up the common people against him: and when they had told their tales, Martius rose up to make them answer. Now, notwithstanding the mutinous people made a marvellous great noise, yet when they saw him, for the reverence they bore unto his valiantness, they quieted themselves, and gave still audience to allege with leisure what he could for his purgation. Moreover, the honestest men of the Antiates, and who most rejoiced in peace, showed by their countenance that they

would hear him willingly, and judge also according to their conscience. Whereupon Tullus, fearing that if he did let him speak, he would prove his innocence to the people, because amongst other things he had an eloquent tongue, besides that the first good service he had done to the people of the Volsces did win him more favour, than these last accusations could purchase him displeasure: and furthermore, the offence they laid to his charge was a testimony of the goodwill they owed him, for they would never have thought he had done them wrong for that they took not the city of Rome, if they had not been very near taking of it, by means of his approach and conduction. For these causes Tullus thought he might no longer delay his pretence and enterprise, neither to tarry for the mutinying and rising of the common people against him: wherefore, those that were of the conspiracy, began to cry out that he was not to be heard, nor that they would not suffer a traitor to usurp tyrannical power over the tribe of the Volsces, who would not yield up his estate and authority. And in saying these words, they all fell upon him, and killed him in the market place, none of the people once offering to rescue him. Howbeit it is a clear case, that this murder was not generally consented unto of the most part of the Volsces: for men came out of all parts to honour his body, and did honourably bury him, setting out his tomb with great store of armour and spoils, as the tomb of a worthy person and great captain. The Romans understanding of his death, showed no other honour or malice, saving that they granted the ladies the request they made: that they might mourn ten months for him, and that was the full time they used to wear blacks for the death of their fathers, brethren, or husbands, according to Numa Pompilius' order, who stablished the same, as we have enlarged more amply in the description of his life. Now Martius being dead, the whole state of the Volsces heartily wished him alive again. For first of all they fell out with the Aeques (who were their friends and confederates) touching pre-eminence and place: and this quarrel grew on so far between them, and frays and murders fell out upon it one with another. After that, the Romans overcame them in battle, in which Tullus was slain in the field, and the flower of all their force was put to the sword: so that they were compelled to accept most shameful conditions of peace, in yielding themselves subject unto the conquerors, and promising to be obedient at their commandment.

# Comparison of Alcibiades with Coriolanus

Now that we have written all the deeds of worthy memory, done by either of them both, we may presently discern that in matters of war, the one has not greatly exceeded the other. For both of them in their charge, were alike hardy and valiant for their persons, as also wise and politic in the wars: unless they will say, that Alcibiades was the better captain, as he that had fought more battles with his enemies, both by sea and land, than ever Coriolanus had done, and had always the victory of his enemies. For otherwise, in this they were much alike: that where they were both present, and had charge and power to command, all things prospered notably, and with good success on the part they were of: and also when they took the contrary side, they made the first have the worse every way. Now for matters of government, the noblemen and honest citizens did hate Alcibiades' manner of rule in the common weal, as of a man most dissolute, and given to flattery: because he ever studied by all devise he could, to curry favour with the common people. So did the Romans malice also Coriolanus' government, for that it was too arrogant, proud, and tyrannical: whereby neither the one nor the other was to be commended. Notwithstanding, he is less to be blamed that seeketh to please and gratify his common people, than he that despiseth and disdaineth them, and therefore offereth them wrong and injury, because he would not seem to flatter them, to win the more authority. For as it is an evil thing to flatter the common people to win credit, even so is it besides dishonesty, and injustice also, to attain to credit and authority, for one to make himself terrible to the people, by offering them wrong and violence.

2 It is true that Martius was ever counted an honest-natured man, plain and simple, without art or cunning: howbeit Alcibiades merely contrary, for he was fine, subtle, and deceitful. And the

greatest fault they ever burdened Alcibiades for, was his malice and deceit, wherewith he abused the ambassadors of the Lacedae-monians, and that he was a let that peace was not concluded, as Thucydides reporteth. Now, though by this act he suddenly brought the city of Athens into wars, yet he brought it thereby to be of greater power, and more fearful to the enemies, by making alliance with the Mantinians and the Argives, who by Alcibiades' practice entered into league with the Athenians. And Martius, as Dionysius the historiographer writeth, did by craft and deceit bring the Romans into wars against the Volsces, causing the Volsces maliciously and wrongfully to be suspected, that went to Rome to see the games played. But the cause why he did it, made the fact so much more foul and wicked. For it was not done for any civil dissension, nor for any jealousy and contention in matters of government, as Alcibiades did: but only following his choleric mood, that would be pleased with no thing, as Dion said, he would needs trouble and turmoil the most part of Italy, and so being angry with his country, he destroyed many other towns and cities that could not help it, nor do withal. This is true also, that Alcibiades' spite and malice did work great mischief and misery to his country: but when he saw they repented them of the injury they had done him, he came to himself, and did withdraw his army. Another time also, when they had banished Alcibiades, he would not yet suffer the captains of the Athenians to run into great errors, neither would he see them cast away by following ill counsel which they took, neither would he forsake them in any danger they put themselves into. But he did the very same that Aristides had done in old time unto Themistocles, for which he was then, and is yet, so greatly praised. For he went unto the captains that had charge then of the army of the Athenians, although they were not his friends, and told them wherein they did amiss, and what they had further to do. Where Martius to the contrary, did first great hurt unto the whole city of Rome, though all in Rome had not generally offended him: yea, and when the best and chiefest part of the city were grieved for his sake, and were very sorry and angry for the injury done him. Furthermore, the Romans sought to appease one only displeasure and despite they had done him, by many ambassa-dors, petitions and requests they made: whereunto he never yielded, while his mother, wife, and children came, his heart was so hardened. And hereby it appeared he was entered into this cruel war (when he would hearken to no peace) of an intent utterly to destroy and spoil his country, and not as though he meant to recover it, or to return thither again. Here was indeed the difference between them: that spials being laid by the Lacedaemonians to kill Alcibiades, for the malice they did bear him, as also for that they were afraid of him, he was compelled to return home again to Athens. Where Martius contrariwise, having been so honourably received and entertained by the Volsces, he could not with honesty forsake them, considering they had done him that honour as to choose him their general, and trusted him so far, as they put all their whole army and power into his hands: and not as the other, whom the Lacedaemonians rather abused, than used him, suffering him to go up and down their city (and afterwards in the midst of their camp) without honour or place at all. So that in the end Alcibiades was compelled to put himself into the hands of Tisaphernes: unless they will say that he went thither of purpose to him, with intent to save the city of Athens from utter destruction, for the desire he had to return home again.

3   Moreover, we read of Alcibiades, that he was a great taker, and would be corrupted with money: and when he had it, he would most licentiously and dishonestly spend it. Where Martius in contrary manner would not so much as accept gifts lawfully offered him by his captains, to honour him for his valiantness. And the cause why the people did bear him such ill will for the controversy they had with the nobility about clearing of debts grew for that they knew well enough it was not for any gain or benefit he had got thereby, so much as it was for spite and displeasure he thought to do them. Antipater in a letter of his, writing of the death of Aristotle the philosopher, doth not without cause commend the singular gifts that were in Alcibiades, and this inespecially: that he passed all others for winning men's goodwills. Whereas all Martius' noble acts and virtues, wanting that affability, became hateful even to those that received benefit by them, who could not abide his severity and self-will: which causeth desolation (as Plato sayeth) and men to be ill followed, or altogether forsaken. Contrariwise, seeing Alcibiades had a trim entertainment, and a very good grace with him, and could fashion himself in all companies, it was no

marvel if his well-doing were gloriously commended, and himself much honoured and beloved of the people, considering that some faults he did, were oftentimes taken for matters of sport, and toys of pleasure. And this was the cause, that though many times he did great hurt to the commonwealth, yet they did oft make him their general, and trusted him with the charge of the whole city. Where Martius suing for an office of honour that was due to him, for the sundry good services he had done to the state, was notwithstanding repulsed, and put by. Thus do we see, that they to whom the one did hurt, had no power to hate him: and the other that honoured his virtue, had no liking to love his person.

4   Martius also did never any great exploit, being general of his countrymen, but when he was general of their enemies against his natural country: whereas Alcibiades, being both a private person, and a general, did notable service unto the Athenians. By reason whereof, Alcibiades wheresoever he was present, had the upper hand ever of his accusers, even as he would himself, and their accusations took no place against him: unless it were in his absence. Where Martius being present, was condemned by the Romans: and in his person murdered, and slain by the Volsces. But here I cannot say they have done well, nor justly, albeit himself gave them some colour to do it, when he openly denied the Roman ambassadors peace, which after he privately granted, at the request of women. So by this deed of his, he took not away the enmity that was between both people: but leaving war still between them, he made the Volsces (of whom he was general) to lose the opportunity of noble victory. Where indeed he should (if he had done as he ought) have withdrawn his army with their counsel and consent, that had reposed so great affiance in him, in making him their general, if he had made that account of them, as their goodwill towards him did in duty bind him. Or else, if he did not care for the Volsces in the enterprise of this war, but had only procured it of intent to be revenged, and afterwards to leave it off, when his anger was blown over, yet he had no reason for the love of his mother to pardon his country, but rather he should in pardoning his country, have spared his mother, because his mother and wife were members of the body of his country and city, which he did besiege. For in that he uncourteously rejected all public petitions, requests of

ambassadors, entreaties of the bishops and priests, to gratify only the request of his mother with his departure: that was no act so much to honour his mother with, as to dishonour his country by, the which was preserved for the pity and intercession of a woman, and not for the love of itself, as if it had not been worthy of it. And so was this departure a grace, to say truly, very odious and cruel, and deserved no thanks of either party, to him that did it. For he withdrew his army, not at the request of the Romans, against whom he made war, nor with their consent, at whose charge the war was made. And of all his misfortune and ill hap, the austerity of his nature, and his haughty obstinate mind, was the only cause: the which of itself being hateful to the world, when it is joined with ambition, it groweth then much more churlish, fierce, and intolerable. For men that have that fault in nature, are not affable to the people, seeming thereby as though they made no estimation or regard of the people: and yet on the other side, if the people should not give them honour and reverence, they would straight take it in scorn, and little care for the matter. For so did Metellus, Aristides, and Epaminondas, all use this manner: not to seek the goodwill of the common people by flattery and dissimulation, which was indeed because they despised that which the people could give or take away. Yet would they not be offended with their citizens, when they were amerced, and set at any fines, or that they banished them, or gave them any other repulse: but they loved them as well as they did before, so soon as they showed any token of repentance, and that they were sorry for the wrong they had done them, and were easily made friends again with them, after they were restored from their banishment. For he that disdaineth to make much of the people, and to have their favour, should much more scorn to seek to be revenged, when he is repulsed. For, to take a repulse and denial of honour so inwardly to the heart, cometh of no other cause, but that he did too earnestly desire it.

5    Therefore Alcibiades did not dissemble at all, that he was not very glad to see himself honoured, and sorry to be rejected and denied any honour: but also he sought all the means he could to make himself beloved of those amongst whom he lived. Whereas Martius' stoutness, and haughty stomach, did stay him from making much of those that might advance and honour him: and yet his

ambition made him gnaw himself for spite and anger, when he saw he was despised. And this is all that reasonably may be reproved in him: for otherwise he lacked no good commendable virtues and qualities. For his temperance, and clean hands from taking of bribes and money, he may be compared with the most perfect, virtuous, and honest men of all Greece: but not with Alcibiades, who was in that undoubtedly always too licentious and loosely given, and had too small regard of his credit and honesty.

### THE END OF CAIUS MARTIUS CORIOLANUS' LIFE

**PYRRUS**
**MARIUS**

# Life of Pyrrus

It is written, that since Noe's flood, the first king of the Thesprotians, and of the Molossians, was Phaëton, one of those who came with Pelasgus into the realm of Epirus. But some say otherwise, that Deucalion and his wife Pyrra remained there, after they had built and founded the temple of Dodone, in the country of the Molossians. But howsoever it was, a great while after that, Neoptolemus the son of Achilles, bringing thither a great number of people with him, conquered the country, and after him left a succession of kings, which were called after his name, the Pyrrides: because that from his infancy he was surnamed Pyrrus, as much to say as red: and one of his legitimate sons whom he had by Lanassa, the daughter of Cleodes, the son of Hillus, was also named by him Pyrrus. And this is the cause why Achilles is honoured as a god in Epirus, being called in their language, Aspetos, that is to say, mighty, or very great. But from the first kings of that race until the time of Tharrytas, there is no memory nor mention made of them, nor of their power that reigned in the meantime, because they all became very barbarous, and utterly void of civility. Tharrytas was indeed the first that beautified the cities of his country with the Grecian tongue, brought in civil laws and customs, and made his name famous to the posterity that followed. This Tharrytas left a son called Alcetas, of Alcetas came Arymbas, of Arymbas and Troiade his wife, came Aeacides, who married Phthia, the daughter of Menon Thessalian: a famous man in the time of the wars surnamed Lamiacus, and one that had far greater authority than any other of the confederates, after Leosthenes. This Aeacides had two daughters by his wife Phthia, to say, Deidamia and Troiade, and one son called Pyrrus.

2    In his time the Molossians rebelled, drove him out of his kingdom, and put the crown into the hands of the sons of

Neoptolemus. Whereupon all the friends of Aeacides that could be taken, were generally murdered, and slain outright. Androclides and Angelus in the meantime stole away Pyrrus, being yet but a suckling babe (whom his enemies nevertheless eagerly sought for to have destroyed) and fled away with him as fast as possibly they might, with few servants, his nurses and necessary women only to look to the child, and give it suck: by reason whereof their flight was much hindered, so as they could go no great journeys, but that they might easily be overtaken by them that followed. For which cause they put the child into the hands of Androclion, Hippias, and Neander, three lusty young men, whom they trusted with him, and commanded them to run for life to a certain city of Macedon, called Megares: and they themselves in the meantime, partly by entreaty, and partly by force, made stay of those that followed them till night. So as with much ado having driven them back, they ran after them that carried the child Pyrrus, whom they overtook at sunset. And now, weening they had been safe, and out of all danger, they found it clean contrary. For when they came to the river under the town walls of Megares, they saw it so rough and swift, that it made them afraid to behold it: and when they gauged the ford, they found it unpossible to wade through, it was so sore risen and troubled with the fall of the rain, besides that the darkness of the night made everything seem fearful unto them. So as they now that carried the child, thought it not good to venture the passage over of themselves alone, with the women that tended the child: but hearing certain countrymen on the other side, they prayed and besought them in the name of the gods, that they would help them to pass over the child, showing Pyrrus unto them afar off. But the countrymen by reason of the roaring of the river understood them not. Thus they continued a long space, the one crying, the other listening, yet could they not understand one another, till at the last one of the company bethought himself to peel off a piece of the bark of an oak, and upon that he wrote with the tongue of a buckle the hard fortune and necessity of the child. Which he tied to a stone to give it weight, and so threw it over to the other side of the river: others say that he did prick the bark through with the point of a dart which he cast over. The countrymen on the other side of the river, having read what was written, and understanding thereby the present danger the child was in, felled down trees in all the haste they could possibly, bound them together, and so passed over the river. And it fortuned that the first man of them that passed over, and took the child, was called Achilles: the residue of the countrymen passed over also, and took the other that came with the child, and conveyed them over as they came first to hand.

3    And thus having escaped their hands, by easy journeys they came at the length unto Glaucias king of Illyria, whom they found in his house sitting by his wife: and laid down the child in the midst of the floor before him. The king hereupon stayed a long time without uttering any one word, weighing with himself what was best to be done, because of the fear he had of Cassander, a mortal enemy of Aeacides. In the meantime, the child Pyrrus creeping of all four, took hold of the king's gown, and scrawled up by that, and so got up on his feet against the king's knees. At the first, the king laughed to see the child: but after it pitied him again, because the child seemed like an humble suitor that came to seek sanctuary in his arms. Other say that Pyrrus came not to Glaucias, but unto the altar of the familiar gods, along the which he got up on his feet, and embraced it with both his hands. Which Glaucias imagining to be done by god's providence, presently delivered the child to his wife, gave her the charge of him, and willed her to see him brought up with his own. Shortly after, his enemies sent to demand the child of him: and moreover, Cassander caused two hundred talents to be offered him, to deliver the child Pyrrus into his hands. Howbeit Glaucias would never grant thereunto, but contrarily, when Pyrrus was come to twelve years old, brought him into his country of Epirus with an army, and stablished him king of the realm again. Pyrrus had a great majesty in his countenance, but yet indeed more fearful than friendly. He had also no teeth in his upper jaw that stood distinctly one from another, but one whole bone throughout his gum, marked a little at the top only, with certain rifts in the place where the teeth should be divided. Men held opinion also, that he did heal them that were sick of the spleen, by sacrificing a white cock, and touching the place of the spleen on the left side of them that were sick, softly with his right foot, they lying on their backs: and there was not so poor nor simple a man that craved this remedy of him, but he gave it him, and took the cock he sacrificed,

for reward of the remedy, which pleased him very well. They say also that the great toe of his right foot had some secret virtue in it. For when he was dead, and that they had burnt all parts of his body, and consumed it to ashes, his great toe was whole, and had no hurt at all. But of that we will write more hereafter.

4   Now, when he was seventeen years of age, thinking himself sure enough of his kingdom, it chanced him to make a journey into Illyria, where he married one of Glaucias' daughters, with whom he had been brought up. But his back was no sooner turned, but the Molossians rebelled again against him, and drove out his friends and servants, and destroyed all his goods, and yielded themselves unto his adversary Neoptolemus. King Pyrrus having thus lost his kingdom, and seeing himself forsaken on all sides, went to Demetrius (Antigonus' son) that had married his sister Deidamia, who in her young age was assured to Alexander, the son of Alexander the Great and of Roxane, and was called his wife. But when all that race was brought to wicked end, Demetrius then married her, being come to full and able age. And in that great battle which was stricken near to the city of Hipsus, where all the kings fought together, Pyrrus being then but a young man, and with Demetrius, put them all to flight that fought with him, and was worthily reputed for the valiantest prince amongst them all. Furthermore, when Demetrius was overcome, and had lost the battle, Pyrrus never forsook him, but faithfully did keep for him the cities of Greece, which he put into his hands. And afterwards when peace was concluded betwixt Demetrius and Ptolomie, Pyrrus was sent an hostage for Demetrius into the realm of Egypt: where he made Ptolomie know (both in hunting, and in other exercises of his person) that he was very strong, hard, and able to endure any labour. Furthermore perceiving that Berenice, amongst all King Ptolomie's wives, was best beloved and esteemed of her husband, both for her virtue and wisdom: he began to entertain and honour her above all the rest. For he was a man that could tell how to humble himself towards the great (by whom he might win benefit) and knew also how to creep into their credit: and in like manner was he a great scorner and despiser of such as were his inferiors. Moreover, for that he was found marvellous honourable and of fair condition, he was preferred before all other young princes, to be the husband of

Antigona, the daughter of Queen Berenice, whom she had by
Philip, before she was married unto Ptolomie.

5    From thenceforth growing, through the alliance of that marriage, more and more into estimation and favour by means of
his wife Antigona, who showed herself very virtuous and loving
towards him, he found means in the end to get both men and
money to return again into the realm of Epirus, and to conquer it:
so was he then very well received of the people, and the better, for
the malice they bore to Neoptolemus, because he dealt both hardly
and cruelly with them. That notwithstanding, Pyrrus fearing lest
Neoptolemus would repair unto some of the other kings, to seek
aid against him, thought good to make peace with him. Whereupon it was agreed between them, that they should both together
be kings of Epirus. But in process of time, some of their men
secretly made strife again between them, and set them at defiance
one with another: and the chiefest cause as it is said, that angered
Pyrrus most, grew upon this. The kings of Epirus had an ancient
custom of great antiquity, after they had made solemn sacrifice
unto Jupiter Martial (in a certain place in the province of Molosside, called Passaron), to take their oath, and to be sworn to the
Epirotes, that they would reign well and justly, according to the
laws and ordinances of the country: and to receive the subjects'
oaths interchangeably also, that they would defend and maintain
them in their kingdom, according to the laws in like manner. This
ceremony was done in the presence of both the kings, and they
with their friends did both give and receive presents each of other.
At this meeting and solemnity, among other, one Gelon, a most
faithful servant and assured friend unto Neoptolemus, who besides
great shows of friendship and honour he did unto Pyrrus, gave him
two pair of draught oxen, which one Myrtilus a cupbearer of
Pyrrus being present and seeing, did crave of his master. But Pyrrus
denied to give them unto him, whereat Myrtilus was very angry.
Gelon perceiving that Myrtilus was angry, prayed him to sup with
him that night. Now some say, he sought to abuse Myrtilus,
because he was fair and young: and began to persuade him after
supper to take part with Neoptolemus, and to poison Pyrrus.
Myrtilus made as though he was willing to give ear to this
persuasion, and to be well pleased withal. But in the meantime, he

went and told his master of it, by whose commandment he made Alexicrates, Pyrrus' chief cupbearer, to talk with Gelon about this practice, as though he had also given his consent to it, and was willing to be partaker of the enterprise. This did Pyrrus to have two witnesses, to prove the pretended poisoning of him. Thus Gelon being finely deceived, and Neoptolemus also with him, both imagining they had cunningly spun the thread of their treason, Neoptolemus was so glad of it, that he could not keep it to himself, but told it to certain of his friends. And on a time going to be merry with his sister, he could not keep it in, but must be prattling of it to her, supposing nobody had heard him but herself, because there was no living creature near them, saving Phoenareta, Samon's wife, the king's chief herdman of all his beasts: and yet she was laid upon a little bed by, and turned towards the wall, so that she seemed as though she had slept. But having heard all their talk, and nobody mistrusting her, the next morning she went to Antigona King Pyrrus' wife, and told her every word what she had heard Neoptolemus say to his sister. Pyrrus hearing this, made no countenance of anything at that time. But having made sacrifice unto the gods, he bade Neoptolemus to supper to his house, where he slew him, being well informed before of the goodwill the chiefest men of the realm did bear him, who wished him to dispatch Neoptolemus, and not to content himself with a piece of Epirus only, but to follow his natural inclination, being born to great things: and for this cause therefore, this suspicion falling out in the meanwhile, he prevented Neoptolemus, and slew him first.

6    And furthermore, remembering the pleasures he had received of Ptolomie and Berenice, he named his first son by his wife Antigona, Ptolomie, and having built a city in the Prescque, an Isle of Epirus, did name it Berenicida. When he had done that, imagining great matters in his head, but more in his hope, he first determined with himself how to win that which lay nearest unto him: and so took occasion by this means, first to set foot into the Empire of Macedon. The eldest son of Cassander, called Antipater, put his own mother Thessalonica to death, and drove his brother Alexander out of his own country, who sent to Demetrius for help, and called in Pyrrus also to his aid. Demetrius being troubled with other matters, could not so quickly go thither. And Pyrrus being

arrived there, demanded for his charge sustained, the city of
Nymphaea, with all the sea coasts of Macedon: and besides all that,
certain lands also that were not belonging to the ancient crown and
revenues of the kings of Macedon, but were added unto it by force
of arms, as Ambracia, Acarnania, and Amphilochia. All these the
young King Alexander leaving unto him, he took possession
thereof, and put good garrisons into the same in his own name: and
conquering the rest of Macedon in the name of Alexander, put
his brother Antipater to great distress. In the meantime King
Lysimachus lacked no goodwill to help Antipater with his force,
but being busied in other matters, had not the mean to do it.
Howbeit knowing very well that Pyrrus in acknowledging the
great pleasures he had received of Ptolomie, would deny him
nothing, he determined to write counterfeit letters to him in
Ptolomie's name, and thereby instantly to pray and require him to
leave off the wars begun against Antipater, and to take of him
towards the defraying of his charges, the sum of three hundred
talents. Pyrrus opening the letters, knew straight that this was but a
fetch and devise of Lysimachus. For King Ptolomie's common
manner of greeting of him, which he used at the beginning of
his letters, was not in them observed: 'To my son Pyrrus, health.'
But in those counterfeit was, 'King Ptolomie, unto King Pyrrus,
health.' Whereupon he presently pronounced Lysimachus for a
naughty man: nevertheless, afterwards he made peace with Antipater, and they met together at a day appointed, to be sworn upon
the sacrifices unto the articles of peace. There were three beasts
brought to be sacrificed, a goat, a bull, and a ram: of the which, the
ram fell down dead of himself before he was touched, whereat all
the bystanders fell a-laughing. But there was a soothsayer, one
Theodotus, that persuaded Pyrrus not to swear: saying, that this
sign and token of the gods did threaten one of the three kings with
sudden death. For which cause Pyrrus concluded no peace.

7   Now Alexander's wars being ended, Demetrius notwithstanding came to him, knowing well enough at his coming that
Alexander had no more need of his aid, and that he did it only but
to fear him. They had not been many days together, but the one
began to mistrust the other, and to spy all the ways they could to
entrap each other: but Demetrius embracing the first occasion

offered, prevented Alexander, and slew him, being a young man, and proclaimed himself king of Macedon in his room. Now Demetrius had certain quarrels before against Pyrrus, because he had overrun the country of Thessalie: and furthermore, greedy covetousness to have the more (which is a common vice with princes and noblemen) made, that being so near neighbours, the one stood in fear and mistrust of the other, and yet much more after the death of Deidamia. But now that they both occupied all Macedon between them, and were to make division of one self kingdom, now, I say, began the matter and occasion of quarrel to grow the greater between them. Whereupon Demetrius went with his army to set upon the Aetolians, and having conquered the country, left Pantauchus his lieutenant there with a great army: and himself in person in the meantime, marched against Pyrrus, and Pyrrus on the other side against him. They both missed of meeting, and Demetrius going on further on the one side, entered into the realm of Epirus, and brought a great spoil away with him: Pyrrus on the other side marched on, till he came to the place where Pantauchus was. To whom he gave battle, and it was valiantly fought out between the soldiers of either party, but specially between the two generals. For doubtless, Pantauchus was the valiantest captain, the stoutest man, and of the greatest experience in arms, of all the captains and soldiers Demetrius had. Whereupon, Pantauchus trusting in his strength and courage, advanced himself forwards, and lustily challenged the combat of Pyrrus. Pyrrus on the other side being inferior to no king in valiantness, nor in desire to win honour, as he that would ascribe unto himself the glory of Achilles, more for the imitation of his valiancy, than for that he was descended of his blood, passed through the midst of the battle unto the first rank, to buckle with Pantauchus. Thus they began to charge one another, first with their darts, and then coming nearer, fought with their swords, not only artificially, but also with great force and fury: until such time as Pyrrus was hurt in one place, and he hurt Pantauchus in two, the one near unto his throat and the other in his leg: so as in the end Pyrrus made him turn his back, and threw him to the ground, but nevertheless killed him not. For, so soon as he was down, his men took him, and carried him away. But the Epirotes encouraged by the victory of their king, and the admiration of his valiantness, stuck to it so lustily, that in the end

they broke the battle of the Macedonian footmen: and having put
them to flight, followed them so lively, that they slew a great
number of them, and took five thousand prisoners.

8    This overthrow did not so much fill the hearts of the Macedonians with anger, for the loss they had received, nor with the hate
conceived against Pyrrus, as it won Pyrrus great fame and honour,
making his courage and valiantness to be wondered at of all such as
were present at the battle that saw him fight, and how he laid about
him. For they thought that they saw in his face the very life and
agility of Alexander the Great, and the right shadow as it were,
showing the force and fury of Alexander himself in that fight. And
where other kings did but only counterfeit Alexander the Great in
his purple garments, and in numbers of soldiers and guards about
their persons, and in a certain fashion and bowing of their necks a
little, and in uttering his speech with an high voice, Pyrrus only was
like unto him, and followed him in his martial deeds and valiant
acts. Furthermore for his experience and skill in warlike discipline,
the books he wrote himself thereof, do amply prove and make
manifest. Furthermore they report, that King Antigonus being
asked, whom he thought to be the greatest captain, made answer,
Pyrrus, so far forth as he might live to be old, speaking only of the
captains of his time. But Hannibal generally said, Pyrrus was the
greatest captain of experience and skill in wars of all other, Scipio
the second, and himself the third: as we have written in the life of
Scipio. So it seemeth that Pyrrus gave his whole life and study to the
discipline of wars, as that which indeed was princely and meet for a
king, making no reckoning of all other knowledge. And furthermore touching this matter, they report that he being at a feast one
day, a question was asked him, whom he thought to be the best
player of the flute, Python or Cephesias: whereunto he answered,
that Polyperchon in his opinion was the best captain, as if he would
have said, that was the only thing a prince should seek for, and
which he ought chiefly to learn and know. He was very gentle and
familiar with his friends, easy to forgive when any had offended
him, and marvellous desirous to requite and acknowledge any
courtesy or pleasure by him received. And that was the cause why
he did very impatiently take the death of Aeropus, not so much for
his death (which he knew was a common thing to every living

creature) as for that he was angry with himself he had deferred the time so long, that time itself had cut him off from all occasion and means to requite the courtesies he had received of him. True it is that money lent, may be repayed again unto the heirs of the lender: but yet it grieveth an honest nature, when he cannot recompense the goodwill of the lender, of whom he has received the good turn. Another time Pyrrus being in the city of Ambracia, there were certain of his friends that gave him counsel to put a naughty man out of the city that did nothing but speak ill of him. But he answered, 'It is better,' quoth he, 'to keep him here still, speaking ill of us but to a few: than driving him away, to make him speak ill of us everywhere.' Certain youths were brought before him on a time, who making merry together, drinking freely, were bold with the king to speak their pleasure of him in very undutiful sort. So, Pyrrus asking them whether it was true they said so or no: 'It is true, and it please your grace,' said one of them, 'we said it indeed, and had not our wine failed us, we had spoken a great deal more.' The king laughed at it, and pardoned them.

9   After the death of Antigona, he married many wives to increase his power withal, and to get more friends. For he married the daughter of Autoleon king of Paeonia, and Bircenna the daughter of Bardillis, king of Illyria, and Lanassa, the daughter of Agathocles, tyrant of Syracusa, that brought him for her dower the Isle of Corfu, which her father had taken. By Antigona his first wife, he had a son called Ptolomie; by Lanassa, another called Alexander; and by Bircenna, another (the youngest of all) called Helenus: all which, though they were martial men by race and natural inclination, yet were they brought up by him in wars, and therein trained as it were even from their cradle. They write, that one of his sons being but a boy, asked him one day to which of them he would leave his kingdom: Pyrrus answered the boy, 'To him that hath the sharpest sword.' That was much like the tragical curse wherewith Oedipus cursed his children:

> Let them (for me) divide both goods, yea rents and land,
>   With trenchant sword and bloody blows, by force of
>                                                  mighty hand.

So cruel, hateful, and beastly is the nature of ambition and desire of rule.

10   But after this battle, Pyrrus returned home again to his
country, full of honour and glory, his heart highly exalted, and his
mind thoroughly contented. And as at his return the Epirotes his
subjects called him an eagle, he answered them: 'If I be an eagle, it
is through you that I am so, for your weapons are the wings that
have raised me up.' Shortly after, being advertised that Demetrius
was fallen sick, and in great danger of death, he suddenly went into
Macedon, only to invade it, and to make prey thereof: howbeit he
had indeed almost taken the whole realm, and made himself lord of
all without stroke stricken. For he came as far as the city of Edessa,
and found no resistance: but rather to the contrary, many of the
country willingly came to his camp, and submitted themselves.
The danger Demetrius was in to lose his realm, did move him
more than the disease and sickness of his body. And on the other
side, his friends, servants and captains, having gathered a great
number of men of war together in marvellous short time, marched
with great speed towards Pyrrus, being earnestly bent to do some
exploit against him: who being come into Macedon but to make a
road only upon them, would not tarry them, but fled, and flying,
lost part of his men, because the Macedonians followed him hard,
and set upon him by the way. But now, though they had driven
Pyrrus thus easily out of Macedon, Demetrius for all that did not
make light account of him: but pretending greater things (as to
recover the lands and dominions of his father, with an army of an
hundred thousand fighting men, and of five hundred sail which he
put to the sea), would not stand to make wars against Pyrrus,
neither yet leave the Macedonians (whilst he was absent) so
dangerous a neighbour, and so ill to deal withal. But lacking leisure
to make wars with Pyrrus, concluded a peace with him, to the end
he might with the more liberty set upon the other kings. Thus
now, the peace concluded betwixt Demetrius and Pyrrus, the
other kings and princes began to find out Demetrius' intent, and
why he had made so great preparation; and being afraid thereof,
wrote unto Pyrrus by their ambassadors, that they wondered how
he could let go such opportunity and occasion, and to tarry till
Demetrius might with better leisure make wars upon him. And
why he chose rather to tarry and fight with him for the altars,
temples and sepulchres of the Molossians, when he should be of
greater power, and have no wars elsewhere to trouble him, than

now that he might easily drive him out of Macedon, having so many things in hand, and being troubled as he was in other places. And considering also that very lately he had taken one of his wives from him, with the city of Corfu. For Lanassa misliking that Pyrrus loved his other wives better then her (they being of a barbarous nation), got her unto Corfu: and desiring to marry some other king, sent for Demetrius, knowing that he of all other kings would soonest be won thereunto. Whereupon Demetrius went thither, and married her, and left a garrison in his city of Corfu.

11    Now these other kings that did advertise Pyrrus in this sort, themselves did trouble Demetrius in the meanwhile: who tracted time, and yet went on with his preparation notwithstanding, for on the one side, Ptolomie entered Greece with a great army by sea, where he caused the cities to revolt against him. And Lysimachus on the other side also, entering into high Macedon by the country of Thracia, burnt and spoiled all as he went. Pyrrus also arming himself with them, went unto the city of Berroea, imagining (as afterwards it fell out) that Demetrius going against Lysimachus would leave all the low country of Macedon naked, without garrison or defence. And the selfsame night that Pyrrus departed, he imagined that King Alexander the Great did call him, and that also he went unto him, and found him sick in his bed, of whom he had very good words and entertainment: insomuch as he promised to help him thoroughly. And Pyrrus imagined also that he was so bold to demand of him again: 'How, my lord, can you help me, that lie sick in your bed?' And that Alexander made answer: 'With my name only.' And that moreover he suddenly therewithal got up on his horse Nisea, and rode before Pyrrus to guide him the way. This vision he had in his dream, which made him bold, and furthermore encouraged him to go on with his enterprise. By which occasion, marching forward with all speed, in few days he ended his intended journey to the city of Berroea, which suddenly he took at his first coming to it: the most part of his army he laid in garrison there, the residue he sent away under the conduct of his captains here and there, to conquer the cities thereabouts. Demetrius having intelligence hereof, and hearing also an ill rumour that ran in his camp amongst the Macedonians, durst not lead them any further, for fear lest (when he should come near

to Lysimachus, being a Macedonian king by nation, and a prince esteemed for a famous captain) they would shrink from him, and take Lysimachus' part: for this cause therefore he turned again upon the sudden against Pyrrus, as against a strange prince, and ill beloved of the Macedonians. But when he came to encamp near him, many coming from Berroea into his camp, blew abroad the praises of Pyrrus, saying, that he was a noble prince, invincible in wars, and one that courteously entreated all those he took to his party: and amongst those, there were other that were no natural Macedonians born, but set on by Pyrrus, and feigned themselves to be Macedonians, who gave out, that now occasion was offered to set them at liberty from Demetrius' proud and stately rule, and to take King Pyrrus' part, that was a courteous prince, and one that loved soldiers and men of war. These words made the most part of Demetrius' army very doubtful, insomuch as the Macedonians looked about, to see if they could find out Pyrrus to yield them-selves unto him. He had at that present left off his headpiece: by mean whereof, perceiving he was not known, he put it on again, and then they knew him afar off, by the sight of his goodly fair plume, and the goat's horns which he carried on the top of his crest. Whereupon there came a great number of Macedonians to his part, as unto their sovereign lord and king, and required the watchword of him. Others put garlands of oaken boughs about their heads, because they saw his men crowned after that sort. And some were so bold also, as to go to Demetrius himself, and tell him, that in their opinions he should do very well and wisely to give place to fortune, and refer all unto Pyrrus. Demetrius hereupon, seeing his camp in such uproar, was so amazed, that he knew not what way to take, but stole away secretly, disguised in a threadbare cloak, and a hood on his head to keep him from knowledge. Pyrrus forthwith seized upon his camp, took all that he found, and was presently proclaimed in the field, King of Macedon.

12    Lysimachus on the other side, came straight thither after him, and said that he had helped to chase Demetrius out of his realm, and therefore claimed half the kingdom with him. Wherefore, Pyrrus not trusting the Macedonians too far as yet, but rather standing in doubt of their faith, granted Lysimachus his desire, and thereupon divided all the cities and provinces of the realm of

Macedon between them. This partition was profitable for them both at that present, and stood then to good purpose to pacify the war, that otherwise might suddenly have risen between them. But shortly after, they found that this partition was no end of their enmity, but rather a beginning of quarrel and dissension between them. For they whose avarice and insatiable greedy appetite, neither the sea, the mountains, nor the inhabitable deserts could contain, nor yet the confines that separate Asia from Europe determine: how should they be content with their own, without usurping others, when their frontiers join so near together, that nothing divides them? Sure it is not possible. For to say truly, they are willingly together by the ears, having these two cursed things rooted in them: that they continually seek occasion how to surprise each other, and either of them envies his neighbour's well doing. Howbeit in appearance they use these two terms of peace and wars, as they do money: using it as they think good, not according to right and justice, but for their private profit. And truly they are men of far greater honesty, that make open war, and avow it, than those that disguise and colour the delay of their wicked purpose, by the holy name of justice or friendship. Which Pyrrus did truly then verify. For desiring to keep Demetrius down from rising another time, and that he should not revive again as escaped from a long dangerous disease: he went to aid the Grecians against him, and was at Athens, where they suffered him to come into the castle, and do sacrifice there unto the goddess Minerva. But coming out of the castle again the same day, he told the Athenians he was greatly beholding unto them for their courtesy, and the great trust they had reposed in him: wherefore to requite them again, he gave them counsel, never to suffer prince nor king from thenceforth to enter into their city, if they were wise, nor once open their gates unto them. So, after that he made peace with Demetrius, who within short time being gone to make wars in Asia, Pyrrus yet once again (persuaded thereunto by Lysimachus) caused all Thessalie to rise against him, and went himself to set upon those garrisons which Demetrius had left in the cities of Greece, liking better to continue the Macedonians in war, than to leave them in peace: besides that himself also was of such a nature, as could not long continue in peace. Demetrius thus in the end being utterly overthrown in Syria, Lysimachus seeing himself free from fear on that side, and being at good leisure, as having nothing to trouble him otherwise, went straight to make war upon Pyrrus, who then remained near unto the city of Edessa, and meeting by the way with the convoy of victuals coming towards him, set upon the conductors, and rifled them wholly. By this means, first he distressed Pyrrus for want of victuals: then he corrupted the princes of Macedon with letters and messengers, declaring unto them, what shame they sustained to have made a stranger their king (whose ancestors had ever been their vassals and subjects) and to have turned all those out of Macedon, that had been familiar friends of King Alexander the Great. Many of the Macedonians were won by these persuasions, which fact so feared Pyrrus, that he departed out of Macedon with his men of war, the Epirotes, and other his confederates: and so lost Macedon by the selfsame means he won it. Kings and princes therefore must not blame private men, though they change and alter sometime for their profit: for therein they do but follow the example of princes, who teach them all disloyalty, treason, and infidelity, judging him most worthy of gain, that least observes justice and equity.

13 So Pyrrus being come home again to his kingdom of Epirus, forsaking Macedon altogether, fortune made him happy enough, and indeed he had good means to live peaceably at home, without any trouble, if he could have contented himself only with the sovereignty over his own natural subjects. But thinking, that if he did neither hurt other, nor that other did hurt him, he could not tell how to spend his time, and by peace he should pine away for sorrow, as Homer said of Achilles:

> He languished and pined by taking ease and rest:
> And in the wars where travail was, he liked ever best.

And thus seeking matter of new trouble, fortune presented him this occasion. About this time, the Romans by chance made war with the Tarentines, who could neither bear their force, nor yet devise how to pacify the same, by reason of the rashness, folly, and wickedness of their governors, who persuaded them to make Pyrrus their general, and to send for him for to conduct these wars: because he was less troubled at that time, than any of the other kings about them, and was esteemed of every man also to be a noble soldier, and famous captain. The elders and wise men of the city utterly misliked that counsel: but some of them were put to silence, through the noise and fury of the people, who cried for wars. Some other seeing them checked and taken up by the multitude in this manner, would no more repair to their common assemblies. Among the rest, there was one Meton, an honest worshipful citizen, who when the day was come that the people should conclude in council, the decree for the calling in of Pyrrus, all the people of Tarentum being assembled, and set in the theatre, this Meton put an old withered garland of flowers upon his head, and carrying a torch in his hand as though he had been drunk, and having a woman minstrel before him playing on a pipe, went dancing in this goodly array through the midst of the whole assembly. And there (as it happens commonly in every hurly burly of people that will be masters themselves, and where no good order is kept) some of them clapped their hands, other burst out in a laughter, and every man suffered him to do what he lust: but they all cried out to the woman minstrel, to play on and spare not, and to Meton himself, that he should sing, and come forward. So Meton made show as though he prepared himself unto it: and when they had given silence to hear him sing, he spoke unto them with a loud voice in this manner: 'My lords of Tarentum, ye do well sure, not to forbid them to play and to be merry that are so disposed, whilst they may lawfully do it: and if ye be wise, every of you also (as many as you be) will take your liberty whilst you may enjoy it. For when King Pyrrus shall be in this city, you shall live I warrant ye after another sort, and not as ye now do.' These words of Meton moved many of the Tarentines, and suddenly there ran a rumour through all the assembly, that he had said truly. But they that had offended the Romans, fearing if peace were made, that they should be delivered into their hands, they checked the people, asking them if they were such fools, as would abide to be mocked and played withal to their teeth: and with those words all ran upon Meton, and drove him out of the theatre. The decree thus confirmed by voices of the people, they sent ambassadors into Epirus, to carry presents unto King Pyrrus, not only from the Tarentines, but from other Grecians also that dwelt in Italy, saying that they stood in need of a wise and skilful captain, that was reputed famous in martial discipline. And as to the rest, for numbers of good soldiers, they had men enough in Italy, and were able to bring an army into the field, of the Lucanians, the Messapians, the Samnites, and Tarentines, of twenty thousand horse, and three hundred thousand footmen being all assembled together. These words of the ambassadors did not only lift up Pyrrus' heart, but made the Epirotes also marvellous desirous to go this journey.

14   There was in King Pyrrus' court one Cineas Thessalian, a man of great understanding, and that had been Demosthenes the orator's scholar, who seemed to be the only man of all other in his time in common reputation, to be most eloquent, following the lively image and shadow of Demosthenes' passing eloquence. This Cineas Pyrrus ever entertained about him, and sent him ambassador to the people and cities thereabouts: where he verified Euripides' words:

> As much as trenchant blades in mighty hands may do,
> So much can skill of eloquence achieve and conquer too.

And therefore Pyrrus would often say, that Cineas had won him more towns with his eloquence, than himself had done by the sword: for which he did greatly honour and employ him in all his chief affairs. Cineas perceiving that Pyrrus was marvellously bent to these wars of Italy, finding him one day at leisure, discoursed with him in this sort: 'It is reported, and it please your majesty, that the Romans are very good men of war, and that they command many valiant and warlike nations: if it please the gods we do overcome them, what benefit shall we have of that victory?' Pyrrus answered him again: 'Thou doest ask me a question that is manifest of itself. For when we have once overcome the Romans, there can neither Grecian nor barbarous city in all the country withstand us, but we shall straight conquer all the rest of Italy with ease: whose greatness, wealth, and power, no man knoweth better then thyself.' Cineas pausing a while, replied: 'And when we have taken Italy, what shall we do then?' Pyrrus not finding his meaning yet, said unto him: 'Sicilia as thou knowest, is hard adjoining to it, and doth as it were offer itself unto us, and is a marvellous populous and rich land, and easy to be taken: for all the cities within the island are one against another, having no head that governs them, since Agathocles died, more than orators only that are their counsellors, who will soon be won.' 'Indeed it is likely which your grace speaketh,' quoth Cineas, 'but when we have won Sicilia, shall then our wars take end?' 'If the gods were pleased,' said Pyrrus, 'that victory were achieved, the way were then broad open for us to attain great conquests. For who would not afterwards go into Africa, and so to Carthage, which also will be an easy conquest, since Agathocles secretly flying from Syracusa, and having passed the seas with a few ships, had almost taken it? And that once conquered, it is most certain there durst not one of all our enemies that now do daily vex and trouble us, lift up their heads or hands against us' 'No surely,' said Cineas: 'for it is a clear case, that with so great a power we may easily recover the realm of Macedon again, and command all Greece besides, without let of any. But when we have all in our hands, what shall we do in the end?' Then Pyrrus laughing, told him again: 'We will then, good Cineas, be quiet, and take our ease, and make feasts every day, and be as merry one with another as we can possible.' Cineas having brought him to that point, said again to him: 'My lord, what letteth us now to be quiet, and merry together, if we enjoy that presently without further travel and trouble, which we will now go seek for abroad, with such shedding of blood, and so manifest danger? And yet we know not whether ever we shall attain unto it, after we have both suffered, and caused other to suffer, infinite sorrows and troubles.' These last words of Cineas did rather offend Pyrrus, than make him to alter his mind: for he was not ignorant of the happy state he should thereby forgo, yet could he not leave off the hope of that he did so much desire.

15   So he sent Cineas before unto the Tarentines, with three thousand footmen: and afterwards the Tarentines having sent him great store of flatbottoms, galleys, and of all sorts of passengers, he shipped into them twenty elephants, three thousand horsemen, and two and twenty thousand footmen, with five hundred bowmen and slings. All things thus ready, he weighed anchors, and hoist sails, and was no sooner in the main sea, but the north wind blew very roughly, out of season, and drove him to leeward. Notwithstanding, the ship which he was in himself, by great toil of the pilots and mariners turning to windward, and with much ado and marvellous danger recovered the coast of Italy. Howbeit the rest of his fleet were violently dispersed here and there, whereof some of them failing their course into Italy, were cast into the seas of Libya, and

Sicilia. The others not able to recover the point of Apulia, were benighted, and the sea being high wrought, by violence cast them upon the shore, and against the rocks, and made shipwrecks of them, the *Admiral* only reserved, which through her strength, and the greatness of her burden, resisted the force of the sea that most violently beat against her. But afterwards, the wind turning and coming from the land, the sea cruelly raking over the height of her forecastle, in fine brought her in manifest peril of opening, and splitting, and in danger to be driven from the coast, putting her out again to the mercy of the winds, which changed every hour. Wherefore Pyrrus casting the peril every way, thought best to leap into the sea. After him forthwith leapt his guard, his servants, and other his familiar friends, venturing their lives to save him. But the darkness of the night, and rage of the waves (which the shore breaking, forced so to rebound back upon them), with the great noise also, did so hinder their swimming, that it was even day before they could recover any land, and yet was it by means that the wind fell. As for Pyrrus, he was so sea-beaten, and wearied with the waves, that he was able to do no more: though of himself he had so great a heart, and stout a courage, as was able to overcome any peril. Moreover, the Messapians (upon whose coast the storm had cast him) ran out to help him, and diligently laboured in all they could possible to save him, and received also certain of his ships that had escaped, in which were a few horsemen, about two thousand footmen, and two elephants.

16   With this small force, Pyrrus marched on his journey to go by land unto Tarentum: and Cineas being advertised of his coming, went with his men to meet him. Now when he was come to Tarentum, at the first he would do nothing by force, nor against the goodwill of the inhabitants: until such time as his ships that had escaped the dangers of the sea, were all arrived, and the greatest part of his army come together again. But when he had all his army he looked for, seeing that the people of Tarentum could neither save themselves, nor be saved by any other, without straight order and compulsion, because they made their reckoning that Pyrrus should fight for them, and in the meantime they would not stir out of their houses from bathing themselves, from banqueting, and making good cheer: first of all he caused all the parks and places of

show to be shut up, where they were wont to walk and disport
themselves, in any kind of exercise, and as they walked, to talk of
wars as it were in pastime, and to fight with words, but not to come
to the blows. And further he forbade all feastings, mummeries,
and such other like pleasures, as at that time were out of season.
He trained them out also to exercise their weapons, and showed
himself very severe in musters, not pardoning any whose names
were billed to serve in the wars: insomuch as there were many
(which unacquainted with such rough handling and government)
forsook the city altogether, calling it a bondage, not to have liberty
to live at their pleasure. Furthermore, Pyrrus having intelligence
that Levinus the Roman consul came against him with a great
puissant army, and that he was already entered into the land of
Lucania, where he destroyed and spoiled all the country before
him: albeit the Tarentines' aid of their confederates was not as yet
come, he thought it a great shame to suffer his enemies' approach
so near him, and therefore taking that small number he had,
brought them into the field against Levinus. Howbeit he sent a
herald before to the Romans, to understand of them, if (before they
entered into this war) they could be content the controversies they
had with all the Grecians dwelling in Italy, might be decided by
justice, and therein to refer themselves to his arbitrament, who of
himself would undertake the pacification of them. Whereunto the
consul Levinus made answer, that the Romans would never allow
him for a judge, neither did they fear him for an enemy. Wherefore
Pyrrus going on still, came to lodge in the plain which is between
the cities of Pandosia and of Heraclea: and having news brought
him that the Romans were encamped very near unto him on the
other side of the river of Siris, he took his horse, and rode to the
river's side to view their camp. So having thoroughly considered
the form, the situation, and the order of the same, the manner of
charging their watch, and all their fashions of doing, he wondered
much thereat. And speaking to Megacles, one of his familiars about
him, he said: 'This order, Megacles,' quoth he, 'though it be of
barbarous people, yet is it not barbarously done, but we shall
shortly prove their force.' After he had thus taken this view, he
began to be more careful than he was before, and purposed to tarry
till the whole aid of their confederates were come together, leaving
men at the river's side of Siris, to keep the passage, if the enemies

ventured to pass over: as they did indeed. For they made haste to
prevent the aid that Pyrrus looked for, and passed their footmen
over upon a bridge, and their horsemen at divers fords of the river:
insomuch as the Grecians fearing lest they should be compassed in
behind, drew back. Pyrrus advertised thereof, and being a little
troubled therewithal, commanded the captains of his footmen
presently to put their bands in battle ray, and not to stir till they
knew his pleasure: and he himself in the meantime marched on
with three thousand horse, in hope to find the Romans by the river
side, as yet out of order, and utterly unprovided. But when he saw
afar off a greater number of footmen with their targets ranged in
battle, on this side the river, and their horsemen marching towards
him in very good order, he caused his men to join close together,
and himself first began the charge, being easy to be known from
other, if it had been no more but his passing rich glistering armour
and furniture, and withal, for that his valiant deeds gave manifest
proof of his well deserved fame and renown. For, though he
valiantly bestirred his hands and body both, repulsing them he
encountered withal in fight, yet he forgot not himself, nor ne-
glected the judgment and foresight, which should never be
wanting in a general of an army: but as though he had not fought
at all, quietly and discreetly gave order for everything, riding to and
fro, to defend and encourage his men in those places where he saw
them in most distress. But even in the hottest of the battle,
Leonatus Macedonian spied an Italian, a man of arms, that followed Pyrrus up and down where he went, and ever kept in
manner of even hand with him, to set upon him. Wherefore he
said to Pyrrus: 'My lord, do you not see that barbarous man there
upon a bay horse with white feet? Sure he looketh as though he
meant to do some notable feat and mischief with his own hands:
for his eye is never off you, but waiteth only upon you, being sharp
set to deal with yourself and none other, and therefore take heed of
him.' Pyrrus answered him, 'It is impossible, Leonatus, for a man to
avoid his destiny: but neither he, nor any other Italian whatsoever,
shall have any joy to deal with me.' And as they were talking thus
of the matter, the Italian taking his spear in the midst, and setting
spurs to his horse, charged upon Pyrrus, and ran his horse through
and through with the same. Leonatus at the selfsame instant served
the Italian's horse in the like manner, so as both their horses fell

dead to the ground. Howbeit Pyrrus' men that were about him, saved him presently, and slew the Italian in the field, although he fought it out right valiantly. The Italian's name was Oplacus, born in the city of Ferentum, and was captain of a band of men of arms.

17   This mischance made King Pyrrus look the better to himself afterwards, and seeing his horsemen gave back, sent presently to hasten his footmen forward, whom he straight set in order of battle: and delivering his armour and cloak to one of his familiars called Megacles, and being hidden as it were in Megacles' armour, returned again to the battle against the Romans, who valiantly resisted him, so that the victory depended long in doubt. For it is said, that both the one side and the other did chase, and was chased, above seven times in that conflict. The changing of the king's armour served very well for the safety of his own person, howbeit it was like to have marred all, and to have made him lose the field. For many of his enemies set upon Megacles, that ware the king's armour: and the party that slew him dead, and threw him stark to the ground, was one Dexius by name, who quickly snatched off his headpiece, took away his cloak, and ran to Levinus the consul, crying out aloud, that he had slain Pyrrus, and withal showed forth the spoils he supposed to have taken from him. Which being carried about through all the bands, and openly showed from hand to hand, made the Romans marvellous joyful, and the Grecians to the contrary, both afraid and right sorrowful: until such time as Pyrrus hearing of it, went and passed along all his bands bareheaded and bare-faced, holding up his hand to his soldiers, and giving them to understand with his own voice, that it was himself. The elephants in the end were they indeed that won the battle, and did most distress the Romans: for, their horses seeing them afar off, were sore afraid, and durst not abide them, but carried their masters back in despite of them. Pyrrus at the sight thereof, made his Thessalian horsemen to give a charge upon them whilst they were in this disorder, and that so lustily, as they made the Romans flee, and sustain great slaughter. For Dionysius writeth, that there died few less than fifteen thousand Romans at that battle. But Hieronymus speaketh only of seven thousand. And of Pyrrus' side, Dionysius writeth, there were slain thirteen thousand. But Hieronymus saith less than four thousand: howbeit they were all of

the best men of his army, and those whom most he trusted. King
Pyrrus presently hereupon also took the Romans' camp, which
they forsook, and won many of their cities from their alliance,
spoiled, and overcame much of their country. Insomuch as he
came within six and thirty mile of Rome, whither came to his aid,
as confederates of the Tarentines, the Lucanians and the Samnites,
whom he rebuked because they came too late to the battle. Howbeit a man might easily see in his face, that he was not a little glad
and proud to have overthrown so great an army of the Romans
with his own men, and the aid of the Tarentines only.

18    On the other side, the Romans' hearts were so great, that they
would not depose Levinus from his consulship, notwithstanding
the loss he had received: and Caius Fabricius said openly, that they
were not the Epirotes that had overcome the Romans, but Pyrrus
had overcome Levinus: meaning thereby, that this overthrow
chanced unto them, more through the subtlety and wise conduction of the general, than through the valiant feats and worthiness of
his army. And hereupon they speedily supplied their legions again
that were minished, with other new soldiers in the dead men's
place, and levied a fresh force besides, speaking bravely and fiercely
of this war, like men whose hearts were nothing appalled. Whereat
Pyrrus marvelling much, thought good first to send to the Romans,
to prove if they would give any ear to an offer of peace, knowing
right well that the winning of the city of Rome was no easy matter
to compass or attain, with that strength he presently had: and also
that it would be greatly to his glory, if he could bring them to peace
after this his valiant victory. And hereupon he sent Cineas to
Rome, who spoke with the chiefest of the city, and offered presents
to them and their wives, in the behalf of the king his master.
Howbeit, neither man nor woman would receive any at his hands,
but answered all with one voice: that if the peace might be general
to all, they all privately would be at the king's commandment, and
would be glad of his friendship. Moreover, when Cineas had
talked in open audience before the senate of many courteous
offers, and had delivered them profitable capitulations of peace,
they accepted none, nor showed any affection to give ear unto
them, although he offered to deliver them their prisoners home
again without ransom, that had been taken at the battle, and

promised also to aid them in the conquest of Italy, requiring no other recompense at their hands, saving their goodwills only to his master, and assurance for the Tarentines, that they should not be annoyed for anything past, without demand of other matter. Nevertheless in the end, when they had heard these offers, many of the senators yielded, and were willing to make peace: alleging that they had already lost a great battle, and how they looked for a greater, when the force of the confederates of Italy should join together with King Pyrrus' power. But Appius Claudius, a famous man, who came no more to the senate, nor dealt in matters of state at all by reason of his age, and partly because he was blind: when he understood of King Pyrrus' offers, and of the common bruit that ran through the city, how the senate were in mind to agree to the capitulations of peace propounded by Cineas, he could not abide, but caused his servants to carry him in his chair upon their arms unto the senate door; his sons and sons-in-law taking him in their arms, carried him so into the senate house. The senate made silence to honour the coming in of so notable and worthy a personage: and he so soon as they had set him in his seat, began to speak in this sort:

19 'Hitherunto with great impatience, my lords of Rome, have I borne the loss of my sight, but now, I would I were also as deaf as I am blind, that I might not (as I do) hear the report of your dishonourable consultations determined upon in senate, which tend to subvert the glorious fame and reputation of Rome. What is now become of all your great and mighty brags you blazed abroad, through the whole world? That if Alexander the Great himself had come into Italy, in the time that our fathers had been in the flower of their age, and we in the prime of our youth, they would not have said everywhere that he was altogether invincible, as now at this present they do: but either he should have left his body slain here in battle, or at the least wise have been driven to flee, and by his death or flying should greatly have enlarged the renown and glory of Rome? You plainly show it now, that all these words spoken then, were but vain and arrogant vaunts of foolish pride, considering that you tremble for fear of the Molossians and Chaonians, who were ever a prey to the Macedonians: and that ye are afraid of Pyrrus also, who all his life time served and followed one of the guard unto Alexander the Great, and now is come to

make wars in these parts, not to aid the Grecians inhabiting in Italy, but to flee from his enemies there about his own country, offering you to conquer all the rest of Italy with an army, wherewith he was nothing able to keep a small part of Macedon only for himself. And therefore you must not persuade yourselves, that in making peace with him, you shall thereby be rid of him: but rather shall you draw others to come and set upon you besides. For they will utterly despise you, when they shall hear ye are so easily overcome, and that you have suffered Pyrrus to escape your hands, before you made him feel the just reward of his bold presumptuous attempt upon you: carrying with him for a further hire, this advantage over you, that he hath given a great occasion both to the Samnites and Tarentines, hereafter to mock and deride you.' After that Appius had told this tale unto the senate, everyone through the whole assembly desired rather war than peace. They dispatched Cineas away thereupon with this answer, that if Pyrrus sought the Romans' friendship, he must first depart out of Italy, and then send unto them to treat of peace: but so long as he remained there with his army, the Romans would make wars upon him, with all the force and power they could make, yea although he had over-thrown and slain ten thousand such captains as Levinus was. They say that Cineas, during the time of his abode at Rome, entreating for this peace, did curiously labour to consider and understand the manners, order, and life of the Romans, and their common weal, discoursing thereof with the chiefest men of the city: and how afterwards he made ample report of the same unto Pyrrus, and told him amongst other things, that the senate appeared to him a council house of many kings. And furthermore (for the number of people) that he feared greatly they should fight against such a serpent, as that which was in old time in the a marshes of Lerne, of which, when they had cut off one head, seven other came up in the place: because the consul Levinus had now levied another army, twice as great as the first was, and had left at Rome also, many times as many good able men to carry armour.

20 After this, there were sent ambassadors from Rome unto Pyrrus, and amongst other, Caius Fabricius, touching the state of the prisoners. Cineas told the king his master, that this Fabricius was one of the greatest men of account in all Rome, a right honest

man, a good captain, and a very valiant man of his hands, yet poor indeed he was notwithstanding. Pyrrus taking him secretly aside, made very much of him, and amongst other things, offered him both gold and silver, praying him to take it, not for any dishonest respect he meant towards him, but only for a pledge of the goodwill and friendship that should be between them. Fabricius would none of his gift: so Pyrrus left him for that time. Notwithstanding, the next morning thinking to fear him, because he had never seen elephant before, Pyrrus commanded his men, that when they saw Fabricius and him talking together, they should bring one of his greatest elephants, and set him hard by them, behind a hanging: which being done, at a certain sign by Pyrrus given, suddenly the hanging was pulled back, and the elephant with his trunk was over Fabricius' head, and gave a terrible and fearful cry. Fabricius softly giving back, nothing afraid, laughed and said to Pyrrus smiling: 'Neither did your gold, O king, yesterday move me, nor your elephant today fear me.' Furthermore, whilst they were at supper, falling in talk of divers matters, specially touching the state of Greece and the philosophers there, Cineas by chance spoke of Epicurus, and rehearsed the opinions of the Epicurians touching the gods and government of the commonwealth, how they placed man's chief felicity in pleasure, how they fled from all office and public charge, as from a thing that hinders the fruition of true felicity: how they maintained that the gods were immortal, neither moved with pity nor anger, and led an idle life full of all pleasures and delights, without taking any regard of men's doings. But as he still continued this discourse, Fabricius cried out aloud, and said: 'The gods grant that Pyrrus and the Samnites were of such opinions, as long as they had wars against us.' Pyrrus marvelling much at the constancy and magnanimity of this man, was more desirous a great deal to have peace with the Romans, than before, and privately prayed Fabricius very earnestly, that he would treat for peace, whereby he might afterwards come and remain with him, saying that he would give him the chief place of honour about him, amongst all his friends. Whereunto Fabricius answered him softly: 'That were not good, O king, for yourself,' quoth he: 'for your men that presently do honour and esteem you, by experience if they once knew me, would rather choose me for their king, than yourself.' Such was Fabricius' talk, whose words

Pyrrus took not in ill part, neither was offended with them at all, as a tyrant would have been: but did himself report to his friends and familiars the noble mind he found in him, and delivered him upon his faith only, all the Roman prisoners: to the end that if the senate would not agree unto peace, they might yet see their friends, and keep the feast of Saturn with them, and then to send them back again unto him. Which the senate established by decree, upon pain of death to all such as should not perform the same accordingly.

21    Afterwards Fabricius was chosen consul, and as he was in his camp, there came a man to him that brought him a letter from King Pyrrus' physician, written with his own hands: in which the physician offered to poison his master, so he would promise him a good reward for ending the wars without further danger. Fabricius detesting the wickedness of the physician, and having made Q. Aemilius his colleague, and fellow consul also, to abhor the same, wrote a letter unto Pyrrus, and bade him take heed, for there were that meant to poison him. The contents of his letter were these: 'Caius Fabricius and Quintus Aemylius consuls of Rome, unto King Pyrrus, greeting. You have, O king, made unfortunate choice, both of your friends and of your enemies, as shall appear unto you by reading of this letter, which one of yours hath written unto us: for you make wars with just and honest men, and do yourself trust altogether the wicked and unfaithful. Hereof there-fore we have thought good to advertise you, not in respect to pleasure you, but for fear lest the misfortune of your death might make us unjustly to be accused: imagining that by treachery of treason, we have sought to end this war, as though by valiantness we could not otherwise achieve it.' Pyrrus having read this letter, and proved the contents thereof true, executed the physician as he had deserved: and to requite the advertisement of the consuls, he sent Fabricius and the Romans their prisoners, without paying of ransom, and sent Cineas again unto them, to prove if he could obtain peace. Howbeit the Romans, because they would neither receive pleasure of their enemies, and least of all reward, for that they consented not unto so wicked a deed, did not only refuse to take their prisoners of free gift, but they sent him again so many Samnites and Tarentines. And furthermore, for peace and his friendship, they would give no ear to it, before the wars were

ended, and that he had sent away his army again by sea, into his kingdom of Epirus. Wherefore Pyrrus seeing no remedy, but that he must needs fight another battle, after he had somewhat refreshed his army, drew towards the city of Asculum, where he fought the second time with the Romans: and was brought into a marvellous ill ground for horsemen, by a very swift-running river, from whence came many brooks and deep marshes, insomuch as his elephants could have no space nor ground to join with the battle of the footmen, by reason whereof there was a great number of men hurt and slain on both sides. And in the end, the battle being fought out all day long, the dark night did sever them: but the next morning, Pyrrus to win the advantage to fight in the plain field, where he might prevail with the force of his elephants, sent first certain of his bands to seize upon the naughty ground they had fought on the day before. And by this policy having brought the Romans into the plain field, he thrust in amongst his elephants, store of shot and slingmen, and then made his army march (being very well set in order) with great fury against his enemies. They missing the other day's turnings and places of retire, were now compelled to fight all on a front in the plain field: and striving to break into the battle of Pyrrus' footmen before the elephants came, they desperately pressed in upon their enemies' pikes with their swords, not caring for their own persons what became of them, but only looked to kill and destroy their enemies. In the end notwithstanding, after the battle had held out very long, the Romans lost it, and they first began to break and flee on that side where Pyrrus was, by reason of the great force and fury of his charge, and much more through the violence of the elephants: against which, the Roman's valiantness nor courage could aught prevail, but that they were driven to give them place (much like the rage of surging waves, or terrible trembling of the earth) rather then tarry to be trodden under feet, and overthrown by them, whom they were not able to hurt again, but be by them most grievously martyred, and their troubles thereby yet nothing eased. The chase was not long, because they fled but into their camp: and Hieronymus the historiographer writeth, that there died six thousand men of the Romans, and of Pyrrus' part about three thousand five hundred and five, as the king's own chronicles do witness. Nevertheless, Dionysius maketh no mention of two battles given near unto the city of Asculum, nor that the Romans were certainly overthrown: howbeit he confirmeth that there was one battle only that continued until sunset, and that they scarcely severed also when night was come on, Pyrrus being hurt on the arm with a spear, and his carriage robbed and spoiled by the Samnites besides. And further, that there died in this battle, above fifteen thousand men, as well of Pyrrus' side, as of the Romans' part: and that at the last, both the one and the other did retire. And some say, that it was at that time Pyrrus answered one, who rejoiced with him for the victory they had won: 'If we win another of the price,' quoth he, 'we are utterly undone.' For indeed then had he lost the most part of his army he brought with him out of his realm, and all his friends and captains in manner every one, or at the least there lacked little of it: and besides that, he had no means to supply them with other from thence, and perceived also that the confederates he had in Italy began to wax cold. Where the Romans to the contrary, did easily renew their army with fresh soldiers, which they caused to come from Rome as need required, much like unto a lively spring, the head whereof they had at home in their country; and they fainted not at all for any losses they received, but rather were they so much the more hotly bent, stoutly determining to abide out the wars, what ever betide.

22 And thus whilst Pyrrus was troubled in this sort, new hopes and new enterprises were offered unto him, that made him doubtful what to do. For even at a clap came ambassadors to him out of Sicilia, offering to put into his hands the cities of Syracusa, of Agrigentum, and of the Leontines, and beseeching him to aid them to drive the Carthaginians out of the isle, thereby to deliver them from all the tyrants. And on the other side also, news was brought him from Greece, how Ptolomie surnamed the lightning was slain, and all his army overthrown in battle against the Gauls, and that now he should come in good hour for the Macedonians, who lacked but a king. Then he cursed his hard fortune that presented him all at once such sundry occasions to do great things: and as if both enterprises had been already in his hand, he made his account that of necessity he must lose one of them. So, long debating the matter with himself, which of the two ways he should conclude upon, in the end he resolved, that by the wars of Sicilia, there was

good mean to attain to the greater matters, considering that Africa was not far from them. Wherefore, disposing himself that way, he sent Cineas thither immediately to make his way, and to speak to the towns and cities of the country as he was wont to do: and in the meantime left a strong garrison in the city of Tarentum, to keep it at his devotion, wherewith the Tarentines were very angry. For they made request unto him, either to remain in their country to maintain wars with them against the Romans (which was their meaning why they sent for him), or else if he would needs go, at the least wise to leave their city in as good state as he found it. But he answered them again very roughly, that they should speak no more to him in it, and that they should not choose but tarry his occasion. And with this answer took ship, and sailed towards Sicilia: where so soon he was arrived, he found all that he hoped for, for the cities did willingly put themselves into his hands. And where necessity of battle was offered him to employ his army, nothing at the beginning could stand before him. For, with thirty thousand footmen, two thousand five hundred horsemen, and two hundred sail which he brought with him, he drove the Carthaginians before him, and conquered all the country under their obedience. Now at that time, the city of Erix was the strongest place they had: and there were a great number of good soldiers within it to defend it. Pyrrus determined to prove the assault of it, and when his army was ready to give the charge, he armed himself at all pieces from top to toe, and approaching the walls, vowed unto Hercules to give him a solemn sacrifice, with a feast of common plays, so that he would grant him grace to show himself unto the Grecians inhabiting in Sicilia, worthy of the noble ancestors from whence he came, and of the great good fortune he had in his hands. This vow ended, he straight made the trumpets sound to the assault, and caused the barbarous people that were on the walls, to retire with force of his shot. Then when the scaling ladders were set up, himself was the first that mounted on the wall, where he found divers of the barbarous people that resisted him. But some he threw over the walls on either side of him, and with his sword slew many dead about him, himself not once hurt: for the barbarous people had not the heart to look him in the face, his countenance was so terrible. And this doth prove that Homer spoke wisely, and like a man of experience, when he said, that valiantness only amongst all other moral virtues is that which hath sometimes certain furious motions and divine provocations, which make a man besides himself. So the city being taken, he honourably performed his vowed sacrifice to Hercules, and kept a feast of all kinds and sorts of games and weapons.

23 There dwelt a barbarous people at that time about Messina, called the Mamertines, who did much hurt to the Grecians thereabouts, making many of them pay tax and tribute: for they were a great number of them, and all men of war and good soldiers, and had their name also of Mars, because they were martial men, and given to arms. Pyrrus led his army against them, and overthrew them in battle: and put their collectors to death, that did levy and exact the tax, and razed many of their fortresses. And when the Carthaginians required peace and his friendship, offering him ships and money, pretending greater matters, he made them a short answer, that there was but one way to make peace and love between them, to forsake Sicilia altogether, and to be contented to make Mare Libycum the border betwixt Greece and them. For his good fortune, and the force he had in his hands, did set him aloft, and further allured him to follow the hope that brought him into Sicilia, aspiring first of all unto the conquest of Libya. Now, to pass him over thither he had ships enough, but he lacked oars and mariners: wherefore when he would press them, then he began to deal roughly with the cities of Sicilia, and in anger compelled and severely punished them that would not obey his commandment. This he did not at his first coming, but contrarily had won all their goodwills, speaking more courteously to them than any other did, and showing that he trusted them altogether, and troubled them in nothing. But suddenly being altered from a popular prince unto a violent tyrant, he was not only thought cruel and rigorous, but that worst of all is, unfaithful and ingrateful: nevertheless, though they received great hurt by him, yet they suffered it, and granted him any needful thing he did demand. But when they saw he began to mistrust Thaenon and Sostratus, the two chief captains of Syracusa, and they who first caused him to come into Sicilia, who also at his first arrival delivered the city of Syracusa into his hands, and had been his chief aiders in helping him to compass that he had done in Sicilia: when I say, they saw he would no more carry them with

him, nor leave them behind him for the mistrust he had of them, and that Sostratus fled from him, and absented himself, fearing lest Pyrrus would do him some mischief: and that Pyrrus moreover, had put Thaenon to death, mistrusting that he would also have done him some harm. Then all things fell out against Pyrrus, not one after another, nor by little and little, but all together at one instant, and all the cities generally hated him to the death, and did again some of them confederate with the Carthaginians, and others with the Mamertines, to set upon him. But when all Sicilia was thus bent against him, he received letters from the Samnites and Tarentines, by which they advertised him, how they had much ado to defend themselves within their cities and strongholds, and that they were wholly driven out of the field: wherefore they earnestly besought him speedily to come to their aid. This news came happily to him, to cloak his flying, that he might say it was not for despair of good success in Sicilia that he went his way: but true it was indeed, that when he saw he could no longer keep it, than a ship could stand still among the waves, he sought some honest shadow to colour his departing. And that surely was the cause why he returned again into Italy. Nevertheless, at his departure out of Sicily, they say that looking back upon the isle, he said to those that were about him: 'O what a goodly field for a battle, my friends, do we leave to the Romans and Carthaginians, to fight the one with the other?' And verily so it fell out shortly after, as he had spoken.

24   But the barbarous people conspiring together against Pyrrus, the Carthaginians on the one side watching his passage, gave him battle on the sea, in the very strait itself of Messina, where he lost many of his ships, and fled with the rest, and took the coast of Italy. And there the Mamertines on the other side, being gone thither before, to the number of eighteen thousand fighting men, durst not present him battle in open field, but tarried for him in certain straits of the mountains, and in very hard places, and so set upon his rearward, and disordered all his arms. They slew two of his elephants, and cut off a great number of his rearward, so as he was compelled himself in person to come from his vanguard, to help them against the barbarous people, which were lusty valiant men, and old trained soldiers. And there Pyrrus caught a blow on his head with a sword, and was in great danger: insomuch as he was

forced to retire out of the press and fight, which did so much the more encourage his enemies. Among which there was one more adventurous then the rest, a goodly man of personage, fair armed in white armour, who advancing himself far before his company, cried out to the king with a bold and fierce voice, and challenged him to fight with him if he were alive. Pyrrus being mad as it were with this bravery, turned again with his guard, in spite of his men, hurt as he was. And besides that he was all on afire with choler, and his face all bloody and terrible to behold, he went through his men, and came at the length to this barbarous villain that had challenged him: and gave him such a blow on his head with all his force and power, that what by the strength of his arm, and through the goodness of the temper and mettle of the sword, the blow clave his head right in the midst, down to the shoulders: so that his head being thus divided, the one part fell on the one shoulder, and the other part on the other. This matter suddenly stayed the barbarous people, and kept them from going any further, they were so afraid and amazed both to see so great a blow with one's hand, and it made them think indeed that Pyrrus was more than a man. After that, they let him go, and troubled him no more. Pyrrus holding on his journey, arrived at the length in the city of Tarentum, with twenty thousand footmen, and three thousand horse. And with these (joining thereto the choicest picked men of the Tarentines) he went incontinently into the field to seek out the Romans, who had their camp within the territories of the Samnites, which were then in very hard state.

25   For their hearts were killed, because that in many battles and encounters with the Romans, they were ever overthrown. They were very angry besides with Pyrrus, for that he had forsaken them, to go his voyage unto Sicilia, by reason whereof there came no great number of soldiers into his camp. But notwithstanding, he divided all his strength into two parts, whereof he sent the one part into Lucania, to occupy one of the Roman consuls that was there, to the end he should not come to aid his companion: and with the other part he went himself against Manius Curius, who lay in a very strange place of advantage near to the city of Benevento, attending the aid that should come to him out of Lucania, besides also that the soothsayers (by the signs and tokens of the birds and sacrifices) did

counsel him not to start from thence. Pyrrus to the contrary, desiring to fight with Manius before his aid came unto him, which he looked for out of Lucania, took with him the best soldiers he had in all his army, and the warlikest elephants, and marched away in the night, supposing to steal upon Manius on the sudden, and give an assault unto his camp. Now Pyrrus having a long way to go, and through a woody country, his lights and torches failed him, by reason whereof many of his soldiers lost their way, and they lost a great deal of time also, before they could again be gathered together: so as in this space the night was spent, and the day once broken, the enemies perceived plainly how he came down the hills. This at the first sight made them muse a while, and put them in a little fear: nevertheless Manius having had the signs of the sacrifices favourable, and seeing that occasion did press him to it, went out into the field, and set upon the forward of his enemies, and made them turn their backs. The which feared all the rest in such wise, that there were slain a great number of them in the field, and certain elephants also taken. This victory made Manius Curius leave his strength, and come into the plain field, where he set his men in battle ray, and overthrew his enemies by plain force on the one side: but on the other he was repulsed by violence of the elephants, and compelled to draw back into his own camp, wherein he had left a great number of men to guard it. So when he saw them upon the ramparts of his camp all armed, ready to fight, he called them out, and they coming fresh out of places of advantage to charge upon the elephants, compelled them in a very short time to turn their backs, and flee through their own men, whom they put to great trouble and disorder: so as in the end, the whole victory fell upon the Romans' side, and consequently by means of that victory, followed the greatness and power of their empire. For the Romans being grown more courageous by this battle, and having increased their force, and won the reputation of men unconquerable, immediately after conquered all Italy besides, and soon after that, all Sicilia.

26   To this end as you see, came King Pyrrus' vain hope he had to conquer Italy and Sicilia, after he had spent six years continually in wars, during which time his good fortune decayed, and his army consumed. Notwithstanding, his noble courage remained always invincible, what losses soever he had sustained: and moreover

whilst he lived, he was ever esteemed the chiefest of all the kings and princes in his time, as well for his experience and sufficiency in wars, as also for the valiantness and hardiness of his person. But what he won by famous deeds, he lost by vain hopes: desiring so earnestly that which he had not, as he forgot to keep that which he had. Wherefore Antigonus compared him unto a dice player that casts well, but cannot use his luck. Now having brought back again with him into Epirus eight thousand footmen, and five hundred horsemen, and being without money to pay them, he devised with himself to seek out some new war to entertain those soldiers, and keep them together. Wherefore upon a new aid of certain of the Gauls being come unto him, he entered into the realm of Macedon (which Antigonus, Demetrius' son held at that time) with intent only to make a foray, and to get some spoil in the country. But when he saw that he had taken divers holds, and moreover, that two thousand men of war of the country came and yielded themselves unto him, he began to hope of better success, than at the first he looked for. For upon that hope he marched against King Antigonus' self, whom he met in a very straight valley, and at his first coming, gave such a lusty charge upon his rearward, that he put all Antigonus' army in great disorder. For Antigonus had placed the Gauls in the rearward of his army to close it in, which were a convenient number, and did valiantly defend the first charge: and the skirmish was so hot, that the most of them were slain. After them, the leaders of the elephants perceiving they were environed on every side, yielded themselves and their beasts. Pyrrus seeing his power to be now increased with such a supply, trusting more to his good fortune, than any good reason might move him, thrust further into the battle of the Macedonians, who were all afraid, and troubled for the overthrow of their rearward, so as they would not once base their pikes, nor fight against him. He for his part holding up his hand, and calling the captains of the bands by their names, straightways made all the footmen of Antigonus' turn wholly to his side: who flying, saved himself with a few horsemen, and kept certain of the cities in his realm upon the sea coast. But Pyrrus in all his prosperity, judging nothing more to redound to his honour and glory, than the overthrow of the Gauls, laid aside their goodliest and richest spoils, and ordered up the same in the temple of Minerva Itonida, with this inscription:

When Pyrrus had subdued the puissant Gauls in fields,
He caused of their spoils to make these targets, arms,
                                        and shields
The which he hanged up, in temple all on high,
Before Minerva (goddess here) in sign of victory.
When he'had overcome the whole and huge host
The which Antigonus did bring, into his country's coast.
No marvel should it seem, though victory he won,
Since valiantness brings victory, and evermore hath done:
And valiantness always hath constantly kept place,
From age to age, and time to time, in Aeacus his race.

Immediately after this battle, all the cities of the realm of
Macedon yielded unto him: but when he had the city of Aeges in
his power, he used the inhabitants thereof very hardly, and
specially because he left a great garrison of the Gauls there which
he had in pay. This nation is extreme covetous, as then they
showed themselves: for they spared not to break up the tombs
wherein the kings of Macedon lay buried there, took away all the
gold and silver they could find, and afterwards with great
insolency cast out their bones into the open wind. Pyrrus was told
of it, but he lightly passed it over, and made no reckoning of it:
either because he deferred it till another time, by reason of the
wars he had then in hand: or else for that he durst not meddle
with punishing of these barbarous people at that time. But
whatsoever the matter was, the Macedonians were very angry
with Pyrrus, and blamed him greatly for it. Furthermore, having
not yet made all things sure in Macedon, nor being fully possessed
of the same, new toys and hope came into his head, and, mocking
Antigonus, said he was a mad man to go apparelled in purple like
a king, when a poor cloak might become him like a private man.
Now, Cleonymus king of Sparta being come to procure him to
bring his army into the country of Lacedaemon, Pyrrus was very
willing to it. This Cleonymus was of the blood royal of Sparta, but
because he was a cruel man, and would do all things by authority,
they loved him not at Sparta, nor trusted him at all: and therefore
did they put him out, and made Areus king, a very quiet man.
And this was the oldest quarrel Cleonymus had against the
commonwealth of Sparta: but besides that, he had another private
quarrel, which grew upon this cause. In his old years, Cleonymus

had married a fair young lady called Chelidonida, which was also
of the blood royal, and the daughter of Leotychides. This lady
being fallen extremely in love with Acrotatus, King Areus' son, a
goodly young gentleman, and in his lusty youth, she greatly vexed
and dishonoured her husband Cleonymus, who was over head
and ears in love and jealousy with her: for there was not one in all
Sparta, but plainly knew that his wife made none account of him.
And thus his home sorrows, being joined with his outward
common griefs, even for spite, desiring a revenge, in choler he
went to procure Pyrrus to come unto Sparta, to restore him again
to his kingdom. Hereupon he brought him into Lacedaemonia
forthwith, with five and twenty thousand footmen, two thousand
horse, and four and twenty elephants: by which preparation,
though by nothing else, the world might plainly see, that Pyrrus
came with a mind not to restore Cleonymus again unto Sparta,
but of intent to conquer for himself (if he could) all the country of
Peloponnesus. For in words he denied it to the Lacedaemonians
themselves, who sent ambassadors unto him when he was in the
city of Megalipolis, where he told them that he was come into
Peloponnesus, to set the towns and cities at liberty which
Antigonus kept in bondage: and that his true intent and meaning
was to send his young sons into Sparta (so they would be
contented) to the end they might be trained after the Laconian
manner, and from their youth have this advantage above all other
kings, to have been well brought up. But feigning these things,
and abusing those that came to meet him on his way, they took no
heed of him, till he came within the coast of Laconia, into the
which he was no sooner entered, but he began to spoil and waste
the whole country. And when the ambassadors of Sparta reproved
and found fault with him, for that he made wars upon them in
such sort, before he had openly proclaimed it, he made them
answer: 'No more have you yourselves used to proclaim that,
which you purposed to do to others.' Then one of the ambassadors called Mandricidas, replied again unto him in the Laconian
tongue: 'If thou be a god, thou wilt do us no hurt, because we
have not offended thee: and if thou be a man, thou shalt meet
with another that shall be better than thyself.'

27    Then he marched directly to Sparta, where Cleonymus gave him counsel even at the first, to assault it. But he would not so do, fearing (as they said) that if he did it by night, his soldiers would sack the city: and said it should be time enough to assault it the next day at broad daylight, because there were but few men within the town, and beside they were very ill provided. And furthermore, King Areus himself was not there, but gone into Creta to aid the Gortynians, who had wars in their own country. And doubtless, that only was the saving of Sparta from taking, that they made no reckoning to assault it hotly: because they thought it was not able to make resistance. For Pyrrus camped before the town, thoroughly persuaded with himself, that he should find none to fight with him: and Cleonymus' friends and servants also did prepare his lodging there, as if Pyrrus should have come to supper to him, and lodged with him. When night was come, the Lacedaemonians counselled together, and secretly determined to send away their wives and little children into Creta. But the women themselves were against it, and there was one among them called Archidamia, who went into the senate house with a sword in her hand, to speak unto them in the name of all the rest, and said: that they did their wives great wrong, if they thought them so faint-hearted, as to live after Sparta were destroyed. Afterwards it was agreed in council, that they should cast a trench before the enemy's camp, and that at both the ends of the same they should bury carts in the ground unto the midst of the wheels, to the end that being fast set in the ground, they should stay the elephants, and keep them from passing further. And when they began to go in hand withal, there came wives and maids unto them, some of them their clothes girt up round about them, and others all in their smocks, to work at this trench with the old men, advising the young men that should fight the next morning, to rest themselves in the meanwhile. So the women took the third part of the trench to task, which was six cubits broad, four cubits deep, and eight hundred foot long as Philarchus saith: or little less as Hieronymus writeth. Then when the break of day appeared, and the enemies removed to come to the assault, the women themselves fetched the weapons which they put into the young men's hands, and delivered them the task of the trench ready made, which they before had undertaken, praying them valiantly to keep and defend it, telling them withal,

how great a pleasure it is to overcome the enemies, fighting in view and sight of their native country, and what great felicity and honour it is to die in the arms of his mother and wife, after he hath fought valiantly like an honest man, and worthy of the magnanimity of Sparta. But Chelidonida being gone aside, had tied a halter with a riding knot about her neck, ready to strangle and hang herself, rather than to fall into the hands of Cleonymus, if by chance the city should come to be taken.

28 Now Pyrrus marched in person with his battle of footmen, against the front of the Spartans, who being a great number also, did tarry his coming on the other side of the trench: the which, besides that it was very ill to pass over, did let the soldiers also to fight steadily in order of battle, because the earth being newly cast up, did yield under their feet. Wherefore, Ptolomie King Pyrrus' son, passing all along the trench side with two thousand Gauls, and all the choice men of the Chaonians, essayed if he could get over to the other side at one of the ends of the trench where the carts were: which being set very deep into the ground, and one joined unto another, they did not only hinder the assailants, but the defendants also. Howbeit in the end, the Gauls began to pluck off the wheels of these carts, and to draw them into the river. But Acrotatus, King Areus' son, a young man, seeing the danger, ran through the city with a troop of three hundred lusty youths besides, and went to enclose Ptolomie behind before he espied him, for that he passed a secret hollow way till he came even to give the charge upon them: whereby they were enforced to turn their faces towards him, one running in another's neck, and so in great disorder were thrust into the trenches, and under the carts: insomuch as at the last, with much ado, and great bloodshed, Acrotatus and his company drove them back, and repulsed them. Now the women and old men, that were on the other side of the trench, saw plainly before their face, how valiantly Acrotatus had repulsed the Gauls. Wherefore, after Acrotatus had done this exploit, he returned again through the city unto the place from whence he came, all on a gore blood, courageous and lively, for the victory he came newly from. The women of Sparta thought Acrotatus far more noble and fairer to behold, than ever he was: so that they all thought Chelidonida happy to have such a friend and lover. And there were certain old

men that followed him, crying after him, 'Go thy way Acrotatus, and enjoy thy love Chelidonida: beget noble children of her unto Sparta.' The fight was cruel on that side where Pyrrus was, and many of the Spartans fought very valiantly. Howbeit amongst other, there was one named Phillius, who after he had fought long, and slain many of his enemies with his own hands, that forced to pass over the trench: perceiving that his heart fainted for the great number of wounds he had upon him, called one of them that were in the rank next behind him, and giving him his place, fell down dead in the arms of his friends, because his enemies should not have his body.

29   In the end, the battle having continued all the day long, the night did separate them: and Pyrrus being laid in his bed, had this vision in his sleep. He thought he struck the city of Lacedaemon with lightning, and that he utterly consumed it: whereat he was so passing glad, that even with the very joy he awaked, and thereupon forthwith commanded his captains to make their men ready to the assault: and told his dream unto his familiars, supposing that out of doubt it did betoken he should in that approach take the city. All that heard it, believed it was so, saving one Lysimachus: who to the contrary, said that this vision liked him not, because the places smitten with lightning are holy, and it is not lawful to enter into them: by reason whereof he was also afraid, that the gods did signify unto him, that he should not enter into the city of Sparta. Pyrrus answered him: 'That,' said he, 'is a matter disputable to and fro in an open assembly of people, for there is no manner of certainty in it. But furthermore, every man must take his weapon in his hand, and set this sentence before his eyes:

> A right good sign it is, that he would hazard life
> In just defence of master's cause with spear and bloody knife.'

Alluding unto Homer's verses, which he wrote for the defence of his country. And saying thus, he rose, and at the break of day led his army unto the assault. On the other side also, the Lacedaemonians with a marvellous courage and magnanimity, far greater than their force, bestirred themselves wonderfully to make resistance, having their wives by them that gave them their weapons wherewith they fought, and were ready at hand to give meat and drink to them that need, and did also withdraw those that were hurt to cure them. The

Macedonians likewise for their part, endeavoured themselves with all their might to fill up the trench with wood and other things, which they cast upon the dead bodies and armours, lying in the bottom of the ditch: and the Lacedaemonians again laboured all that they could possible to let them. But in this great broil, one perceived Pyrrus a-horseback to have leapt the trench, passed over the strength of the carts, and make force to enter into the city. Wherefore those that were appointed to defend that part of the trench, cried out straight: and the women fell a-shrieking and running, as if all had been lost. And as Pyrrus passed further, striking down with his own hands all that stood before him, a Cretan shot at him, and struck his horse through both sides: who leaping out of the press for pain of his wound, dying, carried Pyrrus away, and threw him upon the hanging of a steep hill, where he was in great danger to fall from the top. This put all his servants and friends about him in a marvellous fear, and therewithal the Lacedaemonians seeing them in this fear and trouble ran immediately unto that place, and with force of shot drove them all out of the trench. After this retire, Pyrrus caused all assault to cease, hoping the Lacedaemonians in the end would yield, considering there were many of them slain in the two days past, and all the rest in manner hurt. Howbeit, the good fortune of the city (whether it were to prove the valiantness of the inhabitants themselves, or at the least to show what power they were of even in their greatest need and distress, when the Lacedaemonians had small hope left) brought one Aminias Phocian from Corinth, one of King Antigonus' captains, with a great band of men, and put them into the city to aid them: and straight after him, as soon as he had entered, King Areus arrived also on the other side from Creta, and two thousand soldiers with him. So the women went home to their houses, making their reckoning that they should not need any more to trouble themselves with wars. They gave the old men liberty also to go and rest themselves, who being past all age to fight, for necessity's sake yet were driven to arm themselves, and take weapon in hand: and in order of battle placed the new-come soldiers in their rooms.

30 Pyrrus understanding that new supplies were come, grew to greater stomach than before, and enforced all that he could, to win the town by assault. But in the end, when to his cost he found that

he won nothing but blows, he gave over the siege, and went to spoil all the country about, determining to lie there in garrison all the winter. He could not for all this avoid his destiny. For there rose a sedition in the city of Argos between two of the chiefest citizens, Aristeas and Aristippus: and because Aristeas thought that King Antigonus did favour his enemy Aristippus, he made haste to send first unto Pyrrus, whose nature and disposition was such, that he did continually heap hope upon hope, ever taking the present prosperity for an occasion to hope after greater to come. And if it fell out he was a loser, then he sought to recover himself, and to restore his loss, by some other new attempts. So that neither for being conqueror, nor overcome, he would ever be quiet, but always troubled some, and himself also: by reason whereof, he suddenly departed towards Argos. But King Areus having laid ambushes for him in divers places, and occupied also the straitest and hardest passages, by the which he was to pass, gave a charge upon the Gauls and Molossians, which were in the tail of his army. Now, the selfsame day Pyrrus was warned by a soothsayer, who sacrificing had found the liver of the sacrificed beast infected: that it betokened the loss of some most near unto him. But when he heard the noise of the charge given, he thought not of the forewarning of his soothsayer, but commanded his son to take his household servants with him, and to go thither: as he himself in the meantime with as great haste as he could, made the rest of his army march, to get them quickly out of this dangerous way. The fray was very hot about Ptolomie Pyrrus' son, for they were all the chief men of the Lacedaemonians with whom he had to do, led by a valiant captain called Evalcus. But as he fought valiantly against those that stood before him, there was a soldier of Creta called Oraesus, born in the city of Aptera, a man very ready of his hand, and light of foot, who running along by him, struck him such a blow on his side, that he fell down dead in the place. This prince Ptolomie being slain, his company began straight to flee: and the Lacedaemonians followed the chase so hotly, that they took no heed of themselves, until they saw they were in the plain field far from their footmen. Wherefore Pyrrus, unto whom the death of his son was newly reported, being afire with sorrow and passion, turned suddenly upon them with the men of arms of the Molossians, and being the first that came unto them, made a marvellous slaughter among them. For, notwithstanding that everywhere before that time he was terrible and invincible, having his sword in his hand: yet then he did show more proof of his valiantness, strength, and courage, than he had ever done before. And when he had set spurs to his horse against Evalcus to close with him, Evalcus turned on the toe side, and gave Pyrrus such a blow with his sword, that he missed little the cutting of his bridle hand: for he cut indeed all the reins of the bridle asunder. But Pyrrus straight ran him through the body with his spear, and lighting off from his horse, he put all the troop of the Lacedaemonians to the sword that were about the body of Evalcus, being all chosen men. Thus the ambition of the captains was cause of that loss unto their country for nothing, considering that the wars against them were ended.

31   But Pyrrus having now as it were made sacrifice of these poor bodies of the Lacedaemonians, for the soul of his dead son, and fought thus wonderfully also to honour his funerals, converting a great part of his sorrow for his death into anger and wrath against the enemies, he afterwards held on his way directly towards Argos. And understanding that King Antigonus had already seized the hills that were over the valley, he lodged near unto the city of Nauplia: and the next morning following sent a herald unto Antigonus, and gave him defiance, calling him wicked man, and challenged him to come down into the valley to fight with him, to try which of them two should be king. Antigonus made him answer, that he made wars as much with time, as with weapon: and furthermore, that if Pyrrus were weary of his life, he had ways open enough to put himself to death. The citizens of Argos also sent ambassadors unto them both, to pray them to depart, since they knew that there was nothing for them to see in the city of Argos, and that they would let it be a neuter, and friend unto them both. King Antigonus agreed unto it, and gave them his son for hostage. Pyrrus also made them fair promise to do so too, but because he gave no caution nor sufficient pledge to perform it, they mistrusted him the more. Then there fell out many great and wonderful tokens, as well unto Pyrrus, as unto the Argives. For Pyrrus having sacrificed oxen, their heads being stricken off from their bodies, they thrust out their tongues, and licked up their own blood. And within the city of Argos, a sister of the temple of Apollo Lycias, called Apollonide, ran through the streets, crying out that she saw the city full of murder, and blood

running all about, and an eagle that came unto the fray, howbeit she vanished away suddenly, and nobody knew what became of her.

32    Pyrrus then coming hard to the walls of Argos in the night, and finding one of the gates called Diamperes opened by Aristeas, he put in his Gauls: who possessed the market place, before the citizens knew anything of it. But because the gate was too low to pass the elephants through with their towers upon their backs, they were driven to take them off, and afterwards when they were within, to put them on in the dark, and in tumult: by reason whereof they lost much time, so that the citizens in the end perceived it, and ran incontinently unto the castle of Aspides, and into other strong places of the city. And therewithal, they sent with present speed unto Antigonus, to pray him to come and help them, and so he did: and after he was come hard to the walls, he remained without with the scouts, and in the meantime sent his son with his chiefest captains into the town, who brought a great number of good soldiers and men of war with them. At the same time also arrived Areus, king of Sparta, with a thousand of the Cretans, and most lusty Spartans: all which joining together, came to give a charge upon the Gauls that were in the market place, who put them in a marvellous fear and hazard. Pyrrus entering on that side also of the city called Cylarabis, with terrible noise and cries, when he understood that the Gauls answered him not lustily and courageously, he doubted straight that it was the voice of men distressed, and that had their hands full. Wherefore, he came on with speed to relieve them, thrusting the horsemen forwards that marched before him, with great danger and pain, by reason of holes, and sinks, and water conduits, whereof the city was full. By this mean there was a wonderful confusion amongst them, as may be thought fighting by night, where no man saw what he had to do, nor could hear what was commanded, by reason of the great noise they made, straying here and there up and down the streets, the one scattered from the other: neither could the captains set their men in order, as well for the darkness of the night, as also for the confused tumult that was all the city over, and for that the streets also were very narrow. And therefore they remained on both sides without doing anything, looking for daylight: at the dawning whereof, Pyrrus perceived the castle of Aspides, full of his armed enemies. And furthermore,

suddenly as he was come into the market place, amongst many other goodly common works set out to beautify the same, he spied the images of a bull and a wolf in copper, the which fought one with another. This sight made him afraid, because at that present he remembered a prophecy that had been told him, that his end and death should be, when he saw a wolf and a bull fight together. The Argives report, that these images were set up in the market place, for the remembrance of a certain chance that had happened in their country. For when Danaus came thither first, by the way called Pyramia (as one would say, land sown with corn) in the country of Thyreatide, he saw as he went a wolf fight with a bull: whereupon he stayed to see what the end of their fight would come to, supposing the case in himself, that the wolf was of his side, because that being a stranger as he was, he came to set upon the natural inhabitants of the country. The wolf in the end obtained the victory: wherefore Danaus making his prayer unto Apollo Lycias, followed on his enterprise, and had so good success, that he drove Gelanor out of Argos, who at that time was king of the Argives. And thus you hear the cause why they say these images of the wolf and bull were set up in the market place of Argos.

33 Pyrrus being half discouraged with the sight of them, and also because nothing fell out well according to his expectation, thought best to retire: but fearing the straitness of the gates of the city, he sent unto his son Helenus, whom he had left without the city with the greatest part of his force and army, commanding him to overthrow a piece of the wall that his men might the more readily get out, and that he might receive them, if their enemies by chance did hinder their coming out. But the messenger whom he sent was so hasty and fearful, with the tumult that troubled him in going out, that he did not well understand what Pyrrus said unto him, but reported his message quite contrary. Whereupon the young prince Helenus taking the best soldiers he had with him, and the rest of his elephants, entered into the city to help his father, who was now giving back: and so long as he had room to fight at ease, retiring still, he valiantly repulsed those that set upon him, turning his face oft unto them. But when he was driven unto the street that went from the market place to the gate of the city, he was kept in with his own men that entered at the same gate to help him. But they could not

hear when Pyrrus cried out, and bade them go back, the noise was so great: and though the first had heard him, and would have gone back, yet they that were behind, and did still thrust forward into the press, did not permit them. Besides this, moreover, the biggest of all the elephants by misfortune fell down overthwart the gate, where he grinding his teeth did hinder those also, that would have come out and given back. Furthermore, another of the elephants that were entered before into the city, called Nicon (as much to say, as conquering), seeking his governor that was stricken down to the ground from his back with terrible blows, ran upon them that came back upon him, overthrowing friends and foes one in another's neck, till at the length having found the body of his master slain, he lift him up from the ground with his trunk, and carrying him upon his two tushes, returned back with great fury, treading all under feet he found in his way. Thus every man being thronged and crowded up together in this sort, there was not one that could help himself: for it seemed to be a mass and heap of a multitude, and one whole body shut together, which sometime thrust forward, and sometime gave back, as the sway went. They fought not so much against their enemies, who set upon them behind: but they did themselves more hurt, than their enemies did. For if any drew out his sword, or based his pike, he could neither scabbard the one again, nor lift up the other, but thrust it full upon his own fellows that came in to help them, and so killed themselves one thrusting upon another.

34   Wherefore Pyrrus seeing his people thus troubled and harried to and fro, took his crown from his head which he ware upon his helmet, that made him known of his men afar off, and gave it unto one of his familiars that was next unto him: and trusting then to the goodness of his horse, flew upon his enemies that followed him. It fortuned that one hurt him with a pike, but the wound was neither dangerous nor great: wherefore Pyrrus set upon him that had hurt him, who was an Argian born, a man of mean condition, and a poor old woman's son, whose mother at that present time was got up to the top of the tiles of a house, as all other women of the city were, to see the fight. And she perceiving that it was her son whom Pyrrus came upon, was so affrighted to see him in that danger, that she took a tile, and with both her hands cast it upon Pyrrus. The tile falling off from his head by reason of his headpiece, lighted full in the nape of

his neck, and broke his neck bone asunder: wherewith he was suddenly so benumbed, that he lost his sight with the blow, the reins of his bridle fell out of his hand, and himself fell from his horse to the ground, by Licymmias' tomb, before any man knew what he was, at the least the common people. Until at the last there came one Zopyrus, that was in pay with Antigonus, and two or three other soldiers also that ran straight to the place, and knowing him, dragged his body into a gate, even as he was coming again to himself out of this trance. This Zopyrus drew out a Slavon sword he wore by his side, to strike off his head. But Pyrrus cast such a grim countenance on him between his eyes, that made him so afraid, and his hand so to shake therewith: that being thus amazed, he did not strike him right in the place where he should have cut off his head, but killed him under his mouth about his chin, so that he was a great while ere he could strike off his head. The matter was straight blown abroad amongst divers: whereupon Alcyoneus running thither, asked for the head that he might know it again. But when he had it, he ran presently unto his father withal, and found him talking with his familiar friends, and cast Pyrrus' head before him. Antigonus looking upon it, when he knew it, laid upon his son with his staff, and called him cruel murderer, and unnatural barbarous beast: and so hiding his eyes with his cloak, wept for pity (remembering the fortune of his grandfather Antigonus, and of his father Demetrius), and then caused Pyrrus head and body to be honourably burnt and buried. Afterwards Alcyoneus meeting Helenus (King Pyrrus' son) in very poor state, muffled up with a poor short cloak, used him very courteously with gentle words, and brought him to his father. Antigonus seeing his son bringing of him, said unto him: 'This part now, my son, is better then the first, and pleaseth me a great deal more. But yet thou hast not done all thou shouldest: for thou shouldest have taken from him his beggarly cloak he weareth, which doth more shame us that are the gainers, than him that is the loser.' After he had spoken these words, Antigonus embraced Helenus, and having apparelled him in good sort, sent him home with honourable convoy into his realm of Epirus. Furthermore, seizing all Pyrrus' camp and army, he courteously received all his friends and servants.

THE END OF PYRRUS' LIFE

# Life of Caius Marius

It is not known what was the third name of Caius Marius, no more than of Quintius Sertorius, who had all Spain in his hands at one time: nor of Lucius Mummius, he that destroyed the city of Corinth. For this name of Achaicus, that was given unto Mummius, of Africanus unto Scipio, and of Numidicus unto Metellus, were all surnames given them by reason of the conquests they won. By this reason Posidonius thinketh to overcome them that say, that the third name the Romans have, is their proper name: as Camillus, Marcellus, Cato. For if it fell out so, said he, then it must needs follow that they which have two names, should have no proper name. But on the other side also, he doth not consider that by the like reason he should say, that women have no names: for there is not a woman in Rome that is called by her first name, which Posidonius judgeth to be the proper name of the Romans. And that of the other two, the one is the common name of all the house or family, as of the Pompeians, of the Manlians, and of the Cornelians, like as the Heraclides and the Pelopides are amongst the Grecians: and the other is a surname taken of the deeds, or of the nature, form, or shape of the body, or of some other like accident, as are these surnames: Macrinus, Torquatus, and Sylla. Even as amongst the Grecians likewise, Mnemon, which signifieth having good memory; Grypos, having a crooked nose; Callinicos, conquering. But as for that, the diversity of custom would deliver objection sufficient to the contrary, to him that listed.

2   And furthermore, as touching the favour of Marius' face, we have seen an image of his in marble at Ravenna, a city of the Gauls, which doth lively represent that rough severity of nature and manner which they say was in him. For being born a rough man by nature, and given to the wars, and having followed the same altogether from his youth, more than the civil life, when he came

to authority, he could not bridle his anger and choleric nature. And they say furthermore, that he never learned the Greek tongue, nor used it in any matters of weight: as though it had been a mockery to study to learn the tongue, the masters whereof lived in bondage under others. After his second triumph, in the dedication of a certain temple, he made Greek plays to show the Romans pastime, and came into the theatre; howbeit he did but sit down only, and went his way straight. Wherefore methinks, that as Plato was wont to say oft unto Xenocrates the philosopher, who was of a currish nature, had his head ever occupied, and too severe: 'Xenocrates, my friend, I pray thee do sacrifice to the Graces.' So if any man could have persuaded Marius to have sacrificed to the Muses, and to the Grecian Graces: (that is to say, that he had known the Greek tongue), to so many famous and glorious deeds as he did, both in peace and wars, he had not joined so unfortunate and miserable an end as he made, through his choler and extreme ambition, at such years, and through an insatiable covetousness, which like boisterous winds made him to make shipwreck of all, in a most cruel, bloody, and unnatural age. The which is easily known in reading the discourse of his doings.

3    First of all he was of a mean house, born of poor parents, by father and mother that got their livings by sweat of their brows. His father, as himself, was called Caius: Fulcinia was his mother. And this was the cause why he began so late to haunt the city, and to learn the civility and manners of Rome, having been brought up always before in a little poor village called Cirroeaton, within the territory of the city of Arpos: where he led a hard country life, in respect of those that lived pleasantly and finely in the cities, but otherwise well reformed, and nearest unto the manners of the ancient Romans. The first journey he made unto the wars, was against the Celtiberians in Spain, under Scipio African, when he went to besiege the city of Numantia: where his captains in short time found that he was a better soldier, than any other of his companions. For he did marvellous easily receive the reformation of manners, and the discipline of wars, which Scipio advanced amongst his soldiers that were ill trained before, and given over to all pleasure. And they say, that in the sight of his general he fought hand to hand with one of his enemies, and slew him: upon which

occasion, Scipio to make him love him, did offer him many courtesies and pleasures. But specially one day above the rest, having made him sup with him at his table, someone after supper falling in talk of captains that were in Rome at that time, one that stood by Scipio asked him (either because indeed he stood in doubt, or else for that he would curry favour with Scipio) what other captain the Romans should have after his death, like unto him. Scipio having Marius by him, gently clapped him upon his shoulder, and said: 'Peradventure this shall be he.' Thus happily were they both born, the one to show from his youth that one day he should come to be a great man, and the other also for wisely conjecturing the end, by seeing of the beginning.

4 Well, it fortuned so, that these words of Scipio (by report) above all things else put Marius in a good hope, as if they had been spoken by the oracle of some god, and made him bold to deal in matters of state and commonwealth: where, by means of the favour and countenance Caecilius Metellus gave him (whose house his father and he had always followed and honoured) he obtained the office of tribuneship. In this office he preferred a law touching the manner how to give the voices in election of the magistrates, which did seem to take from the nobility the authority they had in judgment. And therefore the consul Cotta stepped up against it, and persuaded the senate to resist that law, and not suffer it to be authorised, and therewithal presently to call Marius before them to yield reason of his doing. So was it agreed upon in the senate. Now Marius coming into the senate, was not abashed at anything, as some other young man would have been that had but newly begun to enter into the world as he did: and having no other notable calling or quality in him, saving his virtue only to commend him, but taking boldness of himself (as the noble acts he afterwards did, gave show of his valour) he openly threatened the consul Cotta to send him to prison, if he did not presently withdraw the conclusion he had caused to be resolved upon. The consul then turning himself unto Caecilius Metellus, asked him how he liked it. Metellus standing up, spoke in the behalf of the consul: and then Marius calling a sergeant out, commanded him to take Metellus self, and to carry him to prison. Metellus appealed to the other tribunes, but never a one would take his matter in hand: so that

the senate when all was done, were compelled to call back the conclusion that before was taken. Then Marius returning with great honour into the market place among the assembly of the people, caused this law to pass and be authorised: and every man held opinion of him that he would prove a stout man, and such a one, as would not stoop for any fear, nor shrink for bashfulness, but would beard the senate in favour of the people. Notwithstanding, he shortly after changed opinion, and altered the first, by another act he made. For when another went about to have a law made, to distribute corn unto every citizen without payment of any penny, he was vehemently against it, and overthrew it: so that thereby he came to be alike honoured and esteemed of either party, as he that would neither pleasure the one, nor the other, to the prejudice of the commonwealth.

5    After he had been tribune, he sued for the chiefest office of Aedilis. Of the aediles there are two sorts: the first is called *aedilitas curulis*, so named because of certain chairs that have crooked feet, upon which they sit when they give audience. The other is of less dignity, and that is called *aedilitas popularis*: and when they have chosen the first and greater Aedilis at Rome, they presently proceed the same day also in the market place unto election of the lesser. Marius seeing plainly that he was put by the chiefest of the aediles, turned again straight yet to demand the second: but this was misliked in him, and they took him for too bold, too shameless, and too presumptuous a man. So that in one self day he had two denials and repulses, which never man but himself before had. And nevertheless, all this could not cut his comb, but shortly after he sued also for the praetorship, and he lacked but little of the denial of that: yet in the end, being last of all chosen, he was accused to have bribed the people, and bought their voices for money. And surely amongst many other, this presumption was very great, that they saw a man of Cassius Sabacon within the bars where the election is made, running to and fro among them that gave their voices, because this Sabacon was Marius' very great friend. The matter came before the judges, and Sabacon was examined upon it. Whereunto he answered, that for the great extreme heat he felt, he was very dry, and asked for cold water to drink, and that this man had brought him some in a pot where he was: howbeit that he

went his way as soon as ever he had drunk. This Sabacon was afterwards put out of the senate by the next censors, and many judge that he was worthy of this infamy, for that he was perjured in judgment, or because he was so subject and given to his pleasure. Caius Herennius was also called for a witness against Marius: but he did allege for his excuse, that the law and custom did dispense with the patron, to be a witness against his follower and client, and he was quit by the judges – for the Romans always call those patrons, who take the protection of meaner than themselves into their hands – saying, that Marius' predecessors, and Marius himself, had ever been followers of the house of the Herennians. The judges received his answer, and allowed thereof. But Marius spoke against it, alleging, that since he had received this honour to bear office in the commonwealth, he was now grown from this base condition, to be any more a follower of any man: the which was not true in all. For every office of a magistrate doth not exempt him that has the office, nor yet his posterity, to be under the patronage of another, nor doth discharge him from the duty of honouring them: but of necessity he must be a magistrate, which the law doth permit to sit in the crooked chair called *curulis*, that is to say, carried upon a chariot through the city. But notwithstanding that at the first hearing of this cause, Marius had but ill success, and that the judges were against him all they could: yet in the end for all that, at the last hearing of his matter, Marius, contrary to all men's opinions, was discharged, because the judges' opinions with and against him fell to be of like number.

6    He used himself very orderly in his office of praetorship, and after his year was out, when it came to divide the provinces by lot, Spain fell unto him, which is beyond the river of Baetis: where it is reported that he scoured all the country thereabouts of thieves and robbers, which notwithstanding was yet very cruel and savage, for the rude, barbarous, and uncivil manner and fashion of life of the inhabitants there. For the Spaniards were of opinion even at that time, that it was a goodly thing to live upon theft and robbery. At his return to Rome out of Spain, desiring to deal in matters of the commonwealth, he saw that he had neither eloquence nor riches, which were the two means, by the which those that were at that time in credit and authority, did carry the people even as they

would. Notwithstanding, they made great account of his constancy and noble mind they found in him, of his great pains and travel he took continually, and of the simplicity of his life: which were causes to bring him to honour and preferment, insomuch as he married very highly. For he married Julia, that was of the noble house of the Caesars, and aunt unto Julius Caesar: who afterwards came to be the chiefest man of all the Romans, and who by reason of that alliance between them, seemed in some things to follow Marius, as we have written in his life. Marius was a man of great temperance and patience, as may be judged by an act he did, putting himself into the hands of surgeons. For his shanks and legs were full of great swollen veins, and being angry because it was no pleasant thing to behold, he determined to put himself into the hands of surgeons to be cured. And first, laying out one of his legs to the surgeon to work upon, he would not be bound as others are in the like case: but patiently abode all the extreme pains a man must of necessity feel being cut, without stirring, groaning, or sighing, still keeping his countenance, and said never a word. But when the surgeon had done with his first leg, and would have gone to the other, he would not give it him: 'Nay,' said he, 'I see the cure is not worth the pain I must abide.'

7 Afterwards, Caecilius Metellus the consul, being appointed to go into Africa to make war with King Iugurthe, took Marius with him for one of his lieutenants. Marius being there, seeing notable good service to be done, and good occasion to show his manhood, was not of mind in this voyage to increase Metellus' honour and reputation, as other lieutenants did: and thought that it was not Metellus that called him forth for his lieutenant, but fortune herself that presented him a fit occasion to raise him to greatness, and (as it were) did lead him by the hand into a goodly field, to put him to the proof of that he could do. And for this cause therefore, he endeavoured himself to show all the possible proofs of valiantness and honour he could. For, the wars being great continually there, he never for fear refused any attempt or service, how dangerous or painful soever it were, neither disdained to take any service in hand, were it never so little: but exceeding all other his fellows and companions in wisdom and foresight, in that which was to be done, and striving with the meanest soldiers in living hardly and

painfully, won the goodwill and favour of every man. For to say truly, it is a great comfort and refreshing to soldiers that labour, to have companions that labour willingly with them. For they think, that their company labouring with them, doth in manner take away the compulsion and necessity. Furthermore, it pleaseth the Roman soldier marvellously to see the general eat openly of the same bread he eateth, or that he lieth on a hard bed as he doth, or that himself is the first man to set his hand to any work when a trench is to be cast, or their camp to be fortified. For they do not so much esteem the captains that honour and reward them, as they do those that in dangerous attempts labour, and venture their lives with them. And further, they do far better love them that take pains with them, than those that suffer them to live idly by them. Marius performing all this, and winning thereby the love and goodwills of his soldiers, he straight filled all Libya and the city of Rome with his glory, so that he was in every man's mouth. For they that were in the camp in Africa, wrote unto them that were at Rome, that they should never see the end of these wars against this barbarous king, if they gave not the charge unto Marius, and chose him consul.

8   These things misliked Metellus very much, but specially the misfortune that came upon Turpilius, did marvellously trouble him: which fell out in this sort. Turpilius was Metellus' friend, yea he and all his parents had followed Metellus in this war, being master of the works in his camp. Metellus made him governor over the city of Vacca, a goodly great city: and he using the inhabitants of the same very gently and courteously, mistrusted nothing, till he was fallen into the hands of his enemies through their treason. For they had brought King Iugurthe into their city unknowing to him, howbeit they did him no hurt, but only begged him of the king, and let him go his way safe. And this was the cause why they accused Turpilius of treason. Marius being one of his judges in the council, was not contented to be bitter to him himself, but moved many of the council besides to be against him. So that Metellus by the voices of the people, was driven against his will to condemn him to suffer as a traitor: and shortly after it was found, and proved, that Turpilius was wrongfully condemned and put to death. To say truly, there was not one of the council but were very sorry with Metellus, who marvellous impatiently took the death of the poor

innocent. But Marius contrarily rejoiced, and took it upon him that he pursued his death, and was not ashamed to make open vaunts, that he had hanged a fury about Metellus' neck, to revenge his friend's blood, whom he guiltless had caused to be put to death. After that time they became mortal enemies. And they say, that one day Metellus to mock him withal, said unto him: 'O good man, thou wilt leave us then, and return to Rome to sue for the consulship, and canst thou not be contented to tarry to be consul with my son?' Now his son at that time was but a boy. But whatsoever the matter meant, Marius left him not so, but laboured for leave all he could possible. And Metellus after he had used many delays and excuses, at the length gave him leave, twelve days only before the day of election of the consuls. Wherefore Marius made haste, and in two days and a night came from the camp to Utica upon the sea side, which is a marvellous way from it: and there before he took ship, did sacrifice unto the gods, and the soothsayer told him, that the gods by the signs of his sacrifices, did promise him uncredible prosperity, and so great, as he himself durst not hope after. These words made Marius heart greater. Whereupon he hoist sail, and having a passing good gale of wind in the poop of the ship, passed the seas in four days, and being landed, rode post to Rome. When he was arrived, he went to show himself unto the people: who were marvellous desirous to see him. And being brought by one of the tribunes of the people unto the pulpit for orations, after many accusations which he objected against Metellus, in the end he besought the people to choose him consul, promising that within few days he would either kill, or take King Iugurthe prisoner.

9   Whereupon he was chosen consul without any contradiction. And so soon as he was proclaimed, he began immediately to levy men of war, causing many poor men that had nothing, and many slaves also, to be enrolled against the order of ancient custom: where other captains before him did receive no such manner of men, and did no more suffer unworthy men to be soldiers, than they did allow of unworthy officers in the commonwealth: in doing the which every one of them that were enrolled, left their goods behind them, as a pledge of their good service abroad in the wars. Yet this was not the matter that made Marius to be most

hated, but they were his stout proud words, full of contempt of others, that did chiefly offend the noblemen in the city. For he proclaimed it everywhere abroad as it were, that his consulship was a spoil he had gotten of the effeminate rich noblemen through his valiantness, and that the wounds which he had upon his body for service of the commonwealth, and not the monuments of the dead, nor the images and statues of others, were those that recommended him to the people, nor wear his strength. And ofttimes naming Albinus, and otherwhile Bestia, both noblemen, and of great houses, who having been generals of the Roman army, had very ill fortune in the country of Libya, he called them cowards, and simple soldiers, asking them that were about him, if they did not think that their ancestors would rather have wished to have left their children that came of them like unto himself, than such as they had been: considering that they themselves had won honour and glory, not for that they were descended of noble blood, but through their deserved virtue and valiant deeds. Now Marius spoke not these words in a foolish bravery, and for vainglory only, to purchase the ill will of the nobility for nothing: but the common people being very glad to see him shame and despite the senate, and measuring always the greatness of his courage with his haughty fierce words, they egged him forward still not to spare the nobility, and to reprove the great men, so that he ever held with the commonalty.

10 And furthermore, when he was passed over again into Africa, it spited Metellus to the heart, because that he having ended all the war, that there remained almost no more to take or win, Marius should come in that sort to take away the glory and triumph out of his hands, having sought to rise and increase by unthankfulness towards him. He would not come to him therefore, but went another way, and left the army with Rutilius one of his lieutenants, to deliver the same unto him. Howbeit the revenge of this ingratitude lighted in the end upon Marius' own neck. For Sylla took out of Marius' hands the honour of ending this war, even as Marius had taken it from Metellus. But how, and after what sort, I will repeat it in few words, because we have written the particularities more at large in the life of Sylla. Bocchus king of high Numidia, was father-in-law unto King Iugurthe, unto whom

he gave no great aid, whilst he made wars with the Romans, because he hated his unfaithfulness, and feared lest he would make himself greater than he was: but in the end, after Iugurthe had fled, and wandered up and down in every place, he was constrained of very necessity to cast his last hope and anchor upon him, as his final refuge, and so repair unto him. King Bocchus received him rather for shame, because he durst not punish him, than for any love or goodwill he bore him: and having him in his hands, seemed openly to entreat Marius for him, and secretly to write the contrary unto him. But in the meantime, he practised treason under hand, and sent privily for Lucius Sylla, who then was quaestor (to say, high treasurer) under Marius, and of whom he had received certain pleasures in those wars. Sylla trusting to this barbarous king, went at his sending for to him. But when he was come, King Bocchus repented him of his promise, and altered his mind, standing many days in doubt with himself how to resolve, whether he should deliver King Iugurthe, or keep Sylla himself: yet at the last he went on with his purpose and intended treason, and delivered King Iugurthe alive into Sylla's hands. And this was the first original cause of the pestilent and mortal enmity that grew afterwards betwixt Marius and Sylla, and was like to have utterly overthrown the city of Rome, and to have razed the foundation of the empire unto the ground. For many envying the glory of Marius, gave it out everywhere, that this act of the taking of King Iugurthe appertained only unto Sylla: and Sylla himself caused a ring to be made, which he ware commonly, and had graven upon the stone of the same, how Bocchus delivered Iugurthe into his hands. And afterwards he made it always his seal to despite Marius withal, who was an ambitious and proud man, and could abide no companion to be partaker of the glory of his doings: and Sylla did it specially at the procurement of enemies and ill willers, who gave the glory of the beginning and chief exploits of this war, unto Metellus, and the last and final conclusion unto Sylla, to the end that the people should not have Marius in so great estimation and good opinion, as they had before.

11   But all this envy, detraction, and hatred against Marius, was soon after extinguished and trodden under foot, by reason of the great danger that fell upon all Italy out of the West: and they never

spoke of it afterwards, knowing that the commonwealth stood in need of a good captain, and that they began to look about, and consider who should be that great wise pilot, that might save and preserve it from so exceeding dangerous storm of wars. For there was not a nobleman of all the ancient houses of Rome, that durst undertake to offer himself to demand the consulship: but Marius being absent, was chosen consul the second time. For Iugurthe was no sooner taken, but news came to Rome of the coming down of the Teutons, and of the Cimbres, the which would not be believed at the first, by reason of the infinite number of the fighting men which was said to be in their company, and for the uncredible force and power of armies which was justified to come also: but afterwards they knew plainly, that the rumour that ran abroad was less, than the truth fell out indeed. For they were three hundred thousand fighting men all armed, who brought with them also another multitude as great (or more) of women and children: which wandered up and down seeking countries and towns to dwell and live in, as they heard say the Gauls had done in old time, who leaving their own country, came, and had possessed the best part of Italy, which they had taken away from the Thuscans. Now to say truly, no man knew of what nation they were, nor from whence they came: as well for that they had no friendship with any other people, as also because they came out of a far country, as a cloud of people that was spread all over Gaul and Italy. It was doubted much that they came out of Germany, dwelling about the north sea: and this they conjectured by view of the greatness of their bodies, and also for that they had dark blue eyes and red hair, besides that the Germans in their tongue do call thieves and robbers, Cimbri. Others say that Celtica, for the great length and largeness of the country, stretching itself from the coast of the great Ocean sea and from the north parts, drawing towards the marshes Moeotides, and the East runneth into Scythia, or Tartaria Pontica: and that for neighbourhood these two nations joined together, and went out of their country, not that they made this great voyage all at one time, but at many sundry times, marching yearly in the spring further and further into the country. And thus by continuance of time, they passed by force of arms through all the firm land of Europe: and that for this cause, although they had many particular names according to the diversity of their nations, yet all this mass and multitude of people gathered together, were called notwithstanding, the army of the Celtoscythes, as who would say, the Celtotartares. Others hold opinion that the nation of the Cimmerians, who were known in old time for ancient Grecians, the one part of them were not very great in respect of the whole, the which being fled (or driven out of their country for some civil dissension) were compelled by the Tartars to pass beyond the marshes Moeotides, into the countries of Asia, under the conduction of a captain called Ligdamis. But the residue of them which were a far greater number, and more warlike men, they dwelt in the furthest parts of the earth, adjoining unto the great Ocean sea, in a dark shadowed country, covered with wonderful forests, of such length, and so great and thick, and the trees so high, that the sun can have no power upon the ground, and they join hard upon the great forest of Hercynia. And furthermore, they are under such a climate, where the pole is of such a height by the inclination of the circles equidistant, which they call Parallels, that it is not far from the point that answereth directly to the plummet upon the head of the inhabitants: and where the days are equinoctial, they do divide all their time in two parts, the which giveth Homer occasion to feign, that when Ulysses would call upon the dead, he went into the country of the Cimmerians, as into the country of hell. And this is the cause why they say these barbarous people left their own countries to come into Italy, which from the beginning were called Cimmerians, and afterwards they say (and not without great likelihood) that they were surnamed Cimbres: howbeit that is spoken rather by a likely conjecture, than by any assured truth of history. And as for the multitude of men, the most part of historiographers do write, that they were rather more, than less than we have spoken of: and that they were so hardy and valiant, that nothing could stand before them, they did so great things by the strength of their hands where they fought with any, so violently and so suddenly, that they seemed to be like a lightning fire all about where they came. By means whereof, they met with no man that durst resist them, but scraped together and carried away all that they found, hand over head: and there were many Roman captains appointed governors to keep that which the Romans held in Gaul beyond the mountains, who with great armies were shamefully overthrown by them. The cowardliness of those whom they had overcome, was the chiefest cause that moved them to direct their journey to Rome. For when they had vanquished the first they fought withal, and got great riches also, they were so fleshed by this, that they determined to stay nowhere before they had first destroyed Rome, and sacked all Italy.

12 The Romans hearing of this out of all parts, sent for Marius to give him the conduction and leading of these wars, and chose him consul the second time: notwithstanding that it was directly against the law, that did expressly forbid any man to be chosen being absent, and until also a certain time appointed had passed between the vacation and election, before they could choose him officer twice in one office. Some alleged this law, of intent to hinder the election. But the people repulsed them, objecting to the contrary, that this was not the first time the law had given place to the benefit of the commonwealth, and that the occasion offered to abrogate the law at that present was no less, than former occasions by the which they chose Scipio consul, against the course and time appointed by the law, not for any fear they stood in to lose their own country, but for the desire they had to destroy the country of the Carthaginians, by reason whereof the people proceeded to election. And Marius bringing home his army again out of Libya into Italy, took possession of his consulship the first day of January (on which day the Romans begin their year) and therewithal made his triumph into the city of Rome, showing that to the Romans, which they thought never to have seen: and that was, King Iugurthe prisoner, who was so subtle a man, and could so well frame himself unto his fortune, and with his craft and subtlety was of so great courage besides, that none of his enemies ever hoped to have had him alive. But it is said, that after he was led in this triumph, he fell mad straight upon it. And the pomp of triumph being ended, he was carried into prison, where the sergeants for haste to have the spoil of him, tore his apparel by force from off his back: and because they would take away his rich gold earrings that hung at his ears, they pulled away with them the tip of his ear, and then cast him naked to the bottom of a deep dungeon, his wits being altogether troubled. Yet when they did throw him down, laughing he said: 'O Hercules, how cold are your stoves.' He lived there yet six days, fighting with hunger, and desiring always to prolong his miserable life unto the last hour: the

which was a just deserved punishment for his wicked life. In this triumph were carried (as they say) three thousand and seven hundred pound weight in gold, and of silver nuggets, five thousand seven hundred and lxxv pound weight: and more in gold and ready coin, eight and twenty thousand and seven hundred crowns. After this triumph, Marius caused the senate to assemble within the capitol, where he entered into the company with his triumphing robe, either because he forgot it, or else of too gross and uncivil arrogancy: but perceiving that all the assembly misliked of it, he rose suddenly, and took his long consul's gown, and then returned quickly again into his place.

13   Furthermore Marius departing to go to the wars, thought to train his army by the way, and to harden his soldiers unto labour, causing them to run every way, making great long journeys, compelling each soldier to carry his own furniture, and to prepare him necessary victuals to find himself withal: so that ever after they made a proverb of it, and called such as were painful and willing to do that which they were commanded without grudging, Marius' mules. Other notwithstanding, do show another cause and beginning of this proverb. For they say, that Scipio lying at the siege of the city of Numantia, would not only take view of the armour and horses of service that were in his army, but also of the mules and other beasts of burden, because he would see how they were kept and furnished. So Marius brought his horse and mule to the muster which he kept himself, fat, fair, and very well dressed, and his mule's hair so slick and smooth, and therewithal so lusty and trim, as none of the rest were like unto them. Scipio took great pleasure to see these beasts so well kept, and in so good plight: insomuch as he spoke of it afterwards many a time and oft. And upon his words, this manner of talk was taken up ever after, and became a common proverb: when they mean to mock any man that is painful, and given to sore labour, making as though they would praise him, they call him Marius' mule.

14   Furthermore, it was a happy turn for Marius (in mine opinion) that these barbarous people (like in force to the beating back of the raging seas) turned their first fury towards Spain: and that he in the mean space had time and leisure to train and exercise his soldiers, to make them bold, and withal, himself to be thoroughly known

amongst them. For when by little and little they had learned not to offend, nor disobey, then they found his rough commanding, and sharp severity in punishing such as slack their duty, both profitable and very necessary, besides that it was also just and reasonable. Again, his great fury, his sharp words, and his fierce looks, after they had a while been used to them, by little and little they seemed nothing so fearful to them, as to their enemies. But the thing that pleased the soldiers more then all the rest, was his justice and upright dealing: whereof they report such an example: Marius had a nephew of his in his camp called Caius Lusius, who had charge of men in the army. This Lusius was taken for a marvellous honest man, saving that he had this foul vice in him, that he would be suddenly in love with fair young boys: and as at that time he fell in love with a trim young stripling, called Trebonius, that served under him, and having many times lewdly enticed him, and never could obtain his purpose, at the last sent for him one night by his servant. The young man might not disobey his captain being sent for, but presently went unto him. When he was come into his tent, and that his captain did strive with all his force to do him villainy, he drew out his sword, and killed him in the place. And this was done when Marius was out of his camp: who so soon as he returned, caused the marshal to bring the young man before him. Many stepped forth straight to accuse him, but no man to defend him. Wherefore he boldly began to tell his tale himself, and to name many witnesses, who had both seen and known how his dead captain had oftentimes offered him dishonour, and how that he had continually resisted his abominable motion, and would never yield himself unto him, for any gift or present he could offer him. Wherefore Marius commending him greatly, and being very glad of it, caused presently one of those crowns to be brought unto him, which are used to be given to them that in a day of battle have done some valiant deed, and he himself did crown Trebonius withal, as one that had done a noble act, and at such a time, as good and honest examples were requisite. This judgment of Marius being carried to Rome, stood him to great good purpose towards the obtaining of his third consulship: besides also that they looked for the coming back of these barbarous people about the spring, with whom the Roman soldiers would not fight under any other captain than Marius. Howbeit they came not so soon again as they looked for them, but Marius passed over also the year of his third consulship. So time coming about again for the election of new consuls, and his companion also being dead, he was driven to go himself unto Rome, leaving the charge of his camp in his absence unto Manius Acilius. At that time there were many noblemen that sued for the consulship: but Lucius Saturninus, one of the tribunes, who had the commonalty under his girdle as he would himself, more than any of the other tribunes, and being won underhand by Marius, made many orations, in the which he persuaded the people to choose Marius consul the fourth time. Marius to the contrary, seemed to refuse it, saying that he would none of it, though the people chose him. Whereupon Saturninus called him traitor, crying out, that his refusal in such a danger and time of necessity, was an apparent part to bewray the commonwealth. It was found straight that this was a gross pact betwixt Saturninus and Marius, by such as could see day at a little hole. Nevertheless, the people considering that their present troubles required Marius' skill and good fortune in the wars, they made him consul the fourth time, and joined Catulus Luctatius consul with him, a man that was greatly honoured of the nobility, and not misliked also of the common people.

15  Marius having news of the approaching of the barbarous people, passed over the Alps with great speed, and fortifying his camp by the river of Rhone, he brought great provision of all kinds of victuals thither with him, lest being straited by lack thereof, he should be forced to come to battle at any other time, but even as he would himself, and as it should seem good unto him. And where before that time the transporting of victuals unto his camp by sea was very long and dangerous, and a marvellous great charge besides, he made it very short and easy by this means. The mouth of the river of Rhone had gathered together so much mud, and such store of sand, which the waves of the sea had cast on heaps together, that the same was become very high and deep: so as the banks made the entry into it very narrow, hard, and dangerous for great ships of burden that came from the sea. Marius considering this matter, set his men a work while they had nothing to do, and made them dig a large trench and deep channel, into the which he turned a great part of the river, and carried it to a convenient place

of the coast, where the water fell into the sea by an open gulf, whereby he made it able to carry the greatest ships that were: and besides that, it was in a very still quiet place, not being troubled with winds nor waves. The channel carrieth yet his name, and is called Marius' channel or trench. These barbarous people divided themselves into two armies to pass into Italy, so that it fell out to the one part, which were the Cimbres, to go through high Germany, and to force that passage which Catulus kept: and unto the other part, which were the Teutons and Ambrons, to pass through the country of the Genouesians by the sea side against Marius. Now the Cimbres having the greater compass to fetch about, stayed longer, and remained behind: but the Teutons and the Ambrons going their way first, had in few days dispatched their journey they had to go, to bring them to the camp where the Romans lay, unto whom they presented themselves by infinite numbers, with terrible faces to behold, and their cries and voices far contrary unto other men's. They took in a marvellous deal of ground in length to camp upon, and so came forth to defy Marius, and provoke him to battle in open field.

16 Marius made no reckoning of all their bragging defiances, but kept his men together within his camp, taking on terribly with them that would rashly take upon them to move aught to the contrary, and which through impatience of choler would needs go forth to fight, calling them traitors to their country. 'For,' said he, 'we are not come to fight for our private glory, neither to win two triumphs nor victories for ourselves: but we must seek by all means to divert and put by this great shower of wars from us, and this lightning and tempest, that it overcome not all Italy.' These words he spoke unto the private captains which were under him, as unto men of havior and quality. But as for the common soldiers, he made them stand upon the trenches of his camp, one after another, to behold the enemies, and to acquaint themselves with sight of their faces, their countenance, and marching, and not to be afraid of their voices to hear them speak, which were wonderful, both strange and beastly: and also that they might know the fashion of their weapons, and how they handled them. And by this order and ordinary viewing of them, in time he made the things that seemed fearful unto his men at the first sight, to be afterwards very familiar:

so that they made no more wondering at them. For he judged, the thing which indeed is true, that a rare and new matter never seen before, for lack of judgment and understanding, makes things unknown to us more horrible and fearful than they are: and to the contrary, that custom takes away a great deal of fear, and terror of those things, which by nature are indeed fearful. The which was seen then by experience. For they being daily acquainted to look upon these barbarous people, it did not only diminish some part of the former fear of the Roman soldiers: but furthermore they whetting their choler with the fierce intolerable threats and brags of these barbarous brutish people, did set their hearts afire to fight with them, because they did not only waste and destroy all the country about them, but besides that, came to give assault even unto their camp with such a boldness, that the Roman soldiers could no longer suffer them, and they let not to speak words that came to Marius' ears himself. 'What cowardliness hath Marius ever known in us, that he keeps us thus from fighting, and under lock and key as it were, in the guard of porters, as if we were women? Let us therefore show ourselves like men, and go ask him if he look for any other soldiers beside ourselves to defend Italy: and if he have determined to employ us as pioneers only, when he would cast a trench to rid away the mud, or to turn a river contrary. For therein hath he only hitherunto employed us in great labour, and they are the notable works he hath done in his two consulships, whereof he maketh his boast unto them at Rome. Is he afraid they should take him, as they did Carbo and Caepio, whom the enemies have overthrown? He must not be afraid of that: for he is a captain of another manner of valour and reputation than they were, and his army much better then theirs was. But howsoever it be, yet were it much better in proving to lose something, than to be idle, and to suffer our friends and confederates to be destroyed and sacked before our eyes.'

17   Marius was marvellous glad to hear his men complain thus, and did comfort them, and told them that he did nothing mistrust their courage and valiantness: howbeit that through the counsel of certain prophecies and oracles of the gods, he did expect time and place fit for victory. For he ever carried a Syrian woman in a litter about with him called Martha, with great reverence, whom they

said had the spirit of prophecy in her: and that he did ever sacrifice unto the gods by her order, and at such time as she willed him to do it. This Syrian woman went first to speak with the senate about these matters, and did foretell and prognosticate what should follow. But the senate would not hear her, and made her to be driven away. Whereupon she went unto the women, and made them see proof of some things she vaunted of, and specially Marius' wife, at whose feet she was set one day in an assembly of the common plays, to see swordplayers fight for life and death: for she told her certainly which of them should overcome. Whereupon this lady sent her unto her husband Marius, who made great reckoning of her, and carried her even in a litter with him wheresoever he went. She was always at Marius' sacrifices, apparelled in a gown of purple in grain, clasped to her with clasps, and held a spear in her hand wound all about with nosegays, and garlands of flowers tied on with laces. This manner of geste made many doubt whether Marius showed this woman openly, believing indeed that she had the gift of prophecy: or else that knowing the contrary, he made as though he did believe it, to help her feigning. But that which Alexander the Myndian wrote touching vultures, is a thing greatly to be wondered at. For he said there were two of them followed Marius in his wars, and that they ever showed themselves and missed not, when he should win any great battle, and that they did know them by Latin collars they ware about their necks, which the soldiers had tied about them, and afterwards let them go where they would: by reason whereof, they did know the soldiers again, and it seemed also that they did salute them, and were very glad when they saw them, and persuaded themselves, that it was a sign and token of good luck to follow. Many signs and tokens were seen before the battle: howbeit all the rest were ordinary sights, saving that which was reported to be seen at Tudertum, and Ameria, two cities of Italy. For they say there were seen spears and targets in the night, burning like fire in the element, which first were carried up and down here and there, and then met together, even as men move and stir that fight one with another: until at the length, the one giving back, and the other following after, they all vanished away, and consumed towards the West. About the selfsame time also, there came from the city of Pessinunta, Batabaces, the chief priest of the great mother of the gods, who brought news, that the goddess had spoken to him within her sanctuary, and told him that the victory of this war should fall out on the Romans' side. The senate believed it, and ordained that they should build a temple unto that goddess, to give her thanks for the victory which she did promise them. Batabaces also would have presented himself unto the people in open assembly, to tell them as much. But there was one Aulus Pompeius, a tribune, that would not suffer him to do it, calling him tumbler, or juggler, and violently thrust him behind the pulpit for orations: but the mischance that fell upon Pompeius afterwards, made them the more to believe Batabaces' words. For Pompeius the tribune no sooner came home unto his house, but a great vehement ague took him, whereof he died the seventh day after, as all the world could witness.

18    Now the Teutons perceiving that Marius stirred not at all out of his camp, they proved to assault him: howbeit they were so well received with shot and slings, that after they had lost certain of their men, they gave it over, and determined to go further, persuading themselves that they might easily pass the Alps without danger. Wherefore trussing up all their baggage, they passed by Marius' camp: at which time it appeared more certainly than before, that they were a marvellous great multitude of people, by the length of time which they took to pass their way. For it is said they were passing by his camp, six days continually together. And as they came raking by the Roman's camp, they asked them in mockery, if they would write or send home anything to their wives, for they would be with them ere it were long. When they were all passed and gone, and that they continued on their journey still, Marius also raised his camp, and went and followed them fair and softly foot by foot, and ever kept hard at their tail as near as he could, always fortifying his camp very well, and ever choosing strong places of situation and advantage to lodge in, that they might be safe in the night time. Thus they marched on in this sort, until they came unto the city of Aix, from whence they had not far to go, but they entered straight into the mountains of the Alps. Wherefore Marius prepared now to fight with them: and chose out a place that was very strong of situation to lodge his camp in, howbeit there lacked water. And they say he did it of purpose, to the end to

quicken his men's courage the more thereby. Many repined at it, and told him that they should stand in great danger to abide marvellous thirst if they lodged there. Whereunto he made answer: showing them the river that ran hard by the enemy's camp, saying withal that they must go thither and buy drink with their blood. The soldiers replied again: 'And why then do ye not lead us thither, whilst our blood is yet moist?' He gently answered them again: 'Because the first thing we do, we must fortify our camp.'

19  The soldiers, though they were angry with him, yet they obeyed him, but the slaves having neither drink for themselves, nor for their cattle, gathered together a great troop of them, and went towards the river: some of them carrying axes, other hatchets, other swords and spears, with their pots to carry water, determining to fight with the barbarous people, if otherwise they could not come by it. A few of the barbarous people at the first fought with them, because the most part of their company were at dinner, after they had bathed, and others were still in the bath washing themselves, finding in that place many springs of hot natural baths. Thus the Romans found many of the barbarous people making merry, and taking their pleasure about these baths, for the great delight they took to consider the pleasantness of the place: but when they heard the noise of them that fought, they began to run one after another unto the place from whence the noise came. Wherefore it was a hard thing for Marius any longer to keep the Roman soldiers in from going to their help, for that they feared their slaves should have been slain of the barbarous people: and moreover, because the valiantest soldiers of their enemies called the Ambrons (who before had overcome Manlius and Caepio, two Roman captains with their armies, and that made of themselves thirty thousand fighting men) ran to arms, being very heavy of their bodies, as having filled their bellies well, but otherwise valiant and courageous fellows, and more lively than they were wont to be, by reason of the wine they had drunk. They ran not furiously to fight out of order, neither did they cry out confusedly, but marching all together in good array, making a noise with their harness all after one sort, they oft rehearsed their own name, 'Ambrons, Ambrons, Ambrons': which was, either to call one another of them, or else to fear the Romans with their name only. The Italians also on the other side, being

the first that came down to fight with them, were the Ligurians, dwelling upon the coast of Genuoa, who hearing this noise and cry of theirs, plainly understanding them, answered them again with the like noise and cry, 'Ligurians, Ligurians, Ligurians', saying that it was the true surname of all their nation. And so before they joined together, this cry was redoubled many a time on either side: and the captains of both parts made their soldiers cry out all together, contending for envy one against another, who should cry it out loudest. This contention of crying, inflamed the soldiers' courages the more. Now the Ambrons having the river to pass, were by this means put out of order, and before they could put themselves in battle ray again, after they had passed the river, the Ligurians ran with great fury to set upon the foremost: and after them, to aid the Ligurians that had begun the charge, the Romans themselves fell also upon the Ambrons, coming down from the places of advantage upon these barbarous people, and compelled them by this means to turn their backs, and flee. So the greatest slaughter they made, fortuned upon the bank of the river, whereinto they thrust one another in such sort, that all the river ran blood, being filled with dead bodies. And they that could get over the river again, and were on the other side, durst not gather together any more to stand to defence: so as the Romans slew them, and drove them into their camp, even unto their carriage. Then their women came out against them with swords and axes in their hands, grinding their teeth: and crying out for sorrow and anger, they charged as well on their own people that fled, as upon them that chased them: the one as traitors, and the other as enemies. Furthermore, they thrust themselves amongst them that fought, and strove by force to pluck the Roman's targets out of their hands, and took hold of their naked swords bare-handed, abiding with an invincible courage to be hacked and mangled with their swords. And thus was the first battle given (as they say) by the river's side, rather by chance unlooked for, than by any set purpose, or through the general's counsel.

20   Now the Romans, after they had overcome the most part of the Ambrons, retiring back by reason the night had overtaken them, did not (as they were wont after they had given such an overthrow) sing songs of victory and triumph, nor make good cheer in their tents one with another, and least of all sleep (which

is the best and sweetest refreshing for men that have fought happily): but contrarily, they watched all that night with great fear and trouble, because their camp was not trenched and fortified, and because they knew also that there remained almost innumerable thousands of barbarous people, that had not yet fought: besides also, that the Ambrons that had fled and escaped from the overthrow, did howl out all night with loud cries, which were nothing like men's lamentations and sighs, but rather like wild beasts bellowing and roaring. So that the bellowing of such a great multitude of beastly people, mingled together with threats and wailings, made the mountains thereabouts and the running river to rebound again of the sound and echo of their cries marvellously: by reason whereof, all the valley that lay between both, thundered to hear the horrible and fearful trembling. This made the Roman soldiers afraid, and Marius himself in some doubt: because they looked to have been fought withal the same night, being altogether troubled and out of order. Notwithstanding, the barbarous people did not assault them that night, nor the next day following, but only prepared themselves unto battle. And in the meantime Marius knowing that there was above the place where they were camped, certain caves and little valleys covered with wood, he secretly sent Claudius Marcellus thither with three thousand footmen well armed, and commanded him to keep close in ambush, until he saw that the barbarous people were fighting with him, and that then he should come and set upon their rearward. The residue of his army, they supped when time came, and after supper reposed themselves. The next morning at the break of day, Marius brought his men into the field out of his fort: where he put them in order of battle, sending his horsemen before to draw the enemies out to skirmish. The Teutons seeing them come, had not the patience to tarry till the Romans were come down into the plain field to fight without advantage, but arming themselves in haste, and in rage, ran up the hill to the Romans where they stood in battle ray. Marius taking good regard to that they did, sent here and there unto the private captains, charging them they should not stir, and only to temporise and forbear, until the enemies came within a stone's cast of them: and that they should then throw their darts at them, and afterwards draw their swords, and repulse the barbarous people with their shields. For he did foresee before, that when they should climb up

against the hill (upon the hanging whereof the Romans had set
their battle) that their blows would not be of great force, nor their
order and ranks could stand close together to any effect or purpose:
because they could not have sure footing, nor march assuredly, but
would easily be thrown backward if they were never so little
repulsed, by reason of the hanging of the hill. Marius gave this
order unto his folk, and therewithal was himself the first man that
put it in execution: for he was as trim a warrior, and as valiant a
soldier, as any man in all his army: besides, not one amongst them
all would venturee further, and be more bold than himself.

15   So when the Romans had resisted them, and stayed them
suddenly, going with fury to have won the hill, perceiving themselves to be repulsed, they gave back by little and little, until they
came into the field: and then began the foremost of them to gather
together, and to put themselves in battle ray upon the plain, when
suddenly they heard the noise and charging of them that were in
the tail of their army. For Claudius Marcellus failed not to take the
occasion when it was offered him, because that the noise of their
first charge coming up against the hills thereabouts, under the
which he lay in ambush, gave him advertisement thereof: whereupon he caused his men presently to show, and running with great
cries, came to give a charge upon those which were in the tail of
the barbarous people, putting the hindmost to the sword. They
made their fellows whose backs were next unto them, to turn their
faces, and so from man to man, till at the length, in short time all
their battle began to waver in disorder: and they made no great
resistance, when they saw they were so charged before and behind,
but began straight to flee for life. The Romans following them hard
at the heels, killed and took prisoners above a hundred thousand of
them, and took moreover their carts, their tents and all their
carriage. Which the whole army by consent agreed to present unto
Marius, excepting nothing, saving that which was embezzled and
conveyed away under hand. Now, though this was a marvellous
honourable and right noble present, yet they thought it not a
recompense sufficient for that he had deserved, for the valour he
had showed of a famous captain in leading of his army, and for the
good order he kept in this war: so happy thought they themselves
to have escaped so great a danger. Notwithstanding, some writers

do not agree, that the spoil of the barbarous people was given unto Marius: nor that there were also so great a number of men slain as we have spoken of. But they say, that after this battle the Marssilians did enclose their vines, with hedges made of dead men's bones: and that the bodies being rotten and consumed upon the fields through the great rain that fell upon them the winter following, the ground waxed so fat, and did soak the grease so deep in the same, that the summer following they did bear an incredible quantity of all sorts of fruits. And by this means were Archilocus' words proved true, that the arable land doth wax fat with such rottenness or putrefaction. And it is said also, that of ordinary after great battles, there falleth great store of rain. Either it is by mean of some god that pouring down pure rain water doth purify, wash, and cleanse the ground, defiled and polluted with man's blood: or else it happeneth by natural cause. For that the overthrow of so many dead bodies, and of the blood spilt, engendereth a moist, gross, and heavy vapour, which doth thicken the air (that by nature is changeable, and easy to alter) from a very small or little beginning, unto an exceeding great change.

22 After this battle, Marius caused the harness and spoils of the barbarous people to be laid aside, that were left whole and fair to sight, to beautify and enrich the pomp of his triumph. Then he caused the rest to be gathered together on a great heap, and laid upon a stack of wood, to make a noble sacrifice unto the gods, all his army being armed about him, crowned with garlands of triumph, and himself apparelled in a long gown of purple, according to the custom of the Romans in such a case, and holding a torch burning in both his hands, which he first lifted up unto heaven. And as he was turning down the torch to put fire to the stack of wood, they saw some of his friends a good way off a-horseback, coming post unto him: then suddenly there was a great silence made of all the assembly, every man desirous to hear what good news they had brought. When they were come and lighted off their horses, they ran straight to embrace Marius, and brought him news that he was chosen consul the fifth time: and presented him the letters sent him from Rome confirming the same. And thus, this new joy falling out besides the victory, the private soldiers did show the great joy and pleasure they took in both, with great shouts and beating upon their

harness: and the captains also, they crowned Marius again with new garlands of laurel which they put about his head, and that done, he put fire under the stack of wood, and ended his sacrifice.

23    But that which never suffereth men quietly to enjoy the good hap of any victory clearly, but in this mortal life doth ever mingle the ill with the good, be it either fortune or spite of fatal destiny, or else the necessity of the natural causes of earthly things, did shortly after this great joy bring news unto Marius, of his companion Catulus Luctatius the other consul, who was like a cloud in a fair bright day, and brought the city of Rome again into a new fear and trouble. For Catulus that went against the Cimbres, thought it was not for him to keep the straits of the mountains, in hope to let the barbarous people for passing: because that in so doing, he had been compelled to divide his army into many parts, and had weakened himself very much if he had taken that course. Wherefore coming a little on this side the Alps towards Italy, he planted himself upon the river of Athesis, and built a bridge upon it, to pass and repass over his men when he would, and set up at either end of the bridge two strong forts well fortified, that he might more commodiously help the places on the other side of the river, if the barbarous people by chance would offer to force them, after they had got out of the straits of the mountains. Now, these barbarous people had such a glory in themselves, and disdained their enemies so much, that more to show their force and boldness, than of any necessity that compelled them, or for any benefit they got by it, they suffered it to snow upon them being stark naked, and did climb up to the top of the mountains, through great heaps of ice and snow. And when they were at the very top of all, they laid their long broad targets under their bodies, and lay all along upon them, sliding down the steep high rocks, that had certain hangings over of an infinite height. In the end, they came to camp near unto the Romans by the river side, and considered how they might pass it over: and began to fill it up, tearing down (like giants) great hills of earth which they found thereabouts, brought thither great trees which they pulled up whole by the roots, threw in great pieces of rocks which they broke, and whole towers of earth after them, to stop and break the course of the river. But besides all this, they threw great timber into the river, which being carried down the

stream, came with such a force, and hit against the posts of the bridge so violently, that they shaked the Romans' bridge marvellously. Whereupon many of the soldiers of the great camp were afraid, and forsaking it, began to retire. But then did Catulus, like a perfect good captain, show that he made less account of his own private honour and estimation, than he did of the general honour of all his soldiers. For, seeing that he could not persuade his men by any reason to tarry, and that in this fear they dislodged in disorder against his will, he himself commanded the standard bearer of the Eagle to march on, and ran to the foremost that went their way, and marched himself before them all, to the intent that the shame of this retire should altogether light upon him, and not upon his country, and that it might appear the Romans did follow their captain, and not flee away. The barbarous people therefore assaulting the fort at the end of the bridge of the river of Athesis, took it, and all the men that were in it. And because the Romans defended it like valiant men, and had lustily ventured their lives to the death for defence of their country, the barbarous people let them go upon composition, which they swore to keep faithfully, by their bull of copper. This bull afterwards was taken when they lost the battle, and carried (as they say) into Catulus Luctatius' house, as the chiefest thing of the victory. Furthermore, the barbarous people finding the country open without any defence, scattered here and there, and destroyed all where they came.

24 Whereupon the Romans sent for Marius to Rome to go against them: and after he was arrived, every man thought he should have entered in triumph, because also the senate did grant it him very willingly. But he would not do it, either because he would not deprive his soldiers and the captains that had fought under him, of any part of the honour that was due unto them, they being absent: or because that he would warrant the people from the present danger they were in, by laying aside the glory of his former victories, into the hands of the good fortune of Rome, in certain hope to take it again afterwards, by a more honourable and perfect confirmation of the second. Wherefore, after he had made an oration to the people and senate according to the time, he went his way immediately towards Catulus Luctatius, whose coming did comfort him much: and sent also for his army that was yet in Gaul

beyond the mountains. And after his army was come, he passed the river of Po, to keep the barbarous people from hurting Italy on this side the Po. Now, the Cimbres still deferred to give battle because they looked for the Teutons, and said, that they marvelled much what they meant to tarry so long: either because they knew not indeed of their overthrow, or else for that they would not seem to know it, because they handled them cruelly that brought the news of their deaths. At the length, they sent unto Marius to ask him lands and towns sufficient to keep them and their brethren. Marius asked their ambassadors what brethren they meant. They answered, that they were the Teutons. Whereat the bystanders began to laugh, and Marius finely mocked them, saying: 'Care not for those brethren,' said he, 'for we have given them ground enough, which they will keep forever.' These ambassadors found his mock straight, and began to revile and threaten him, that the Cimbres should presently make him repent it, and the Teutons so soon as they arrived. 'Why,' said Marius unto them again, 'they are come already: and there were no honesty in you, if you could go your way and not salute them, since they are your brethren.' And as he spoke these words, he commanded his men to bring him the kings of the Teutons bound and chained, that had been taken within the mountains of the Alps by the Sequani.

25    The Cimbres understanding this by report of their ambassadors, presently marched towards Marius, who stirred not at all, but only fortified and kept his camp. They say that it was for this battle that Marius first invented the new devise he brought in for the dart which the Romans were wont always to throw against the enemies at the first charge. For before, the staff of the dart was fastened unto the iron, and the iron unto the staff, with two little iron pins that passed through the wood: and then Marius left one of the iron pins as it was before, and taking away the other, put a little thin pin of wood, easy to be broken, in place of the same, making it craftily, to the end that when the dart was thrown, and stuck in the enemy's target, it should not stand right forward, but bow downwards towards the iron, that the wooden pin being broken, the staff of the dart should hang downwards, holding yet by the iron pin running quite through at the point. So Boeorix king of the Cimbres, coming near to Marius' camp with a small number of

horsemen, sent him defiance, and willed him to appoint a day and place for battle, that they might try it out, who should be owners of the country. Whereunto Marius made answer, that it was not the manner of the Romans to counsel with their enemies, of the time and place when they should give battle: but nevertheless, he would not stick to pleasure the Cimbres so much. And thus they agreed between them, that it should be the third day following, in the plain of Verselles, which was very commodious for the horsemen of the Romans: and also for the barbarous people to put out at will their great number of fighting men. So both armies failed not to meet according to appointment, but appeared ranged in battle, the one before the other. Catulus Luctatius the other consul had in his camp twenty thousand and three hundred soldiers: and Marius had in his camp two and thirty thousand fighting men, which he placed in the two wings of the battle, shutting in Catulus with his men in the midst. As Sylla writeth it, who was present at the same, saying that Marius did it of malice, for the hope he had to overthrow his enemies with the two wings of the battle, to the end that the whole victory should light upon his two wings, and that Catulus and his men in the midst should have no part thereof. For he could not so much as front the enemy, because that commonly when the front of a battle is of such a breadth, the two wings are ever stretched out before, and is made like the crescent of a moon, where the midst is thickest and farthest in. And it is written also in other stories, that Catulus himself, accusing the malice of Marius, because he did so, spoke it to excuse his own dishonour. As for the Cimbres, the troops of their footmen coming out of their forts leisurely, did put themselves into a squadron, as broad as long, for in every side they occupied almost thirty furlong: but their horsemen which were fifteen thousand, marched before in sumptuous furniture. For they had helmets on their heads, fashioned like wild beast's necks, and strange beavers or buffs to the same, and ware on their helmets great high plumes of feathers, as they had been wings: which to sight made them appear taller and bigger men than they were. Furthermore, they had good cuirasses on their backs, and carried great white targets before them: and for weapons offensive, every man had two darts in his hand to bestow afar off, and when they came to hand strokes, they had great heavy swords which they fought withal near hand.

26    But at that time they did not march directly in rank against the army of the Romans, but turned a little on the right hand, meaning to enclose the Romans between them and their footmen that were on the left hand. The Roman captains found their policy straight, but they could not keep their soldiers back: for there was one that cried, the enemies fled, and immediately all the rest began to run after. In the meantime, the footmen of the barbarous people that were like to a sea before them, came forwards still: and then Marius having washed his hands, and lifting them up to heaven, promised, and vowed a solemn sacrifice unto the gods of a hundred oxen. Catulus also made a vow, lifting up his hands to heaven in like manner, that he would build a temple unto fortune for that day: and it is reported, that Marius having sacrificed, when they showed him the entrails of the beasts sacrificed: he cried out aloud, 'The victory is mine.' But when they came to give the charge, Marius had a great misfortune happened him, poured upon him by God's justice, who turned his craft against himself, as Sylla writeth: for there rose very credibly so great a dust, that both armies lost the sight one of another. And hereupon Marius being the first that ran to begin the charge, and having placed his men about him, missed to meet with his enemies: and being passed beyond their battle, wandered a great while up and down the field, whilst the barbarous people fought against Catulus. So that the greatest fury of the battle was against Catulus and his army: in the which, Sylla writeth he was himself, and sayeth, that the heat and the sun which was full in the Cimbres' faces, did the Romans marvellous pleasure at that time. For the barbarous people being very hard brought up to away with cold (because they were born and bred in a cold country, shadowed altogether with woods and trees as we have said) were to the contrary very tender against the heat, and did melt with sweating against the sun, and gaped straight for breath, putting their targets before their faces: for it was also in the heart of summer, about the seven and twenty day of the month of July, that this battle was given: and this dust also made the Romans the bolder, and kept them that they could not see the innumerable multitude of their enemies far from them. And every man running to set upon them that came against them, they were joined together in fight, before that the sight of their enemies could make them afraid. And furthermore, they were so good soldiers, and so

able to take pains, that how extreme soever the heat was, no man was seen sweat nor blow, though they ran at the first to set upon them: and this hath Catulus Luctatius himself left in writing unto the praise of his soldiers.

27 So were the most part of the barbarous people, and specially of the best soldiers, slain in the field. And because they should not open nor break their ranks, the foremost ranks were all tied and bound together with girdles, leather thongs, and long chains of iron: and they that fled, were chased and followed into their camp by the Romans, where they met with horrible and fearful things to behold. For, their wives being upon the top of their carts, apparelled all in black, slew all those that fled, without regard of persons: some their fathers, other their husbands or their brethren, and strangling the little young babes with their own hands, they cast them under the cart wheels, and between the horse legs, and afterwards slew themselves. And they say, that there was a woman hanged at the end of a cart ladder, having hanged up two of her children by the necks at her heels. And that the men also, for lack of a tree to hang themselves on, tied slipping halters about their necks, unto the horns and feet of the oxen, and that they did prick them afterwards with goads to make them fling and leap so long, that dragging them all about, and treading them under feet, at the length they killed them. Now, though numbers were slain by this means, yet were there three score thousand of them taken prisoners, and the number of them that were slain, came to twice as many more. In this manner Marius' soldiers spoiled the camp of the Cimbres: but the spoils of dead men that were slain in the field, with their ensigns and trumpets, were all brought (as it is said) unto Catulus' camp, which was a plain testimony to show that Catulus and his soldiers had won the field. Strife rising thus between the soldiers of both camps about it, that the matter might be tried friendly between them, they made the ambassadors of Parma their arbitrators, who were by chance at that time in the army. Catulus Luctatius' soldiers led the ambassadors to the place where the overthrow was given, showing them the enemies' bodies pierced through with their pikes, which were easy to be known, because Catulus had made them grave his name upon their pikes. For all this, Marius went away with the honour of this great victory, as

well for the first battle he was alone, when he overthrew the Teutons and the Ambrons, as for his great calling, having been consul five times. And furthermore, the common people at Rome called him the third founder of the city of Rome thinking themselves now delivered from as great a danger, as before time they had been from the ancient Gauls. And every man feasting at home with his wife and children, offered the best dishes of meat they had to supper, unto the gods, and unto Marius: and would needs have him alone to triumph for both victories. But he would not in any case, but triumphed into the city with Catulus Luctatius, meaning to show himself courteous and moderate in so great prosperity: and peradventure also fearing Catulus' soldiers, who were in readiness and prepared (if Marius would have deprived their captain of that honour) to let him also of his triumph.

28   And thus you see how he passed his fifth consulship. After that, he made more earnest suit for the sixth consulship, than ever any other did for his first: seeking the peoples' goodwills by all the fair means he could to please them, humbling himself unto them, not only more than became his estate and calling, but directly also against his own nature, counterfeiting a courteous popular manner, being clean contrary to his disposition. His ambition made him timorous to deal in matters of the state concerning the city. For that courage and boldness which he had in battle against the enemy, he lost it quite when he was in an assembly of people in the city: and was easily put out of his bias, with the first blame or praise he heard given him. And though they report, that on a time when he made a thousand Camerines free of the city of Rome, because they had done valiant service in the wars, that there were some that did accuse him, saying, that it was a thing done against all law: he answered them, that for the noise of the armour, he could not hear the law. Notwithstanding, it seemeth that indeed he was greatly afraid of the fury of the people in an assembly of the city. For in time of wars, he ever stood upon his reputation and authority, knowing that they had need of him: but in peace and civil government, because he would rather be the chiefest man than the honestest man, he would creep into the people's bosoms to get their favour and goodwill. And thus through his evil behaviour, he brought all the nobility generally to be his enemies. But he feared

nor mistrusted none so much, as he did Metellus, for the great
unthankful part he remembered he had played him: and the rather
also, because he knew him to be a just and true-dealing man,
and one that was ever against these people-pleasers and flatterers.
Marius therefore practised all the ways he could, to get Metellus to
be banished Rome. Wherefore, to compass his intent, he fell in
friendship with Glaucia, and one Saturninus, two of the most
boldest, most desperate, and most hardbrained young men, that
were in all Rome: who had all the rabblement of rogues and
beggars, and such tumultuous people at their commandment, by
whose means he made new popular laws, and caused the soldiers
to be called home out of the wars, and mingled them with the
people of the city in common assemblies, to trouble and vex
Metellus. Moreover Rutilius, an honest and true writer (howbeit
an enemy unto Marius) writeth, that he obtained his sixth consulship by corruption of money, which he caused to be distributed
amongst the tribes of the people: and that he bought it for ready
money to put by Metellus, and to have Valerius Flaccus not for his
fellow and companion in the consulship, but rather for a minister
of his will. There was never Roman to whom the people granted
the consulship six times, except it were unto Valerius Corvinus
only. But for him, they say that there was five and forty years
between his first consulship and the last. Where Marius since the
first year of his consulship, continued five years together by good
fortune one after another.

29  But in his last consulship, he won himself great hate and
malice, because he did many foul faults to please Saturninus withal:
as amongst others, when he bore with Saturninus, who murdered
Nonius his competitor in the tribuneship. Afterwards when
Saturninus was chosen tribune of the people, he preferred a law for
distribution of the lands among the common people, and unto that
law he had specially added one article: that all the lords of the senate
should come openly to swear, that they should keep and observe
from point to point that which the people by their voices should
decree, and should not deny it in any jot. But Marius in open
senate, made as though he would withstand this article, saying, that
neither he nor any other wise man of judgment would take this
oath: for said he, if the law be evil, then they should do the senate

open wrong to compel them by force to grant it, and not of their own goodwills. But he spoke not that, meaning to do as he said: for it was but a bait he had laid for Metellus only, which he could hardly escape. For, imagining that to tell a fine lie, was a piece of virtue, and of a good wit, he was thoroughly resolved with himself, not to pass for anything he had spoken in the senate. And to the contrary also, knowing well enough that Metellus was a grave wise man, who esteemed that to be just and true (as Pindarus said) is the beginning and foundation of great virtue, he thought he would outreach him, making him affirm before the senate that he would not swear, knowing also that the people would hate him deadly, if he would refuse afterwards to swear. And so indeed it happened. For Metellus having assured them then that he would not swear, the senate broke up upon it. And shortly after, Saturninus the tribune calling the senators unto the pulpit for orations, to compel them to swear before the people, Marius went thither to offer himself to swear. Whereupon the people making silence, listened attentively to hear what he would say. But Marius not regarding his large promise and brags made before the senate, said then, his neck was not so long, that he would prejudice the commonwealth in a matter of so great importance: but that he would swear, and obey the law, if it were a law. This shifting subtlety he added to it, to cloak and cover his shame: and when he had said so, he took his oath. The people seeing him swear, were marvellous glad, and praised him with clapping of their hands: but the nobility hanging down their heads were ashamed of him, and were marvellous angry in their hearts with him, that he had so cowardly and shamefully gone from his word. Thereupon all the senate took their oaths, one after another against their wills, because they were afraid of the people. Saving Metellus, whom neither parents' nor friends' persuasion and entreaty could once move to swear, for any punishment that Saturninus had imposed upon them, which refused to take the oath, but continued one man still according to his nature, and would never yield unto it, offering to abide any pain, rather than to be brought to consent to a dishonest matter unbeseeming his estate. And thereupon went out of the assembly, and talking with them that did accompany him, told them, that to do evil, it was too easy a thing: and to do good without danger, it was also a common matter: but to do well with danger, that was the part of an honest and virtuous man. Saturninus then commanded the consuls by edict of the people, that they should banish Metellus by sound of trumpet, with special commandment, that no man should let him have fire nor water, nor lodge him privately nor openly. The common people, they were ready to have fallen upon him: and to have killed him: but the noblemen being offended for the injury they had offered him, gathered together about him to save him, if any would offer him violence. Metellus himself was so good a man, that he would not any civil dissension should rise for his sake: and therefore he absented himself from Rome, wherein he did like a wise man. 'For,' said he, 'either things will amend, and the people then repenting themselves of the wrong they have done me, will call me home again: or else things standing as they do now, it shall be best for me to be furthest off. But for his travel in his exile, how much he was beloved and honoured, and how sweetly he passed his time studying philosophy in the city of Rhodes, shall be declared more at large in his life.

30 Now on the other side, Marius to recompense the pleasure Saturninus had done him, being driven to let him have his will in all things, did not foresee what an intolerable plague he brought unto the commonwealth, giving the bridle to a desperate man, who every way, by force, by sword and murder, plainly sought to usurp tyrannical power, with the utter destruction and subversion of the whole common weal. And so bearing reverence of the one side unto the nobility, and desiring on the other side to gratify the common people, he played a shameful part, and showed himself a double-dealing man. For one night the nobility and chiefest citizens coming to his house, to persuade him to bridle Saturninus' insolence and boldness, at the selfsame time also Saturninus going thither to speak with him, he caused him to be let in at a back door, the noblemen not being privy to his coming. And so Marius telling the nobility, and then Saturninus, that he was troubled with a looseness of his body, under this pretence whipped up and down, now to the one, then to the other, and did nothing else but set them further out one against another, than they were before. Nevertheless, the senate being marvellous angry with his naughty double dealing, and the order of knights taking part with the senate, Marius in the end was compelled to arm the people in the

market place, to suppress them that were up, and drove them into the Capitol: where for lack of water, they were compelled to yield themselves at the length, because he had cut off the pipes and conduits by the which the water ran unto the capitol. By reason whereof, they being unable to continue any longer, called Marius unto them, and yielded themselves to him, under the assurance of the faith of the common people. But although Marius did what he could possible to his uttermost power to save them, he could not prevail, nor do them pleasure: for they were no sooner come down into the market place, but they were all put to death. Whereupon he having now purchased himself the ill will of the people and nobility both, when time came about that new censors should be chosen, every man looked that he would have been one of the suitors: howbeit he sued not for it, for fear of repulse, but suffered others to be chosen of far less dignity and calling than himself. Wherein notwithstanding he gloried, saying that he would not sue to be censor, because he would not have the ill will of many, for examining too straitly their lives and manners.

31    Again, a decree being preferred to repeal Metellus' banishment, Marius did what he could possible by word and deed to hinder it: howbeit, seeing in the end he could not have his will, he let it alone. The people having thus willingly revoked Metellus' banishment, Marius' heart would not serve him to see Metellus return again, for the malice he bore him: wherefore, he took the seas to go into Cappadocia and Galatia, under colour to pay certain sacrifices to the mother of the gods, which he had vowed unto her. But this was not the very cause that made him to undertake this journey, for he had another secret meaning in it. For his nature not being framed to live in peace, and to govern civil matters, and having attained to his greatness by arms, and supposing that his glory and authority consumed and decreased altogether living idly in peace, he sought to devise new occasion of wars, hoping if he could stir up the kings of Asia, and specially Mithridates (who without his procurement was feared much, that one day he would make wars against the Romans) that he should then undoubtedly without let of any man be chosen general to make wars with him: and withal also, that by that means he should have occasion to fill the city of Rome with new triumphs, and his house with the spoils

of the great kingdom of Ponte, and with the riches of the king. Now Mithridates disposing himself to entertain Marius, with all the honour and courtesies he could possibly show him, Marius in the end notwithstanding would not once give him a good look, nor a courteous word again, but churlishly said unto Mithridates at his departure from him: 'Thou must determine one of these two, King Mithridates: either to make thyself stronger then the Romans, or else to look to do what they command thee, without resistance.' These words amazed Mithridates, who had heard say before that the Romans would speak their minds freely: howbeit he never saw nor proved it before, until that time.

32   After Marius was returned unto Rome, he built a house near unto the market place, because he would not (as he said himself) that such as came unto him should trouble themselves in going far to bring him home to his house: or else for that he thought this would be an occasion that divers would come to salute him, as they did other senators. Howbeit that was not the cause indeed, but the only cause was, for that he had no natural grace nor civility to entertain men courteously that came unto him, and that he lacked behaviour besides to rule in a commonwealth: and therefore in time of peace they made no more reckoning of him, than they did of an old rusty harness or implement that was good for nothing, but for the wars only. And for all other that professed arms as himself did, no man grieved him so much to be called forward to office and state before himself, as Sylla did. For he was ready to burst for spite, to see that the noblemen did all what they could to prefer Sylla, for the malice and ill will they bore him: and that Sylla's first rising and preferment grew, by the quarrels and contentions he had with him. And specially when Bocchus king of Numidia was proclaimed by the senate, a friend and confederate of the Roman people, he offered up statues of victories, carrying tokens of triumph, into the temple of the Capitol: and placed near unto them also, an image of gold of King Iugurthe, which he delivered by his own hands unto Sylla. And this made Marius stark mad for spite and jealousy, and could not abide that another should take upon him the glory of his doings: insomuch as he determined to pluck those images down, and to carry them away by force. Sylla on the other side stomached Marius, and would not suffer him to take them out of the place

where they were: so that this civil sedition had taken present effect, had not the wars of their confederates fallen out between, and restrained them for a time. For the best soldiers and most warlike people of all Italy, and of greatest power, they all together rose against the Romans, and had well near overthrown their whole empire. For they were not only of great force, and power, and well armed: but their captains also, for valiantness and skill, did in manner equal the worthiness of the Romans.

33   For this war fell out wonderfully, by reason of the calamity and misfortune that happened in it: but it won Sylla as much fame and reputation, as it did Marius shame and dishonour. For he showed himself very cold and slow in all his enterprises, still delaying time, either because age had mortified his active heat, and killed that quick ready disposition of body that was wont to be in him, being then above three score and five year old: or else as he said himself, because he was waxen gouty, and had ache in his veins and sinews, that he could not well stir his body, and that for shame, because he would not tarry behind in this war, he did more than his years could away withal. Notwithstanding, as he was, yet he won a great battle, wherein were slain six thousand of their enemies: and so long as the wars endured, he never gave them advantage of him, but patiently suffered them sometime to entrench him, and to mock him, and give him vile words, challenging him out to fight, and yet all this would not provoke him. It is said also, that Pompedius Silo, who was the chiefest captain of reputation and authority the enemies had, said unto Marius on a time: 'If thou be Marius, so great a captain as they say thou art, leave thy camp, and come out to battle.' 'Nay,' said Marius to him again, 'If thou be a great captain, pluck me out by the ears, and compel me to come to battle.' Another time when the enemies gave them occasion to a great charge upon them with advantage, the Romans were faint-hearted, and durst not set upon them. Wherefore, after both the one and the other were retired, Marius caused his men to assemble, and spoke unto them in this sort: 'I cannot tell which of the two I should reckon most cowards: you yourselves, or your enemies: for they durst not once see your backs, nor you them in the faces.' In the end notwithstanding, he was compelled to resign his charge, being able to serve no longer for the weakness and debility of his body.

34 Now, all the rebels of Italy being put down, many at Rome (by
the orators' means) did sue to have the charge of the wars against
Mithridates: and among them, a tribune of the people called
Sulpitius (a very bold and rash man), beyond all men's hope and
opinion preferred Marius, and persuaded them to give him the
charge of these wars, with title and authority of vice-consul. The
people thereupon were divided into two parts: for the one side
stood for Marius, and the other would have Sylla take the charge,
saying, that Marius was to think now upon the hot baths at Baies, to
look to cure his old body, brought low with rheum and age, as
himself said. For Marius had a goodly stately house in those parts
near unto the mount of Misene, which was far more fine and
curiously furnished, than became a captain that had been in so many
foughten battles and dangers. They say that Cornelia afterwards
bought that fine house for the sum of seven thousand five hundred
crowns, and shortly after also, Lucullus bought it again for two
hundred and fifty thousand crowns: to so great excess was vanity and
curiosity grown in very short time at Rome. Notwithstanding all
this, Marius too ambitiously striving like a passioned young man
against the weakness and debility of his age, never missed day but he
would be in the field of Mars to exercise himself among the young
men, showing his body disposed and ready to handle all kind of
weapons, and to ride horses: albeit that in his latter time he had no
great health of body, because he was very heavy and sad. There were
that liked that passing well in him, and went of purpose into the field
to see the pains he took, striving to excel the rest. Howbeit those of
the better sort were very sorry to see his avarice and ambition,
considering specially, that being of a poor man become very rich,
and of a right mean person a great estate, that he could not now
contain his prosperity within reasonable bounds, nor content himself to be esteemed and honoured, quietly enjoying all he had won,
and which at that present he did possess: but as if he had been very
poor and needy, after he had received such great honour and
triumphs, would yet carry out his age so stoutly, even into
Cappadocia, and unto the realm of Pont, to go fight there against
Archelaus and Neoptolemus, lieutenants of King Mithridates. Indeed he alleged some reasons to excuse himself, but they were
altogether vain: for he said that he desired in person to bring up his
son in exercise of arms, and to teach him the discipline of wars.

35   That discovered the secret hidden plague, which of long time hath lurked in Rome, Marius specially having now met with a fit instrument and minister to destroy the commonwealth, which was, the insolent and rash Sulpitius: who altogether followed Saturninus' doings, saving that he was found too cowardly and faint-hearted in all his enterprises, and for that did Marius justly reprove him. But Sulpitius, because he would not dally nor delay time, had ever six hundred young gentlemen of the order of knights, whom he used as his guard about him, and called them the guard against the senate. And one day as the consuls kept their common assembly in the market place, Sulpitius coming in armed upon them, made them both take their heels, and get them packing: and as they fled, one of the consuls' sons being taken tardy, was slain. Sylla being the other consul, and perceiving that he was followed hard at hand unto Marius' house, ran into the same against the opinion of all the world: whereof they that ran after him not being aware, passed by the house. And it is reported that Marius himself conveyed Sylla safely out at a back door, and that he being escaped thus, went unto his camp. Notwithstanding, Sylla himself in his commentaries doth not say, that he was saved in Marius' house when he fled: but that he was brought thither to his consent unto a matter which Sulpitius would have forced him unto against his will, presenting him naked swords on every side. And he writeth also, that being thus forcibly brought unto Marius' house, he was kept there in this fear, until such time as returning into the market place, he was compelled to revoke again the adjournment of justice, which he and his companion by edict had commanded. This done, Sulpitius then being the stronger, caused the commission and charge of this war against Mithridates to be assigned unto Marius by the voice of the people. Therefore Marius giving order for his departure, sent two of his colonels before to take the army of Sylla: who having won his soldiers' hearts before, and stirred them up against Marius, brought them on with him directly towards Rome, being no less then five and thirty thousand fighting men: who setting upon the captains Marius had sent unto them, slew them in the field. In revenge whereof, Marius again in Rome put many of Sylla's friends and followers to death, and proclaimed open liberty by sound of trumpet, to all slaves and bondmen that would take arms for him: but there were never but three only that

offered themselves. Whereupon, having made a little resistance unto Sylla when he came into Rome, he was soon after compelled to run his way. Marius was no sooner out of the city, but they that were in his company forsaking him, dispersed themselves here and there being dark night: and Marius himself got to a house of his in the country, called Salonium, and sent his son to one of his father-in-law Mutius' farms not far from thence, to make some provision for victuals. But Marius in the meantime, went before to Ostia, where one of his friends, Numerius, had prepared him a ship, in the which he embarked immediately, not tarrying for his son, and hoist sail, having only Granius his wife's son with him. In the meantime the younger Marius being at his father-in-law Mutius' farm, stayed so long in getting of provision, in trussing of it up, and carrying it away, that broad daylight had like to have discovered him: for the enemies had advertisement whither he was gone, whereupon certain horsemen were sent thither supposing to have found him. But the keeper of the house having an inkling of their coming, and preventing them also before they came, suddenly yoked his oxen to the cart which he loaded with beans, and hid this younger Marius under the same. And pricking the oxen forward with his goad, set out, and met them as he went towards the city, and delivered Marius in this sort into his wife's house: and there taking such things as he needed, when the night following came, went towards the sea, and took ship, finding one cross-sailed, bound towards Africa.

36 Marius the father sailing on still, had a very good wind to point along the coast of Italy: notwithstanding, being afraid of one Geminius, a chief man of Terracine, who hated him to the death, he gave the mariners warning thereof betimes, and willed them to take heed of landing at Terracine. The mariners were very willing to obey him, but the wind stood full against them coming from the main, which raised a great storm, and they feared much that their vessel which was but a boat, would not brook the seas, besides that he himself was very sick in his stomach, and sore sea beaten: notwithstanding, at the length, with the greatest difficulty that might be, they recovered the coast over against the city of Circees. In the meantime, the storm increased still, and their victuals failed them: whereupon they were compelled to land, and

went wandering up and down not knowing what to do, nor what way to take. But as it falls out commonly in suchlike cases of extremity, they thought it always the best safety for them, to flee from the place where they were, and to hope of that which they saw not: for if the sea were their enemy, the land was so likewise. To meet with men, they were afraid: and not to meet with them on the other side lacking victuals, was indeed the greater danger. Nevertheless, in the end they met with herdmen that could give them nothing to eat, but knowing Marius, warned him to get him out of the way as soon as he could possible, because it was not long since that there passed by a great troop of horsemen that sought him all about. And thus being brought unto such perplexity, that he knew not where to bestow himself, and specially for that the poor men he had in his company were almost starved for hunger, he got out of the highway notwithstanding, and sought out a very thick wood where he passed all that night in great sorrow, and the next morning being compelled by necessity, determined yet to employ his body before all his strength failed. Thus he wandered on along the sea coast, still comforting them that followed him the best he could, and praying them not to despair, but to refer themselves to him, even until the last hope, trusting in certain prophecies which the soothsayers had told him of long time before. For when he was but very young, and dwelling in the country, he gathered up in the lap of his gown, the eyrie of an eagle, in the which were seven young eagles: whereat his father and mother much wondering, asked the soothsayers what that meant. They answered, that their son one day should be one of the greatest men in the world, and that out of doubt he should obtain seven times in his life the chiefest office of dignity in his country. And for that matter, it is said that so indeed it came to pass. Other hold opinion, that such as were about Marius at that time, in that present place, and elsewhere, during the time of his flying, they hearing him tell this tale, believed it, and afterwards put it down in writing, as a true thing, although of truth it is both false and feigned. For they say, that the eagle never gets but two young ones: by reason whereof it is maintained also, that the poet Musaeus hath lied, in that which he hath written in these verses:

> The eagle lays three eggs, and two she hatcheth forth:
> But yet she bringeth up but one, that anything is worth.

Howsoever it was, it is certain that Marius many times during the time of his flying said, that he was assured he should come unto the seventh consulship.

37 When they were come near now to the city of Minturnes, about two mile and a half from it, they might perceive a troop of horsemen coming by the sea side, and two ships on the sea that fell upon the coast by good hap. Wherefore they all began to run (so long as they had breath and strength) towards the sea, into the which they threw themselves, and got by swimming unto one of the ships where Granius was: and they crossed over unto the isle that is right against it called Enaria. Now for Marius, who was heavy and sick of body, two of his servants helped to hold him up always above water, with the greatest pain and difficulty in the world: and at the last they laboured so thoroughly, that they put him into the other ship at the selfsame present, when the horsemen came unto the sea side, who cried out aloud to the mariners, to land again, or else throw Marius overboard: and then to go where they would. Marius on the other side humbly besought them with tears, not so to do: whereby the masters of the ship in a short space were in many minds whether to do it, or not to do it. In the end notwithstanding, they answered the horsemen they would not throw him over the board: so the horsemen went their way in a great rage. But as soon as they were gone, the masters of the ship changing mind, drew towards land, and cast anchor about the mouth of the river of Liris, where it leaveth her banks, and makes great marshes: and there they told Marius he should do well to go a-land to eat somewhat, and refresh his sea-sick body, till the wind served them to make sail, which doubtless, said they, will be at a certain hour when the sea wind falls and becomes calm, and that there riseth a little wind from the land, engendered by the vapours of the marshes, which will serve the turn very well to take seas again. Marius following their counsel, and thinking they had meant good faith, was set a-land upon the river's bank and there laid him down upon the grass, nothing suspecting that which happened after to him. For the mariners presently taking their ship again, and hoisting up their anchors, sailed straight away, and fled, judging it no honesty for them to have delivered Marius into the hands of his enemies, nor safety for themselves to have saved him.

Marius finding himself all alone, and forsaken of every man, lay on
the ground a great while, and said never a word: yet at the length
taking heart a little to him, got up once again on his feet, and
painfully wandered up and down, where was neither way nor path
at all, overthwart deep marshes and great ditches, full of water and
mud, till he came at the length to a poor old man's cottage,
dwelling there in these marshes, and falling at his feet, besought
him to help to save and succour a poor afflicted man, with promise
that one day he would give him a better recompense than he
looked for, if he might escape this present danger wherein he was.
The old man whether for that he had known Marius aforetime, or
that seeing him (by conjecture only) judged him to be some great
personage, told him that if he meant but to lay down and rest
himself a little, his poor cabin would serve that turn reasonably
well: but if he meant to wander thus, to flee his enemies that
followed him, he would then bring him into a more secret place,
and further off from noise. Marius prayed him that he would so
much do for him: and the good man brought him into the marsh,
unto a low place by the river's side, where he made him lie down,
and then covered him with a great deal of reed and bent, and other
such light things as could not hurt him.

38   He had not long been there, but he heard a great noise
coming towards the cabin of the poor old man: for Geminius of
Terracine had sent men all about to seek for him, whereof some by
chance came that way, and put the poor man in a fear, and
threatened him that he had received and hidden an enemy of the
Romans. Marius hearing that, rose out of the place where the old
man had laid him, and stripping himself stark naked, went into a
part of the marsh where the water was full of mire and mud, and
there was found of those that searched for him: who taking him
out of the slime all naked as he was, carried him into the city of
Minturnes, and delivered him there into the governor's hands.
Open proclamation was made by the senate through all Italy, that
they should apprehend Marius, and kill him wheresoever they
found him. Notwithstanding, the governors and magistrates of
Minturnes thought good first to consult thereupon amongst themselves, and in the meantime they delivered him into the safe
custody of a woman called Fannia, whom they thought to have

been a bitter enemy of his, for an old grudge she had to him, which was this: Fannia sometime had a husband called Tinnius, whom she was willing to leave for that they could not agree, and required her dower of him again, which was very great. Her husband again said, she had played the whore. The matter was brought before Marius in his sixth consulship, who had given judgment upon it. Both parties being heard, and the law prosecuted on either side, it was found that this Fannia was a naughty woman of her body, and that her husband knowing it well enough before he married her, yet took her with her faults, and long time lived with her. Wherefore Marius being angry with them both, gave sentence that the husband should repay back her dower, and that for her naughty life, she should pay four farthings. This notwithstanding, when Fannia saw Marius, she grudged him not for that, and least of all had any revenging mind in her towards him, but contrarily did comfort and help him what she could with that she had. Marius thanked her marvellously for it, and bade her hope well: because he met with good luck as he was coming to her house, and in this manner. As they were leading of him, when he came near to Fannia's house, her door being open, there came an ass running out to go drink at a conduit, not far from thence: and meeting Marius by the way, looked upon him with a lively joyful countenance, first of all stopping suddenly before him, and then beginning to bray out aloud, and to leap and skip by him. Whereupon Marius straight conjecturing with himself, said, that the gods did signify unto him, that he should save himself sooner by water than by land, because that the ass leaving him, ran to drink, and cared not to eat. So when he had told Fannia this tale, he desired to rest, and prayed them to let him alone, and to shut the chamber door to him.

39 But the magistrates of the city having consulted together about him, in the end resolved they must defer no longer time, but dispatch him out of the way presently. Now when they were agreed upon it, they could not find a man in the city that durst take upon him to kill him: but a man of arms of the Gauls, or one of the Cimbres (for we find both the one and the other in writing) that went thither with his sword drawn in his hand. Now, that place of the chamber wherein Marius lay was very dark, and as it is

reported, the man of arms thought he saw two burning flames come out of Marius' eyes, and heard a voice out of that dark corner, saying unto him: 'O fellow, thou, darest thou come to kill Caius Marius?' The barbarous Gaul hearing these words, ran out of the chamber presently, casting his sword in the midst of the floor, and crying out these words only: 'I cannot kill Caius Marius.' This made the Minturnians afraid in the city at the first, but afterwards it moved them to compassion. So they were angry with themselves, and did repent them that they converted their counsel to so cruel and unkind a deed, against one that had preserved all Italy: and to deny him aid in so extreme necessity, it was too great a sin. 'Therefore let us let him go,' said they to themselves, 'where he will, and suffer him take his fortune appointed him elsewhere: and let us pray to the gods to pardon this offence of ours, to have thrust Marius naked and beggarly out of our city.' For these considerations, the Minturnians went all together to Marius where he was, and stood about him, determining to see him safely conducted unto the sea side. Now though every man was ready and willing to pleasure him, some with one thing, some with another, and that they did hasten him all they could possible, yet they were a good while a-going thither, because there was a wood called Marica, that lay right in their way between their city and the sea coast: which they greatly reverence, and think it a sacrilege to carry anything out of that wood, that was once brought into it. On the other side, to leave to go through this wood, and to compass it round about, it would ask a marvellous long time. So they standing all in doubt what they should do, one of the ancientest men of the city spoke aloud unto them, and said: that there was no way forbidden them, that went about to save Marius' life. Then Marius himself being the foremost man, taking up some of the fardels which they carried with him, to pleasure him in the ship, went through the wood.

40    All other things necessary being thus readily prepared for him with like goodwill, and specially the ship which one Bellaeus had ordained for him, he caused all this story to be painted in a table at large, which he gave unto the temple, out of the which he departed when he took ship. After he was departed thence, the wind by good fortune carried him into the Isle of Enaria, where he found Granius

and some other of his friends, with whom he took sea again, and pointed towards Africa. But lacking water, they were compelled to land in Sicilia, in the territory of the city of Erix: where by chance there lay a Roman quaestor, who kept that coast. Marius being landed there, escaped very narrowly that he was not taken of him: for he slew sixteen of his men that came out with him to take water. So Marius getting him thence with all speed, crossed the seas, until he arrived in the Isle of Menynge, where he first understood that his son was saved with Cethegus, and that they were both together gone to Hiempsal king of the Numidians to beseech him of aid. This gave him a little courage, and made him bold to pass out of that isle, into the coast of Carthage. Now at that time, Sextilius a Roman praetor was governor of Africa, unto whom Marius had never done good nor hurt, and therefore he hoped, that for pity only he might perhaps have help at his hand. Howbeit he was no sooner landed with a few of his men, but a sergeant came straight and said unto him: 'Sextilius, praetor and governor of Libya, doth forbid thee to land in all this province: otherwise he telleth thee, that he will obey the senate's commandment, and pursue thee as an enemy of the Romans.' Marius hearing this commandment, was so angry and sorry both, that he could not readily tell what answer to make him, and paused a good while, and said never a word, still eyeing the sergeant with a grim look: until he asked him, what answer he would make, to the praetor's commandment. Marius then fetching a deep sigh from his heart, gave him this answer: 'Thou shalt tell Sextilius, that thou hast seen Caius Marius banished out of his country, sitting amongst the ruins of the city of Carthage.' By this answer, he wisely laid the example of the ruin and destruction of that great city of Carthage, before Sextilius' eyes, and the change of his fortune, to warn Sextilius that the like might fall upon him. In the meantime, Hiempsal king of the Numidians, not knowing how to resolve, did honourably entreat young Marius and his company. But when they were willing to go their way, he always found new occasion to stay them, and was very glad to see that he started not for any opportunity or good occasion that was offered: notwithstanding, there fortuned a happy mean unto them, whereby they saved themselves. And this it was. This Marius the younger being a fair complexioned young man, it pitied one of the king's concubines to see him so hardly dealt withal. This pity of hers was a

shadow to cloak the love she bore him: but Marius would not
hearken at the first to her enticements, and refused her. Yet in the
end, perceiving that there was no other way for him to escape
thence, and considering that she did all things for their avail, more
diligently and lovingly than she would have done, if she had not
meant further matter unto him, than only to enjoy the pleasure of
him, he then accepted her love and kindness, so as at the length she
taught him a way how to fly, and save himself and his friends.
Hereupon he went to his father, and after they had embraced and
saluted each other, going along the sea side they found two
scorpions fighting together. Marius took this for an ill sign: whereupon they quickly took a fisher boat, and went into the Isle of
Cercina, which is no great distance off from firm land. They had no
sooner hoist up anchor, but they saw the horsemen which King
Hiempsal had sent unto the place from whence they were departed:
and that was one of the greatest dangers that Marius ever escaped.

41    In the meantime there was news at Rome, that Sylla made war
against King Mithridates' lieutenants: and furthermore, that the
consuls being up in arms the one against the other, Octavius won
the battle, and being the stronger had driven out Cinna, who
sought to have usurped tyrannical power, and had made Cornelius
Merula consul in his place: and that Cinna on the other side levied
men out of other parts of Italy, and made wars upon them that
were in Rome. Marius hearing of this dissension, thought good to
return as soon as he could possible into Italy. And assembling
certain horsemen of the nation of the Maurusians in Africa, and
certain Italians that had saved themselves there, unto the number
of a thousand men in all, he took sea, and landed in a haven of
Thuscane called Telamon: and being landed, proclaimed by sound
of trumpet, liberty to all slaves and bondmen that would come to
him. So the labourers, herdmen, and neatherds of all that march,
for the only name and reputation of Marius, ran to the sea side
from all parts: of the which he having chosen out the stoutest and
lustiest of them, won them so by fair words, that having gathered a
great company together in few days, he made forty sail of them.
Furthermore, knowing that Octavius was a marvellous honest
man, that would have no authority otherwise than law and reason
would: and that Cinna to the contrary was suspected of Sylla, and

that he sought to bring in change and innovation to the commonwealth, he determined to join his force with Cinna. So Marius sent
first unto Cinna, to let him understand that he would obey him as
consul, and be ready to do all that he should command him. Cinna
received him, and gave him the title and authority of vice-consul,
and sent him sergeants to carry axes and rods before him, with all
other signs of public authority. But Marius refused them, and said,
that pomp became not his miserable fortune: for he ever went in a
poor threadbare gown, and had let his hair grow still after he was
banished, being above three score and ten year old: and had a sober
gait with him, to make men pity him the more that saw him. But
under all this counterfeit pity of his, he never changed his natural
look, which was ever more fearful and terrible, than otherwise.
And where he spoke but little, and went very demurely and
soberly, that showed rather a cankered courage within him, than a
mind humbled by his banishment.

42   Thus when he had saluted Cinna, and spoken to the soldiers,
he then began to set things abroach, and made a wonderful change
in few days. For first of all, with his ships he cut off all the victuals
by sea, and robbed the merchants that carried corn and other
victuals to Rome: so that in a short space he was master purveyor
for all necessary provision and victuals. After this he went along
the coast, and took all the cities upon the sea side, and at the length
won Ostia also by treason, put the most part of them in the town
to the sword, and spoiled all their goods: and afterwards making a
bridge upon the river of Tiber, took from his enemies all hope to
have any manner of provision by sea. That done, he went directly
towards Rome with his army, where first he won the hill called
Ianiculum through Octavius' fault: who overthrew himself in his
doings, not so much for lack of reasonable skill of wars, as through
his unprofitable curiosity and strictness in observing the law. For
when divers did persuade him to set the bondmen at liberty to
take arms for defence of the commonwealth, he answered, that he
would never give bondmen the law and privilege of a Roman
citizen, having driven Caius Marius out of Rome to maintain
the authority of the law. But when Caecilius Metellus was come
to Rome the son of that Metellus Numidicus, that having begun
the wars in Libya against King Iugurthe, was put out by Marius,

the soldiers forsook Octavius immediately, and came unto him, because they took him to be a better captain, and desired also to have a leader that could tell how to command them, to save the city, and the commonwealth. For they promised to fight valiantly, and persuaded themselves that they should overcome their enemies, so that they had a skilful and valiant captain that could order them. Metellus misliking their offer, commanded them in anger to return again unto the consul: but they for spite went unto their enemies. Metellus on the other side, seeing no good order taken in the city to resist the enemies, got him out of Rome. But Octavius being persuaded by certain soothsayers and Chaldean sacrificers, who promised him all should go well with him, tarried still in Rome. For that man being otherwise as wise as any Roman of his time, and one that dealt as uprightly in his consulship, not carried away with flattering tales, and one also that followed the ancient orders and customs as infallible rules and examples, neither breaking nor omitting any part thereof, methinks yet had this imperfection, that he frequented the soothsayers, wise men, and astronomers, more than men skilful in arms and government. Wherefore, before that Marius himself came into the city, Octavius was by force plucked out of the pulpit for orations, and slain presently by Marius' soldiers, whom he had sent before into the city. And it is said also, that when he was slain, they found a figure of a Chaldean prophecy in his bosom: and here is to be noted a great contrariety in these two notable men, Octavius and Marius. The first lost his life by trusting to soothsaying: and the second prospered, and rose again, because he did not despise the art of divination.

43   The state of Rome standing then in this manner, the senate consulting together, sent ambassadors unto Cinna and Marius, to pray them to come peaceably into Rome: and not to imbrue their hands with the blood of their citizens. Cinna sitting in his chair as consul, gave them audience, and made them a very reasonable and courteous answer. Marius standing by him, spoke never a word but showed by his sour look that he would straight fill Rome with murder and blood. So when the ambassadors were gone, Cinna came into Rome environed with a great number of soldiers: but Marius stayed suddenly at the gate, speaking partly in anger, and partly in mockery, that he was a banished man, and driven out of

his country by law. And therefore if they would have him come into Rome again, they should first by a contrary decree abolish and revoke that of his banishment, as if he had been a religious observer of the laws, and as though Rome had at that present enjoyed their freedom and liberty. Thus he made the people assemble in the market place to proceed to the confirmation of his calling home again. But before three or four tribes had time to give their voices, disguising the matter no longer, and showing plainly that he meant not to be lawfully called home again from exile, he came into Rome with a guard about him, of the veriest rascals, and most shameless slaves, called the Bardiaeians, who came to him from all parts: and they for the least word he spoke, or at the twinkling of his eye, or at a nod of his head made to them, slew many men through his commandment, and at the length slew Ancharius a senator (that had been praetor) at Marius' feet with their swords, because only that Marius did not salute him when he came one day to speak with him. After this murder, they continued killing all them that Marius did not salute, and speak unto: for that was the very sign he had given them, to kill them openly in the streets before every man, so that his very friends were afraid of being murdered, when they came to salute him. Thus being a great number of men slain, Cinna in the end began to be satisfied, and to appease his anger. But Marius' anger and insatiable desire of revenge increased more: and more, so that he spared not one if he suspected him never so little: and there was neither town nor highway, that was not full of scouts and spies, to hunt them out that hid themselves and fled. Then experience taught them, that no friend is faithful, and to be trusted, if fortune especially frown never so little: for there were very few that did not bewray their friends that fled to them for succour. And therefore do Cornutus' servants so much the more deserve praise, who having secretly hidden their master in his house, did hang up the dead body of some common person by the neck, and having put a gold ring on his finger, they showed him to the Bardiaeians, Marius' guard, and buried him instead of their own master, without suspicion of any man that it was a feigned thing: and so Cornutus being hidden by his servants, was safely conveyed into the country of Gaul.

44    Mark Anthony the orator had also found out a faithful friend,

yet was he unfortunate. This faithful friend of his was a poor simple man, who having received one of the chiefest men of Rome into his house to keep him close there, he being desirous to make him the best cheer he could with that little he had, sent one of his men to the next tavern to fetch wine, and tasting the wine more curiously then he was wont to do, he called for better. The drawer asked him, why the new ordinary wine would not serve him, but he must needs have of the best and dearest: the foolish fellow simply answered him (telling him as his familiar friend) that his master did feast Mark Anthony, who was hidden very secretly in his house. He was no sooner gone with his wine, and his back turned, but the vile traitorous drawer ran unto Marius, who was set at supper when he came. The drawer being brought to him, promised him to deliver Mark Anthony into his hands. Marius hearing that, was so jocund, that he cried out, and clapped his hands together for joy: and would have risen from the board, and gone thither himself in person, had not his friends kept him back. But he sent Annius one of his captains thither with a certain number of soldiers, and commanded them to bring him his head quickly. So they went thither, and when they were come to the house which the drawer had brought them to, Annius tarried beneath at the door, and the soldiers went up the stairs into the chamber, and finding Anthony there, they began to encourage one another to kill him, not one of them having the heart to lay hands upon him. For Anthony's tongue was as sweet as a siren, and had such an excellent grace in speaking, that when he began to speak unto the soldiers, and to pray them to save his life, there was not one of them so hard-hearted, as once to touch him, no not only to look him in the face, but looking downwards, fell a-weeping. Annius perceiving they tarried long, and came not down, went himself up into the chamber, and found Anthony talking to his soldiers, and them weeping, his sweet eloquent tongue had so melted their hearts: but he rating them, ran furiously upon him, and struck off his head with his own hands. And Catulus Luctatius also, that had been consul with Marius, and had triumphed over the Cimbres with him, seeing himself in this peril, set men to entreat Marius for him: but his answer was ever, he must needs die. So Catulus locked himself into a little chamber, and made a great fire of charcoal to be kindled, and with the smoke thereof choked himself. Now after their heads were cut off, they threw out the naked bodies into the streets, and trod them under their feet: the which was not only a pitiful, but a fearful sight to all that saw them. But after all this yet, there was nothing that grieved the people so much, as the horrible lechery and abominable cruelty of this guard of the Bardiaeians, who coming into men's houses by force, after they had slain the masters, defiled their young children, and ravished their wives and maids, and no man would once reprove their cruelty, lechery, and insatiable avarice: until Cinna and Sertorius in the end set upon them as they slept in their camp, and slew them every one.

45    But in this extremity, as if all things had been restored unto their first estate, news came again from all parts to Rome, that Sylla having ended his war against King Mithridates, and recovered the provinces which he had usurped, returned into Italy with a great power. This caused these evils and unspeakable miseries to cease a little, because the wicked doers of the same looked they should have wars on their backs ere it were long. Whereupon Marius was chosen consul the seventh time. He going out of his house openly the first day of January, being the beginning of the year, to take possession of his consulship, caused one Sextus Lucinus to be thrown down headlong from the rock Tarpeian, which seemed to be a great sign and certain token of the evils and miseries, that fell out afterwards the selfsame year upon them of their faction, and unto all the city beside. But Marius being sore broken with his former troubles, and his mind oppressed with extreme sorrow and grief, could not now at this last time of need pluck up his heart to him again, when he came to think of this new toward war that threatened him, and of the dangers, griefs, and troubles he should enter into, more great and perilous than any he had passed before. For through the great experience he had in wars, he trembled for fear when he began to think of it, considering that he had to fight, not with Octavius, nor with Merula, captains of a company of rebels gathered together: but with a noble Sylla, that had driven him out of Rome before, and that came now from driving the puissant king Mithridates unto the furthest part of the realm of Pont, and of the sea Euxinum. Thus, deeply weighing and considering the same, and specially when he looked back upon his long

time of banishment, how vagabondlike he wandered up and down in other countries, and remembered the great misfortunes he had passed, and the sundry dangers he fell so often into, being pursued still by sea and by land, it grieved him to the heart, and made him so unquiet, that he could not sleep in the night, or if he slept, had fearful dreams that troubled him, and still he thought he heard a voice buzzing in his ears:

A lion's very den, is dreadful to behold:
Though he himself be gone abroad, and be not therein hold.

But fearing most of all that he should no more sleep and take his rest, he gave himself to make unreasonable banquets, and to drink more then his years could bear, seeking to win sleep by this means, to avoid care the better. But at the length there came one from the sea, that gave him certain intelligence of all: and that was an increase of a new fear unto him. And thus he being now extremely troubled, partly for fear of the thing to come, and partly also for the over heavy burden of his present ill, there needed but little more aggravation, to fall into the disease whereof he died, which was a pleurisy: as Posidonius the philosopher writeth, who sayeth plainly that he went into his chamber when he was sick, and spoke unto him about matters of his ambassade, for the which he came to Rome. Yet another historiographer Caius Piso writeth, that Marius walking one day after supper with his friends, fell in talk of his fortune from the beginning of his life, telling them at large how often fortune had turned with and against him: concluding, that it is no wise man's part to trust her any more. So when he had done, he took his leave of them, and laid him down upon his bed, where he lay sick seven days together, and on the seventh day died. Some write that his ambition appeared plainly, by a strange raving that took him in his head during his sickness. For he thought that he made wars with Mithridates, and showed in his bed all his gestures and movings of his body, as if he had been in a battle, crying the selfsame cries out aloud, which he was wont to cry when he was in the extremest fight. The desire he had to have taken this charge in hand against Mithridates, was so deeply settled in his mind through extreme ambition and jealousy that possessed him, that being then three score and ten year old, after he had been the first man that ever was chosen seven times consul in Rome, and also after that he had got a world of goods and riches together that might have sufficed many kings, yet for all this he died for sorrow, lamenting his hard fortune, as if he had died before his time, and before that he had done and ended that which he had desired.

46   But this was clean contrary unto that the wise Plato did, when he drew near to his death. For he gave God thanks for his fatal end and good fortune. First, for that he had made him a reasonable man, and no brute beast: secondly, a Greek and no barbarous man: and furthermore, for that he was born in Socrates' time. It is reported also, that one Antipater of Tharsis, calling to mind a little before his death the good fortune he had in his life time, did not forget among other things, to tell of the happy navigation he made, coming from his country unto Athens: which did witness that he put upon the file of his good accounts for a singular great grace, all favour fortune had shown him, and that he kept it in perpetual memory, being the only and most assured treasure a man can have, to keep those gifts that nature or fortune do bestow upon him. But contrariwise, unthankful fools unto God and nature both, do forget with time the memory of their former benefits, and laying up nothing, nor keeping it in perpetual memory, are always void of goods and full of hope, gaping still for things to come and leaving in the meantime the things present, though reason persuadeth them the contrary. For fortune may easily let them of the thing to come, but she cannot take that from them which is already past: and yet they utterly forget the certain benefit of fortune, as a thing nothing belonging unto them, and dream always of that which is uncertain. And sure it chanceth to them by great reason. For, having gathered outward goods together, and locking them up before they have built and laid a sure grounded foundation of reason through good learning, they cannot afterwards fill nor quench their insatiable greedy covetous mind. Thus ended Marius his life, the seventeenth day of his seventh consulship, whereof all the city of Rome was not a little glad, and took heart again unto them, supposing they had then been delivered from a bloody cruel tyranny. But within few days after they knew it to their cost, that they had changed an old master taken out of the world, for a younger that came but newly to them: such extreme unnatural cruelties and murders did Marius the younger commit, after the

death of his father Marius, murdering in manner all the chiefest noblemen of Rome. At the first, they took him for a valiant and hardy young man, whereupon they named him the son of Mars: but shortly after his deeds did show the contrary, and then they called him the son of Venus. In the end he was shut in, and besieged by Sylla in the city of Perusia, where he did what he could possible to save his life, but all was in vain: and lastly, seeing no way to escape, the city being taken, he slew himself with his own hands.

## THE END OF CAIUS MARIUS' LIFE

# NICIAS
# CRASSUS

# Life of Nicias

I have reason (as I think) to compare Nicias with Crassus, and the
events that happened to the one in Parthia, with those that befell
the other in Sicily: yet am I to pray them that shall happen to read
my writings, not to think me in intermeddling with those matters
(in the describing and reporting whereof, Thucydides hath gone
beyond himself, both for variety and liveliness of narration, as also
in choice and excellent words) to have the like intent and opinion,
that Timaeus the historiographer had. Who, hoping by the gravity
and life of his words and reports, to darken the glory of Thucydides,
and make Philistus (in comparison of himself) appear ignorant, and
without any grace of historical narration, hath in his history of
purpose sought occasion to enter into the describing of those
battles by sea and by land, and the report of those speeches and
orations, which are delivered by them with great judgment and
eloquence. Wherein he cometh as near them whom he contends
to pass, as doth the footman to the Lydian coach, as saith Pindarus:
and besides shows himself fond and of small judgment, or as
Diphilus saith,

A lubber laden with Sicilian grease.

And in divers places, he falleth into Xenarchus' follies. As where
he saith, that he thinks it was an evil token for the Athenians, that
Nicias the captain (whose name was derived of this word *Nice*,
signifying victory) dissuaded their attempts against Sicily: and that
by the throwing down and mangling of the Hermes (to say, the
images of Mercury) it was foreshowed that they should receive
great overthrows by the general of the Syracusans, called Hermocrates, the son of Hermon. And further, that it was not unlikely
that Hercules did favour the Syracusans, by reason of the goddess
Proserpina (protector and defender of the city of Syracusa), to
requite her for that she gave him Cerberus the dog, porter of

hell: and that he did malice the Athenians besides, because they
took the Aegestaeans' part (who came of the Troyans, whom he
much hated), for breaking their promise and faith with him, whose
city himself had overthrown in revenge of the wrong that
Laomedon King of Troy had offered him. Howbeit Timaeus
shows as much wit and judgment, in delivering us such toys in an
history, as he does in correcting the style of Philistus, or in
condemning and railing of Plato and Aristotle. But in my fancy,
this ambition and contention to write or to speak more clerkly
then others, showeth always a base envious mind, like a scholar full
of his school points. But when it striveth with things that are past
all challenge and correcting, then is it extreme folly and madness.
Since therefore I may not pass over nor omit certain things, which
Thucydides and Philistus have already set down, and especially
those wherein they lay open Nicias' nature and qualities, which the
variety of his successes and fortune did cover, I must lightly touch
them, and report so much as is necessary and convenient, lest men
condemn me, for sloth and negligence. And in the rest I have
endeavoured to gather and propound things not commonly
marked and known, which I have collected as well out of sundry
men's works and ancient records, as out of many old antiquities:
and of them all compiled a narration, which will serve (I doubt not)
to decipher the man and his nature.

2   Of Nicias therefore may be said that which Aristotle hath
written of him: that there were three famous citizens of Athens,
very honest men, and which favoured the commonalty with a
natural fatherly love: Nicias the son of Niceratus, Thucydides the
son of Milesius, and Theramenes the son of Agnon. But of the
three, this last was of smallest account: for he is flouted as a foreigner
born in the Isle of Ceos, and challenged besides for inconstant and
irresolute in matters of state and government: and inclining sometimes to one faction, sometime to another, he was called
Cothurnus, a kind of buskin indifferently serving for both legs, and
in old time was used of common players of tragedies. Of the other
two, Thucydides being the elder, did many good acts in favour of
the nobility against Pericles, who always took part with the inferior
sort. Nicias that was the younger, had reasonable estimation in
Pericles' lifetime: for he was joined captain with him, and

oftentimes also had charge by himself alone without him. After Pericles' death, the nobility raised him to great authority, to be as a strong bulwark for them, against Cleon's insolency and boldness: and withal, he had the love of the people, to advance and prefer him. Now this Cleon in truth could do much with the people, he did so flatter and dandle them, like an old man, still feeding their humour with gain: but yet they themselves whom he thus flattered, knowing his extreme covetousness, impudency, and boldness, preferred Nicias before him, because his gravity was not severe nor odious, but mingled with a kind of modesty, that he seemed to fear the presence of the people, which made them thereby the more to love and esteem him. For being (as he was) of a fearful and mistrustful nature and disposition, in wars he cloaked his fear with good fortune, which ever favoured him alike in all his journeys and exploits that he took in hand where he was captain. Now being much afraid of accusers, this timorous manner of proceeding in the city was found to be popular, whereby he won him the goodwill of the people: and by means thereof rose daily more and more, because the people commonly fear those that hate them, and advance them that fear them. For the greatest honour nobility can do to the commonalty, is to show that they do not despise them.

3 Now Pericles, who through his perfect virtue only, and force of his great eloquence, ruled the whole state and commonwealth of Athens, he needed no counterfeit colour, nor artificial flattering of the people, to win their favour and goodwills: but Nicias lacking that, and having wealth enough, sought thereby to creep into the people's favour. And where Cleon would entertain the Athenians with pleasant toys and devices, and could feed the people's humour that way, Nicias finding himself no fit man to work by such encounter, crept into the people's favour with liberality, with charges of common plays, and with suchlike sumptuousness, exceeding in cost and pleasant sports not only all those that had been before him, but such also as were in his time. There yet remain monuments of his consecrating unto the gods: as the image of Pallas in the castle of Athens, the gilt being worn off: and the chapel which is under the festival table of Bacchus: for he many times had the chief prize in Bacchus' dances, and never went away without some game. And touching this matter, there goeth a report that at certain plays

whereof Nicias defrayed the charges, one of his men came forth upon the players' stage before the people, apparelled like Bacchus: and being a goodly tall young man, without any hair on his face, the Athenians took such pleasure to see him so attired, that they made a clapping of their hands a long time together for joy. Therewithal Nicias stood up, and told them, that it were a shame for him to leave the body of a man in bondage, that openly was esteemed as a god: and thereupon forthwith made this young slave a free man. Men write also of certain sumptuous and devout acts he did in the Isle of Delos, where the dancers and singers which the cities of Greece sent thither to sing rhymes and verses in the honour of Apollo, were wont before to arrive disorderly: and the cause was, for the numbers of people that ran to see them, who made them sing straight without any order, and landing in haste out of their ships, they left their apparel, and put on such vestments as they should wear in procession, and their garlands of flowers on their heads, all at one present time. But Nicias, being commanded to go thither to present the singers of Athens, landed first in the Isle of Renia, hard adjoining to the Isle of Delos, with his singers, his beasts for sacrifice, and with all the rest of his train, carrying a bridge with him, which he had caused to be made at Athens, upon measure taken of the channel betwixt the one and the other isle, set out with pictures and tables, with gilding, with nosegays and garlands of triumph, and with excellent wrought tapestry: which in the night he set up upon the channel, being not very broad, and the next morning by break of the day caused his singers to pass over upon it, singing all the way as they went in his procession so nobly set forth, even unto the very temple of Apollo. And when the sacrifice, the feast, and games that were to be played were finished, he gave a goodly palm tree of copper, which he offered up to Apollo, bought lands besides that cost him ten thousand drachmas, which he consecrated also unto the god patron of the isle: and ordained, that the profits of the same should be yearly bestowed by the Delians, upon an open sacrifice and feast, in the which they should pray to their god for the health and prosperity of Nicias: and so caused it to be written and graven upon a pillar he left in Delos, as a perpetual monument and keeper of his offering and foundation. Afterwards, this copper palm tree being broken by winds, it fell upon the great image of the Naxians' gift, and threw it down to the ground.

4  Surely in this ceremony and act of his, there was a marvellous
pomp, and great show of popular ambition: neverthelesss he that
shall consider of his life and actions, may easily persuade himself that
above all he did it of very pure zeal and devotion, and secondly, to
give pleasure and pastime to the people. For by Thucydides' report
of him, he was one that feared the gods with trembling, and was
wholly given to religion. We find written in one of the dialogues of
Pasiphoon, that Nicias did sacrifice daily to the gods, and kept a
soothsayer continually in his house, giving out abroad, that it was to
counsel with him what should happen about the affairs of the
commonwealth: but in truth it was to enquire of his own business,
and specially of his mines of silver. For he had many great mines
about Laurion side, that were very profitable to him: but withal
they dug with great danger, and he was driven continually to keep
marvellous number of slaves at work there. The most part of Nicias'
riches was in ready money, and thereby he had many cravers and
hangers on him, whom he gave money unto: for he gave as well
unto wicked people that might do mischief, as unto them that
deserved reward, and were worthy of his liberality. Thus was his
fear a rent to the wicked, as his liberality was also a revenue to the
good: and hereof the comical poets do deliver us ancient testimony.
For Teleclides speaking of a certain informer saith thus:

> Charicles did refuse to give one mina for to stay
> The bruiting of his secret birth, conveyed close away:
> But Nice, the son of Nicerate, did willingly bestow
> A brace of minas double told. And though I well do know
> The cause of his so doing, yet I will not him bewray:
> For why? The man is my good friend, and wise I dare well say.

And he, whom Eupolis mocketh in his comedy entitled *Maricas*,
bringing a plain simple man upon the stage, doth ask him:

THE INFORMER
> How long is it ago since thou didst speak with Nicias?

THE PLAIN MAN
> I saw him standing even right now upon the market place.

THE INFORMER
> This man affirms he saw him there. And wherefore should he say
> He saw him, but of some intent his lewdness to bewray?
> Now sirs, ye see how Nicias here is taken in the trip,
> For all his walking close in clouds to give the privy slip.

THE AUTHOR

> O foolish folk, suppose ye that so good a man as he,
> In any fault or shameful fact will tardy taken be?

And Cleon threatening, in the comedy of Aristophanes intitled *The Knights*, saith these words:

> The orators if by the throat I take,
> Then sure I am, that Nicias straight will quake.

Phrynichus self also telleth us glancingly, that he was so timorous and easy to be frayed, when he said speaking of another man:

> A good stout man (I know full well) he was,
> And not a coward like to Nicias.

5    Now Nicias being thus timorous of nature, and fearing to give any little occasion to the orators to accuse him, kept himself so warily, that he neither durst eat nor drink with any man in the city, nor yet put forth himself in company to talk, or pass the time amongst them, but altogether avoided such sports and pleasures. For when he was in office, he would never out of the council house, but still busied himself in dispatching causes, from morning till night, and was ever the first that came, and last that went away. And when he had no matter of state in hand, then was he very hardly to be spoken withal, and would offer no access unto him, but kept close in his house: and some of his friends did ever answer them that came to his gate, and prayed them to pardon him, saying, that he was busy then about affairs of the commonwealth. One Hieron, whom Nicias had brought up in his house, and had himself taught him both learning and music, was his greatest procurer and instrument to keep him from speech with any man, and brought him to this reputation of greatness and gravity. This Hieron (as it is reported) was the son of Dionysius Chalcus, of whom they find certain poetical works at this day: who being captain of a certain number of men that were sent to dwell in Italy, did build there the city of Thuries. Hieron I say did serve his turn, and helped him secretly to enquire what he would understand of the soothsayers, and gave out these words among the people: that Nicias led too miserable and painful a life, for the overgreat care he took to serve the commonwealth: insomuch as, though he were in his hot house to wash him, or at his table at meat, his mind ran still

of some matters about the commonwealth, and to serve the state, did neglect his own private affairs: so that he scant began to sleep and take rest, when others commonly had slept their first sleep, and that he looked like nobody. Furthermore, that he was grown crabbed and uncourteous, even to such as before had been his familiar friends. 'So that,' said he, 'he loseth them together with his goods, and all for service of the commonwealth: where others grow rich and win friends by the credit they have to be heard of the people, and can make merry among them, and sport with the matters of state which they have in their hands.' Now in truth, such was Nicias' life, that he might truly say that which Agamemnon spoke of himself in the tragedy of Euripides, called *Iphigenie in Aulide*:

> In outward show of stately pomp all others I exceed,
> And yet the people's underling I am in very deed.

6   And Nicias perceiving that the people in some things did serve their turns with the experience of them that were eloquent, and wiser than others, although they yet mistrusted their sufficiency, and had a special eye to them, plucking down their courage, by taking their authority from them: as for proof the condemnation of Pericles, the banishment of Damon, and the mistrust they had of Antiphon Rhamnusian, and moreover by that they did unto Paches (that took the Isle of Lesbos), who being brought before the judges in open council to give up an account of his charge, drew out his sword, and slew himself in presence of them all. Nicias I say, remembering these examples, sought ever to flee from these offices, which were either too great, or too small, and when he accepted any, had special regard to work surely, and to venture nothing. Whereby all his enterprises that he took in hand, as we may easily conjecture, prospered marvellous well: but yet he imputed nothing to his own wisdom, nor yet to his virtue and sufficiency, but thanked fortune ever for all, and praying diligently to the gods, contented himself to lessen his glory, and that only to avoid envy. As the event of things falling out even in his time do sufficiently witness unto us. For the city of Athens having sustained many great losses and overthrows, he was never a party, nor had ought to do in any of them. As once for example: the Athenians were overcome in Thracia by the Chalcidonians, howbeit it was under the leading of

Calliades and Xenophon, who were their captains. Another time, the loss they had in Aetolia under the charge of Demosthenes. Moreover at Delium, a city of Boeotia, where they lost a thousand men at one conflict, Hippocrates then being there general. And as touching the plague, the greatest number laid the fault thereof to Pericles, who by reason of wars kept the men that came out of the country, within the walls of the city of Athens: and so by changing of air, and their wonted manner of life, they fell into it. Now with none of all these great troubles and misfortunes was Nicias ever burdened: but contrariwise he being captain took the Isle of Cythera, which the Lacedaemonians inhabited, being an excellent place for situation to molest and destroy the country of Laconia. He won divers cities again that had rebelled in Thracia, and brought them once more under the obedience of Athens. At his first coming, having shut in the Megarians within their walls, he took the Isle of Minoa: and at his departure thence, shortly after won the haven of Nisea also. Furthermore, landing in the country of the Corinthians, he overcame them that offered him battle, and slew a great number, and among others Lycophron the captain. At this battle he chanced to forget to bury two of his men that were slain, whose bodies could not be found in gathering up of the rest: howbeit soon as he heard of it, he caused all his fleet to stay, and sent an herald to the enemies, to pray leave to fetch away those two bodies. Now, though by law of arms they that sent to ask leave to take away their dead to bury them, did thereby lose the honour of their victory, and were barred to set up any mark or token of triumph, because it seemed by the suit, that they which had them in their power were conquerors, and not the petitioners that made request for them, which otherwise need not to have made demand of them, Nicias notwithstanding was contented rather to forsake the honour of his victory, than to leave the bodies of two of his countrymen in the field without burial. So, after he had destroyed all the coast of Laconia, and had overcome certain Lacedaemonians that came against him in battle, he took the city of Thyrea, which the Aeginetes kept at that time, whom he brought prisoners unto Athens.

7   And when the Peloponnesians had prepared great armies both by sea and by land to besiege the fort of Pyle, the which

Demosthenes the captain had fortified: battle being given by sea, it
chanced there remained four hundred natural citizens of Sparta
within the Isle of Spacteria. Now the Athenians thought it a noble
exploit of them (as indeed it was), to take those four hundred alive:
howbeit the siege was very sore, because they lacked water even in
the midst of summer, and were forced to fetch a marvellous
compass to bring victuals to their camp, which when winter should
be once comen would be very dangerous, and almost an impossible
thing to do. Whereupon, they then became sorry, and repented
them much that they had sent away the ambassadors of the
Lacedaemonians, which came to them to treat of peace, and that
they had (through Cleon's procurement) suffered them to depart
in that sort without resolution taken: who was against them
altogether, only to do Nicias a despite, being his enemy, and did
earnestly solicit the matter the Lacedaemonians requested. This
was the cause why Cleon persuaded the Athenians, to refuse their
offer of peace. But when the people saw that this siege drew out in
length, and that their camp suffered grievous wants and necessities,
then fell they out with Cleon, and he again burdened Nicias,
saying that through his fear he would let the besieged Spartans
escape, and that if he had been captain, they should not have held
out so long. Thereupon the Athenians said aloud to Cleon: 'And
why doest not thou go thither yet to take them?' Moreover Nicias
self also rising up, openly gave him his authority to take this Pyle,
and bade him levy as many soldiers as he would to go thither, and
not to brag with such impudent words where was no danger, but
to do some notable service to the commonwealth. Cleon at the
first shrank back, being amazed withal, little thinking they would
have taken him so suddenly at his word. But in the end, perceiving
the people urged him to it, and that Nicias also was importunate
with him, ambition so inflamed him, that he not only took the
charge upon him, but in a bravery said, that within twenty days
after his departure he would either put all the Spartans to
the sword, or bring them prisoners unto Athens. The Athenians
hearing Cleon say so, had more lust to laugh a good, than to
believe that he spoke: for it was their manner ever to laugh at his
anger and folly. For it is reported of him, that the people on a time
being solemnly assembled in council early in the morning, to hear
what Cleon would say, and having tarried long for him, at the

length he came with a garland on his head, and prayed the assembly
to dismiss the court till the next morning: 'For,' quoth he, 'I shall
not be at leisure today, because I have sacrificed, and do feast also
certain strangers my friends that are come to see me.' So the people
burst out in a laughing, and broke up the assembly.

8    This notwithstanding, fortune favoured him at that time, and he
handled himself so well in this charge with Demosthenes, that he
took all the Spartans that they besieged, within the time he had
appointed, saving such as were slain: and having made them yield,
brought them prisoners to Athens. This fell out greatly to Nicias'
shame and reproach. For it appeared not only a casting away of his
shield, but worse than that, a voluntary forsaking of his province
upon a base timorous mind, giving his enemy occasion thereby to
do some noble exploit, depriving himself of his honourable charge.
Wherefore Aristophanes mocketh him again, in his comedy of
*Birds*, saying:

> It is no time to sleep and linger still,
> As Nicias doth, without good cause or skill.

Also in another place of his comedy of *Plowmen* he says:

> I fain would follow husbandry. Who lets thee? Marry you.
> A thousand drachmas I will give to be discharged now
> Of office in the common weal. Content, so shall we have
> Two thousand drachmas just, with those that Nicias lately gave.

But herein Nicias did great hurt to the commonwealth, suffering
Cleon in that sort to grow to credit and estimation. For after that
victory, Cleon grew to so haughty a mind and pride of himself, that
he was not to be dealt withal: whereupon fell out the occasion of
the great miseries that happened to the city of Athens, which most
grieved Nicias of all other. For Cleon amongst other things took
away the modesty and reverence used before in public orations to
the people: he of all other was the first that cried out in his orations,
that clapped his hand on his thigh, threw open his gown, and flung
up and down the pulpit as he spoke. Of which example afterwards
followed all licentiousness, and contempt of honesty, the which all
the orators and counsellors fell into, that dealt in matters of state and
commonwealth, and was in the end the overthrow of all together.

9    In that very time began Alcibiades to grow to credit, by practice
in the state, who was not altogether so corrupt, neither simply evil:
but as they say of the land of Egypt, that for the fatness and lustiness
of the soil,

It bringeth forth both wholesome herbs, and also noisome weeds.

Even so Alcibiades' wit excelling either in good or ill, was the
cause and beginning of great change and alteration. For it fell out,
that after Nicias was rid of Cleon, he could not yet bring the city of
Athens again to peace and quietness. For when the commonwealth
began to grow to some rest and reasonable good order, then was
it again brought into wars, through Alcibiades' extreme fury of
ambition. And thus it began. The only peacebreakers and disturbers
of common quiet generally throughout Greece, were these two
persons, Cleon and Brasidas: for war cloaked the wickedness of the
one, and advanced the valiantness of the other, giving to either
occasion to do great mischiefs and also opportunity to work many
noble exploits. Now Cleon and Brasidas being both slain together
at a battle fought by Amphipolis, Nicias straight perceiving the
Spartans had long desired peace, and that the Athenians were no
more so hotly given to the wars, but that both the one and the other
had their hands full, and were willing to be quiet, devised what
means he might use to bring Sparta and Athens to reconciliation
again, and to rid all the cities of Greece also from broil and misery
of war, that thenceforth they might all together enjoy a peaceable
and happy life. The rich men, the old men, and the husbandmen,
he found very willing to hearken to peace: and talking privately also
with divers others, he had so persuaded them that he cooled them
for being desirous of wars. Whereupon, putting the Spartans in
good hope that all were inclined to peace, if they sought it, the
Spartans believed him, not only for that they had found him at
other times very soft and courteous, but also because he was careful
to see that their prisoners of Sparta (who had been taken at the fort
of Pyle) were gently entreated, and had made their miserable
captivity more tolerable. So peace was concluded between the
Spartans and the Athenians for a year, during which abstinence,
they frequenting one another again, and beginning to taste the
sweetness and pleasures of peace, and the safety of free access one to
see another's friends that were strangers, began then to wish that

they might still continue in peace and amity together, without effusion of blood of either party, and took great delight in their dances, to hear them sing such songs:

> And let my spear lie overgrown with dusty spiders' webs.

They did also with great joy and gladness remember him which said, that in peace no sound of trumpet, but the crowing of the cock doth wake them that be asleep: and on the other side they cursed and took on with them that said it was predestined, the war should continue thrice nine years. And so, upon a meeting together to talk of many matters, they made an universal peace throughout all Greece. Now most men thought that surely all their sorrows and miseries were come to an end, and there was no talk of any man but of Nicias, saying: that he was a man beloved of the gods, who for his devotion towards them, had this special gift given him, that the greatest blessing that could come unto the world, was called after his name. For to confess a truth, every man was certainly persuaded that this peace was Nicias' work, as the war was Pericles' procurement, who upon light causes persuaded the Grecians to run headlong into most grievous calamities: and Nicias on the other side had brought them to become friends, and to forget the great hurts the one had received of the other in former wars. And even to this present day, that peace is called Nicium, as who would say, Nicias' peace.

10   The capitulations of the peace were thus agreed upon: that of either side they should alike deliver up the cities and lands which each had taken from other in time of wars, together with the prisoners also: and that they should first make restitution, whose lot it was to begin. Nicias (according to Theophrastus' report) for ready money secretly bought the lot, that the Lacedaemonians might be the first that should make restitution. And when the Corinthians and Boeotians that disliked of this peace, sought by the complaints they made to renew the war again, Nicias then persuaded both the Athenians and Lacedaemonians, that they should add for strength unto their country, the alliance and peace offensive and defensive made between them, for a more sure knot of friendship, whereby they might be the better assured the one of the other, and also the more dreadful to their enemies that should

rebel against them. These things went clean against Alcibiades'
mind: who besides that he was ill born for peace, was enemy also
unto the Lacedaemonians, for that they sought to Nicias, and
made none account of him, but despised him. Here was the
occasion that caused Alcibiades to prove from the beginning what
he could do to hinder this peace, wherein he prevailed nothing.
Yet shortly after, Alcibiades perceiving that the Athenians liked
not so well of the Lacedaemonians as they did before, and that
they thought themselves injured by them, because they had lately
made league with the Boeotians without their privity, and had not
wholly rendered up the cities of Panactum and Amphipolis
according to the conditions articled between them, began then to
enlarge and aggravate the people's complaints, and to make them
offended with every one of them. And furthermore he procured
ambassadors from the city of Argos to come to Athens, and so
handled the matter, that the Athenians made league offensive and
defensive with them. While the matters were thus in hand, there
came to Athens also ambassadors from Lacedaemon, with full
power and authority to set all things at stay, and to compound all
controversies: who having first spoken with the senate, propounded things unto them both very honest and reasonable.
Whereupon, Alcibiades being afraid that they letting the people
understand so much, should thereby bring them to yield to what
they desired, he finely deceived the poor ambassadors by this
devise. He promised upon his oath to help them in that they went
about, so far forth as they would not confess themselves to have
absolute power from the ephors, making them to believe it was
the only way to bring their matters to pass. The ambassadors
giving credit to his words, relied upon him, and so forsook Nicias.
Whereupon Alcibiades brought them before the people being
set in council, and there demanded openly of them, whether
they had full power and authority to accord all matters yea or no.
Whereunto they made him answer with a loud voice, that they
had not. Thereupon Alcibiades, contrary both to their expectation, and his own oath and promise made unto them, began to
call the council to witness whether they did not in open senate say
the contrary, and so advised the people not to trust nor give credit
unto such men, as were openly taken with so manifest a lie, and
that in one self matter would one while say one thing, another

while another. It boots not to ask whether the ambassadors were much amazed to hear Alcibiades' words: for Nicias himself wist not what to say to the matter, the suddenness of the cause did so confuse and grieve him, being a thing he least looked for. Now the people they were so moved besides, that they became indifferent whether to have sent for the ambassadors of Argos presently to have made league with them or not: but there fell out an earth-quake upon this matter, that greatly served Nicias' turn, and broke up the assembly. The people meeting again in council the next morning, Nicias with all that he could do, or say, could scant withhold them from making league with the Argives: and to get leave in the meantime to go to the Lacedaemonians, promising he would make all well again. Thereupon, Nicias going to Sparta, was received and honoured there like a noble man, and as one whom they thought well affected towards them: but for the rest, he prevailed nothing, and being overcome by those that favoured the Boeotians, returned again to Athens as he departed thence. Where he was not only ill welcomed home, and worse esteemed, but was also in danger of his person, through the fury of the people, that at his request and counsel had redelivered such men prisoners, and so great a number of them. For indeed, the prisoners which Cleon had brought to Athens from the fort of Pyle, were all of the chiefest houses of Sparta, and their kinsmen and friends were the noblest men of the city. Notwithstanding, the people in the end did none other violence to him, saving that they chose Alcibiades their captain, and made league with the Elians, and Mantinians (which had revolted from the Lacedaemonians) and with the Argives also: and sent pirates to the fort of Pyle, to spoil the country of Laconia. Upon these occasions the Athenians fell again into wars.

11 Now when the quarrel and controversy was greatest between Nicias and Alcibiades, the *ostracismon* (to wit, the banishment for a time) came in, by the which the people banished for ten years any such of their citizens as they thought either of too great authority, or that was most envied for his wealth and substance. Alcibiades and Nicias were then not a little perplexed, considering their present danger, being sure that the one of them two should not fail but be banished by this next banishment. For the people hated Alcibiades' life, and were afraid of his valiantness: as we have more

amply declared in the description of his life. And for Nicias, his wealth made him to be envied, besides they misliked his strange manner of dealing, being no more familiar nor conversant with the people than he was, and counted him too stately: moreover they hated him also, because in many matters he had spoken directly against the thing the people desired, and had enforced them against their wills to agree to that which was profitable for themselves. In fine, to speak more plainly, there fell out great strife between the young men that would have wars, and the old men that coveted peace, some desirous to banish Nicias, and some others Alcibiades: but

> Where discord reigns in realm or town,
> The wicked win the chief renown.

And so fell it out then. For the Athenians being divided in two factions, gave authority to certain of the most impudent and insolent persons that were in all the city: and among them was one Hyperbolus of the town of Perithus, a man of no havior nor value, why he should be bold: but yet one that grew to some credit and power, dishonouring his country by the honour they gave him. Now Hyperbolus thinking himself free at that time from any danger of banishment (having rather deserved the gallows), hoping that if one of them two were banished, he should match him well enough that remained behind, showed openly, that he was glad of their discord and variance, and busily stirred up the people against them both. Nicias and Alcibiades being acquainted with his wicked practices, having secretly talked together, joined both their factions in one: whereby they brought it so to pass, that neither of them were banished, but Hyperbolus self for ten years. Which matter for the present time made the people very merry, though afterwards it grieved them much, seeing their ordinance of the *ostracismon* blemished by the unworthiness of the person: which punishment was an honour unto him. For this banishment was thought a meet punishment for Thucydides, Aristides, and suchlike men of account as they, or their like: but for Hyperbolus, it was thought too great an honour, and too manifest an occasion of glory to be given to him, that for his wickedness had the selfsame punishment, which was to be inflicted upon the chiefest estates for their greatness. And the comical poet Plato himself saith in a place:

Although his lewd behaviour did deserve as much or more,
Yet was not that the punishment he should have had therefore.
The Ostracie devised was for men of noble fame,
And not for varlets, whose lewd life deserved open shame.

After this Hyperbolus, there was never man banished with the *ostracismon*. For himself was the last, as Hipparchus Cholargian, and nearest kinsman to the tyrant, was the first. Sure fortune is a very uncertain thing, and without conceit of reason. For had Nicias frankly put himself to the hazard of this banishment against Alcibiades, one of these two things must needs have happened him: either to have remained in the city with victory, his adversary being banished: or being convict by his banishment to have escaped those extreme miseries and calamities the which he afterwards fell into, besides the fame he had won of a wise captain, though he had been overcome. I know notwithstanding that Theophrastus writeth, how Hyperbolus not Nicias, was banished through the dissension that fell betwixt Phaeax and Alcibiades: albeit most writers agree with that I have told you before.

12    Now the ambassadors of the Egestans and Leontines being come to Athens, to persuade the Athenians to attempt the conquest of Sicilia, Nicias being against it, was overcome by Alcibiades' craft and ambition. For he, before they were called to council, had already through false surmises filled the people's heads with a vain hope and persuasion of conquest. Insomuch as the young men meeting in places of exercise, and the old men also in artificers' shops, and in their compassed chairs, or half circles where they sat talking together, were every one occupied about drawing the platform of Sicily, telling the nature of the Sicilian sea, and reckoning up the havens and places looking towards Africa. For they made not their account that Sicily should be the end of their wars, but rather the storehouse and armoury for all their munition and martial provision to make war against the Carthaginians, and to conquer all Africa, and consequently all the Africa seas, even to Hercules' pillars. Now all their minds being bent to wars, when Nicias spoke against it, he found very few men of quality to stand by him. For the rich, fearing lest the people would think they did it to avoid charge, and the cost they should be at about these wars, they held their peace, though indeed not contented withal: yet would not Nicias

leave still to counsel them to the contrary. But when they had
passed the decree in council for the enterprise of Sicily, and that the
people had chosen him chief captain, with Alcibiades and
Lamachus, to follow the same, at the next session of the council
held in the city, Nicias rose up again, to see if he could turn the
people from this journey with all the protestations he could possibly
make, burdening Alcibiades, that for his own ambition and private
commodity, he brought the commonwealth into so far and dangerous a war. But all his words prevailed not. Himself before all others
was thought the meetest man for this charge, partly because of his
experience, but chiefly for that they knew he would handle their
matters with greater safety, when his timorous foresight should be
joined with Alcibiades' valiantness, and with Lamachus' softness;
which indeed most confirmed the election. Now after the matter
thus debated, Demostratus one of the orators that most procured
the Athenians to undertake this enterprise stepped forth, and said:
'It were good that Nicias left off, and set aside all these excuses and
devises, and preferred a decree, that the people should thoroughly
authorise the captains that were chosen, to set forward and execute
what they thought good, as well here as there, and so persuaded the
people to pass and authorise it.'

13   Yet it is said that the priests objected many things to hinder
the journey. But Alcibiades also having suborned certain soothsayers, alleged in like case some ancient oracles that said, the
Athenians should have great honour from Sicily: and, further had
enticed certain pilgrims, who said they were but nearly come from
the oracle of Jupiter Ammon, and had brought this oracle thence,
'That the Athenians should take all the Syracusans.' But worst of
all, if any knew of contrary signs or tokens to come, they held their
peace, lest it should seem they intermeddled to prognosticate evil
for affection's sake, seeing that the signs themselves, which were
most plain and notorious, could not remove them from the
enterprise of this journey. As for example, the hacking and cutting
of the Hermes, and images of Mercury, which in one night were
all to be mangled, saving one image only called the Hermes of
Andocides, which was given and consecrated in old time by the
tribe of the Aegeides, and was set up directly over against a
citizen's house called Andocides. Furthermore, the chance that

happened by the altar of the twelve gods, where a man leaping suddenly upon it, after he had gone round about it, cut off his genitories with a stone. And in a temple also in the city of Delphes, where was a little image of Minerva of gold, set upon a palm tree of copper, which the city of Athens had given of the spoils won of the Medes, upon that palm tree sat certain crows many days together, and never left pecking and jobbing at the fruit of it which was all of gold, until they made the same to fall from the tree. But the Athenians said, that the Delphians (whom the Syracusans had subdued) had finely feigned this devise. There was a prophecy also that commanded them to bring one of Minerva's nuns to Athens, that was in the city of Clazomenes. So they sent for this nun called Hesychia, which is, rest: and it seemeth it was that which the gods by this prophecy did counsel them unto, that for that time they should be quiet. Meton the astronomer having charge in the army levied for the war of Sicily, being afraid of this prophecy, or otherwise misliking the celestial signs, and success of the journey, feigned himself mad, and set his house afire. Others say he counterfeited not madness, but did one night indeed set his house afire, and that the next morning looking ruefully on it, he went into the market place as a man brought to pitiful state, to sue to the people, that in consideration of his great misfortune happened him, they would discharge his son of the voyage, who was to take charge of a galley at his own cost, and ready to make sail. Moreover, the familiar spirit of wise Socrates that did use to tell him before what should happen, told him then that this journey would fall out to the destruction of Athens. Socrates told it to certain of his very familiar friends: and from them the rumour became common. And this also troubled a number of them, for the unlucky days on the which they did embark. For they were the very days on the which the women celebrated the feast and yearday of Adonis' death: and there were also in divers parts of the city, images of dead men carried to burial, and women following them, mourning and lamenting. So that such as did put any confidence in those signs, said they misliked it much, and that they were afraid lest the same signified, that all the preparation of this army (the which was set out with such pomp and bravery) would come to nothing.

14   Now for Nicias, that he spoke against this war in open council, whilst they were deliberating upon it, and that he was not carried away with any vain hope, nor puffed up with the glory of so honourable a charge to make him change his mind, therein surely he showed himself an honest man, wise, and constant. But when he saw plainly that he could by no persuasions remove the people from the enterprise of this war, neither yet by suit nor entreaty get himself discharged from being a captain thereof, but that they would in any case make him one of the heads of the army, then was it out of time to be fearful, and still giving back, turning his head so oft like a child to look upon his galley behind him, and ever to be telling that no reason could be heard in determining of this journey. For indeed this was enough to discourage his companions, and to mar all at their first setting out: where, to say truly, he should suddenly have set upon his enemies, and have gone to it with a lusty courage, to have assayed fortune. But he took a clean contrary course. For when Lamachus thought good at their first coming to go straight to Syracusa, and to give them battle as near the walls as might be, and that Alcibiades on the other side was of opinion first of all to go about to win the cities that were in league with the Syracusans, and after that they had made them rebel, then to go against the Syracusans themselves, Nicias to the contrary spoke in council, and thought it better to go on fair and softly, descrying the coasts of Sicily round about to view their galleys and preparation, and so to return straight to Athens again, leaving only a few of their men with the Egestans, to help to defend them. But this from the beginning marvellously cooled the courage of the soldiers, and quite discouraged them. Shortly after also, the Athenians having sent for Alcibiades to answer to certain accusations, Nicias remaining captain with Lamachus (the other captain in sight, but Nicias self in power and authority the lieutenant general of all the army) still used delays, running up and down, and spending time so long in consultation, till the soldiers were left without both hope and courage: and the fear the enemy had of them at their first coming to see so great an army, was now in manner clean gone. Yet Alcibiades being in the army, before he was sent for from Athens, they went with three score galleys to Syracusa, of the which they placed fifty in battle ray out of the haven, and sent the other ten into the haven to discover: which approaching near the city, caused an herald to

make open proclamation, that they were come thither to restore the Leontines to their lands and possessions, and took a ship of the enemies, in the which among other things they found tables, wherein were written the names of all the inhabitants of Syracusa, according to their tribes and houses. These tables were kept far from the city, in the temple of Jupiter Olympian, but at that time they had sent for them to know the number of men of service, and of age to bear weapon. The same tables being taken by the Athenians, and carried to the generals of the army, the soothsayers seeing this long roll of names, at the first misliked it, fearing lest the prophecy had been fulfilled, which promised them, that the Athenians one day should take all the Syracusans. Howbeit it is reported this prophecy came to pass in another exploit, when Callippus Athenian having slain Dion, won also the city of Syracusa.

15   Now when Alcibiades was gone from the camp, Nicias bore all the sway and commanded the whole army. For Lamachus, though otherwise he was a stout man, an honest man, and very valiant of his hands, and one that would not spare himself in time of need, nevertheless he was so poor and miserable, that even when he was in state of a general, and gave up an account of his expenses, he would not stick to put into his books, so much for a gown, and so much for a pair of pantofles. Where Nicias' authority and reputation contrariwise was of another manner of cut, as well for other respects, as for his riches, and for the honour of many noble things which he had done before. As one namely which they tell of him, that on a time being a captain with others, and sitting in council with his companions in the council house at Athens, about the dispatch of certain causes, he spoke unto Sophocles the poet, then present amongst them, and bade him speak first and say his opinion, being the oldest man of all the whole company. Sophocles answered him again: 'Indeed I confess I am the oldest man, but thou art the noblest man, and him whom every man regards best.' So having at that time Lamachus under him, a better captain and man of war than himself was, yet by being so slow to employ the army under his charge by deferring of time still, and hovering about Sicily as far from his enemies as he could, he first gave the enemies time and leisure to be bold without fear of him. And then going to besiege Hybla, being but a pelting little town,

and raising the siege without taking of it, he fell into so great a contempt with every man, that from thenceforth no man almost made any more reckoning of him. At last, he retired unto Catana with his army, without any other exploit done, saving that he took Hyccara, a baggage village of the barbarous people, and where it is said Lais the courtesan was born, and that being then a young girl, she was sold among other prisoners, and afterwards carried into Peloponnesus.

16   And in fine, the summer being far spent, Nicias was informed that the Syracusans had taken such courage to them, that they would come and enterprise the charge upon them first: and that their horsemen were approached already before his camp, to skirmish with them, asking the Athenians in mockery, if they were come into Sicily to dwell with the Catanians, or to restore the Leontines to their lands again. Hereupon with much ado, Nicias determined to go to Syracusa, and because he would camp there in safety, and at ease without hazard, he sent one of Catana before to Syracusa, to tell them (as if he had been a spy) that if they would suddenly come and set upon the camp of the Athenians and take all their carriage, he wished them to come with all their power to Catana at a day certain which he would appoint them. 'For the Athenians,' said he, 'for the most part are within the city, wherein there are certain citizens, which favouring the Syracusans, have determined so soon as they hear of their coming, to keep the gates of the city, and at the same time also to set the Athenians' ships afire:' and how there were also a great number in the city of this confederacy, that did but look every hour for their coming. And this was the noblest stratagem of war, that Nicias showed all the time he was in Sicily. For by this devise he made the Syracusans come into the field with all their power, so that they left their city without guard: and he himself departing in the meantime from Catana with all his fleet, won the haven of Syracusa at his ease, and chose out a place to camp in, where his enemies could not hurt him: in the which he was both the stronger, and might without let or difficulty set upon them with that, wherein he most trusted. The Syracusans returning straight from Catana, and offering him battle hard by the walls of Syracusa, he came out into the field, and overthrew them. There were not many of the Syracusans slain at

this battle, because their horsemen did hinder the chase: but Nicias breaking up the bridges upon the river, gave Hermocrates occasion to mock him. For, comforting and encouraging the Syracusans, he told them Nicias deserved to be laughed at, because he did what he could that he might not fight, as if he had not purposely come from Athens to Syracusa to fight. This notwithstanding, he made the Syracusans quake for fear: for where they had then fifteen captains, they chose out three only, to whom the people were sworn, that they would suffer them to have full power and authority to command and take order for all things. The temple of Jupiter Olympian was hard by the Athenians' camp, which they would gladly have taken, for that it was full of rich jewels and offerings of gold and silver, given unto the temple aforetime. But Nicias of purpose still drove off time, and delayed so long, till the Syracusans at last sent a good garrison thither to keep it safe: thinking with himself, that if his soldiers came to take and spoil the temple, his country should be nothing the richer by it, and himself besides should bear all the blame of sacrilege. So, having obtained victory without profit (which ran straight through Sicily), within few days after he returned unto the city of Naxos, where he lay all the winter, consuming a wonderful mass of victuals with so great an army, for the doing of things of small moment, upon certain Sicilians that yielded to him. The Syracusans in the meantime being in heart again, and courageous, returned to Catana, where they spoiled and overran all the country, and burnt the camp of the Athenians. Herefore every man blamed Nicias much, because through his long delay, and protracting of time to make all things sure, he let slip sundry occasions of notable exploits, wherein good service might have been done. Yet when he would do a thing indeed, he did it so thoroughly as no man could take exception to his doings, for that he brought it to so good a pass: and once taking it in hand, he did execute it with all speed though he was both slow to determine and a coward to enterprise.'

17   Now when he removed his army to return to Syracusa, he brought it so orderly, and also with such speed and safety, that he was come by sea to Thapsus, had landed and taken the fort of Epipolis, before the Syracusans had any intelligence of it, or could possibly help it. For the choice men of the Syracusans being set out

against him hoping to have stopped his passage, he overthrew them, took three hundred prisoners and made their horsemen flee, which before were thought invincible. But that which made the Syracusans most afraid, and seemed most wonderful also to the other Grecians, was this: that in a very short space he had almost environed Syracusa with a wall, which was as much in compass about as the walls of Athens, and worse to perform, by reason of the woody country, and for the sea also that beateth upon the walls, besides that there were divers marshes hard by it: and yet (sick as he was of the stone) he had almost finished it. And sure good reason it is that we attribute the fault of the not finishing of it, unto his sickness. For mine own part I wonder marvellously both of the care and diligence of the captain, and of the valiantness and dexterity of the soldiers, which appeareth by the notable feats they did. For Euripides after their overthrow and utter ruin, made a funeral epitaph in verse, and saith thus:

> Eight times our men did put the men of Syracusa to flight,
> So long as with indifferency the gods did use their might.

But we find it written, that the Syracusans were not only eight times, but many times more overthrown by them: a time at length there was indeed, that both the gods and fortune fought against them, even when the Athenians were of greatest power.

18  Now Nicias in his own person was ever in the greatest and most weighty affairs, striving with his sickly body. Howbeit one day when his disease grew sore upon him, he was compelled to be lodged in his camp with a few of his men: and Lamachus in the meantime alone having charge of the whole army, fought with the Syracusans, who then had brought a wall from the city, unto the wall with the which the Athenians had purposed to have shut them in, to keep that they should not compass it round. And because the Athenians commonly were the stronger in these skirmishes, they many times over rashly followed the chase of their enemies that fled. As it chanced one day that Lamachus went so far, that he was left alone to encounter a company of horsemen of the city, before whom Callicrates marched foremost, a valiant man of his hands, who challenged Lamachus hand to hand. Lamachus abode him, and in the conflict was first hurt: but he gave Callicrates also such a wound therewithal, that they both fell down dead presently in the

place. At that time the Syracusans being the stronger side, took up his body, and carried it away with them: but they spurred cut for life to the Athenians' camp, where Nicias lay sick, without any guard or succour at all: nevertheless, Nicias rose with speed out of his bed, and perceiving the danger he was in, commanded certain of his friends to set the wood afire which they had brought within the trenches of the camp, to make certain devices for battery, and the engines of timber also that were already made. That devise only stayed the Syracusans, saved Nicias, and the strength of their camp, together with all the silver and carriage of the Athenians. For the Syracusans perceiving afar off, betwixt them and the strength of their camp, such a great flame as rose up in the air, upon sight of it turned tail straight, and made towards their city. Things falling out thus, Nicias being left sole captain of the army without any companion, in great hope notwithstanding to do some good, divers cities of Sicily yielded unto him, ships fraught with corn came out of every quarter to his camp, and many submitted themselves, for the good success he had in all his doings. Furthermore the Syracusans also sent to parle with him of peace, being out of hope that they were able to defend their city any longer against him. Gylippus also a captain of the Lacedaemonians, coming to aid the Syracusans, understanding by the way how the city of Syracusa was shut in with a wall round about, and in great distress, held on his voyage notwithstanding, not with any hope to defend Sicily (supposing the Athenians had won the whole country) but with intent nevertheless to help the cities of Italy if he could possibly. For it was a common rumour abroad, that the Athenians had won all, and that their captain for his wisdom and good fortune was invincible. Nicias himself now contrary to his wonted wisdom and foresight, trusting altogether to the good success which he saw to follow him, but specially believing the reports that were told him of Syracusa, and the news that were brought him thence by some of themselves, which came secretly unto him, persuading himself that within few days he should have Syracusa by composition, took no care to withstand Gylippus' coming hither, neither sent any men to keep him from landing in Sicily. By which negligence, Gylippus landed in a passenger, without Nicias' knowledge: so small reckoning they made of him, and so much did they fondly despise him. Gylippus being thus landed far from Syracusa, began

to gather men of war together, before the Syracusans themselves
knew of his landing, or looked for his coming: insomuch as they
had already appointed the assembly of a council to determine the
articles and capitulations of peace, which they should conclude
upon with Nicias. Moreover, there were some that persuaded
they should do well to make haste to conclude the peace, before
the enclosure of Nicias' wall was altogether finished, which then
lacked not much to perform, having all the stuff for the purpose
brought even ready to the place.

19 But as these things were even thus a-doing, arrived one
Gongylus at Syracusa, that came from Corinth with a galley. At
whose landing, the people upon the pier flocking about him, to
hear what news, he told them that Gylippus would be there before
it were long, and that there came certain other galleys after to their
aid. The Syracusans would hardly believe him, until there came
another messenger also sent from Gylippus self of purpose, that
willed them to arm, and come to him into the field. Thereupon
the Syracusans being marvellously revived, went all straight and
armed themselves. And Gylippus was no sooner come into
Syracusa, but he presently put his men in battle ray, to set upon the
Athenians. Nicias for his part had likewise also set the Athenians in
order of battle, and ready to fight. When both the armies were
now approached near each to other, Gylippus threw down his
weapons, and sent a herald unto Nicias to promise them life and
baggage to depart safely out of Sicily. But Nicias would make the
herald none answer to that message. Howbeit there were certain
of his soldiers that in mockery asked the herald, if for the coming
of a poor cape and wand of Lacedaemon, the Syracusans thought
themselves strengthened so much, that they should despise the
Athenians, which not long before kept three hundred Lacedaemonians prisoners in irons, far stronger and more hair on their
heads, than Gylippus had, and had also sent them home to their
citizens at Lacedaemon. And Timaeus writeth also, that the
Sicilians themselves made no reckoning of Gylippus, neither then,
nor at any time after. After, because they saw his extreme covetousness and misery: and then, for that he came so meanly
apparelled, with a threadbare cape, and a long bush of hair, which
made them scorn him. Yet in another place he saith, that so soon

as Gylippus arrived in Sicily, many came to him out of every quarter with very good will, like birds wondering at an owl. This second report seemeth truer than the first: for they swarmed about him, because in this cape and wand they saw the tokens and the majesty of the city and seigniory of Sparta. Thucydides also saith, that it was Gylippus only that did all there. And much like doth Philistus self, a Syracusan, confess, who was present then in prison and saw all things that were done. Notwithstanding, at the first battle the Athenians had the upper hand, and slew a number of the Syracusans, among the which Gongylus the Corinthian was one. But the morning following, Gylippus made them know the skill and experience of a wise captain. For, with the selfsame weapons, with the same men, with the same horses, and in the same places, changing only the order of his battle, he overthrew the Athenians: and (fighting with them still) having driven them even into their camp, he set the Syracusans a-work to build up a wall overthwart (with the very selfsame stones and stuff which the Athenians had brought and laid there for the finishing of their enclosure) to cut off the other, and to keep it from going forward, that it joined not together. So, all that the Athenians had done before until that present, was utterly to no purpose. Things standing in these terms, the Syracusans being courageous again, began to arm galleys, and running up and down the fields with their horsemen and slaves, took many prisoners. Gylippus on the other side, went in person to and fro through the cities of Sicily, persuading and exhorting the inhabitants in such sort, that they all willingly obeyed him, and took arms by his procurement. Nicias seeing things thus fall out, fell to his old trade again, and considering the change of his state and former good luck, his heart beginning to faint, wrote straight to the Athenians to send another army into Sicily, or rather to call that home which he had there, but in any case to give him leave to return, and to discharge him of his office, for cause of his sickness.

20    The Athenians were indifferent before he wrote, to send aid thither: howbeit the envy the nobility bore unto Nicias' good fortune, did ever cause some delay that they sent not, until then, and then they determined to send with speed. So Demosthenes was named to be sent away immediately after winter, with a great navy. In the midst of winter, Eurymedon went to Nicias, and

carried him both money and news, that the people had chosen some of them for his companions in the charge, which were already in service with him, to wit, Euthydemus and Menander. Now Nicias in the meantime being suddenly assailed by his enemies, both by sea and land, though at the first he had fewer galleys in number than they, yet he budged divers of theirs and sunk them. But by land again, he could not aid his men in time, because Gylippus at the first onset had taken a fort of his called Plemmyrion, within the which lay the store and tackle for many galleys, and a great mass of ready money which was wholly lost. Besides, in the same conflict also were many men slain, and many taken prisoners. Yet further, the greatest matter of weight was, that thereby he took from Nicias the great commodity he had to bring his victuals safely by sea to his camp. For while the Athenians kept this fort, they might at their pleasure bring victuals without danger to their camp, being covered with the same: but when they had lost it, then it was hard for them so to do, because they were ever driven to fight with the enemies, that lay at anchor before the fort. Furthermore the Syracusans did not think that their army by sea was overthrown, because their enemies were the stronger, but for that their men had followed the Athenians disorderedly: and therefore were desirous once again to venture, in better sort and order than before. But Nicias by no means would be brought to fight again, saying, that it were a madness, looking for such a great navy and a new supply as Demosthenes was coming withal, rashly to fight with a fewer number of ships than they, and but poorly furnished. But contrarily, Menander and Euthydemus, newly promoted to the state of captains with Nicias, being pricked forwards with ambition against the two other captains (Nicias, and Demosthenes that was then coming) desired to prevent Demosthenes, in performing some notable service before his arrival, and thereby also to excel Nicias' doings. Howbeit, the cloak they had to cover their ambition withal was, the honour and reputation of the city of Athens, the which (said they) were shamed and dishonoured forever, if they now should show themselves afraid of the Syracusans, who provoked them to fight. Thus brought they Nicias against his will to battle, in the which the Athenians were slain and overcome, by the good counsel of a Corinthian pilot called Ariston. For the left wing of their battle (as Thucydides writeth) was clearly overthrown, and they lost a great number of their men. Whereupon Nicias was wonderfully perplexed, considering on the one side that he had taken marvellous pains, whilst he was sole captain of the whole army: and on the other side, for that he had committed a foul fault, when they had given him companions.

21   But as Nicias was in this great despair, they descried Demosthenes upon a pier of the haven, with his fleet bravely set out and furnished, to terrify the enemies. For he had three score and thirteen galleys, and in them he brought five thousand footmen well armed and appointed, and of darters, bowmen, and hurlers with slings about three thousand, and the galleys trimmed and set forth with goodly armours, numbers of ensigns, and with a world of trumpets, hautboys, and such marine music, and all set out in this triumphant show, to fear the enemies the more. Now thought the Syracusans themselves again in a peck of troubles, perceiving they strove against the stream, and consumed themselves to no purpose, when by that they saw there was no likelihood to be delivered from their troubles. And Nicias also rejoiced, that so great aid was come, but his joy held not long. For so soon as he began to talk with Demosthenes of the state of things, he found him bent forthwith to set upon the Syracusans, and to hazard all with speed, that they might quickly take Syracusa, and so dispatch away home again. Nicias thought this more haste than good speed, and feared much this foolhardiness. Whereupon he prayed him to attempt nothing rashly, nor desperately: and persuaded him that it was their best way to prolong the war against the enemies, who were without money, and therefore would soon be forsaken of their confederates. And besides if they came once to be pinched for lack of victuals, that they would then quickly seek to him for peace, as they had done afore time. For there were many within Syracusa that were Nicias' friends, who wished him to abide time: for they were weary of war, and waxed angry also with Gylippus. So that if they were but straited a little more with want of victuals, they would yield straight. Nicias delivering these persuasions somewhat darkly, and keeping somewhat also from utterance, because he would not speak them openly, made his colleagues think he spoke it for cowardliness, and that he returned again to his former delays to keep all in security, by

which manner of proceeding he had from the beginning killed the hearts of his army, for that he had not at his first coming set upon the enemies, but had protracted time so long, till the courage of his soldiers was cold and done, and himself also brought into contempt with his enemies. Whereupon the other captains (his colleagues and companions with him in the charge) Euthydemus and Menander, stuck to Demosthenes' opinion: whereunto Nicias was also forced against his will to yield. So Demosthenes the selfsame night taking the footmen, went to assault the fort of Epipolis: where, before his enemies heard anything of his coming, he slew many of them, and made the rest flee that offered resistance. But not content with this victory, he went further, till he fell upon the Boeotians. They gathering themselves together were the first that resisted the Athenians, basing their pikes with such fury and loud cries, that they caused the former to retire, and made all the rest of the assailants afraid and amazed. For the foremost flying back, came full upon their companions: who taking them for their enemies, and their flight for a charge, resisted them with all their force, and so mistaking one another, both were wounded and slain, and the hurt they meant unto their enemies, did unfortunately light upon their own fellows. For this multitude meeting thus confusedly together, what through their great fear, and what for that they could not discern one another in the night, the which was neither so dark that they could not see at all, nor yet so clear as they might certainly judge by sight what they were that met them: (for then the moon declined apace, and the small light it gave was diffused with the number of men that ran to and fro) the fear they had of the enemy made them mistrust their friends. All these troubles and disadvantages had the Athenians, and beside, the moon on their backs, which causing the shadow to fall forward, did hide their number, and glistering of armour: and contrarily, the enemies' targets, glaring in their eyes by the reflection of the moon that shone upon them, increased their fear, and making them seem a greater number and better appointed than they were indeed. At last, the enemies giving a lusty charge upon them on every side, after they once began to give back and turn tail, some were slain by their enemies, others by their own company, and others also broke their necks falling from the rocks. The rest that were dispersed abroad in the fields, were the next morning every man of them put to the sword by the horsemen. So, the account made, two thousand Athenians were slain, and very few of them escaped by flight, that brought their armours back again.

22    Wherefore Nicias that always mistrusted it would thus come to pass, was marvellously offended with Demosthenes, and condemned his rashness. But he excusing himself as well as he could, thought it best to embark in the morning betimes, and so to hoist sail homewards. 'For,' said he, 'we must look for no new aid from Athens, neither are we strong enough with this army to overcome our enemies: and though we were, yet must we of necessity avoid the place we are in, because (as it is reported) it is always unwholesome for an army to camp in.' And then specially most contagious, by reason of the autumn and season of the year, as they might plainly see by experience. For many of their people were already sick, and all of them in manner had no mind to tarry. Nicias in no case liked the motion of departing thence, because he feared not the Syracusans, but rather the Athenians, for their accusations and condemnation. And therefore in open council he told them, that as yet he saw no such danger to remain: and though there were, yet that he had rather die of his enemies' hands, than to be put to death by his own countrymen. Being therein of a contrary mind to Leo Byzantine, who after that said to his citizens: 'I had rather suffer death by you, than to be slain with you.' And furthermore, as for removing their camp to some other place, they should have leisure enough to determine of that matter as they thought good. Now when Nicias had delivered this opinion in council, Demosthenes having had ill luck at his first coming, durst not contrary it. And the residue also supposing that Nicias stuck not so hard against their departure, but that he relied upon the trust and confidence he had of some within the city, they all agreed to Nicias. But when news came that there was a new supply come unto the Syracusans, and that they saw the plague increased more and more in their camp, then Nicias self thought it best to depart thence, and gave notice to the soldiers to prepare themselves to ship away.

23    Notwithstanding, when they had put all things in readiness for their departure, without any knowledge of the enemy, or suspicion thereof, the moon began to eclipse in the night, and suddenly to lose her light, to the great fear of Nicias and divers

others, who through ignorance and superstition quaked at such sights. For, touching the eclipse and darkening of the sun, which is ever at any conjunction of the moon, every common person then knew the cause to be the darkness of the body of the moon betwixt the sun and our sight. But the eclipse of the moon itself, to know what doth darken it in that sort, and how being at the full it doth suddenly lose her light, and change into so many kind of colours, that was above their knowledge, and therefore they thought it very strange, persuading themselves that it was a sign of some great mischiefs the gods did threaten unto men. For Anaxagoras, the first that ever determined and delivered anything, for certain and assured, concerning the light and darkness of the moon, his doctrine was not then of any long continuance, neither had it the credit of antiquity, nor was generally known, but only to a few, who durst not talk of it but with fear even to them they trusted best. And the reason was, for that the people could not at that time abide them that professed the knowledge of natural philosophy, and enquired of the causes of things: for them they called then Μετεωρολέσχης, as much to say, as curious enquirers, and tattlers of things above the reach of reason, done in heaven and in the air. Because the people thought they ascribed that which was done by the gods only, unto certain natural and necessary causes, that work their effects not by providence nor will, but by force and necessary consequences. For these causes was Protagoras banished from Athens, and Anaxagoras put in prison: from whence Pericles had much ado to procure his delivery. And Socrates also, though he did not meddle with that part of philosophy, was notwithstanding put to death for the suspicion thereof. In fine, the doctrine of Plato being received and liked, as well for his virtuous life, as also for that he submitted the necessity of natural causes unto the controlment and disposition of divine power, as unto a more excellent and supreme cause, took away all the ill opinion which the people had of such disputations, and gave open passage and free entry unto the mathematical sciences. And therefore Dion, one of Plato's scholars and friends, an eclipse of the moon chancing even at the very same time that he was weighing up his anchors to sail from Zacynthe, to make war with the tyrant Dionysius, being nothing afraid nor troubled therewithal, made sail notwithstanding, and when he came to Syracusa, drove out the tyrant. But then it fell out unfortunately for Nicias, who had no expert nor skilful soothsayer: for the party which he was wont to use for that purpose, and which took away much of his superstition, called Stilbides, was dead not long before. For this sign of the eclipse of the moon (as Philochorus saith) was not hurtful for men that would flee, but contrarily very good: 'For,' said he, 'things that men do in fear, would be hidden, and therefore light is an enemy unto them.' But this notwithstanding, their custom was not to keep themselves close above three days in such eclipses of the moon and sun, as Autoclides self prescribeth in a book he made of such matters: where Nicias bore them then in hand, that they should tarry the whole and full revolution of the course of the moon, as though he had not seen her straight clear again, after she had once passed the shadow and darkness of the earth.

24    But all other things laid aside and forgotten, Nicias disposed himself to sacrifice unto the gods: until such time as the enemies came again as well to besiege their forts, and all their camp by land, as also to occupy the whole haven by sea. For they had not only put men aboard into their galleys able to wear armour, but moreover young boys into fisher boats and other light barks, with the which they came to the Athenians, and shamefully reviled them, to procure them to fight: among the which there was one of a noble house, called Heraclides, whose boat being forwarder than his companions, was in danger of taking by a galley of the Athenians, that rowed against him. Pollichus his uncle being afraid of it, launched forward with ten galleys of Syracusa for his rescue, of the which himself was captain. The other galleys doubting also lest Pollichus should take hurt, came on likewise amain: so that there fell out a great battle by sea, which the Syracusans won, and slew Eurymedon the captain, and many other. This made the soldiers of the Athenians so afraid, that they began to cry out, it was no longer tarrying there, and that there was none other way but to depart thence by land. For after the Syracusans had won that battle, they had straight shut up the haven mouth. Nicias could not consent to such a retire. For, said he, it would be too great a shame for them to leave their galleys and other ships to the enemy, considering the number not to be much less then two hundred: but he thought good rather to arm a hundred and ten galleys with the best and

valiantest of their footmen and darters that were in the army, because the other galleys had spent their oars. And for the rest of the army, Nicias forsaking their great camp and walls (which reached as far as the temple of Hercules) did set them in battle ray upon the pier of the haven. Insomuch that the Syracusans, which until that day could not perform their wonted sacrifices unto Hercules, did then send their priests and captains thither to do them.

25 The soldiers being embarked into the galleys, the priests and soothsayers came and told the Syracusans, that undoubtedly the signs of the sacrifices did promise them a noble victory, so that they gave no charge, but only stood upon their defence: for so did Hercules ever overcome, defending, when he was assailed. With this good hope the Syracusans rowed forward, and there was such a hot and cruel battle by sea, as had not been in all this war before: the which was as dreadful to them that stood on the shore to behold it, as it was mortal unto them that fought it, seeing the whole conflict, and what alteration fell out beyond all expectation. For the Athenians did as much hurt themselves by the order they kept in their fight, and by the ranks of their ships, as they were hurt by their enemies. For they had placed all their great ships together, fighting with the heavy against the enemies that were light and swift, which came on on every side of them, whirling stones at them which were sharp to wound how ver they lighted: whereas the Athenians only casting their darts, and using their bows and slings, by means of their rowing up and down could not lightly aim to hit with the head. That manner of fight, Aristo a Corinthian (an excellent ship master) had taught the Syracusans, who was himself slain valiantly fighting, when they were conquerors. The Athenians thereupon being driven to fight, having sustained marvellous slaughter and overthrow (their way to flee by sea being also clearly taken from them), and perceiving moreover that they could hardly save themselves by land, were then so discouraged, as they made no longer resistance, when their enemies came hard by them and carried away their ships, before their faces. Neither did they ask leave to take up their dead men's bodies to bury them, taking more pity to forsake their diseased and sore wounded companions, than to bury them that were already slain. When they considered all these things, they thought their own state more

miserable than theirs, which were to end their lives with much
more cruelty, than was their misery present.

26   So they being determined to depart thence in the night,
Gylippus perceiving the Syracusans through all the city disposed
themselves to sacrifice to the gods, and to be merry, as well for the
joy of their victory, as also for Hercules' feast, thought it bootless
to persuade them, and much less to compel them, to take arms
upon a sudden, to set upon their enemies that were departing.
Howbeit Hermocrates devising with himself how to deceive
Nicias, sent some of his friends unto him with instructions, to tell
him that they came from such as were wont to send him secret
intelligence of all things during this war: and willed him to take
heed not to depart that night, lest he fell into the ambushes which
the Syracusans had laid for him, having sent before to take all the
straits and passages, by the which he should pass. Nicias being
overreached by Hermocrates' craft and subtlety, stayed there that
night, as though he had been afraid to fall within the danger of his
enemies' ambush. Thereupon, the Syracusans the next morning
by peep of day hoist sail, got the straits of Nicias' passage, stopped
the rivers' mouths, and broke up the bridges: and then cast their
horsemen in a squadron in the next plain fields adjoining, so that
the Athenians had no way left to escape, and pass by them,
without fighting. At last notwithstanding, having stayed all that
day and the next night following, they put themselves in journey,
and departed with great cries and lamentations, as if they had gone
from their natural country, and not out of their enemies' land: as
well for the great distress and necessity wherein they were (lacking
all things needful to sustain life), as also for the extreme sorrow
they felt to leave their sore wounded companions and diseased
kinsmen and friends behind them, that could not for their weakness follow the camp, but specially for that they looked for some
worse matter to fall to themselves, than that which they saw
present before their eyes to be happened to their fellows. But of all
the most pitiful sights to behold in that camp, there was none
more lamentable nor miserable, than the person of Nicias self:
who being tormented with his disease, and waxen very lean and
pale, was also unworthily brought to extreme want of natural
sustenance, even when he had most need of comfort, being very

sickly. Yet notwithstanding his weakness and infirmity, he took great pains, and suffered many things, which the soundest bodies do labour much to overcome and suffer: making it appear evidently to every man, that he did not abide all that pains for any respect of himself, or desire that he had to save his own life, so much as for their sakes in that he yielded not unto present despair. For where the soldiers for very fear and sorrow burst out into tears and bitter wailing, Nicias self showed, that if by chance he were forced at any time to do the like, it was rather upon remembrance of the shame and dishonour that came into his mind, to see the unfortunate success of this voyage, instead of the honour and victory they hoped to have brought home, than for any other respect. But if to see Nicias in this misery, did move the lookers on to pity, yet did this much more increase their compassion, when they remembered Nicias' words in his orations continually to the people, to break this journey, and to dissuade them from the enterprise of this war. For then they plainly judged him not to have deserved these troubles. Yet furthermore, this caused the soldiers utterly to despair of help from the gods, when they considered with themselves, that so devout and godly a man as Nicias (who left nothing undone that might tend to the honour and service of the gods) had no better success, than the most vile and wicked persons in all the whole army.

27  All this notwithstanding, Nicias strained himself in all that might be, both by his good countenance, his cheerful words, and his kind using of every man, to let them know that he fainted not under his burden, nor yet did yield to this his misfortune and extreme calamity. And thus travelling eight days journey outright together, notwithstanding that he was by the way continually set upon, wearied, and hurt, yet he ever maintained his bands, and led them whole in company until that Demosthenes, with all his bands of soldiers' was taken prisoner, in a certain village called Polyzelios: where remaining behind, he was environed by his enemies in fight, and seeing himself so compassed in, drew out his sword, and with his own hands thrust himself through, but died not of it, because his enemies came straight about him, and took hold of him. The Syracusans thereupon went with speed to Nicias, and told him of Demosthenes' case. He giving no credit to them, sent presently

certain of his horsemen thither to understand the truth: who brought him word that Demosthenes and all his men were taken prisoners. Then he besought Gylippus to treat of peace, to suffer the poor remain of the Athenians to depart out of Sicily with safety, and to take such hostages for the sure payment of all such sums of money the Syracusans had disbursed by means of this war, as should like himself: which he promised he would cause the Athenians to perform and satisfy unto them. Howbeit the Syracusans would in no wise hearken to peace, but cruelly threatening and reviling them that made motion hereof, in rage gave a new onset upon him, more fiercely then ever before they had done. Nicias being then utterly without any kind of victuals, did notwithstanding hold out that night, and marched all the next day following (though the enemies' darts still flew about their ears) until he came to the river of Asinarus, into the which the Syracusans did forcibly drive them. Some others of them also dying for thirst, entered the river of themselves, thinking to drink. But there of all others was the most cruel slaughter of the poor wretches, even as they were drinking: until such time as Nicias falling down flat at Gylippus' feet, said thus unto him: 'Since the gods have given thee, Gylippus, victory, show mercy, not to me that by these miseries have won immortal honour and fame, but unto these poor vanquished Athenians: calling to thy remembrance, that the fortunes of war are common, and how that the Athenians have used you Lacedaemonians courteously, as often as fortune favoured them against you.' Gylippus beholding Nicias, and persuaded by his words, took compassion of him (for he knew he was a friend unto the Lacedaemonians at the last peace concluded betwixt them, and furthermore thought it great honour to him, if he could carry away the two captains or generals of his enemies prisoners), showed him mercy, gave him words of comfort, and moreover commanded besides that they should take all the residue prisoners. But his commandment was not known in time to all: insomuch as there were many more slain than taken, although some private soldiers saved divers notwithstanding by stealth. Now the Syracusans having brought all the prisoners that were openly taken into a troop together, first unarmed them, then taking their weapons from them hung them up upon the goodliest young trees that stood upon the river's side in token of triumph. And so putting on triumphing garlands upon their heads, and having trimmed their

own horses in triumphant manner, and also shorn all the horses of
their enemies, in this triumphing sort they made their entry into the
city of Syracusa, having gloriously ended the most notable war that
ever was amongst the Greeks one against another, and attained also
the noblest victory that could be achieved, and that only by force of
arms and valiancy.

28  So at their return, a council and assembly was held at Syracusa,
by the citizens and their confederates: in the which, Eurycles one
of the orators, (a practiser in public causes) first made petition, that
the day on the which they had taken Nicias, might forever
thenceforth be kept holy day, without any manner of work or
labour, but only to do sacrifice to the gods: and that the feast should
be called, Asinarus' feast, after the name of the river where the
overthrow was given. This victory was had the six and twenty day
of the month of July. And as touching the prisoners, that the
confederates of the Athenians and their slaves should be openly
sold by the drum: and that the natural Athenians which were free
men, and their confederates of the country of Sicily, should be
clapped in irons, and laid in prison, the captains only excepted,
whom they should put to death. The Syracusans confirmed this
decree. And when the captain Hermocrates went about to persuade them that to be merciful in victory, would be more honour
unto them, than the victory itself, they thrust him back with great
tumult. And furthermore, when Gylippus made suit that for the
captains of the Athenians, he might carry them alive with him to
Sparta, he was not only shamefully denied, but most vilely abused,
so lusty were they grown upon this victory, beside also that in the
time of the war they were offended with him, and could not
endure his strait severe Laconian government. Timaeus saith
moreover, that they accused him of covetousness and theft, which
vice he inherited from his father. For Cleandrides his father was
convict for extortion, and banished Athens. And Gylippus self
having stolen thirty talents out of a thousand which Lysander sent
to Sparta by him, and having hid them under the cusinges of his
house, being bewrayed, was compelled with shame to flee his
country, as we have more amply declared in the life of Lysander.
So Timaeus writeth, that Nicias and Demosthenes were not stoned
to death by the Syracusans, as Thucydides and Philistus report, but

that they killed themselves, upon word sent them by Hermocrates (before the assembly of the people was broken up) by one of his men whom the keepers of the prison let in unto them: howbeit their bodies were cast out at the jail door, for every man to behold. I have heard there is a target at this present to be seen in a temple at Syracusa, which is said to be Nicias' target, covered all over with gold and purple silk, passing finely wrought together.

29    As for the other prisoners of the Athenians, the most of them died of sickness, and of ill handling in the prison: where they had no more allowed them to live withal but two dishfuls of barley for their bread, and one of water for each man a day. Indeed many of them were conveyed away, and sold for slaves: and many also that escaped unknown as slaves, were also sold for bondmen, whom they branded in the forehead with the print of a horse, who notwithstanding besides their bondage endured also this pain. But such, their humble patience and modesty did greatly profit them. For either shortly after they were made free men, or if they still continued in bondage, they were gently entreated, and beloved of their masters. Some of them were saved also for Euripides' sake. For the Sicilians liked the verses of this poet better, than they did any other Grecian's verses of the midst of Greece. For if they heard any rhymes or songs like unto his, they would have them by heart, and one would present them to another with great joy. And therefore it is reported, that divers escaping this bondage, and returning again to Athens, went very lovingly to salute Euripides, and to thank him for their lives: and told him how they were delivered from slavery, only by teaching them those verses which they remembered of his works. Others told him also, how that after the battle, they escaping by flight, and wandering up and down the fields, met with some that gave them meat and drink to sing his verses. And this is not to be marvelled at, weighing the report made of a ship of the city of Camus, that on a time being chased in thither by pirates, thinking to save themselves within their ports, could not at the first be received, but had repulse: howbeit being demanded whether they could sing any of Euripides' songs, and answering that they could, were straight suffered to enter, and come in.

30    The news of this lamentable overthrow was not believed at the first, when they heard of it at Athens. For a stranger that landed

in the haven of Piraea, went and sat him down (as the manner is) in a barber's shop, and thinking it had been commonly known there, began to talk of it. The barber hearing the stranger tell of such matter, before any other had heard of it, ran into the city as fast as he could, and going to the governors told the news openly before them all. The magistrates thereupon did presently call an assembly, and brought the barber before them: who being demanded of whom he heard these news, could make no certain report. Whereupon being taken for a forger of news, that without ground had put the city in fear and trouble, he was presently bound and laid on a wheel, whereon they use to put offenders to death, and so was there tormented a great time, until at last there arrived certain men in the city, who brought too certain news thereof, and told everything how the overthrow came. So as in fine they found Nicias' words true, which now they believed, when they saw all those miseries light fully upon them, which he long before had prognosticated unto them.

### THE END OF NICIAS' LIFE

# Life of Marcus Crassus

Marcus Crassus was the son of a censor, who had also received the honour of triumph: but himself was brought up in a little house with two other of his brethren, which were both married in their father's and mother's life time, and kept house together. Whereupon it came to pass, that he was a man of such sober and temperate diet, that one of his brethren being deceased, he married his wife by whom he had children. For women, he lived as continent a life as any Roman of his time: notwithstanding, afterwards being of riper years, he was accused by Plotinus to have deflowered one of the vestal nuns called Licinia. But in truth the cause of that suspicion grew thus. Licinia had a goodly pleasant garden hard by the suburbs of the city, wherewith Crassus was marvellously in love, and would fain have had it good cheap: and upon this only occasion was often seen in speech with her, which made the people suspect him. But for as much as it seemed to the judges that his covetousness was the cause that made him follow her, he was cleared of the incest suspected, but he never left following of the nun, till he had got the garden of her.

2   The Romans say there was but that only vice of covetousness in Crassus, that drowned many other goodly virtues in him: for mine own opinion, methinks he could not be touched with that vice alone without others, since it grew so great, as the note of that only did hide and cover all his other vices. Now to set out his extreme covetous desire of getting, naturally bred in him, they prove it by two manifest reasons. The first, his manner and means he used to get: and the second, the greatness of his wealth. For at the beginning he was not left much more worth, than three hundred talents. And during the time that he dealt in the affairs of the commonwealth, he offered the tenths of all his goods wholly unto Hercules, kept open house for all the people of Rome, and gave also to every

citizen of the same as much corn as would keep him three months:
and yet when he went from Rome to make war with the Parthians,
himself being desirous to know what all he had was worth, found
that it amounted to the sum of seven thousand one hundred talents.
But if I may with licence use evil speech, writing a truth: I say he
got the most part of his wealth by fire and blood, raising his greatest
revenue of public calamities. For when Sylla had taken the city of
Rome, he made portsale of the goods of them whom he had put to
death, to those that gave most, terming them his booty, only for
that he would the nobility, and greatest men of power in the city,
should be partakers with him of this iniquity: and in this open sale
Crassus never left taking of gifts, nor buying of things of Sylla
for profit. Furthermore, Crassus perceiving that the greatest decay
commonly of the buildings in Rome came by fire, and falling down
of houses, through the overmuch weight by numbers of storeys
built one upon another, bought bondmen that were masons, carpenters, and these devisers and builders, and of those he had to
the number of five hundred. Afterwards, when the fire took any
house, he would buy the house while it was a-burning, and the
next houses adjoining to it, which the owners sold for little, being
then in danger as they were, and a-burning: so that by process of
time, the most part of the houses in Rome came to be his. But
notwithstanding that he had so many slaves to his workmen, he
never built any house from the ground, saving his own house
wherein he dwelt: saying, that such as delighted to build, undid
themselves without help of any enemy. And though he had many
mines of silver, many ploughs, and a number of hinds and plough-
men to follow the same, yet all that commodity was nothing, in
respect of the profit his slaves and bondmen brought him daily in.
As readers, scriveners, goldsmiths, bankers, receivers, stewards of
household, carvers, and other such officers at the table, taking pains
himself to help them when they were learners, and to instruct them
what they should do: and to be short, he thought the greatest care a
good householder ought to have, was to see his slaves or servants
well taught, being the most lively cattle and best instruments of a
man's house. And surely therein his opinion was not ill, at the least
if he thought as he spoke: that all things must be done by servants,
and his servants must be ruled by him. For we see that the art and
skill to be a good husband, when it consisteth in government of

things without life or sense, is but a base thing, only tending to gain: but when it dependeth upon good order and government of men, methinks then it is to know how to govern well a commonwealth. But as his judgment was good in the other, so was it very bad in this: that he thought no man rich, and wealthy, that could not maintain a whole army with his own proper goods. For the war (as King Archidamus was wont to say) is not made with any certainty of expense: and therefore there must no sufficiency of riches be limited for the maintenance of the same. But herein Marius and he differed far in opinion: who having allowed every Roman fourteen acres land (called with them *iugera*), understanding that some were not pleased, but would have more, made them this answer: 'The gods forbid any Roman should think that land little, which indeed is enough to suffice for his maintenance.'

3    This notwithstanding, Crassus was courteous to strangers, for his house was open to them all, and he lent his friends money without interest: but when they broke day of payment with him, then would he roundly demand his money of them. So, his courtesy to lend many times without interest, did more trouble them, than if he had taken very great usury. Indeed when he bade any man to come to his table, his fare was but even ordinary, without all excess: but his fine and cleanly service, and the good entertainment he gave every man that came to him, pleased them better, than if he had been more plentiful of diet and dishes. As for his learning and study, he chiefly studied eloquence, and that sort specially that best would serve his turn to speak in open presence: so that he became the best spoken man in Rome of all his time, and by his great industry and diligent endeavour excelled all them that even by nature were most apt unto it. For some say, he had never so small nor little a cause in hand, but he always came prepared, having studied his case before for pleading: and oftentimes also when Pompey, Caesar, and Cicero refused to rise, and speak to matters, Crassus would defend every cause if he were requested. And therefore was he generally beloved and well thought of, because he showed himself painful, and willing to help every man. Likewise was his gentleness marvellously esteemed, because he saluted everybody courteously, and made much of all men: for, whomsoever he met in the streets that spoke to him as he passed

and saluted him, were he never so mean, he would speak to him again, and call him by his name. It is said also he was very well studied in stories, and indifferently seen in philosophy, specially in Aristotle's works, which one Alexander did read unto him, a man that became very gentle and patient of nature, by using of Crassus' company: for it were hard to say, whether Alexander was poor when he came to Crassus or made poor while he was with him. Of all his friends he would ever have Alexander abroad with him, and while they were abroad, would lend him a hat to cover his head by the way: but so soon as they were returned, he would call for it again. O wonderful patience of a man! To see that he making profession of philosophy as he did, the poor man being in great poverty, did not place poverty in things indifferent. But hereof we will speak more hereafter.

4    Cinna and Marius being now of greater power, and coming on directly towards Rome, every man suspected straight their coming was for no good to the commonwealth, but as appeared plainly, for the death and destruction of the noblest men of Rome. For it so fell out indeed, that they slew all the chief men they found in the city, among whom Crassus' father and his brother were of the number, and himself being at that time but young, escaped the present danger only by flight. Furthermore, Crassus hearing that they laid wait to take him, and that the tyrants sought him in every place, took three of his friends in his company, and ten servants only, and fled into Spain with all possible speed, where he had been with his father before, and had got some friends when he was praetor, and ruled that country. Nevertheless, seeing everybody afraid, and mistrusting Marius' cruelty as if he had been at their doors, he durst not bewray himself to any man, but went into the fields, and hid him in a great cave being within the land of one Vibius Piciacus by the sea side, from whence he sent a man of his to this Piciacus, to feel what goodwill he bore him, but specially for that his victuals began to fail him. Vibius hearing that Crassus was safe, and had escaped, became very glad of it: and understanding how many persons he had with him, and into what place he was got, went not himself to see him, but called one of his slaves (who was his receiver and occupied that ground for him) and bringing him near the place where Crassus was, commanded him every night to

provide meat for supper, to bring it ready dressed to this rock whereunder was the cave, and make no words of it, neither be inquisitive for whom it was, for if he did, he should die for it: and otherwise, for keeping the thing secret as he commanded, he promised to make him a free man. This cave is not far from the sea side, and is closed in round about with two rocks that meet together, which receive a soft cool wind into them. When ye are entered into the cave, it is of a great height within, and in the hollows thereof are many other caves of great receipt one within another, and besides that, it neither lacketh light nor water: for there is a well of passing good water running hard by the rock, and the natural rifts of the rocks also receiving the light without, where they meet together, do send it inward into the cave. So that in the day time it is marvellous light, and hath no damp air, but very pure and dry, by reason of the thickness of the rock, which sendeth all the moistness and vapour into that springing well.

5   Crassus keeping close in this cave, Vibius' receiver brought victuals thither daily to relieve him, and his company, but saw not them he brought it to, nor could understand what they were: and yet they saw him plainly, observing the hour and time of his coming when he brought the same. He provided them no more than would even necessarily serve their turn, and yet plenty sufficient to make good cheer withal: for Vibius was bent to entertain Crassus as honourably as he could possible, insomuch as he considered he was a young man, and therefore reason would he should offer him some occasion to take such pleasure and delight as his youth required. For to relieve his necessity only, he thought that rather a part of fear, than any show of love towards him. One day he took two fair young damsels, and brought them with him to the sea side: and when he came to the cave, showed them where they should get up, and bade them not be afraid. Crassus at the first, when he saw the young wenches, was afraid he had been be-wrayed: yet he asked them what they were, and whom they sought. They being instructed by Vibius what they should say, answered, that they sought their master that was hidden there. Then Crassus knew this was Vibius' mirth to show him courtesy: so he received them into his cave, and kept them as long as he lay there, letting Vibius understand by them what he lacked. Fenestella

writeth, that he saw one of them when she was an old woman, and that he had heard her tell him this tale many a time with great delight.

6  In fine, Crassus (after he had laid hidden in this cave eight months) understanding that Cinna was dead, came out: and so soon as he made himself to be known, there repaired a great number of soldiers unto him, of whom he only chose two thousand five hundred, and with them passed by many cities, and sacked one called Malaca, as divers do write, but he flatly denied it, and stoutly contraried them that affirmed it. And afterwards having gotten ships together, went into Africa, to Metellus Pius, a man of great fame, and that had already gotten a great army together. Howbeit he tarried not long with Metellus, but jarring with him, went unto Sylla, who welcomed and honoured him as much as any that he had about him. Sylla afterwards arriving in Italy, intending to employ all the young nobility he had in his company, gave every one of them charge under him, and sent Crassus into the country of the Marsians, to levy men of war there. Crassus desiring certain bands of Sylla to aid him, being driven to pass by his enemies, Sylla answered him angrily again: 'I give thee thy father, thy brother, thy friends and kinsmen to aid thee, whom they most wickedly have slain and murdered, and whose deaths I pursue with hot revenge of main army, upon those bloody murderers that have slain them.' Crassus being nettled with these words, departed thence presently, and stoutly passing through his enemies, levied a good number of soldiers: and was ever after ready at Sylla's commandment in all his wars. Here began first (as they say) the strife and contention betwixt him and Pompey. For Pompey being younger than Crassus, and born of a wicked father in Rome, whom the people more hated than ever they did man, came yet to great honour by his valiancy, and by the notable acts he did in the wars at that time. So that Sylla did Pompey that honour many times, which he seldom did unto them that were his elders, nor yet unto those that were his equals: as to rise up when he came towards him, to put off his cap, to call him imperator, as much as lieutenant general. And this galled Crassus to the heart, although he had no wrong in that Pompey was taken before him, because he had no experience in matters of war at that time, and also because

these two vices that were bred in him, misery and covetousness, drowned all his virtue and well doing. For at the sack of the city of Tuder, which he took, he privily got the most part of the spoil to himself, whereof he was accused before Sylla. Yet in the last battle of all this civil war (which was the greatest and most dangerous of all other) even before Rome itself, the wing that Sylla led was repulsed and overthrown: but Crassus that led the right wing, overcame his enemies, followed them in chase till midnight, sent Sylla word of his victory, and demanded victuals for his men. But then again he ran into as great defame, for buying or begging the confiscate goods of the outlaws appointed to be slain, for little or nothing. And it is said also, that he made one an outlaw in the country of the Brutians, without Sylla's privity or commandment, only to have his goods. But Sylla being told of it, would never after use him in any open service. Surely this is a strange thing, that Crassus self being a great flatterer of other, and could creep into any man's favour, was yet himself easy to be won through flattery of any man that would seek him that way. Furthermore it is said of him that he had this property: that though himself was as extremely covetous as might be, yet he bitterly reproved and utterly misliked them that had his own humour of avarice.

7 Pompey's honour that he attained unto daily, by bearing great charge and rule in the wars, did greatly trouble Crassus: both because he obtained the honour of triumph before he came to be senator, and also that the Romans commonly called him, Pompeius Magnus, to say, Pompey the Great. Crassus being in place on a time when one said that saw Pompey coming, 'See, Pompey the Great is come.' 'And how great I pray ye?' said he scornfully. 'Howbeit despairing that he could not attain to match him in the wars, he gave himself unto the affairs of the city: and by his pains and industry of pleading, and defending men's causes, by lending of money to them that needed, and by helping of them that sued for any office, or demanded anything else of the people, he attained in the end to the like estimation and authority that Pompey was come unto by his many noble victories. And there was one notable thing in either of them. For Pompey's fame and power was greater in Rome, when himself was absent: and contrariwise when he was there present, Crassus oftentimes was better esteemed than he.

Pompey carried a great majesty and gravity in his manner of life, would not be seen often of the people, but kept from repairing to open places, and would speak but in few men's causes, and that unwillingly: all to keep his favour and credit whole for himself, when he stood in need to employ the same. Where Crassus' diligence was profitable to many, because he kept continually in the market place, and was easy to be repaired unto by any man that required his help, daily following those exercises, endeavouring himself to pleasure every man: so that by this easy access and familiarity, for favour and goodwill he grew to exceed the gravity and majesty of Pompey. But as for the worthiness of their persons, their eloquence of speech, and their good grace and countenance: in all those (it is said) Pompey and Crassus were both alike. And this envy and emulation never carried Crassus away with any open malice and ill will. For though he was sorry to see Pompey and Caesar honoured above him, yet the worm of ambition never bred malice in him. No, though Caesar when he was taken by pirates in Asia (as he was once) and being kept prisoner cried out aloud: 'O Crassus, what joy will this be to thee, when thou shalt hear I am in prison.' This notwithstanding, they were afterwards good friends, as it appears. For Caesar being ready on a time to depart out of Rome for praetor into Spain, and not being able to satisfy his creditors that came flocking all at once about him, to stay and arrest his carriage, Crassus in that time of need forsook him not, but became his surety for the sum of eight hundred and thirty talents. In fine, all Rome being divided into three factions, to wit, of Pompey, Caesar, and Crassus (for as for Cato, the estimation they had of his fidelity was greater than his authority: and his virtue more wondered at than practised), insomuch as the gravest and wisest men took part with Pompey, the liveliest youths, and likeliest to run into desperate attempts, they followed Caesar's hope. Crassus keeping the midst of the stream, was indifferent to them both, and oftentimes changed his mind and purpose. For in matters of government in the common weal, he neither showed himself a constant friend, nor a dangerous enemy: but for gain, was easily made friend or foe. So that in a moment they saw him praise and reprove, defend and condemn, the same laws, and the same men. His estimation grew more, through the people's fear of him, than for any goodwill they bore him. As appeareth by the answer that one Sicinius (a very busy headed man, and one that troubled every governor of the common weal in his time) made to one that asked him, why he was not busy with Crassus amongst the rest: and how it happened that he so escaped his hands? 'O', said he, 'he carries hay on his horn.' The manner was then at Rome, if any man had a cursed bullock that would strike with his horn, to wind hay about his head, that the people might beware of him when they met him.

8    The commotion of fencers, which some call Spartacus' war, their wasting and destroying of Italy, came upon this occasion. In the city of Capua, there was one Lentulus Batiatus, that kept a great number of fencers at unrebated foils, whom the Romans call *gladiatores*, whereof the most part were Gauls and Thracians. These men were kept locked up, not for any fault they had committed, but only for the wickedness of their master that had bought them, and compelled them by force, one to fight with another at the sharp. On a time two hundred of them were minded to steal away: but their conspiracy being bewrayed, three score and eighteen of them entered into a cook's house, and with the spits and kitchen knives, which there they got, went quite out of the city. By the way they fortuned to meet with carts laden with fencers' weapons, that were brought from Capua going to some other city: those they also took by force, and arming themselves therewith, got them then to a strong place of situation. Where amongst themselves they chose three captains, and one Spartacus a Thracian born (and of those countrymen that go wandering up and down with their herds of beasts, never staying long in a place) they made their general. This Spartacus was not only valiant, but strong made withal, and endued with more wisdom and honesty, than is commonly found in men of his state and condition: and for civility and good understanding, a man more like to the Grecians, than any of his countrymen commonly be. It is reported, that when Spartacus came first to Rome to be sold for a slave, there was found as he slept, a snake wound about his face. His wife seeing it, being his own countrywoman, and a wise woman besides, possessed with Bacchus' spirit of divination, said plainly that it did signify, that one day he should be of great power, much dread, and have very good success. This same woman prophetess was then with him, and followed him likewise when he fled.

9    Now first they overthrew certain soldiers that came out of Capua against them, thinking to take them: and stripping them of their armour and weapons, made them glad to take the fencers' weapons, which they threw away as vile and unseemly. After that, the Romans sent Clodius praetor against them, with three thousand men. Who besieged them in their fort, situate upon a hill that had a very steep and narrow ascent unto it, and kept the passage up to them: all the rest of the ground round about it, was nothing but high rocks hanging over, and upon them great store of wild vines. Of them the bondmen cut the strongest strips, and made thereof ladders, like to these ship ladders of ropes, of such a length and so strong, that they reached from the top of the hill even to the very bottom: upon those they all came safely down, saving one that tarried above to throw down their armour after them, who afterwards by the same ladder saved himself last of all. The Romans mistrusting no such matter, these bondmen compassed the hill round, assailed them behind, and put them in such a fear with the sudden onset, as they fled upon it every man, and so was their camp taken. Thereupon divers herdmen and shepherds that kept cattle hard by the hill, joined with the Romans that fled, being strong and hardy men: of which some they armed, and others they used as scouts and spials to discover. Upon this overthrow was sent another captain from Rome, called Publius Varinus, against these bondmen: who first overcame Furius, the lieutenant of Varinus, in battle, and two thousand of his men: and after that again they slew one Cossinius, and overthrew a great army of his, being joined with P. Varinus as his fellow and counsellor. Spartacus having intelligence that Cossinius was bathing himself at a place called the salt pits, had almost taken him tardy, having much ado by flight to save himself: notwithstanding, Spartacus won all his carriage at that time, and having him hard in chase, took his whole camp with great slaughter of his men, among whom Cossinius self was slain. Spartacus having thus now in sundry battles and encounters overcome the praetor himself, P. Varinus, and at the length taken his sergeants from him that carried the axes before him, and his own horse whereon he rode himself, was grown then to such a power, as he was dreaded of every man. Yet all this notwithstanding, Spartacus wisely considering his own force, thinking it not good to tarry till he might overcome the power of the Romans, marched

with his army towards the Alps, taking it their best way after they had passed them over, every man to repair home to his own country, some into Gaul, the rest into Thracia. But his soldiers trusting to their multitude, and persuading themselves to do great things, would not obey him therein, but went again to spoil and overrun all Italy. The senate of Rome being in a great perplexity, not only for the shame and dishonour that their men should be overcome in that sort by slaves and rebels, but also for the fear and danger all Italy stood in besides, sent both the consuls together, Gellius and Lentulus, as unto as difficult and dangerous a war, as any that could have happened unto them. This Gellius, one of the consuls, setting suddenly upon a band of the Germans, which in bravery and contempt as it were, dispersed themselves from their camp, put them to the sword every man. Lentulus, his colleague and fellow consul on the other side, compassed in Spartacus round with a great army, but Spartacus charged his lieutenants that led the army, gave them battle, overthrew them, and took all their carriage. Hereupon, marching on still with his army towards the Alps, Cassius the praetor and governor of Gaul about the Po, came against him with an army of ten thousand men. Spartacus joined battle with him, and overcame him. Cassius having lost a great number of his men, with great difficulty saved himself by flying.

10 The senate hearing of Cassius' overthrow, were marvellously offended with the consuls, and sent commandment unto them, to leave off the war: and thereupon gave the whole charge thereof unto Marcus Crassus, who was accompanied in this journey with many noble young gentlemen of honourable houses, both for that he was marvellously esteemed, and also for the goodwill they bore him. Now went Crassus from Rome, and camped in Romania, tarrying Spartacus' coming, who was marching thitherward. He sent Mummius one of his lieutenants with two legions, to fetch a compass about to entrap the enemy behind, straitly commanding him to follow Spartacus' rearward, but in no case to offer him skirmish nor battle. But Mummius notwithstanding this strait commandment, seeing some hope given him to do good, set upon Spartacus, who gave him the overthrow, slew numbers of his men, and more had slain, saving that certain of them saved themselves by flight, having only lost their armour and weapons. Hereupon

Crassus was grievously offended with Mummius, and receiving his soldiers that fled, gave them other armour and weapons: but yet upon sureties, that they should keep them better thenceforth, than they had before done. Now Crassus of the five hundred that were in the first ranks, and that first fled, them he divided into fifty times ten, and out of every one of those he put one of them to death as the lot fell out: renewing again the ancient discipline of the Romans to punish cowardly soldiers, which of long time before had not been put in use. For it is a kind of death that bringeth open shame withal, and because it is done in the face of the camp, it maketh all the residue afraid to see the terror of this punishment. Crassus having done execution in this sort upon his men, led his army against Spartacus: who still drew back, until he came to the sea side through the country of the Lucanians, where he found in the strait of the Far of Messina, certain pirates' ships of Cilicia, and there determined to go into Sicilia. And having put two thousand men into Sicily, he then revived the war there of the slaves, which was but in manner newly ended, and lacked small provocation to begin it again. But these pirates having promised Spartacus to pass him over thither, and also taken gifts of him, deceived him, and broke their promise. Whereupon Spartacus returning back again from the sea side, went and camped within a little isle of the Rhegians. Crassus coming thither to seek him, and perceiving that the nature of the place taught him what he should do, determined with a wall to choke up the bar or channel entering into this little island, both to keep his men occupied from idleness, and his enemies also from victual. This was a marvellous hard and long piece of work, notwithstanding Crassus finished it beyond all men's expectation in a very short time, and brought a trench from one side of the sea to the other overthwart this bar, which was three hundred furlongs in length, fifteen foot broad, and so many in height: and upon the top of this trench built a high wall, of a marvellous strength, whereof Spartacus at the first made light account, and laughed at it. But when pillage began to fail him, and travelling all about the isle for victuals, perceiving himself to be shut in with this wall, and that there was no kind of victuals to be had within all the compass of the isle, he then took the vantage of a rough boisterous night, the wind being very great, when it snowed exceedingly, set his men a-work, and filled up a piece of the trench (being of a small breadth) with earth, stones, and boughs of trees, whereupon he passed over the third part of his army.

11 Crassus at the first then became afraid, lest Spartacus would have taken his way directly toward Rome: but he was soon put out of that fear, when he heard they were fallen out together, and that a great number of them rebelling against Spartacus, went and camped by themselves by the lake of Lucania, which water by report had this variable property, that at certain times it changeth and becometh very sweet, and at some other times again so salt and brackish, as no man can drink it. Crassus going to set upon them, drove them beyond the lake, but could kill no great number of them, nor follow them very far, because Spartacus came presently to the rescue with his army, who stayed the chase. Crassus had written letters before to the senate, to call Lucullus home out of Thracia, and Pompey out of Spain, whereof he then repented him, and made all the possible speed he could to end this war, before either of them came thither: knowing, that which of them so ever came to his help, to him would the people give the honour of ending this war, and not to himself. Wherefore he first determined to assail them that had revolted from Spartacus, and camped by themselves: who were led by Caius Canicius, and another called Castus. So Crassus sent six thousand footmen before to take a hill, commanding them to lie as close as they could, that their enemies might not discover them: and so they did, and covered their morians and headpieces as well as might be, from being seen. Nevertheless they were discovered by two women doing sacrifice for the safety of their army: and thereupon were all in great hazard of casting away, had not Crassus been, who came in time to their aid, and gave the enemies the cruellest battle that ever they fought in all that war. For there were slain of the slaves at that battle, twelve thousand and three hundred, of which, two only were found hurt in the backs, and all the rest slain in the place of their ranks, valiantly fighting where they were set in battle ray. Spartacus after this overthrow, drew towards the mountains of Petelie, whither Quintus, one of Crassus' lieutenants, and Scrofa his treasurer followed him, still skirmishing with his rearward all the way: yet in fine, Spartacus turned suddenly upon them, made the Romans flee that still harried his men in that sort,

and hurt Scrofa Crassus' treasurer so sore that he hardly escaped with life. But the vantage they had of the Romans by this overthrow, fell out in the end to the utter destruction of Spartacus. For his men thereby, being the most of them fugitive bondmen, grew to such a stoutness and pride of themselves, that they would no more flee from fight, neither yet would they any longer obey their leaders and captains: but by the way as they went, they compassed them in with their weapons, and told them, that they should go back again with them whether they would or not, and be brought through Lucania against the Romans. All this made for Crassus as he wished, for he had received news that Pompey was coming, and that divers were suitors for him at Rome to be sent in this journey, saying, that the last victory of this war was due to him, and that he would dispatch it at a battle, as soon as he came thither. Crassus therefore seeking occasion to fight, lodged as near the enemy as he could, and made his men one day cast a trench, which the bondmen seeking to prevent, came with great fury, and set upon them that wrought. Whereupon fell out a hot skirmish, and still supplies came on of either side: so that Spartacus in the end perceiving he was forced unto it, put his whole power in battle ray. And when he had set them in order, and that they brought him his horse he was wont to fight on, he drew out his sword, and before them all slew the horse dead in the place, saying: 'If it be my fortune to win the field, I know I shall have horse enough to serve my turn: and if I chance to be overcome, then shall I need no more horses.' After that, he flew in among the Romans, thinking to attain to fight with Crassus, but he could not come near him: yet he slew with his own hands two Roman centurions that resisted him. In the end, all his men he had about him forsook him and fled, so as Spartacus was left alone among his enemies: who valiantly fighting for his life, was cut in pieces. Now though Crassus' fortune was very good in this war, and that he had showed himself a noble and valiant captain, venturing his person in any danger, yet he could not keep Pompey from the honour of ending this war: for the slaves that escaped from this last battle where Spartacus was slain, fell into Pompey's hands, who made an end of all those rebellious rascals. Pompey hereupon wrote to the senate, that Crassus had overcome the slaves in battle, but that he himself had pulled up that war even by the very roots. After this

Pompey made his entry into Rome, and triumphed for his victory of Sertorius, and the conquest of Spain. Crassus also sued not for the great triumph, neither thought he the small ovation triumph afoot, which they granted him, any honour unto him, for over-coming a few fugitive bondmen. But for this small triumph, whereby it was called *ovatio*, how much it differeth from the great triumph, see Marcellus' life, where we have at large discoursed thereof.

12 Now Pompey being called to be consul, Crassus, though he stood in good hope to be chosen consul with him, did yet notwithstanding pray his friendship and furtherance. Pompey was very willing to help him, and was ever desirous to make Crassus beholding to him: whereupon he dealt friendly for him, and spoke openly in the assembly of the city, that he would no less thank the people to appoint Crassus his companion and fellow consul with him, than for making himself consul. But notwithstanding they were both consuls together in office, their friendship held not, but were ever at jar, and the one against the other. So by means of their disagreement, they passed all the time of their consulship without any memorable act done: saving that Crassus made a great sacrifice to Hercules, and kept an open feast for the people of Rome of a thousand tables, and gave to every citizen corn to find him three months. But in the end of their consulship, at a common council held, there was a knight of Rome called Onatius Aurelius (a man not greatly known, for that he had no dealings in the state, and kept most in the country), who getting up to the pulpit for orations, told the people what a vision he had seen in his dream. 'Jupiter,' said he, 'appearing to me this night, willed me to tell you openly, that we should not put Crassus and Pompey out of their office, before they were reconciled together.' He had no sooner spoken the words, but the people commanded them to be friends. Pompey sat still, and said never a word to it. But Crassus rose, and took Pompey by the hand, and turning him to the people, told them aloud: 'My lords of Rome, I do nothing unworthy of myself, to seek Pompey's friendship and favour first, since you yourselves have called him the Great, before he had any hair upon his face, and that ye gave him the honour of triumph, before he was senator.'

13    And this is all that Crassus did of any account in his consulship. When he was censor also, he passed it over without any act
done. For he reformed not the senate, mustered not the men of
war, nor took any view or estimate of the people's goods: although
Luctatius Catulus was his colleague and fellow censor, as gentle a
person as any of that time that lived in Rome. Now Crassus at the
first entry into his office of censor, going about a cruel and violent
act, to bring Egypt to pay tribute to the Romans, Catulus did
stoutly withstand him: whereby dissension falling out between
them, they both did willingly resign their office. In that great
conspiracy of Catiline, which in manner overthrew the whole state
and commonwealth of Rome, Crassus was had in some jealousy
and mistrust: because there was one of the confederates that named
him for one of them, howbeit they gave no credit unto him. Yet
Cicero in an oration of his, doth plainly accuse Crassus and Caesar,
as confederates with Catiline: howbeit this oration came not forth
till they were both dead. And in the oration he made also, when his
office and authority of consul ceased, he said that Crassus came
one night to him, and showed him a letter touching Catiline,
certainly confirming the conspiracy then in examination. For
which cause Crassus ever after hated him: and that he did not
openly revenge it, the let was by mean of his son. For Publius
Crassus much favouring eloquence, and being given to his book,
bore great goodwill unto Cicero: in such sort, that upon his
banishment he put on changed garments as Cicero did, and procured many other youths to do the like also, and in fine, persuaded
his father to become his friend.

14    Caesar now returning to Rome from the province he had in
government, intended to sue for the consulship: and perceiving that
Pompey and Crassus were again at a jar, thought thus with himself,
that to make the one of them his friend to further his suit, he should
but procure the other his enemy: and minding therefore to attain
his desire with the favour of them both, sought first the means to
make them friends, and persuaded with them, that by their controversy the one seeking the other's undoing, they did thereby but
make Cicero, Catulus and Cato of the greater authority, who of
themselves were of no power, if they two joined in friendship
together: for making both their friends and factions one, they might

rule the state and commonwealth even as they would. Caesar having by his persuasion reconciled Crassus and Pompey, joining their three powers in one, made themselves unvincible, which afterwards turned to the destruction of the people and senate of Rome. For he made them not only greater than they were before, the one by the other's means: but himself also of great power through them. For when they began to favour Caesar, he was straight chosen consul without any denial: and so behaved himself in the consulship, that at the length they gave him charge of great armies, and then sent him to govern the Gauls: which was, as a man may say, even themselves to put him into the castle that should keep all the city in subjection: imagining that they two should make spoil and good booty of the rest, since they had procured him such a government. Now for Pompey, the cause that made him commit this error was nothing else, but his extreme ambition. But as for Crassus, besides his old vice of covetousness rooted in him, he added to that a new avarice and desire of triumphs and victories, which Caesar's fame for prowess and noble acts in wars did thoroughly kindle in him, that he being otherwise his better in all things, might not yet in that be his inferior: which fury took such hold as it never left him, till it brought him unto an infamous end, and the commonwealth to great misery. Thus Caesar being come out of his province of Gaul unto Luca, divers Romans went thither to see him, and among other, Pompey and Crassus. They having talked with him in secret, agreed among them to devise to have the whole power of Rome in their hands: so that Caesar should keep his army together, and Crassus and Pompey should take other provinces and armies to them. Now to attain to this, they had no way but one: that Pompey and Crassus should again sue the second time to be consuls, and that Caesar's friends at Rome should stand with them for it, sending also a sufficient number of his soldiers to be there at the day of choosing the consuls.

15 Thereupon Pompey and Crassus returned to Rome to that end, but not without suspicion of their practice: for there ran a rumour in the city, that their meeting of Caesar in Luca, was for no good intent. Whereupon, Marcellinus and Domitius asked Pompey in open senate, if he meant to make suit to be consul. Pompey answered them: peradventure he did, peradventure he did

not. They asking him again the same question: he answered, he
would sue for the good men, not for the evil. Pompey's answers
were thought very proud and haughty. Howbeit Crassus answered
more modestly, that if he saw it necessary for the commonwealth,
he would sue to be consul: if not, that he would not stand for
it. Upon these words, some were so bold to make suit for the
consulship, as Domitius among other. But afterwards Pompey and
Crassus standing openly for it, all the rest left off their suit for fear
of them, Domitius only excepted: whom Cato so prayed and
entreated, as his kinsman and friend, that he made him to seek it.
For he persuaded him, that it was to fight for the defence of their
liberty, and how that it was not the consulship Crassus and Pompey
looked after, but that they went about to bring in a tyranny: and
that they sued not for the office, but to get such provinces and
armies into their hands as they desired, under colour and countenance of the consulship. Cato ringing these words into their ears,
and believing it certainly to be true as he said, brought Domitius as
it were by force into the market place, where many honest men
joined with them, because they wondered what the matter meant
that these two noblemen should sue the second time to be consuls,
and why they made suit to be joined together, and not to have any
other with them, considering there were so many other worthy
men, meet to be companion with either of them both in that
office. Pompey fearing he should be prevented of his purpose, fell
to commit great outrage and violence. As amongst other, when the
day came to choose the consuls, Domitius going early in the
morning before day, accompanied with his friends to the place
where the election should be, his man that carried the torch before
him was slain, by some whom Pompey had laid in wait, and many
of his company hurt, and among others, Cato. And having thus
dispersed them, he beset a house round about whither they fled for
succour, and enclosed them there, until they were both chosen
consuls together. Shortly after they came with force to the pulpit
for orations, and drove Cato out of the market-place, and slew
some of them that resisted and would not fly. They also then
prolonged Caesar's government of the Gauls for five years more,
and procured for themselves by decree of the people, the countries
of Syria and Spain. Again, when they drew lots together, Syria fell
to Crassus, and Spain to Pompey.

16 Every man was glad of their fortune. For the people on the one side were: loth Pompey should go far from Rome: and himself also loving his wife well, was glad he had occasion to be so near her, that he might remain the most of his time at Rome. But Crassus of all other rejoiced most at his hap, that he should go into Syria: and it appeared plainly that he thought it was the happiest turn that ever came to him, for he would ever be talking of the journey, were he in never so great or strange company. Furthermore, being among his friends and familiars, he would give out such fond boasts of it, as no young man could have made greater vaunts: which was clean contrary to his years and nature, having lived all his lifetime as modestly, and with as small ostentation as any man living. But then forgetting himself too much, had such fond conceits in his head, as he not only hoped after the conquest of Syria, and of the Parthians, but flattered himself that the world should see all that Lucullus had done against King Tigranes, and Pompey against King Mithridates, were but trifles (as a man would say) to that he intended. For he looked to conquer the Bactrians, the Indians, and the great Ocean sea toward the east, though in the decree passed by the people there was no mention made of any wars against the Parthians. Now every man saw Crassus' ambition and greedy desire of honour: insomuch as Caesar self wrote unto Crassus out of Gaul, commending his noble intent and forwardness, and wished him to go through therewith. But Atteius one of the tribunes being bent against Crassus to withstand his departure (having divers other confederates with him to further his purpose, who much misliked that any man of a bravery and lustiness should make war with any nation or people that had no way offended the Romans, but were their friends and confederates), Crassus fearing this conspiracy, prayed Pompey to assist and accompany him out of the city, because he was of great authority and much reverenced of the people, as it appeared then. For, though multitudes of people were gathered together of purpose to let Crassus of his departure, and to cry out upon him, yet when they saw Pompey go before him, with a pleasant smiling countenance, they quieted themselves, and made a lane for them, suffering them to pass on, and said nothing. This notwithstanding, Atteius the tribune stepped before them, and commanded Crassus he should not depart the city, with great protestations if he did the contrary. But

perceiving Crassus still held on his way notwithstanding, he commanded then one of the officers to lay hold of him, and to arrest him: howbeit the other tribunes would not suffer the officer to do it. So the sergeant dismissed Crassus. Then Atteius running towards the gate of the city, got a chafing-dish with coals, and set it in the midst of the street. When Crassus came against it, he cast in certain perfumes, and made sprinklings over it, pronouncing horrible curses, and calling upon terrible and strange names of gods. The Romans say that those manner of curses are very ancient, but yet very secret, and of so great force as he that is once cursed with that curse can never escape it, nor he that useth it doth ever prosper after it. And therefore few men do use it, and never but upon urgent occasion. But then they much reproved Atteius, for using of these dreadful ceremonies and extreme curses, which were much hurtful to the commonwealth, although he for his country's sake had thus cursed Crassus.

17   Crassus setting forward notwithstanding, sailed on, and arrived at Brundusium, when winter storms had not left the seas, and he had lost many of his ships: howbeit he landed his army, and marched through the country of Galatia. There he found King Deiotarus, a very old man and yet building a new city: and to taunt him prettily, said unto him: 'What, O king, begin you to build now in the afternoon?' To whom the king of the Galatians again smiling made answer: 'And truly, sir captain, you go not very early (methinks) to make war with the Parthians.' For indeed Crassus was three score and upward, and yet his face made him seem older than he was. But to our story again. Crassus being come into the country, had as good luck as he looked for: for he easily built a bridge upon the river of Euphrates, and passed his army over it without any let or trouble. So entering into Mesopotamia, received many cities, that of goodwill yielded themselves unto him. Howbeit there was one city called Zenodotia, whereof Appolonius was tyrant, where Crassus lost a hundred of his men: thereupon he brought his whole army thither, took it by force, sacked their goods, and sold the prisoners by the drum. The Greeks called this city Zenodotia, and for winning of the same Crassus suffered his men to call him Imperator, to say, sovereign captain: which turned to his shame and reproach, and made him to be thought of a base

mind, as one that had small hope to attain to great things, making such reckoning of so small a trifle. Thus when he had bestowed seven thousand of his footmen in garrison, in those cities that had yielded unto him, and about a thousand horsemen, he returned back to winter in Syria. Thither came his son Publius Crassus to him out of Gaul from Julius Caesar, who had given him such honours, as generals of Rome did use to give to valiant soldiers for reward of their good service: and brought unto his father a thousand men of arms, all choice men. This methinks was the greatest fault Crassus committed in all his enterprise of that war. For when he should presently have gone on still, and entered into Babylon and Seleucia (cities that were ever enemies unto the Parthians), he tracted time, and gave them leisure to prepare to encounter his force when he should come against them. Again they found great fault with him for spending of his time when he lay in Syria, seeming rather to lead a merchant's life, than a chieftain's. For he never saw his army, nor trained them out to any martial exercise, but fell to counting the revenue of the cities, and was many days busily occupied weighing of the gold and silver in the temple of the goddess Hierapolis. And worse than that: he sent to the people, princes, and cities about him, to furnish him with a certain number of men of war, and then he would discharge them for a sum of money. All these things made him to be both ill spoken of, and despised of everybody. The first token of his ill luck that happened to him, came from this goddess Hierapolis, whom some suppose to be Venus, other say Iuno, and others, that she is the mother and chief cause that giveth beginning of moisture to everything that cometh forth and hath a being, and taught men the original cause also of every good thing. For as Crassus the father and son both were coming out of the temple, Crassus the younger fell first on his face, and the father afterwards upon his son.

18 Likewise as he was gathering his garrisons together, calling them out of the cities into the field, there came ambassadors unto him from Arsaces, king of the Parthians: who delivered him their message in few words, and told him, that if this army he brought came from the Romans to make war with their master, then that he would have no peace nor friendship with them, but would make mortal wars against them. Further, if it were (as he had heard say)

that Crassus against the people's minds of Rome, for his own covetous desire and peculiar profit, was come in a jollity to make war with the Parthians, and to invade their country, then in that respect Arsaces would deal more favourably, in consideration of Crassus' years, and was contented also to suffer his men to depart with life and goods, whom he took rather to be in prison, than in garrison within his cities. Thereto Crassus courageously answered, that he would make them answer in the city of Seleucia. Therewith Vagises, one of the eldest ambassadors, fell a-laughing, and showing Crassus the palm of his hand, told him thus: 'Hair will sooner grow in the palm of my hand, Crassus, than you will come to Seleucia.' In this sort the ambassadors took their leave of Crassus, and returned to their King Hyrodes, telling him he was to prepare for war. In the mean space, certain of Crassus' soldiers whom he had left in garrison in the cities of Mesopotamia, having escaped marvellous dangerously and with great difficulty, brought him news of importance, having themselves seen the wonderful great camp of the enemy and their manner of fight in the assaults they made to the cities where they lay in garrison. And, as it falleth out commonly among men escaped from any danger, making things more fearful and dangerous than they be indeed, they reported that it was impossible by flying to save themselves, if they did follow in chase: neither to overtake them also if they fled. And further, that they had such kind of arrows as would fly swifter than a man's eye could discern them, and would pierce through anything they hit, before a man could tell who shot them. Besides, for the horsemen's weapons they used, that they were such, as no armour could possibly hold out: and their armours on the other side made of such a temper and metal, as no force of anything could pierce them through. The Romans hearing these news, fell from their former stoutness and courage, being borne in hand before, that the Parthians differed nothing at all from the Armenians and Cappadocians, whom Lucullus had overcome and spoiled so oft, that he was weary withal: and they had already made account, that their greatest pains in this war, was but the tediousness of the journey they had to make, and the trouble they should have to follow those men that would not abide them. But then contrary to expectation, they looked to come to strokes, and to be lustily fought withal. Hereupon, divers captains and head officers that had charge in the army (among whom Cassius the treasurer was one) advised Crassus to stay, and to deliberate in council to know whether he were best to go on, or to remain where he was. The soothsayers themselves did partly let Crassus understand, that the gods showed no good tokens in all their sacrifices, and were hardly to be pacified. But Crassus gave no ear to them, neither would hear any other that told him as much, but only listened to them that counselled him to make haste.

19 Yet Crassus' chiefest comfort and encouragement, was of Artabazes, king of Armenia, who came to his camp with six thousand horse, which were but only the king's cornet and guard. Again he promised him other ten thousand horsemen all armed and barbed, and thirty thousand footmen which he kept continually in pay, and counselled Crassus to enter the Parthians' country upon Armenia's side, because his camp should not only have plenty of victuals, which he would send him out of his country, but for that he should also march in more safety, having a country full of mountains and woods before him, very ill for horsemen, which was the only strength and force of the Parthians. Crassus coldly thanked Artabazes for his goodwill, and all his noble offer of aid: yet told him he would take his journey through Mesopotamia, where he had left many good soldiers of the Romans. And thus departed the king of Armenia from him. But now as Crassus was passing his army upon the bridge he had made over the river of Euphrates, there fell out sudden strange and terrible cracks of thunder, with fearful flashes of lightning full in the soldiers' faces: moreover, out of a great black cloud came a wonderful storm and tempest of wind upon the bridge, that the marvellous force thereof overthrew a great part of the bridge and carried it quite away. Besides all this, the place where he appointed to lodge, was twice stricken with two great thunder claps. One of his great horse in like case, being bravely furnished and set out, took the bit in his teeth, and leapt into the river with his rider on his back, who were both drowned, and never seen after. They say also, that the first eagle and ensign that was to be taken up when they marched, turned back of itself, without any hands laid upon it. Further it fortuned that as they were distributing the victuals unto the soldiers, after they had all passed over the bridge, the first thing that was given

them, was salt and water lentils, which the Romans take for a token
of death and mourning, because they use it at the funerals of the
dead. After all this, when Crassus was exhorting his soldiers, a word
escaped his mouth that troubled the army marvellously. For he told
them that he had broken the bridge which he had made over the
river of Euphrates of purpose, because there should not a man of
them return back again. Where indeed when he had seen that they
took this word in ill part, he should have called it in again, or have
declared his meaning, seeing his men so amazed thereat: but he
made light of it, he was so wilful. In the end he made ordinary
sacrifice for the purging of his army: and when the soothsayer gave
him the entrails of the beast that was sacrificed, they fell out of his
hands. Crassus perceiving that the bystanders were troubled withal,
fell a-laughing, and told them, 'You see what age is: yet shall you
not see my sword fall out of my hand.'

20    So having ended his sacrifice, he began to march forward into
the country by the river's side, with seven legions of footmen, and
little lack of four thousand horse, and in manner as many shot and
slings lightly armed. There returned to him certain of his scouts
that had viewed the country, and told him there was not an enemy
to be seen in the field: howbeit that they had found the track of a
marvellous number of horse, which seemed as they were returned
back. Then Crassus first of all began to hope well: and his soldiers
also, they fell to despise the Parthians, thinking certainly that they
would not come to battle with them. Yet Cassius his treasurer ever
persuaded him the contrary, and thought it better for him to
refresh his army a little in one of the cities where he had his
garrison, until such time as he heard more certain news of the
enemies: or else that he would march directly towards Seleucia by
the river's side, which lay fit for him to victual himself easily by
boats that would always follow his camp, and should be sure
besides that the enemies could not environ him behind, so that
having no way to set upon them but before, they should have
none advantage of them.

21    Crassus going about then to consult of the matter, there came
one Ariamnes unto him, a captain of the Arabians, a fine subtle
fellow, which was the greatest mischief and evil, that fortune could
send to Crassus at that present time, to bring him to utter ruin and

destruction. For there were some of Crassus' soldiers that had
served Pompey before in that country, who knew him very well,
and remembered that Pompey had done him great pleasures:
whereupon they thought that he bore great goodwill to the
Romans. But Ariamnes had been laboured at that time by the king
of Parthia's captains, and was won by them to deceive Crassus, and
to entice him all he could, to draw him from the river and the
woody country, and to bring him into the plain field, where they
might compass him in with their horsemen: for they meant
nothing less than to fight with the Romans at the sword's point.
This barbarous captain Ariamnes coming to Crassus, did highly
praise and commend Pompey, as his good lord and benefactor (for
he was an excellent spoken man) and extolled Crassus' army,
reproving him that he came so slowly forward, tracting time in that
sort as he did, preparing himself as though he had need of armour
and weapon, and not of feet and hands swift and ready against the
enemies: who (for the chiefest of them) had of long time occupied
themselves to flee with their best moveables, towards the deserts of
Scythia and Hyrcania. 'Therefore if you determine,' said he, 'to
fight, it were good you made haste to meet them, before the king
have gathered all his power together. For now you have but
Surena and Sillaces, two of his lieutenants against you, whom he
hath sent before to stay you that you follow him not: and for the
king himself, be bold, he meaneth not to trouble you.' But he lied
in all. For King Hyrodes had divided his army in two parts at the
first, whereof himself took the one, and went to spoil the realm of
Armenia, to be revenged of King Artabazes: and with the other he
sent Surena against the Romans, not for any contempt he had of
Crassus (for it was not likely he would disdain to come to battle
with him, being one of the chiefest noble men of Rome, and to
think it more honourable to make war with King Artabazes in
Armenia) but I think rather he did it of purpose to avoid the greater
danger, and to keep far off, that he might with safety see what
would happen, and therefore sent Surena before to hazard battle,
and to turn the Romans back again. For Surena was no mean man,
but the second person of Parthia next unto the king: in riches,
reputation, valour, and experience in wars, the chiefest of his time
among all the Parthians, and for execution, no man like him.
Surena, when he did but remove into the country only with his

household, had a thousand camels to carry his sumpters, and two hundred coaches of courtesans, a thousand men of arms armed at all pieces, and as many more besides lightly armed: so that his whole train and court made above ten thousand horse. Further, by the tenure of that land he had by succession from his ancestors, his office was at the first proclaiming of any king, to put the royal crown or diadem upon the king's head. Moreover, he had restored King Hyrodes that then reigned to his crown, who had been before driven out of his realm: and had won him also the great city of Seleucia, himself being the first man that scaled the walls, and overthrew them with his own hands that resisted him. And though he was under thirty years of age, yet they counted him a wise man, as well for his counsel, as his experience, which were the means whereby he overcame Crassus. Who through his rashness and folly at the first, and afterwards for very fear and timorousness, which his misfortune had brought him unto, was easy to be taken and entrapped, by any policy or deceit.

22   Now this barbarous captain Ariamnes having then brought Crassus to believe all that he said, and drawn him by persuasion from the river of Euphrates, unto a goodly plain country, meeting at the first with very good way, but after with very ill, because they entered into sands where their feet sunk deep, and into desert fields where was neither tree nor water, nor any end of them that they could discern by eye, so that not only extreme thirst, and miserable way, marvellously amazed the Romans, but the discomfort of the eye also, when they could see nothing to stay their sight upon: that, above all the rest, wrought their extreme trouble. For neither far nor near any sight of tree, river, brook, mountain, grass, or green herb appeared within their view, but in truth an endless sea of desert sands on every side, round about their camp. Then began they to suspect that they were bewrayed. Again, when news came that Artabazes king of Armenia, was kept in his country with a great war King Hyrodes: made upon him, which kept him that he could not according to his promise come to aid him, yet that he wished him to draw towards Armenia, that both their armies being joined together they might the better fight with King Hyrodes if not, that he would always keep the woody country, marching in those valleys and places where his horsemen might be safe, and about the

mountains: Crassus was so wilful, as he would write no answer to it, but angrily told the messenger, that he had no leisure then to hearken to the Armenians, but that afterwards he would be revenged well enough of Artabazes' treason. Cassius his treasurer was much offended with Crassus for this answer: howbeit perceiving he could do no good with him, and that he took everything in evil part, he said unto him, he would tell him no more. Notwithstanding, taking Ariamnes this captain of the Arabians aside, he rebuked him roundly, and said: 'O thou wretch, what cursed devil hath brought thee to us, and how cunningly hast thou bewitched and charmed Crassus: that thou hast made him bring his army into this endless desert, and to trace this way fitter for an Arabian captain of thieves, than for a general and consul of the Romans?' Ariamnes being crafty and subtle, speaking gently unto Cassius, did comfort him, and prayed him to have patience, and going and coming by the bands, seeming to help the soldiers, he told them merrily: 'O my fellows, I believe you think to march through the country of Naples, and look to meet with your pleasant springs, goodly groves of wood, your natural baths, and the good groves round about to refresh you, and do not remember that you pass through the deserts of Arabia and Assyria.' And thus did this barbarous captain entertain the Romans a while: but afterwards he dislodged betimes, before he was openly known for a traitor, and yet not without Crassus' privity, whom he bore in hand, that he would go set some broil and tumult in the enemy's camp.

23 It is reported that Crassus the very same day came out of his tent not in his coat armour of scarlet (as the manner was of the Roman generals), but in a black coat: howbeit, remembering himself, he straight changed it again. It is said moreover, that the ensign-bearers when they should march away, had much ado to pluck their ensigns out of the ground, they stuck so fast. But Crassus scoffing at the matter, hastened them the more to march forward, compelling the footmen to go as fast as the horsemen, till a few of their scouts came in, whom they had sent to discover: who brought news how the enemies had slain their fellows, and what ado they had themselves to escape with life, and that they were a marvellous great army, and well appointed to give them battle. This news made all the camp afraid, but Crassus self more than the

rest, so as he began to set his men in battle ray, being for haste in manner besides himself. At the first following Cassius' mind, he set his ranks wide, casting his soldiers into a square battle, a good way asunder one from another, because he would take in as much of the plain as he could, to keep the enemies from compassing them in, and so divided the horsemen into the wings. Yet afterwards he changed his mind again, and straited the battle of his footmen, fashioning it like a brick, more long than broad, making a front, and showing their faces every way. For there were twelve cohorts or ensigns embattled on either side, and by every cohort a company of horse, because there should be no place left without aid of horsemen, and that all his battle should be alike defended. Then he gave Cassius the leading of one wing, his son Publius Crassus the other, and himself led the battle in the midst. In this order they marched forward, till they came to a little brook called Balissus, where there was no great store of water, but yet happily lighted on for the soldiers, for the great thirst and extreme heat they had abidden all that painful way, where they had met with no water before. There the most part of Crassus' captains thought best to camp all night, that they might in the meantime find means to know their enemies what number they were, and how they were armed, that they might fight with them in the morning. But Crassus yielding to his son's and his horsemen's persuasion, who entreated him to march on with his army, and to set upon the enemy presently, commanded that such as would eat, should eat standing, keeping their ranks. Yet on the sudden, before this commandment could run through the whole army, he commanded them again to march, not fair and softly as when they go to give battle, but with speed, till they spied the enemies, who seemed not to the Romans at the first to be so great a number, neither so bravely armed as they thought they had been. For, concerning their great number, Surena had of purpose hid them, with certain troops he sent before: and to hide their bright armours, he had cast cloaks and beasts' skins upon them. But when both the armies approached near the one to the other, and that the sign to give charge was lift up in the air: first they filled the field with a dreadful noise to hear. For the Parthians do not encourage their men to fight with the sound of a horn, neither with trumpets nor hautboys, but with great kettle drums hollow within, and about them

they hang little bells and copper rings, and with them they all make
a noise everywhere together, and it is like a dead sound, mingled as
it were with the braying or bellowing of a wild beast, and a fearful
noise as if it thundered, knowing that hearing is one of the senses
that soonest moveth the heart and spirit of any man, and maketh
him soonest besides himself.

24 The Romans being put in fear with this dead sound, the
Parthians straight threw the clothes and coverings from them that
hid their armour, and then showed their bright helmets and
cuirasses of Margian tempered steel, that glared like fire, and their
horses barbed with steel and copper. And Surena also, general of
the Parthians, who was as goodly a personage, and as valiant, as any
other in all his host, though his beauty somewhat effeminate, in
judgment showed small likelihood of any such courage: for he
painted his face, and ware his hair after the fashion of the Medes,
contrary to the manner of the Parthians, who let their hair grow
after the fashion of the Tartares, without combing or tricking of
them, to appear more terrible to their enemies. The Parthians at
the first thought to have set upon the Romans with their pikes, to
see if they could break their first ranks. But when they drew near
and saw the depth of the Romans' battle standing close together,
firmly keeping their ranks, then they gave back, making as though
they fled, and dispersed themselves. But the Romans marvelled
when they found it contrary, and that it was but a device to
environ them on every side. Whereupon Crassus commanded his
shot and light armed men to assail them, which they did: but they
went not far, they were so beaten in with arrows, and driven to
retire to their force of the armed men. And this was the first
beginning that both feared and troubled the Romans, when they
saw the vehemence and great force of the enemies' shot, which
broke their armours, and ran through anything they hit, were it
never so hard or soft. The Parthians thus still drawing back, shot all
together on every side, not aforehand, but at adventure: for the
battle of the Romans stood so near together, as if they would, they
could not miss the killing of some. These bowmen drew a great
strength, and had big strong bows, which sent the arrows from
them with a wonderful force. The Romans by means of these bows
were in hard state. For if they kept their ranks, they were griev-

ously wounded: again if they left them, and sought to run upon the Parthians to fight at hand with them, they saw they could do them but little hurt, and yet were very likely to take the greater harm themselves. For, as fast as the Romans came upon them, so fast did the Parthians flee from them, and yet in flying continued still their shooting: which no nation but the Scythians could better do than they, being a matter indeed most greatly to their advantage. For by their flight they best do save themselves, and fighting still, they thereby shun the shame of that their flying.

25   The Romans still defended themselves, and held it out, so long as they had any hope that the Parthians would leave fighting when they had spent their arrows, or would join battle with them. But after they understood that there were a great number of camels laden with quivers full of arrows, where the first that had bestowed their arrows fetched about to take new quivers: then Crassus seeing no end of their shot, began to faint, and sent to Publius his son, willing him in any case to charge upon the enemies, and to give an onset, before they were compassed in on every side. For it was on Publius' side that one of the wings of the enemy's battle was nearest unto them, and where they rode up and down to compass them behind. Whereupon Crassus' son taking thirteen hundred horsemen with him (of the which, a thousand were of the men of arms whom Julius Caesar sent) and five hundred shot, with eight ensigns of footmen having targets, most near to the place where himself then was, he put them out in breadth, that wheeling about they might give a charge upon them that rode up and down. But they seeing him coming, turned straight their horse and fled, either because they met in a marsh, or else of purpose to beguile this young Crassus, enticing him thereby as far from his father as they could. Publius Crassus seeing them fly, cried out, 'These men will not abide us', and so spurred on for life after them: so did Censorinus and Megabacchus with him (the one a senator of Rome, a very eloquent man, the other a stout courageous valiant man of war), both of them Crassus' well approved friends, and in manner of his own years. Now the horsemen of the Romans being trained out thus to the chase, their footmen also would not abide behind, nor show themselves to have less hope, joy, and courage, than their horsemen had. For they thought all had been won, and

that there was no more to do, but to follow the chase: till they were
gone far from the army, and then they found the deceit. For the
horsemen that fled before them, suddenly turned again, and a
number of others besides came and set upon them. Whereupon
they stayed, thinking that the enemies perceiving they were so
few, would come and fight with them hand to hand. Howbeit they
set out against them their men at arms with their barbed horse, and
made their light horsemen wheel round about them, keeping none
order at all: who galloping up and down the plain, whirled up the
sand hills from the bottom with their horse feet, which raised such
a wonderful dust, that the Romans could scarce see or speak one to
another. For they being shut up into a little room, and standing
close one to another, were sore wounded with the Parthians'
arrows, and died of a cruel lingering death, crying out for anguish
and pain they felt: and turning and tormenting themselves upon
the sand, they broke the arrows sticking in them. Again, striving by
force to pluck out the forked arrow heads, that had pierced far into
their bodies through their veins and sinews, thereby they opened
their wounds wider, and so cast themselves away. Many of them
died thus miserably martyred: and such as died not, were not able
to defend themselves. Then when Publius Crassus prayed and
besought them to charge the men at arms with their barbed horse,
they showed him their hands fast nailed to their targets with
arrows, and their feet likewise shot through and nailed to the
ground: so as they could neither flee, nor yet defend themselves.
Thereupon himself encouraging his horsemen, went and gave a
charge, and did valiantly set upon the enemies, but it was with too
great disadvantage, both for offence, and also for defence. For
himself and his men with weak and light staves, broke upon them
that were armed with cuirasses of steel, or stiff leather jacks. And
the Parthians in contrary manner with mighty strong pikes gave
charge upon these Gauls, which were either unarmed, or else but
lightly armed. Yet those were they in whom Crassus most trusted,
having done wonderful feats of war with them. For they received
the Parthians' pikes in their hands, and took them about the
middles, and threw them off their horse, where they lay on the
ground, and could not stir for the weight of their harness: and there
were divers of them also that lighting from their horse, lay under
their enemies' horse bellies, and thrust their swords into them.

Their horse flinging and bounding in the air for very pain threw their masters under feet, and their enemies one upon another, and in the end fell dead among them. Moreover, extreme heat and thirst did marvellously cumber the Gauls, who were used to abide neither of both: and the most part of their horse were slain, charging with all their power upon the men at arms of the Parthians, and so ran themselves in upon the points of their pikes. At the length, they were driven to retire towards their footmen, and Publius Crassus among them, who was very ill by reason of the wounds he had received. And seeing a sand hill by chance not far from them, they went thither, and setting their horse in the midst of it, compassed it in round with their targets, thinking by this means to cover and defend themselves the better from the barbarous people: howbeit they found it contrary. For the country being plain, they in the foremost ranks did somewhat cover them behind, but they that were behind, standing higher than they that stood foremost (by reason of the nature of the hill that was highest in the midst) could by no means save themselves, but were all hurt alike, as well the one as the other, bewailing their own misery and misfortune, that must needs die without revenge, or declaration of their valiancy. At that present time there were two Grecians about Publius Crassus, Hieronymus and Nicomachus, who dwelt in those quarters in the city of Carres: they both counselled P. Crassus to steal away with them, and to flee to a city called Ischnes, that was not far from thence, and took the Romans' part. But P. answered them, that there was no death so cruel as could make him forsake them, that died for his sake. When he had so said, wishing them to save themselves, he embraced them, and took his leave of them: and being very sore hurt with the shot of an arrow through one of his hands, commanded one of his gentlemen to thrust him through with a sword, and so turned his side to him for the purpose. It is reported Censorinus did the like. But Megabacchus slew himself with his own hands, and so did the most part of the gentlemen that were of that company. And for those that were left alive, the Parthians got up the sand hill, and fighting with them, thrust them through with their spears and pikes, and took but five hundred prisoners. After that, they struck off Publius Crassus' head, and thereupon returned straight to set upon his father Crassus, who was then in this state.

26 Crassus the father, after he had willed his son to charge the
enemies, and that one brought him word he had broken them, and
pursued the chase: and perceiving also that they that remained in
their great battle, did not press upon him so near as they did before,
because that a great number of them were gone after the other for
rescue, he then began to be lively again, and keeping his men close,
retired with them the best he could by a hill's side, looking ever
that his son would not be long before that he returned from the
chase. But Publius seeing himself in danger, had sent divers messengers to his father, to advertise him of his distress, whom the
Parthians intercepted and slew by the way: and the last messengers
he sent, escaping very hardly, brought Crassus news, that his son
was but cast away, if he did not presently aid him, and that with a
great power. These news were grievous to Crassus in two respects:
first for the fear he had, seeing himself in danger to lose all, and
secondly for the vehement desire he had to go to his son's help.
Thus he saw in reason all would come to nought, and in fine
determined to go with all his power, to the rescue of his son. But
in the meantime the enemies were returned from his son's overthrow, with a more dreadful noise and cry of victory, than ever
before: and thereupon their deadly sounding drums filled the air
with their wonderful noise. The Romans then looked straight for a
hot alarm. But the Parthians that brought Publius Crassus' head
upon the point of a lance, coming near to the Romans, showed
them his head, and asked them in derision, if they knew what
house he was of, and who were his parents: 'For it is not likely,'
said they, 'that so noble and valiant a young man should be the son
of so cowardly a father, as Crassus.' The sight of Publius Crassus'
head killed the Romans' hearts more, than any other danger they
had been in at any time in all the battle. For it did not set their
hearts afire as it should have done, with anger and desire of
revenge: but far otherwise, made them quake for fear, and struck
them stark dead to behold it. Yet Crassus self showed greater
courage in this misfortune, than he before had done in all the war
beside. For riding by every band he cried out aloud: 'The grief
and sorrow of this loss, my fellows, is no man's but mine, mine
only: but the noble success and honour of Rome remaineth still
unvincible, so long as you are yet living. Now, if you pity my loss
of so noble and valiant a son, my good soldiers, let me entreat you

to turn your sorrow into fury: make them dearly buy the joy they have gotten: be revenged of their cruelty, and let not my misfortune fear you. For why? Aspiring minds sometime must needs sustain loss. Lucullus overcame not Tigranes, nor Scipio Antiochus, but their blood did pay for it. Our ancestors in old time lost a thousand ships, yea in Italy divers armies and chieftains for the conquest of Sicilia: yet for all the loss of them, at the length they were victorious over them, by whom they were before vanquished. For the empire of Rome came not to that greatness it now is at, by good fortune only, but by patience and constant suffering of trouble and adversity, never yielding or giving place to any danger.'

27    Crassus using these persuasions to encourage his soldiers for resolution, found that all his words wrought none effect: but contrarily, after he had commanded them to give the shout of battle, he plainly saw their hearts were done, for that their shout rose but faint, and not all alike. The Parthians on the other side, their shout was great, and lustily they rang it out. Now when they came to join, the Parthians' archers a-horseback compassing in the Romans upon the wings, shot an infinite number of arrows at their sides. But their men at arms giving charge upon the front of the Romans' battle with their great lances, compelled them to draw into a narrow room, a few excepted, that valiantly, and in desperate manner, ran in among them, as men rather desiring so to die, than to be slain with their arrows, where they could do the Parthians almost no hurt at all. So were they soon dispatched, with the great lances that ran them through, head, wood and all, with such a force, as oftentimes they ran through two at once. Thus when they had fought the whole day, night drew on, and made them retire, saying they would give Crassus that night's respite, to lament and bewail his son's death: unless that otherwise he wisely looking about him thought it better for his safety to come and offer himself to King Arsaces' mercy, than to tarry to be brought unto him by force. So the Parthians camping hard by the Romans, were in very good hope to overthrow him the next morning. The Romans on the other side had a marvellous ill night, making no reckoning to bury their dead, nor to dress their wounded men, that died in miserable pain: but every man bewailed his hard fortune, when

they saw not one of them could escape, if they tarried till the morning. On the other side, to depart in the night through that desert, their wounded men did grieve them much. Because, to carry them so away, they knew it would let their flight: and yet to leave them so behind, their pitiful cries would give the enemies knowledge of their departure. Now, though they all thought Crassus the only author of their misery, yet were they desirous to see his face, and to hear him speak. But Crassus went aside without light, and laid him down with his head covered, because he would see no man, showing thereby the common sort an example of unstable fortune: and the wise men, a good learning to know the fruits of ill counsel and vain ambition, that had so much blinded him, as he could not be content to command so many thousands of men, but thought (as a man would say) himself the meanest of all other, and one that possessed nothing, because he was accounted inferior unto two persons only, Pompey and Caesar. Notwithstanding, Octavius, one of his chieftains, and Cassius the treasurer, made him rise, and sought to comfort him the best they could. But in the end, seeing him so overcome with sorrow, and out of heart, that he had no life nor spirit in him, they themselves called the captains and centurions together, and sat in council for their departure, and so agreed that there was no longer tarrying for them. Thus of their own authority at the first they made the army march away, without any sound of trumpet or other noise. But immediately after, they that were left hurt and sick, and could not follow, seeing the camp remove, fell a-crying out and tormenting themselves in such sort, that they filled the whole camp with sorrow, and put them out of all order, with the great moan and loud lamentation: so as the foremost rank that first dislodged, fell into a marvellous fear, thinking they had been the enemies that had come and set upon them. Then turning oft, and setting themselves in battle ray, one while loading their beasts with the wounded men, another while unloading them again, they were left behind, saving three hundred horsemen that scaped, who came about midnight to the city of Carres. Ignatius their captain called to the watch on the walls, and spoke in the Latin tongue. Who answering, he willed them to tell Coponius, governor of the town, that Crassus had fought a great battle with the Parthians, and said no more, neither told what he was: but rode on still, till he came to the

bridge which Crassus had made over Euphrates. Yet this word
Ignatius gave to the watch to tell Coponius, served Crassus' turn
very well. For Coponius thought by this great haste of his, and the
short confused speech he made, passing on his way, that he had no
good news to tell them: wherefore he straight armed his soldiers,
and understanding that Crassus was returning back, went to meet
him, and brought him and his army into the city of Carres.

28    The Parthians knew well enough of the removing of the
Romans' camp, but yet would not follow them in the night, but
the next morning entering into their camp where they lay, slew all
that were left behind, which were about four thousand men: and
riding after them that were gone, took many stragglers in the plain.
Among them there was Barguntinus, one of Crassus' lieutenants,
who strayed in the night out of the army with four whole ensigns,
and having lost his way, got to a hill, where the Parthians besieged
him, slew him and all his company, though he valiantly there
defended himself: yet twenty of them only escaped, who with their
swords drawn in their hands, running forward with their heads
thrust in among the thickest of the Parthians: they wondering at
their desperation, opened of themselves, and suffered them to
march on towards the city of Carres. In the meantime false news
was brought to Surena, how Crassus with all the chiefest men of his
host was fled, and that the great number that were received into
the city of Carres were men of all sorts gathered together, and not
a man of any quality or estimation. Surena thereupon thinking he
had lost the honour of his victory, yet standing in some doubt of it,
because he would know the truth, that he might either besiege the
city of Carres, or pursue after Crassus, sent one of his interpreters to
the walls of the city, charging him to call for Crassus, or Cassius,
and to tell them that Surena would parle with them. The interpreter did as he was commanded. Word was brought to Crassus,
and he accepted parlance. Shortly after also, thither came certain
soldiers of the Arabians from the camp of the Parthians, who knew
Crassus and Cassius very well by sight, having divers times seen
them in their camp before the battle. These Arabians seeing Cassius
upon the walls, told him, that Surena was contented to make peace
with them, and to let them go safely, as his master's good friends, so
that they would surrender Mesopotamia into the king of Parthia's

hands, and how they thought that was the best way for both parties, rather than to be enforced unto it by extremity. Cassius thought this a good offer, and told them, that they must appoint the day and place, where Crassus and Surena should meet to talk together of the matter. The Arabians made answer they would do it: and so departed.

29 Surena hearing this, was glad he had them at such advantage, where he might besiege them. The next day he brought all his army before the city of Carres. There the Parthians marvellously reviled the Romans, and told them, they must deliver them Crassus and Cassius bound hands and feet, if they would have any grace or peace with them. The Romans were marvellously offended that they were thus deceived, and told Crassus, that it was no boot any longer to look for aid of the Armenians, but presently to flee: howbeit to keep it secret in any wise from any of the Carrenians, till the very hour of their departure. Yet Crassus self had told it to Andromachus, the veriest traitor and villain in all the city, whom he had chosen to be his guide. This traitor Andromachus advertised the enemies in every point of their purpose and departure. But because the Parthians do never use to fight in the night, and that it was a hard matter to bring them to it, and again that Crassus departed in the night time, Andromachus was afraid lest the Romans would win such ground before the Parthians, as they could not possibly overtake him the next day. Therefore of purpose he sometime brought them one way, other while another way, and at the last, brought them into a great bog or marsh, full of deep holes and ditches, and where they must needs make many turns and returns before they could get out again, and yet very hardly. Whereupon, some in the army began to mistrust, that Andromachus meant no good to turn and toss them up and down in that sort, and therefore would follow him no more: insomuch as Cassius among others, returned towards the city of Carres again, from whence they came. And when his guides (who were Arabians) counselled him to tarry there, till the moon were out of the sign of Scorpio, he answered them, 'I fear the sign of Sagittary more.' So as soon as he could, he took his way towards Assyria with five hundred horsemen. And other of the army also having faithful guides, recovered a country of the mountains, called

Sinnaca, and retired into a safe place before the break of day: and they were about five hundred men, whom Octavius a nobleman had in charge. But the day stole upon Crassus, hunting up and down yet in the marsh, in those ill-favoured places, into the which Andromachus that traitor had of purpose brought him, having with him four ensigns of footmen all with targets, and very few horsemen, and five sergeants that carried the axes and rods before him: with whom, with much ado and great labour, he got into the right way, when the enemies were almost upon him, and that he was within twelve furlong of joining with Octavius. There in haste he had gotten a hill, which was not so steep for horsemen, neither of such strength as the other hills were, called Sinnaces, yet under them, and joining to them by a long hill that runneth along the plain, so as Octavius plainly saw the danger Crassus was in. Thereupon he first ran down the hills with a few of his men that followed him: but after also came all the rest, saying they were cowards if they should tarry behind. At their coming they gave such a hot onset upon the Parthians that they made them give back from that hill: and compassing Crassus in the midst of them, covering him round with their targets, they spoke nobly, that never arrow of the Parthians should touch the body of their general, before they were slain one after another, and that they had fought it out to the last man in his defence.

30    Hereupon Surena perceiving the Parthians were not so courageous as they were wont to be, and that if night came upon them, and that the Romans did once recover the high mountains, they could never possibly be met withal again, he thought cunningly to beguile Crassus once more by this devise. He let certain prisoners go of purpose, before whom he made his men give out this speech. That the king of Parthia would have no mortal war with the Romans: but far otherwise, he rather desired their friendship, by showing them some notable favour, as to use Crassus very courteously. And to give colour to this bruit, he called his men from fight: and going himself in person towards Crassus, with the chiefest of the nobility of his host, in quiet manner, his bow unbent, he held out his right hand, and called Crassus to talk with him of peace, and said unto him: though the Romans had felt the force and power of their king, it was against his will, for he could

do no less but defend himself: howbeit that now he was very willing and desirous to make them taste of his mercy and clemency, and was contented to make peace with them, and to let them go safely where they would. All the Romans besides Crassus were glad of Surena's words. But Crassus that had been deceived before by their crafty fetches and devices, considering also no cause apparent to make them change thus suddenly, would not hearken to it, but first consulted with his friends. Howbeit the soldiers they cried out on him to go, and fell at words with him, saying: that he cared not though they were all slain, and that himself had not the heart only to come down and talk with the enemies that were unarmed. Crassus proved first to pacify them by fair means, persuading them to bear a little patience but till night, which was at hand, and then they might safely depart at their pleasure, and recover the mountains and strait passages, where their enemies could not follow them: and pointing them the way with his finger, he prayed them not to be faint-hearted, nor to despair of their safety, seeing they were so near it. But in the end Crassus perceiving they fell to mutiny, and beating of their harness did threaten him if he went not, fearing then they would do him some villainy: went towards the enemy, and coming back a little, said only these words: 'O Octavius, and you Petronius, with all you Roman gentlemen that have charge in this army, you all see now how against my will I am enforced to go to the place I would not, and can witness with me, how I am driven with shame and force. Yet I pray you if your fortunes be to escape this danger, that ye will report wheresoever you come, that Crassus was slain, not delivered up by his own soldiers into the hands of the barbarous people, as I am, but deceived by the fraud and subtlety of his enemies.'

31 Octavius would not tarry behind on the hill, but went down with Crassus: but Crassus sent away his officers that followed him. The first that came from the Parthians unto Crassus were two mongrel Grecians who dismounting from their horse saluted him, and prayed him to send some of his men before, and Surena would show them, that both himself and his train came unarmed towards him. Crassus thereto made them answer, that if he had made any account of his life, he would not have put himself into their hands. Notwithstanding he sent two brethren before, called the Roscians,

to know what number of men, and to what end they met so many together. These two brethren came no sooner to Surena, but they were stayed: and himself in the meantime kept on his way a-horseback, with the noblest men of his army. Now when Surena came near to Crassus: 'Why, how now,' quod he, 'what meaneth this? A consul and lieutenant general of Rome afoot, and we a-horseback? Therewithal he straight commanded one of his men to bring him a horse. Crassus answered Surena again: in that, they neither of both offended, following the use and manner of their country, when any meeting is made for treaty of peace. Surena replied: as for the treaty of peace, that was already agreed upon between the King Hyrodes and the Romans: howbeit that they were to go to the river, and there to set down the articles in writing. 'For you Romans,' said he, 'do not greatly remember the capitulations you have agreed upon.' With those words he gave him his right hand. As Crassus was sending for a horse: 'You shall not need,' said Surena, 'for look, the king doth present you this. And straight one was brought him with a steel saddle richly gilt, upon the which his gentlemen mounted Crassus immediately, and following him behind, lashed his horse to make him run the swifter. Octavius seeing that, first laid hand on the bridle, then Petronius colonel of a thousand footmen: and after them, all the rest of the Romans also gathered about Crassus to stay the horse, and to take him from them by force, that pressed him on of either side. So they thrust one at another at the first very angrily, and at the last fell to blows. Then Octavius drew out his sword, and slew one of the barbarous noblemen's horsekeepers: and another came behind him, and slew Octavius. Petronius had no target, and receiving a blow on his cuirass, lighted from his horse, and had no hurt: and on the other side came Pomaxathres, one of the Parthians, and slew Crassus. Some say notwithstanding, that Pomax-athres slew him not, but another, yet that he cut off his head and his hand after he fell dead to the ground. But all these reports are rather conjectures, than any certainty. For as for them that were there, some of them were slain in the field fighting for Crassus, and other saved themselves by flying to the hill. The Parthians followed them, and told them that Crassus had paid the pain he had deserved: and for the rest, that Surena bade them come down with safety. Then some of them yielded to their enemies: and other dispersed themselves when night came, and of them very few escaped with life. Other being followed and pursued by the Arabians were all put to the sword. So as it is thought there were slain in this overthrow, about twenty thousand men, and ten thousand taken prisoners.

32 Surena had now sent Crassus' head and his hand unto Hyrodes, the king his master, into Armenia: and gave out a bruit as far as the city of Seleucia, that he brought Crassus alive, and that he had prepared a sight to laugh at, which he called his triumph. Among the Roman prisoners there was one called Caius Pacianus, who was very like Crassus: him they clothed in woman's apparel of the Parthians, and had taught him to answer, when any called him Crassus, or lord captain. Him they put a-horseback, and had many trumpets before him, and sergeants upon camels' backs, that carried axes before them, and bundles of rods, and many purses tied to the bundles of rods, and Romans' heads newly cut off, tied to the axes: and after him followed all the strumpets and women minstrels of Seleucia, who went singing of songs of mockery and derision, of Crassus' womanish cowardliness. Now for these open shows, everyone might see them: but besides that sight, Surena having called the senate of Seleucia together, laid before them Aristides' books of ribaldry, entitled *The Milesians*, which was no fable, for they were found in a Roman's fardell or truss, called Rustius. This gave Surena great cause to scorn and despise the behaviour of the Romans, which was so far out of order, that even in the wars they could not refrain from doing evil, and from the reading of such vile books. Then the senators of Seleucia found that Aesop was a wise man, who said, that every man carried a sack on his neck, and that they put other men's faults at the sack's mouth, and their own towards the bottom of the sack. When they considered that Surena had put the book of the lasciviousness of the Milesians at the sack's mouth, and a long tale of the Parthians' vain pleasures and delights in the bottom of the sack, carrying such a number of carts laden with naughty packs in his army as he did, which seemed an army of eremites and field mice. For in the forward and foremost ranks, all appeared terrible and cruel, being only lances, pikes, bows, and horse: but all they ended afterwards in the rearward with a train of harlots, instruments of music, dancing, singing, banqueting, and

rioting all night with courtesans. I will not deny but Rustius deserved blame: but yet withal I say, that the Parthians were shameless to reprove these books of the vanities of the Milesians, considering that many of their kings, and of the royal blood of the Arsacides, were born of the Ionian and Milesian courtesans.

33   Things passing thus in this sort, King Hyrodes had made peace and league with Artabazes king of Armenia, who gave his sister in marriage unto Pacorus, King Hyrodes' son, and made great feasts one to another: in the which were many Greek verses sung, Hyrodes self understanding well the Greek tongue, and Artabazes was so perfect in it, that he himself made certain tragedies, orations, and stories, whereof some are yet extant at this day. The same night Crassus' head was brought, the tables being all taken up, Jason a common player of interludes (born in the city of Tralles) came before the kings, and recited a place of the tragedy of the *Bacchantes* of Euripides, telling of the misfortune of Agave, who struck off his son's head. And as every man took great pleasure to hear him, Sillaces coming into the hall, after his humble duty first done to the king, delivered him Crassus' head before them all. The Parthians seeing that, fell a-clapping of their hands, and made an outcry of joy. The gentlemen ushers by the king's commandment, did set Sillaces at the table. Jason casting off his apparel representing Pentheus' person, gave it to another player to put on him, and counterfeiting the Bacchantes possessed with fury, began to rehearse these verses, with a gesture, tune and voice of a man mad, and beside himself:

> Behold, we from the forest bring a stag now newly slain,
> A worthy booty and reward beseeming well our pain.

This marvellously pleased the company: and specially singing these verses afterwards, where the chorus both asked, and answered himself:

> Who struck this stag?
> None else but I thereof may brag.

Pomaxathres hearing them dispute about the matter, being set at the table with others, rose straight, and went and took the head himself, to whom of right it belonged to say those words, and not unto the player that spoke them. King Hyrodes liked this sport marvellously, and rewarded Pomaxathres according to the manner of the country in such a case: and to Jason he also gave a talent. Such was the success of Crassus' enterprise and voyage, much like unto the end of a tragedy. But afterwards, Hyrodes' cruelty, and Surena's foul perjury and craft, were in the end justly revenged upon them both, according to their deserts. For King Hyrodes envying Surena's glory, put Surena to death. And Hyrodes fell into a disease that became a dropsy, after he had lost his son Pacorus, who was slain in a battle by the Romans. Phraates his second son, thinking to set his father forwards, gave him drink of the juice of aconitum. The dropsy received the poison, and one drove the other out of Hyrodes' body, and set him a-foot again. Phraates perceiving his father to amend upon it, to make short work, with his own hands strangled him.

# Comparison of Crassus with Nicias

But now to proceed to the comparison: first, Nicias' goods were more justly got, and with less reproach, than Crassus' wealth: for otherwise a man cannot give any great praise to mineral works, the which are wrought by lewd and ill-disposed barbarous fellows kept in irons, and toiled to death in unwholesome and pestilent places. But being compared unto Crassus' buying of confiscate goods at Sylla's hands, and ungentlemanly bargains of houses afire, or in danger thereof, surely Nicias' trade will appear the better way of getting. For as openly did Crassus avow usury, as tillage. And again for other faults, wherewith Crassus many times was burdened, and which he stoutly denied: as, that he took money of men having matters before the senate at Rome, to win favour for their side: and that he preferred matters to the prejudice of the confederates of the Romans, only for his private profit: and therefore curried favour with ladies, and generally sought to cloak all foul offenders: of all these faults was Nicias never so much as once suspected. For he to the contrary, was mocked of everybody, because for fear he maintained wicked doers by gifts: which perhaps would not have becomed Pericles, nor Aristides, and yet was meet for Nicias, who was born a timorous natured man, and never had courage in him. Whereof Lycurgus the orator did vaunt afterwards to the people, being accused that he redeemed detractors with money: 'I am glad,' said he, 'that I having dealt thus long in affairs of the state, it is found I have rather given than taken.' And now touching expenses: Nicias was thought the better and more civil citizen. For his charge and cost was, in dedicating some goodly image to the gods, or in making of public plays or pastimes to recreate the people. But all the money he spent that way, and all that he was worth besides, was nothing comparable, and but a small part of that Crassus bestowed in an open feast he made at Rome: feasting so many thousands at one time, and did find and maintain them also for a certain time after. Now I cannot but wonder at those men, that deny vice to be an inequality and disagreement of manners, repugnant in itself, seeing men may honestly spend that which is naughtily gotten.

2 Thus much for their goods. For Nicias' doings in the common weal, he did nothing maliciously, cruelly, nor unjustly, neither anything of self-will or stomach, but rather dealt plainly and simply. For he was deceived by trusting of Alcibiades, and never came to speak before the people, but with great fear. Crassus, on the other side, was reproved for his inconstancy and lightness, for that he would easily change friends or enemies: and he himself denied not, that he came to be consul the second time by plain force and cruelty, having hired two murderers to kill Cato and Domitius. And in the assembly the people held for dividing of the provinces, many men were hurt, and four were slain in the market-place: and more than that, Crassus himself (which we have forgotten to write in his life) gave one Lucius Annalius so sore a blow on the face with his fist, for speaking against him, that he sent him going with blood about his ears. But as Crassus in those things was very fierce and cruel, so Nicias' womanish behaviour on the other side, and faint heart in matters of the commonwealth, humbling himself to the meanest and most vile persons, deserveth great reproach. Where Crassus in this respect showed himself assuredly of a noble mind, not contending with men of small account, as with Cleon, or Hyperbolus, but would give no place to Caesar's fame and glory, nor yet to Pompey's three triumphs, but sought to go even with them in power and authority: and had immediately before exceeded Pompey's power, in the dignity of censor. For magistrates, and governors of the common weal, should make themselves to be honoured, but not envied, killing envy by the greatness of their power. But if it were so that Nicias preferred quietness, and the safety of his person above all things else, and that he feared Alcibiades in the pulpit for orations, the Lacedaemonians in the fort of Pyle, and Perdiccas in Thracia, he had liberty and scope enough to repose himself in the city of Athens, and might have forborne the dealing in matters, and (as rhetoricians say) have put a hood of quietness upon his head very well. For doubtless, concerning his desire to make peace, it was a

godly mind in him, and an act worthy of a noble person, to bring that to pass he did, appeasing all war: wherein Crassus certainly was not to be compared to him, though he had joined all the provinces to the empire of Rome, that reach unto the Caspian sea, and to the great ocean of the Indians.

3 But on the other side also, when one hath to deal with people that can discern when a man ruleth according to equity and justice, and that he seeth he is in the prime of his credit and authority, he must not then for lack of courage suffer wicked men to step in his room, nor give occasion to prefer such to authority in the common weal, as are unworthy for that place and countenance: neither should allow such any credit, as are altogether of no credit nor trust, as Nicias did: who was the only occasion that Cleon, being before but a prattling orator, was chosen general. Neither do I also commend Crassus, for that in the war against Spartacus he made haste to give him battle more rashly then safely or considerately. For his ambition spurred him forward, because he was afraid lest Pompey's coming should take from him the glory of all that he had done in that war, as Mummius took from Metellus the honour of the winning of Corinth. But besides all this, Nicias' fact therein was without the compass of reason, and can no way be excused. For he did not resign his honour and office of general to Cleon his enemy, when there was hope of good success, or little peril: but fearing the danger of the journey, he was contented to save one, and took no care besides for the commonwealth. Which Themistocles showed not, in the time of the war against the Persians. For he, to keep Epicydes an orator (a man of no reckoning beside his eloquence, and extremely covetous) from being chosen general of Athens, lest he should have overthrown the common weal, secretly bribed him with money to leave off his suit. And Cato also, when he saw the state of Rome in greatest danger, sued to be tribune of the people for the commonwealth's sake. And Nicias in contrary manner, reserving himself to make war with the city of Minoa, or with the Isle of Cythera, or with the poor unfortunate Melians, if there fell out afterwards occasion to fight against the Lacedaemonians, then away went his captain's cloak, and he left the ships, the army, and munition to the charge and government of Cleon's rashness and small experience of war,

when the necessity of the service required the wisest and most expert captain. The which he did, not despising the means to make him honoured, but it was a plain drawing back, at time of need, to defend his country. Wherefore, afterwards he was compelled against his will to be general, to make wars in Sicilia with the Syracusans: because the people thought he was not so earnest to dissuade the journey, for that he thought it not meet for the commonwealth, but because through his sloth and cowardliness he would make his country lose so good an opportunity to conquer Sicily. Yet was this a great testimony of his honesty and trust they had in him: who though he ever hated war, and did flee from the offices of honour and charge in the commonwealth, his country-men notwithstanding did always choose him, as the most experienced person, and meetest man of the city. Now Crassus in contrary manner desiring nothing else but to be general, could never attain to it, but in the war of the bondmen: and yet was it for lack of another: (for Pompey, Metellus, and both the Lucullus were then abroad in the wars), although he was otherwise of great estimation and authority. Howbeit it seemeth to me, that his friends that loved him best, thought him (as the comical poet saith)

A good man any way else, but in wars.

His ambition notwithstanding and covetous desire of rule, did nothing benefit the Romans. For the Athenians sent Nicias to the war against his will: but Crassus led the Romans thither against their wills. So that the commonwealth fell into misery by the one, and the other through the commonwealth was brought into misery: and yet therein there is rather cause to praise Nicias, than to blame Crassus.

4    For Nicias like a wise man, and a captain of great experience, could never so much as be brought to think they should conquer Sicily: and therefore dissuaded his countrymen from the journey, and would give no place to the vain hope of the people of Athens. But Crassus taking upon him to make wars with the Parthians, as though it had been an easy matter to overcome them, found himself deceived, yet did he aspire to great things. For as Julius Caesar had conquered and subdued to the imperial crown of Rome, all the countries of the West parts, to say, the Gauls, the

Germans, and England, even so did Crassus' desire to go towards
the east parts, to conquer all to the great west sea of the Indians, and
to subdue all the regions of Asia, whereunto Pompey and Lucullus
aspired, being both very noble personages, and such as ever
courteously behaved themselves to all men: notwithstanding, provoked thereunto with the like desire that Crassus had. For when
the charge of the wars in the east parts was assigned to Pompey, by
decree and order of the people, the senate utterly misliked it, and
were against it all they could. When news were brought to Rome
that Julius Caesar in battle had overthrown and slain three hundred
thousand Germans, Cato persuading with the senate, was yet still
of this mind, that Caesar should be delivered into the hands of his
enemies whom he had overcome, for to be punished: thereby to
turn the sharp revenge and wrath of the gods from Rome, upon
him only, that was the unjust breaker of the peace. This notwithstanding, the people making none account of Cato's persuasions,
made common feasts and processions fifteen days together, and
open sacrifices to the gods with great joy through the city, to thank
them for this famous victory. How glad may we think would they
have been, and how many days would they have feasted and
sacrificed, if Crassus had written from Babylon of his victory, and
that he had conquered all the realms of the Medes, of the Persians,
of the Hyrcanians, of Suse, and of the Bactrians, and that he had
made new governments and provinces to the empire of Rome?

    If a man will needs do wrong and injustice,

as Euripides saith to them, that cannot live in peace, and be
contented with their own, he must not then stick at trifles (as
razing of a castle of Scandia, or of a city of Menda, or chasing of the
Aeginetes being out of their own natural country, and hiding
themselves like birds without nests, in another bird's hole), but
must dearly sell the wrong he doth, and not lightly condemn
justice, as a thing of small account. For they that will commend the
intent of Alexander the Great in his voyage, for the conquests he
made in the East, and do dispraise Crassus' voyage, do not well to
judge of the beginning, by the events and success of the end.

5    For executing of their offices, Nicias did many noble exploits.
For he overthrew his enemies in divers battles, and had almost

taken the city of Syracusa: and sure they can not justly blame him for all the misfortunes that chanced in the war of Sicilia, but partly the plague was a cause of it, and partly also the envy of those towards him that remained at Athens. Whereas Crassus ran into so many errors, and committed such foul parts in all his voyage, that he gave fortune no leisure to do him good: so that I wonder not so much that his folly was overcome by the power of the Parthians, as that it could overcome the good fortune of the Romans. Since it so falleth out then, that they both came to like unfortunate end, Nicias prognosticating before what things should happen by art and rule of divination, and Crassus contrarily disdaining to observe anything, sure it falleth out hard in judgment, which of them two proceeded with most safety. Yet according to the best approved opinions, a fault committed of fear is more excusable, than of rashness and folly to break any ancient law or custom. For their deaths, Crassus' end deserved least reproach. For he against his will did yield himself, and was neither bound nor mocked, but only persuaded by his friends, and through his enemies' fraud and treason most traitorously deceived: where Nicias cowardly and dishonourably hoping to save his life, trusting to the mercy of his enemies, made his death more infamous.

# ALEXANDER
# JULIUS CAESAR

# Life of Alexander the Great

Having determined in this volume to write the life of King Alexander, and of Julius Caesar, that overcame Pompey: having to speak of many things, I will use none other preface, but only desire the readers not to blame me though I do not declare all things at large, but briefly touch divers, chiefly in those their noblest acts and most worthy of memory. For they must remember, that my intent is not to write histories, but only lives. For, the noblest deeds do not always show men's virtues and vices, but oftentimes a light occasion, a word, or some sport makes men's natural dispositions and manners appear more plain, than the famous battles won, wherein are slain ten thousand men, or the great armies or cities won by siege or assault. For like as painters or drawers of pictures, which make no account of other parts of the body, do take the resemblances of the face and favour of the countenance, in the which consisteth the judgment of their manners and disposition, even so they must give us leave to seek out the signs and tokens of the mind only, and thereby show the life of either of them, referring you unto others to write the wars, battles, and other great things they did.

2  It is certain that Alexander was descended from Hercules by Caranus, and that of his mother's side, he came of the blood of the Aeacides by Neoptolemus. They say also, that King Philip his father when he was a young man, fell in fancy with his mother Olympias, which at that time also was a young maiden, and an orphan without father or mother, in the Isle of Samothracia, where they were both received into the mystery and fraternity of the house of the religious: and that afterwards, he did ask her in marriage of her brother Arymbas, with whose consent they were married together. The night before they lay in wedded bed, the bride dreamed that lightning fell into her belly, and that withal,

there was a great light fire that dispersed itself all about into divers flames. King Philip her husband also, shortly after he was married, dreamed that he did seal his wife's belly, and that the seal wherewith he sealed left behind the print of a lion. Certain wizards and soothsayers told Philip that this dream gave him warning to look straitly to his wife. But Aristander Telmesian answered again, that it signified his wife was conceived with child, for that they do not seal a vessel that hath nothing in it: and that she was with child with a boy, which should have a lion's heart. It is reported also, that many times as she lay asleep in her bed, there was seen a serpent lying by her, the which was the chiefest cause (as some presuppose) that withdrew Philip's love and kindness from her, and caused him that he lay not so oft with her, as before he was wont to do: either for that he feared some charm or enchantment, or else for that he thought himself unmeet for her company, supposing her to be beloved of some god. Some do also report this after another sort, as in this manner: that the women in those parts of long time have been commonly possessed with the spirit of Orpheus, and the divine fury of Bacchus, whereupon they are called Clodones, and Mimallones (as much as warlike, and fierce), and do many things like unto the women of Edonia, and Thracia, dwelling about the mountain Aemus. Hereby it appeareth, that this word *threskeuin* (signifying in the Greek tongue, too superstitiously given to the ceremonies of the gods) came from them. For Olympias above other women, loving to be inspired with such divine madness and fury, did celebrate their solemn sacrifices with a certain horrible and barbarous manner. For in these dances to Bacchus, she carried a great number of tame snakes about her, the which gliding upon the ivy wherewith the women were dressed in those ceremonies, and winding themselves about the little javelins they had in their hands, and the garlands about their heads, thereby they made men the more afraid of them.

3   Whereupon Philip after this dream, sent Chaero Megalopolitan unto the oracle of Apollo at Delphes, to enquire what it signified. Answer was given him, that he should do sacrifice unto Jupiter Hammon, and honour him above all gods: and that he had lost one of his eyes, with the which he peeping in at a cranny of his chamber door, saw the god in form of a snake lie by his wife. Furthermore,

Olympias (as Eratosthenes writeth) bidding her son farewell when he went to conquer Asia, after she had secretly told him alone, by whom he was begotten, she prayed him to be valiant, and to show himself worthy his son, that begat him. Others tell also, that she was angry with this report, saying: 'Will Alexander never leave to make me suspected of Juno?' So it is, that Alexander was born on the sixth day of the month of Hecatombaeon (in English, June), which the Macedonians call Lous. On the very same day, the temple of Diana in the city of Ephesus was burnt, as Hegesias Magnesian doth witness, whose cry and exclamation was so terrible and cold, that it was enough to have quenched that fire. It is not to be wondered at, that Diana suffered her temple to be burnt, being like a midwife busy about Alexander's birth. But this is true, that all the priests, magicians and soothsayers, which were at that time in Ephesus, judging that this did prognosticate some marvellous great misfortune to come, like men bestraught of their wits, they ran up and down the city, smiting of their faces, and crying that some great plague and mischief was born that day unto Asia. Shortly after that King Philip had won the city of Potidaea, three messengers came to him the same day that brought him great news. The first, that Parmenio had won a notable battle of the Illyrians: the second, that his horse only won the bell and prize at the Olympian games: and the third, that his wife had brought him a son called Alexander. Philip being marvellous glad to hear these news, the soothsayers did make his joy yet greater, assuring him that his son which was born with three victories all together, should be invincible.

4   Now for his stature and personage, the statues and images made of him by Lysippus do best declare it, for that he would be drawn of no man but him only. Divers of his successors and friends did afterwards counterfeit his image, but that excellent workman Lysippus only, of all other the chiefest, hath perfectly drawn and resembled Alexander's manner of holding his neck, somewhat hanging down towards the left side, and also the sweet look and cast of his eyes. But when Apelles painted Alexander holding lightning in his hand, he did not show his fresh colour, but made him somewhat black and swarter, than his face indeed was: for naturally he had a very fair white colour, mingled also with read, which chiefly appeared in his face and in his breast. I remember I read also

in the commentaries of Aristoxenus, that his skin had a marvellous good savour, and that his breath was very sweet, insomuch that his body had so sweet a smell of itself, that all the apparel he ware next unto his body, took thereof a passing delightful savour, as if it had been perfumed. And the cause hereof peradventure might be, the very temperature and constitution of his body, which was hot and burning like fire. For Theophrastus is of opinion, that the sweet savour cometh by means of the heat that dryeth up the moisture of the body. By which reason also it appeareth, that the dry and hot countries parched with heat of the sun, are those that deliver unto us the best spices: because that the sun drieth up the moisture of the outward parts, as a matter of corruption. This natural heat that Alexander had, made him (as it appeareth) to be given to drink, and to be hasty. Even from his childhood they saw that he was given to be chaste. For though otherwise he was very hot and hasty, yet was he hardly moved with lust or pleasure of the body, and would moderately use it. But on the other side, the ambition and desire he had of honour, showed a certain greatness of mind and noble courage, passing his years. For he was not (as his father Philip) desirous of all kind of glory: who like a rhetorician had a delight to utter his eloquence, and stamped in his coins the victories he had won at the Olympian games, by the swift running of his horse and coaches. For when he was asked one day (because he was swift of foot) whether he would assay to run for victory at the Olympian games: 'I could be content,' said he, 'so I might run with kings.' And yet to speak generally, he misliked all such contention for games. For it seemeth that he utterly misliked all wrestling and other exercise for prize, where men did use all their strength: but otherwise he himself made certain festival days and games of prize, for common stage players, musicians, and singers, and for the very poets also. He delighted also in hunting of divers kinds of beasts, and playing at the staff.

5   Ambassadors being sent on a time from the king of Persia, whilst his father was in some journey out of his realm: Alexander familiarly entertaining of them, so won them with his courteous entertainment (for that he used no childish questions unto them, nor asked them trifling matters, but what distance it was from one place to another, and which way they went into the high countries

of Asia, and of the king of Persia himself, how he was towards his enemies, and what power he had), that he did ravish them with delight to hear him, insomuch that they made no more account of Philip's eloquence and sharp wit, in respect of his son's courage and noble mind to attempt great enterprises. For when they brought him news that his father had taken some famous city, or had won some great battle, he was nothing glad to hear it, but would say to his playfellows: 'Sirs, my father will have all. I shall have nothing left me to conquer with you, that shall be aught worth.' For he delighting neither in pleasure nor riches, but only in valiantness and honour, thought, that the greater conquests and realms his father should leave him, the less he should have to do for himself. And therefore, seeing that his father's dominions and empire increased daily more and more, perceiving all occasion taken from him to do any great attempt, he desired no riches nor pleasure, but wars and battles, and aspired to a seigniory where he might win honour. He had divers men appointed him (as it is to be supposed) to bring him up, as schoolmasters, governors, and grooms of his chamber to attend upon him: and among those, Leonidas was the chiefest man that had the government and charge of him, a man of a severe disposition, and a kinsman also unto the Queen Olympias. He misliked to be called a master or tutor, though it be an office of good charge, whereupon the others called him Alexander's governor, because he was a nobleman, and allied to the prince. But he that bore the name of his schoolmaster, was Lysimachus, an Acarnanian born, who had no other manner of civility in him, saving that he called himself Phoenix, Alexander Achilles, and Philip Peleus: and therefore he was well thought of, and was the second person next unto Leonidas.

6   At what time Philonicus Thessalian had brought Bucephal the horse to sell unto King Philip, asking thirteen talents, they went into the field to ride him. The horse was found so rough and churlish that the riders said he would never do service, for he would let no man get up on his back, nor abide any of the gentlemen's voices about King Philip, but would yerke out at them. Thereupon Philip being afraid, commanded them to carry him away as a wild beast, and altogether unprofitable: the which they had done, had not Alexander that stood by said, 'O gods, what

a horse do they turn away, for lack of skill and heart to handle him.'
Philip heard what he said, but held his peace. Alexander oft
repeating his words, seeming to be sorry that they should send back
the horse again: 'Why,' said Philip, 'doest thou control them that
have more experience than thou, and that know better than thou
how to handle a horse?' Alexander answered, 'And yet methinks I
should handle him better than all they have done.' 'But if thou
canst not, no more than they,' replied Philip, 'what wilt thou
forfeit for thy folly?' 'I am content,' quoth Alexander, 'to jeopard
the price of the horse.' Every man laughed to hear his answer: and
the wager was laid between them. Then ran Alexander to the
horse, and took him by the bridle, and turned him towards the sun.
It seemed that he had marked (as I suppose) how mad the horse was
to see his own shadow, which was ever before him in his eye, as he
stirred to and fro. Then Alexander speaking gently to the horse,
and clapping him on the back with his hand, till he had left his fury
and snorting, softly let fall his cloak from him, and lightly leaping
on his back, got up without any danger, and holding the reins of
the bridle hard, without striking or stirring the horse, made him to
be gentle enough. Then when he saw that the fury of the horse was
past, and that he began to gallop, he put him to his full career, and
laid on spurs and voice a-good. Philip at the first with fear
beholding his son's agility, lest he should take some hurt, said never
a word: but when he saw him readily turn the horse at the end of
his career, in a bravery for that he had done, all the lookers on gave
a shout for joy. The father on the other side (as they say) fell
a-weeping for joy. And when Alexander was lighted from the
horse, he said unto him kissing his head: 'O son, thou must needs
have a realm that is meet for thee, for Macedon will not hold thee.'

7   Furthermore, considering that of nature he was not to be won
by extremity, and that by gentle means and persuasion he could
make him do what he would, he ever sought rather to persuade
than command him in anything he had to do. Now Philip putting
no great affiance in his schoolmasters of music and humanity, for
the instruction and education of his son, whom he had appointed
to teach him, but thinking rather that he needed men of greater
learning than their capacities would reach unto: and that as
Sophocles saith,

He needed many reins, and many bits at once:

he sent for Aristotle (the greatest philosopher in his time, and best learned) to teach his son, unto whom he gave honourable stipend. For Philip having won and taken before, the city of Stagyra, where Aristotle was born, for his sake he built it again, and replenished it with inhabitants which fled away, or otherwise were in bondage. He appointed them, for a school house and dwelling place, the pleasant house that is by the city of Mieza. In that place are yet seen seats of stone which Aristotle caused to be made, and close walks to walk in the shadow. It is thought also, that Alexander did not only learn of Aristotle moral philosophy and humanity, but also he heard of him other more secret, hard, and grave doctrine, which Aristotle's scholars do properly call Acroamata, or Epoptica, meaning things speculative, which requireth the master's teaching to understand them, or else are kept from common knowledge: which sciences they did not commonly teach. Alexander being passed into Asia, and hearing that Aristotle had put out certain books of that matter, for the honour's sake of philosophy, he wrote a letter unto him, somewhat too plain, and of this effect. 'Alexander unto Aristotle, greeting: Thou hast not done well to put forth the Acroamatical sciences. For wherein shall we excel other, if those things which thou hast secretly taught us, be made common to all? I do thee to understand, that I had rather excel others in excellency of knowledge, than in greatness of power. Farewell.' Whereunto Aristotle to pacify this his ambitious humour, wrote unto him again, that these books were published, and not published. For to say truly, in all his treatises which be called μετὰ τὰ φυσικά, there is no plain instruction profitable for any man, neither to pick out by himself, nor yet to be taught by any other, than Aristotle himself, or his scholars. So that it is written as a memorial for them that have been entered and brought up in the Peripatetic sect and doctrine.

8    It seemeth also, that it was Aristotle above all other, that made Alexander take delight to study physic. For Alexander did not only like the knowledge of speculation, but would exercise practice also, and help his friends when they were sick: and made besides certain remedies, and rules to live by: as appeareth by his letters he wrote, that of his own nature he was much given to his book, and

desired to read much. He learned also the *Iliades* of Homer, of Aristotle's correction, which they call τὴν ἐκ τοῦ νάρθηκος, the corrected, as having passed under the rule: and laid it every night under his bed's head with his dagger, calling it (as Onesicrates writeth) the institution of martial discipline. And when he was in the high countries of Asia, where he could not readily come by other books, he wrote unto Harpalus to send them to him. Harpalus sent him the histories of Philistus, with divers tragedies of Euripides, Sophocles, and Aeschylus, and certain hymns of Telestus and Philoxenus. Alexander did reverence Aristotle at the first, as his father, and so he termed him: because from his natural father he had life, but from him, the knowledge to live. But afterwards he suspected him somewhat, yet he did him no hurt, neither was he so friendly to him as he had been: whereby men perceived that he did not bear him the goodwill he was wont to do. This notwithstanding, he left not that zeal and desire he had to the study of philosophy, which he had learned from his youth, and still continued with him. For he showed divers testimonies thereof. As, the honour he did unto Anaxarchus the philosopher; the fifty talents which he sent unto Xenocrates, Dandamis, and Calanus, of whom he made great account.

9   When King Philip made war with the Bizatines, Alexander being but sixteen year old, was left his lieutenant in Macedon, with the custody and charge of his great seal: at what time he also subdued the Medarians which had rebelled against him, and having won their city by assault, he drove out the barbarous people, and made a colony of it of sundry nations, and called it Alexandropolis, to say, the city of Alexander. He was with his father at the battle of Chaeronea against the Grecians, where it was reported, that it was he that gave charge first of all upon the holy band of the Thebans. Furthermore, there was an old oak seen in my time, which the countrymen commonly call Alexander's oak, because his tent or pavilion was fastened to it: and not far from thence is the charnel house, where those Macedonians were buried that were slain at the battle. For these causes, his father Philip loved him very dearly, and was glad to hear the Macedonians call Alexander king, and himself their captain. Howbeit the troubles that fell out in his court afterwards, by reason of Philip's new marriages and loves, bred

great quarrel and strife amongst the women: for the mischief of dissension and jealousy of women doth separate the hearts of kings one from another, whereof was chiefest cause, the sharpness of Olympias, who being a jealous woman, fretting, and of a revenging mind, did incense Alexander against his father. But the chiefest cause that provoked Alexander, was Attalus at the marriage of Cleopatra, whom Philip married a maiden, falling in fancy with her when himself was past marriage. This was the matter: Attalus being uncle unto this Cleopatra, fell drunk at the marriage, and having in his cups, he persuaded the Macedonians that were at the feast, to pray to the gods, that they might have a lawful heir of Philip and Cleopatra, to succeed him in the kingdom of Macedon. Alexander being in a rage therewith threw a cup at his head, and said unto him: 'Why, traitor, what am I? Dost thou take me for a bastard?' Philip seeing that, rose from the board, and drew out his sword, but by good fortune for them both, being troubled with choler and wine, he fell down on the ground. Then Alexander mocking him, 'Lo,' said he to the Macedonians, 'here is the man that prepared to go out of Europe into Asia, and stepping only from one bed to another, ye see him laid along on the ground.' After this great insolence, he took his mother Olympias away with him, and carrying her into his country of Epirus, he left her there, and himself afterwards went into Illyria. In the meantime, Demartus Corinthian, a friend of King Philip's and very familiar with him, came to see him. Philip when he had courteously welcomed him, asked him how the Grecians did agree together. 'Truly, O king,' quod he, 'it imports you much to enquire of the agreement of the Grecians, when your own court is so full of quarrel and contention.' These words nipped Philip in such sort, and caused him to know his fault, that through Demaratus' means, whom he sent to persuade Alexander to return, Alexander was made to come back again.

10   Now when Pexodorus, a prince of Caria, desiring for necessity's sake to enter in league and friendship with Philip, offered his eldest daughter in marriage unto Aridaeus King Philip's son, and had sent Aristocritus ambassador into Macedon for that purpose, the friends of Alexander and his mother began again to inveigle him with new reports and suspicions, how Philip by this great

marriage would advance Aridaeus to his utter undoing, and leave him his heir in the kingdom. Alexander being nettled therewith sent one Thessalus a player of tragedies into Caria to Pexodorus: to persuade him to leave Aridaeus, that was a bastard and a fool, and rather to make alliance with Alexander. This offer pleased Pexodorus far better, to have Alexander his son-in-law, than Aridaeus. Philip understanding this, went himself into Alexander's chamber, taking Philotas with him (the son of Parmenio) one of his familiars, and bitterly took up Alexander, telling him that he had a base mind, and was unworthy to be left his heir after his death, if he would cast himself away, marrying the daughter of a Carian, that was a slave and subject of a barbarous king. Thereupon he wrote letters unto Corinth, that they should send Thessalus bound unto him. And furthermore, he banished out of Macedon, Harpalus, Nearchus, Phrygius, and Ptolomy, his son's companions: whom Alexander afterwards called home again, and placed them in great authority about him. Shortly after, Pausanias sustaining villainy by the counsel and commandment of Attalus and Cleopatra, craving justice of Philip, and finding no amends, he converted all his anger against him, and for spite slew him himself. Of this murder, most men accused Queen Olympias, who (as it is reported) allured this young man, having just cause of anger, to kill him. And Alexander also went not clear from suspicion of this murder. For some say, that Pausanias after this villainy was done him, complained unto Alexander, and told him how he had been abused: who recited these verses to him of Euripides, in the tragedy of *Medea*, where she said in anger, that she would be revenged:

> Both of the bridegroom and the bride,
> And of the father-in-law.

Notwithstanding, afterwards he caused diligent search to be made, and all them to be severely punished that were of the conspiracy: and was angry also that his mother Olympias had cruelly slain Cleopatra.

2 So he came to be king of Macedon at twenty years of age, and found his realm greatly envied and hated of dangerous enemies, and every way full of danger. For, the barbarous nations that were near neighbours unto Macedon, could not abide the bondage of strangers, but desired to have their natural kings. Neither had

Philip time enough to bridle and pacify Greece, which he had conquered by force of arms: but having a little altered the governments, had through his insolency left them all in great trouble and ready to rebel, for that they had not long been acquainted to obey. Thereupon Alexander's council of Macedon, being afraid of the troublesome time, were of opinion, that Alexander should utterly forsake the affairs of Greece, and not to follow them with extremity, but that he should seek to win the barbarous people by gentle means, that had rebelled against him, and wisely to remedy these new stirs. But he far otherwise determined to establish his safety by courage and magnanimity: persuading himself, that if they saw him stoop and yield at the beginning, how little so ever it were, every one would be upon him. Thereupon, he straight quenched all the rebellion of the barbarous people, invading them suddenly with his army, by the river of Danuby, where in a great battle he overthrew Syrmus, king of the Triballians. Furthermore, having intelligence that the Thebans were revolted, and that the Athenians also were confederate with them, to make them know that he was a man, he marched with his army towards the strait of Thermopiles, saying that he would make Demosthenes the orator see (who in his orations, while he was in Illyria, and in the country of the Triballians, called him child) that he was grown a stripling passing through Thessaly, and should find him a man before the walls of Athens. When he came with his army unto the gates of Thebes, he was willing to give them of the city occasion to repent them: and therefore only demanded Phoenix and Prothytes, authors of the rebellion. Furthermore, he proclaimed by trumpet, pardon and safety unto all them that would yield unto him. The Thebans on the other side, demanded of him Philotas and Antipater, two of his chiefest servants, and made the crier proclaim in the city, that all such as would defend the liberty of Greece, should join with them. Then did Alexander leave the Macedonians at liberty to make war with all cruelty. Then the Thebans fought with greater courage and desire than they were able, considering that their enemies were many against one. And on the other side also, when the garrison of the Macedonians which were within the castle of Cadmia, made a sally upon them, and gave them charge in the rearward, then they being environed of all sides, were slain in manner every one of them, their city taken, destroyed, and razed even to the hard ground. This he did, specially to make all the rest of the people of Greece afraid by example of this great calamity and misery of the Thebans, to the end none of them should dare from thenceforth once to rise against him. He would cloak this cruelty of his under the complaints of his confederates, the Phocians and Plateians: who complaining to him of the injuries the Thebans had offered, could not deny them justice. Notwithstanding, excepting the priests and the religious, and all such as were friends unto any of the lords of Macedon, all the friends and kinsmen of the poet Pindarus, and all those that had dissuaded them which were the rebels, he sold all the rest of the city of Thebes for slaves, which amounted to the number of thirty thousand persons, besides them that were slain at the battle, which were six thousand more.

12    Now amongst the other miseries and calamities of the poor city of Thebes there were certain Thracian soldiers, who having spoiled and defaced the house of Timoclea, a virtuous lady and of noble parentage, they divided her goods among them: and their captain having ravished her by force, asked her, whether she had anywhere hidden any gold or silver. The lady told him, she had. Then leading him into her garden, she brought him unto a well, where she said she had cast all her jewels and precious things, when she heard the city was taken. The barbarous Thracian stooped to look into the well: she standing behind him, thrust him in, and then threw stones enough on him, and so killed him. The soldiers when they knew it, took and bound her, and so carried her unto Alexander. When Alexander saw her countenance, and marked her gait, he supposed her at the first to be some great lady, she followed the soldiers with such a majesty and boldness. Alexander then asking her what she was, she answered, that she was the sister of Theagenes, who fought a battle with King Philip before the city of Chaeronea, where being general he was slain, valiantly fighting for the defence of the liberty of Greece. Alexander wondering at her noble answer and courageous deed, commanded no man should touch her nor her children, and so freely let her go whether she would.

13    He made league also with the Athenians, though they were very sorry for their miserable fortune. For the day of the solemn feast of their mysteries being come, they left it off, mourning for

the Thebans: courteously entertaining all those, that flying from Thebes came to them for succour. But whether it was for that his anger was past him, following therein the nature of lions, or because that after so great an example of cruelty, he would show a singular clemency again, he did not only pardon the Athenians of all faults committed, but did also counsel them to look wisely to their doings, for their city one day should command all Greece, if he chanced to die. Men report, that certainly he oftentimes repented him that he had dealt so cruelly with the Thebans, and the grief he took upon it was cause that he afterwards showed himself more merciful unto divers others. Afterwards also he did blame the fury of Bacchus, who to be revenged of him, made him kill Clitus at the table being drunk, and the Macedonians also to refuse him to go any further to conquer the Indians, which was an imperfection of his enterprise, and a minishing also of his honour. Besides, there was never Theban afterwards, that had escaped the fury of his victory, and did make any petition to him, but he had his suit. Thus was the state of Thebes as you have heard.

14   Then the Grecians having assembled a general council of all the states of Greece within the straits of Peloponnesus, there it was determined that they would make war with the Persians. Whereupon they chose Alexander general for all Greece. Then divers men coming to visit Alexander, as well philosophers as governors of states, to congratulate with him for his election, he looked that Diogenes Sinopian (who dwelt at Corinth) would likewise come as the rest had done: but when he saw he made no reckoning of him, and that he kept still in the suburbs of Corinth, at a place called Cranium, he went himself unto him, and found him laid all along in the sun. When Diogenes saw so many coming towards him, he sat up a little, and looked full upon Alexander. Alexander courteously spoke unto him, and asked him, if he lacked anything. 'Yea,' said he, 'that I do: that thou stand out of my sun a little.' Alexander was so well pleased with this answer, and marvelled so much at the great boldness of this man, to see how small account he made of him, that when he went his way from him, Alexander's familiars laughing at Diogenes, and mocking him, he told them: 'Masters, say what you list: truly if I were not Alexander, I would be Diogenes.' Alexander being desirous to hear what the oracle of Apollo Delphian would

say unto him touching the success of his journey into Asia, he went unto the city of Delphes. It chanced so, that he came thither in the days which they call unfortunate, on which days no man used to ask Apollo anything. This notwithstanding, he sent first unto the nun which pronounced the oracles, to pray her to come to him. But she refused to come, alleging the custom which forbade her to go. Thereupon, Alexander went thither himself in person, and brought her out by force into the temple. She seeing then that he would not be denied, but would needs have his will, told him, 'My son, for that I see, thou art invincible.' Alexander hearing that, said he desired no other oracle, and that he had as much as he looked for. Afterwards when he was even ready to go on with his voyage, he had divers signs and tokens from the gods: and amongst other, an image of the poet Orpheus made of cypress, in the city of Lebethres, in those days did sweat marvellously. Many men fearing that sign, Aristander the soothsayer bade Alexander be of good cheer, and hope well, for he should obtain noble victories that should never be forgotten, the which should make the poets and musicians sweat to write and sing them.

15    Then, for his army which he led with him, they that do set down the least number, say that they were thirty thousand footmen, and five thousand horsemen: and they that say more, do write, four and thirty thousand footmen, and four thousand horsemen. Aristobulus writeth, that Alexander had no more but three score and ten talents to pay his soldiers with: and Duris writeth, that he had no more provision of victuals, than for thirty days only. And Onesicritus saith moreover, that he did owe two hundred talents. Now, notwithstanding that he began this war with so small ability to maintain it, he would never take ship before he understood the state of his friends, to know what ability they had to go with him, and before he had given unto some lands, and unto other a town, and to others again, the custom of some haven. Thus by his bounty having in manner spent almost the revenues of the crown of Macedon, Perdiccas asked him: 'My lord, what will you keep for yourself?' 'Hope,' said he. 'Then,' quoth Perdiccas again, 'we will also have some part, since we go with you.' And so refused the revenue which the king had given him for his pension. Many others did also the like. But such as were contented to take his liberality, or would ask

him anything, he gave them very frankly, and in such liberality spent all the revenue he had. With this desire and determination, he went on to the strait of Hellespont, and going to the city of Ilium, he did sacrifice unto Diana, and made funeral effusions unto the demigods (to wit, unto the princes which died in the war of Troia, whose bodies were buried there) and specially unto Achilles, whose grave he anointed with oil, and ran naked round about it with his familiars, according to the ancient custom of funerals. Then he covered it with nosegays and flowers, saying, that Achilles was happy, who while he lived had a faithful friend, and after his death an excellent herald to sing his praise. When he had done, and went up and down the city to see all the monuments and notable things there, one asked him, if he would see Paris' harp. He answered again, he would very fain see Achilles' harp, who played and sung upon it all the famous acts done by valiant men in former times.

16    In the meantime, Darius king of Persia, having levied a great army, sent his captains and lieutenants to tarry Alexander at the river of Granicus. There was Alexander to fight of necessity, being the only bar to stop his entry into Asia. Moreover, the captains of his council about him, were afraid of the depth of this river, and of the height of the bank on the other side, which was very high and steep, and could not be won without fighting. And some said also, that he should have special care of the ancient regard of the month, because the kings of Macedon did never use to put their army into the field in the month of Dason, which is June. 'For that,' said Alexander, 'we will remedy soon: let them call it the second month, Artemisium', which is May. Furthermore Parmenio was of opinion, that he should not meddle the first day, because it was very late. Alexander made answer again, that Hellespont would blush for shame, if he were now afraid to pass over the river, since he had already come over an arm of the sea. Thereupon he himself first entered the river with thirteen guidons of horsemen, and marched forwards against an infinite number of arrows which the enemies shot at him as he was coming up the other bank, which was very high and steep, and worst of all, full of armed men and horsemen of the enemies: which stayed to receive him in battle ray, thrusting his men down into the river, which was very deep, and ran so swift, that it almost carried them down the stream:

insomuch that men thought him more rash than wise, to lead his men with such danger. This notwithstanding, he was so wilfully bent that he would needs over, and in the end with great ado recovered the other side, specially because the earth slid away, by reason of the mud. So when he was over, he was driven to fight pell mell one upon another, because his enemies did set upon the first that were passed over, before they could put themselves into battle ray, with great cries, keeping their horses very close together, and fought first with their darts, and afterwards came to the sword when their darts were broken. Then many of them set upon him alone, for he was easily to be known above the rest by his shield and the hinder part of his helmet, about the which there hung from the one side to the other, a marvellous fair white plume. Alexander had a blow with a dart on his thigh, but it hurt him not. Thereupon Roesaces and Spithridates, both two chief captains of the Persians, setting upon Alexander at once, he left the one, and riding straight to Roesaces, who was excellently armed, he gave him such a blow with his lance, that he broke it in his hand, and straight drew out his sword. But so soon as they two had closed together, Spithridates coming at the side of him, raised himself upon his stirrups and gave Alexander with all his might such a blow of his head with a battle axe, that he cut the crest of his helmet, and one of the sides of his plume, and made such a gash, that the edge of his battle axe touched the very hair of his head. And as he was lifting up his hand to strike Alexander again, great Clitus preventing him, thrust him through with a partisan: and at the very same instant, Roesaces also fell dead from his horse with a wound which Alexander gave him with his sword. Now whilst the horsemen fought with such fury, the squadron of the battle of footmen of the Macedonians had passed the river, and both the battles began to march one against the other. The Persians stuck not manfully to it any long time, but straight turned their backs and fled, saving the Grecians which took pay of King Darius: they drew together upon a hill, and craved mercy of Alexander. But Alexander setting upon them, more of will than discretion, had his horse killed under him, being thrust through the flank with a sword. This was not Bucephal, but another horse he had. All his men that were slain or hurt at this battle, were hurt amongst them valiantly fighting against desperate men. It is reported that there were slain at this first battle, twenty thousand footmen of these barbarous people, and two thousand five hundred horsemen. Of Alexander's side, Aristobulus writeth, that there were slain four and thirty men in all, of the which twelve of them were footmen. Alexander to honour their valiantness, caused every one of their images to be made in brass by Lysippus. And because he would make the Grecians partakers of this victory, he sent unto the Athenians three hundred of their targets, which he had won at the battle, and generally upon all the other spoils, he put this honourable inscription: 'Alexander the son of Philip, and the Grecians, excepting the Lacedaemonians, have won this spoil upon the barbarous Asians.' As for plate of gold or silver, also purple silks, or other such precious ware which he gat among the Persians, he sent them all unto his mother, a few except.

17    This first victory of Alexander brought such a sudden change amongst the barbarous people in Alexander's behalf, that the city self of Sardis, the chief city of the empire of the barbarous people, or at the least through all the low countries and coasts upon the sea, they yielded straight unto him, saving the cities of Halicarnassus and Miletum, which did still resist him: howbeit at length he took them by force. When he had also conquered all thereabouts, he stood in doubt afterwards what he were best to determine. Sometime he had a marvellous desire, wholly to follow Darius wheresoever he were, and to venture all at a battle. Another time again, he thought it better first to occupy himself in conquering of these low countries, and to make himself strong with the money and riches he should find among them, that he might afterwards be the better able to follow him. In the country of Lydia near unto the city Xanthum, they say there is a spring that broke of itself, and overflowing the banks about it, cast out a little table of copper from the bottom, upon the which were graved certain characters in old letters, which said that the kingdom of the Persians should be destroyed by the Grecians. This did further so encourage Alexander, that he made haste to clear all the sea coast, even as far as Cilicia and Phoenicia. But the wonderful good success he had, running along all the coast of Pamphilia, gave divers historiographers occasion to set forth his doings with admiration saying that it was one of the wonders of the world, that the fury of the sea, which unto all other was extreme rough, and many times would swell over the tops of the high rocks

upon the cliffs, fell calm unto him. And it appeareth that Menander himself in a comedy of his doth witness this wonderful happiness of Alexander, when merrily he sayeth:

> O great Alexander, how great is thy state!
> For thou with thyself mayst thus justly debate.
> 'If any man living I list for to call,
> He cometh and humbly before me doth fall.
> And if through the surges my journey do lie,
> The waves give me way, and the sea becomes dry.'

Yet Alexander himself simply writeth in his epistles (without any great wonder) that by sea he passed a place called the ladder, and that to pass there, he took ship in the city of Phaselides. There he remained many days, and when he saw the image of Theodectes Phaselitan, standing in the market place, he went in a dance thither one evening after supper, and cast flowers and garlands upon his image, honouring the memory of the dead, though it seemed but in sport, for that he was his companion when he lived by means of Aristotle and his philosophy.

18   After that he overcame also the Pisidians, who thought to have resisted him, and conquered all Phrygia besides. There in the city of Gordius, which is said to be the ancient seat of King Midas, he saw the chariot that is so much spoken of, which is bound with the bark of a cornel tree; and it was told him for a truth, of the barbarous people, that they believed it as a prophecy, that whosoever could undo the band of that bark, was certainly ordained to be king of all the world. It is commonly reported, that Alexander proving to undo that band, and finding no ends to undo it by, they were so manyfold wreathed one within the other, he drew out his sword, and cut the knot in the midst. So that then many ends appeared. But Aristobulus writeth, that he had quickly undone the knot by taking the bolt out of the axtree, which holdeth the beam and body of the chariot, and so severed them asunder. Departing thence, he conquered the Paphlagonians and Cappadocians, and understood of the death of Memnon, that was Darius' general of his army by sea, and in whom was all their hope to trouble and withstand Alexander: whereupon he was the bolder to go on with his determination to lead his army into the high countries of Asia. Then did King Darius himself come against Alexander, having

levied a great power at Susa, of six hundred thousand fighting men, trusting to that multitude, and also to a dream, the which his wizards had expounded rather to flatter him, than to tell him truly. Darius dreamed that he saw all the army of the Macedonians on a fire, and Alexander serving of him in the selfsame attire that he himself wore when he was one of the chamber unto the late king his predecessor: and that when he came into the temple of Belus, he suddenly vanished from him. By this dream it plainly appeared, that the gods did signify unto him, that the Macedonians should have noble success in their doings, and that Alexander should conquer all Asia, even as King Darius had done, when he was but Asgandes unto the king: and that shortly after, he should end his life with great honour.

19 This furthermore made him bold also, when he saw that Alexander remained a good while in Cilicia, supposing it had been for that he was afraid of him. Howbeit it was by reason of a sickness he had, the which some say he got by extreme pains and travail, and others also, because he washed himself in the river of Cydnus, which was cold as ice. Howsoever it came, there was none of the other physicians that durst undertake to cure him, thinking his disease incurable, and no medicines to prevail that they could give him, and fearing also that the Macedonians would lay it to their charge, if Alexander miscarried. But Philip Acarnanian, considering his master was very ill, and bearing himself of his love and goodwill towards him, thought he should not do that became him, if he did not prove (seeing him in extremity and danger of life) the utmost remedies of physic, what danger so ever he put himself into: and therefore took upon him to minister physic unto Alexander, and persuaded him to drink it boldly if he would quickly be whole, and go to the wars. In the meantime, Parmenio wrote him a letter from the camp, advertising him, that he should beware of Philip his physician, for he was bribed and corrupted by Darius, with large promises of great riches, that he would give him with his daughter in marriage, to kill his master. Alexander when he had read this letter, laid it under his bed's head, and made none of his nearest familiars acquainted therewith. When the hour came that he should take his medicine, Philip came into his chamber with other of the king's familiars, and brought a cup in his hand with the potion he

should drink. Alexander then gave him the letter, and withal, cheerfully took the cup of him, showing no manner of fear or mistrust of anything. It was a wonderful thing and worth the sight, how one reading the letter, and the other drinking the medicine both at one instant, they looked one upon another, howbeit not both with like cheerful countenance. For Alexander looked merrily upon him, plainly showing the trust he had in his physician Philip, and how much he loved him: and the physician also beheld Alexander, like a man perplexed and amazed, to be so falsely accused, and straight lift up his hands to heaven, calling the gods to witness that he was innocent, and then came to Alexander's bedside, and prayed him to be of good cheer, and boldly to do as he would advise him. The medicine beginning to work, overcame the disease, and drove for the time, to the lowest parts of his body, all his natural strength and powers: insomuch as his speech failed him, and he fell into such a weakness, and almost swooning, that his pulse did scant beat, and his senses were well near taken from him. But that being past, Philip in few days recovered him again. Now, when Alexander had got some strength, he showed himself openly unto the Macedonians: for they would not be pacified, nor persuaded of his health, until they had seen him.

20   In King Darius' camp, there was one Amyntas a Macedonian, and banished out of his country, who knew Alexander's disposition very well. He finding that Darius meant to meet with Alexander within the straits and valleys of the mountains, besought him to tarry rather where he was, being a plain open country round about him, considering that he had a great host of men to fight with a few enemies, and that it was most for his advantage to meet with him in the open field. Darius answered him again, that he was afraid of nothing, but that he would fly before he could come to him. Amyntas replied, 'For that, O king, I pray you fear not: for I warrant you upon my life he will come to you, yea and is now onwards on his way coming towards you.' All these persuasions of Amyntas could not turn Darius from making his camp to march towards Cilicia. At the selfsame time also, Alexander went towards Syria to meet with him. But it chanced one night, that the one of them missed of the other, and when day was come, they both returned back again: Alexander being glad of this hap, and making

haste to meet with his enemy within the straits. Darius also seeking to win Alexander's lodging from whence he came, and to bring his army out of the straits, began then to find the fault and error committed, for that he had shut himself up in the straits, (holden in on the one side with the mountain, and on the other with the sea, and the river of Pindarus that ran between both) and that he was driven to disperse his army into divers companies, in a stony and ill-favoured country, ill for horsemen to travel, being on the contrary side a great advantage for his enemies, which were excellent good footmen, and but few in number. But now, as fortune gave Alexander the field as he would wish it to fight for his advantage, so could he tell excellently well how to set his men in battle ray to win the victory. For albeit that Alexander had the less number by many than his enemy, yet he had such policy and cast with him, that he foresaw all, and would not be environed: for he did put out the right wing of his battle a great deal further, than he did his left wing, and fighting himself in the left wing in the foremost ranks, he made all the barbarous people flee that stood before him: howbeit, he was hurt on his thigh with a blow of a sword. Chares writeth, that Darius self did hurt him, and that they fought together man to man. Notwithstanding Alexander self writing of this battle unto Antipater sayeth, that indeed he was hurt on the thigh with a sword, howbeit it did put him in no danger: but he writeth not that Darius did hurt him. Thus having won a famous victory, and slain above a hundred and ten thousand of his enemies, he could not yet take Darius, because he fled, having still four or five furlongs vantage before him: howbeit he took his chariot of battle wherein he fought, and his bow also. Then he returned from the chase, and found the Macedonians sacking and spoiling all the rest of the camp of the barbarous people, where there was infinite riches (although they had left the most part of their carriage behind them in the city of Damas, to come lighter to the battle), but yet reserved for himself all King Darius' tent, which was full of a great number of officers, of rich moveables, and of gold and silver. So, when he was come to the camp, putting off his armour, he entered into the bath and said: 'Come on, let us go and wash off the sweat of the battle in Darius' own bath.' 'Nay,' replied one of his familiars again, 'in Alexander's bath: for the goods of the vanquished are rightly the vanquishers'.' When he came into the bath, and saw the basins and ewers, the

boxes, and phials for perfumes, all of clean gold, excellently
wrought, all the chamber perfumed passing sweetly, that it was like
a paradise, then going out of his bath, and coming into his tent,
seeing it so stately and large, his bed, the table, and supper, and all
ready in such sumptuous sort, that it was wonderful, he turned him
unto his familiars and said: 'This was a king indeed, was he not,
think ye?'

21  As he was ready to go to his supper, word was brought him,
that they were bringing unto him amongst other ladies taken
prisoners, King Darius' mother and his wife, and two of his
daughters unmarried: who having seen his chariot and bow, burst
out into lamentable cries, and violent beating of themselves
thinking Darius had been slain. Alexander paused a good while
and gave no answer, pitying more their misfortune, than rejoicing
at his own good hap. Then he presently sent one Leonatus unto
them, to let them understand, that Darius was alive, and that they
should not need to be afraid of Alexander, for he did not fight with
Darius, but for his kingdom only: and as for them, that they
should have at his hands all that they had of Darius before, when
he had his whole kingdom in his hands. As these words pleased the
captive ladies, so the deeds that followed, made them find his
clemency to be no less. For first he suffered them to bury as many
of the Persian lords as they would, even of them that had been
slain in the battle, and to take as much silks of the spoils, jewels,
and ornaments, as they thought good to honour their funerals
with: and also did lessen no part of their honour, nor of the
number of their officers and servants, nor of any jot of their estate
which they had before, but did allow them also greater pensions,
than they had before. But above all, the princeliest grace, and most
noble favour that Alexander showed unto these captive princesses,
which had always lived in honourable fame and chastity, was this:
that they never heard word, or so much as any suspicion that
should make them afraid to be dishonoured or deflowered, but
were privately among themselves unvisited or repaired unto by
any man, but of their own, not as if they had been in a camp of
their enemies, but as if they had been kept in some close monas-
tery: although Darius' wife (as it is written) was passing fair, Darius
also was a goodly prince, and that his daughters likewise did

resemble their father and mother. Alexander thinking it more princely for a king, as I suppose, to conquer himself, than to overcome his enemies, did neither touch them nor any other, maid or wife, before he married them, Barsine only excepted, who being left Memnon's widow (general of King Darius by sea) was taken by the city at Damas. She being excellently well learned in the Greek tongue, and of good entertainment (being the daughter of Artabazus, who came of a king's daughter), Alexander was bold with her by Parmenio's procurement (as Aristobulus writeth), who enticed him to embrace the company of so excellent a woman, and passing fair besides. Furthermore, beholding the other Persian ladies besides which were prisoners, what goodly fair women they were, he spoke it pleasantly, that the ladies of Persia made men's eyes sore to behold them. Notwithstanding, preferring the beauty of his continency, before their sweet fair faces, he passed by without any spark of affection towards them, more than if they had been images of stone without life.

22   To confirm this, Philoxenus whom he had left his lieutenant in the low countries upon the sea coast, wrote unto him on a time, that one Theodorus a merchant of Tarentum, had to sell two goodly young boys, marvellous fair: and therefore that he sent unto him to know his pleasure, if he would buy them. Therewith he was so offended, that many times he cried out aloud: 'O, my friends, what villainy has ever Philoxenus seen in me, that he should devise (having nothing to do there) to purchase me such infamy?' Whereupon he wrote unto him from the camp, with reproachful words, that he should send that vile Tarentin merchant Theodorus and his merchandise to the devil. He sharply punished also one Agnon, that wrote unto him he would buy a young boy called Crobylus (who for beauty bore the only name in Corinth), and bring him to him. Another time also, when he heard that Damon and Timotheus Macedonians, under Parmenio's charge, had deflowered two of the soldiers' wives that were strangers, and waged of him, he wrote unto Parmenio to look unto it, and to examine the matter. And if he found them guilty of the rape, that then he should put them both to death, as brute beasts born to destroy mankind. And in that letter he wrote thus of himself: 'For myself,' said he, 'I have neither seen, nor desired to see Darius' wife: neither have I suffered

any speech of her beauty before me.' Moreover he said, that he did understand that he was mortal by these two things: to wit, sleep, and lust: for, from the weakness of our nature proceedeth sleep and sensuality. He was also no greedy gut, but temperate in eating, as he showed by many proofs: but chiefly in that he said unto the princess Ada, whom he adopted for his mother, and made her queen of Caria. For when (for the love she bore him) she daily sent him sundry delicate dishes of meat, tarts, and marchpanes, and besides the meat itself, the pastlers and cooks to make them, which were excellent workmen, he answered that he could not tell what to do with them, for he had better cooks than those, appointed him by his governor Leonidas, to wit: for his dinner, to rise before day, and to march by night: and for his supper, to eat little at dinner. 'And my governor,' said he, 'would oftentimes open the chests where my bedding and apparel lay, to see if my mother had put any fine knacks or conceits among them.'

23   Furthermore, he was less given to wine, than men would have judged. For he was thought to be a greater bibber than he was, because he sat long at the board, rather to talk than drink. Forever when he drank, he would propound some tedious matter, and yet but when he was at leisure. For having matters to do, there was neither feast, banquet, play, marriage, nor any pastime that could stay him, as they had done other captains. The which appeareth plainly by the shortness of his life, and by the wonderful and notable deeds he did, in that little time he lived. When he had leisure, after he was up in the morning, first of all he would do sacrifice to the gods, and then would go to dinner, passing away all the rest of the day in hunting, writing something, taking up some quarrel between soldiers, or else in studying. If he went any journey of no hasty business, he would exercise himself by the way as he went, shooting in his bow, or learning to get up or out of his chariot suddenly, as it ran. Oftentimes also for his pastime he would hunt the fox, or catch birds, as appeareth in his book of remembrances for every day. Then when he came to his lodging, he would enter into his bath, and rub and anoint himself: and would ask his pantelers and carvers if his supper were ready. He would ever sup late, and was very curious to see, that every man at his board were alike served, and would sit long at the table, because

he ever loved to talk, as we have told you before. Otherwise he was as noble a prince and gracious to wait upon, and as pleasant, as any king that ever was. For he lacked no grace nor comeliness to adorn a prince, saving that he would be something over busy in glorying in his own deeds, much like unto a bragging soldier: neither was he contented himself to please his own humour that way, but would also suffer his familiars to soothe him even to his teeth. And this was many times the destruction of honest men about him, the which would neither praise him in his presence, hating the flatterers, nor yet durst say less of the praises which they gave him. For of the first they were ashamed, and by the second they fell in danger. After supper, he would wash himself again, and sleep until noon the next day following, and oftentimes all day long. For himself, he was nothing curious of dainty dishes: for when any did send him rare fruits, or fish, from the countries near the sea side, he would send them abroad unto his friends, and seldom keep anything for himself. His table notwithstanding was always very honourably served, and did still increase his fare, as he did enlarge his conquests: till it came to the sum of ten thousand drachmas a day. But there he stayed, and would not exceed that sum, and moreover commanded all men that would feast him, that they should not spend above that sum.

24  After this battle of Issus, he sent unto the city of Damas, to take all the gold and silver, the carriage, and all the women and children of the Persians which were left there, where the men of arms of the Thessalians sped them full well. For therefore did he send them thither, because he saw that they had fought valiantly at the day of the battle: and so were the rest of his army also well stored with money. There the Macedonians having tasted first of the gold, silver, women, and barbarous life, as dogs by scent do follow the track of beasts, even so were they greedy to follow after the goods of the Persians. First Alexander thought it best to win all the sea coast. Thither came the kings of Cyprus, and Phoenicia, and delivered up to him the whole island and all Phoenicia, saving only the city of Tyre. That city he besieged seven months together by land, with great bulwarks and divers engines of battery, and by sea, with two hundred galleys. During this siege, Alexander dreamed one night, that Hercules held out his hand unto him over

the walls of the city, and called him by his name: and there were
divers Tyrians also that dreamed it likewise, that Apollo told them
that he would go unto Alexander, because he was not pleased with
their doings in the city. Thereupon they bound his image (which
was of a wonderful bigness) with great chains, and nailed him
down fast to the base, as if he had been a traitor that would have
yielded himself unto their enemies, and called him Alexandrine, as
much as favouring Alexander. Alexander had there also another
dream. For he dreamed that he saw a satyr afar off sporting with
him, and when he thought to have come near to have taken him,
he still escaped from him: until at the length, after he had run a
good while after him, and entreated him, he fell into his hands.
The soothsayers being asked what this dream should signify,
answered probably, by dividing Satyros into two, and then it is Σὰ
τύρος: which signifieth, the city of Tyre shall be thine. And they
do yet show unto this day, the fountain where Alexander thought
he saw the satyr. Continuing this siege, he went to make war with
the Arabians, that dwell upon the mountain Antiliban, where he
was in great danger of being cast away, only because he heard his
tutor Lysimachus that followed him, say boastingly, that he was
not inferior, nor older than Phoenix. For when they came at the
foot of the mountain, they left their horses, and went up afoot: and
Alexander was of so courteous a nature, that be would not leave
his tutor Lysimachus behind him (who was so weary that he could
go no further) but because it was dark night, and for that the
enemies were not far from them, he came behind to encourage his
tutor, and in manner to carry him. By this means, unawares, he
was far from his army with very few men about him, and
benighted besides: moreover it was very cold, and the way was
very ill. At the length, perceiving divers fires which the enemies
had made, some in one place, and some in another, trusting to his
valiantness, having always provided remedy in extremity, when
the Macedonians were distressed, himself ever putting to his own
hand, he ran unto them that had made the fires next him, and
killing two of the barbarous people that lay by the fire side, he
snatched away a fire brand, and ran with it to his own men, who
made a great fire. At this the barbarous people were so afraid, that
they ran their way as fast as they could. Other also thinking to
come and set upon him, he slew them every man, and so lay there

that night, himself and his men without danger. Thus Chares reporteth this matter.

25 Now for the siege of Tyre, that fell out thus. Alexander caused the most part of his army to take rest, being overharried and wearied with so many battles as they had fought: and sent a few of his men only to give assault unto the city, to keep the Tyrians occupied, that they should take no rest. One day the soothsayer Aristander sacrificing unto the gods, having considered of the signs of the entrails of the beasts, did assure them that were present, that the city should be taken by the latter end of the month. Everybody laughed to hear him: for that day was the very last day of the month. Alexander seeing him amazed, as one that could not tell what to say to it, seeking ever to bring those tokens to effect, which the soothsayers did prognosticate, commanded them that they should not reckon that day the thirty day, but the seven and twenty, and immediately upon it, made the trumpet sound the alarm, and give a hotter assault to the wall, than he had thought to have done before. They fought valiantly on both sides, in so much as they that were left in the camps could not keep in, but must needs run to the assault to help their companions. The Tyrians seeing the assault so hot on every side, their hearts began to fail them, and by this means was the city taken the selfsame day. Another time also, when Alexander was before Gaza, the chief city of Syria, there fell a clod of earth upon his shoulder, out of the which there flew a bird into the air. The bird lighting upon one of the engines of his battery, was caught with the nets made of sinews which covered over the ropes of the engines. Aristander did prognosticate, that it signified he should be hurt in his shoulder, notwithstanding, that he should yet take the town. And indeed so it came to pass. When he sent great presents of spoils which he won at the sack of this city, unto his mother Olympias, Cleopatra, and divers others of his friends, among other things, he sent unto Leonidas his governor, five hundred talents' weight of frankincense, and a hundred talents' weight of myrrh: remembering the hope he put him into when he was a child. For, as Alexander was upon a day sacrificing unto the gods, he took both his hands full of frankincense to cast into the fire, to make a perfume thereof. When his governor Leonidas saw him, he said thus unto him: 'When thou

hast conquered the country where these sweet things grow, then be liberal of thy perfume: but now, spare that little thou hast at this present.' Alexander calling to mind at that time his admonition, wrote unto him in this sort: 'We do send thee plenty of frankincense and myrrh, because thou shouldest no more be a niggard unto the gods.'

26    There was brought unto him a little coffer also, which was thought to be the preciousest thing and the richest, that was gotten of all the spoils and riches taken at the overthrow of Darius. When he saw it, he asked his familiars that were about him, what they thought fittest, and the best thing to be put into it. Some said one thing, some said another thing: but he said, he would put the *Iliades* of Homer into it, as the worthiest thing. This is confirmed by the best historiographers. Now if that which the Alexandrians report upon Heraclides' words, be true, then it appeareth that he did profit himself much by Homer in this journey. For it is reported that when he had conquered Egypt, he determined to build a great city, and to replenish it with a great number of Grecians, and to call it after his name. But as he was about to enclose a certain ground, which he had chosen by the advice of his engineers and work-masters, the night before he had a marvellous dream, that he saw an old man standing before him, full of white hairs, with an honourable presence, and coming towards him said these verses:

> Within the foaming sea there lies a certain island, right
> Against the shore of Egypt, which of ancient Pharos hight.

As soon as he rose the next morning, he went to see this Isle of Pharos, the which at that time was a little above the mouth of the river of Nylus, called Canobia, howbeit it is now joined unto firm land, being forced by man's hand. This he thought the meetest place that could be, to build the city which he had determined. For it is as a tongue or a great bar of earth, broad enough, that separateth a great lake on the one side, and the sea on the other, the which doth join hard to a great haven. Then he said that Homer was wonderful in all his things, but that amongst others, he was an excellent architecture: and commanded, that straight they should cast the platform of the city, according to the situation of the place. Now they found at that time no chalk, nor white earth there to mark withal, wherefore they were driven to take meal, and with that did mark out upon the earth being black, the compass of the town that was round and circular, and being divided into two equal parts, either of them resembled the skirts and fashion of the Macedonian cloak. Alexander liked this draft passingly well. But there rose upon the sudden out of the river or lake, such an infinite multitude of great fowl of all sorts, that they covered the element as it had been a cloud, and lighting within this circuit, did eat up all the meal, and left not a crumb. Alexander liked not these signs. Notwithstanding, his soothsayers bade him not be discouraged, for they told him it was a sign that he should build a city there, so plentiful of all things, that he should maintain all sorts of people. Then he commanded them, unto whom he had given the charge of the building, that they should go forward with their work, and he himself in the meantime, took his journey to go visit the temple of Jupiter Hammon. The journey was long, and there were many troubles by the way, but two dangers above all the rest most special. The first, lack of water, because they had to travel many days' journey through a great desert. The second was, the danger of the rising of the south wind by the way, to blow the sand abroad, which was of a wonderful length. And it is reported, that on a time there rose such a tempest in that desert, that blew up whole hills of sand, which slew fifty thousand men of Cambyses' army. Every man in Alexander's train did know these dangers very well: howbeit it was hard to dissuade Alexander from anything which he had a desire unto. For, fortune favouring him in all his attempts, made him constant and resolute in his determinations: and his noble courage besides, made him invincible in all things he took in hand, insomuch as he did not only compel his enemies, but he had power also of time and place.

27 In that voyage, instead of these former dangers spoken of, he had many helps, the which are supposed were sent him from the gods, by the oracles that followed afterwards. For in a certain sort, they have believed the oracles that were written of him. First of all, the wonderful water and great showers that fell from the element did keep him from fear of the first danger, and did quench their thirst, and moistened the dryness of the sand in such sort, that there came a sweet fresh air from it. Furthermore, when the marks were hidden from the guides to show them the way, and that they

wandered up and down, they could not tell where, there came crows unto them that did guide them flying before them: flying fast when they saw them follow them, and stayed for them when they were behind. But Callisthenes writeth a greater wonder than this, that in the night time, with the very noise of the crows, they brought them again into the right way which had lost their way. Thus Alexander in the end, having passed through this wilderness, he came unto the temple he sought for: where the prophet or chief priest saluted him from the god Hammon, as from his father. Then Alexander asked him, if any of the murderers that had killed his father, were left alive. The priest answered him, and bade him take heed he did not blaspheme, for his father was no mortal man. Then Alexander again rehearsing that he had spoken, asked him, if the murderers that had conspired the death of Philip his father were all punished. After that, he asked him touching his kingdom, if he would grant him to be king over all the world. The god answered him by the mouth of his prophet, he should: and that the death of Philip was fully revenged. Then did Alexander offer great presents unto the god, and gave money large to the priests, and ministers of the temple. This is that the most part of writers do declare, touching Alexander's demand, and the oracles given him. Yet did Alexander himself write unto his mother, that he had secret oracles from the god, which he would only impart unto her, at his return into Macedon. Others say also, that the prophet meaning to salute him in the Greek tongue to welcome him the better, would have said unto him, 'O Paidion, as much as 'Dear son': but that he tripped a little in his tongue, because the Greek was not his natural tongue, and placed an s for an n in the latter end, saying, 'O Pai Dios, to wit, 'O son of Jupiter': and that Alexander was glad of that mistaking. Whereupon there ran a rumour straight among his men, that Jupiter had called him his son. It is said also, that he heard Psammon the philosopher in Egypt, and that he liked his words very well, when he said that god was king of all mortal men: 'For,' quoth he, 'he that commandeth all things, must needs be god.' But Alexander self spoke better, and like a philosopher, when he said: that god generally was father to all mortal men, but that particularly he did elect the best sort for himself.

28  To conclude, he showed himself more arrogant unto the barbarous people, and made as though he certainly believed that he had been begotten of some god: but unto the Grecians he spoke more modestly of divine generation. For in a letter he wrote unto the Athenians touching the city of Samos, he said: 'I gave ye not that noble free city, but it was given you at that time by him whom they called my lord and father': meaning Philip. Afterwards also being stricken with an arrow, and feeling great pain of it: 'My friends,' said he, 'this blood which is spilt, is man's blood, and not as Homer said:

No such as from the immortal gods doth flow.'

And one day also in a marvellous great thunder, when every man was afraid, Anaxarchus the rhetorician being present, said unto him: 'O thou son of Jupiter, wilt thou do as much?' 'No,' said he, laughing on him, 'I will not be so fearful to my friends, as thou would'st have me: disdaining the service of fish to my board, because thou seest not princes' heads served in.' And the report goeth also, that Alexander upon a time sending a little fish unto Hephestion, Anaxarchus should say as it were in mockery, that they which above others seek for fame with great trouble and hazard of life, have either small pleasure in the world, or else as little as others have. By these proofs and reasons alleged, we may think that Alexander had no vain nor presumptuous opinion of himself, to think that he was otherwise begotten of a god, but that he did it in policy to keep other men under obedience, by the opinion conceived of his godhead.

29  Returning out of Phoenicia into Egypt, he made many sacrifices, feasts, and processions in honour of the gods, sundry dances, tragedies, and suchlike pastimes goodly to behold: not only for the sumptuous setting out of them, but also for the goodwill and diligence of the setters forth of them, which strived every one to exceed the other. For the kings of the Cyprians were the setters of them forth, as at Athens they draw by lot a citizen of every tribe of the people, to defray the charges of these pastimes. These kings were very earnest who should do best, but specially Nicocreon, king of Salamina in Cyprus: and Pasicrates, lord of the city of Soles. For it fell to their lot to furnish two of the

excellentest players. Pasicrates furnished Athenodorus, and Nicocreon Thessalus: whom Alexander loved singularly well, though
he made no show of it, until that Athenodorus was declared victor
by the judges deputed to give sentence. For when he went from
the plays, he told them he did like the judges' opinion well,
notwithstanding, he would have been contented to have given the
one half of his realm, not to have seen Thessalus overcome.
Athenodorus being condemned upon a time by the Athenians,
because he was not in Athens at the feasts of Bacchus, when the
comedies and tragedies were played, and a fine set of his head for
his absence, he besought Alexander to write unto them in his
behalf, that they would release his penalty. Alexander would not
so do, but sent thither his money whereof he was condemned, and
paid it for him of his own purse. Also when Lycon Scarphian, an
excellent stage player, had pleased Alexander well, and did foist in
a verse in his comedy, containing a petition of ten talents, Alexander laughing at it, gave it him. Darius at that time wrote unto
Alexander, and unto certain of his friends also, to pray him to take
ten thousand talents for the ransom of all those prisoners he had in
his hands, and for all the countries, lands and signories on their side
the river of Euphrates, and one of his daughters also in marriage,
that from thenceforth he might be his kinsman and friend. Alexander imparted this to his council. Amongst them Parmenio said
unto him: 'If I were Alexander,' quoth he, 'surely I would accept
this offer.' 'So would I indeed,' quoth Alexander again, 'if I were
Parmenio.' In fine, he wrote again unto Darius, that if he would
submit himself, he would use him courteously: if not, that then he
would presently march towards him.

30    But he repented him afterwards, when King Darius' wife was
dead with child: for without dissimulation it grieved him much,
that he had lost so noble an occasion to show his courtesy and
clemency. This notwithstanding, he gave her body honourable
burial, sparing for no cost. Amongst the eunuchs of the queens
chamber, there was one Tireus taken prisoner, among the women:
who stealing out of Alexander's camp, taking his horseback, rode
unto Darius to bring him news of the death of his wife. Then
Darius beating of his head, and weeping bitterly, cried out aloud:
'Oh gods! what wretched hap have the Persians, that have not only

had the wife and sister of their king taken prisoners even in his lifetime, but now that she is dead also in travail of child, she hath been deprived of princely burial!' Then spoke the eunuch to him, and said: 'For her burial, most gracious king, and for all due honour that might be wished her, Persia hath no cause to complain of her hard fortune. For neither did Queen Statira your wife whilst she lived prisoner, nor your mother, nor daughters, want any part or jot of their honour they were wont to have before, saving only to see the light of your honour, the which god Oromasdes grant to restore again (if it be his will) unto your majesty: neither was there any honour wanting at her death (to set forth her stately funerals) that might be gotten, but more, was lamented also with the tears of your enemies. For Alexander is as merciful in victory, as he is valiant in battle.' Darius hearing the eunuch's words, being vexed in mind for very grief, took the eunuch aside into the secretest place of his tent, and said unto him: 'If thou be not, with the misfortune of the Persians, become a Macedonian, but do in thy heart acknowledge Darius for thy sovereign lord and master, I pray thee, and do also conjure thee, by the reverence thou bearest unto this bright light of the sun, and to the right hand of the king, that thou do tell me truly. Are these the least evils which I lament in Statira, her imprisonment and death? And did she not in her life make us more miserable by her dishonour, than if we had dishonourably fallen into the hands of a cruel enemy? For, what honest communication I pray thee, can a young victorious prince have with his enemy's wife a prisoner, having done her so much honour as he hath done?' Darius going on with these speeches, Tireus the eunuch fell down on his knees, and besought him not to say so, neither to blemish the virtue of Alexander in that sort, nor yet so to dishonour his sister and wife deceased, and thereby also to deprive himself of the greatest comfort he could wish to have in this calamity, which was, to be overcome by an enemy that had greater virtues than a man could possibly have: but rather that he should wonder at Alexander's virtue, who had showed himself chaster to the ladies, than valiant against the Persians. And therewithal, the eunuch confirmed the great honesty, chastity, and noble mind of Alexander, by many great and deep oaths. Then Darius coming out among his friends again, holding up his hands unto the heavens, made this prayer unto the gods: 'O heavenly

gods, creators of men, and protectors of kings and realms: first, I
beseech you grant me, that restoring the Persians again to their
former good state, I may leave the realm unto my successors, with
that glory and fame I received it of my predecessors: that obtaining
victory, I may use Alexander with that great honour and courtesy,
which he hath in my misery showed unto those I loved best in
the world. Or otherwise, if the time appointed be come, that the
kingdom of Persia must needs have end, either through divine
revenge, or by natural change of earthly things, then, good gods
yet grant, that none but Alexander after me, may sit in Cyrus'
throne.' Divers writers do agree, that these things came even thus
to pass.

31    Now Alexander having conquered all Asia on this side of the
river of Euphrates, he went to meet with Darius, that came down
with ten hundred thousand fighting men. It was told him by some
of his friends to make him laugh, that the slaves of his army had
divided themselves in two parts, and had chosen them a general of
either part, naming the one Alexander, and the other Darius: and
that at the first, they began to skirmish only with clods of earth,
and afterwards with fists, but at the last, they grew so hot, that they
came to plain stones and staves, so that they could not be parted.
Alexander hearing that, would needs have the two generals fight
hand to hand one with the other: and Alexander self did arm him
that was called Alexander, and Philotas the other which was called
Darius. All the army thereupon was gathered together to see this
combat between them, as a thing that did betoken good or ill luck
to some. The fight was sharp between them, but in the end, he
that was called Alexander overcame the other: and Alexander to
reward him, give him twelve villages, with privilege to go after
the Persian manner. Thus it is written by Eratosthenes. The great
battle that Alexander fought with Darius, was not (as many writers
report) at Arbeles, but at Gausameles, which signifieth in the
Persian tongue, the house of the camel. For some one of the
ancient kings of Persia that had escaped from the hands of his
enemies, flying upon a drumbledary camel, lodged him in that
place, and therefore appointed the revenues of certain villages to
keep the camel there. There fell out at that time an eclipse of the
moon, in the month called Boedromion (now August) about the

time that the feast of the mysteries was celebrated at Athens. The
eleventh night after that, both their armies being in sight of the
other, Darius kept his men in battle ray, and went himself by torch
light viewing his bands and companies. Alexander on the other
side whilst his Macedonian soldiers slept, was before his tent with
Aristander the soothsayer, and made certain secret ceremonies and
sacrifices unto Apollo. The ancient captains of the Macedonians,
specially Parmenio, seeing all the valley betwixt the river of
Niphates and the mountains of the Gordieians, all on a bright light
with the fires of the barbarous people, and hearing a dreadful noise
as of a confused multitude of people that filled their camp with the
sound thereof, they were amazed, and consulted, that in one day it
was in manner unpossible to fight a battle with such an incredible
multitude of people. Thereupon they went unto Alexander after
he had ended his ceremonies, and did counsel him to give battle
by night, because the darkness thereof should help to keep all fear
from his men, which the sight of their enemies would bring them
into. But then he gave them this notable answer: 'I will not steal
victory,' quoth he. This answer seemed very fond and arrogant to
some, that he was so pleasant, being near so great danger. Howbeit
others think that it was a present noble courage, and a deep
consideration of him, to think what should happen thereby to give
Darius no manner of occasion (if he were overcome) to take heart
again, and to prove another battle, accusing the darkness of the
night as cause of his overthrow as he had done at the first conflict,
imputing his overthrow to the mountains, the straits, and the sea.
'For,' said he, 'Darius will never leave to make wars with us for
lack of men, nor munition, having so large a realm as he hath, and
such a world of people besides: but then he will no more hazard
battle, when his heart is done, and all hope taken from him, and
that he seeth his army at noondays overthrown by plain battle.'

32   After his captains were gone from him, he went into his tent,
and laid him down to sleep, and slept all that night more soundly
than he was wont to do before: insomuch as the lords and princes of
his camp coming to wait upon him at his uprising, marvelled when
they found him so sound asleep, and therefore of themselves they
commanded the soldiers to eat. Afterwards, perceiving that time
came fast upon them, Parmenio went into Alexander's chamber,

and coming to his bed's side, called him twice or thrice by his name, till at the last he waked him, and asked him how it chanced that he slept so long, like one that had already overcome, and that did not think he should fight as great and dangerous a battle as ever he did in his life. 'Why,' said Alexander, laughing on him: 'doest thou not think we have already overcome, being troubled no more with running after Darius up and down a country utterly destroyed, as we should otherwise have been compelled to have done, if he would not have come to battle, and destroyed the country before us?' Now Alexander did not only show himself before the battle, but even at the very instant of battle, a noble man of courage, and of great judgment. For Parmenio leading the left wing of his battle, the men of arms of the Bactrians gave such a fierce onset upon the Macedonians, that they made them give back: and Mazeus also, King Darius' lieutenant, sent certain troops of horsemen out of their battle, to give charge upon them that were left in the camp to guard the carriage. Parmenio being amazed with either of both attempts, sent immediately to advertise Alexander, that all their camp and carriage would be lost, if he did not send presently to aid the rearward. When these news came to Alexander from Parmenio, he had already given the signal of battle unto his men for to give charge. Whereupon he answered the messenger that brought him these news, that he should tell Parmenio he was a mad man and out of his wits, not remembering that if they won the battle, they should not only save their own carriage, but also win the carriage of their enemies: and if it were their chance to lose it, then that they should not need to care for their carriage, nor for their slaves, but only to think to die honourably, valiantly fighting for his life. Having sent this message unto Parmenio, he put on his helmet. The rest of his armour for his body, he had put it on before in his tent, which was, a Sicilian cassock, and upon that a brigandine made of many folds of canvas with eyelet holes, which was got among the spoils at the battle of Issus. His headpiece was as bright as silver, made by Theophilus the armourer: his collar suitlike to the same, all set full of precious stones, and he had a sword by his side, marvellous light, and of excellent temper, which the king of the Citieians had given him, using commonly to fight with his sword at any set battle. His coat armour was marvellous rich, and of sumptuous workmanship, far above all the rest he ware. It was of the workmanship of Hellicon, the which the Rhodians gave him for a present, and this he commonly wore when he went to battle. Now when he did set his men in battle ray, or made any oration unto them, or did ride along the bands to take view of them, he always used to ride upon another horse to spare Bucephal, because he was then somewhat old: notwithstanding, when he meant indeed to fight, then Bucephal was brought unto him, and as soon as he was got up on his back, the trumpet sounded, and he gave charge.

33  Then, after he had made long exhortations to encourage the men of arms of the Thessalians, and the other Grecians also, and when they had all promised him they would stick to him like men, and prayed him to lead them, and give charge upon the enemies, he took his lance in his left hand, and holding up his right hand unto heaven, besought the gods (as Callisthenes writeth) that if it were true, he was begotten of Jupiter, that it would please them that day to help him, and to encourage the Grecians. The soothsayer Aristander was then a-horseback hard by Alexander, apparelled all in white, and a crown of gold on his head, who showed Alexander when he made his prayer, an eagle flying over his head, and pointing directly towards his enemies. This marvellously encouraged all the army that saw it, and with this joy, the men of arms of Alexander's side, encouraging one another, did set spurs to their horse to charge upon the enemies. The battle of the footmen of the Persians began a little to give way, and before the foremost could come to give them charge, the barbarous people turned their backs, and fled. The chase was great, Alexander driving them that fled upon the midst of their own battle, where Darius self was in person. He spied him afar off over the foremost rank in the midst of his battle, being a goodly tall prince, standing in a chariot of war, compassed in round with great troops of horsemen, all set in goodly ordinance to receive the enemy. But when they saw Alexander at hand with so grim a look, chasing them that fled, through those that yet kept their ranks, there fell such a fear among them, that the most part dispersed themselves. Notwithstanding, the best and most valiantest men fought it out to the death before their king, and falling dead one upon another, they did let them that the enemies could not so well follow Darius. For they lying one by another on the ground, drawing on to the last gasp, did yet take both men and

horses by the legs to hinder them. Darius then seeing nothing but
terror and destruction before his eyes, and that the bands which he
had set before him for safeguard, came back upon him, so as he
could not devise how to turn his chariot forward nor backward, the
wheels were so hindered and stayed with the heaps of dead bodies,
and that the horse also being set upon and hid in manner in this
conflict, fell to leaping and plunging for fear, so that the charioteers
could no longer guide nor drive them: he got up upon a mare that
lately had foal, and so saved himself flying upon her. And yet had he
not thus escaped, had not Parmenio once again sent unto Alexander
to pray him to come and aid him, because there was yet a great
squadron whole together that made no countenance to flee. Somewhat there was in it, that they accused Parmenio that day to have
dealt but slackly and cowardly, either because his age had taken his
courage from him, or else for that he envied Alexander's greatness
and prosperity, who against his will became over-great, as Callisthenes said. In fine, Alexander was angry with the second message,
and yet told not his men truly the cause why, but feigning that he
would have them leave killing, and because also night came on, he
caused the trumpet sound retreat, and so went towards his army,
whom he thought to be in distress. Notwithstanding, news came to
him by the way, that in that place also, they had given the enemies
the overthrow, and that they fled every way for life.

34 The battle having this success, every man thought that the
kingdom of the Persians was utterly overthrown, and that Alexander
likewise was become only king of all Asia: whereupon he made
sumptuous sacrifices unto the gods, and gave great riches, houses,
lands and possessions unto his friends and familiars. Furthermore, to
show his liberality also unto the Grecians, he wrote unto them, that
he would have all tyrannies suppressed throughout all Greece, and
that all the Grecians should live at liberty under their own laws.
Particularly also he wrote unto the Plataeians, that he would re-edify
their city again, because their predecessors in time past, had given
their country unto the Grecians, to fight against the barbarous
people for the defence of the common liberty of all Greece. He sent
also into Italy unto the Grotonians, part of the spoil, to honour the
memory of the valiantness and goodwill of Phayllus their citizen,
who in the time of the wars with the Medes (when all the Grecians

that dwelt in Italy had forsaken their natural countrymen of Greece itself, because they thought they could not otherwise escape) went with a ship of his unto Salamina, which he armed and set forth at his own charges, because he would be at the battle and partake also of the common danger with the Grecians: such honour did Alexander bear unto prowess, that he loved to reward and remember the worthy deeds of men.

35    Then Alexander marching with his army into the country of Babylon, they all yielded straight unto him. When he came into the country of the Ecbatanians, he marvelled when he saw an opening of the earth, out of the which there came continual sparks of fire as out of a well: and that hard by also the earth spewed out continually a kind of mawnd or chalky clay somewhat liquid, of such abundance, as it seemed like a lake. This maund or chalk is like unto a kind of lime or clay, but it is so easy to be set afire, that not touching it with any flame, by the brightness only of the light that cometh out of the fire, it is set afire, and doth also set the air afire which is between both. The barbarous people of that country, being desirous to show Alexander the nature of that Naptha, scattered the street that led to his lodging, with some of it. Then the day being shut in, they fired it at one of the ends, and the first drops taking fire, in the twinkling of an eye, all the rest from one end of the street to the other was of a flame, and though it was dark and within night, lightened all the place thereabout. Alexander being in bath at that time, and waited upon by a page called Steven (a hard-favoured boy, but yet that had an excellent sweet voice to sing), one Athenophanes an Athenian, that always anointed and bathed the king, and much delighted him with his pleasant conceits, asked him if he would see the trial of this Naptha upon Steven: for if the fire took, and went not out, then he would say it had a wonderful force, and was unquenchable. The page was contented to have it proved upon him. But so soon as they had laid it on him, and did but touch it only, it took straight of such a flame, and so fired his body, that Alexander himself was in a marvellous perplexity withal. And sure had it not been by good hap, that there were many by ready with vessels full of water to put into the bath, it had been impossible to have saved the boy from being burnt to nothing: and yet so he escaped narrowly, and besides was sick long

after. Now some apply this Naptha unto the fable of Medea, saying that therewith she rubbed the crown and lawn she gave unto the daughter of Creon at her marriage, so much spoken of in the tragedies. For neither the crown nor the lawn could cast fire of themselves, neither did the fire light by chance. But by oiling them with this Naptha she wrought a certain aptness to receive more forcibly the operation of the fire, which was in place where the bride sat. For the beams which the fire casteth out, have over some bodies no other force, but to heat and lighten them. But such as have an oily dry humour, and thereby a sympathy and proportionable conformity with the nature of the fire, it easily enflameth and setteth afire, by the forcible impression of his beams. Howbeit they make a great question of the cause of this natural force of Naptha,* or whether this liquid substance and moist humour that taketh fire so easily, doth come of the earth that is fatty and apt to conceive fire. For this country of Babylon is very hot, insomuch as oftentimes barley being put into the ground, it bloweth it up again, as if the earth by vehement inflammation had a strong blast to cast it out: and men in the extremest heat of the summer, do sleep there, upon great leather budgets filled full of fresh water. Harpalus, whom Alexander left there his lieutenant and governor of that country, desiring to set forth and beautify the gardens of the king's palace and walks of the same, with all manner of plants of Greece, he brought all the rest to good pass, saving ivy only, which the earth could never abide, but it ever died, because the heat and temper of the earth killed it, and the ivy of itself liketh fresh air and a cold ground. This digression is somewhat from the matter, but peradventure the reader will not think it troublesome, how hard soever he find it, so it be not over tedious.

36    Alexander having won the city of Susa, he found within the castle four thousand talents in ready coin, gold and silver, besides other infinite treasure and inestimable, amongst the which (it is said) he found to the value of five thousand talents weight of purple Hermiona silk† which they had safe locked up and kept the space

---

* In this place there lack of certain lines in the Greek original.
† It seemeth that he meaneth of silk dyed in purple, whereof the best that was in Europe was made in the city of Hermiona, in Laconia.

of two hundred years save ten, and yet the colour kept as fresh as if it had been newly made. Some say that the cause why it was so well kept, came by means of the dying of it, with honey, in silks which before had been dyed red, and with white oil in white silks. For, there are silks seen of that colour of as long a time, that keep colour as well as the other. Dino writeth furthermore, that the kings of Persia made water to be brought from the rivers of Nylus and Ister (otherwise called Danubie) which they did lock up with their other treasure for a confirmation of the greatness of their empire, and to show that they were lords of the world.

37   The ways to enter into Persia being very hard of passage, and in manner unpassable (both for the illness of the ways, as also for the guard that kept them, which were the choicest men of Persia), Darius also being fled thither, there was one that spoke the Greek and Persian tongue (whose father was born in the country of Lycia, and his mother a Persian) that guided Alexander into Persia, by some compass fetched about not very long, according to the oracle's answer of Alexander given by the mouth of Nun Pythias, when he was a child: that a Lycian should guide and lead him against the Persians. There was then great slaughter made in Persia of the prisoners that were taken. For Alexander himself writeth, that he commanded the men should be put to the sword, thinking that the best way to serve his turn. It is said also, that there he found a marvellous treasure of gold and silver in ready money, as he had done before in the city of Susa: the which he carried away with all the rest of the king's rich wardrobe, and with it laded ten thousand mules, and five thousand camels. Alexander entering into the castle of the chief city of Persia, saw by chance a great image of Xerxes lie on the ground, the which unawares was thrown down by the multitude of the soldiers that came in, thronging one upon another. Thereupon he stayed, and spoke unto it as if it had been alive, saying: 'I cannot tell whether I should pass by thee, and let thee lie, for the war thou madest sometime against the Grecians: or whether I should lift thee up, respecting the noble mind and virtues thou haddest.' In the end, when he had stood mute a long time, considering of it, he went his way: and meaning to refresh his weary army, because it was the winter quarter, he remained there four months together. The

report goeths, that the first time that Alexander sat under the cloth of state of King Darius, all of rich gold, Demarathus Corinthian (who first began to love him even in his father Philip's time) burst out in tears for joy, good old man, saying that the Grecians long time dead before, were deprived of this blessed hap: to see Alexander set in King Xerxes' princely chair.

38   After that, preparing again to go against Darius, he would needs make merry one day, and refresh himself with some banquet. It chanced so, that he with his companions was bidden to a private feast privately, where was assembled some fine courtesans of his familiars who with their friends tarried at the banquet. Amongst them was that famous Thais, born in the country of Attica, and then concubine to Ptolomy, King of Egypt after Alexander's death. She finely praising Alexander, and partly in sporting wise, began to utter matter in affection of her country, but yet of greater importance than became her mouth: saying, that that day she found herself fully recompensed to her great good liking, for all the pains she had taken, travelling through all the countries of Asia, following of his army, now that she had this favour and good hap to be merry and pleasant, in the proud and stately palace of the great kings of Persia. But yet it would do her more good, for a recreation, to burn Xerxes' house with the fire of joy, who had burnt the city of Athens: and herself to give the fire to it, before so noble a prince as Alexander. Because ever after it might be said, that the women following his camp had taken more noble revenge of the Persians, for the wrongs and injury they had done unto Greece, than all the captains of Greece that ever were had done, either by land or sea. When she had said, Alexander's familiars about him clapped their hands, and made great noise for joy, saying that it were as good a deed as could be possible, and persuaded Alexander unto it. Alexander yielding to their persuasions, rose up, and putting a garland of flowers upon his head, went foremost himself: and all his familiars followed after him, crying and dancing all about the castle. The other Macedonians hearing of it also, came thither immediately with torches' light and great joy, hoping that this was a good sign that Alexander meant to return again into Macedon, and not to dwell in the country of the barbarous people, if he did burn and destroy the king's castle. Thus, and in this sort it was

thought to be burnt. Some writers think otherwise: that it was not
burnt with such sport, but by determination of the council. But
howsoever it was, all they grant, that Alexander did presently
repent him, and commanded the fire to be quenched straight.

39   For his liberality, that goodwill and readiness to give, increased
with his conquests: and when he did bestow gifts of any, he would
besides his gift ever give them good countenance, on whom he
bestowed his grace and favour. And here I will recite a few
examples thereof. Aristo being colonel of the Paeonians, having
slain one of his enemies, he brought him his head, and said: 'Such a
present, O king, by us, is ever rewarded with a cup of gold.' 'Yea,'
quoth Alexander, smiling upon him, 'with an empty cup. But I
drink to thee this cup full of good wine, and do give thee cup and
all.' Another time, he met with a poor Macedonian that led a mule
laden with gold of the king's: and when the poor mule was so weary
that she could no longer carry her burden, the muleteer put it upon
his own back, and loaded himself withal, carrying it so a good pretty
way: howbeit in the end being overladen, was about to throw it
down on the ground. Alexander perceiving it, asked him what
burden he carried. When it was told him: 'Well,' quoth he to the
muleteer, 'be not weary yet, but carry it into the tent, for I give it
thee.' To be short, he was angrier with them that would take
nothing of him, than he was with those that would ask him
somewhat. He wrote also unto Phocion, that he would take him
no more for his friend, if he would refuse his gifts. It seemed that he
had given nothing unto a young boy called Serapion (who ever did
serve them the ball that played at tennis) because he asked him
nothing. Wherefore, the king playing on a time, this young boy
threw the ball to others that played with him, and not to himself.
The king marvelling at it, at the length said unto him: 'Why, my
boy, doest thou not give me the ball?' 'Because your majesty doth
not ask it me,' quoth he. Alexander then understanding his meaning, laughed at the boy, and did much for him afterwards. There
was attending on him also one Proteas, a pleasant conceited man,
and that could slent finely. It chanced upon some occasion that
Alexander fell out with him: whereupon some of his friends were
intercessors to the king for him, and besought him to pardon him:
and Proteas himself also being present, craved pardon with tears in

his eyes. Alexander thereupon forgave him. Then pleasantly replied Proteas, 'I desire it may please your grace, that I may receive some testimony to assure me I am in your favour.' Thereupon the king straight commanded one to give him five talents. The goods and riches he gave unto his familiars and guard about him, were very great, as it appeareth plainly by a letter which his mother Olympias wrote unto him, to this effect: 'I know thou sparest not to give thy friends large gifts, and that thou makest much of them: but thereby thou makest them king's fellows, they get many friends, and leave the post alone without any.' His mother did many times write suchlike matters unto him, the which Alexander kept very secret, saving one day when he opened one of them; Hephaestion being present drew near, and read the letter with him, as he was wont to do. Alexander did let him alone, but when he had read it, he plucked the seal of arms from his finger, wherewith he did use to seal his letters, and put it to Hephaestion's mouth. He gave also unto the son of Mazeus (that was the chiefest man about Darius) a second government, besides that which he had before, and greater than the first. This young nobleman refused it saying: 'Why, and it please your grace, before there was but one Darius, but you now make many Alexanders.' He gave unto Parmenio also, Bagoas' house, where (as is reported) he found a thousand talents' worth of the spoils and goods of the Susians. He wrote also unto Antipater, that he should keep a guard about his person, for he had many enemies that lay in wait for him. He did send also many goodly presents unto his mother, but withal he wrote unto her, that she would meddle no more with his matters nor gifts, taking upon her the office of a captain. She storming at it, he patiently did brook her anger. Antipater another time, writing a long letter unto him against his mother Olympias, when he had read it over: 'Lo,' said he, 'Antipater knoweth not, that one tear of the mother's eye will wipe out ten thousand such letters.'

40    Furthermore, Alexander perceiving on a time, that his friends became very dissolute and licentious in diet and life, and that Agnon Teian had his corked shoes nailed with silver nails, that Leonatus also caused divers camels to be laden amongst his carriage with powder of Egypt, to put upon him when he wrestled or used any other exercise of body: and that also they carried after Philotas,

toils for chase and hunting, of a hundred furlong long, and that there were also that used precious perfumes and sweet savours when they bathed themselves, more than there were that rubbed themselves with plain oil, and that they had fine chamberlains to rub them in the bath, and to make their beds soft and delicate: he wisely and courteously rebuked them and said: 'I marvel,' said he, 'that you which have fought in so often and great battles, do not remember that they which travail, do sleep more sweet and soundly, than they that take their ease and do nothing: and that you do not mark, that comparing your life with the manner of the life of the Persians, to live at pleasure is a vile thing, and to travail is princely. And how I pray you, can a man take pain to dress his own horse, or to make clean his lance or helmet, that for slothful curiosity's sake, disdaineth to rub his own body with his fine fingers? Are you ignorant, that the type of honour in all our victory consisteth, in scorning to do that which we see them do, whom we have vanquished and overcome?' To bring them therefore by his example, to acquaint themselves with hardness, he took more pains in wars and in hunting, and did hazard himself more dangerously, than ever he had done before. Whereupon an ambassador of Lacedaemon being present to see him fight with a lion, and to kill him, said unto him: 'Truly your grace hath fought well with this lion, and tried which of you two should be king.' Craterus after that, caused this hunting to be set up in the temple of Apollo in Delphes: where are the images of the lion, of the dogs, and of the king fighting with the lion, and of himself also that came to help him, all those images being of copper, some made by Lysippus, the rest by Leochares.

41 Thus Alexander did put himself unto all jeopardies, as well to exercise his strength and courage, as also to allure his men to do the like. This notwithstanding, his friends and familiars having wealth at will, as men exceeding rich, they would needs live delicately and at ease, and would take no more pains, misliking utterly to go up and down the countries to make war here and there: and thereupon began a little to find fault with Alexander, and to speak evil of him. Which at the first Alexander took quietly, saying, that it was honour for a king to suffer himself to be slandered and ill spoken of, for doing of good. And yet the least good turns he did unto his

friends, did show his hearty love and honour he bore them, as shall appear unto you by some examples that follow. Peucestas being bitten by a bear, did let his friends understand it by letters, but he wrote nothing thereof unto Alexander. Alexander was offended therewith, and wrote unto him thus: 'Send me word at the least yet how thou doest, and whether any of thy fellows did forsake thee at the hunting, to the end they may be punished.' Hephaestion being absent about certain business he had, Alexander wrote unto him, that as they were hunting a beast called *ichnewmon*, Craterus unfortunately crossing Perdiccas' dart, was stricken through both his thighs. Peucestas being cured of a great disease, Alexander wrote unto Alexippus his physician that had cured him, and gave him thanks. Craterus also being sick, he dreamed of him one night, and therefore made certain sacrifices for the recovery of his health, and sent unto him, willing him to do the like. And when the physician Pausanias meant to give him a drink of Elleborum, he wrote letters unto him, telling him what danger he was in, and prayed him to be careful how he received that medicine. He did also put Ephialtes and Cissus in prison, who brought him the first news of Harpalus' flying, because they did wrongfully accuse and slander him. When he had commanded there should be a bill made of all the old men's names, and diseased persons that were in his camp, to send them home again into their country, there was one Eurylochus Aegeian that made his name be billed among the sick persons, and it was found afterwards that he was not sick, and confessed that he did it only to follow a young woman called Telesippa, with whom he was in love, who was returning homewards towards the sea side. Alexander asked him, whether this woman were free or bond: he answered him, that she was a courtesan free born. Then said Alexander unto Eurylochus, 'I would be glad to further thy love, yet I cannot force her to tarry: but seek to win her by gifts and fair words to be contented to tarry, since she is a free woman.'

42   It is a wonderful thing to see what pains he would take, to write for his friends, even in such trifles as he did. As, when he wrote into Cilicia for a servant of Seleucus that was fled from his master, sending strait commandment, that they should carefully lay for him. And by another letter he commendeth Peucestas, for that he had stayed and taken one Nicon, a slave of Craterus. And by one other

letter also unto Megabizus, touching another bondman that had taken sanctuary in a temple: he commanded him also to seek to entice him out of the sanctuary, to lay hold on him if he could, but otherwise not to meddle with him in any case. It is said also, that at the first when he used to sit in judgment to hear criminal causes, whilst the accuser went on with his complaint and accusation, he always used to lay his hand upon one of his ears to keep that clean from the matter of accusation, thereby reserving it to hear the purgation and justification of the person condemned. But afterwards, the number of accusations that were brought before him, did so provoke and alter him, that he did believe the false accusations, by the great number of the true that were brought in. But nothing put him more in rage, than when he understood they had spoken ill of him: and then he was so fierce, as no pardon would be granted, for that he loved his honour, more than his kingdom or life. Then at that time he went against Darius, thinking that he meant to fight again: but understanding that Bessus had taken him, then he gave the Thessalians leave to depart home into their country, and gave them two thousand talents, over and above their ordinary pay. Alexander had then a marvellous long, hard, and painful journey in following of Darius: for eleven days, he rode three thousand three hundred furlong, insomuch as the most part of his men were even weary, and done, for lack of water. It chanced him one day to meet with certain Macedonians that carried (upon mules) goat skins full of water, which they had fetched from a river. They seeing Alexander in manner dead for thirst, being about noon, ran quickly to him, and in a headpiece brought him water. Alexander asked them, to whom they carried this water. They answered him again, that they carried it to their children, but yet we would have your grace to live: for though we lose them, we may get more children. When they had said so, Alexander took the helmet with water, and perceiving that men of arms that were about him, and had followed him, did thrust out their necks to look upon this water, he gave the water back again unto them that had given it him, and thanked them, but drank none of it. 'For,' said he, 'if I drink alone, all these men here will faint.' Then they seeing the noble courage and courtesy of Alexander, cried out that he should lead them: and therewithal began to spur their horses, saying, that they were not weary nor athirst, nor did think themselves mortal, so long as they had such a king.

43   Every man was alike willing to follow Alexander, yet had he
but three score only that entered with him into the enemies' camp.
There, passing over much gold and silver which was scattered
abroad in the market place, and going also by many chariots full of
women and children, which they found in the fields, flying away at
all adventure, they ran upon the spur until they had overtaken the
foremost that fled, thinking to have found Darius amongst them.
But at the length, with much ado, they found him laid along in a
coach, having many wounds upon his body, some of darts and some
spears. So, he being almost at the last cast, called for some drink, and
drank cold water, which Polystratus gave him. To whom when he
had drunk, he said: 'This is my last mishap, my friend, that having
received this pleasure, I cannot requite thee: howbeit Alexander
will recompense thee, and the gods Alexander, for the liberality and
courtesy which he hath showed unto my wife and children, whom
I pray thee embrace for my sake.' At these last words, he took
Polystratus by the hand, and so gave up the ghost. Alexander came
immediately after, and plainly showed that he was sorry for his
death and misfortune: and undoing his own cloak, he cast it upon
the body of Darius. After that, having by good hap got Bessus into
his hands, he tore him in pieces with two high straight trees which
he bowed downwards, and tied his legs to each of them: so that
when the trees were let go, they gave a sudden cruel jerk up and
carried either tree a piece of his body with it. Then Alexander
having given Darius' corse princely burial, and embalmed him, he
sent it unto his mother, and received his brother Exathres for one of
his friends.

44   From thence he went into the country of Hyrcania with all
the flower of his army, where he saw the gulf of the sea Caspium,
which he thought of no less greatness than the sea of Pontus,
howbeit calmer than the other seas be. He could not then
certainly find out what it was, nor from whence it came: but of
likelihood he thought it was some breaking out of the lake or
marsh of Meotin. Yet some ancient natural philosophers seemed
to know truly what it was. For many years before Alexander's
voyage and conquest, they wrote, that of the four chiefest gulfs of
the sea that cometh from the Ocean, and do enter within main
land, that which is most northerly is the sea Caspium, which they

call also Hyrcanium. As Alexander went through the country, certain barbarous people suddenly set upon them that led Bucephal his horse, and took him: but with that he was in such a rage, that he sent a herald into their country to proclaim open wars upon them, and that he would put man, woman, and child to the sword, if they brought him not his horse again. Whereupon, when his horse was returned home, and that they yielded up their cities and forts into his hands: he did use them all very courteously, and moreover did give them money for the ransom of his horse, which they restored.

45 Departing thence, he entered into the country of Parthia. There having leisure enough, he began to apparel himself after the fashion of the barbarous people, because he thought thereby the better to win the hearts of the countrymen, framing himself unto their own fashions: or else to try the hearts of the Macedonians, to see how they would like the manner of the Persians (which he meant to bring them unto) in reverencing of him as they did their king, by little and little acquainting them to allow the alteration and change of his life. This notwithstanding, he would not at the first take up the apparel of the Medes, which was very strange, and altogether barbarous. For he went not without breeches, nor did wear a long gown trailing on the ground, nor a high coptanct hat, but took a mean apparel betwixt the Medes and the Persians, more modest then theirs, and more costly than the last: and yet at the first he did not wear it, but when he would talk with the barbarous people, or else privately among his friends and familiars. Afterwards notwithstanding, he showed himself openly to the people in that apparel, when he gave them audience. This sight grieved the Macedonians much: but they had his virtues in such admiration, that they thought it meet in some things he should take his own pleasure, since he had been often hurt in the wars, and not long before had his leg broken with an arrow, and another time, had such a blow with a stone full in his neck, that it made him spur blind a great while after, and yet nevertheless he never eschewed any bodily danger. For he passed over the river of Orexartes, which he took to be Tanais, and having in battle overthrown the Scythians, he followed them in chase above a hundred furlong, notwithstanding that at that instant he had a looseness of body.

46   Thither came unto him (as it is reported) the queen of the Amazons, as many writers do testify: among the which are these, Clitarchus, Polycritus, Onesicritus, Antigenes, and Hister. But Chares, Ptolomy, Anticlides, and Philon Theban, Philip the historiographer, Hecateus Eretrian, Philip Chalcidian, and Duris Samian, all these do write that it was not true: and it seemeth also that Alexander self doth confirm it. For, writing all things particularly unto Antipater as they happened unto him, he wrote unto him that the king of Scythia offered him his daughter in marriage: but there he maketh no mention at all of any Amazon. It is also said, that Onesicritus long time after that did read unto King Lysimachus the fourth book of his history, where he did speak of the Amazon. Lysimachus smiling, said unto him: 'Why, and where was I then?' But for that matter, to credit or not credit it, Alexander's estimation thereby is neither impaired nor advanced.

47   Furthermore, Alexander fearing that the Macedonians, being weary with this long war, would go no further, he left all the rest of his army behind, and took only twenty thousand footmen, and three thousand horsemen of the choicest men of his army, and with them invaded the country of Hyrcania. There he made an oration unto them, and told them, that the barbarous people of Asia had but seen them as it were in a dream, and if they should now return back into Macedon, having but only stirred them, and not altogether subdued Asia, the people offended with them, would set upon them as they went home, as if they were no better than women. Nevertheless, he gave any man leave to return that would, protesting therewith against them that would go, how they did forsake him, his friends, and those who had so good hearts towards him, as to follow him in so noble a journey, to conquer the whole earth unto the Macedonians. This self matter is reported thus in a letter which Alexander wrote unto Antipater: and there he writeth furthermore, that having made this oration unto them, they all cried out, and bade him lead them into what part of the world he would. When they had granted their goodwills, it was no hard matter afterwards, to win the rest of the common sort who followed the example of the chiefest. Thereupon he did frame himself the more to live after the fashion of the country there, and interchangeably also to bring the men of that country unto the

manner of the Macedonians: being persuaded, that by this mixture and interchange of manners one with another, he should by friendship more than force, make them agree lovingly together, when that he should be so far from the country of Persia. For this purpose therefore, he chose thirty thousand of their children of that country, and set them to learn the Greek tongue, and to be brought up in the discipline of wars, after the Macedonians' manner: and gave them schoolmasters and captains to train them in each faculty. And for the marrying of Roxane, he fancied her, seeing her at a feast where he was: which fell out as well for his turn, as if he had with better advice and counsel loved her. For the barbarous people were very proud of this match when they saw him make alliance with them in this sort, insomuch as they loved him better than they did before, because they saw in those things he was always so chaste and continent, that notwithstanding he was marvellously in love with her, yet he would not dishonourably touch this young lady, before he was married unto her. Furthermore, Alexander considering that of the two men which he loved best, Hephaestion liked well of his match, and went apparelled as himself did, and that Craterus contrarily did still use the Macedonian manner, he dealt in all affairs with the barbarous people by Hephaestion, and with the Grecians and Macedonians by Craterus. To be short, he loved the one, and honoured the other: saying, that Hephaestion loved Alexander, and Craterus loved the king. Hereupon these two persons bore one another grudge in their hearts, and oftentimes broke out in open quarrel: insomuch as on a time being in India, they drew their swords and fought together, and divers of their friends ran to take part with either side. Thither came Alexander self also, who openly before them all, bitterly took up Hephaestion, and called him fool and bedlam, saying: 'Doest thou not know, that whatsoever he be that should take Alexander from thee, he should never live?' Privately also, he sharply rebuked Craterus, and calling them both before him, he made them friends together, swearing by Jupiter Hammon, and by all the other gods, that he loved them two of all men living, nevertheless if ever he found that they fell out together again, they should both die for it, or him at the least that first began to quarrel. So ever after that, they say, there was never foul word nor deed between them, not so much as in sport only.

48   There was also one Philotas, the son of Parmenio, a man of
great authority among the Macedonians, who next unto Alexander
was the most valiantest man, the patientest to abide pain, the
liberalest, and one that loved his men and friends better than any
nobleman in the camp whatsoever. Of him it is reported, that a
friend of his came to him on a time to borrow money: and he
commanded straight one of his men to let him have it. His purse
bearer answered him, that he had none. 'Why,' said his master,
'doest thou tell me so? Hast thou not plate and apparel to sell or
gage to help him to some?' Howbeit otherwise, he had such a pride
and glory to show his riches, to apparel himself so sumptuously,
and to be more fine and prinked than became a private man, that
this made him to be hated: because he took upon him to be a
great man and to look big on the matter, which became him ill
favouredly, and therefore every man, through his own folly, fell in
misliking with him. Insomuch as his own father said one day unto
him: 'Son, I pray thee be more humble and lowly.' This Philotas
had long before been complained upon unto Alexander, because
that when the carriage of King Darius' army (which was in the city
of Damas) was taken after the battle of Cilicia, among many
prisoners that were taken and brought unto Alexander's camp,
there was one Antigona, a passing fair young courtesan, born in the
city of Pidna. Philotas found means to get her, and like a young
man that was in love with her, making merry with her at the table,
fondly let fall brave words and boasts of a soldier, saying, that what
notable things were done, they were done by himself and his
father: and called Alexander at every word, young man, and said
that by their means he held his name and kingdom. This courtesan
told one of his friends what he said, and that friend told another
friend, and so went from man to man (as commonly it doth) till at
the length it came to Craterus' ears. He took the courtesan, and
brought her unto Alexander, unto whom she told as much as she
had said before. Alexander bade her still make much of Philotas,
and to tell him every word what he said of him.

49   Philotas knowing nothing that he was thus circumvented, did
ever frequent her company, and would be bold commonly to
speak many foolish and indiscreet words against the king, sometime in anger, and sometime again in a bravery. Alexander this

notwithstanding, though he had manifest proof and cause to accuse Philotas, yet he dissembled it for that time, and would not be known of it: either for that he knew Parmenio loved him, or else for that he was afraid of their great power and authority. About that time there was one Limnus Chalaestrian a Macedonian, that laid great and secret wait to kill Alexander: and being in love with a young man called Nicomachus, enticed him to help him to do this deed. The young man wisely denied it, and told the same to his brother called Balinus. He went unto Philotas, and prayed him to bring them both before Alexander, for they had a matter of great importance to impart unto him. Philotas would not let him speak with the king (but why, no man could tell) telling them that the king had greater matters in hand, and was not at leisure. Then they went unto another, and he brought them unto Alexander, unto whom first they opened the treason of Limnus conspired against him: and by the way they told also, how they had been twice before with Philotas, who would not let them come in, nor speak with them. That angered Alexander greatly, and he was the more offended also when Limnus was slain by him whom he sent to apprehend him, resisting him for that he would not be taken: and thought that by his death he had lost a great means to come to the light of this treason and conspiracy. Then Alexander frowning upon Philotas, brought all his enemies upon his back, that of long time had hated him. For they began to speak boldly, that it was time for the king to look about him, for it was not to be supposed that this Limnus Chalaestrian of himself durst have entered into that treason, but rather that he was a minister, and a chief instrument, set on by a greater personage then he: and therefore that it stood Alexander upon to examine them straiter, which had cause to keep this treason secret. After Alexander once gave ear unto such words and vehement presumptions, there was straight brought in a thousand accusations against Philotas. Thereupon he was apprehended, and in the presence of divers lords and familiars of the king, put to the torture, Alexander self being behind a hanging, to hear what he would say. It is reported, that when he heard how faintly and pitifully he besought Hephaestion to take pity of him, he said unto himself: 'Alas, poor Philotas, thou that hath so faint a heart, how durst thou take upon thee so great matters?' In fine, Philotas was put to death, and immediately after he was executed, Alexander sent also with speed unto the realm of Media to kill Parmenio, who was his lieutenant there, and one that had served King Philip his father in his greatest affairs, and who only of all other the old servants of his father had procured Alexander to take in hand the conquest of Asia: and who also of three sons which he brought out with him, had seen two of them die before him, and afterwards was slain himself with the third. This cruelty of Alexander made his friends afraid of him, and specially Antipater: who secretly sent ambassadors unto the Aetolians, to make league with them, because they themselves also were afraid of Alexander, for that they had put the Oeniades to death. Alexander hearing that, said, that he himself, and not the sons of the Oeniades, would be revenged of the Aetolians.

50   Not long after that, followed the murder of Clitus, the which to hear it simply told, would seem much more cruel than the death of Philotas. But reporting the cause and the time together in which it chanced: it will be found that it was not of set purpose, but by chance, and unfortunately, that Alexander being overcome with wine, did unluckily wreak his anger upon Clitus. The manner of his misfortune was this: there came certain men of the low countries from the sea side, that brought apples of Greece unto Alexander. Alexander wondering to see them so green and fair, sent for Clitus to show him them, and to give him some of them. Clitus by chance did sacrifice at that time unto the gods, and left his sacrifice to go unto Alexander: howbeit there were three wethers that followed him, on whom the accustomed sprinklings had been done already to have sacrificed them. Alexander understanding that, told it to his soothsayers, Aristander, and Cleomantis Laconian, who both did answer him, that it was an ill sign. Alexander thereupon gave order straight, that they should do sacrifice for the health of Clitus, and specially for that three days before he dreamed one night that he saw Clitus in a mourning gown, sitting amongst the sons of Parmenio, the which were all dead before. This notwithstanding, Clitus did not make an end of his sacrifice, but came straight to supper to the king, who had that day sacrificed unto Castor and Pollux. At this feast there was old drinking, and all the supper time there were certain verses sung and made by a poet, called Pranichus (or as others say, of one

Pierion), against certain captains of the Macedonians, which had not long before been overcome by the barbarous people, and only to shame them, and to make the company laugh. With these verses, ancient men that were at this feast, became much offended, and grew angry with the poet that made them, and the minstrel that sung them. Alexander on the other side, and his familiars, liked them very well, and commanded the minstrel to sing still. Clitus therewithal being overtaken with wine, and besides of a churlish nature, proud and arrogant, fell into greater choler, and said: that it was neither well nor honestly done in that sort to speak ill of those poor Macedonian captains (and specially amongst the barbarous people their enemies), which were far better men than they that laughed them to scorn, although their fortune much worse then theirs. Alexander then replied, and said, that saying so, he pleaded for himself, calling cowardliness misfortune. Then Clitus standing up, said again: 'But yet this my cowardliness saved thy life, that callest thyself the son of the gods, when thou turnedst thy back from Spithridates' sword: and the blood which these poor Macedonians did shed for thee, and the wounds which they received of their bodies fighting for thee, have made thee so great, that thou disdainest now to have King Philip for thy father, and wilt needs make thyself the son of Jupiter Hammon.'

51 Alexander being moved with these words, straight replied: 'O villain, thinkest thou to scape unpunished for these proud words of thine, which thou usest continually against me, making the Macedonians rebel against Alexander?' Clitus answered again, 'Too much are we punished, Alexander, for our pains and service to receive such reward: nay, most happy think we them that long since are dead and gone, not now to see the Macedonians scourged with rods of the Medes, and compelled to curry favour with the Persians, to have access unto their king.' Thus Clitus boldly speaking against Alexander, and Alexander again answering and reviling him, the gravest men sought to pacify this stir and tumult. Alexander then turning himself unto Xenodochus Cardian, and Artemius Colophonian: 'Do you not think,' said he, 'that the Grecians are amongst the Macedonians, as demigods that walk among brute beasts?' Clitus for all this would not give over his impudence and malapertness, but cried out, and bade Alexander

speak openly what he had to say, or else not to bid free men come to sup with him that were wont to speak frankly: if not, to keep with the barbarous slaves that honoured his Persian girdle and long white garment. Then could Alexander no longer hold his choler, but took an apple that was upon his table, and threw it at Clitus, and looked for his sword, the which Aristophanes, one of his guard that waited on him, had of purpose taken from him. And when every man came straight about him to stay him, and to pray him to be contented, he immediately rose from the board, and called his guard unto him in the Macedonian tongue (which was a sign of great trouble to follow after it), and commanded a trumpeter to sound the alarm. But he drawing back, would not sound: whereupon Alexander struck him with his fist. Notwithstanding, the trumpeter was greatly commended afterwards, for that he only kept the camp that they rose not. All this could not quiet Clitus, whereupon his friends with much ado thrust him out of the hall: but he came in again at another door, and arrogantly and unreverently rehearsed this verse of the poet Euripides, out of *Andromache*'s tragedy:

> Alas for sorrow, evil ways
> Are into Greece crept nowadays.

Then Alexander taking a partisan from one of his guard, as Clitus was coming towards him, and had lift up the hanging before the door, he ran him through the body, so that Clitus fell to the ground, and fetching one groan, died presently. Alexander's choler had left him straight, and he became marvellous sorrowful: and when he saw his friends round about him say never a word, he plucked the partisan out of his body, and would have thrust it into his own throat.

52 Howbeit his guard about him caught him by the hands, and carried him perforce into his chamber: and there he did nothing all that night but weep bitterly, and the next day following, until such time as he was able to cry no more, but lying on the ground, only lay sighing. His friends hearing his voice no more, were afraid, and came into his chamber by force to comfort him. But Alexander would hear none of them, saving Aristander the soothsayer, who remembered him of his dream he had of Clitus before, which was a prognostication of that which had happened: whereby it appeared

that it was his destiny before he was born. This seemed to comfort Alexander. Afterwards they brought in Callisthenes the philosopher, a kinsman of Aristotle's, and Anaxarchus born in Abdera. Of these two, Callisthenes sought by gentle talk, not moving any matter offensive, to comfort Alexander's sorrow. But Anaxarchus that from the beginning had taken a way by himself in the study of philosophy, being accounted a brainsick man, and one that despised his companions, he coming into Alexander's chamber also with him, cried out at the door as he came in: 'See, yonder is Alexander the Great whom all the world looks upon, and is afraid of. See where he lies, weeping like a slave on the ground, that is afraid of the law, and of the reproach of men: as if he himself should not give them law, and stablish the bounds of justice or injustice, since he hath overcome to be lord and master, and not to be subject and slave to a vain opinion. Knowest thou not that the poets say, that Jupiter hath Themis, to wit, right and justice placed of either hand on him? What signifieth that, but all that the prince doth, is wholly right, and just?' These words of Anaxarchus did comfort the sorrowful heart of King Alexander at that time, but therewithal, they made Alexander's manners afterwards more fierce and dissolute. For, as he thereby did marvellously grow in favour with the king, even so did he make the company of Callisthenes (who of himself was not very pleasant, because of his gravity and sourness) much more hateful and misliked than before. It is written also that there was certain talk one night at King Alexander's board touching the seasons of the year, and temperateness of the air, and that Callisthenes was of their opinion which maintained, that the country they were in at that time was much colder, and the winter also sharper than in Greece. Anaxarchus held the contrary opinion, and stiffly maintained it, in so much as Callisthenes said unto him: 'And yet must thou grant, that it is colder here than there. For there, all the winter time thou couldest go with a single cloak on thy back only, and here thou must have three or four garments upon thee when thou art at thy board.'

53    This galled Anaxarchus to the quick, and made him more angry than before: and for the other rhetoricians and flatterers, they did also hate him, because they saw him followed of young men for his eloquence, and beloved also of old men for his honest life, the

which was very grave, modest, and contented with his own, desiring no man's else. Whereby men found, that the reason he alleged for following of Alexander in this voyage, was true: for he said that he came to be an humble suitor to the king to restore his banished citizens into their country again, and to replenish their city with inhabitants. Now, though his estimation made him chiefly to be envied, yet did he himself give his enemies occasion to accuse him. For oftentimes being invited by the king to supper, either he would not come, or if he came, he would be mute, and say nothing, showing by his gravity and silence, that nothing pleased him that was either said or done. Whereupon Alexander self said on a time unto him:

> I cannot think that person wise,
> That in his own case hath no eyes.

It is reported of him also, that being at supper on a time with the king, divers requesting him to make an oration on the sudden in commendation of the Macedonians, he made such an eloquent oration upon that matter, that all they that heard him rose from the board, and clapping their hands for joy, cast nosegays and flowers upon him. But yet Alexander at that time said unto him that which the poet Euripides said:

> It is no mastery to be eloquent,
> In handling of a plenteous argument.

'Nay, but utter then thy eloquence in reproving of the Macedonians, that hearing their faults, they may learn to amend.' Then Callisthenes changing copy, spoke boldly many things against the Macedonians: declaring, that the dissension amongst the Grecians did increase King Philip's power, alleging these verses:

> Where discord reigns in realm or town,
> Even wicked folk do win renown.

But by this occasion, he purchased himself great ill will of the Macedonians: insomuch, as Alexander self said at that time, that he had not so much showed his eloquence, as the malice he bore unto the Macedonians.

54    Hermippus the historiographer writeth, that one Straebus a clerk of Callisthenes did afterwards tell it unto Aristotle in this sort:

and that Callisthenes seeing King Alexander offended with him, did recite these verses of Homer three or four times as he went:

> Patroclus who far passed thee,
> Was slain as thou art like to be.

And therefore very wisely said Aristotle, that Callisthenes was eloquent, but not wise. For like a philosopher, he stoutly stood against kneeling to the king, and said that openly, which the noblest and ancientest men among the Macedonians durst but whisper one in another's ear, though they did all utterly mislike it: whereby he did yet deliver Greece from open shame, and Alexander from a greater, bringing him from that manner of adoration of his person. This notwithstanding, he undid himself because he would seem rather by presumption to bring him to it, than by reason to persuade him. Chares Mitylenian hath written, that Alexander having drunk at a certain feast where he happened to be, reached his cup unto one of his friends, who after he had taken it of him, rose up first on his feet, and drank also, turning him towards the gods, and first making solemn reverence, he went and kissed Alexander, and then sat him down again. All the rest that were at the feast, did the like one after another, and Callisthenes also, who took the cup when it came to his turn (the king not looking on him, but talking with Hephaestion), after he had drunk, came to the king to kiss him as others had done. Howbeit one Demetrius called Phidon, said unto the king: 'Kiss him not, I pray your grace, for he of all men hath done you no reverence.' Alexander turned his head aside, and would not kiss him. Then cried Callisthenes out aloud: 'Well,' quoth he, 'then I will go my way, with less than others, by a kiss.'

55 And thus began Alexander's grudge first against Callisthenes, by means whereof Hephaestion was credited the better, when he said that Callisthenes had promised him to reverence Alexander, although that he had broken promise. After him also Lysimachus, Agnon, and divers others began to play their parts against him, saying, that this sophister went bragging up and down, as if he had destroyed a whole tyranny, and that all the young men followed him to honour him, as if among so many thousand soldiers, never a man of them had so noble a heart as he. And therefore, when the treason of Hermolaus against Alexander's person was discovered, they found the accusation probable, the which some false detractors

had informed against Callisthenes: who had answered Hermolaus that asked him, how he could come to be famous above all men, thus: 'In killing the famousest person.' And to animate him to go forward with this treason, he had told him further, that he should not be afraid of a golden bed, but remember that he had to do with a man, which was sometime sick and hurt as other men were. This notwithstanding, there was never a one of Hermolaus' confederates, that would once name Callisthenes, what torments soever they abided, to bewray who were their companions. And Alexander self also writing of this treason immediately after, unto Craterus, Attalus, and Alcetas, said, that their servants which had been racked and put to the torture, did constantly affirm that they only had conspired his death, and no man else was privy unto it. But afterwards, he sent another letter unto Antipater, wherein he directly accused Callisthenes, and said, that his servants had already been stoned to death by the Macedonians, howbeit that he himself would afterwards also punish the master, and those that had sent unto him, and that had received the murderers into their cities, who came of purpose to kill him. And therein he plainly showed the ill will he bore unto Aristotle, for that Callisthenes had been brought up with him, being his kinsman, and the son of Hero, Aristotle's niece. Some say, that Alexander trussed Callisthenes up. Others again report, that he died of sickness in prison. Nevertheless Chares writeth, that Callisthenes was kept prisoner seven months together, because he should have had his judgment in open council even in the presence of Aristotle himself: howbeit, being very fat, he was eaten in the end by lice, and so died, about the time that Alexander was hurt fighting against the Mallians Oxydracians, in the conquest of India; but these things chanced a good while after.

56   Demaratus Corinthian being very old, had a great desire to go see Alexander: and when he had seen him, he said that the Grecians which were dead long before, were deprived of that bliss and happiness, that they could not see Alexander sit in the royal seat of King Darius. Howbeit, he did not long enjoy the king's goodwill unto him, for he died of a sickness soon after he came unto his camp, and Alexander did honour his funerals: for all the army in their armour did cast up a mount of earth fashioned like a tomb, which was a great compass about, and four score cubits high.

His ashes afterwards were brought with an honourable convoy, unto the sea side, in a chariot with four horses richly set out.

57 Alexander being ready to take his journey to go conquer India, perceiving that his army was very heavy and unwildsom to remove, for the wonderful carriage and spoils they had with them, the carts one morning being laden, he first burnt his own carriage, and next his friends', and then commanded that they should also set the carriage of the Macedonians afire, which counsel seemed more dangerous to be resolved of, than the proof of the execution fell out difficult. For there are very few of them that were angry therewith, and the most part of them (as if they had been secretly moved by some god) with loud cries of joy, one of them gave unto another such necessary things as they had need of, and afterwards of themselves did burn and spoil all the rest. This made Alexander much more rigorous than he was before, besides that he was already become cruel enough, and without mercy or pardon, did sharply punish every man that offended. For having commanded Menander, one of his friends, to keep him a stronghold, he put him to death, because he would not remain there. Furthermore, he himself slew Orsodates (a captain of the barbarous people) with a dart, for that he rebelled against him. About that time, there was an ewe that had eaned a lamb, which had upon her head, the form and purple colour of the king's hat, after the Persian manner, called tiara, having two stones hanging on each side of it. Alexander abhorred this monstrous sign, insomuch as he purged himself by certain Babylonian priests, which he always carried about with him for that purpose, and said unto his friends, that this monster did not so much move him for respect of himself, as it did for them, fearing that the gods after his death had predestined the force and power of his kingdom to fall into the hands of some base cowardly person. This notwithstanding, another sign and token which chanced in the neck of that, did take away this fear and discouragement he had. For a Macedonian called Proxenus, that had charge of the king's carriage, as he digged in a certain place by the river of Oxus, to set up the king's tent and his lodging, he found a certain fat and oily vein, which after they had drawn out the first, there came out also another clearer, which differed nothing, neither in smell, taste, nor savour, from natural oil, having the gloss and fatness so like, as

there could be discerned no difference between them: the which
was so much more to be wondered at, because that in all that
country there were no olives. They say also, that the water of the
river self of Oxus is very soft, and maketh their skins fat, which
wash or bathe themselves therein. And yet it appeareth by that
which Alexander self wrote unto Antipater, that he was very glad
of it, putting that amongst the greatest signs which the gods had
sent unto him. The soothsayers did interpret this wonder, that it
was a sign, that he should have a noble, but yet a painful voyage:
for the gods, said they, have given oil unto men to refresh their
weariness.

58    And truly so did he sustain many dangers in those wars, and
was oftentimes hurt in fight. But the greatest loss he had of his men,
was for lack of victuals, and by the infection of the air. For he,
striving to overcome fortune by valiantness, and her force by virtue,
thought nothing impossible for a valiant man, neither anything
able to withstand a noble heart. It is reported, that when he went
to besiege a stronghold which Sisimethres kept, being thought
unsaultable, and that his soldiers were in despair of it, he asked one
Oxyarthes, what heart Sisimethres had. Oxyarthes answered him,
that he was the veriest coward in the world. 'O, that is well,' quoth
Alexander: 'then it is to be won, if that be true thou saist, since the
captain of the piece is but a coward.' So he took it of a sudden, by
putting Sisimethres in a great fear. After that also, he did besiege
another piece of as great strength and difficulty to assault as the
other, and making the young soldiers of the Macedonians to go to
the assault, he called one of them unto him, whose name also was
Alexander, unto whom he said thus: 'Alexander, this day thou must
fight like a man, and it be but for thy name sake.' The young man
did not forget his words, for he fought so valiantly, that he was slain,
for whom Alexander was very sorry. Another time when his men
were afraid, and durst not come near unto the city of Nisa to assault
it, because there ran a very deep river hard by the walls, he came to
the river's side, and said: 'Oh, what a coward am I, that never
learned to swim!' And so prepared himself to swim over upon his
shield. After he had caused them to retire from the assault, there
came ambassadors unto him from the cities besieged, to crave
pardon of him. They wondered at him at the first, when they saw

him armed, without any pomp or other ceremony about him: but much more, when a chair was brought him to sit down on, that he commanded the oldest man amongst them, called Acuphis, to take it to him, and sit him down. Acuphis marvelling at Alexander's great courtesy, asked him what they should do for him, thenceforth to be his good friends. 'I will,' said Alexander, 'that they from whom thou comest as ambassador unto us, do make thee their king: and withal that they do send me a hundred of their best men for hostages.' Acuphis, smiling, answered him again: 'But I shall rule them better, O king, if I send you the worst, and not the best.'

59  There was a king called Taxiles, a very wise man, who had a great country in India, no less in bigness and circuit than all Egypt, and as full of good pasture and fruits as any country in the world could be: who came on a time to salute Alexander, and said unto him: 'What should we need, Alexander, to fight, and make wars one with another, if thou comest not to take away our water, and our necessary commodity to live by: for which things, men of judgment must needs fight? As for other goods, if I be richer than thou, I am ready to give thee of mine, and if I have less, I will not think scorn to thank thee, if thou wilt give me some of thine.' Alexander being pleased to hear him speak thus wisely, embraced him, and said unto him: 'Thinkest thou this meeting of ours can be without fight, for all these goodly fair words? No, no, thou hast won nothing by that: for I will fight and contend with thee in honesty and courtesy, because thou shalt not exceed me in bounty and liberality.' So Alexander taking divers gifts of him, but giving more unto Taxiles, he drank to him one night at supper, and said, 'I drink to thee a thousand talents in gold.' This gift misliked Alexander's friends: but in recompense thereof, he won the hearts of many of those barbarous lords and princes of that country. There was a certain number of soldiers of the Indians, the warlikest men of all that country: who being mercenary soldiers, were ever entertained in service of the great free cities, which they valiantly defended, and did great hurt unto Alexander in divers places. Alexander having made peace with them in a city where they were kept in, when they came abroad upon surety of this peace which they had made, he met with them as they went their way, and put them all to the sword. There was but this only fault, to blemish the

honour of his noble deeds in all his wars: for in all things else, he showed mercy and equity. Furthermore, the grave philosophers and wise men of India did greatly trouble him also. For they reproved the kings and princes of the Indians for that they yielded unto Alexander, and procured the free cities to take arms against him. But by their occasion, he took divers of their cities.

60    For King Porus, Alexander self writeth in his epistles, all his acts at large which he did against him. For he saith, that both their camps lying on either side of the river of Hydaspes, King Porus set his elephants upon the bank of the river with their heads towards their enemies, to keep them from passing over: and that he himself did continually make a noise and tumult in his camp, to acquaint his men not to be afraid of the barbarous people. Furthermore, that in a dark night when there was no moonlight, he took part of his footmen, and the choice of his horsemen, and went far from his enemies to get over into a little island. When he was come into the island, there fell a wonderful shower of rain, great winds, lightnings and thunders upon his camp, insomuch as he saw many of his men burnt by lightning in this little island. This notwithstanding, he did not leave to get over to the other side of the river. The river being swollen with the great flood of rain that fell the night before, overflowing the banks, it did eat into the ground where the water ran: so that Alexander when he had passed over the river, and was come to the other side, found himself in very ill case, for that he could hardly keep his feet, because the earth was very slippery under him, and the rage of the water had eaten into it, and broke it down on every side. It is written of him, that then he said unto the Athenians: 'O Athenians, could ye think that I could take such pains, and put myself into so many dangers, only to be praised of you?' Thus Onesicritus reporteth it. But Alexander self writeth, that they left their rafters or great pieces of timber pinned together whereupon they had passed over the stream of the main river: and that they waded through the other arm or gut of the water which had broken the earth, up to their breasts with their harness on their backs. Furthermore, when he had passed over both waters, he rode with his horsemen twenty furlongs before the battle of his footmen, thinking that if his enemies came to give him charge with their men of arms, that he was the stronger: and if they would also advance

their footmen forward, that his footmen also should come time enough. One of the twain fell out as he had guessed. For, a thousand horsemen, and three score chariots armed with his enemies, gave him charge before their great company, whom he overthrew, and took all their chariots, and slew four hundred of the men of arms in the field. King Porus then knowing by those signs that Alexander was there in person, and had passed over the river, he marched towards him with all his army in battle ray, saving a few which he left behind to resist the Macedonians, if they showed force to pass over the river. Alexander being afraid of the great multitude of his enemies, and of the terror of the elephants, did not give charge upon the midst of the battle, but being himself in the left wing, gave charge upon the corner of the enemies' left wing, and also commanded them that were in the right wing to do the like. So, both the ends of the enemies' army were broken and put to flight: and they that fled, ran unto the elephants, and gathered themselves together about them. Thus the battle being begun, the conflict continued long, insomuch as the enemies were scantly all overthrown by three of the clock in the afternoon. Many writers do agree, that Porus was four cubits and a shaft length higher and bigger than the elephant, although the elephant was very great, and as big as a horse: and besides that the elephant did show great wit and care, to save the king his master. For whilst he perceived his master was strong enough, he lustily repulsed those which came to assail him: but when he found that he began to faint, having many wounds upon his body, and arrows sticking in it, then being afraid lest his master should fall down from his back, he softly fell on his knees, and gently taking his darts and arrows with his trunk, which he had in his body, he plucked them all from him one after another. Porus being taken, Alexander asked him, how he should handle him. 'Princely,' answered Porus. Alexander asked him again, if he would say anything else. 'I comprehend all,' said he, 'in this word princely.' Thereupon Alexander did not only leave him his provinces and realms, whereof before he was king, by the name of his lieutenant, but gave him many other countries also. When he had subdued all the free people, of the which there were fifteen several nations, five thousand of no small cities, besides an infinite number of villages, and thrice as many other countries, he made Philip one of his friends, his lieutenant of all those countries.

61   His horse Bucephal died at this battle, not in the field, but afterwards whilst he was in cure for the wounds he had on his body: but as Onesicritus saith, he died even worn for very age. Alexander was as sorry for his death, as if he had lost any of his familiar friends: and for proof thereof, he built a great city in the place where his horse was buried, upon the river of Hydaspes, the which he called after his name, Bucephalia. It is reported also, that having lost a dog of his called Peritas, which he had brought up of a whelp, and loved very dearly, he built also a city, and called it after his name. Sotion writeth, that he heard it reported thus of Potamon Lesbian.

62   This last battle against King Porus killed the Macedonians' hearts, and made them that they had no desire to go any further to conquer India. For, finding that they had such ado to overcome them, though they were but twenty thousand footmen, and two thousand horse, they spoke ill of Alexander when he went about to compel them to pass over the river of Ganges, understanding by the countrymen that it was two and thirty furlong over, and a hundred fathom deep: and how that the bank of the river was full of soldiers, horsemen, and elephants. For it was reported, that the kings of the Gangarides and the Praesians were on the other side with four score thousand horsemen, two hundred thousand footmen, eight thousand chariots or carts of war well armed, and six thousand elephants of war. This was no fable, nor frivolous tale. For a king called Androcottus (who reigned not long after) gave unto Seleucus, five hundred elephants at one time, and conquered all India with six hundred thousand fighting men. Alexander then offended with his men's refusal, kept close in his tent for certain days, and lay upon the ground, saying that he did not thank them for all that they had done thitherunto, unless they passed over the river of Ganges also: and that to return back again, it was as much to confess that he had been overcome. At the length, when he saw and considered that there was great reason in his friends' persuasions which laboured to comfort him, and that his soldiers came to the door of his tent, crying and lamenting, humbly beseeching him to lead them back again, in the end he took pity of them, and was contented to return. This notwithstanding, before he departed from those parts, he put forth many vain and false

devices to make his name immortal among that people. He made armours of greater proportion than his own, and mangers for horses, higher than the common sort: moreover, he made bits also far heavier than the common sort, and made them to be thrown and scattered abroad in every place. He built great altars also in honour of the gods, the which the kings of the Praesians have in great veneration at this day: and passing over the river, do make sacrifices there, after the manner of the Grecians. Androcottus at that time was a very young man, and saw Alexander himself, and said afterwards, that Alexander had well near taken and won all the country, the king which then reigned was so hated of all his subjects, for his wicked life, and base parentage he came of.

63 Departing thence, he went to see the great sea Oceanum, and made divers boats with oars, in the which he easily went down the rivers at his pleasure. Howbeit, this his pleasant going by water, was not without war: for he would land oftentimes, and did assail cities, and conquered all as he went. Yet in assailing the city of Mallians (which they say are the warlikest men of all the Indians), he was almost slain there. For, having with darts repulsed the enemies from the wall, he himself was the first man that set foot on a ladder to get up, the which broke as soon as ever he was gotten upon the rampart. Then the barbarous people coming together against the wall, did throw at him from beneath, and many times lighted upon him. Alexander having few of his men about him, made no more ado, but leaped down from the wall in the midst of his enemies, and by good hap lighted on his feet. His harness making a great noise with the fall, the barbarous people were afraid, thinking they had seen some light or spirit go before him: so that at the first they all betook them to their legs, and ran scatteringly here and there. But after that, when they came again to themselves, and saw that he had but two gentlemen only about him, they came and set upon him of all hands, and fought with him at the sword or push of the pike, and so hurt him very sore through his armour: but one among the rest, being somewhat further off, gave him such a terrible blow with an arrow, that he struck him through his curirass, and shot him in at the side under his breast. The blow entered so into his body, that he fell down on one of his knees. Whereupon, he that had stricken him with his arrow, ran suddenly to him with a scimitar drawn in

his hand. Howbeit Peucestas and Limnaeus stepped before him, and were both hurt: Limnaeus was slain presently, and Peucestas fought it out, till at the length, Alexander self slew the barbarous man with his own hand, after he had many grievous wounds upon his body. At the length he had a blow with a dart on his neck that so astonished him, that he leaned against the wall looking upon his enemies. In the mean time, the Macedonians compassing him round about, took him, and carried him into his tent half in a swound, and was past knowledge: whereupon, there ran a rumour straight in the camp, that Alexander was dead. They had much ado to cut the arrow asunder that was of wood: so his cuirass being plucked off with great pain, yet were they to pluck the arrow head out of his body, which stuck in one of his bones: the which as it is reported, was four fingers long, and three fingers broad. So that when they plucked it out, he swounded so oft, that he was almost dead. This notwithstanding, he overcame the danger, and escaped. Being very weak, he kept diet a long time to recover himself, and never came out of his tent: until he heard the Macedonians cry, and make great noise about his tent, desirous to see him. Then he put on a night gown, and came out amongst them all: and after he had done sacrifice unto the gods for recovery of his health, he went on his journey again, and in the same did conquer many great countries, and took divers goodly cities.

64    He did also take ten of the wise men of the country, which men do all go naked, and therefore are called Gymnosophistae (to wit, philosophers of India), who had procured Sabbas to rebel against him, and had done great hurt unto the Macedonians. And because they were taken to be the sharpest and readiest of answer he did put them (as he thought) many hard questions, and told them he would put the first man to death, that answered him worst, and so the rest in order: and made the eldest among them judge of their answers. The question he asked the first man, was this:

1. Whether the dead or the living, were the greater number. He answered, the living. 'For the dead,' said he, 'are no more men.'

2. The second man he asked: whether the earth or the sea brought forth most creatures. He answered, the earth. 'For the sea,' said he,' is but a part of the earth.'

3. To the third man: which of all beasts was the subtlest. 'That,' said he, 'which man hitherto never knew.'

4. To the fourth: why did he make Sabbas rebel? 'Because,' said he, 'he should live honourably, or die vilely.'

5. To the fifth, which he thought was first, the day or the night? He answered, the day, by a day. The king finding his answer strange, added to this speech: 'Strange questions must needs have strange answers.'

6. Coming to the sixth man, he asked him, how a man should come to be beloved: 'If he be a good man,' said he, 'not terrible.'

7. To the seventh, how a man should be a god? 'In doing a thing,' said he, 'impossible for a man.'

8. To the eighth, which was the stronger: life or death? 'Life,' said he, 'that suffereth so many troubles.'

9. And unto the ninth and last man: how long a man should live? 'Until,' said he, 'he think it better to die, than to live.'

When Alexander had heard these answers, he turned unto the judge, and bade him give his judgment upon them. The judge said, they had all answered one worse than another. 'Then shalt thou die first,' said Alexander, 'because thou hast given such sentence.' 'Not so, O king,' quoth he, 'if thou wilt not be a liar: because thou saidst, that thou wouldst kill him first, that had answered worst.'

65 In fine, Alexander did let them go with rewards. He sent Onesicritus also unto the other wise men of the Indians, which were of greatest fame among them, and that led a solitary and quiet life, to pray them to come unto him. This Onesicritus the philosopher, was Diogenes the Cynic's scholar. It is reported, that Calanus one of these wise men, very sharply and proudly bade him put off his clothes, to hear his words naked: or otherwise that he would not speak to him, though he came from Jupiter himself. Yet Dandamis answered him more gently. For he having learned what manner of men Socrates, Pythagoras and Diogenes were, said: that they seemed to have been wise men, and well born, notwithstanding that they had reverenced the law too much in their life time. Others write notwithstanding, that Dandamis said nothing else, but asked why

Alexander had taken so painful a journey in hand, as to come into India. For Calanus (whose right name otherwise was Sphines), King Taxiles persuaded him to go unto Alexander: who because he saluted those he met, in the Indian tongue, saying Cale, as much to say, as God save ye, the Grecians named him Calanus. It is reported, that this Calanus did show Alexander a figure and similitude of his kingdom, which was this. He threw down before him a dry sere piece of leather, and then put his foot upon one of the ends of it. The leather being trodden down on that side, rose up in all parts else; and going up and down withal still treading upon the sides of the leather, he made Alexander see, that the leather being trodden down on the one side, did rise up of all sides else, until such time as he put his foot in the midst of the leather, and then all the whole leather was plain alike. His meaning thereby, was to let Alexander understand, that the most part of his time he should keep in the midst of his country, and not to go far from it.

66    Alexander continued seven months travelling upon the rivers, to go see the great sea Oceanum. Then he took ship, and sailed into a little island called Scyllustis, howbeit others call it Psitulcis. There he landed, made sacrifices unto the gods, and viewed the greatness and nature of the sea Oceanum, and all the situation of the coast upon that sea, as far as he could go. Then he made his prayers unto the gods, that no conqueror living after him should go beyond the bounds of his journey and conquest, and so returned homeward. He commanded his ships should fetch a compass about, and leave India on the right hand: and made Nearchus admiral of all his fleet, and Onesicritus chief pilot. He himself in the meantime went by land through the country of the Orites, and there he found great scarcity of victuals, and lost many of his men: so that he carried not out of India the fourth part of his men of war which he brought thither, which were in all, six score thousand footmen, and fifteen thousand horsemen. Some of them died of grievous diseases, others by ill diet, others by extreme heat and drought, and the most of them by hunger, travelling through this barren country, where the poor men lived hardly, and had only a few sheep which they fed with sea fish, that made their flesh savour very ill-favouredly. At the length, when in three score days'

journey he had painfully travelled through this country, he then entered into the country called Gedrosia, where he found great plenty of all kind of victuals, which the governors, kings, and princes, neighbours unto the same, did send unto him.

67   After he had refreshed his army there a little, he went through the country of Carmania, where he continued seven days together banqueting, going still through the country. For night and day, he was feasting continually with his friends upon a scaffold longer than broad, rising up of height, and drawn with eight goodly horse. After that scaffold followed divers other chariots covered over, some with goodly rich arras, and purple silk, others with trim fresh boughs which they renewed at every field's end: and in those were Alexander's other friends and captains with garlands of flowers upon their heads, which drank and made merry together. In all this army, there was neither helmet, pike, dart, nor target seen: but gold and silver bowls, cups, and flagons in the soldiers' hands, all the way as they went, drawing wine out of great pipes and vessels which they carried with them, one drinking to another, some marching in the fields going forward, and others also set at the table. About them were the minstrels playing and piping on their flutes and shawms, and women singing and dancing, and fooling by the way as they went. In all this dissolute marching through the country, and in the midst of their drunkenness, they mingled with it sport: that every man did strive to counterfeit all the insolencies of Bacchus, as if god Bacchus himself had been there in person, and had led the mummery. When he came unto the king's castle of Gedrosia, he stayed there also certain days to refresh his army with feasting and banqueting. It is said, that one day when he had drunk hard, he went to see the games for dancing: and amongst them, the games which a young man called Bagoas had set forth (with whom Alexander fell in liking), and bore the bell. This Bagoas being in his dancing garments, came through the theatre, and sat him down by Alexander. The Macedonians were so glad of it, that they shouted and clapped their hands for joy, crying out aloud, to kiss him: so that in fine he took him in his arms, and kissed him, before them all.

68   Thither came Nearchus his admiral unto him: who made report what he had seen and done in this navigation. Alexander was so glad of that, as he was desirous to sail by sea himself: and so, entering into the sea Oceanum by the mouth of Euphrates, with a great fleet of ships, to compass in all the coasts of Arabia and Africa, and thence into Mare Mediterraneum, by the straits of the pillars of Hercules. To this intent he built a great number of ships in the city of Thapsacus, and sent for mariners, shipmasters, and pilots, out of all parts. But now, the difficulty of the journey which he took upon him for the conquest of India, the danger he was in when he fought with the Mallians, and the number of his men which he lost besides which was very great, all these things considered together, making men believe that he should never return with safety, they made all the people which he had conquered bold to rise against him, and gave his governors and lieutenants of provinces occasion to commit great insolencies, robberies, and exactions of people. To be short, it put all his kingdom in broil and sedition. Insomuch as Olympias and Cleopatra rising against Antipater, they divided his government between them: Olympias choosing for her, the kingdom of Epirus, and Cleopatra, the kingdom of Macedon. Which when Alexander had heard, he said his mother was the wisest: for the realm of Macedon would never have suffered a woman to reign over them. Thereupon he sent Nearchus back again to the sea, determining to fill all the sea coasts with war. As he travelled through the countries far from the sea, he put his captains and governors to death, which had revolted against him: and of those he slew Oxyarthes, one of Abulites' sons, by his own hand, running him through with a pike. And when Abulites self also had brought Alexander iij thousand talents only, without any other provision made for victuals for his army, he made him put the money before his horse, which would not once touch it. Then said he unto him: 'I pray thee to what purpose serveth this provision?' And therewithal immediately committed him to prison.

69   As he came through the country of Persia, he first renewed the old custom there, which was: that as often times as the kings did return home from any far journey, they gave unto every woman a crown apiece. It is said therefore that for this cause, some of their natural kings many times did not return again into their

country: and that Ochus amongst others did not so much as once return back again, willingly banishing himself out of his country, of niggardliness, because he would not be at this charge. After that, Cyrus' tomb (king of Persia) being found and broken up, he put him to death that did it, although he were a Macedonian of the city of Pella (and none of the meanest), called Polymachus. When he had read the inscription written upon it in the Persian tongue, he would needs also have it written in the Greek tongue: and this it was: 'O man, what so thou art, and whencesoever thou comest, for I know thou shalt come: I am Cyrus that conquered the empire of Persia. I pray thee envy me not for this little earth that covereth my body.' These words pierced Alexander's heart, when he considered the uncertainty of worldly things. There also, Calanus the Indian philosopher, having had a flux a little while, prayed that they would make him a stack of wood, such as they use to burn dead bodies on, and then rode thither a-horseback: and after he had made his prayer unto the gods, he cast those sprinklings upon him, which were used to be sprinkled at the funerals of the dead. Then cutting off a lock of his hair before he went up on the woodstack, he bade all the Macedonians that were there farewell, and shook them by the hands, praying them that day to be merry, and drink freely with the king, whom he would see shortly after in the city of Babylon. When he had said these words, he laid him down upon the woodstack, covered his face, and never stirred hand nor foot, nor quinched when the fire took him, but did sacrifice himself in this sort, as the manner of his country was, that the wise men should so sacrifice themselves. Another Indian also, who followed Julius Caesar, did the like many years after in the city of Athens: and there is his tomb yet to be seen, commonly called the Indian's tomb.

70 When Alexander came from seeing this sacrifice of Calanus, he did bid divers of his friends and captains to supper to him: and there did bring forth a crown for a reward unto him that drank best. He that drank most of all other, was one Promachus, that drank four gallons of wine, and won the crown, worth a talent: but he lived not above three days after. And of other also that fell in sport to quaffing, who should drink most, there died of them (as Chares writeth) one and forty persons: of an extreme cold that took them

in their drunkenness and wine. When they were in the city of Susa, he married certain of his friends, and himself also married Statira, one of King Darius' daughters, disposing also of the other Persian ladies (according to their estate and birth) unto his best friends. He made also a solemn feast of common marriages amongst the Macedonians, of them that had been married before: at which feast, it is written, that nine thousand persons sitting at the boards, he gave unto every one of them a cup of gold to offer wine in honour of the gods. And there also amongst other wonderful gifts, he did pay all the debts the Macedonians owed unto their creditors, the which amounted unto the sum of ten thousand talents saving a hundred and thirty less. Whereupon Antigenes with one eye, falsely putting in his name amongst the number of the debtors, and bringing in one that said he had lent him money, Alexander caused him to be paid. But afterwards, when it was proved to his face, that there was no such matter, Alexander then was so offended with him, that he banished him his court, and deprived him of his captainship, notwithstanding that he had before showed himself a valiant man in the wars. For when he was but a young man, he was shot into the eye, before the city of Perinthe, which King Philip did besiege: and at that present time they would have plucked the arrow out of his eye, but he never fainted for it, neither would suffer them to pull it out, before he had first driven his enemies within the walls of their city. He took this infamy very inwardly, and he was so sorry for it, that every man might see he was like to die for sorrow. Then Alexander fearing he should die, did pardon him, and bade him besides keep the money which was given him.

71   Now the thirty thousand young boys which Alexander had left to the government of captains, to train and exercise them in the discipline of war, they being grown strong men, and lusty youths, excellently well trained and ready in arms: Alexander rejoiced when he saw them. This notwithstanding did much discourage the Macedonians, and made them greatly afraid, because they thought that from henceforth the king would make less account of them. For when Alexander would have sent the sick and impotent persons, which had been maimed in the wars, into the low country, to the sea side, they answered him, that so doing he should do them great wrong, to send these poor men from him in

that sort (after they had done him all the service they could) home to their country and friends, in worse case than he took them from thence. And therefore they said, if he would send away some, let him send them all away as men unserviceable, specially since he had now such goodly young dancers about him, with whom he might go conquer the world. Alexander was marvellously offended with their proud words, insomuch that in his anger he reviled them all, put away his ordinary guard, and took other Persians in their place, making some the guard about his own person, others his ushers, heralds, and ministers to execute his will and commandment. The poor Macedonians seeing Alexander thus waited on, and themselves so shamefully rejected, they let fall their stoutness, and after they had communed of the matter together, they were ready to tear themselves for spite and malice. In fine, when they had laid their heads together, they consented to go unto his tent and without weapons, naked in their shirts to yield themselves unto him, weeping and howling, beseeching him to do with them what pleased him, and to use them like wretched unthankful creatures. But Alexander, though his anger was now somewhat pacified, did not receive them the first time, neither did they also go their ways, but remained there two days and nights together, in this pitiful state, before the door of his tent, lamenting unto him, and calling him their sovereign and king: until that he came himself out of his tent the third day, and seeing the poor wretches in this grievous and pitiful state, he himself fell a-weeping a long time. So, after he had a little rebuked them, he called them courteously, and gave the impotent and sick persons leave to depart home, rewarding them very honourably. Furthermore, he wrote unto Antipater his lieutenant, that he should always give them the highest place in all common sports and assemblies, and that they should be crowned with garlands of flowers. Moreover, he commanded that the orphans whose parents were slain in the wars, should receive the pay of their fathers.

72 After Alexander was come unto the city of Ecbatana, in the kingdom of Medea, and that he had dispatched his weightiest causes, he gave himself again unto public sports, feasts, and pastimes, for that there were newly come unto him out of Greece, three thousand excellent masters and devisers of such sports.

About that time it chanced, that Hephaestion fell sick of an ague. But he being a young man of war, did not regard his mouth as he should have done, but having spied opportunity that his physician Glaucus was gone unto the theatre, to see the sports and pastimes, he went to dinner, and ate a roasted capon whole, and drank a great pot full of wine, which he had caused to be set in water: whereupon his fever took him so sorely, that he lived not long after. Alexander unwisely took the chance of his death, and commanded all the hairs of his horse and mules to be presently shorn in token of mourning, and that all the battlements of the walls of cities should also be overthrown, and hung up poor Glaucus his physician upon a cross, and commanded that no minstrel should be heard play of any kind of instrument within his camp: until that there was brought him an oracle from Jupiter Hammon, commanding that Hephaestion should be worshipped and sacrificed unto, as a demigod. In the end, to pass over his mourning and sorrow, he went unto the wars, as unto a hunting of men, and there subdued the people of the Cossaeians, whom he plucked up by the roots, and slew man, woman, and child. And this was called the sacrifice of Hephastion's funerals. Alexander furthermore being desirous to bestow ten thousand talents' cost upon his obsequies and funerals, and also to exceed the charge by the rareness and excellency of workmanship, amongst all other excellent workmasters, he desired one Stasicrates, for he had ever passing invention, and his work was always stately and sumptuous in any new things he took in hand. For he talking one day with Alexander, told him, that of all the mountains he knew in the world, he thought there was none more excellent to resemble the statue or image of a man, than was Mount Atho in Thracia: and that if it were his pleasure, he would make him the noblest and most durable image, that should be in the world, which in his left hand should hold a city to contain ten thousand persons, and out of his right hand, there should run a great river into the sea. Yet Alexander would not hearken to him, but then was talking with other workmen of more strange inventions, and far greater cost.

73    Now as he was ready to take his journey to go unto Babylon, Nearchus his admiral came again unto him from the great sea Oceanum, by the river of Euphrates, and told him, how certain

Chaldean soothsayers came unto him, who did warn him that he should not go into Babylon. Howbeit Alexander made no reckoning of it, but went on. But when he came hard to the walls of Babylon, he saw a great number of crows fighting and killing one of another, and some of them fell down dead hard by him. Afterwards being told him that Apollodorus the governor of the city of Babylon, having sacrificed unto the gods, to know what should happen to him, he sent for the soothsayer Pythagoras, to know of him if it were true. The soothsayer denied it not. Then Alexander asked him, what signs he had in the sacrifice. He answered, that the liver of the beast had no head. 'O gods,' said Alexander then, 'this is an ill sign.' Notwithstanding he did Pythagoras no hurt, but yet he repented him that he did not believe Nearchus' words. For this respect therefore Alexander lay much abroad in the country from Babylon, and did take his pleasure rowing up and down the river of Euphrates. Yet had he many other ill signs and tokens one upon another, that made him afraid. For there was a tame ass that killed one of the greatest and goodliest lions in all Babylon, with one of his feet. Another time when Alexander had put off his clothes, to be anointed to play at tennis, when he should put on his apparel again, the young gentleman that played with him, found a man set in his chair of estate, having the king's diadem on his head, and his gown on his back, and said never a word. Then they asked him what he was. It was long before he made them answer, but at the length coming to himself, he said his name was Dionysius, born in Messina: and being accused for certain crimes committed, he was sent from the sea thither, where he had been a long time prisoner, and also that the god Serapis had appeared unto him, and undone his irons, and that he commanded him to take the king's gown and his diadem, and to sit him down in his chair of estate, and say never a word.

74 When Alexander heard it, he put him to death according to the counsel of his soothsayers: but then his mind was troubled, and feared that the gods had forsaken him, and also grew to suspect his friends. But first of all, Alexander feared Antipater and his sons, above all other. For one of them called Iolas, was his first cupbearer: and his brother called Cassander, was newly come out of Greece unto him. The first time that Cassander saw some of the barbarous

people reverencing Alexander, he having been brought up with the liberty of Greece, and had never seen the like before, fell into a loud laughing very unreverently. Therewith King Alexander was so offended, that he took him by the hair of his head with both his hands, and knocked his head and the wall together. Another time also when Cassander did answer some that accused his father Antipater: King Alexander took him up sharply, and said unto him: 'What saist thou?' said he. 'Dost thou think that these men would have gone so long a journey as this, falsely to accuse thy father, if he had not done them wrong?' Cassander again replied unto Alexander, and said, that that was a manifest proof of their false accusation, for that they did now accuse him being so far off, because they thought they could not suddenly be disproved. Alexander thereat fell a-laughing a good, and said, 'Lo, these are Aristotle's quiddities to argue *pro* and *contra*: but this will not save you from punishment, if I find that you have done these men wrong.' In fine, they report that Cassander took such an inward fear and conceit upon it, that long time after when he was king of Macedon, and had all Greece at his commandment, going up and down the city of Delphes, and beholding the monuments and images that are there, he found one of Alexander, which put him into such a sudden fear, that the hairs of his head stood upright, and his body quaked in such sort, that it was a great time before he could come to himself again.

75    Now after that Alexander had left his trust and confidence in the gods, his mind was so troubled and afraid, that no strange thing happened unto him (how little so ever it was) but he took it straight for a sign and prediction from the gods, so that his tent was always full of priests and soothsayers that did nothing but sacrifice and purify, and tend unto divinements. So horrible a thing is the mistrust and contempt of the gods, when it is begotten in the hearts of men, and superstition also so dreadful, that it filleth the guilty consciences and fearful hearts like water distilling from above: as at that time it filled Alexander with all folly after that fear had once possessed him. This notwithstanding, after that he had received some answers touching Hephaestion from the oracle of Jupiter Hammon, he left his sorrow, and returned again to his banquets and feasting. For he did sumptuously feast Nearchus, and one day when

he came out of his bath according to his manner, being ready to go to bed, Medius one of his captains besought him to come to a banquet to him at his lodging. Alexander went thither, and drank there all that night and the next day, so that he got an ague by it. But that came not (as some write) by drinking up Hercules' cup all at a draught: neither for the sudden pain he felt between his shoulders, as if he had been thrust into the back with a spear. For all these were thought to be written by some, for lies and fables, because they would have made the end of this great tragedy lamentable and pitiful. But Aristobulus writeth, that he had such an extreme fever and thirst withal, that he drank wine, and after that fell a-raving, and at the length died the thirty day of the month of June.

76    In his household book of things passed daily, it is written, that his fever being upon him, he slept in his hothouse on the eighteenth day of June. The next morning after he was come out of his hothouse, he went into his chamber, and passed away all that day with Medius, playing at dice: and at night very late, after he had bathed himself and sacrificed unto the gods, he fell to meat, and had his fever that night. And the twenty day also, bathing himself again, and making his ordinary sacrifice to the gods, he did sit down to eat within his stove, hearkening unto Nearchus that told him strange things he had seen in the great sea Oceanum. The one and twenty day also having done the like as before, he was much more inflamed than he had been, and felt himself very ill all night, and the next day following in a great fever: and on that day he made his bed to be removed, and to be set up by the fish ponds, where he communed with his captains touching certain rooms that were void in his army, and commanded them not to place any men that were not of good experience. The three and twenty day, having an extreme fever upon him, he was carried unto the sacrifices, and commanded that his chiefest captains only should remain in his lodging, and that the other meaner sort, as centiniers or lieutenants of bands, that they should watch and ward without. The four and twenty day, he was carried unto the other palace of the kings, which is on the other side of the lake, where he slept a little, but the fever never left him: and when his captains and noblemen came to do him humble reverence, and to see him, he lay speechless. So did he the five and twenty day also: insomuch as the Macedonians thought he was

dead. Then they came and knocked at the palace gate, and cried out unto his friends and familiars, and threatened them, so that they were compelled to open them the gate. Thereupon the gates were opened, and they coming in their gowns went unto his bedside to see him. That self day Python and Seleucus were appointed by the king's friends to go to the temple of the god Serapis, to know if they should bring King Alexander thither. The god answered them, that they should not remove him from thence. The eight and twenty day at night Alexander died.

77   Thus it is written word for word in manner, in the household book of remembrance. At that present time, there was no suspicion that he was poisoned. Yet they say, that six years after, there appeared some proof that he was poisoned. Whereupon his mother Olympias put many men to death, and cast the ashes of Iolas into the wind, that was dead before, for that it was said he gave him poison in his drink. They that think it was Aristotle that counselled Antipater to do it, by whose means the poison was brought, they say that Agnothemis reported it, having heard it of King Antigonus' own mouth. The poison (as some say) was cold as ice, and falleth from a rock in the territory of the city of Nonacris, and it is gathered as they would gather a dew into the horn of the foot of an ass, for there is no other kind of thing that will keep it, it is so extreme cold and piercing. Others defend it, and say, that the report of his poisoning is untrue: and for proof thereof they allege this reason, which is of no small importance, that is: that the chiefest captains fell at great variance after his death, so that the corpse of Alexander remained many days naked without burial, in a hot dry country and yet there never appeared any sign or token upon his body, that he was poisoned, but was still a clean and fair corpse as could be. Alexander left Roxane great with child, for the which the Macedonians did her great honour: but she did malice Statira extremely, and did finely deceive her by a counterfeit letter she sent, as if it had come from Alexander, willing her to come unto him. But when she was come, Roxane killed her and her sister, and then threw their bodies into a well, and filled it up with earth, by Perdiccas' help and consent. Perdiccas came to be king immediately after Alexander's death, by means of Aridaeus, whom he kept about him for his guard and safety. This Aridaeus, being

born of a common strumpet and common woman, called Phillina, was half lunatic, not by nature nor by chance: but, as it is reported, put out of his wits when he was a young towardly boy, by drinks which Olympias caused to be given him; and thereby continued frantic.

## THE END OF ALEXANDER'S LIFE

# Life of Julius Caesar

At what time Sylla was made lord of all, he would have had Caesar put away his wife Cornelia, the daughter of Cinna dictator: but when he saw, he could neither with any promise nor threat bring him to it, he took her jointure away from him. The cause of Caesar's ill will unto Sylla, was by means of marriage: for Marius the elder married his father's own sister, by whom he had Marius the younger, whereby Caesar and he were cousin germanes. Sylla being troubled in weighty matters, putting to death so many of his enemies, when he came to be conqueror, he made no reckoning of Caesar: but he was not contented to be hidden in safety, but came and made suit unto the people for the priesthoodship that was void, when he had scant any hair on his face. Howbeit he was repulsed by Sylla's means, that secretly was against him. Who, when he was determined to have killed him, some of his friends told him, that it was to no purpose to put so young a boy as he to death. But Sylla told them again, that they did not consider that there were many Marians in that young boy. Caesar understanding that, stole out of Rome, and hid himself a long time in the country of the Sabynes, wandering still from place to place. But one day being carried from house to house, he fell into the hands of Sylla's soldiers, who searched all those places, and took them whom they found hidden. Caesar bribed the captain, whose name was Cornelius, with two talents which he gave him. After he had escaped them thus, he went unto the sea side, and took ship, and sailed into Bithynia to go unto King Nicomedes. When he had been with him a while, he took sea again, and was taken by pirates about the Isle of Pharmacusa: for those pirates kept all upon that sea coast, with a great fleet of ships and boats.

2   They asking him at the first twenty talents for his ransom, Caesar laughed them to scorn, as though they knew not what a

man they had taken, and of himself promised them fifty talents. Then he sent his men up and down to get him this money, so that he was left in manner alone among these thieves of the Cilicians (which are the cruellest butchers in the world) with one of his friends, and two of his slaves only: and yet he made so little reckoning of them, that when he was desirous to sleep, he sent unto them to command them to make no noise. Thus was he eight and thirty days among them, not kept as prisoner, but rather waited upon by them as a prince. All this time he would boldly exercise himself in any sport or pastime they would go to. And other while also he would write verses, and make orations, and call them together to say them before them: and if any of them seemed as though they had not understood him, or passed not for them, he called them blockheads, and brute beasts, and laughing, threatened them that he would hang them up. But they were as merry with the matter as could be, and took all in good part, thinking that this his bold speech came through the simplicity of his youth. So when his ransom was come from the city of Miletum, they being paid their money, and he again set at liberty, he then presently armed, and manned out certain ships out of the haven of Miletum, to follow those thieves, whom he found yet riding at anchor in the same island. So he took the most of them, and had the spoil of their goods, but for their bodies, he brought them into the city of Pergamum, and there committed them to prison, whilst he himself went to speak with Junius, who had the government of Asia, as unto whom the execution of these pirates did belong, for that he was praetor of that country. But this praetor having a great fancy to be fingering of the money, because there was good store of it, answered, that he would consider of these prisoners at better leisure. Caesar leaving Junius there, returned again unto Pergamum, and there hung up all these thieves openly upon a cross, as he had oftentimes promised them in the isle he would do, when they thought he did but jest.

3    Afterwards when Sylla's power began to decay, Caesar's friends wrote unto him, to pray him to come home again. But he sailed first unto Rhodes, to study there a time under Apollonius the son of Molon, whose scholar also Cicero was, for he was a very honest man, and an excellent good rhetorician. It is reported that Caesar

had an excellent natural gift to speak well before the people, and besides that rare gift, he was excellently well studied, so that doubtless he was counted the second for eloquence in his time, and gave place to the first, because he would be the first and chiefest man of war and authority, being not yet come to the degree of perfection to speak well, which his nature could have performed in, because he was given rather to follow wars and to manage great matters, which in the end brought him to be lord of all Rome. And therefore in a book he wrote against that which Cicero made in the praise of Cato, he prayeth the readers not to compare the style of a soldier with the eloquence of an excellent orator, that had followed it the most part of his life.

4 When he was returned again unto Rome, he accused Dolabella for his ill behaviour in the government of his province, and he had divers cities of Greece that gave in evidence against him. Notwithstanding Dolabella at the length was dismissed. Caesar, to requite the goodwill of the Grecians, which they had showed him in his accusation of Dolabella, took their cause in hand, when they did accuse Publius Antonius before Marcus Lucullus, praetor of Macedon: and followed it so hard against him in their behalf, that Antonius was driven to appeal before the tribunes at Rome, alleging, to colour his appeal withal, that he could have no justice in Greece against the Grecians. Now Caesar immediately won many men's goodwills at Rome, through his eloquence in pleading of their causes: and the people loved him marvellously also, because of the courteous manner he had to speak to every man, and to use them gently, being more ceremonious therein, than was looked for in one of his years. Furthermore, he ever kept a good board, and fared well at his table, and was very liberal besides: the which indeed did advance him forward, and brought him in estimation with the people. His enemies judging that this favour of the common people would soon quail, when he could no longer hold out that charge and expense, suffered him to run on, till by little and little he was grown to be of great strength and power. But in fine, when they had thus given him the bridle to grow to this greatness, and that they could not then pull him back, though indeed in sight it would turn one day to the destruction of the whole state and commonwealth of Rome, too late they found, that

there is not so little a beginning of anything, but continuance of time will soon make it strong, when through contempt there is no impediment to hinder the greatness. Thereupon, Cicero like a wise shipmaster that feareth the calmness of the sea, was the first man that mistrusting his manner of dealing in the commonwealth, found out his craft and malice, which he cunningly cloaked under the habit of outward courtesy and familiarity. 'And yet,' said he, 'when I consider how finely he combeth his fair bush of hair, and how smooth it lieth, and that I see him scratch his head with one finger only, my mind gives me then, that such a kind of man should not have so wicked a thought in his head, as to overthrow the state of the commonwealth.' But this was long time after that.

5    The first show and proof of the love and goodwill which the people did bear unto Caesar, was: when he sued to be tribune of the soldiers (to wit, colonel of a thousand footmen) standing against Caius Pompilius, at what time he was preferred and chosen before him. But the second and more manifest proof than the first, was at the death of his aunt Julia, the wife of Marius the elder. For being her nephew, he made a solemn oration in the market-place in commendation of her, and at her burial did boldly venture to show forth the images of Marius: the which was the first time that they were seen after Sylla's victory, because that Marius and all his confederates had been proclaimed traitors and enemies to the commonwealth. For when there were some that cried out upon Caesar for doing of it, the people on the other side kept a stir, and rejoiced at it, clapping of their hands, and thanked him, for that he had brought as it were out of hell, the remembrance of Marius' honour again into Rome, which had so long time been obscured and buried. And where it had been an ancient custom of long time, that the Romans used to make funeral orations in praise of old ladies and matrons when they died, but not of young women, Caesar was the first that praised his own wife with funeral oration when she was dead, the which also did increase the people's goodwills the more, seeing him of so kind and gentle nature. After the burial of his wife, he was made treasurer, under Antistius Vetus praetor, whom he honoured ever after: so that when himself came to be praetor, he made his son to be chosen treasurer. Afterwards, when he was come out of that office, he married his third wife Pompeia, having

a daughter by his first wife Cornelia, which was married unto Pompey the Great. Now for that he was very liberal in expenses, buying (as some thought) but a vain and short glory of the favour of the people (where indeed he bought good cheap the greatest things that could be), some say, that before he bore any office in the commonwealth, he was grown in debt, to the sum of thirteen hundred talents. Furthermore, because he was made overseer of the work, for the highway going unto Appius, he disbursed a great sum of his own money towards the charges of the same. And on the other side, when he was made Aedilis, for that he did show the people the pastime of three hundred and twenty couple of sword players, and did besides exceed all other in sumptuousness in the sports and common feasts which he made to delight them withal (and did as it were drown all the stately shows of others in the like, that had gone before him), he so pleased the people, and won their love therewith, that they devised daily to give him new offices for to requite him.

6 At that time there were two factions in Rome, to wit, the faction of Sylla, which was very strong and of great power, and the other of Marius, which then was under foot and durst not show itself. But Caesar, because he would renew it again, even at that time when he being Aedilis, all the feasts and common sports were in their greatest ruff, he secretly caused images of Marius to be made, and of victories that carried triumphs, and those he set up one night within the Capitol. The next morning when every man saw the glistering of these golden images excellently well wrought, showing by the inscriptions, that they were the victories which Marius had won upon the Cimbres, everyone marvelled much at the boldness of him that durst set them up there, knowing well enough who it was. Hereupon, it ran straight through all the city, and every man came thither to see them. Then some cried out upon Caesar, and said it was a tyranny which he meant to set up, by renewing of such honours as before had been trodden under foot, and forgotten, by common decree and open proclamation: and that it was no more but a bait to gage the people's goodwills, which he had set out in the stately shows of his common plays, to see if he had brought them to his lure, that they would abide such parts to be played, and a new alteration of things to be made. They of

Marius' faction on the other side, encouraging one another, showed themselves straight a great number gathered together, and made the mount of the Capitol ring again with their cries and clapping of hands: insomuch as the tears ran down many of their cheeks for very joy, when they saw the images of Marius, and they extolled Caesar to the skies, judging him the worthiest man of all the kindred of Marius. The senate being assembled thereupon, Catulus Luctatius one of the greatest authority at that time in Rome, rose, and vehemently inveighed against Caesar, and spoke that then which ever since has been noted much: that Caesar did not now covertly go to work, but by plain force sought to alter the state of the commonwealth. Nevertheless, Caesar at that time answered him so that the senate was satisfied. Thereupon they that had him in estimation did grow in better hope than before, and persuaded him, that hardily he should give place to no man, and that through the goodwill of the people, he should be better than all they, and come to be the chiefest man of the city.

7   At that time, the chief bishop Metellus died, and two of the notablest men of the city, and of greatest authority (Isauricus and Catulus) contended for his room: Caesar notwithstanding their contention, would give neither of them both place, but presented himself to the people, and made suit for it as they did. The suit being equal betwixt either of them, Catulus, because he was a man of greater calling and dignity than the other, doubting the uncertainty of the election, sent unto Caesar a good sum of money, to make him leave off his suit. But Caesar sent him word again, that he would lend a greater sum than that to maintain the suit against him. When the day of the election came, his mother bringing him to the door of his house, Caesar weeping, kissed her, and said: 'Mother, this day thou shalt see thy son chief bishop of Rome, or banished from Rome.' In fine, when the voices of the people were gathered together, and the strife well debated, Caesar won the victory, and made the senate and noblemen all afraid of him, for that they thought that thenceforth he would make the people do what he thought good. Then Catulus and Piso fell flatly out with Cicero, and condemned him, for that he did not bewray Caesar, when he knew that he was of conspiracy with Catiline, and had opportunity to have done it. For when Catiline was bent and

determined, not only to overthrow the state of the commonwealth, but utterly to destroy the empire of Rome, he scaped out of
the hands of justice for lack of sufficient proof, before his full
treason and determination was known. Notwithstanding he left
Lentulus and Cethegus in the city, companions of his conspiracy:
unto whom, whether Caesar did give any secret help or comfort, it
is not well known. Yet this is manifest, that when they were
convinced in open senate, Cicero being at that time consul, asking
every man's opinion in the senate, what punishment they should
have, and every one of them till it came to Caesar, gave sentence
they should die, Caesar then rising up to speak, made an oration
(penned and premeditated before) and said, that it was neither
lawful, nor yet their custom did bear it, to put men of such nobility
to death (but in an extremity) without lawful indictment and
condemnation. And therefore, that if they were put in prison in
some city of Italy, where Cicero thought best, until that Catiline
were overthrown, the senate then might at their pleasure quietly
take such order therein, as might best appear unto their wisdoms.

8 This opinion was thought more gentle, and withal was uttered
with such a passing good grace and eloquence, that not only they
which were to speak after him did approve it: but such also as had
spoken to the contrary before, revoked their opinion and stuck to
his, until it came to Cato and Catulus to speak. They both did
sharply inveigh against him, but Cato chiefly: who in his oration
made Caesar suspected to be of the conspiracy, and stoutly spoke
against him, insomuch that the offenders were put into the hands of
the officers to be put to death. Caesar coming out of the senate, a
company of young men which guarded Cicero for the safety of his
person, did set upon him with their swords drawn. But some say,
that Curio covered Caesar with his gown, and took him out of their
hands. And Cicero self, when the young men looked upon him,
beckoned with his head that they should not kill him, either fearing
the fury of the people, or else that he thought it too shameful and
wicked a part. But if that were true, I marvel why Cicero did not
put it into his book he wrote of his consulship. But certainly they
blamed him afterwards, for that he took not the opportunity offered
him against Caesar, only for overmuch fear of the people, that loved
him very dearly. For shortly after, when Caesar went into the

senate, to clear himself of certain presumptions and false accusations objected against him, and being bitterly taunted among them, the senate keeping him longer than they were wont, the people came about the council house, and called out aloud for him, bidding them let him out. Cato then fearing the insurrection of the poor needy persons, which were they that put all their hope in Caesar, and did also move the people to stir, did persuade the senate to make a frank distribution of corn unto them, for a month. This distribution did put the commonwealth to a new charge of five hundred and fifty myriads. This counsel quenched a present great fear, and did in happy time scatter and disperse abroad the best part of Caesar's force and power, at such time as he was made praetor, and that for respect of his office he was most to be feared.

9   Yet all the time he was officer, he never sought any alteration in the commonwealth, but contrarily he himself had a great misfortune fell in his own house, which was this. There was a young nobleman of the order of the patricians, called Publius Clodius, who lacked neither wealth nor eloquence, but otherwise as insolent and impudent a person, as any was else in Rome. He became in love with Pompeia Caesar's wife, who misliked not withal: notwithstanding she was so straitly looked to, and that Aurelia (Caesar's mother) an honest gentlewoman had such an eye of her, that these two lovers could not meet as they would, without great peril and difficulty. The Romans do use to honour a goddess which they call the good goddess, as the Grecians have her whom they call Gynaecia, to wit, the goddess of women. Her, the Phrygians do claim to be peculiar unto them, saying, that she is King Midas' mother. Howbeit the Romans hold opinion, that it is a nymph of wood, married unto god Faunus. The Grecians, they say also, that she was one of the mothers of the god Bacchus, whom they dare not name. And for proof hereof, on her feast day, the women make certain tabernacles of vine twigs, and leaves of vine branches, and also they make as the tale goes, a holy dragon for this goddess, and do set it by her: besides, it is not lawful for any man to be present at their sacrifices, no not within the house itself where they are made. Furthermore, they say that the women in the sacrifices do many things amongst themselves, much like unto the ceremonies of Orpheus. Now when the time of this feast came, the

husband (whether he were praetor or consul) and all his men and
the boys in the house, do come out of it, and leave it wholly to his
wife, to order the house at her pleasure, and there the sacrifices and
ceremonies are done the most part of the night, and they do besides
pass the night away in songs and music.

10    Pompeia, Caesar's wife, being that year to celebrate this feast,
Clodius who had yet no hair on his face, and thereby thought he
should not be bewrayed, disguised himself in a singing wench's
apparel, because his face was very like unto a young wench. He
finding the gates open, being secretly brought in by her chamber
maid that was made privy unto it, she left him, and ran to Pompeia
her mistress, to tell her that he was come. The chambermaid tarried
long before she came again, insomuch as Clodius being weary
waiting for her where she left him, he took his pleasure, and went
from one place to another in the house, which had very large rooms
in it, still shunning the light, and was by chance met withal by one
of Aurelia's maids, who taking him for a woman, prayed her to
play. Clodius refusing to play, the maid pulled him forward, and
asked him what he was: Clodius then answered her, that he tarried
for Abra one of Pompeia's women. So, Aurelia's maid knowing
him by his voice, ran straight where the lights and ladies were,
and cried out, that there was a man disguised in woman's apparel.
The women therewith were so amazed, that Aurelia caused them
presently to leave off the ceremonies of the sacrifice, and to hide
their secret things, and having seen the gates fast locked, went
immediately up and down the house with torch light to seek out
this man: who at the last was found out in the chamber of
Pompeia's maid, with whom he hid himself. Thus Clodius being
found out, and known of the women, they thrust him out of the
doors by the shoulders. The same night the women told their
husbands of this chance as soon as they came home. The next
morning, there ran a great rumour through the city, how Clodius
had attempted a great villainy, and that he deserved, not only to be
punished of them whom he had slandered, but also of the commonwealth and the gods. There was one of the tribunes of the people
that did indict him, and accuse him of high treason to the gods.
Furthermore, there were also of the chiefest of the nobility and
senate, that came to depose against him, and burdened him with

many horrible and detestable facts, and specially with incest committed with his own sister, which was married unto Lucullus. Notwithstanding, the people stoutly defended Clodius against their accusations: and this did help him much against the judges, which were amazed, and afraid to stir the people. This notwithstanding, Caesar presently put his wife away, and thereupon being brought by Clodius' accuser to be a witness against him, he answered, he knew nothing of that they objected against Clodius. This answer being clean contrary to their expectation that heard it, the accuser asked Caesar, why then he had put away his wife: 'Because I will not,' said he, 'that my wife be so much as suspected.' And some say, that Caesar spoke truly as he thought. But others think, that he did it to please the common people, who were very desirous to save Clodius. So Clodius was discharged of this accusation, because the most part of the judges gave a confused judgment, for the fear they stood one way of the danger of the common people if they condemned him, and for the ill opinion of the other side of the nobility, if they did quit him.

11    The government of the province of Spain being fallen unto Caesar for that he was praetor, his creditors came and cried out upon him, and were importunate of him to be paid. Caesar being unable to satisfy them, was compelled to go unto Crassus, who was the richest man of all Rome, and that stood in need of Caesar's boldness and courage to withstand Pompey's greatness in the commonwealth. Crassus became his surety unto his greediest creditors for the sum of eight hundred and thirty talents: whereupon they suffered Caesar to depart to the government of his province. In his journey it is reported, that passing over the mountains of the Alps, they came through a little poor village that had not many households, and yet poor cottages. There, his friends that did accompany him, asked him merrily, if there were any contending for offices in that town, and whether there were any strife there amongst the noblemen for honour. Caesar speaking in good earnest, answered: 'I cannot tell that,' said he, 'but for my part, I had rather be the chiefest man here, than the second person in Rome.' Another time also when he was in Spain, reading the history of Alexander's acts, when he had read it, he was sorrowful a good while after, and then burst out in weeping. His friends

seeing that, marvelled what should be the cause of his sorrow. He answered them, 'Do ye not think,' said he, 'that I have good cause to be heavy, when King Alexander being no older than myself is now, had in old time won so many nations and countries: and that I hitherunto have done nothing worthy of myself?'

12 Therefore when he was come into Spain, he was very careful of his business, and had in few days joined ten new ensigns more of footmen, unto the other twenty which he had before. Then marching forward against the Callaecians and Lusitanians, he conquered all, and went as far as the great sea Oceanum, subduing all the people which before knew not the Romans for their lords. There he took order for pacifying of the war, and did as wisely take order for the establishing of peace. For he did reconcile the cities together, and made them friends one with another, but specially he pacified all suits of law and strife betwixt the debtors and creditors, which grew by reason of usury. For he ordained that the creditors should take yearly two parts of the revenue of their debtors, until such time as they had paid themselves: and that the debtors should have the third part to themselves to live withal. He having won great estimation by this good order taken, returned from his government very rich, and his soldiers also full of rich spoils, who called him Imperator, to say sovereign captain.

13 Now the Romans having a custom, that such as demanded honour of triumph, should remain a while without the city, and that they on the other side which sued for the consulship, should of necessity be there in person, Caesar coming unhappily at that very time when the consuls were chosen, he sent to pray the senate to do him that favour, that being absent, he might by his friends sue for the consulship. Cato at the first did vehemently inveigh against it, vouching an express law forbidding the contrary. But afterwards, perceiving that notwithstanding the reasons he alleged, many of the senators (being won by Caesar) favoured his request: yet he cunningly sought all he could to prevent them, prolonging time, dilating his oration until night. Caesar thereupon determined rather to give over the suit of his triumph, and to make suit for the consulship: and so came into the city, and had such a devise with him, as went beyond them all, but Cato only. His devise was this: Pompey and Crassus, two of the greatest personages of the city of

Rome, being at jar together, Caesar made them friends, and by that means got unto himself the power of them both: for, by colour of that gentle act and friendship of his, he subtly (unawares to them all) did greatly alter and change the state of the commonwealth. For it was not the private discord between Pompey and Caesar, as many men thought, that caused the civil war: but rather it was their agreement together, who used all their powers first to overthrow the state of the senate and nobility, and afterwards they fell at jar one with another. But Cato, that then foresaw and prophesied many times what would follow, was taken but for a vain man: but afterwards they found him a wiser man, than happy in his counsel.

14    Thus Caesar being brought unto the assembly of the election, in the midst of these two noble persons, whom he had before reconciled together, he was there chosen consul, with Calphurnius Bibulus, without gainsaying or contradiction of any man. Now when he was entered into his office, he began to put forth laws meeter for a seditious tribune of the people, than for a consul, because by them he preferred the division of lands, and distributing of corn to every citizen, gratis, to please them withal. But when the noblemen of the senate were against his devise, he desiring no better occasion, began to cry out, and to protest, that by the overhardness and austerity of the senate, they drove him against his will to lean unto the people: and thereupon having Crassus on the one side of him, and Pompey on the other, he asked them openly in the assembly, if they did give their consent unto the laws which he had put forth. They both answered, they did. Then he prayed them to stand by him against those that threatened him with force of sword to let him. Crassus gave him his word, he would. Pompey also did the like, and added thereunto, that he would come with his sword and target both, against them that would withstand him with their swords. These words offended much the senate, being far unmeet for his gravity, and indecent for the majesty and honour he carried, and most of all uncomely for the presence of the senate whom he should have reverenced: and were speeches fitter for a rash light-headed youth, than for his person. Howbeit the common people on the other side, they rejoiced. Then Caesar because he would be more assured of Pompey's power and friendship, he gave him his daughter Julia in marriage, which was made sure before

unto Servilius Caepio, and promised him in exchange Pompey's wife, the which was sure also unto Faustus the son of Sylla. And shortly after also, Caesar self did marry Calphurnia the daughter of Piso, whom he caused to be made consul, to succeed him the next year following. Cato then cried out with open mouth, and called the gods to witness, that it was a shameful matter, and not to be suffered, that they should in that sort make havoc of the empire of Rome, by such horrible bawdy matches, distributing among themselves through those wicked marriages, the governments of the provinces, and of great armies. Calphurnius Bibulus, fellow-consul with Caesar, perceiving that he did contend in vain, making all the resistance he could to withstand this law, and that oftentimes he was in danger to be slain with Cato, in the market-place and assembly, he kept close in his house all the rest of his consulship. When Pompey had married Julia, he filled all the market-place with soldiers, and by open force authorised the laws which Caesar made in the behalf of the people. Furthermore, he procured that Caesar had Gaul on this side, and beyond the Alps, and all Illyria, with four legions granted him for five years. Then Cato standing up to speak against it, Caesar bade his officers lay hold of him, and carry him to prison, thinking he would have appealed unto the tribunes. But Cato said never a word, when he went his way. Caesar perceiving them, that not only the senators and nobility were offended, but that the common people also for the reverence they bare unto Cato's virtues, were ashamed, and went away with silence, he himself secretly did pray one of the tribunes that he would take Cato from the officers. But after he had played this part, there were few senators that would be president of the senate under him, but left the city, because they could not away with his doings. And of them, there was an old man called Considius, that on a time boldly told him, the rest durst not come to council, because they were afraid of his soldiers. Caesar answered him again: 'And why then doest not thou keep thee at home, for the same fear?' Considius replied, 'Because my age taketh away fear from me: for having so short a time to live, I have no care to prolong it further.' The shamefullest part that Caesar played while he was consul, seemeth to be this: when he chose P. Clodius tribune of the people, that had offered his wife such dishonour, and profaned the holy ancient mysteries of the women, which were celebrated in his own house.

Clodius sued to be tribune to no other end, but to destroy Cicero: and Caesar self also departed not from Rome to his army, before he had set them together by the ears, and driven Cicero out of Italy.

15   All these things they say he did, before the wars with the Gauls. But the time of the great armies and conquests he made afterwards, and of the war in the which he subdued all the Gauls (entering into another course of life far contrary unto the first), made him to be known for as valiant a soldier and as excellent a captain to lead men, as those that afore him had been counted the wisest and most valiantest generals that ever were, and that by their valiant deeds had achieved great honour. For whosoever would compare the house of the Fabians, of the Scipios, of the Metellians, yea those also of his own time, or long before him, as Sylla, Marius, the two Lucullians, and Pompey self,

Whose fame ascendeth up unto the heavens:

it will appear that Caesar's prowess and deeds of arms, did excel them all together. The one, in the hard countries where he made wars: another, in enlarging the realms and countries which he joined unto the empire of Rome: another, in the multitude and power of his enemies whom he overcame: another, in the rudeness and austere nature of men with whom he had to do, whose manners afterwards he softened and made civil: another, in courtesy and clemency which he used unto them whom he had conquered: another, in great bounty and liberality bestowed upon them that served under him in those wars: and in fine, he excelled them all in the number of battles he had fought, and in the multitude of his enemies he had slain in battle. For in less then ten years' war in Gaul he took by force and assault above eight hundred towns: he conquered three hundred several nations: and having before him in battle thirty hundred thousand soldiers, at sundry times he slew ten hundred thousand of them, and took as many more prisoners.

16   Furthermore, he was so entirely beloved of his soldiers, that to do him service (where otherwise they were no more than other men in any private quarrel) if Caesar's honour were touched, they were invincible, and would so desperately venture themselves, and with such fury, that no man was able to abide them. And this appeareth plainly by the example of Acilius, who in a battle by sea

before the city of Marselles, boarding one of his enemy's ships, one cut off his right hand with a sword, but yet he forsook not his target which he had in his left hand, but thrust it in his enemies' faces, and made them flee, so that he won their ship from them. And Cassius Scaeva also, in a conflict before the city of Dyrrachium, having one of his eyes put out with an arrow, his shoulder stricken through with a dart, and his thigh with another, and having received thirty arrows upon his shield, he called to his enemies, and made as though he would yield unto them. But when two of them came running to him, he clave one of their shoulders from his body with his sword, and hurt the other in the face: so that he made him turn his back, and at the length saved himself, by means of his companions that came to help him. And in Britain also, when the captains of the bands were driven into a marsh or bog full of mire and dirt, and that the enemies did fiercely assail them there, Caesar then standing to view the battle, he saw a private soldier of his thrust in among the captains, and fought so valiantly in their defence, that at the length he drove the barbarous people to fly, and by his means saved the captains, which otherwise were in great danger to have been cast away. Then this soldier being the hindmost man of all the captains, marching with great pain through the mire and dirt, half swimming and half a-foot, in the end got to the other side, but left his shield behind him. Caesar wondering at his noble courage, ran to him with joy to embrace him. But the poor soldier hanging down his head, the water standing in his eyes, fell down at Caesar's feet, and besought him to pardon him, for that he had left his target behind him. And in Africa also, Scipio having then one of Caesar's ships, and Granius Petronius aboard on her amongst other, not long before chosen treasurer, he put all the rest to the sword but him, and said he would give him his life. But Petronius answered him again, that Caesar's soldiers did not use to have their lives given them, but to give others their lives: and with those words he drew his sword, and thrust himself through.

17  Now Caesar's self did breed this noble courage and life in them. First, for that he gave them bountifully, and did honour them also, showing thereby, that he did not heap up riches in the wars to maintain his life afterwards in wantonness and pleasure, but that he did keep it in store, honourably to reward their valiant

service: and that by so much he thought himself rich, by how much he was liberal in rewarding of them that had deserved it. Furthermore, they did not wonder so much at his valiantness in putting himself at every instant in such manifest danger, and in taking so extreme pains as he did, knowing that it was his greedy desire of honour that set him afire, and pricked him forward to do it: but that he always continued all labour and hardiness, more than his body could bear, that filled them all with admiration. For, concerning the constitution of his body, he was lean, white, and soft-skinned, and often subject to headache, and otherwhile to the falling sickness (the which took him the first time, as it is reported, in Corduba, a city of Spain), but yet therefore yielded not to the disease of his body, to make it a cloak to cherish him withal, but contrarily, took the pains of war as a medicine to cure his sick body fighting always with his disease, travelling continually, living soberly, and commonly lying abroad in the field. For the most nights he slept in his coach or litter, and thereby bestowed his rest, to make him always able to do something: and in the daytime, he would travel up and down the country to see towns, castles, and strong places. He had always a secretary with him in his coach, who did still write as he went by the way, and a soldier behind him that carried his sword. He made such speed the first time he came from Rome, when he had his office, that in eight days he came to the river of Rhone. He was so excellent a rider of horse from his youth, that holding his hands behind him, he would gallop his horse upon the spur. In his wars in Gaul, he did further exercise himself to indict letters as he rode by the way, and did occupy two secretaries at once with as much as they could write: and as Oppius writeth, more than two at a time. And it is reported, that Caesar was the first that devised friends might talk together by writing ciphers in letters, when he had no leisure to speak with them for his urgent business, and for the great distance besides from Rome. How little account Caesar made of his diet, this example doth prove it. Caesar supping one night in Milan with his friend Valerius Leo, there was served sparage to his board, and oil of perfume put into it instead of salad oil. He simply ate it, and found no fault, blaming his friends that were offended: and told them, that it had been enough for them to have abstained to eat of that they misliked, and not to shame their friend, and how that he lacked good manner that found fault with his friend. Another time as he travelled through the country, he was driven by foul weather on the sudden to take a poor man's cottage, that had but one little cabin in it, and that was so narrow, that one man could but scarce lie in it. Then he said to his friends that were about him: 'Greatest rooms are meetest for greatest men, and the most necessary rooms, for the sickest persons.' And thereupon he caused Oppius that was sick to lie there all night: and he himself, with the rest of his friends, lay without doors, under the easing of the house.

18 The first war that Caesar made with the Gauls, was with the Helvetians and Tigurinians, who having set fire of all their good cities, to the number of twelve, and four hundred villages besides, came to invade that part of Gaul which was subject to the Romans, as the Cimbri and Teutons had done before: unto whom for valiantness they gave no place, and they were also a great number of them (for they were three hundred thousand souls in all), whereof there were a hundred, four score and ten thousand fighting men. Of those, it was not Caesar himself that overcame the Tigurinians, but Labienus his lieutenant, that overthrew them by the river of Arax. But the Helvetians themselves came suddenly with their army to set upon him, as he was going towards a city of his confederates. Caesar perceiving that, made haste to get him some place of strength, and there did set his men in battle ray. When one brought him his horse to get up on which he used in battle, he said unto them: 'When I have overcome mine enemies, I will then get up on him to follow the chase, but now let us give them charge.' Therewith he marched forward afoot, and gave charge: and there fought it out a long time, before he could make them flee that were in battle. But the greatest trouble he had, was to distress their camp, and to break their strength which they had made with their carts. For there, they that before had fled from the battle, did not only put themselves in force, and valiantly fought it out, but their wives and children also fighting for their lives to the death, were all slain, and the battle was scant ended at midnight. Now if the act of this victory was famous, unto that he also added another as notable, or exceeding it. For of all the barbarous people that had escaped from battle, he gathered together again above a hundred thousand of them, and compelled them to return

home into their country which they had forsaken, and unto their towns also which they had burnt, because he feared the Germans would come over the river of Rhine, and occupy that country lying void.

19    The second war he made, was defence of the Gauls against the Germans: although before, he himself had caused Ariovistus their king to be received for a confederate of the Romans. Notwithstanding, they were grown very unquiet neighbours, and it appeared plainly, that having any occasion offered them to enlarge their territories, they would not content them with their own, but meant to invade and possess the rest of Gaul. Caesar perceiving that some of his captains trembled for fear, but specially the young gentlemen of noble houses of Rome, who thought to have gone to the wars with him, as only for their pleasure and gain, he called them to counsel, and commanded them that were afraid, that they should depart home, and not put themselves in danger against their wills, if they had such womanish faint hearts to shrink when he had need of them. And for himself, he said, he would set upon the barbarous people, though he had left him but the tenth legion only, saying, that the enemies were no valianter than the Cimbri had been, nor that he was a captain inferior unto Marius. This oration being made, the soldiers of the tenth legion sent their lieutenants unto him, to thank him for the good opinion he had of them: and the other legions also fell out with their captains, and all of them together followed him many days' journey with goodwill to serve him, until they came within two hundred furlongs of the camp of the enemies. Ariovistus' courage was well cooled, when he saw Caesar was come, and that the Romans came to seek out the Germans, where they thought, and made account, that they durst not have abidden them: and therefore nothing mistrusting it would have come so to pass, he wondered much at Caesar's courage, and the more when he saw his own army in amaze withal. But much more did their courages fall, by reason of the foolish women prophesiers they had among them, which did foretell things to come: who, considering the waves and trouble of the rivers, and the terrible noise they made running down the stream, did forewarn them not to fight, until the new moon. Caesar having intelligence thereof, and perceiving that the barbarous people

thereupon stirred not, thought it best then to set upon them, being discouraged with this superstitious fear, rather than losing time, he should tarry their leisure. So he did skirmish with them even to their forts, and little hills where they lay, and by this means provoked them so, that with great fury they came down to fight. There he overcame them in battle, and followed them in chase, with great slaughter, three hundred furlong, even unto the river of Rhine: and he filled all the fields thitherto with dead bodies and spoils. Howbeit Ariovistus flying with speed, got over the river of Rhine, and escaped with a few of his men. It is said that there were slain four score thousand persons at this battle.

20   After this exploit, Caesar left his army amongst the Sequanes to winter there: and he himself in the meantime, thinking of the affairs at Rome, went over the mountains into Gaul about the river of Po, being part of his province which he had in charge. For there, the river called Rubico divideth the rest of Italy from Gaul on this side the Alps. Caesar lying there, did practise to make friends in Rome, because many came thither to see him: unto whom he granted their suits they demanded, and sent them home also, partly with liberal reward, and partly with large promises and hope. Now during all this conquest of the Gauls, Pompey did not consider how Caesar interchangeably did conquer the Gauls with the weapons of the Romans, and won the Romans again with the money of the Gauls. Caesar being advertised that the Belgae (which were the warlikest men of all the Gauls, and that occupied the third part of Gaul) were all up in arms, and had raised a great power of men together, he straight made towards them with all possible speed, and found them spoiling and overrunning the country of the Gauls, their neighbours, and confederates of the Romans. So he gave them battle, and they fighting cowardly, he overthrew the most part of them which were in a troop together, and slew such a number of them, that the Romans passed over deep rivers and lakes afoot, upon their dead bodies, the rivers were so full of them. After this overthrow, they that dwelt nearest unto the sea side, and were next neighbours unto the Ocean, did yield themselves without any compulsion or fight: whereupon, he led his army against the Nervians, the stoutest warriors of all the Belgae. They dwelling in the wood country, had conveyed their

wives, children and goods, into a marvellous great forest, as far
from their enemies as they could: and being about the number of
six score thousand fighting men and more, they came one day and
set upon Caesar, when his army was out of order, and fortifying of
his camp, little looking to have fought that day. At the first charge,
they broke the horsemen of the Romans, and compassing in the
twelfth and seventh legion, they slew all the centurions and
captains of the bands. And had not Caesar self taken his shield on
his arm, and flying in amongst the barbarous people, made a lane
through them that fought before him, and the tenth legion also
seeing him in danger, run unto him from the top of the hill where
they stood in battle, and broken the ranks of their enemies, there
had not a Roman escaped alive that day. But taking example of
Caesar's valiantness, they fought desperately beyond their power,
and yet could not make the Nervians flee, but they fought it out to
the death, till they were all in manner slain in the field. It is written
that of three score thousand fighting men, there escaped only but
five hundred: and of four hundred gentlemen and councillors of
the Romans, but three saved.

21   The senate understanding it at Rome, ordained that they
should do sacrifice unto the gods, and keep feasts and solemn
processions fifteen days together without intermission, having
never made the like ordinance at Rome for any victory that ever
was obtained, because they saw the danger had been marvellous
great, so many nations rising as they did in arms together against
him: and further, the love of the people unto him made his victory
much more famous. For when Caesar had set his affairs at a stay in
Gaul, on the other side of the Alps, he always used to lie about the
river of Po in the winter time, to give direction for the establishing
of things at Rome, at his pleasure. For, not only they that made suit
for offices at Rome were chosen magistrates, by means of Caesar's
money which he gave them, with the which, bribing the people,
they bought their voices, and when they were in office, did all that
they could to increase Caesar's power and greatness, but the
greatest and chiefest men also of the nobility, went unto Luke unto
him. As Pompey, Crassus, Appius, praetor of Sardinia, and Nepos,
proconsul in Spain. Insomuch that there were at one time, six score
sergeants carrying rods and axes before the magistrates, and above

two hundred senators besides. There they fell in consultation, and determined that Pompey and Crassus should again be chosen consuls the next year following. Furthermore, they did appoint, that Caesar should have money again delivered him to pay his army, and besides, did prorogue the time of his government, five years further. This was thought a very strange and an unreasonable matter unto wise men. For they themselves that had taken so much money of Caesar, persuaded the senate to let him have money of the common treasure, as though he had had none before: yea to speak more plainly, they compelled the senate unto it, sighing and lamenting to see the decrees they passed. Cato was not there then, for they had purposely sent him before into Cyprus. Howbeit Faonius that followed Cato's steps, when he saw that he could not prevail, nor withstand them, he went out of the senate in choler, and cried out amongst the people, that it was a horrible shame. But no man did hearken to him: some for the reverence they bore unto Pompey and Crassus, and others favouring Caesar's proceedings, did put all their hope and trust in him: and therefore did quiet themselves, and stirred not.

22   Then Caesar returning into Gaul beyond the Alps unto his army, found there a great war in the country. For two great nations of Germany had not long before passed over the river of Rhine, to conquer new lands: and the one of these people were called Ipes, and the other Tenterides. Now touching the battle which Caesar fought with them, he himself doth describe it in his commentaries, in this sort. That the barbarous people having sent ambassadors unto him, to require peace for a certain time, they notwithstanding, against law of arms, came and set upon him as he travelled by the way, insomuch as eight hundred of their men of arms overthrew five thousand of his horsemen, who nothing at all mistrusted their coming. Again, that they sent him other ambassadors to mock him once more: but that he kept them, and therewith caused his whole army to march against them, thinking it a folly and madness to keep faith with such traitorous barbarous breakers of leagues. Canutius writeth, that the senate appointing again to do new sacrifice, processions, and feasts, to give thanks to the gods for this victory, Cato was of contrary opinion, that Caesar should be delivered into the hands of the barbarous people, for to purge their city and

commonwealth of this breach of faith, and to turn the curse upon
him, that was the author of it. Of these barbarous people, which
came over the Rhine (being about the number of four hundred
thousand persons), they were all in manner slain, saving a very few
of them, that flying from the battle got over the river of Rhine
again, who were received by the Sicambrians, another people of
the Germans. Caesar taking this occasion against them, lacking no
goodwill of himself besides, to have the honour to be counted the
first Roman that ever passed over the river of Rhine with an army,
he built a bridge over it. This river is marvellous broad, and
runneth with great fury. And in that place specially where he built
his bridge, for there it is of a great breadth from one side to the
other, and it hath so strong and swift a stream besides, that men
casting down great bodies of trees into the river (which the stream
bringeth down with it) did with the great blows and force thereof
marvellously shake the posts of the bridge he had set up. But to
prevent the blows of those trees, and also to break the fury of the
stream, he made a pile of great wood above the bridge a good way,
and did forcibly ram them in to the bottom of the river, so that
in ten days' space, he had set up and finished his bridge of the
goodliest carpenters' work, and most excellent invention to see to,
that could be possibly thought or devised.

23   Then passing over his army upon it, he found none that durst
any more fight with him. For the Swevians, which were the
warlikest people of all Germany, had got themselves with their
goods into wonderful great valleys and bogs, full of woods and
forests. Now when he had burnt all the country of his enemies, and
confirmed the league with the confederates of the Romans, he
returned back again into Gaul after he had tarried eighteen days at
the most in Germany, on the other side of the Rhine. The journey
he made also into England, was a noble enterprise, and very
commendable. For he was the first that sailed the west Ocean with
an army by sea, and that passed through the sea Atlanticum with his
army, to make war in that so great and famous island, (which many
ancient writers would not believe that it was so indeed, and did
make them vary about it, saying that it was but a fable and a lie): and
was the first that enlarged the Roman empire, beyond the earth
inhabitable. For twice he passed over the narrow sea against the

firm land of Gaul, and fighting battles there, did hurt his enemies
more than enrich his own men: because, of men hardily brought
up, and poor, there was nothing to be gotten. Whereupon his war
had not such success as he looked for, and therefore taking pledges
only of the king, and imposing a yearly tribute upon him, to be paid
unto the people of Rome, he returned again into Gaul. There he
was no sooner landed, but be found letters ready to be sent over the
sea unto him: in the which he was advertised from Rome, of the
death of his daughter, that she was dead with child by Pompey. For
the which, Pompey and Caesar both were marvellous sorrowful:
and their friends mourned also, thinking that this alliance which
maintained the commonwealth (that otherwise was very tickle) in
good peace and concord, was now severed, and broken asunder,
and the rather likely, because the child lived not long after the
mother. So the common people at Rome took the corpse of Julia, in
despite of the tribunes, and buried it in the field of Mars.

24 Now Caesar being driven to divide his army (that was very
great) into sundry garrisons for the winter time, and returning again
into Italy as he was wont, all Gaul rebelled again, and had raised
great armies in every quarter to set upon the Romans, and to assay if
they could distress their forts where they lay in garrison. The
greatest number and most warlike men of these Gauls, that entered
into action of rebellion, were led by one Ambiorix: and first did set
upon the garrisons of Cotta, and Titurius, whom they slew, and all
the soldiers they had about them. Then they went with three score
thousand fighting men to besiege the garrison which Quintus
Cicero had in his charge, and had almost taken them by force,
because all the soldiers were every man of them hurt: but they were
so valiant and courageous, that they did more than men (as they say)
in defending of themselves. These news being come to Caesar, who
was far from thence at that time, he returned with all possible speed,
and levying seven thousand soldiers, made haste to help Cicero that
was in such distress. The Gauls that did besiege Cicero, understanding of Caesar's coming, raised their siege incontinently, to go and
meet him: making account that he was but a handful in their hands,
they were so few. Caesar to deceive them, still drew back, and
made as though he fled from them, lodging in places meet for a
captain that had but a few to fight with a great number of his

enemies, and commanded his men in no wise to stir out to skirmish with them, but compelled them to raise up the ramparts of his camp, and to fortify the gates, as men that were afraid, because the enemies should the less esteem of them: until that at length he took opportunities by their disorderly coming to assail the trenches of his camp (they were grown to such a presumptuous boldness and bravery), and then sallying out upon them, he put them all to flight with slaughter of a great number of them.

25 This did suppress all the rebellions of the Gauls in those parts, and furthermore, he himself in person went in the midst of winter thither, where he heard they did rebel; for that there was come a new supply out of Italy of three whole legions in their room, which he had lost: of the which, two of them Pompey lent him, and the other legion, he himself had levied in Gaul about the river of Po. During these stirs, broke forth the beginning of the greatest and most dangerous war that he had in all Gaul, the which had been secretly practised of long time by the chiefest and most warlike people of that country, who had levied a wonderful great power. For everywhere they levied multitudes of men, and great riches besides, to fortify their strongholds. Furthermore the country where they rose, was very ill to come unto, and specially at that time being winter, when the rivers were frozen, the woods and forests covered with snow, the meadows drowned with floods, and the fields so deep of snow, that no ways were to be found, neither the marshes nor rivers to be discerned, all was so overflown and drowned with water: all which troubles together were enough (as they thought) to keep Caesar from setting upon the rebels. Many nations of the Gauls were of this conspiracy, but two of the chiefest were the Arvernians and Carnutes: who had chosen Vercingentorix for their lieutenant general, whose father the Gauls before had put to death, because they thought he aspired to make himself king.

26 This Vercingentorix dividing his army into divers parts, and appointing divers captains over them, had gotten to take his part, all the people and countries thereabout, even as far as they that dwell towards the sea Adriatic,* having further determined (under-

* Some say, that in this place is to be read in the Greek πρὸς τὸν Ἄραριν, which is the river Saone.

standing that Rome did conspire against Caesar) to make all Gaul
rise in arms against him. So that if he had but tarried a little longer,
until Caesar had entered into his civil wars, he had put all Italy in as
great fear and danger, as it was when the Cimbri did come and
invade it. But Caesar, that was very valiant in all assays and dangers
of war, and that was very skilful to take time and opportunity, so
soon as he understood the news of the rebellion, he departed with
speed, and returned back the selfsame way which he had gone,
making the barbarous people know, that they should deal with an
army invincible, and which they could not possibly withstand,
considering the great speed he had made with the same, in so sharp
and hard a winter. For where they would not possibly have
believed, that a post or courier could have come in so short a time
from the place where he was, unto them, they wondered when
they saw him burning and destroying the country, the towns and
strong forts where he came with his army, taking all to mercy that
yielded unto him, until such time as the Hedvi took arms against
him, who before were wont to be called the brethren of the
Romans, and were greatly honoured of them. Wherefore Caesar's
men when they understood that they had joined with the rebels,
they were marvellous sorry, and half discouraged. Thereupon
Caesar, departing from those parts, went through the country of
the Lingones, to enter the country of the Burgonians, who were
confederates of the Romans, and the nearest unto Italy on that side,
in respect of all the rest of Gaul. Thither the enemies came to set
upon him, and to environ him of all sides, with an infinite number
of thousands of fighting men. Caesar on the other side tarried their
coming, and fighting with them a long time, he made them so
afraid of him, that at length he overcame the barbarous people. But
at the first, it seemeth notwithstanding, that he had received some
overthrow: for the Arvernians showed a sword hanged up in one
of their temples, which they said they had won from Caesar.
Insomuch as Caesar self coming that way by occasion, saw it, and
fell a-laughing at it. But some of his friends going about to take it
away, he would not suffer them, but bade them let it alone, and
touch it not, for it was a holy thing.

27 Notwithstanding, such as at the first had saved themselves by
fleeing, the most of them were got with their king into the city of

Alexia, the which Caesar went and besieged, although it seemed inexpugnable, both for the height of the walls, as also for the multitude of soldiers they had to defend it. But now during this siege, he fell into a marvellous great danger without, almost incredible. For an army of three hundred thousand fighting men of the best men that were among all the nations of the Gauls, came against him, being at the siege of Alexia, besides them that were within the city, which amounted to the number of three score and ten thousand fighting men at the least: so that perceiving he was shut in betwixt two so great armies, he was driven to fortify himself with two walls, the one against them of the city, and the other against them without. For if those two armies had joined together, Caesar had been utterly undone. And therefore, this siege of Alexia, and the battle he won before it, did deservedly win him more honour and fame, than any other. For there, in that instant and extreme danger, he showed more valiantness and wisdom, than he did in any battle he fought before. But what a wonderful thing was this? That they of the city never heard anything of them that came to aid them, until Caesar had overcome them: and furthermore, that the Romans themselves which kept watch upon the wall that was built against the city, knew also no more of it than they, but when it was done, and that they heard the cries and lamentations of men and women in Alexia, they perceived on the other side of the city such a number of glistering shields of gold and silver, such store of bloody corselets and armours, such a deal of plate and moveables, and such a number of tents and pavilions after the fashion of the Gauls, which the Romans had gotten of their spoils in their camp. Thus suddenly was this great army vanished, as a dream or vision, where the most part of them were slain that day in battle. Furthermore, after that they within the city of Alexia had done great hurt to Caesar, and themselves also, in the end, they all yielded themselves. And Vercingentorix (he that was their king and captain in all this war) went out of the gates excellently well armed, and his horse furnished with rich caparison accordingly, and rode round about Caesar, who sat in his chair of estate. Then lighting from his horse, he took off his caparison and furniture, and unarmed himself, and laid all on the ground, and went and sat down at Caesar's feet, and said never a word. So Caesar at length committed him as a prisoner taken in the wars, to lead him afterwards in his triumph at Rome.

28  Now Caesar had long time determined to destroy Pompey,
and Pompey him also. For Crassus being killed amongst the
Parthians, who only did see, that one of them two must needs fall,
nothing kept Caesar from being the greatest person, but because he
destroyed not Pompey, that was the greater: neither did anything
let Pompey to withstand that it should not come to pass, but
because he did not first overcome Caesar, whom only he feared.
For till then, Pompey had not long feared him, but always before
set light by him, thinking it an easy matter for him to put him
down when he would, if he had brought him to that greatness he
was come unto. But Caesar contrarily, having had that drift in his
head from the beginning, like a wrestler that studieth for tricks to
overthrow his adversary, he went far from Rome, to exercise
himself in the wars of Gaul, where he did train his army, and
presently by his valiant deeds did increase his fame and honour. By
these means became Caesar as famous as Pompey in his doings, and
lacked no more to put his enterprise in execution, but some
occasions of colour, which Pompey partly gave him, and partly
also the time delivered him, but chiefly, the hard fortune and ill
government at that time of the commonwealth of Rome. For they
that made suit for honour and offices, bought the voices of the
people with ready money, which they gave out openly to usury,
without shame or fear. Thereupon, the common people that had
sold their voices for money, came to the market-place at the day of
election, to fight for him that had hired them: not with their
voices, but with their bows, slings, and swords. So that the
assembly seldom time broke up, but that the pulpit for orations was
defiled and sprinkled with the blood of them that were slain in the
market-place, the city remaining all that time without government
of magistrate, like a ship left without a pilot. Insomuch, as men of
deep judgment and discretion seeing such fury and madness of the
people, thought themselves happy if the commonwealth were no
worse troubled, than with the absolute state of a monarchy and
sovereign lord to govern them. Furthermore, there were many
that were not afraid to speak it openly, that there was no other help
to remedy the troubles of the commonwealth, but by the authority
of one man only, that should command them all: and that this
medicine must be ministered by the hands of him, that was the
gentlest physician, meaning covertly Pompey. Now Pompey used

many fine speeches, making semblance as though he would none of it, and yet cunningly underhand did lay all the irons in the fire he could, to bring it to pass, that he might be chosen dictator. Cato finding the mark he shot at, and fearing lest in the end the people should be compelled to make him dictator, he persuaded the senate rather to make him sole consul, that contenting himself with that more just and lawful government, he should not covet the other unlawful. The senate following his counsel, did not only make him consul, but further did prorogue his government of the provinces he had. For he had two provinces, all Spain and Africa, the which he governed by his lieutenants: and further, he received yearly of the common treasure to pay his soldiers a thousand talents.

29   Hereupon Caesar took occasion also to send his men to make suit in his name for the consulship, and also to have the government of his provinces prorogued. Pompey at the first held his peace. But Marcellus and Lentulus (that otherwise hated Caesar) withstood them, and to shame and dishonour him, had much needless speech in matters of weight. Furthermore, they took away the freedom from the colonies which Caesar had lately brought unto the city of Novum Comum in Gaul towards Italy, where Caesar not long before had lodged them. And moreover, when Marcellus was consul, he made one of the senators in that city to be whipped with rods, who came to Rome about those matters: and said, he gave him those marks, that he should know he was no Roman citizen, and bade him go his way, and tell Caesar of it. After Marcellus' consulship, Caesar setting open his coffers of the treasure he had got among the Gauls, did frankly give it out amongst the magistrates at Rome, without restraint or spare. First, he set Curio the tribune clear out of debt: and gave also unto Paul the consul a thousand five hundred talents, with which money he built that notable palace by the market-place, called Paul's Basilic, in the place of Fulvius' Basilic. Then Pompey being afraid of this practice, began openly to procure, both by himself and his friends, that they should send Caesar a successor: and moreover, he sent unto Caesar for his two legions of men of war which he had lent him, for the conquest of Gaul. Caesar sent him them again, and gave every private soldier, two hundred and fifty silver drachmas. Now, they that brought these two legions back from Caesar, gave out ill and seditious words

against him among the people, and did also abuse Pompey with
false persuasions and vain hopes, informing him that he was marvellously desired and wished for in Caesar's camp: and that though in
Rome, for the malice and secret spite which the governors there did
bear him, he could hardly obtain that he desired, yet in Gaul he
might assure himself, that all the army was at his commandment.
They added further also, that if the soldiers there did once return
over the mountains again into Italy, they would all straight come to
him, they did so hate Caesar, because he wearied them with too
much labour and continual fight, and withal, for that they suspected
he aspired to be king. These words breeding security in Pompey,
and a vain conceit of himself, made him negligent in his doings, so
that he made no preparation for war, as though he had no occasion
to be afraid: but only studied to thwart Caesar in speech, and to
cross the suits he made. Howbeit Caesar passed not of all this. For
the report went, that one of Caesar's captains which was sent to
Rome to prosecute his suit, being at the senate door, and hearing
that they denied to prorogue Caesar's time of government which
he sued for, clapping his hand upon his sword, he said, 'If you will
not grant it him, this shall give it him.'

30 Notwithstanding, the requests that Caesar propounded, carried
great semblance of reason with them. For he said, that he was
contented to lay down arms, so that Pompey did the like: and that
both of them as private persons should come and make suit of their
citizens to obtain honourable recompense: declaring unto them,
that taking arms from him, and granting them unto Pompey, they
did wrongfully accuse him in going about to make himself a tyrant,
and in the meantime to grant the other means to be a tyrant. Curio
making these offers and persuasions openly before the people, in
the name of Caesar, he was heard with great rejoicing and clapping
of hands, and there were some that cast flowers and nosegays upon
him when he went his way, as they commonly use to do unto any
man, when he hath obtained victory, and won any games. Then
Antonius one of the tribunes, brought a letter sent from Caesar,
and made it openly to be read in despite of the consuls. But Scipio
in the senate, Pompey's father-in-law, made this motion: that if
Caesar did not dismiss his army by a certain day appointed him, the
Romans should proclaim him an enemy unto Rome. Then the

consuls openly asked in the presence of the senators, if they thought it good that Pompey should dismiss his army: but few agreed to that demand. After that again they asked, if they liked that Caesar should dismiss his army: thereto they all in manner answered, 'Yea, yea.' But when Antonius requested again that both of them should lay down arms, then they were all indifferently of his mind. Notwithstanding, because Scipio did insolently behave himself, and Marcellus also, who cried that they must use force of arms, and not men's opinions, against a thief, the senate rose straight upon it without further determination, and men changed apparel through the city because of this dissension, as they use to do in a common calamity.

31   After that, there came other letters from Caesar, which seemed much more reasonable: in the which he requested that they would grant him Gaul, that lieth between the mountains of the Alps and Italy, and Illyria, with two legions only, and then that he would request nothing else, until he made suit for the second consulship. Cicero the orator, that was newly come from his government of Cilicia, travailed to reconcile them together, and pacified Pompey the best he could: who told him, he would yield to anything he would have him, so he did let him alone with his army. So Cicero persuaded Caesar's friends to be contented, to take those two provinces, and six thousand men only, that they might be friends and at peace together. Pompey very willingly yielded unto it, and granted them. But Lentulus the consul would not agree to it, but shamefully drove Curio and Antonius out of the senate: whereby they themselves gave Caesar a happy occasion and colour, as could be, stirring up his soldiers the more against them, when he showed them these two notable men and tribunes of the people that were driven to fly, disguised like slaves, in a carrier's cart. For, they were driven for fear to steal out of Rome, disguised in that manner.

32   Now at that time, Caesar had not in all about him, above five thousand footmen, and three thousand horsemen: for the rest of his army he left on the other side of the mountains to be brought after him by his lieutenants. So, considering that for the execution of his enterprise, he should not need so many men of war at the first, but rather suddenly stealing upon them, to make them afraid with his valiantness, taking benefit of the opportunity of time, because he

should more easily make his enemies afraid of him, coming so
suddenly when they looked not for him, than he should otherwise
distress them, assailing them with his whole army, in giving them
leisure to provide further for him, he commanded his captains and
lieutenants to go before, without any other armour than their
swords, to take the city of Ariminum (a great city of Gaul, being
the first city men come to, when they come out of Gaul) with as
little bloodshed and tumult, as they could possible. Then committing that force and army he had with him, unto Hortensius one of
his friends, he remained a whole day together, openly in the sight
of every man, to see the sword players handle their weapons before
him. At night he went into his lodging, and bathing his body a
little, came afterwards into the hall amongst them, and made merry
with them a while, whom he had bidden to supper. Then when it
was well forward night, and very dark, he rose from the table, and
prayed his company to be merry, and no man to stir, for he would
straight come to them again: howbeit he had secretly before
commanded a few of his trustiest friends to follow him, not all
together, but some one way, and some another way. He himself in
the meantime took a coach he had hired, and made as though he
would have gone some other way at the first, but suddenly he
turned back again towards the city of Ariminum. When he was
come unto the little river of Rubicon, which divideth Gaul on this
side the Alps from Italy, he stayed upon a sudden. For, the nearer
he came to execute his purpose, the more remorse he had in his
conscience, to think what an enterprise he took in hand: and his
thoughts also fell out more doubtful, when he entered into consideration of the desperateness of his attempt. So he fell into many
thoughts with himself, and spoke never a word, waving sometime
one way, sometime another way, and often times changed his
determination, contrary to himself. So did he talk much also with
his friends he had with him, amongst whom was Asinius Pollio,
telling them what mischiefs the beginning of this passage over that
river would breed in the world, and how much their posterity and
them that lived after them, would speak of it in time to come. But
at length, casting from him with a noble courage, all those perilous
thoughts to come, and speaking these words which valiant men
commonly say, that attempt dangerous and desperate enterprises,
'A desperate man fears no danger: come on', he passed over the

river, and when he was come over, he ran with his coach and never
stayed, so that before daylight he was within the city of Ariminum,
and took it. It is said, that the night before he passed over this river,
he dreamed a damnable dream, that he carnally knew his mother.

33    The city of Ariminum being taken, and the rumour thereof
dispersed through all Italy, even as if it had been open war both by
sea and land, and as if all the laws of Rome, together with the
extreme bounds and confines of the same, had been broken up, a
man would have said, that not only the men and women for fear,
as experience proved at other times, but whole cities themselves
leaving their habitations, fled from one place to another through all
Italy. And Rome itself also was immediately filled with the flowing
repair of all the people their neighbours thereabouts, which came
thither from all parts like droves of cattle, that there was neither
officer nor magistrate that could any more command them by
authority, neither by any persuasion of reason bridle such a confused and disorderly multitude: so that Rome had in manner
destroyed itself for lack of rule and order. For in all places, men
were of contrary opinions, and there were dangerous stirs and
tumults everywhere: because they that were glad of this trouble,
could keep in no certain place, but running up and down the city,
when they met with others in divers places, that seemed either to
be afraid or angry with this tumult (as otherwise it is impossible in
so great a city), they flatly fell out with them, and boldly threatened
them with that that was to come. Pompey himself, who at that
time was not a little amazed, was yet much more troubled with the
ill words some gave him on the one side, and some on the other.
For some of them reproved him, and said that he had done wisely,
and had paid for his folly, because he had made Caesar so great and
strong against him and the commonwealth. And other again did
blame him, because he had refused the honest offers and reasonable
conditions of peace, which Caesar had offered him, suffering
Lentulus the consul to abuse him too much. On the other side,
Phaonius spoke unto him, and bade him stamp on the ground with
his foot: for Pompey being one day in a bravery in the senate, said
openly: let no man take thought for preparation of war, for when
he listed, with one stamp of his foot on the ground, he would fill all
Italy with soldiers. This notwithstanding, Pompey at that time had

greater number of soldiers than Caesar: but they would never let him follow his own determination. For they brought him so many lies, and put so many examples of fear before him, as if Caesar had been already at their heels, and had won all: so that in the end he yielded unto them, and gave place to their fury and madness, determining (seeing all things in such tumult and garboyle) that there was no way but to forsake the city, and thereupon commanded the senate to follow him, and not a man to tarry there, unless he loved tyranny more than his own liberty and the commonwealth.

34 Thus the consuls themselves, before they had done their common sacrifices accustomed at their going out of the city, fled every man of them. So did likewise the most part of the senators, taking their own things in haste, such as came first to hand, as if by stealth they had taken them from another. And there were some of them also that always loved Caesar, whose wits were then so troubled and besides themselves, with the fear they had conceived, that they also fled, and followed the stream of this tumult, without manifest cause or necessity. But above all things, it was a lamentable sight to see the city itself, that in this fear and trouble was left at all adventure, as a ship tossed in storm of sea, forsaken of her pilots, and despairing of her safety. This their departure being thus miserable, yet men esteemed their banishment (for the love they bore unto Pompey) to be their natural country, and reckoned Rome no better than Caesar's camp. At that time also Labienus, who was one of Caesar's greatest friends, and had been always used as his lieutenant in the wars of Gaul, and had valiantly fought in his cause, he likewise forsook him then, and fled unto Pompey. But Caesar sent his money and carriage after him, and then went and encamped before the city of Corfinium, the which Domitius kept, with thirty cohorts or ensigns. When Domitius saw he was besieged, he straight thought himself but undone, and despairing of his success, he bade a physician, a slave of his, give him poison. The physician gave him a drink which he drank, thinking to have died. But shortly after, Domitius hearing them report what clemency and wonderful courtesy Caesar used unto them he took, repented him then that he had drunk this drink, and began to lament and bewail his desperate resolution taken to die. The physician did comfort

him again, and told him, that he had taken a drink only to make him sleep, but not to destroy him. Then Domitius rejoiced, and went straight and yielded himself unto Caesar: who gave him his life, but he notwithstanding stole away immediately, and fled unto Pompey. When these news were brought to Rome, they did marvellously rejoice and comfort them that still remained there: and moreover there were of them that had forsaken Rome, which returned thither again.

35   In the meantime, Caesar did put all Domitius' men in pay, and he did the like through all the cities, where he had taken any captains, that levied men for Pompey. Now Caesar having assembled a great and dreadful power together, went straight where he thought to find Pompey himself. But Pompey tarried not his coming, but fled into the city of Brundusium, from whence he had sent the two consuls before with that army he had, unto Dyrrachium: and he himself also went thither afterwards, when he understood that Caesar was come, as you shall hear more amply hereafter in his life. Caesar lacked no goodwill to follow him, but wanting ships to take the seas, he returned forthwith to Rome: so that in less then three score days, he was lord of all Italy, without any blood shed. Who when he was come to Rome, and found it much quieter than he looked for, and many senators there also, he courteously entreated them, and prayed them to send unto Pompey, to pacify all matters between them, upon reasonable conditions. But no man did attempt it, either because they feared Pompey for that they had forsaken him, or else for that they thought Caesar meant not as he spoke, but that they were words of course, to colour his purpose withal. And when Metellus also, one of the tribunes, would not suffer him to take any of the common treasure out of the temple of Saturn, but told him that it was against the law: 'Tush,' said he, 'time of war and law are two things. If this that I do,' quoth he, 'do offend thee, then get thee hence for this time: for war cannot abide this frank and bold speech. But when wars are done, and that we are all quiet again, then thou shalt speak in the pulpit what thou wilt: and yet I do tell thee this of favour, impairing so much my right, for thou art mine, both thou and all them that have risen against me, and whom I have in my hands.' When he had spoken thus unto Metellus, he went to the temple

door where the treasure lay, and finding no keys there, he caused smiths to be sent for, and made them break open the locks. Metellus thereupon began again to withstand him, and certain men that stood by praised him in his doing: but Caesar at length speaking bigly to him, threatened him he would kill him presently, if he troubled him any more, and told him furthermore, 'Young man,' quoth he, 'thou knowest it is harder for me to tell it thee, than to do it.' That word made Metellus quake for fear, that he got him away roundly: and ever after that, Caesar had all at his commandment for the wars.

36 From thence he went into Spain, to make war with Petreius and Varro, Pompey's lieutenants: first to get their armies and provinces into his hands which they governed, that afterwards he might follow Pompey the better, leaving never an enemy behind him. In this journey he was oftentimes himself in danger, through the ambushes that were laid for him in divers strange sorts and places, and likely also to have lost all his army for lack of victuals. All this notwithstanding, he never left following of Pompey's lieutenants, provoking them to battle, and entrenching them in, until he had gotten their camp and armies into his hands, albeit that the lieutenants themselves fled unto Pompey.

37 When Caesar returned again to Rome, Piso his father-in-law gave counsel to send ambassadors unto Pompey, to treat of peace. But Isauricus, to flatter Caesar, was against it. Caesar being then created dictator by the senate, called home again all the banished men, and restored their children to honour, whose fathers before had been slain in Sylla's time: and did somewhat cut off the usuries that did oppress them, and besides, did make some such other ordinances as those, but very few. For he was dictator but eleven days only, and then did yield it up of himself, and made himself consul, with Servilius Isauricus, and after that determined to follow the wars. All the rest of his army he left coming on the way behind him, and went himself before with six hundred horse, and five legions only of footmen, in the winter quarter, about the month of January, which after the Athenians, is called Posideon. Then having passed over the sea Ionium, and landed his men, he won the cities of Oricum and Apollonia. Then he sent his ships back again unto Brundusium, to transport the rest of his soldiers that could not

come with that speed he did. They as they came by the way (like men whose strength of body, and lusty youth, was decayed), being wearied with so many sundry battles as they had fought with their enemies, complained of Caesar in this sort. 'To what end and purpose doth this man hale us after him, up and down the world, using us like slaves and drudges? It is not our armour, but our bodies that bear the blows away: and what, shall we never be without our harness of our backs, and our shields on our arms? Should not Caesar think, at the least when he seeth our blood and wounds, that we are all mortal men, and that we feel the misery and pains that other men do feel? And now even in the dead of winter, he putteth us unto the mercy of the sea and tempest, yea which the gods themselves cannot withstand: as if he fled before his enemies, and pursued them not.' Thus spending time with this talk, the soldiers still marching on, by small journeys came at length unto the city of Brundusium. But when they were come, and found that Caesar had already passed over the sea, then they straight changed their complaints and minds. For they blamed themselves, and took on also with their captains, because they had not made them make more haste in marching: and sitting upon the rocks and cliffs of the sea, they looked over the main sea, towards the realm of Epirus, to see if they could discern the ships returning back, to transport them over.

38    Caesar in the meantime being in the city of Apollonia, having but a small army to fight with Pompey, it grieved him for that the rest of his army was so long a-coming, not knowing what way to take. In the end he followed a dangerous determination, to embark unknown in a little pinnace of twelve oars only, to pass over the sea again unto Brundusium: the which he could not do without great danger, considering that all that sea was full of Pompey's ships and armies. So he took ship in the night apparelled like a slave, and went aboard upon this little pinnace, and said never a word, as if he had been some poor man of mean condition. The pinnace lay in the mouth of the river of Anius, the which commonly was wont to be very calm and quiet, by reason of a little wind that came from the shore, which every morning drove back the waves far into the main sea. But that night, by ill fortune, there came a great wind from the sea that overcame the land wind, insomuch as the force

and strength of the river fighting against the violence of the rage and waves of the sea, the encounter was marvellous dangerous, the water of the river being driven back, and rebounding upward, with great noise and danger in turning of the water. Thereupon the master of the pinnace seeing he could not possibly get out of the mouth of this river, bade the mariners to cast about again, and to return against the stream. Caesar hearing that, straight discovered himself unto the master of the pinnace, who at first was amazed when he saw him: but Caesar then taking him by the hand said unto him, 'Good fellow, be of good cheer, and forwards hardily: fear not, for thou hast Caesar and his fortune with thee.' Then the mariners forgetting the danger of the storm they were in, laid on load with oars, and laboured for life what they could against the wind, to get out of the mouth of this river. But at length, perceiving they laboured in vain, and that the pinnace took in abundance of water, and was ready to sink, Caesar then to his great grief was driven to return back again. Who when he was returned unto his camp, his soldiers came in great companies unto him, and were very sorry, that he mistrusted he was not able with them alone to overcome his enemies, but would put his person in danger, to go fetch them that were absent, putting no trust in them that were present.

39   In the meantime Antonius arrived, and brought with him the rest of his army from Brundusium. Then Caesar finding himself strong enough, went and offered Pompey battle, who was passingly well lodged, for victualling of his camp both by sea and land. Caesar on the other side, who had no great plenty of victuals at the first, was in a very hard case: insomuch as his men gathered roots, and mingled them with milk, and ate them. Furthermore, they did make bread of it also, and sometime when they skirmished with the enemies, and came along by them that watched and warded, they cast of their bread into their trenches, and said, that as long as the earth brought forth such fruits, they would never leave besieging of Pompey. But Pompey straitly commanded them, that they should neither carry those words nor bread into their camp, fearing lest his men's hearts would fail them, and that they would be afraid, when they should think of their enemies' hardness, with whom they had to fight, if they were weary with no pains, no more than brute beasts. Caesar's

men did daily skirmish hard to the trenches of Pompey's camp, in the which Caesar had ever the better, saving once only, at what time his men fled with such fear, that all his camp that day was in great hazard to have been cast away. For Pompey came on with his battle upon them, and they were not able to abide it, but were fought with, and driven into their camp, and their trenches were filled with dead bodies, which were slain within the very gate and bulwarks of their camp, they were so valiantly pursued. Caesar stood before them that fled, to make them to turn head again: but he could not prevail. For when he would have taken the ensigns to have stayed them, the ensign bearers threw them down on the ground: so that the enemies took two and thirty of them, and Caesar's self also scaped hardly with life. For striking a great big soldier that fled by him, commanding him to stay, and turn his face to his enemy, the soldier being afraid, lift up his sword to strike at Caesar. But one of Caesar's pages preventing him, gave him such a blow with his sword, that he struck off his shoulder. Caesar that day was brought unto so great extremity, that, if Pompey had not either for fear, or spiteful fortune, left off to follow his victory, and retired into his camp, being contented to have driven his enemies into their camp, returning to his camp with his friends, he said unto them: 'The victory this day had been our enemies', if they had had a captain, that could have told how to have overcome.' So when he was come to his lodging, he went to bed, and that night troubled him more, than any night that ever he had. For still his mind ran with great sorrow of the foul fault he had committed in leading of his army, of self-will to remain there so long by the sea side, his enemies being the stronger by sea: considering that he had before him a goodly country, rich and plentiful of all things, and goodly cities of Macedon and Thessaly, and had not the wit to bring the war from thence, but to lose his time in a place where he was rather besieged of his enemies for lack of victuals, than that he did besiege them by force of arms. Thus, fretting and chafing to see himself so straited with victuals, and to think of his ill luck, he raised his camp, intending to go set upon Scipio, making account, that either he should draw Pompey to battle against his will, when he had not the sea at his back to furnish him with plenty of victuals: or else that he should easily overcome Scipio, finding him alone, unless he were aided.

40 This remove of Caesar's camp did much encourage Pompey's army and his captains, who would needs in any case have followed after him, as though he had been overcome, and had fled. But for Pompey himself, he would in no respect hazard battle, which was a matter of so great importance. For finding himself well provided of all things necessary to tarry time, he thought it better to draw this war out in length, by tract of time, the rather to consume this little strength that remained in Caesar's army: of the which, the best men were marvellous well trained and good soldiers, and for valiantness, at one day's battle, were incomparable. But on the other side again, to remove here and there so oft, and to fortify their camp where they came, and to besiege any wall, or to keep watch all night in their armour, the most part of them could not do it, by reason of their age, being then unable to away with that pains, so that the weakness of their bodies did also take away the life and courage of their hearts. Furthermore, there fell a pestilent disease among them that came by ill meats hunger drove them to eat: yet was not this the worst. For besides, he had no store of money, neither could tell how to come by victuals: so that it seemed in all likelihood, that in very short time he would come to nothing.

41 For these respects, Pompey would in no case fight, and yet had he but Cato only of his mind in that, who stuck in it the rather, because he would avoid shedding of his countrymen's blood. For when Cato had viewed the dead bodies slain in the camp of his enemies, at the last skirmish that was between them, the which were no less then a thousand persons, he covered his face, and went away weeping. All other but he, contrarily fell out with him, and blamed him, because he so long refrained from battle: and some pricked him forward, and called him Agamemnon, and king of kings, saying, that he delayed this war in this sort, because he would not leave his authority to command them all, and that he was glad always to see so many captains round about him, which came to his lodging to honour him, and wait upon him. And Faonius also, a harebrained fellow, frantically counterfeiting the round and plain speech of Cato, made as though he was marvellous angry, and said: 'Is it not great pity, that we shall not eat this year of Tusculum figs, and all for Pompey's ambitious mind to reign alone?' And Afranius, who not long before was but lately come out

of Spain (where, because he had but ill success, he was accused of treason, that for money he had sold his army unto Caesar), he went busily asking, why they fought not with that merchant, unto whom they said he had sold the province of Spain?. So that Pompey with these kind of speeches, against his will, was driven to follow Caesar, to fight with him. Then was Caesar at the first marvellously perplexed, and troubled by the way, because he found none that would give him any victuals, being despised of every man, for the late loss and overthrow he had received. But after that he had taken the city of Gomphes in Thessaly, he did not only meet with plenty of victuals to relieve his army with, but he strangely also did rid them of their disease. For the soldiers meeting with plenty of wine, drinking hard, and making merry, drove away the infection of the pestilence. For they disposed themselves unto dancing, masquing, and playing the Baccherians by the way: insomuch that drinking drunk they overcame their disease, and made their bodies new again.

42   When they both came into the country of Pharsalia, and both camps lay before the other:, Pompey returned again to his former determination, and the rather, because he had ill signs and tokens of misfortune in his sleep. For he thought in his sleep that when he entered into the theatre, all the Romans received him with great clapping of hands. Whereupon, they that were about him grew to such boldness and security, assuring themselves of victory, that Domitius, Spinther, and Scipio, in a bravery contended between themselves for the chief bishopric which Caesar had. Furthermore, there were divers that sent unto Rome to hire the nearest houses unto the market-place, as being the fittest places for praetors and consuls: making their account already, that those offices could not scape them incontinently after the wars. But besides those, the young gentlemen and Roman knights were marvellous desirous to fight, that were bravely mounted, and armed with glistering gilt armours, their horses fat and very finely kept, and themselves goodly young men, to the number of seven thousand, where the gentlemen of Caesar's side were but one thousand only. The number of his footmen also were much after the same reckoning. For he had five and forty thousand against two and twenty thousand.

43 Wherefore Caesar called his soldiers together, and told them how Cornificius was at hand, who brought two whole legions, and that he had fifteen ensigns led by Calenus, the which he made to stay about Megara and Athens. Then he asked them if they would tarry for that aid or not, or whether they would rather themselves alone venture battle. The soldiers cried out to him, and prayed him not to defer battle, but rather to devise some fetch to make the enemy fight as soon as he could. Then as he sacrificed unto the gods, for the purifying of his army, the first beast was no sooner sacrificed, but his soothsayer assured him that he should fight within three days. Caesar asked him again, if he saw in the sacrifices, any lucky sign, or token of good luck. The soothsayer answered, 'For that, thou shalt answer thyself, better than I can do: for the gods do promise us a marvellous great change, and alteration of things that are now, unto another clean contrary. For if thou beest well now, doest thou think to have worse fortune hereafter? And if thou be ill, assure thyself thou shalt have better.' The night before the battle, as he went about midnight to visit the watch, men saw a great firebrand in the element, all of alight fire, that came over Caesar's camp, and fell down in Pompey's. In the morning also when they relieved the watch, they heard a false alarm in the enemies' camp, without any apparent cause: which they commonly call, a sudden fear, that makes men besides themselves. This notwithstanding, Caesar thought not to fight that day, but was determined to have raised his camp from thence, and to have gone towards the city of Scotusa: and his tents in his camp were already overthrown, when his scouts came in with great speed, to bring him news that his enemies were preparing themselves to fight.

44 Then he was very glad, and after he had made his prayers unto the gods to help him that day, he set his men in battle ray, and divided them into three squadrons: giving the middle battle unto Domitius Calvinus, and the left wing unto Antonius, and placed himself in the right wing, choosing his place to fight in the tenth legion. But seeing that against that his enemies had set all their horsemen, he was half afraid when he saw the great number of them, and so brave besides. Wherefore he closely made six ensigns to come from the rearward of his battle, whom he had laid as an ambush behind his right wing, having first appointed his

soldiers what they should do, when the horsemen of the enemies came to give them charge. On the other side, Pompey placed himself in the right wing of his battle, gave the left wing unto Domitius, and the middle battle unto Scipio his father-in-law. Now all the Roman knights (as we have told you before) were placed in the left wing, of purpose to environ Caesar's right wing behind, and to give their hottest charge there, where the general of their enemies was: making their account, that there was no squadron of footmen how thick soever they were, that could receive the charge of so great a troop of horsemen, and that at the first onset, they should overthrow them all, and march upon their bellies. When the trumpets on either side did sound the alarm to the battle, Pompey commanded his footmen that they should stand still without stirring, to receive the charge of their enemies, until they came to throwing of their darts. Wherefore Caesar afterwards said, that Pompey had committed a foul fault, not to consider that the charge which is given running with fury, besides that it giveth the more strength also unto their blows, doth set men's hearts also afire: for the common hurling of all the soldiers that run together, is unto them as a box of the ear that sets men afire. Then Caesar making his battle march forward to give the onset, saw one of his captains (a valiant man, and very skilful in war, in whom he had also great confidence) speaking to his soldiers that he had under his charge, encouraging them to fight like men that day. So he called him aloud by his name, and said unto him: 'Well, Caius Crassinius, what hope shall we have today? How are we determined, to fight it out manfully?' Then Crassinius casting up his hand, answered him aloud: 'This day, O Caesar, we shall have a noble victory, and I promise thee ere night thou shalt praise me alive or dead.' When he had told him so, he was himself the foremost man that gave charge upon his enemies, with his band following of him, being about six score men, and making a lane through the foremost ranks, with great slaughter he entered far into the battle of his enemies: until that valiantly fighting in this sort, he was thrust in at length in the mouth with a sword, that the point of it came out again at his neck.

45   Now the footmen of both battles being come to the sword, the horsemen of the left wing of Pompey did march as fiercely also,

spreading out their troops, to compass in the right wing of Caesar's battle. But before they began to give charge, the six ensigns of footmen which Caesar had laid in ambush behind him, they began to run full upon them, not throwing away their darts far off as they were wont to do, neither striking their enemies on the thighs nor on the legs, but to seek to hit them full in the eyes, and to hurt them in the face, as Caesar had taught them. For he hoped that these lusty young gentlemen that had not been often in the wars, nor were used to see themselves hurt, and the which, being in the prime of their youth and beauty, would be afraid of those hurts, as well for the fear of the present danger to be slain, as also for that their faces should not forever be deformed. As indeed it came to pass, for they could never abide that they should come so near their faces, with the points of their darts, but hung down their heads for fear to be hit with them in their eyes, and turned their backs, covering their face, because they should not be hurt. Then, breaking of themselves, they began at length cowardly to fly, and were occasion also of the loss of all the rest of Pompey's army. For they that had broken them, ran immediately to set upon the squadron of the footmen behind, and slew them. Then Pompey seeing his horsemen from the other wing of his battle, so scattered and dispersed, flying away, forgot that he was any more Pompey the Great which he had been before, but rather was like a man whose wits the gods had taken from him, being afraid and amazed with the slaughter sent from above, and so retired into his tent speaking never a word, and sat there to see the end of this battle. Until at length all his army being overthrown, and put to flight, the enemies came, and got up upon the ramparts and defence of his camp, and fought hand to hand with them that stood to defend the same. Then as a man come to himself again, he spoke but this only word: 'What, even into our camp?' So in haste, casting off his coat armour and apparel of a general, he shifted him, and put on such as became his miserable fortune, and so stole out of his camp. Furthermore, what he did after this overthrow, and how he had put himself into the hands of the Egyptians, by whom he was miserably slain, we have set it forth at large in his life.

46 Then Caesar entering into Pompey's camp, and seeing the bodies laid on the ground that were slain, and others also that were

a–killing, said, fetching a great sigh: 'It was their own doing, and against my will.' For Caius Caesar, after he had won so many famous conquests, and overcome so many great battles, had been utterly condemned notwithstanding, if he had departed from his army. Asinius Pollio writeth, that he spoke these words then in Latin, which he afterwards wrote in Greek, and sayeth furthermore, that the most part of them which were put to the sword in the camp, were slaves and bondmen, and that there were not slain in all at this battle, above six thousand soldiers. As for them that were taken prisoners, Caesar did put many of them amongst his legions, and did pardon also many men of estimation, among whom Brutus was one, that afterwards slew Caesar himself: and it is reported, that Caesar was very sorry for him, when he could not immediately be found after the battle, and that he rejoiced again, when he knew he was alive, and that he came to yield himself unto him.

47  Caesar had many signs and tokens of victory before this battle: but the notablest of all other that happened to him, was in the city of Tralles. For in the temple of victory, within the same city, there was an image of Caesar, and the earth all about it very hard of itself, and was paved besides with hard stone: and yet some say that there sprang up a palm hard by the base of the same image. In the city of Padua, Caius Cornelius an excellent soothsayer (a countryman and friend of Titus Livius the historiographer) was by chance at that time set to behold the flying of birds. He (as Livy reporteth) knew the very time when the battle began, and told them that were present, 'Even now they gave the onset on both sides, and both armies do meet at this instant.' Then sitting down again to consider of the birds, after he had bethought him of the signs, he suddenly rose up on his feet, and cried out as a man possessed with some spirit, 'O Caesar, the victory is thine.' Every man wondering to see him, he took the crown he had on his head, and made an oath that he would never put it on again, till the event of his prediction had proved his art true. Livy testifieth, that it so came to pass.

48  Caesar afterwards giving freedom unto the Thessalians, in respect of the victory which he won in their country, he followed after Pompey. When he came into Asia, he gave freedom also unto the Gnidians for Theopompus' sake, who had gathered the fables together. He did release Asia also, the third part of the

tribute which the inhabitants paid unto the Romans. Then he came into Alexandria, after Pompey was slain, and detested Theodotus, that presented him Pompey's head, and turned his head at the side because he would not see it. Notwithstanding, he took his seal, and beholding it, wept. Furthermore, he courteously used all Pompey's friends and familiars, who wandering up and down the country, were taken of the king of Egypt, and won them all to be at his commandment. Continuing these courtesies, he wrote unto his friends at Rome, that the greatest pleasure he took of his victory was, that he daily saved the lives of some of his countrymen that bore arms against him. And for the war he made in Alexandria, some say, he need not have done it, but that he willingly did it for the love of Cleopatra: wherein he won little honour, and besides did put his person in great danger. Others do lay the fault upon the king of Egypt's ministers, but specially on Pothinus the eunuch, who bearing the greatest sway of all the king's servants, after he had caused Pompey to be slain, and driven Cleopatra from the court, secretly laid wait all the ways he could, how he might likewise kill Caesar. Wherefore Caesar hearing an inkling of it, began thenceforth to spend all the night long in feasting and banqueting, that his person might be in the better safety. But besides all this, Pothinus the eunuch spoke many things openly not to be borne, only to shame Caesar, and to stir up the people to envy him. For he made his soldiers have the worst and oldest wheat that could be gotten: then if they did complain of it, he told them, they must be contented, seeing they ate at another man's cost. And he would serve them also at the table in treen and earthen dishes, saying, that Caesar had away all their gold and silver, for a debt that the king's father (that then reigned) did owe unto him: which was, a thousand seven hundred and fifty myriads, whereof Caesar had before forgiven seven hundred and fifty thousand unto his children. Howbeit then he asked a million to pay his soldiers withal. Thereto Pothinus answered him, that at that time he should do better to follow his other causes of greater importance, and afterwards that he should at more leisure recover his debt, with the king's goodwill and favour. Caesar replied unto him, and said, that he would not ask counsel of the Egyptians for his affairs, but would be paid: and thereupon secretly sent for Cleopatra which was in the country to come unto him.

49    She only taking Apollodorus Sicilian of all her friends, took a little boat, and went away with him in it in the night, and came and landed hard by the foot of the castle. Then having no other mean to come in to the court, without being known, she laid herself down upon a mattress or flockbed, which Apollodorus her friend tied and bound up together like a bundle with a great leather thong, and so took her up on his back, and brought her thus hampered in this fardel unto Caesar, in at the castle gate. This was the first occasion (as it is reported) that made Caesar to love her: but afterwards, when he saw her sweet conversation and pleasant entertainment, he fell then in further liking with her, and did reconcile her again unto her brother the king, with condition, that they two jointly should reign together. Upon this new reconciliation, a great feast being prepared, a slave of Caesar's that was his barber, the fearfullest wretch that lived, still busily prying and listening abroad in every corner, being mistrustful by nature, found that Pothinus and Achillas did lie in wait to kill his master Caesar. This being proved unto Caesar, he did set such sure watch about the hall, where the feast was made, that in fine, he slew the eunuch Pothinus himself. Achillas on the other side, saved himself, and fled unto the king's camp, where he raised a marvellous dangerous and difficult war for Caesar: because he having then but a few men about him as he had, he was to fight against a great and strong city. The first danger he fell into, was for the lack of water he had: for that his enemies had stopped the mouth of the pipes, the which conveyed the water unto the castle. The second danger he had, was, that seeing his enemies came to take his ships from him, he was driven to repulse that danger with fire, the which burnt the arsenal where the ships lay, and that notable library of Alexandria withal. The third danger was in the battle by sea, that was fought by the tower of Phar: where meaning to help his men that fought by sea, he leapt from the pier, into a boat. Then the Egyptians made towards him with their oars, on every side: but he leaping into the sea, with great hazard saved himself by swimming. It is said, that then holding divers books in his hand, he did never let them go, but kept them always upon his head above water, and swam with the other hand, notwithstanding that they shot marvellously at him, and was driven sometime to duck into the water: howbeit the boat was drowned presently. In fine, the king coming to his men that made war with Caesar, he

went against him, and gave him battle, and won it with great slaughter, and effusion of blood. But for the king, no man could ever tell what became of him after. Thereupon Caesar made Cleopatra his sister, queen of Egypt, who being great with child by him, was shortly brought to bed of a son, whom the Alexandrians named Caesarion.

50 From thence he went into Syria, and so going into Asia, there it was told him that Domitius was overthrown in battle by Pharnaces, the son of King Mithridates, and was fled out of the realm of Ponte, with a few men with him: and that this King Pharnaces greedily following his victory, was not contented with the winning of Bithynia and Cappadocia, but further would needs attempt to win Armenia the Less, procuring all those kings, princes, and governors of the provinces thereabouts, to rebel against the Romans. Thereupon Caesar went thither straight with three legions, and fought a great battle with King Pharnaces, by the city of Zela, where he slew his army, and drove him out of all the realm of Ponte. And because he would advertise one of his friends of the suddenness of this victory, he only wrote three words unto Anitius at Rome: *Veni, Vidi, Vici*: to wit, I came, I saw, I overcame. These three words ending all with like sound and letters in the Latin, have a certain short grace, more pleasant to the ear, than can be well expressed in any other tongue.

51 After this, he returned again into Italy, and came to Rome, ending his year for the which he was made dictator the second time, which office before was never granted for one whole year, but unto him. Then he was chosen consul for the year following. Afterwards he was very ill spoken of, for that his soldiers in a mutiny having slain two praetors, Cosconius and Galba, he gave them no other punishment for it, but instead of calling them soldiers, he named them citizens, and gave unto every one of them a thousand drachmas a man, and great possessions in Italy. He was much misliked also for the desperate parts and madness of Dolabella, for the covetousness of Anitius, for the drunkenness of Antonius and Cornificius, which made Pompey's house be pulled down and builded up again, as a thing not big enough for him, wherewith the Romans were marvellously offended. Caesar knew all this well enough, and would have been contented to have

redressed them: but to bring his matters to pass, he pretended he was driven to serve his turn by such instruments.

52   After the battle of Pharsalia, Cato and Scipio being fled into Africa, King Iuba joined them, and levied a great puissant army. Wherefore Caesar determined to make war with them, and in the midst of winter, he took his journey into Sicily. There, because he would take all hope from his captains and soldiers to make any long abode there, he went and lodged upon the very sands by the sea side, and with the next gale of wind that came, he took the sea with three thousand footmen, and a few horsemen. Then having put them a-land, unawares to them he hoist sail again, to go fetch the rest of his army, being afraid lest they should meet with some danger in passing over: and meeting them mid way, he brought them all into his camp. Where, when it was told him that his enemies trusted in an ancient oracle, which said, that it was predestined unto the family of the Scipios to be conquerors in Africa: either of purpose to mock Scipio the general of his enemies, or otherwise in good earnest to take the benefit of this name (given by the oracle) unto himself, in all the skirmishes and battles he fought, he gave the charge of his army unto a man of mean quality and account, called Scipio Sallutius, who came of the race of Scipio African, and made him always his general when he fought. For he was eftsoons compelled to weary and harry his enemies: for that neither his men in his camp had corn enough, nor his beasts forage, but the soldiers were driven to take sea weeds, called *alga*, and (washing away the brackishness thereof with fresh water, putting to it a little herb called dog's tooth) to cast it so to their horse to eat. For the Numidians (which are light horsemen, and very ready of service) being a great number together, would be on a sudden in every place, and spread all the fields over thereabout, so that no man durst peep out of the camp to go for forage. And one day as the men of arms were staying to behold an African doing notable things in dancing, and playing with the flute, they being set down quietly to take their pleasure of the view thereof, having in the meantime given their slaves their horses to hold, the enemies stealing suddenly upon them, compassed them in round about, and slew a number of them in the field, and chasing the other also that fled, followed them pell mell into their camp. Furthermore had not Caesar himself

in person, and Asinius Pollio with him, gone out of the camp to the rescue, and stayed them that fled, the war that day had been ended. There was also another skirmish where his enemies had the upper hand, in the which it is reported, that Caesar taking the ensign bearer by the collar that carried the eagle in his hand, stayed him by force, and turning his face, told him: 'See, there be thy enemies.'

53   These advantages did lift up Scipio's heart aloft, and gave him courage to hazard battle: and leaving Afranius on the one hand of him, and King Iuba on the other hand, both their camps lying near to other, he did fortify himself by the city of Thapsacus, above the lake, to be a safe refuge for them all in this battle. But whilst he was busy entrenching of himself, Caesar having marvellous speedily passed through a great country full of wood, by bypaths which men would never have mistrusted, he stole upon some behind, and suddenly assailed the other before, so that he overthrew them all, and made them fly. Then following this first good hap he had, he went forthwith to set upon the camp of Afranius, the which he took at the first onset, and the camp of the Numidians also, King Iuba being fled. Thus in a little piece of the day only, he took three camps, and slew fifty thousand of his enemies, and lost but fifty of his soldiers. In this sort is set down the effect of this battle by some writers. Yet others do write also, that Caesar self was not there in person at the execution of this battle. For as he did set his men in battle ray, the falling sickness took him, whereunto he was given, and therefore feeling it coming, before he was overcome withal, he was carried into a castle not far from thence, where the battle was fought, and there took his rest till the extremity of his disease had left him.

54   Now, for the praetors and consuls that escaped from this battle, many of them being taken prisoners, did kill themselves, and others also Caesar did put to death: but he being specially desirous of all men else to have Cato alive in his hands, he went with all possible speed unto the city of Utica, whereof Cato was governor, by means whereof he was not at the battle. Notwithstanding being certified by the way that Cato had slain himself with his own hands, he then made open show that he was very sorry for it, but why or wherefore, no man could tell. But this is true, that Caesar said at that present time: 'O Cato, I envy thy death, because thou

diddest envy my glory, to save thy life.' This notwithstanding, the book that he wrote afterwards against Cato being dead, did show no great affection nor pitiful heart towards him. For how could he have pardoned him, if living he had had him in his hands, that being dead did speak so vehemently against him? Notwithstanding, men suppose he would have pardoned him, if living he had taken him alive, by the clemency he showed unto Cicero, Brutus, and divers others that had borne arms against him. Some report, that he wrote that book, not so much for any private malice he had to his death, as for a civil ambition, upon this occasion. Cicero had written a book in praise of Cato, which he intituled, *Cato*. This book in likelihood was very well liked of, by reason of the eloquence of the orator that made it, and of the excellent subject thereof. Caesar therewith was marvellously offended, thinking that to praise him, of whose death he was author, was even as much as to accuse himself: and therefore he wrote a letter against him, and heaped up a number of accusations against Cato, and entitled the book *Anticaton*. Both these books have favourers unto this day, some defending the one for the love they bore to Caesar, and others allowing the other for Cato's sake.

55   Caesar being now returned out of Afric, first of all made an oration to the people, wherein he greatly praised and commended this his last victory, declaring unto them, that he had conquered so many countries unto the empire of Rome, that he could furnish the commonwealth yearly with two hundred thousand bushels of wheat, and twenty hundred thousand pound weight of oil. Then he made three triumphs, the one for Egypt, the other for the kingdom of Ponte, and the third for Afric: not because he had overcome Scipio there, but King Iuba. Whose son being likewise called Iuba, being then a young boy, was led captive in the show of this triumph. But this his imprisonment fell out happily for him: for where he was but a barbarous Numidian, by the study he fell unto when he was prisoner, he came afterwards to be reckoned one of the wisest historiographers of the Grecians. After these three triumphs ended, he very liberally rewarded his soldiers, and to curry favour with the people, he made great feasts and common sports. For he feasted all the Romans at one time, at two and twenty thousand tables, and gave them the pleasure to see divers sword

players to fight at the sharp, and battles also by sea, for the remembrance of his daughter Julia, which was dead long afore. Then after all these sports, he made the people (as the manner was) to be mustered: and where there were at the last musters before, three hundred and twenty thousand citizens, at this muster only there were but a hundred and fifty thousand. Such misery and destruction had this civil war brought unto the commonwealth of Rome, and had consumed such a number of Romans, not speaking at all of the mischiefs and calamities it had brought unto all the rest of Italy, and to the other provinces pertaining to Rome.

56 After all these things were ended, he was chosen consul the fourth time, and went into Spain to make war with the sons of Pompey: who were yet but very young, but had notwithstanding raised a marvellous great army together, and showed to have had manhood and courage worthy to command such an army, insomuch as they put Caesar himself in great danger of his life. The greatest battle that was fought between them in all this war, was by the city of Munda. For then Caesar seeing his men sorely distressed, and having their hands full of their enemies, he ran into the press among his men that fought, and cried out unto them: 'What, are ye not ashamed to be beaten and taken prisoners, yielding yourselves with your own hands to these young boys?' And so, with all the force he could make, having with much ado put his enemies to flight, he slew above thirty thousand of them in the field, and lost of his own men a thousand of the best he had. After this battle he went into his tent, and told his friends, that he had often before fought for victory, but this last time now, that he had fought for the safety of his own life. He won this battle on the very feast day of the Bacchanalians, in the which men say, that Pompey the Great went out of Rome, about four years before, to begin this civil war. For his sons, the younger escaped from the battle: but within few days after, Diddius brought the head of the elder. This was the last war that Caesar made. But the triumph he made into Rome for the same, did as much offend the Romans, and more, than anything that ever he had done before: because he had not overcome captains that were strangers, nor barbarous kings, but had destroyed the sons of the noblest man in Rome, whom fortune had overthrown. And because he had plucked up his race by the roots, men did not think it

meet for him to triumph so, for the calamities of his country, rejoicing at a thing for the which he had but one excuse to allege in his defence, unto the gods and men: that he was compelled to do that he did. And the rather they thought it not meet, because he had never before sent letters nor messengers unto the commonwealth at Rome, for any victory that he had ever won in all the civil wars: but did always for shame refuse the glory of it.

57   This notwithstanding, the Romans inclining to Caesar's prosperity, and taking the bit in the mouth, supposing that to be ruled by one man alone, it would be a good mean for them to take breath a little, after so many troubles and miseries as they had abidden in these civil wars, they chose him perpetual dictator. This was a plain tyranny: for to this absolute power of dictator, they added this, never to be afraid to be deposed. Cicero propounded before the senate, that they should give him such honours, as were meet for a man: howbeit others afterwards added too, honours beyond all reason. For, men striving who should most honour him, they made him hateful and troublesome to themselves that most favoured him, by reason of the immeasurable greatness and honours which they gave him. Thereupon, it is reported, that even they that most hated him, were no less favourers and furtherers of his honours, than they that most flattered him, because they might have greater occasions to rise, and that it might appear they had just cause and colour to attempt that they did against him. And now for himself, after he had ended his civil wars, he did so honourably behave himself, that there was no fault to be found in him: and therefore methinks, amongst other honours they gave him, he rightly deserved this, that they should build him a temple of clemency, to thank him for his courtesy he had used unto them in his victory. For he pardoned many of them that had borne arms against him, and furthermore, did prefer some of them to honour and office in the commonwealth: as amongst others, Cassius and Brutus, both the which were made praetors. And where Pompey's images had been thrown down, he caused them to be set up again: whereupon Cicero said then, that Caesar setting up Pompey's images again, he made his own to stand the surer. And when some of his friends did counsel him to have a guard for the safety of his person, and some also did offer themselves to serve him, he would

never consent to it, but said, it was better to die once, than always to be afraid of death. But to win himself the love and goodwill of the people, as the honourablest guard and best safety he could have, he made common feasts again, and general distributions of corn. Furthermore, to gratify the soldiers also, he replenished many cities again with inhabitants, which before had been destroyed, and placed them there that had no place to repair unto: of the which the noblest and chiefest cities were these two, Carthage and Corinth; and it chanced so, that like as aforetime they had been both taken and destroyed together, even so were they both set afoot again, and replenished with people, at one self time.

58    And as for great personages, he won them also, promising some of them, to make them praetors and consuls in time to come, and unto others, honours and preferments, but to all men generally good hope, seeking all the ways he could to make every man contented with his reign. Insomuch as one of the consuls called Maximus, chancing to die a day before his consulship ended, he declared Caninius Rebilius consul only for the day that remained. So, divers going to his house (as the manner was) to salute him, and to congratulate with him of his calling and preferment, being newly chosen officer, Cicero pleasantly said, 'Come, let us make haste, and be gone thither, before his consulship come out.' Furthermore, Caesar being borne to attempt all great enterprises, and having an ambitious desire besides to covet great honours, the prosperous good success he had of his former conquests bred no desire in him quietly to enjoy the fruits of his labours, but rather gave him hope of things to come, still kindling more and more in him, thoughts of greater enterprises, and desire of new glory, as if that which he had present, were stale and nothing worth. This humour of his was no other but an emulation with himself as with another man, and a certain contention to overcome the things he prepared to attempt. For he was determined, and made preparation also, to make war with the Persians. Then when he had overcome them, to pass through Hyrcania (compassing in the sea Caspium, and Mount Caucasus) into the realm of Pontus, and so to invade Scythia: and overrunning all the countries and people adjoining unto high Germany, and Germany itself, at length to return by Gaul into Italy, and so to enlarge the Roman Empire round, that it

might be every way compassed in with the great sea Oceanum. But whilst he was preparing for this voyage, he attempted to cut the bar of the strait of Peloponnesus, in the place where the city of Corinth standeth. Then he was minded to bring the rivers of Anienes and Tiber, straight from Rome unto the city of Circees, with a deep channel and high banks cast up on either side, and so to fall into the sea at Terracina, for the better safety and commodity of the merchants that came to Rome to traffic there. Furthermore, he determined to drain and sow all the water of the marshes betwixt the cities of Nomentum and Setium, to make it firm land, for the benefit of many thousands of people: and on the sea coast next unto Rome, to cast great high banks, and to cleanse all the haven about Ostia of rocks and stones hidden under the water, and to take away all other impediments that made the harbour dangerous for ships, and to make new havens and arsenals meet to harbour such ships, as did continually traffic thither. All these things were purposed to be done, but took no effect.

59    But the ordinance of the calendar, and reformation of the year, to take away all confusion of time, being exactly calculated by the mathematicians, and brought to perfection, was a great commodity unto all men. For the Romans using then the ancient computation of the year, had not only such incertainty and alteration of the month and times, that the sacrifices and yearly feasts came by little and little to seasons contrary for the purpose they were ordained: but also in the revolution of the sun (which is called Annus Solaris) no other nation agreed with them in account: and of the Romans themselves, only the priests understood it. And therefore when they listed, they suddenly (no man being able to control them) did thrust in a month, above their ordinary number, which they called in old time, Mercedonius. Some say, that Numa Pompilius was the first that devised this way, to put a month between: but it was a weak remedy, and did little help the correction of the errors that were made in the account of the year, to frame them to perfection. But Caesar committing this matter unto the philosophers, and best expert mathematicians at that time, did set forth an excellent and perfect calendar, more exactly calculated than any other that was before: the which the Romans do use until this present day, and do nothing err as others, in the difference of time. But his enemies

notwithstanding that envied his greatness, did not stick to find fault withal. As Cicero the orator, when one said, 'Tomorrow the star Lyra will rise' 'Yea,' said he,' at the commandment of Caesar,' as if men were compelled so to say and think, by Caesar's edict.

60  But the chiefest cause that made him mortally hated, was the covetous desire he had to be called king: which first gave the people just cause, and next his secret enemies honest colour, to bear him ill will. This notwithstanding, they that procured him this honour and dignity, gave it out among the people, that it was written in the Sibylline prophecies, how the Romans might overcome the Parthians, if they made war with them and were led by a king, but otherwise that they were unconquerable. And furthermore they were so bold besides, that Caesar returning to Rome from the city of Alba, when they came to salute him, they called him king. But the people being offended, and Caesar also angry, he said he was not called king, but Caesar. Then every man keeping silence, he went his way heavy and sorrowful. When they had decreed divers honours for him in the senate, the consuls and praetors accompanied with the whole assembly of the senate, went unto him in the market-place, where he was set by the pulpit for orations, to tell him what honours they had decreed for him in his absence. But he sitting still in his majesty, disdaining to rise up unto them when they came in, as if they had been private men, answered them, that his honours had more need to be cut off, than enlarged. This did not only offend the senate, but the common people also, to see that he should so lightly esteem of the magistrates of the commonwealth: insomuch as every man that might lawfully go his way, departed thence very sorrowfully. Thereupon also Caesar rising, departed home to his house, and tearing open his doublet collar, making his neck bare, he cried out aloud to his friends, that his throat was ready to offer to any man that would come and cut it. Notwithstanding, it is reported, that afterwards to excuse this folly, he imputed it to his disease, saying, that their wits are not perfect which have his disease of the falling evil, when standing of their feet they speak to the common people, but are soon troubled with a trembling of their body, and a sudden dimness and giddiness. But that was not true. For he would have risen up to the senate, but Cornelius Balbus one of his friends (but

rather a flatterer) would not let him, saying: 'What, do you not
remember that you are Caesar, and will you not let them reverence
you, and do their duties?'

61    Besides these occasions and offences, there followed also his
shame and reproach, abusing the tribunes of the people in this sort.
At that time, the feast Lupercalia was celebrated, the which in old
time men say was the feast of shepherds or herdmen, and is much
like unto the feast of the Lycaeians in Arcadia. But howsoever it is,
that day there are divers noblemen's sons, young men (and some of
them magistrates themselves that govern then) which run naked
through the city, striking in sport them they meet in their way, with
leather thongs, hair and all on, to make them give place. And many
noblewomen, and gentlewomen also, go of purpose to stand in
their way, and do put forth their hands to be stricken, as scholars
hold them out to their schoolmaster, to be stricken with the ferula:
persuading themselves that being with child, they shall have good
delivery, and also being barren, that it will make them to conceive
with child. Caesar sat to behold that sport upon the pulpit for
orations, in a chair of gold, apparelled in triumphing manner.
Antonius, who was consul at that time, was one of them that ran
this holy course. So when he came into the market-place, the
people made a lane for him to run at liberty, and he came to Caesar,
and presented him a diadem wreathed about with laurel. Whereupon there rose a certain cry of rejoicing, not very great, done only
by a few, appointed for the purpose. But when Caesar refused the
diadem, then all the people together made an outcry of joy. Then
Antonius offering it him again, there was a second shout of joy, but
yet of a few. But when Caesar refused it again the second time, then
all the whole people shouted. Caesar having made this proof, found
that the people did not like of it, and thereupon rose out of his
chair, and commanded the crown to be carried unto Jupiter in the
Capitol. After that, there were set up images of Caesar in the city
with diadems upon their heads, like kings. Those, the two tribunes,
Flavius and Marullus, went and pulled down: and furthermore,
meeting with them that first saluted Caesar as king, they committed
them to prison. The people followed them rejoicing at it, and called
them Brutes: because of Brutus, who had in old time driven the
kings out of Rome, and that brought the kingdom of one person,

unto the government of the senate and people. Caesar was so offended withal, that he deprived Marullus and Flavius of their tribuneships, and accusing them, he spoke also against the people, and called them Bruti and Cumani, to wit, beasts and fools.

62 Hereupon the people went straight unto Marcus Brutus, who from his father came of the first Brutus, and by his mother of the house of the Servilians, a noble house as any was in Rome, and was also nephew and son-in-law of Marcus Cato. Notwithstanding, the great honours and favour Caesar showed unto him, kept him back that of himself alone, he did not conspire nor consent to depose him of his kingdom. For Caesar did not only save his life, after the battle of Pharsalia when Pompey fled, and did at his request also save many more of his friends besides, but furthermore, he put a marvellous confidence in him. For he had already preferred him to the praetorship for that year, and furthermore was appointed to be consul, the fourth year after that, having through Caesar's friendship obtained it before Cassius, who likewise made suit for the same: and Caesar also, as it is reported, said in this contention, 'Indeed Cassius hath alleged best reason, but yet shall he not be chosen before Brutus.' Some one day accusing Brutus while he practised this conspiracy, Caesar would not hear of it, but clapping his hand on his body, told them, 'Brutus will look for this skin:' meaning thereby, that Brutus for his virtue, deserved to rule after him, but yet, that for ambition's sake, he would not show himself unthankful nor dishonourable. Now they that desired change, and wished Brutus only their prince and governor above all other, they durst not come to him themselves to tell him what they would have him to do, but in the night did cast sundry papers into the praetor's seat where he gave audience, and the most of them to this effect: 'Thou sleepest, Brutus, and art not Brutus indeed.' Cassius finding Brutus' ambition stirred up the more by these seditious bills, did prick him forward, and egg him on the more, for a private quarrel he had conceived against Caesar: the circumstance whereof, we have set down more at large in Brutus' life. Caesar also had Cassius in great jealousy, and suspected him much: whereupon he said on a time to his friends, 'What will Cassius do, think ye? I like not his pale looks.' Another time when Caesar's friends complained unto him of Antonius and Dolabella,

that they pretended some mischief towards him, he answered them again, 'As for those fat men and smooth combed heads,' quoth he, 'I never reckon of them: but these pale-visaged and carrion lean people, I fear them most,' meaning Brutus and Cassius.

63    Certainly, destiny may easier be foreseen, than avoided, considering the strange and wonderful signs that were said to be seen before Caesar's death. For, touching the fires in the element, and spirits running up and down in the night, and also these solitary birds to be seen at noondays sitting in the great market-place, are not all these signs perhaps worth the noting, in such a wonderful chance as happened? But Strabo the philosopher writeth, that divers men were seen going up and down in fire: and furthermore, that there was a slave of the soldiers, that did cast a marvellous burning flame out of his hand, insomuch as they that saw it, thought he had been burnt, but when the fire was out, it was found he had no hurt. Caesar self also doing sacrifice unto the gods, found that one of the beasts which was sacrificed had no heart: and that was a strange thing in nature, how a beast could live without a heart. Furthermore, there was a certain soothsayer that had given Caesar warning long time before, to take heed of the day of the Ides of March (which is the fifteenth of the month), for on that day he should be in great danger. That day being come, Caesar going unto the senate house, and speaking merrily to the soothsayer, told him, 'The Ides of March be come:' 'So be they,' softly answered the soothsayer, 'but yet are they not past.' And the very day before, Caesar supping with Marcus Lepidus, sealed certain letters as he was wont to do at the board: so talk falling out amongst them, reasoning what death was best, he preventing their opinions, cried out aloud, 'Death unlooked for.' Then going to bed the same night as his manner was, and lying with his wife Calpurnia, all the windows and doors of his chamber flying open, the noise awoke him, and made him afraid when he saw such light: but more, when he heard his wife Calpurnia, being fast asleep, weep and sigh, and put forth many fumbling lamentable speeches. For she dreamed that Caesar was slain, and that she had him in her arms. Others also do deny that she had any such dream, as amongst other, Titus Livius writeth, that it was in this sort. The senate having set upon the top of Caesar's house, for an ornament and setting forth of the same, a certain

pinnacle, Calpurnia dreamed that she saw it broken down, and that she thought she lamented and wept for it. Insomuch that Caesar rising in the morning, she prayed him if it were possible, not to go out of the doors that day, but to adjourn the session of the senate, until another day. And if that he made no reckoning of her dream, yet that he would search further of the soothsayers by their sacrifices, to know what should happen him that day. Thereby it seemed that Caesar likewise did fear and suspect somewhat, because his wife Calpurnia until that time, was never given to any fear or superstition: and then, for that he saw her so troubled in mind with this dream she had. But much more afterwards, when the soothsayers having sacrificed many beasts one after another, told him that none did like them, then he determined to send Antonius to adjourn the session of the senate.

64 But in the meantime came Decius Brutus, surnamed Albinus, in whom Caesar put such confidence, that in his last will and testament he had appointed him to be his next heir, and yet was of the conspiracy with Cassius and Brutus: he fearing that if Caesar did adjourn the session that day, the conspiracy would out, laughed the soothsayers to scorn, and reproved Caesar, saying, that he gave the senate occasion to mislike with him, and that they might think he mocked them, considering that by his commandment they were assembled, and that they were ready willingly to grant him all things, and to proclaim him king of all the provinces of the empire of Rome out of Italy, and that he should wear his diadem in all other places, both by sea and land. And furthermore, that if any man should tell them from him, they should depart for that present time, and return again when Calpurnia should have better dreams, what would his enemies and ill willers say, and how could they like of his friends' words? And who could persuade them otherwise, but that they would think his dominion a slavery unto them, and tyrannical in himself? 'And yet if it be so,' said he, 'that you utterly mislike of this day, it is better that you go yourself in person, and saluting the senate, to dismiss them till another time.' Therewithal he took Caesar by the hand, and brought him out of his house. Caesar was not gone far from his house, but a bondman, a stranger, did what he could to speak with him: and when he saw he was put back by the great press and multitude of people that followed him,

he went straight unto his house and put himself into Calpurnia's hands to be kept till Caesar came back again, telling her that he had great matters to impart unto him.

65 And one Artemidorus also born in the Isle of Gnidos, a Doctor of Rhetoric in the Greek tongue, who by means of his profession was very familiar with certain of Brutus' confederates, and therefore knew the most part of all their practices against Caesar, came and brought him a little bill written with his own hand, of all that he meant to tell him. He marking how Caesar received all the supplications that were offered him, and that he gave them straight to his men that were about him, pressed near to him, and said: 'Caesar, read this memorial to yourself, and that quickly, for they be matters of great weight and touch you nearly.' Caesar took it of him, but could never read it, though he many times attempted it, for the number of people that did salute him: but holding it still in his hand, keeping it to himself, went on withal into the senate house. Howbeit other are of opinion, that it was some man else that gave him that memorial, and not Artemidorus, who did what he could all the way as he went to give it Caesar, but he was always repulsed by the people.

66 For these things, they may seem to come by chance: but the place where the murder was prepared, and where the senate were assembled, and where also there stood up an image of Pompey dedicated by himself amongst other ornaments which he gave unto the theatre, all these were manifest proofs that it was the ordinance of some god, that made this treason to be executed, specially in that very place. It is also reported, that Cassius (though otherwise he did favour the doctrine of Epicurus) beholding the image of Pompey, before they entered into the action of their traitorous enterprise, he did softly call upon it, to aid him. But the instant danger of the present time, taking away his former reason, did suddenly put him into a furious passion, and made him like a man half besides himself. Now Antonius, that was a faithful friend to Caesar, and a valiant man besides of his hands, him Decius Brutus Albinus entertained out of the senate house, having begun a long tale of set purpose. So Caesar coming into the house, all the senate stood up on their feet to do him honour. Then part of Brutus' company and confederates stood round about Caesar's chair, and part of them

also came towards him, as though they made suit with Metellus Cimber, to call home his brother again from banishment: and thus prosecuting still their suit, they followed Caesar, till he was set in his chair. Who, denying their petitions, and being offended with them one after another, because the more they were denied, the more they pressed upon him, and were the earnester with him, Metellus at length, taking his gown with both his hands, pulled it over his neck, which was the sign given the confederates to set upon him. Then Casca behind him struck him in the neck with his sword, howbeit the wound was not great nor mortal, because it seemed, the fear of such a devilish attempt did amaze him, and take his strength from him, that he killed him not at the first blow. But Caesar turning straight unto him, caught hold of his sword, and held it hard: and they both cried out, Caesar in Latin: 'O vile traitor Casca, what doest thou?' And Casca in Greek to his brother, 'Brother, help me.' At the beginning of this stir, they that were present, not knowing of the conspiracy, were so amazed with the horrible sight they saw that they had no power to flee, neither to help him, not so much as once to make any outcry. They on the other side that had conspired his death, compassed him in on every side with their swords drawn in their hands, that Caesar turned him nowhere but he was stricken at by some, and still had naked swords in his face, and was hacked and mangled among them, as a wild beast taken of hunters. For it was agreed among them, that every man should give him a wound, because all their parts should be in this murder: and then Brutus himself gave him one wound about his privities. Men report also, that Caesar did still defend himself against the rest, running every way with his body: but when he saw Brutus with his sword drawn in his hand, then he pulled his gown over his head, and made no more resistance, and was driven either casually, or purposedly, by the counsel of the conspirators, against the base whereupon Pompey's image stood, which ran all of a gore blood, till he was slain. Thus it seemed, that the image took just revenge of Pompey's enemy, being thrown down on the ground at his feet, and yielding up his ghost there, for the number of wounds he had upon him. For it is reported, that he had three and twenty wounds upon his body: and divers of the conspirators did hurt themselves, striking one body with so many blows.

67    When Caesar was slain, the senate (though Brutus stood in the midst amongst them as though he would have said somewhat touching this fact) presently ran out of the house, and flying, filled all the city with marvellous fear and tumult. Insomuch as some did shut to their doors, others forsook their shops and warehouses, and others ran to the place to see what the matter was: and others also that had seen it, ran home to their houses again. But Antonius and Lepidus, which were two of Caesar's chiefest friends, secretly conveying themselves away, fled into other men's houses, and forsook their own. Brutus and his confederates on the other side, being yet hot with this murder they had committed, having their swords drawn in their hands, came all in a troop together out of the senate, and went into the market-place, not as men that made countenance to fly, but otherwise boldly holding up their heads like men of courage, and called to the people to defend their liberty, and stayed to speak with every great personage whom they met in their way. Of them, some followed this troop, and went amongst them, as if they had been of the conspiracy, and falsely challenged part of the honour with them: among them was Caius Octavius, and Lentulus Spinther. But both of them were afterwards put to death, for their vain covetousness of honour, by Antonius and Octavius Caesar the younger: and yet had no part of that honour for the which they were put to death, neither did any man believe that they were any of the confederates, or of counsel with them. For they that did put them to death, took revenge rather of the will they had to offend, than of any fact they had committed. The next morning, Brutus and his confederates came into the market-place to speak unto the people, who gave them such audience, that it seemed they neither greatly reproved, nor allowed the fact: for by their great silence they showed, that they were sorry for Caesar's death, and also that they did reverence Brutus. Now the senate granted general pardon for all that was past, and to pacify every man, ordained besides, that Caesar's funerals should be honoured as a god, and established all things that he had done: and gave certain provinces also, and convenient honours unto Brutus and his confederates, whereby every man thought all things were brought to good peace and quietness again.

68    But when they had opened Caesar's testament, and found a liberal legacy of money, bequeathed unto every citizen of Rome,

and that they saw his body (which was brought into the market-place) all bemangled with gashes of swords, then there was no order to keep the multitude and common people quiet, but they plucked up forms, tables, and stools, and laid them all about the body, and setting them afire, burnt the corse. Then when the fire was well kindled, they took the firebrands, and went unto their houses that had slain Caesar, to set them afire. Other also ran up and down the city to see if they could meet with any of them, to cut them in pieces: howbeit they could meet with never a man of them, because they had locked themselves up safely in their houses. There was one of Caesar's friends called Cinna, that had a marvellous strange and terrible dream the night before. He dreamed that Caesar bade him to supper, and that he refused, and would not go: then that Caesar took him by the hand, and led him against his will. Now Cinna hearing at that time, that they burnt Caesar's body in the market-place, notwithstanding that he feared his dream, and had an ague on him besides, he went into the market-place to honour his funerals. When he came thither, one of mean sort asked what his name was? He was straight called by his name. The first man told it to another, and that other unto another, so that it ran straight through them all, that he was one of them that murdered Caesar (for indeed one of the traitors to Caesar, was also called Cinna as himself): wherefore taking him for Cinna the murderer, they fell upon him with such fury, that they presently dispatched him in the market-place. This stir and fury made Brutus and Cassius more afraid, than of all that was past, and therefore within few days after, they departed out of Rome: and touching their doings afterwards, and what calamity they suffered till their deaths, we have written it at large, in the life of Brutus.

69 Caesar died at six and fifty years of age; and Pompey also lived not passing four years more than he. So he reaped no other fruit of all his reign and dominion, which he had so vehemently desired all his life, and pursued with such extreme danger, but a vain name only, and a superficial glory, that procured him the envy and hatred of his country. But his great prosperity and good fortune that favoured him all his lifetime, did continue afterwards in the revenge of his death, pursuing the murderers both by sea and land, till they had not left a man more to be executed, of all them that were actors or counsellors in the conspiracy of his death. Furthermore, of all the

chances that happen unto men upon the earth, that which came to Cassius above all other is most to be wondered at. For he being overcome in battle at the journey of Philippes, slew himself with the same sword, with the which he struck Caesar. Again, of signs in the element, the great comet which seven nights together was seen very bright after Caesar's death, the eight night after was never seen more. Also the brightness of the sun was darkened, the which all that year through rose very pale, and shined not out, whereby it gave but small heat: therefore the air being very cloudy and dark, by the weakness of the heat that could not come forth, did cause the earth to bring forth but raw and unripe fruit, which rotted before it could ripe. But above all, the ghost that appeared unto Brutus showed plainly, that the gods were offended with the murder of Caesar. The vision was thus: Brutus being ready to pass over his army from the city of Abydos to the other coast lying directly against it, slept every night (as his manner was) in his tent, and being yet awake, thinking of his affairs (for by report he was as careful a captain, and lived with as little sleep, as ever man did), he thought he heard a noise at his tent door, and looking towards the light of the lamp that waxed very dim, he saw a horrible vision of a man, of a wonderful greatness and dreadful look, which at the first made him marvellously afraid. But when he saw that it did him no hurt, but stood by his bedside, and said nothing, at length he asked him what he was. The image answered him: 'I am thy ill angel, Brutus, and thou shalt see me by the city of Philippes.' Then Brutus replied again, and said: 'Well, I shall see thee then.' Therewithal, the spirit presently vanished from him. After that time Brutus being in battle near unto the city of Philippes, against Antonius and Octavius Caesar, at the first battle he won the victory, and overthrowing all them that withstood him, he drove them into young Caesar's camp, which he took. The second battle being at hand, this spirit appeared again unto him, but spoke never a word. Thereupon Brutus knowing he should die, did put himself to all hazard in battle, but yet fighting could not be slain. So seeing his men put to flight and overthrown, he ran unto a little rock not far off, and there setting his sword's point to his breast, fell upon it, and slew himself, but yet as it is reported, with the help of his friend, that dispatched him.

## THE END OF CAESAR'S LIFE

# DEMOSTHENES
## CICERO

# Life of Demosthenes

He that made the little book of the praise of Alcibiades, touching the victory he won at the horse race of the Olympian games (were it the poet Euripides as some think, or any other), my friend Sossius, said, that to make a man happy, he must of necessity be born in some famous city. But to tell you what I think hereof, doubtless, true happiness chiefly consisteth in the virtue and qualities of the mind, being a matter of no moment, whether a man be born in a pelting village, or in a famous city: no more than it is for one to be born of a fair or foul mother. For it were a madness to think that the little village of Iulide, being the least part of the Isle of Ceo (the whole island of itself being but a small thing) and that the Isle of Aegina (which is of so small a length, that a certain Athenian on a time made a motion it might be taken away, because it was but as a straw in the sight of the haven of Piraea) could bring forth famous poets, and excellent comediants, and not breed an honest, just, and wise man, and of noble courage. For, as we have reason to think that arts and sciences which were first devised and invented to make some things necessary for men's use, or otherwise to win fame and credit, are drowned and cast away in little poor villages, so are we to judge also, that virtue, like a strong and fruitful plant, can take root, and bring forth in every place, where it is graffed in a good nature, and gentle person, that can patiently away with pains. And therefore if we chance to offend, and live not as we should, we cannot accuse the meanness of our country where we were born, but we must justly accuse ourselves.

2   Surely he that hath taken upon him to put forth any work, or to write any history, into the which he is to thrust many strange things unknown to his country, and which are not ready at his hand to be had, but dispersed abroad in divers places, and are to be gathered out of divers books and authorities: first of all, he must needs remain in some great and famous city thoroughly inhabited,

where men do delight in good and virtuous things, because there are commonly plenty of all sorts of books: and that perusing them, and hearing talk also of many things besides, which other historiographers peradventure have not written of, and which will carry so much more credit, because men that are alive may presently speak of them as of their own knowledge, whereby he may make his work perfect in every point, having many and divers necessary things contained in it. But I myself that dwell in a poor little town, and yet do remain there willingly lest it should become less, whilst I was in Italy, and at Rome, I had no leisure to study and exercise the Latin tongue, as well for the great business I had then to do, as also to satisfy them that came to learn philosophy of me: so that even somewhat too late, and now in my latter time, I began to take my Latin books in my hand. And thereby, a strange thing to tell you, but yet true: I learned not, nor understood matters so much by the words, as I came to understand the words, by common experience and knowledge I had in things. But furthermore, to know how to pronounce the Latin tongue well, or to speak it readily, or to understand the signification, translations, and fine joining of the simple words one with another, which do beautify and set forth the tongue, surely I judge it to be a marvellous pleasant and sweet thing, but withal it requireth a long and laboursome study, meet for those that have better leisure then I have, and that have young years on their backs to follow such pleasure.

3    Therefore, in this present book, which is the fifth of this work, where I have taken upon me to compare the lives of noblemen one with another: undertaking to write the lives of Demosthenes and Cicero, we will consider and examine their nature, manners and conditions, by their acts and deeds in the government of the commonwealth, not meaning otherwise to confer their works and writings of eloquence, neither to define which of them two was sharper or sweeter in his oration. For, as the poet Ion saith,

> In this behalf a man may rightly say,
> The dolphins in their proper soil do play.

The which Caecilius little understanding, being a man very rash in all his doings, hath unadvisedly written and set forth in print, a comparison of Demosthenes' eloquence, with Cicero's. But if it were an easy matter for every man to know himself, then the gods needed have given us no commandment, neither could men have said that it came from heaven. But for my opinion, methinks fortune even from the beginning hath framed in manner one self mould of Demosthenes and Cicero, and hath in their natures fashioned many of their qualities one like to the other: as, both of them to be ambitious, both of them to love the liberty of their country, and both of them very fearful in any danger of wars. And likewise their fortunes seem to me, to be both much alike. For it is hard to find two orators again, that being so meanly born as they, have come to be of so great power and authority as they two, nor that have deserved the ill will of kings and noblemen so much as they have done, nor that have lost their daughters, nor that have been banished their countries, and that have been restored again with honour, and that again have fled, and have been taken again, nor that have ended their lives with the liberty of their country. So that it is hard to be judged, whether nature have made them liker in manners, or fortune in their doings, as if they had both like cunning workmasters strived one with the other, to whom they should make them best resemble. But first of all we must write of the elder of them two.

4   Demosthenes the father of this orator Demosthenes, was as Theopompus writeth, one of the chief men of the city, and they called him Machaeropoeus, to wit, a maker of sword blades, because he had a great shop where he kept a number of slaves to forge them. But touching Aeschynes, the orators report of his mother, who said that she was the daughter of one Gelon (that fled from Athens being accused of treason) and of a barbarous woman that was her mother: I am not able to say whether it be true, or devised of malice to do him despite. Howsoever it was, it is true that his father died, leaving him seven year old, and left him reasonable well: for his goods came to little less than the value of fifteen talents. Howbeit his guardians did him great wrong: for they stole a great part of his goods themselves, and did let the rest run to naught, as having little care of it, for they would not pay his schoolmasters their wages. And this was the cause that he did not learn the liberal sciences which are usually taught unto honest men's sons: and to further that want also, he was but a weakling, and very tender, and therefore his mother would not much let him

go to school, neither his masters also durst keep him too hard to it, because he was but a sickly child at the first, and very weak. And it is reported also, that the surname of Battalus was given him in mockery by other schoolboys his companions, because of his weakness of body. This Battalus (as divers men do report) was an effeminate player on the flute, against whom the poet Antiphanes to mock him, devised a little play. Others also do write of one Battalus, a dissolute orator, and that wrote lascivious verses: and it seemeth that the Athenians at that time did call a certain part of man's body uncomely to be named, Battalus. Now for Argas (which surname men say was also given him) he was so called, either for his rude and beastly manners (because some poets do call a snake Argas) or else for his manner of speech, which was very unpleasant to the ear: for Argas is the name of a poet, that made always bawdy and ill-favoured songs. But hereof enough, as Plato said. ·

5   Furthermore, the occasion (as it is reported) that moved him to give himself to eloquence, was this. Calistratus the orator was to defend the cause of one Oropus before the judges, and every man longed greatly for this day of pleading, both for the excellence of the orator, that then bore the bell for eloquence, as for the matter, and his accusation, which was manifestly known to all. Demosthenes hearing his schoolmasters agree together to go to the hearing of this matter, he prayed his schoolmaster to be so good, as to let him go with him. His master granted him, and being acquainted with the keepers of the hall door where this matter was to be pleaded, he so entreated them, that they placed his scholar in a very good place, where being set at his ease, he might both see and hear all that was done, and no man could see him. Thereupon, when Demosthenes had heard the case pleaded, he was greatly in love with the honour which the orator had got, when he saw how he was waited upon home with such a train of people after him: but yet he wondered more at the force of his great eloquence, that could so turn and convey all things at his pleasure. Thereupon he left the study of all other sciences, and all other exercises of wit and body which other children are brought up in, and began to labour continually, and to frame himself to make orations, with intent one day to be an orator among the rest. His master that taught him rhetoric was Isaeus, notwithstanding that Isocrates also kept a

school of rhetoric at that time: either because that being an orphan he was not able to pay the wages that Isocrates demanded of his scholars, which was ten minas: or rather for that he found Isaeus' manner of speech more proper for the use of the eloquence he desired, because it was more finer, and subtler. Yet Hermippus writeth notwithstanding, that he had read certain books, having no name of any author, which declared that Demosthenes had been Plato's scholar, and that by hearing of him, he learned to frame his pronunciation and eloquence. And he writeth also of one Ctesibius, who reporteth that Demosthenes had secretly read Isocrates' works of rhetoric, and also Alcidamus' books, by means of one Callias Syracusan, and others.

6 Wherefore when he came out of his wardship, he began to put his guardians in suit, and to write orations and pleas against them: who in contrary manner did ever use delays and excuses, to save themselves from giving up any account unto him, of his goods and patrimony left him. And thus, following this exercise (as Thucydides writeth), it prospered so well with him, that in the end he obtained it, but not without great pains and danger: and yet with all that he could do, he could not recover all that his father left him, by a good deal. So having now gotten some boldness, and being used also to speak in open presence, and withal, having a feeling and delight of the estimation that is won by eloquence in pleading, afterwards he attempted to put forward himself, and to practise in matters of state. For, as there goes a tale of one Laomedon an Orchomenian, who having a grievous pain in the spleen, by advice of the physicians was willed to run long courses to help him, and that following their order, he became in the end so lusty and nimble of body, that afterwards he would needs make one to run for games, and indeed grew to be the swiftest runner of all men in his time: even so the like chanced unto Demosthenes. For at the first, beginning to practise oratory for recovery of his goods, and thereby having got good skill and knowledge how to plead, he afterwards took upon him to speak to the people in assemblies, touching the government of the commonwealth, even as if he should have contended for some game of price, and at length did excel all the orators at that time that got up into the pulpit for orations: notwithstanding that when he first ventured to

speak openly, the people made such a noise, that he could scant be heard, and besides they mocked him for his manner of speech that was so strange, because he used so many long confused periods, and his matter he spoke of was so intricate with arguments one upon another, that they were tedious, and made men weary to hear him. And furthermore, he had a very soft voice, an impediment in his tongue, and had also a short breath, the which made that men could not well understand what he meant, for his long periods in his oration were oftentimes interrupted, before he was at the end of his sentence. So that at length perceiving he was thus rejected, he gave over to speak any more before the people, and half in despair withdrew himself into the haven of Piraea. There Eunomus the Thessalian being a very old man, found him, and sharply reproved him, and told him that he did himself great wrong, considering, that having a manner of speech much like unto Pericles, he drowned himself by his faint heart, because he did not seek the way to be bold against the noise of the common people, and to arm his body to away with the pains and burden of public orations, but suffering it to grow feebler, for lack of use and practice.

7    Furthermore, being once again repulsed and whistled at, as he returned home, hanging down his head for shame, and utterly discouraged, Satyrus an excellent player of comedies, being his familiar friend, followed him, and went and spoke with him. Demosthenes made his complaint unto him, that where he had taken more pains than all the orators besides, and had almost even worn himself to the bones with study, yet he could by no means devise to please the people: whereas other orators that did nothing but bib all day long, and mariners that understood nothing, were quietly heard, and continually occupied the pulpit with orations: and on the other side that they made no account of him. Satyrus then answered him, 'Thou sayest true, Demosthenes, but care not for this. I will help it straight, and take away the cause of all this, so thou wilt but tell me without book certain verses of Euripides, or of Sophocles.' Thereupon Demosthenes presently rehearsed some unto him, that came into his mind. Satyrus repeating them after him, gave them quite another grace, with such a pronunciation, comely gesture, and modest countenance becoming the verses, that Demosthenes thought them clean changed. Whereby perceiving

how much the action (to wit, the comely manner and gesture in his oration) doth give grace and comeliness in his pleading, he then thought it but a trifle, and almost nothing to speak of, to exercise to plead well, unless therewithal he do also study to have a good pronunciation and gesture. Thereupon he built him a cellar under the ground, the which was whole even in my time, and he would daily go down into it, to fashion his gesture and pronunciation, and also to exercise his voice, and that with such earnest affection, that oftentimes he would be there two or three months one after another, and did shave his head of purpose, because he durst not go abroad in that sort, although his will was good.

8    And yet he took his theme and matter to declaim upon, and to practise to plead of the matters he had had in hand before, or else upon occasion of such talk as he had with them that came to see him, while he kept his house. For they were no sooner gone from him, but he went down into his cellar, and repeated from the first to the last all matters that had passed between him and his friends in talk together, and alleged also both his own and their answers. And if peradventure he had been at the hearing of any long matter, he would repeat it by himself: and would finely couch and convey it into proper sentences, and thus change and alter every way any matter that he had heard, or talked with others. Thereof came the opinion men had of him, that he had no very quick capacity by nature, and that his eloquence was not natural, but artificially got with extreme labour. And for proof hereof, they make this probable reason, that they never saw Demosthenes make any oration on the sudden, and that oftentimes when he was sat in the assembly, the people would call him by his name, to say his opinion touching the matter of counsel then in hand: howbeit that he never rose upon their call, unless he had first studied the matter well he would speak of. So that all the other orators would many times give him a taunt for it: as Pytheas among other, that taunting him on a time, told him, his reasons smelled of the lamp. 'Yea,' replied Demosthenes sharply again, 'so is there great difference, Pytheas, betwixt thy labour and mine by lamplight.' And himself also speaking to others, did not altogether deny it, but told them plainly, that he did not always write at length all that he would speak, neither did he also offer to speak, before he had made briefs of that he would speak. He

said furthermore, that it was a token the man loved the people well, that he would be careful before what he would say to them. 'For this preparative,' quoth he, 'doth show that he doth honour and reverence them. In contrary manner also, he that passeth not how the people take his words, it is a plain token that he despiseth their authority, and that he lacketh no goodwill (if he could) to use force against them, rather than reason and persuasion.' But yet further to enlarge the proofs, that Demosthenes had no heart to make any oration on the sudden, they do allege this reason: that Demades many times rose upon the sudden to maintain Demosthenes' reasons, when the people otherwhile did reject him: and that Demosthenes on the other side did never rise to make Demades' words good, which he had spoken in his behalf.

9   But now might a man ask again: if Demosthenes was so timorous to speak before the people upon the sudden, what meant Aeschines then to say, that he was marvellous bold in his words? And how chanceth it, that he rising upon the sudden, did presently answer the orator Python Byzantine in the field, that was very lusty in speech (and rough like a vehement running stream) against the Athenians? And how chanced it that Lamachus Myrrinaeian, having made an oration in the praise of Philip and Alexander, kings of Macedon, in the which he spoke all the ill he could of the Thebans, and of the Olynthians, and when he had read and pronounced it in the open assembly of the Olympian games, Demosthenes upon the instant rising up on his feet, declared, as if he had read some history, and pointed as it were with his finger unto all the whole assembly, the notable great service and worthy deeds the which the Chalcidians had done in former times, for the benefit and honour of Greece. And in contrary manner also, what mischief and inconvenience came by means of the flatterers, that altogether gave themselves to curry favour with the Macedonians. With these and suchlike persuasions, Demosthenes made such stir amongst the people, that the orator Lamachus being afraid of the sudden uproar, did secretly convey himself out of the assembly. But yet to tell you what I think, Demosthenes in my opinion fashioning himself even from the beginning, to follow Pericles' steps and example, he thought that for other qualities he had, they were not so requisite for him, and that he would counterfeit his gravity and

sober countenance, and to be wise, not to speak over lightly to
every matter at all adventures: judging, that by that manner of
wisdom he came to be great. And like as he would not let slip any
good occasion to speak, where it might be for his credit, so would
he not likewise over rashly hazard his credit and reputation to the
mercy of fortune. And to prove this true, the orations which he
made upon the sudden without premeditation before, do show
more boldness and courage, than those which he had written and
studied long before, if we may believe the reports of Eratosthenes,
Demetrius Phalerian, and of the other comical poets. For Eratosthenes said, that he would be often carried away with choler and
fury. Demetrius also saith, that speaking one day to the people, he
swore a great oath in rhyme, as if he had been possessed with some
divine spirit, and said,

> By sea and land, by rivers, springs, and ponds.

There are also certain comical poets that do call him Ropoper-
perethra, as who would say, a great babbler that speaketh all things
that cometh to his tongue's end. Another mocked him for too
much affecting a figure of rhetoric called *antitheton*: which is,
opposition, with saying, '*Sic recepit sicut cepit*,' (which signifieth, 'He
took it as he found it.') In the use of this figure Demosthenes much
pleased himself, unless the poet Antiphanes speaketh it of pleasure,
deriding the counsel he gave the people, not to take the Isle of
Halonesus of King Philip, as of gift, but to receive it as their own
restored.

10   And yet everybody did grant, that Demades of his own natural
wit, without art, was invincible: and that many times speaking upon
the sudden, he did utterly overthrow Demosthenes' long studied
reasons. And Aristo, of the Isle of Chio, hath written Theophrastus'
judgment of the orators of that time. Who being asked what
manner of orator he thought Demosthenes, he answered, 'Worthy
of this city.' Then again how he thought of Demades: 'Above this
city,' said he. The same philosopher writeth also, that Polyeuctus
Sphettian (one of those that practised at that time in the commonwealth) gave this sentence: that Demosthenes indeed was a great
orator, but Phocion's tongue had a sharper understanding, because
in few words he comprehended much matter. And to this purpose,
they say that Demosthenes himself said also, that as oft as he saw

Phocion get up into the pulpit for orations to speak against him, he was wont to say to his friends: 'See, the axe of my words rises.' And yet it is hard to judge, whether he spoke that in respect of his tongue, or rather for the estimation he had got, because of his great wisdom: thinking (as indeed it is true) that one word only, the twinkling of an eye, or a nod of his head of such a man (that through his worthiness is attained to that credit) hath more force to persuade, than all the fine reasons and devices of rhetoric.

11    But now for his bodily defects of nature, Demetrius Phalerian writeth, that he heard Demosthenes himself say, being very old, that he did help them by these means. First, touching the stammering of his tongue, which was very fat, and made him that he could not pronounce all syllables distinctly, he did help it by putting of little pebble stones into his mouth, which he found upon the sands by the river's side, and so pronounced with open mouth the orations he had without book. And for his small and soft voice, he made that louder, by running up steep and high hills, uttering even with full breath some orations or verses that he had without book. And further it is reported of him, that he had a great looking glass in his house, and ever standing on his feet before it, he would learn and exercise himself to pronounce his orations. For proof hereof it is reported, that there came a man unto him on a time, and prayed his help to defend his cause, and told him that one had beaten him: and that Demosthenes said again unto him, 'I do not believe this is true thou tellest me, for surely the other did never beat thee.' The plaintiff then thrusting out his voice aloud, said: 'What, hath he not beaten me?' 'Yes, indeed,' quoth Demosthenes then: 'I believe it now, for I hear the voice of a man that was beaten indeed.' Thus he thought, that the sound of the voice, the pronunciation or gesture in one sort or other, were things of force to believe or discredit that a man saith. His countenance when he pleaded before the people, did marvellously please the common sort: but the noblemen, and men of understanding, found it too base and mean, as Demetrius Phalerius said, among others. And Hermippus writeth, that one called Aesion, being asked of the ancient orators, and of those of his time, answered: that every man that had seen them, would have wondered with what honour, reverence, and modesty, they spoke unto the people: howbeit that Demosthenes' orations (whosoever

read them) were too artificial and vehement. And therefore we may easily judge, that the orations Demosthenes wrote are very severe and sharp. This notwithstanding, otherwhile he would give many pleasant and witty answers upon the sudden. As when Demades one day said unto him, 'Demosthenes will teach me': after the common proverb, 'The sow will teach Minerva.' He answered straight again: 'This Minerva not long since, was in Collytus street, taken in adultery.' A certain thief also called Chalcus (as much to say, as of copper) stepping forth to say somewhat of Demosthenes' late sitting up a-nights, and that he wrote and studied the most part of the night by lamp light: 'Indeed,' quoth Demosthenes, 'I know it grieves thee to see my lamp burn all night. And therefore you, my lords of Athens, methinks you should not wonder to see such robberies in your city, considering we have thieves of copper, and the walls of our houses be but of clay.' We could tell you of divers others of his like witty and pleasant answers, but these may suffice for this present: and therefore we will proceed to consider further of his nature and conditions, by his acts and deeds in the affairs of the common-wealth.

12   Now Demosthenes' first beginning when he came to deal in the affairs of the state, was in the time of the war made with the Phocians, as himself reporteth: and as appeareth further in his orations which he made against Philip: of the which, the last were made after the war was ended, and the first do touch also some particular doings of the same. He made the oration against Midias, when he was but thirty-two year old, and was of small countenance and reputation in the commonwealth: the want whereof was the chiefest cause (as I think) that induced him to take money for the injury he had done him, and to let his action fall against him.

> He was not of a mild and gentle mind
> But fierce and hasty to revenge by kind.

But, knowing that it was no small enterprise, nor that could take effect by a man of so small power and authority as himself, to overthrow a man so wealthy, so befriended and so eloquent as Midias, he therefore yielded himself unto those, that did speak and entreat for him. Neither do I think that the three thousand drachmas which he received, could have bridled the bitterness of his nature, if otherwise he had seen any hope or likelihood that he could have prevailed against him. Now at his first coming unto the commonwealth, taking a noble matter in hand to speak against Philip, for the defence and maintenance of the laws and liberties of the Grecians, wherein he handled himself so worthily, that in short space he won him marvellous fame for his great eloquence and plain manner of speech. Thereby he was marvellously honoured also through all Greece, and greatly esteemed with the king of Persia: and Philip himself made more account of him, than of all the orators in Athens, and his greatest foes which were most against him, were driven to confess that they had to do with a famous man. For, in the orations which Aeschines and Hyperides made to accuse him, they write thus of him.

13    And therefore I marvel what Theopompus meant, when he wrote that Demosthenes had a subtle, inconstant mind, and could not long continue with one kind of men, nor in one mind for matters of state. For in contrary manner, in my judgment, he continued constant still to the end, in one self manner and order, unto the which he had betaken himself at the beginning: and that not only he never changed all his lifetime, but to the contrary he lost his life because he would be no changeling. For he did not like Demades, who to excuse himself for that he had oft turned coat in matters of government, said, that he went oftentimes against his own sayings, as matters fell out, but never against the benefit of the commonwealth. And Melanopus also, who was ever against Callistratus, having his mouth stopped many times with money, he would up to the pulpit for orations, and tell the people, that indeed Callistratus, which maintaineth the contrary opinion against me, is mine enemy, and yet I yield unto him for this time: for, the benefit of the commonwealth must carry it. And another also, Nicodemus Messenian, who being first of Cassander's side, took part afterwards with Demetrius, and then said, that he did not speak against himself, but that it was meet he should obey his superiors. They cannot detect Demosthenes with the like, that he did ever halt or yield, either in word or deed: for he ever continued firm and constant in one mind in his orations. Insomuch that Panaetius the philosopher saith, that the most part of all his orations are grounded upon this maxim and principle: that for itself, nothing is to be taken

or accepted, but that which is honest. As, the oration of the crown, the which he made against Aristocrates: that also which he made for the franchise and freedom: and in fine, all his orations against Philip of Macedon. And in all those he doth not persuade his countrymen to take that which is most pleasant, easiest, or most profitable: but he proveth that oftentimes honesty is to be preferred above safety or health. So that, had he in all his orations and doings joined to his honesty, courtesy, and frank speech, valiantness in wars and clean hands from bribery, he might deservedly have been compared, not with Myrocles, Polyeuctus, Hyperides and such other orators, but even with the highest, with Cimon, Thucydides, and Pericles.

14   For Phocion, who took the worst way in government of the commonwealth, because he was suspected that he took part with the Macedonians, yet for valiantness, wisdom and justice, he was ever thought as honest a man as Ephialtes and Aristides. But Demosthenes on the other side (as Demetrius saith) was no man to trust to for wars, neither had he any power to refuse gifts and bribes. For, though he would never be corrupted with Philip king of Macedon, yet he was bribed with gold and silver that was brought from the cities of Susa and Ecbatana, and was very ready to praise and commend the deeds of their ancestors, but not to follow them. Truly, yet was he the honestest man of all other orators in his time, excepting Phocion. And besides, he did ever speak more boldly and plainly to the people then any man else, and would openly contrary their minds, and sharply reprove the Athenians for their faults, as appeareth by his orations. Theopompus also writeth that the people on a time would have had him to accuse a man, whom they would needs have condemned. But he refusing to do it, the people were offended, and did mutiny against him. Thereupon he rising up, said openly unto them: 'My lords Athenians, I will always counsel ye to that which I think best for the benefit of the commonwealth, although it be against your minds: but falsely to accuse one, to satisfy your minds, though you command me, I will not do it.' Furthermore, that which he did against Antiphon, showeth plainly, that he was no people pleaser, and that he did lean more unto the authority of the senate. For when Antiphon was quit by the people in an assembly of the city, Demosthenes

notwithstanding took him, and called him again into the Court of
the Areopagites, and did not pass upon the people's ill will, but
there convinced him for promising Philip of Macedon to burn the
arsenal of Athens: so by sentence of that court he was condemned,
and suffered for it. He did also accuse the nun Theorides for many
lewd parts committed, and amongst others, for that she taught
slaves to deceive their masters: and so following the matter against
her to death, she was condemned, and executed.

15   It is thought also, that he made the oration Apollodorus spoke
against the praetor Timotheus, and proved thereby that he was a
debtor to the commonwealth, and so a naughty man: and that he
wrote those orations also intituled unto Formio and Stephanus, for
the which he was justly reproved. For Formio pleaded against
Apollodorus with the oration which Demosthenes self had made
for him: which was even alike, as if out of one self cutler's shop, he
had sold his enemies swords one to kill another. And for his known
orations, those which he made against Androtion, Timocrates and
Aristocrates, he caused them to give them unto others, when he had
not yet dealt in matters of state. For indeed when he did put them
forth, he was not passing seven or eight and twenty year old. The
oration which he made against Aristogiton, and the other also of
liberty, against Ctesippus the son of Cabrias, he spoke them, as he
saith himself (or as others write), openly unto the people, because
he intended to marry Chabrias' mother. Howbeit he did not, but
married a Samian woman, as Demetrius Magnesius writeth in his
book he made entitled *Synonyma*, and in that he wrote against
Aeschines: where he accuseth him that he dealt falsely when he was
ambassador. It is not known whether it was ever recited or not,
although Idomeneus writeth, that there lacked but thirty voices
only to have quit Aeschines. But in this methinks he spoke not
truly, and doth but conjecture it, by that the one and the other have
said in their orations against the crown, in the which, neither the
one nor the other do say precisely, that this accusation proceeded to
judgment. But let others that list decide this doubt.

16   Now before the war began, it was evident enough, to which
part Demosthenes would incline in the commonwealth: for, he
would never leave to reprove and withstand Philip's doings. Therefore he being more spoken of in Philip's court, than any man else,

he was sent unto him the tenth person with nine others in ambassade. Philip gave them all audience one after another: howbeit he was more careful and circumspect to answer Demosthenes' oration, than all the rest. But otherwise out of that place, he did not Demosthenes so much honour, nor gave him so good entertainment, as to his other companions. For Philip showed more kindness, and gave better countenance, unto Aeschines and Philocrates, than unto him. Wherefore when they did highly praise Philip, and said that he was a well spoken prince, a fair man, and would drink freely, and be pleasant in company, Demosthenes smiled at it, and turned all those things to the worst, saying, that those qualities were nothing commendable nor meet for a king. For, the first was a quality meet for a pleader, the second for a woman, and the third for a sponge.

17    In fine, wars falling out between them, because Philip of the one side could not live in peace, and the Athenians on the other side were still incensed and stirred up by Demosthenes' daily orations. Whereupon, the Athenians first sent into the Isle of Euboea (the which by means of certain private tyrants that had taken the towns, became subject again unto Philip), following a decree Demosthenes had preferred, and so went to expulse the Macedonians again. After that also he caused them to send aid unto the Byzantines, and unto the Perinthians, with whom Philip made war. For he so persuaded the Athenians, that he made them forget the malice they did bear unto those two nations, and the faults which either of both the cities had committed against them in the wars, touching the rebellion of their confederates: and he caused them to send them aid, which kept them from Philip's force and power. Furthermore, going afterwards unto all the great cities of Greece as ambassador, he did so solicit and persuade them, that he brought them all in manner to be against Philip. So that the army which their tribe should find at their common charge, was fifteen thousand footmen, all strangers, and two thousand horsemen, besides the citizens of every city which should also serve in the wars at their charge: and the money levied for the maintenance of this war, was very willingly disbursed. Theophrastus writeth, that it was at that time their confederates did pray that they would set down a certain sum of money, what every city should pay: and that

Crobylus an orator should make answer, that the war had no certain
maintenance, inferring that the charges of war was infinite. Now all
Greece being in arms, attending what should happen, and all these
people and cities being unite in one league together: as, the
Euboeians, the Athenians, the Corinthians, the Megarians, the
Leucadians, and the Corcyriaeians: the greatest matter Demosthenes had to do, was to persuade the Thebans also to enter into this
league, because their country confined and bordered with Attica:
besides, their force and power was of great importance, for that they
carried the fame of all Greece at that time, for the valiantest soldiers.
But it was no trifling matter to win the Thebans, and to make them
break with Philip, who but lately before had bound them unto him
by many great pleasures which he had done to them, in the war of
the Phocians: besides also that betwixt Athens and Thebes, by
reason of vicinity, there fell out daily quarrels and debates, the
which with every little thing were soon renewed.

18    This notwithstanding, Philip being proud of the victory he
had won by the city of Amphisse, when he came and invaded the
country of Elatia, and was entered into Phocide, the Athenians
were then so amazed with it, that no man durst occupy the pulpit
for orations, neither could they tell what way to take. Thus the
whole assembly standing in a doubt with great silence,
Demosthenes only stepped up, and did again give them counsel to
seek to make league and alliance with the Thebans: and so did
further encourage the people, and put them in good hope, as he
was always wont to do. Then with others he was sent ambassador
unto Thebes: and Philip also for his part, sent ambassadors unto the
Thebans, Amyntas and Clearchus, two gentlemen Macedonians,
and with them Daochus, Thessalus, and Thrasydaeus, to answer
and withstand the persuasions of the Athenian ambassadors. Thereupon the Thebans began to advise themselves for the best, and laid
before their eyes the miserable fruits and calamities of war, their
wounds being yet green and uncured, which they got by the wars
of Phocide. Notwithstanding, the great force of Demosthenes'
eloquence (as Theopompus writeth) did so inflame the Thebans'
courage with desire of honour, that it trod under their feet all
manner of considerations, and did so ravish them with the love and
desire of honesty, that they cast at their heels all fear of danger, all

remembrance of pleasures received, and all reason persuading the contrary. This act of an orator was of so great force, that Philip forthwith sent ambassadors unto the Grecians, to entreat for peace, and all Greece was up, to see what would become of this stir. Thus, not only the captains of Athens obeyed Demosthenes, doing all that he commanded them, but the governors also of Thebes, and of all the country of Boeotia besides. And the assemblies also of the council of Thebes were as well governed by him, as the assemblies of Athens, being alike beloved both of the one and the other, and having a like authority to command both: and not undeservedly, as Theopompus saith, but by just desert.

19 But some fatal destiny, and the revolution of times had determined the final end of the liberty of Greece at that time, clean contrary to his purpose and intent. There were also many celestial signs that did foreshow and prognosticate what end should ensue thereof. And among others, Apollo's nun gave these dreadful oracles, and this old prophecy of the Sibyl's was commonly sung in everybody's mouth:

> What time the bloody battle shall be fought at Thermodon,
> God grant I may be far away, or else (to look thereon)
> Have eagles' wings to soar above, among the clouds on high.
> For there the vanquished side shall weep, and conqueror shall die.

Men do report that this Thermodon is a little river of our country of Chaeronea, the which falleth into the river of Cephisus: howbeit at this present time there is never a river nor brook in all our country, that I know, called Thermodon. And I think, that that river which we call now Haemon, was in old time Thermodon: for it runs by the temple of Hercules, where the Grecians lay in camp. And it may be, that because it was filled with dead bodies, and that it ran blood at the day of the battle, it changed her name, and was surnamed Haemon, because *haema* in the Greek tongue, signifieth blood. Yet Duris writeth notwithstanding, that this Thermodon was no river, but that certain men setting up their tent, and trenching it about, found a little image of stone, whereupon were engraven these letters, whereby it appeareth that it was a man called Thermodon, who carried an Amazon hurt in his arms, and that for this image of Thermodon, they do sing such another old oracle as this:

Ye ernes and ravens tarry till the field of Thermodon:
There will be store of carcasses of men to feed upon.

20    This notwithstanding, it is very hard to tell the truth of these things. But Demosthenes trusting to the valiantness and power of the Grecians, and being marvellously encouraged to see such a great number of valiant and resolute men so willing to fight with the enemy, he bade them be of good courage, and not to buzz about such oracles, and to give ear to those prophecies. And furthermore, he told them plainly, that he did mistrust the nun Pythia did lean unto Philip, as favouring him, and did put the Thebans in mind of their Captain Epaminondas, and the Athenians of Pericles, and persuaded them, that those two famous men were always of opinion that such prophecies were no other but a fine cloak for cowards, and that taking no heed to them, they did dispatch their matters according to their own discretion. Until this present time, Demosthenes showed himself always an honest man: but when it came to the battle, he fled like a coward, and did no valiant act anything answerable to the orations whereby he had persuaded the people. For he left his rank, and cowardly cast away his weapons to run the lighter, and was not ashamed at all, as Pythias said, of the words written upon his shield in golden letters, which were, 'Good Fortune'. Now Philip having won the battle, he was at that present so joyful that he fell to commit many fond parts. For after he had drunk well with his friends, he went into the place where the overthrow was given, and there in mockery began to sing the beginning of the decree which Demosthenes had preferred (by the which, the Athenians accordingly proclaimed wars against him), rising and falling with his voice, and dancing it in measure with his foot:

Demosthenes, the son of Demosthenes Paeanian did put forth this.

But afterwards beginning to wax sober, and leaving his drunkenness, and that he had remembered himself what danger he had been in, then his hair stood bolt upright upon his head, considering the force and power of such an orator, that in a piece of a day had enforced him to hazard his realm and life at a battle. Now Demosthenes' fame was so great, that it was carried even to the great king of Persia's court, who wrote unto his lieutenants and governors, that they should feed Demosthenes with money, and should procure to entertain him above all the men in Greece, as he that could best withdraw Philip, and trouble him with the wars and tumults of Greece. And this was afterwards proved by letters found of Demosthenes himself, the which came to King Alexander's hands in the city of Sardis, and by other writings also of the governors and lieutenants of the king of Persia: in the which were named directly the express sums of money which had been sent and given unto him.

21 Now, the Grecians being thus overthrown by battle, the other orators, adversaries unto Demosthenes in the commonwealth, began to set upon him, and to prepare to accuse him. But the people did not only clear him of all the accusations objected against him, but did continue to honour him more than before, and to call him to assemblies, as one that loved the honour and benefit of his country. So that when the bones of their countrymen which were slain at the battle of Chaeronea, were brought to be openly buried according to the custom, the people gave him the honour to make the funeral oration in praise of the dead, and made no show of sorrow or grief for the loss they had received (as Theopompus witnesseth, and doth nobly declare), but rather in contrary manner showed that they did not repent them in following of his counsel, but did honour him that gave it. Demosthenes then did make the funeral oration. But afterwards in all the decrees he preferred to the people, he would never subscribe any, to prevent the sinister luck and misfortune of his name, but did pass it under his friends' names one after another, until he grew courageous again, shortly after that he understood of the death of Philip, who was slain immediately after the victory he won at Chaeronea. And it seemeth this was the meaning of the prophecy or oracle in the two last verses:

> The vanquished bewails his luckless lot,
> And he that wins, with life escapeth not.

22 Now Demosthenes hearing of Philip's death, before the news were openly known, to prevent them, he would put the people again into a good hope of better luck to come. Thereupon he went with a cheerful countenance into the assembly of the council, and told them there, that he had had a certain dream that promised great good hap, and that out of hand unto the Athenians: and immediately after, the messengers arrived that brought certain

news of King Philip's death. Thereupon the Athenians made sacrifices of joy to the gods for this happy news, and appointed a crown unto Pausanias that had slain him. Demosthenes also came abroad in his best gown, and crowned with flowers, seven days after the death of his daughter, as Aeschines reporteth: who reproveth him for it, and noteth him to be a man having little love or charity unto his own children. But indeed Aeschines self deserveth more blame, to have such a tender womanish heart as to believe, that weeping and lamenting are signs of a gentle and charitable nature, condemning them that with patience and constancy do pass away such misfortunes. But now to the Athenians again. I can neither think nor say that they did wisely to show such open signs of joy, as to wear crowns and garlands upon their heads, nor also to sacrifice to the gods for the death of a prince, that behaved himself so princely and courteously unto them in the victories he had won of them. For, though indeed all cruelty be subject to the revenge of the gods, yet is this an act of a vile and base mind, to honour a man, and while he lived to make him free of their city, and now that another hath slain him, they to be in such an exceeding jollity withal and to exceed the bonds of modesty so far, as to ramp in manner with both their feet upon the dead, and to sing songs of victory, as if they themselves had been the men that had valiantly slain him. In contrary manner also, I praise and commend the constancy and courage of Demosthenes, that he leaving the tears and lamentation of his home trouble unto women, did himself in the meantime that he thought was for the benefit of the commonwealth: and in my opinion, I think he did therein like a man of courage, and worthy to be a governor of a commonwealth, never to stoop nor yield, but always to be found stable and constant, for the benefit of the commonwealth, rejecting all his troubles, cares, and affections, in respect of the service of his country, and to keep his honour much more carefully, than common players use to do, when they play the parts of kings and princes, whom we see neither weep nor laugh when they list, though they be on the stage, but when the matter of the play falleth out to give them just occasion. But omitting those reasons, if there be no reason (as indeed there is not) to leave and forsake a man in his sorrow and trouble, without giving him some words of comfort, and rather to devise some matter to assuage his sorrow and to withdraw his mind from that, to think upon some pleasanter things: even as they should keep sore eyes from seeing bright and glaring colours, in offering them green and darker. And from whence can a man take greater comfort for his troubles and griefs at home, when the commonwealth doth well: than to join their private griefs with common joys, to the end, that the better may obscure and take away the worse? But thus far I digressed from my history, enlarging this matter, because Aeschines in his oration touching this matter, did move the people's hearts too much to womanish sorrow. But now to the rest.

23  The cities of Greece being again stirred up by Demosthenes, made a new league again together: and the Thebans also having armed themselves by his practice, did one day set upon the garrison of the Macedonians within their city, and slew many of them. The Athenians prepared also to maintain war on the Thebans' behalf, and Demosthenes was daily at all the assemblies of council, in the pulpit, persuading the people with his orations: and he wrote also into Asia unto the king of Persia's lieutenants and captains, to make war with Alexander on their side, calling him child, and Margites, as much to say, as fool. But after that Alexander having set all his things at stay within his realm, came himself in person with his army, and invaded the country of Boeotia, then fell the pride of the Athenians greatly, and Demosthenes also plied the pulpit no more as he was wont. At length, the poor Thebans being left unto themselves, forsaken of every man, they were compelled themselves alone to bear the brunt of this war, and so came their city to utter ruin and destruction. Thereby the Athenians being in a marvellous fear and perplexity, did suddenly choose ambassadors to send unto this young king, and Demosthenes chiefly among others: who being afraid of Alexander's fury and wrath, durst not go to him, but returned from Mount Cytheron, and gave up the ambassade. But Alexander sent to summon the Athenians, to send unto him ten of their orators, as Idomeneus and Duris both do write: or eight, as the most writers and best historiographers do report, which were these: Demosthenes, Polyeuctus, Ephialtes, Lycurgus, Myrocles, Damon, Callisthenes, and Charidemus. At which time, they write that Demosthenes told the people of Athens, the fable of the sheep and wolves, how that the wolves came on a time, and willed the sheep, if they would have peace

with them, to deliver them their mastiffs that kept them. And so
he compared himself, and his companions that travailed for the
benefit of the country, unto the dogs that keep the flocks of
sheep, and calling Alexander the wolf. 'And so forth,' said he,
'like as you see these corn masters bringing a sample of their corn
in a dish or napkin to show you, and by that little do sell all that
they have: so I think you will all wonder, that delivering of us,
you will also deliver yourselves into the hands of your enemies.'
Aristobulus of Cassandra reporteth this matter thus. Now the
Athenians being in consultation, not knowing how to resolve,
Demades having taken five talents of them whom Alexander
demanded, did offer himself, and promised to go in this
ambassade unto Alexander, and to entreat for them, either because he trusted in the love the king did bear him, or else for that
he thought he hoped he should find him pacified, as a lion glutted
with the blood of beasts which he had slain. Howsoever it
happened, he persuaded the people to send him unto him, and so
handled Alexander, that he got their pardon, and did reconcile
him with the city of Athens.

24    Thereupon Alexander being retired, Demades and his fellows
bore all the sway and authority, and Demosthenes was under foot.
Indeed when Agis king of Lacedaemon, came with his army into
the field, he began a little to rouse himself, and to lift up his head:
but he shrunk choler again soon after, because the Athenians would
not rise with the Lacedaemonians, who were overthrown, and Agis
slain in battle. At that time was the cause of the crown pleaded
against Ctesiphon, and the plea was written a little before the battle
of Chaeronea in the year when Charondas was provost of Athens:
howbeit no sentence was given but ten years after that Aristophon
was provost. This was such an open judgment, and so famous, as
never was any, as well for the great fame of the orators that pleaded
in emulation one of the other, as also for the worthiness of the
judges that gave sentence thereof: who did not leave Demosthenes
to his enemies, although indeed they were of greater power than
he, and were also supported with the favour and goodwill of the
Macedonians: but they did notwithstanding so well quit him, that
Aeschines had not so much as the fifth part of men's voices and
opinions in his behalf. Wherefore immediately after sentence given,

he went out of Athens for shame, and travelled into the country of Ionia, and unto the Rhodes, where he did teach Rhetoric.

25    Shortly after, Harpalus flying out of Alexander's service, came unto Athens, being to be charged with many foul matters he had committed by his exceeding prodigality: and also because he feared Alexander's fury, who was grown severe and cruel, unto his chiefest servants. He coming now amongst the Athenians, with store of gold and silver, the orators being greedy and desirous of the gold and silver he had brought, began straight to speak for him, and did counsel the people to receive and protect a poor suitor that came to them for succour. But Demosthenes gave counsel to the contrary, and bade them rather drive him out of the city, and take heed they brought not wars upon their backs, for a matter that not only was not necessary, but furthermore merely unjust. But within few days after, inventory being taken of all Harpalus' goods, he perceiving that Demosthenes took great pleasure to see a cup of the king's, and considered very curiously the fashion and workmanship upon it, he gave it him in his hand, to judge what it weighed. Demosthenes peasing it, wondered at the great weight of it, it was so heavy: so he asked how many pound weight it weighed. Harpalus smiling, answered him: 'It will weigh thee twenty talents.' So when night was come, he sent him the cup, with the twenty talents. This Harpalus was a very wise man, and found straight by Demosthenes' countenance that he loved money, and could presently judge his nature, by seeing his pleasant countenance, and his eyes still upon the cup. So Demosthenes refused not his gift, and being overcome withal, as if he had received a garrison into his house, he took Harpalus' part. The next morning, he went into the assembly of the people, having his neck bound up with wool and rolls. So when they called him by his name to step up into the pulpit, to speak to the people as he had done before, he made a sign with his head, that he had an impediment in his voice, and that he could not speak. But wise men laughing at his fine excuse, told him it was no sinanche that had stopped his wesill that night as he would make them believe: but it was Harpalus' argentsynanche which he had received, that made him in that case. Afterwards when the people understood that he was corrupted, Demosthenes going about to excuse himself, they would not abide to hear him, but made a noise

and exclamation against him. Thereupon there rose up a pleasant conceited man, that said: 'Why my masters, do ye refuse to it hear a man that hath such a golden tongue?'* The people thereupon did immediately banish Harpalus, and fearing lest King Alexander would require an account of the gold and silver which the orators had robbed and pilfered away among them, they made very diligent search and enquiry in every man's house, excepting Callicles' house, the son of Arrenidas, whose house they would have searched by no means, because he was but newly married, and had his new spouse in his house, as Theopompus writeth.

26 Now Demosthenes desiring to show that he was in fault, preferred a decree, that the court of the Areopagites should hear the matter, and punish them that were found faulty, and therewithal straight offered himself to be tried. Howbeit he was one of the first whom the court condemned in the sum of fifty talents, and for lack of payment, they put him in prison: where he could not endure long, both for the shame of the matter for the which he was condemned, as also for his sickly body. So he broke prison, partly without the privity of his keepers, and partly also with their consent: for they were willing he should make a scape. Some do report that he fled not far from the city: where it was told him that certain of his enemies followed him, whereupon he would have hidden himself from them. But they themselves first called him by his name, and coming to him, prayed him to take money of them, which they had brought him from their houses to help him in his banishment: and that therefore they ran after him. Then they did comfort him the best they could, and persuaded him to be of good cheer, and not to despair for the misfortune that was come unto him. This did pierce his heart the more for sorrow, that he answered them: 'Why, would you not have me be sorry for my misfortune, that compels me to forsake the city where indeed I have so courteous enemies, that it is hard for me to find anywhere so good friends?' So he took his banishment unmanly, and remained the most part of his banishment in the city of Aegina, or at the city

---

* This conceit can hardly be expressed in any other language, than in Greek. For he saith, οὐκ ἀκούετε τοῦ τὴν κυλίκα ἔχοντος: alluding to the verb κύλειν, which signifieth to delight by pleasant speech or sound.

of Troezen, where oftentimes he would cast his eyes towards the country of Attica, and weep bitterly. And some have written certain words he spoke, which showed no mind of a man of courage, nor were answerable to the noble things he was wont to persuade in his orations. For it is reported of him, that as he went out of Athens, he looked back again, and holding up his hands to the castle, said in this sort: 'O Lady Minerva, lady patroness of this city: why doest thou delight in three so mischievous beasts: the owl, the dragon, and the people?' Besides, he persuaded the young men that came to see him, and that were with him, never to meddle in matters of state, assuring them, that if they had offered him two ways at the first, the one to go into the assembly of the people, to make orations in the pulpit, and the other to be put to death presently, and that he had known as he did then, the troubles a man is compelled to suffer that meddles with the affairs of the state, the fear, the envy, the accusations, and troubles in the same, he would rather have chosen the way to have suffered death.

27 So, Demosthenes continuing in his exile, King Alexander died, and all Greece was up again: insomuch as Leosthenes being a man of great valour, had shut up Antipater in the city of Lamea, and there kept him straitly besieged. Then Pytheas and Callimedon, surnamed Carabos, two orators, and both of them banished from Athens, they took part with Antipater, and went from town to town with his ambassadors and friends, persuading the Grecians not to stir, neither to take part with the Athenians. But Demosthenes in contrary manner, joining with the ambassadors sent from Athens into every quarter to solicit the cities of Greece to seek to recover their liberty, he did aid them the best he could, to solicit the Grecians to take arms with the Athenians, to drive the Macedonians out of Greece. And Phylarchus writeth, that Demosthenes encountered with Pytheas' words in an open assembly of the people in a certain town of Arcadia. Pytheas having spoken before him, had said: 'Like as we presume always that there is some sickness in the house whither we do see asses' milk brought, so must that town of necessity be sick, wherein the ambassadors of Athens do enter.' Demosthenes answered him again, turning his comparison against him, that indeed they brought asses' milk, where there was need to recover health: and even so, the ambassadors of Athens were sent,

to heal and cure them that were sick. The people at Athens understanding what Demosthenes had done, they so rejoiced at it, that presently they gave order in the field, that his banishment should be revoked. He that persuaded the decree of his revocation, was called Daemon Paeanian, that was his nephew: and thereupon the Athenians sent him a galley to bring him to Athens, from the city of Aegina. So Demosthenes being arrived at the haven of Piraea, there was neither governor, priest, nor almost any townsman left in the city, but went out to the haven to welcome him home. So that Demetrius Magnesian writeth, that Demosthenes then lifting up his hands unto heaven said, that he thought himself happy for the honour of that journey, that the return from his banishment was far more honourable, than Alcibiades' return in the like case had been. For Alcibiades was called home by force: and he was sent for with the goodwill of the citizens. This notwithstanding, he remained still condemned for his fine: for by the law, the people could not dispense withal, nor remit it. Howbeit they devised a way to deceive the law: for they had a manner to give certain money unto them that did prepare and set out the altar of Jupiter Saviour, for the day of the solemnity of the sacrifice, the which they did yearly celebrate unto him: so they gave him the charge to make this preparation for the sum of fifty talents, being the sum of the fine aforesaid wherein he was condemned.

28    Howbeit, he did not long enjoy the good hap of his restitution to his country and goods. For the affairs of the Grecians were immediately after brought to utter ruin. For the battle of Cranon which they lost, was in the month Munichyon (to wit, July), and in the month Boedromion next ensuing (to wit, August) the garrison of the Macedonians entered into the fort of Munichya. And in the month Pyanepsion (to wit, the October following) Demosthenes died in this manner. When news came to Athens, that Antipater and Craterus were coming thither with a great army, Demosthenes and his friends got out of the town a little before they entered, the people, by Demades' persuasion, having condemned them to die. So, every man making shift for himself, Antipater sent soldiers after them to take them: and of them Archias was captain, surnamed Phygadotheras, as much to say, as a hunter of the banished men. It is reported that this Archias was born in the city of Thuries, and that

he had been sometimes a common player of tragedies: and that
Polus also who was born in the city of Aegines (the excellentest
craftsmaster in that faculty of all men), was his scholar. Yet
Hermippus doth recite him amongst the number of the scholars of
Lacritus the orator. And Demetrius also writeth, that he had been at
Anaximenes' school. Now, this Archias having found the orator
Hyperides in the city of Aegina, and Aristonicus Marathonian, and
Himeraeus the brother of Demetrius the Phalerian, which had
taken sanctuary in the temple of Ajax, he took them out of the
temple by force, and sent them unto Antipater, who was at that
time in the city of Cleones, where he did put them all to death: and
some say, that he did cut off Hyperides' tongue.

29 Furthermore, hearing that Demosthenes had taken sanctuary
in the Isle of Calauria, he took little pinnaces, and a certain number
of Thracian soldiers, and being come thither, he sought to persuade
Demosthenes to be contented to go with him unto Antipater,
promising him that he should have no hurt. Demosthenes had a
strange dream the night before, and thought that he had played a
tragedy contending with Archias, and that he handled himself so
well, that all the lookers on at the theatre did commend him, and
gave him the honour to be the best player: howbeit that otherwise
he was not so well furnished as Archias and his players, and that in
all manner of furniture he did far exceed him. The next morning
when Archias came to speak with him, who using gentle words
unto him, thinking thereby to win him by fair means to leave the
sanctuary, Demosthenes looking him full in the face, sitting still
where he was, without removing, said unto him: 'O Archias, thou
diddest never persuade me when thou playedst a play, neither shalt
thou now persuade me, though thou promise me.' Then Archias
began to be angry with him, and to threaten him. 'O,' said
Demosthenes, 'now thou speakest in good earnest, without dissimulation, as the oracle of Macedon hath commanded thee: for
before, thou spakest in the clouds, and far from thy thought. But I
pray thee stay a while, till I have written somewhat to my friends.'
After he had said so, he went into the temple as though he would
have dispatched some letters, and did put the end of the quill in his
mouth which he wrote withal, and bit it as his manner was when he
did use to write anything, and held the end of the quill in his mouth

a pretty while together: then he cast his gown over his head, and laid him down. Archias' soldiers seeing that, being at the door of the temple, laughing him to scorn (thinking he had done so for that he was afraid to die) called him coward, and beast. Archias also coming to him, prayed him to rise, and began to use the former persuasions to him, promising him that he would make Antipater his friend. Then Demosthenes feeling the poison work, cast open his gown, and boldly looking Archias in the face, said unto him: 'Now when thou wilt, play Creon's part, and throw my body to the dogs, without further grave or burial. For my part, O god Neptune, I do go out of thy temple being yet alive, because I will not profane it with my death: but Antipater, and the Macedonians, have not spared to defile thy sanctuary with blood, and cruel murder.' Having spoken these words, he prayed them to stay him up by his armholes, for his feet began already to fail him, and thinking to go forward, as he passed by the altar of Neptune, he fell down, and giving one gasp, gave up the ghost.

30    Now touching the poison, Aristo reporteth, that he sucked and drew it up into his mouth out of his quill, as we have said before. But one Pappus (from whom Hermippus has taken his history) writeth, that when he was laid on the ground before the altar, they found the beginning of a letter which said: 'Demosthenes unto Antipater', but no more. Now his death being thus sudden, the Thracian soldiers that were at the temple door, reported that they saw him pluck the poison which he put into his mouth, out of a little cloth he had, thinking to them that it had been a piece of gold he had swallowed down. Howbeit a maid of the house that served him, being examined by Archias about it, told him that he had carried it about him a long time, for a preservative for him. Eratosthenes writeth, that he kept this poison in a little box of gold made hollow within, the which he ware as a bracelet about his arm. There are many writers also that do report his death diversely, but to recite them all it were in vain: saving that there was one called Demochares (who was Demosthenes' very friend) said, that he died not so suddenly by poison, but that it was the special favour of the gods (to preserve him from the cruelty of the Macedonians) that so suddenly took him out of his life, and made him feel so little pain. Demosthenes

died the sixteenth day of the month Pynepsion (to wit, October), on the which day they do celebrate at Athens the feast of Ceres, called Tesmophoria, which is the dolefullest feast of all the year: on the which day also, the women remain all day long in the temple of the goddess, without meat or drink. Shortly after, the Athenians to honour him according to his deserts, did cast his image in brass, and made a law besides, that the oldest man of his house should forever be kept within the palace, at the charge of the commonwealth: and engraved these verses also upon the base of his image:

> Hadst thou Demosthenes had strength according to thy heart,
> The Macedons should not have wrought the Greeks such
> woe and smart.

For they that think, that it was Demosthenes himself that made the verses in the Isle of Calauria, before he took his poison, they are greatly deceived.

31 But yet a little before my first coming to Athens, there went a report that such a thing happened. A certain soldier being sent for to come unto his captain, did put such pieces of gold as he had into the hands of Demosthenes' statue, which had both his hands joined together: and there grew hard by it a great plane tree, divers leaves whereof either blown oft by wind by chance, or else put there of purpose by the soldier, covered so this gold, that it was there a long time, and no man found it: until such time as the soldier came again, and found it as he left it. Hereupon this matter running abroad in every man's mouth, there were divers wise men that took occasion of this subject, to make epigrams in the praise of Demosthenes, as one who in his life was never corrupted. Furthermore, Demades did not long enjoy the honour he thought he had newly gotten. For the justice of the gods, revenger of the death of Demosthenes, brought him into Macedon, to receive just punishment by death, of those whom he dishonestly flattered: being before grown hateful to them, and afterwards committed a fault whereby he could not escape. For there were letters of his taken, by the which he did persuade, and pray Perdiccas* to make himself king of Macedon,

* He saith Antigonus, in the life of Phocion.

and to deliver Greece from bondage, saying that it hung but by a thread, and yet it was half rotten, meaning thereby, Antipater. Dinarchus Corinthian accused him, that he wrote these letters: the which so grievously offended Cassander, that first he slew his own son in his arms, and then commanded that they should afterwards kill Demades, making him feel then by those miseries (which are the cruellest that can happen unto man) that traitors bewraying their own country do first of all bewray themselves. Demosthenes had often forewarned him of his end, but he would never believe him. Thus, my friend Sossius, you have what we can deliver you, by reading or report, touching Demosthenes' life and doings.

# Life of Marcus Tullius Cicero

As touching Cicero's mother, whose name was Helvia, it is reported she was a gentlewoman born, and lived always very honestly: but for his father, the reports of him are divers and infinite. For some say that he was born and brought up in a fuller's shop: others report that he came of Tullius Actius, who while he lived was honoured among the Volsces as king, and made very sharp and cruel wars with the Romans. But surely it seems to me, that the first of that name called Cicero, was some famous man, and that for his sake his offspring continued still that surname, and were glad to keep it, though many men scorned it, because *cicer* in English signifieth a rich pease. That Cicero had a thing upon the tip of his nose, as it had been a little wart, much like to a rich pease, whereupon they surnamed him Cicero. But this Cicero, whose life we write of now, nobly answered certain of his friends on a time giving him counsel to change his name, when he first made suit for office, and began to practise in matters of state, that he would endeavour himself to make the name of the Ciceros more noble and famous, than the Scauri, or Catuli. After that, Cicero being made treasurer in Sicily, he gave an offering of certain silver plate unto the gods, and at large engraved on it his two first names, Marcus Tullius: and in place of his third name, he pleasantly commanded the workman to cut out the form and fashion of a rich pease. Thus much they write of his name.

2  Now for his birth, it was said that his mother was brought abed of him without any pain, the third day of January: on which day the magistrates and governors of Rome do use at this present, yearly to make solemn prayers and sacrifices unto the gods, for the health and prosperity of the emperor. Further, it is reported, that there appeared an image to his nurse, that did prognosticate unto her she gave a child suck, which in time to come should do great

good unto all the Romans. Now though such things may seem but dreams and fables unto many, yet Cicero himself shortly after proved this prophecy true: because that when he came of age to learn, he grew so toward, and won such fame among the boys, for his excellent wit and quick capacity. For thereupon came the other boys' fathers themselves to the school to see his face, and to be eye witnesses of the report that went of him, of his sharp and quick wit to learn. But others of the rude and baser sort of men were offended with their sons, because to honour Cicero, they did always put him in the midst between them, as they went in the streets. Cicero indeed had such a natural wit and understanding, as Plato thought meet for learning, and apt for the study of philosophy. For he gave himself to all kind of knowledge, and there was no art, nor any of the liberal sciences, that he disdained: notwithstanding in his first young years he was apter, and better disposed to the study of poetry, than any other. There is a pretty poem of his in verses of eight staves, called *Pontius Glaucus*, extant at this day, the which he made when he was but a boy. After that, being given more earnestly unto this study, he was not only thought the best orator, but the best poet also of all the Romans in his time: and yet doth the excellency of his eloquence, and commendation of his tongue continue, even to this day, notwithstanding the great alteration and change of the Latin tongue. But his poetry hath lost the name and estimation of it, because there were many after him that became far more excellent therein than he.

3    After he had left his childish studies, he became then Philo's scholar, the Academic philosopher, the only scholar of all Clitomachus' scholars, whom the Romans esteemed so much for his eloquence, and loved more for his gentle behaviour and conversation. He gave himself also to be a follower of Mutius Scaevola, who at that time was a great man in Rome, and prince of the senate, and who did also instruct Cicero in the laws of Rome. He did also follow Sylla for a time, in the wars of the Marsians. But when he saw that the commonwealth of Rome fell to civil wars, and from civil wars to a monarchy, then he returned again to his book and contemplative life, and frequented the learned men of Greece, and always studied with them, until Sylla had gotten the upper hand, and that he saw all the commonwealth again at some

stay. About that time, Sylla causing the goods of one that was said to be slain, to be sold by the crier (being one of the outlaws and proscripts, to wit, banished by bills set up on posts), Chrysogonus, one of Sylla's freed bondmen, and in great favour with his master, bought them for the sum of two thousand drachmas. Therewithal the son and heir of the dead person called Roscius, being marvellously offended, he showed that it was too shameful an abuse: for his father's goods amounted to the sum of two hundred and fifty talents. Sylla finding himself thus openly touched with public fraud and deceit, for the only gratifying of his man, he procured Chrysogonus to accuse him, that he had killed his own father. Never an orator durst speak in Roscius' behalf to defend his cause, but shrunk colour, fearing Sylla's cruelty and severity. Wherefore poor Roscius the young man, seeing every man forsake him, had no other refuge but to go to Cicero, whom his friends did counsel and persuade boldly to take upon him the defence of Roscius' cause: for he should never have a happy occasion, nor so noble a beginning to bring himself into estimation, as this. Thereupon Cicero determined to take his cause in hand, and did handle it so well, that he obtained the thing he sued for: whereby he won him great fame and credit. But yet being afraid of Sylla's displeasure, he absented himself from Rome, and went into Greece, giving it out that his travel was for a disease he had upon him. Indeed Cicero was dog lean, a little eater, and would also eat late, because of the great weakness of his stomach: but yet he had a good loud voice, though it was somewhat harsh, and lacked grace and comeliness. Furthermore he was so earnest and vehement in his oration that he mounted still with his voice into the highest tunes: insomuch that men were afraid it would one day put him in hazard of his life.

4 When he came to Athens, he went to hear Antiochus of the city of Ascalona, and fell in great liking with his sweet tongue, and excellent grace, though otherwise he misliked his new opinions in philosophy. For Antiochus had then forsaken the opinions of the new Academic philosophers, and the sect of the Carneades: being moved thereunto, either through the manifest proof of things, or by his certain judgment, or (as some say) for that of an ambition or dissension against the scholars and followers of Clitomachus and Philo, he had reproved the resolutions of the Academics, which he

had of long time defended, only to lean for the most part to the Stoics' opinions. Howbeit Cicero had most affection unto the Academics, and did study that sect more than all the rest, of purpose, that if he saw he were forbidden to practise in the commonwealth at Rome, he would then go to Athens (leaving all pleas and orators in the commonwealth) to bestow the rest of his time quietly in the study of philosophy. At length, when he heard news of Sylla's death, and saw that his body was grown to good state and health by exercise, and that his voice became daily more and more to fill men's ears with a sweet and pleasant sound, and yet was loud enough for the constitution of his body: receiving letters daily from his friends at Rome, that prayed him to return home, and moreover, Antiochus self also earnestly persuading him to practise in the commonwealth, he began again to fall to the study of rhetoric, and to frame himself to be eloquent, being a necessary thing for an orator, and did continually exercise himself in making orations upon any speech or proposition, and so frequented the chief orators and masters of eloquence that were at that time. To this end therefore he went into Asia unto Rhodes, and amongst the orators of Asia, he frequented Xenocles Andramettin, and Dionysius Magnesian, and studied also with Menippus Carian: at Rhodes he heard Apollonius Molon, and the philosopher Posidonius. And it is reported also, that Apollonius wanting the Latin tongue, he did pray Cicero for exercise sake, to declaim in Greek. Cicero was very well contented with it, thinking that thereby his faults should be the better corrected. When he had ended his declamation, all those that were present were amazed to hear him, and every man praised him one after another. Howbeit Apollonius all the while Cicero spoke, did never show any glad countenance: and when he had ended, he stayed a great while and said never a word. Cicero misliking withal, Apollonius at length said unto him: 'As for me Cicero, I do not only praise thee, but more than that, I wonder at thee: and yet I am sorry for poor Greece, to see that learning and eloquence (which were the two only gifts and honour left us) are by thee obtained with us, and carried unto the Romans.'

5   Now Cicero being very well disposed, to go with good hope to practise at Rome, he was a little discouraged by an oracle that

was told him. For, enquiring of the god Apollo Delphian, how he might do to win fame and estimation, the nun Pythias answered him he should obtain it, so that in his doings he would rather follow the disposition of his own nature, than the opinion of the common people. Wherefore when he came to Rome, at the first he proceeded very warily, and discreetly, and did unwillingly seek for any office, and when he did, he was not greatly esteemed: for they commonly called him the Grecian, and scholar, which are two words, the which the artificers (and such base mechanical people at Rome) have ever ready at their tongue's end. Now he being by nature ambitious of honour, and pricked forward also by the persuasion of his father and friends, in the end he began to plead, and there obtained not the chiefest place by little and little, but so soon as he fell to practise, he was immediately esteemed above all the other orators and pleaders in his time, and did excel them all. Yet it is reported notwithstanding, that for his gesture and pronunciation, having the selfsame defects of nature at the beginning, which Demosthenes had, to reform them, he carefully studied to counterfeit Roscius, an excellent comedian, and Aesope also a player of tragedies. Of this Aesope men write, that he playing one day Atrius' part upon a stage (who determined with himself how he might be revenged of his brother Thyestes), a servant by chance having occasion to run suddenly by him, he forgetting himself, striving to show the vehement passion and fury of this king, gave him such a blow on his head with the sceptre in his hand, that he slew him dead in the place. Even so Cicero's words were of so great force to persuade, by means of his grace and pronunciation. For he mocking the orators that thrust out their heads, and cried in their orations, was wont to say that they were like to lame men, who were driven to ride, because they could not go afoot: 'Even so,' said he, 'they cry out, because they cannot speak.' Truly pleasant taunts do grace an orator, and showeth a fine wit: but yet Cicero used them so commonly, that they were offensive unto many, and brought him to be counted a malicious scoffer and spiteful man.

6    He was chosen Treasurer in the time of dearth, when there was great scarcity of corn at Rome: and the province of Sicily fell to his lot. At his first coming thither, the Sicilians misliked him very

much, because he compelled them to send corn unto Rome: but after they had found his diligence, justice, and lenity, they honoured him above any governor that ever was sent from Rome. Now there were divers young gentlemen of Rome of noble houses, who being accused for sundry faults committed in wars against their honour, and martial discipline, had been sent back again unto the praetor of Sicily: for whom Cicero pleaded, and did so excellently defend their cause that they were pardoned every man. Thereupon, thinking well of himself, when his time expired, he went to Rome, and by the way there happened a pretty feast unto him. As he passed through the country of Campania (otherwise called the land of labour), he met by chance with one of the chiefest Romans of all his friends. So falling in talk with him, he asked him what they said of him at Rome, and what they thought of his doings, imagining that all Rome had been full of the glory of his name and deeds. His friend asked him again: 'And where hast thou been Cicero all this while, that we have not seen thee at Rome?' This killed his heart straight, when he saw that the report of his name and doings, entering into the city of Rome as into an infinite sea, was so suddenly vanquished away again, without any other fame or speech. But after that, when he looked into himself, and saw that in reason he took an infinite labour in hand to attain to glory, wherein he saw no certain end whereby to attain unto it, it cut off a great part of the ambition he had in his head. And yet the great pleasure he took to hear his own praise, and to be overmuch given to desire of honour and estimation: those two things continued with him even to his dying day, and did eftsoons make him swerve from justice.

7    Furthermore, when he began thoroughly to practise in the affairs of the state, he thought it an ill thing that artificers and craftsmen should have many sorts of instruments and tools without life, to know the names of every one of them, the places where they should take them, and the use whereto they should employ them: and that a man of knowledge and quality (who doth all things with the help and service of men) should be slothful, and careless, to learn to know the names of his citizens. Therefore he gave himself to know, not only men's names of quality, but the streets also they dwelt in, what part of the city soever it was: their goodly houses in the country, the friends they made of, and the

neighbours whom they companied with. So that when he went abroad into Italy, wheresoever he became, Cicero could show and name his friends' houses. He was not very rich, and yet he had enough to serve his turn: the which made men muse the more at him, and they loved him the better, because he took no fee nor gift for his pleading, what cause soever he had in hand, but then specially, when he defended a matter against Verres. This Verres had been praetor of Sicilia, and had committed many lewd parts there, for the which the Sicilians did accuse him. Cicero taking upon him to defend their cause, made Verres to be condemned, not by pleading, but in manner without pleading, and in this sort. The praetors being his judges, and favouring Verres, had made so many rejornements and delays, that they had driven it off to the last day of hearing. Cicero perceiving then he should not have daylight to speak all that he had to say against him, and that thereby nothing should be done and judged, he rose up, and said, that there needed no further plea in this matter, but only brought forth the witnesses before the judges, and having caused their depositions to be taken, he prayed they would proceed to sentence, according to their evidence given on that behalf. Yet some do report, that Cicero gave many pleasant taunts and girds, in pleading the accusation of the Sicilians against Verres. The Romans do call a boar *verres*. There was one Caecilius, the son of a freed bondman, who was suspected to hold with the superstition of the Jews. This Caecilius would have put by the Sicilians from following the accusation of Verres, and would have had the matter of his accusation only referred to him, for the prosecuting of it against him. Cicero scorning his suit, said unto him: 'What hath a Jew to do with a swine?' This Verres had a son somewhat above twenty years of age, who (as the report went) had a very ill name for his beauty. And therefore when Verres one day thought to mock Cicero, saying that he was too womanly: 'His children,' said he, 'are to be reproved of that secretly at home.' In this accusation, Hortensius the orator durst not directly defend Verres: but touching the condemnation of his fine, he was then contented to answer for him, for he had a Sphinx of ivory given him by Verres for his reward. Thereupon Cicero gave him a pretty nip by the way: but Hortensius not understanding him, said he could no skill of dark speeches. 'Well,' said Cicero, 'yet hast thou a sphinx in thy house.'

8   In the end Verres being condemned, and a fine set on his head to the value of seventy-five myriads, Cicero notwithstanding was suspected to be bribed with money for agreeing to cast him in so small a sum. But yet when he came to be Aedilis, the Sicilians to show themselves thankful to him, both brought and sent him many presents out of Sicily. Of all that he took nothing to his own use, but only bestowed their liberality in bringing down the prices of victuals at Rome. He had a goodly house within the confines of the city of Arpos, a farm also by Naples, and another about the city of Pompeii: but all these were no great things. Afterwards also he had the jointure of his wife Terentia, which amounted to the sum of twelve myriads, and besides all this, there came to him by inheritance, eleven myriads of their denarii. Thereupon he lived very honestly and soberly, without excess, with his familiar friends that loved him, both Grecians and Romans, and would never go to supper till after sunset, not so much for any great business he had, as for the weakness of his stomach. But otherwise he was very curious and careful of his person, and would be rubbed and anointed, and he would use also to walk a certain number of turns by proportion: and so exercising his body in that sort, he was never sick, and besides was always very strong and lusty of body, able to abide great pains and sorrows which he fell into afterwards. He gave his father's chief mansion house to his brother, and went to dwell himself in the mount Palatine: because such as came to wait upon him to do him honour, should not take the pains to go so far to see him. For, he had as many men daily at his gate every morning, as either Crassus had for his wealth, or Pompey for his estimation among the soldiers, both of them being at that time the chiefest men of Rome. Yea furthermore, Pompey's self came unto Cicero, because his orations stood him to great purpose, for the increase of his honour and authority.

9   Now when Cicero came to make suit to be praetor (which is, to be as an ordinary judge) though he had many competitors, and fellow suitors with him, yet was he first chosen afore them all: and he did so honestly behave himself in that office, that they did not so much as once suspect him of bribery or extortion. And for proof hereof, it is reported, that Licinius Macer (a man that of himself was of great power, and yet favoured and supported besides by

Crassus) was accused before Cicero of theft and extortion in his office: but he trusting much to his supposed credit, and to the great suit and labour his friends made for him, went home to his house before sentence proceeded against him (the judges being yet to give their opinions) and there speedily trimmed his beard, and put a new gown upon his back, as though he had been sure to have been quit of his accusation, and then returned again into the market-place. But Crassus went to meet him, and told him all the judges had condemned him. Licinius Macer took such a grief and conceit upon it, that he went home to his house again, laid him down on his bed, and never rose after. This judgment won Cicero great fame, for they praised him exceedingly for the great pains he took, to see justice duly executed. Another called also Vatinius (a bedlam fellow, and one that behaved himself very unreverently to the magistrates in his pleading, and besides had a swollen neck) came very arrogantly one day unto Cicero being in his praetorial seat, and asked him a thing which Cicero would not grant him there, but would think of it at better leisure. Thereupon Vatinius told him, that he would not be scrupulous to grant that, if he were praetor. Cicero turning to him, answered him again: 'No more have I,' said he, 'such a swollen neck as thou hast.' Towards the end of his office, two or three days before his time expired, there was one accused Manilius before him, that he also had robbed the commonwealth. This Manilius was very well beloved of the common people, who were persuaded that he was put in suit, not for any fault he had committed, but only to despite Pompey with, whose familiar friend he was. So he required certain days to answer the matter he was accused of; but Cicero would give him no further respite, but to answer it the next day. The people therewith were marvellously offended, because the other praetors in suchlike cases were wont to give ten days' respite to others. The next morning when the tribunes had brought him before the judges, and also accused him unto them, he besought Cicero to hear him patiently. Cicero made him answer, that having always used as much favour and courtesy as he possibly might by law, unto those that were accused, he thought he should offer Manilius too great wrong, if he should not do the like to him: wherefore, because he had but one day more to continue praetor in office, he had purposely given him that day to make his answer before him. For he thought that to leave his accusation to the hearing of another praetor, he could not have been thought a man that had borne him goodwill, and meant to pleasure him. These words did marvellously change the people's opinion and affection towards him, and every man speaking well of him, they prayed him to defend Manilius' cause. He willingly granted them: and coming from the bench, standing at the bar like an orator to plead for him, he made a notable oration, and spoke both boldly and sharply against the chief men of the city, and those specially that did envy Pompey.

10   This notwithstanding, when he came to sue to be consul, he found as great favour amongst the nobility, as he did with the commonalty. For they did further his suit, for the commonwealth's sake, upon this occasion. The change and alteration of government the which Sylla brought in, was thought strange at the first among the people: but now men by process of time being used to it, it was thoroughly established, and no man misliked it. At that time many men practised to subvert the government, not for the benefit of the commonwealth, but to serve their own covetous minds. For Pompey being then in the East parts, made wars with the kings of Pontus and Armenia, and had not left sufficient force at Rome to oppress these seditious persons, that sought nothing but rebellion. These men had made Lucius Catilina their captain: a desperate man to attempt any great enterprise, subtle, and malicious of nature. He was accused before (besides many other vile faults) for deflowering of his own daughter, and killing his brother: and being afraid to be put in suit for it, he prayed Sylla to put his brother amongst the number of the outlaws (or proscripts) as if he had been then alive. These wicked rebels having chosen them such a captain, were sworn and bound one to another in this manner. They killed a man, and did eat of his flesh together, and had besides corrupted the most part of all the youth. For Catiline their captain suffered every man to take his pleasure, as his youth was inclined unto: as to banquet, to follow harlots, and gave them money largely to bestow in these vain expenses. Furthermore all Thuscan began to rise, and the most part of Gaul also, lying between the Alps and Italy. The city of Rome itself was also in great danger of rising, for the inequality of the goods of the inhabitants. For the noblemen, and of greatest courage, had spent all their lands in plays and feasts, or in

buildings and common works, which they built at their own charge, to curry favour with the common people, that they might obtain the chief offices: so that thereby they became very poor, and their goods were in the hands of mean men and wretches. Thus the state of Rome stood in great hazard of uproar, the which any man might easily have procured, that durst have taken upon him any change or alteration of government, there was then such division among them in the state.

11 Catiline notwithstanding, to provide him of a strong bulwark to prosecute his intent, came to sue to be consul, hoping that he should be chosen with Caius Antonius, a man that of himself was apt neither to do any great good, nor much hurt, and yet that could be a great strength and aid unto him that would attempt anything. Divers noble and wise men foreseeing that, did procure Cicero to sue for the consulship. The people accepted him, and rejected Catiline. Antonius and Cicero thereupon were created consuls, although that Cicero of all the suitors for the consulship was but only a knight's son, and not the son of a senator of Rome.

12 Now, though the common people understood not the secret practice and meaning of Catiline, yet at the beginning of Cicero's consulship, there fell out great trouble and contention in the commonwealth. For they of the one side, whom Sylla had by his ordinances deposed from their dignities and offices in Rome (who were no small men, neither few in number), began to creep into the people's goodwill, alleging many true and just reasons against the tyrannical power of Sylla: howbeit spoken in ill time, when it was out of time to make any change or alteration in the commonwealth. The tribunes on the other side preferred laws and ordinances to further this devise. They preferred the law to choose the Decemviri, with sovereign power and authority through all Italy and Syria, and also through all the countries and provinces which Pompey had newly conquered to the empire of Rome, to sell and release all the lands belonging to the state of Rome, to accuse any man whom they thought good, to banish any man, to restore the colonies with people, to take what money they would out of the treasury, to levy men of war, and to keep them in pay as long as they thought good. For this great and absolute power of the Decemviri, there were many men of great account that favoured this law, but

Antonius chiefly, being colleague and fellow consul with Cicero, for he had good hope to be chosen one of these ten Commissioners: and furthermore, it was thought that he was privy unto Catiline's conspiracy, and that he misliked it not, because he was so much in debt. And this was it that the noblemen most feared of all other things. Thereupon Cicero, to provide first to prevent this danger, granted him the province of the realm of Macedon: and the province of Gaul being offered unto himself, he refused it. By this good turn, he won Antonius like a hired player, making him to promise him that he would assist and aid him for the benefit of the commonwealth, and that he would say no more, than he should will him. When he had brought him to this, and had won him to his mind, he then began to be the bolder, and more stoutly to resist them that were authors of this innovation and new laws. Cicero therefore in open senate, did one day sharply reprove, and inveigh against this law of the Decemviri, which the tribunes would have established. But thereby he did so terrify the authors thereof, that there was not one man durst speak against him. This notwithstanding, the tribunes afterwards attempted once again to have it to pass, and appointed the consuls to appear before the people. Howbeit Cicero being nothing abashed at it, he commanded the senate to follow him. So he did not only overthrow this law of the Decemviri, which the tribunes did prefer: but furthermore they were utterly discouraged and out of hope to bring any of their matters to pass they intended, he struck them so dead with his eloquence.

13   For Cicero only of all men in Rome made the Romans know, how much eloquence doth grace and beautify that which is honest, and how invincible right and justice are, being eloquently set forth: and also how that a man that will be counted a wise governor of a common weal, should always in his doings rather prefer profit, than to seek to curry favour with the common people: yet so to use his words, that the thing which is profitable, may not be also unpleasant. And to prove his sweet and pleasant tongue, may be alleged that which he did in the time of his consulship, touching the placing of men at the theatre to see the pastimes. For before, the knights of Rome did sit mingled one with another amongst the common people, and took their place as they came. The first that

made the difference between them, was Marcus Otho, at that time praetor: who made a law, by the which he appointed several seats for the knights, where they might from thenceforth see the pastimes. The people took this grievously, as a thing done to discountenance them: insomuch that Otho coming afterwards into the theatre, all the common people fell a-whistling at him, to shame him withal. The knights also in contrariwise made him room amongst them, with great clapping of hands, in token of honour. Therewith the people fell a-whistling louder than before, and the knights in like manner to clapping of their hands, and so grew to words one with another, that all the theatre was straight in uproar with it. Cicero understanding it, went thither himself, and calling the people to the temple of the goddess Bellona, he there so sharply reproved them, and therewith so persuaded them, that returning presently to the theatre, they did then welcome and receive Otho with clapping of their hands, and contended with the knights which of them should do him greatest honour.

14 But now again, the rebels of Catiline's conspiracy (who were prettily cooled at the first for the fear they stood in) began to be lusty again, and to gather together, boldly encouraging one another to broach their practice, before Pompey returned, who was said to be on the way towards Rome with his army. But besides them, those soldiers that had served before in the wars under Sylla, being dispersed up and down Italy (but specially the best soldiers among them dwelling in the good towns of Thuscan), did stir up Catiline to hasten the enterprise, persuading themselves that they should once again have goods enough at hand, to spoil and ransack at their pleasure. These soldiers having one Manlius to their captain, that had borne office in the field under Sylla, conspired with Catilin, and came to Rome to assist him in his suit: who purposed once again to demand the consulship, being determined at the election to kill Cicero, in the tumult and hurly-burly. The gods also did plainly show by earthquakes, lightning and thunder, and by vision of spirits that did appear, the secret practice and conspiracy: besides also, there fell out manifest conjectures and proofs by men that came to reveal them, howbeit they had not power sufficient to encounter so noble a man, and of great power as Catilin was. Cicero therefore deferring the day of election,

called Catilin into the senate, and there did examine him of that which was reported of him. Catiline supposing there were many in the senate that had goodwills to rebel, and also because he would show himself ready unto them that were of his conspiracy, he gave Cicero a gentle answer, and said thus, 'What do I offend,' said he, 'if that being two bodies in this town, the one lean and weak, and thoroughly rotten, and hath a head: and the other being great, strong, and of power, having no head, I do give it one?' Meaning under this dark answer, to signify the people and senate. This answer being made, Cicero was more afraid than before, insomuch that he put on a brigantine for the safety of his body, and was accompanied with the chiefest men of Rome, and a great number of young men besides, going with him from his house unto the field of Mars, where the elections were made: and had of purpose left open his jacket loose at the collar, that his brigantine he had on might be seen, thereby to let every man that saw him, know the danger he was in. Every man misliked it when they saw it, and came about him to defend him, if any offered to assail him. But it so came to pass, that by voices of the people, Catilin was again rejected from the consulship, and Syllanus and Muraena chosen consuls.

15   Shortly after this election, the soldiers of Thuscan being joined, which should have come to Catilin, and the day appointed being at hand to broach their enterprise, about midnight there came three of the chiefest men of Rome to Cicero's house (Marcus Crassus, Marcus Marcellus, and Scipio Metellus) and knocking at his gate, called his porter, and bade him wake his master presently, and tell him how they three were at the gate to speak with him, about a matter of importance. At night after supper, Crassus' porter brought his master a packet of letters, delivered him by a stranger unknown, which were directed unto divers persons, among the which one of them had no name subscribed, but was only directed unto Crassus himself. The effect of his letter was, that there should be a great slaughter in Rome made by Catilin, and therefore he prayed him that he would depart out of Rome to save himself. Crassus having read his own letter, would not open the rest, but went forthwith unto Cicero, partly for fear of the danger, and partly also to clear himself of the suspicion they had of him for the

friendship that was betwixt him and Catiline. Cicero counselling with them what was to be done, the next morning assembled the senate very early, and carrying the letters with him, he did deliver them according to their direction, and commanded they should read them out aloud. All these letters, and every one of them particularly, did bewray the conspiracy. Furthermore, Quintus Arrius, a man of authority, and that had been praetor, told openly the soldiers and men of war that were levied in Thuscan. And it was reported also, that Manlius was in the field with a great number of soldiers about the cities of Thuscan, gaping daily to hear news of some change at Rome. All these things being thoroughly considered, a decree passed by the senate, that they should refer the care of the commonwealth unto the consuls, to the end that with absolute authority they might (as well as they could) provide for the safety and preservation thereof. Such manner of decree and authority, was not often seen concluded of in the senate, but in time of present fear and danger.

16 Now Cicero having this absolute power, he referred all foreign matters to Quintus Metellus' charge, and did himself take upon him the care and government of all civil affairs within Rome. On the daytime when he went up and down the town, he had such a troop of men after him, that when he came through the great market-place, he almost filled it with his train that followed him. Thereupon Catiline would no longer delay time, but resolved to go himself unto Manlius where their army lay. But before he departed, he had drawn into his confederacy one Martius, and another called Cethegus, whom he commanded betimes in the morning to go to Cicero's house with short daggers to kill him, pretending to come to salute him, and to give him a good morrow. But there was a noblewoman of Rome, called Fulvia, who went overnight unto Cicero, and bade him beware of that Cethegus, who indeed came the next morning betimes unto him: but being denied to be let in, he began to chafe and rail before the gate. This made him the more to be suspected. In the end Cicero coming out of his house, called the senate to the temple of Jupiter Stator (as much to say, a stayer), which standeth at the upper end of the holy street as they go to the Mount Palatine. There was Catiline with others, as though he meant to clear himself of the suspicion that

went of him: howbeit there was not a senator that would sit down by him, but they did all rise from the bench where Catiline had taken his place. And further, when he began to speak, he could have no audience for the great noise they made against him. So at length Cicero rose, and commanded him to avoid out of Rome: saying, that there must needs be a separation of walls between them two, considering that the one used but words, and the other force of arms. Catiline thereupon immediately departing the city with three hundred armed men, was no sooner out of the precinct of the walls, but he made his sergeants carry axes and bundles of rods before him, as if he had been a consul lawfully created, and did display his ensigns of war, and so went in this order to seek Manlius. When they were joined, he had not much less than twenty thousand men together, with the which he went to practise the towns to rebel. Now open war being thus proclaimed, Antonius, Cicero's colleague and fellow consul, was sent against him to fight with him.

17   In the mean space, Cornelius Lentulus surnamed Sura (a man of a noble house, but of a wicked disposition, and that for his ill life was put off the senate) assembled all the rest which were of Catline's conspiracy, and that remained behind him in Rome, and bade them be afraid of nothing. He was then praetor the second time, as the manner is when any man comes to recover again the dignity of a senator which he had lost. It is reported that this surname of Sura was given him upon this occasion. He being Treasurer in Sylla's dictatorship, did fondly waste and consume a marvellous sum of money of the common treasure. Sylla being offended with him for it, and demanding an account of him before the senate, he carelessly and contemptuously stepped forth, saying he could make him no other account, but showed him the calf of his leg, as children do, when they make a fault at tennis. And thereof it came that ever after that they called him Sura, because *sura* in Latin signifieth, the calf of the leg. Another time also being accused for a lewd part he had committed, he bribed some of the judges with money, and being only quit by two voices more which he had in his favour, he said he had lost his money he had given to one of those two judges, because it was enough for him to be cleared by one voice more. This man being of this disposition, was

first of all incensed by Catiline, and lastly marred by certain wizards and false prognosticators that had mocked him with a vain hope, singing verses unto him which they had feigned and devised, and false prophecies also, which they bore him in hand they had taken out of Sybil's books of prophecy, which said: that there should reign three Cornelii at Rome, of the which, two had already fulfilled the prophecy, Cinna and Sylla, and for the third, fortune laid it upon him, and therefore bade him go through withal, and not to dream it out losing opportunity as Catiline had done.

18    Now this Lentulus undertook no small enterprise, but had an intent with him to kill all the whole senate, and as many other citizens as they could murder, and to set fire of Rome, sparing none but Pompey's sons, whom they would reserve for pledges, to make their peace afterwards with Pompey. For the rumour was very great and certain also, that he returned from very great wars and conquests which he had made in the east countries. So they laid a plot to put their treason in execution, in one of the nights of Saturn's feasts. Further, they had brought flax and brimstone, and a great number of armours and weapons into Cethegus' house. Besides all this provision, they had appointed a hundred men in an hundred parts of the city, to the end that fire being raised in many places at one time, it should the sooner run through the whole city. Other men also were appointed to stop the pipes and water conduits which brought water to Rome, and to kill those also that came for water to quench the fire. In all this stir, by chance there were two ambassadors of the Allobroges, whose country at that time did much mislike of the Romans, and were unwilling to be subject unto them. Lentulus thought these men very fit instruments to cause all Gaul to rebel. Thereupon practising with them, he won them to be of their conspiracy, and gave them letters directed to the council of their country, and in them did promise them freedom. He sent other letters also unto Catilin, and persuaded him to proclaim liberty to all bondmen, and to come with all the speed he could to Rome: and sent with them one Titus of the city of Crotona, to carry these letters. But all their counsels and purposes (like fools that never met together but at feasts, drinking drunk with light women) were easily found out by Cicero: who had a careful eye upon them, and very wisely and discreetly saw through them. For he had

appointed men out of the city to spy their doings, which followed them to see what they intended. Furthermore he spoke secretly with some he trusted (the which others also took to be of the conspiracy), and knew by them that Lentulus and Cethegus had practised with the ambassadors of the Allobroges, and drawn them into their conspiracy. At length he watched them one night so narrowly, that he took the ambassadors, and Titus Crotonian with the letters he carried, by help of the ambassadors of the Allobroges, which had secretly informed him of all before.

19 The next morning by break of day, Cicero assembled the senate in the temple of Concord, and there openly read the letters, and heard the evidence of the witnesses. Further, there was one Junius Syllanus a senator that gave in evidence, that some heard Cethegus say they should kill three consuls, and four praetors. Pisa a senator also, and that had been consul, told in manner the selfsame tale. And Caius Sulpitius a praetor, that was sent into Cethegus' house, reported that he had found great store of darts, armour, daggers and swords new made. Lastly, the senate having promised Titus Crotonian he should have no hurt, so he would tell what he knew of this conspiracy, Lentulus thereby was convinced, and driven to give up his office of praetor before the senate, and changing his purple gown, to take another meet for his miserable state. This being done, Lentulus and his consorts were committed to ward, to the praetors' houses. Now growing towards evening, the people waiting about the place where the senate was assembled, Cicero at length came out, and told them what they had done within. Thereupon he was conveyed by all the people unto a friend's house of his hard by: for that his own house was occupied by the ladies of the city, who were busy solemnly celebrating a secret sacrifice in the honour of the goddess, called of the Romans the good goddess, and of the Grecians Gynaecia, to wit feminine: unto her this yearly sacrifice is done at the consul's house, by the wife or mother of the consul then being, the Vestal nuns being present at it. Now Cicero being come into his neighbour's house, began to bethink him what course he were best to take in this matter. For, to punish the offenders with severity, according to their deserts, he was afraid to do it: both because he was of a courteous nature, as also for that he would not seem to be glad to have occasion to show

his absolute power and authority, to punish (as he might) with rigour, citizens that were of the noblest houses of the city, and that had besides many friends. And contrariwise also, being remiss in so weighty a matter as this, he was afraid of the danger that might ensue of their rashness, mistrusting that if he should punish them with less than death, they would not amend for it, imagining they were well rid of their trouble, but would rather become more bold and desperate than ever they were: adding moreover the sting and spite of a new malice unto their accustomed wickedness, besides that he himself should be thought a coward and timorous man, whereas they had already not much better opinion of him.

20 Cicero being perplexed thus with these doubts, there appeared a miracle to the ladies, doing sacrifice at home in his house. For the fire that was thought to be clean out upon the altar where they had sacrificed, there suddenly rose out of the embers of the rind or barks which they had burnt, a great bright flame, which amazed all the other ladies. Howbeit the Vestal nuns willed Terentia (Cicero's wife) to go straight unto her husband, and to bid him not to be afraid to execute that boldly which he had considered of, for the benefit of the commonwealth: and that the goddess had raised this great flame, to show him that he should have great honour by doing of it. Terentia, that was no timorous nor faint-hearted woman, but very ambitious, and furthermore had got more knowledge from her husband of the affairs of the state, than otherwise she had acquainted him with her housewifery in the house, as Cicero himself reporteth: she went to make report thereof unto him, and prayed him to do execution of those men. The like did Quintus Cicero his brother, and also Publius Nigidius, his friend and fellow student with him in philosophy, and whose counsel also Cicero followed much in the government of the common-wealth. The next morning, the matter being propounded to the arbitrament of the senate, how these malefactors should be punished, Syllanus being asked his opinion first, said that they should be put in prison, and from thence to suffer execution. Others likewise that followed him, were all of that mind, but Caius Caesar, that afterwards came to be dictator, and was then but a young man and began to come forward, but yet such a one as by his behaviour and the hope he had, took such a course, that afterwards

he brought the commonwealth of Rome into an absolute monarchy. For at that time, Cicero had vehement suspicions of Caesar, but no apparent proof to convince him. And some say, that it was brought so near, as he was almost convicted, but yet saved himself. Other write to the contrary, that Cicero wittingly dissembled, that he either heard or knew any signs which were told him against Caesar, being afraid indeed of his friends and estimation. For it was a clear case, that if they had accused Caesar with the rest, he undoubtedly had sooner saved all their lives, than he should have lost his own.

21 Now when Caesar came to deliver his opinion touching the punishment of these prisoners, he stood up and said, that he did not think it good to put them to death, but to confiscate their goods: and as for their persons, that they should bestow them in prison, some in one place, some in another, in such cities of Italy as pleased Cicero best, until the war of Catilin were ended. This sentence being very mild, and the author thereof marvellous eloquent to make it good, Cicero himself added thereunto a counterpiece, inclining unto either of both the opinions, partly allowing the first, and partly also the opinion of Caesar. His friends thinking that Caesar's opinion was the safest for Cicero, because thereby he should deserve less blame for that he had not put the prisoners to death, they followed rather the second. Whereupon Syllanus also recanted that he had spoken, and expounded his opinion: saying, that when he spoke they should be put to death, he meant nothing so, but thought the last punishment a senator of Rome could have, was the prison. But the first that contraried this opinion, was Catulus Luctatius, and after him Cato, who with vehement words enforced Caesar's suspicion, and furthermore filled all the senate with wrath and courage: so that even upon the instant it was decreed by most voices, that they should suffer death. But Caesar stepped up again, and spoke against the confiscation of their goods, misliking that they should reject the gentlest part of his opinion, and that contrariwise they should stick unto the severest only: howbeit because the greatest number prevailed against him, he called the tribunes to aid him, to the end they should withstand it: but they would give no ear unto him.

22 Cicero thereupon yielding of himself, did remit the confiscation of their goods, and went with the senate to fetch the prisoners: who were not all in one house, but every praetor had one of them. So he went first to take C. Lentulus, who was in the Mount Palatine, and brought him through the holy street and the market-place, accompanied with the chiefest men of the city, who compassed him round about, and guarded his person. The people seeing that, quaked and trembled with fear, passed by, and said never a word: and specially the young men, who thought it had been some solemn mystery for the health of their country, that was so accompanied with the chief magistrate, and the noblemen of the city, with terror and fear. So when he had passed through the market-place, and was come to the prison, he delivered Lentulus into the hands of the hangman, and commanded him to do execution. Afterwards also Cethegus, and then all the rest one after another, whom he brought to the prison himself, and caused them to be executed. Furthermore, seeing divers of their accomplices in a troop together in the market-place, who knew nothing what he had done, and watched only till night were come, supposing then to take away their companions by force from the place where they were, thinking they were yet alive: he turned unto them, and spoke aloud, 'They lived.' This is a phrase of speech which the Romans use sometime, when they will finely convey the hardness of the speech, to say 'He is dead.' When night was come, and that he was going homeward, as he came through the market-place, the people did wait upon him no more with silence as before, but with great cries of his praise, and clapping of hands in every place he went, and called him Saviour, and second founder of Rome. Besides all this, at every man's door there were links and torches lighted, that it was as light in the streets, as at noondays. The very women also did put lights out of the tops of their houses to do him honour, and also to see him so nobly brought home, with such a long train of the chiefest men of the city (of the which many of them had ended great wars for the which they had triumphed, and had obtained many famous conquests to the empire of Rome, both by sea and land), confessing between themselves one to another, that the Romans were greatly bound to many captains and generals of armies in their time, for the wonderful riches, spoils, and increase of their power which they had won: howbeit that they

were to thank Cicero only, for their health and preservation, having saved them from so great and extreme a danger. Not for that they thought it so wonderful an act to have stricken dead the enterprise of the conspirators, and also to have punished the offenders by death: but because the conspiracy of Catilin being so great and dangerous an insurrection as ever was any, he had quenched it, and plucked it up by the roots, with so small hurt, and without uproar, trouble, or actual sedition. For, the most part of them that were gathered together about Catiline, when they heard that Lentulus and all the rest were put to death, they presently forsook him: and Catiline himself also fighting a battle with them he had about him, against Antonius the other consul with Cicero, he was slain in the field, and all his army defeated.

23 This notwithstanding, there were many that spoke ill of Cicero for this fact, and meant to make him repent it, having for their heads Caesar (who was already chosen praetor for the year to come), Metellus and Bestia, who should also be chosen tribunes. They, so soon as they were chosen tribunes, would not once suffer Cicero to speak to the people, notwithstanding that he was yet in his office of consul for certain days. And furthermore, to let him that he should not speak unto the people, they did set their benches upon the pulpit for orations, which they call at Rome, *rostra*: and would never suffer him to set foot in it, but only to resign his office, and that done, to come down again immediately. He granted thereunto, and went up to the pulpit upon that condition. So silence being made him, he made an oath, not like unto other consuls' oaths when they resign their office in like manner, but strange, and never heard of before: swearing, that he had saved the city of Rome, and preserved all his country and the empire of Rome from utter ruin and destruction. All the people that were present, confirmed it, and swore the like oath. Wherewithal Caesar and the other tribunes his enemies were so offended with him, that they devised to breed him some new stir and trouble: and amongst others, they made a decree, that Pompey should be sent for with his army to bridle the tyranny of Cicero. Cato (who at that time was also tribune) did him great pleasure in the furtherance of the commonwealth, opposing himself against all their practices, with the like authority and power that they had, being a tribune and

brother with them, and of better estimation than they. So that he did not only easily break all their devises, but also in a goodly oration he made in a full assembly of the people, he so highly praised and extolled Cicero's consulship unto them, and the things he did in his office, that they gave him the greatest honours that ever were decreed or granted unto any man living. For by decree of the people he was called, Father of the Country, as Cato himself had called him in his oration: the which name was never given to any man, but only unto him, and also he bore greater sway in Rome at that time, than any man beside him.

24 This notwithstanding, he made himself envied and misliked of many men, not for any ill act he did, or meant to do, but only because he did too much boast of himself. For he never was in any assembly of people, senate, or judgment, but every man's head was full still to hear the sound of Catulus and Lentulus brought in for sport, and filling the books and works he compiled besides full of his own praises: the which made his sweet and pleasant style tedious, and troublesome to those that heard them, as though this misfortune ever followed him to take away his excellent grace. But now, though he had this worm of ambition, and extreme covetous desire of honour in his head, yet did he not malice or envy any other's glory, but would very frankly praise excellent men, as well those that had been before him, as those that were in his time. And this appeareth plainly in his writings. They have written also certain notable words he spoke of some ancient men in old time: as of Aristotle, that he was like a golden flowing river; and of Plato, that if Jupiter himself would speak, he would speak like him; and of Theophrastus, he was wont to call him his delight; and of Demosthenes' orations, when one asked him on a time which of them he liked best: 'The longest,' said he. There be divers writers also, who to show that they were great followers of Demosthenes, do follow Cicero's saying in a certain epistle he wrote unto one of his friends, wherein he said that Demosthenes slept in some of his orations: but yet they forget to tell how highly he praised him in that place, and that he calls the orations which he wrote against Antonius (in the which he took great pains, and studied more than all the rest) Philippians; to follow those which Demosthenes wrote against Philip king of Macedon. Furthermore, there was not a

famous man in all his time, either in eloquence or in learning, whose fame he hath not commended in writing or otherwise in honourable speech of him. For he obtained of Caesar, when he had the empire of Rome in his hands, that Cratippus the Peripatetic philosopher was made citizen of Rome. Further, he procured that by decree of the court of the Areopagites, he was entreated to remain at Athens, to teach and instruct the youth there, for that he was a great honour and ornament unto their city. There are extant also of Cicero's epistles unto Herodes, and others unto his son, willing him to follow Cratippus in his study and knowledge. He wrote another letter also unto Gorgias the rhetorician, and forbade him his son's company, because he understood he enticed him to drunkenness, and to other great dishonesty. Of all his epistles he wrote in Greek, there is but that only written in choler, and another which he wrote unto Pelops Byzantine. And for that he wrote to Gorgias, he had great reason to be offended with him, and to taunt him in his letter: because (as it seemed) he was a man of very lewd life and conversation. But in contrary manner, writing as he did to Pelops, finding himself grieved with him, for that he was negligent in procuring the Byzantines to ordain some public honours in his behalf: that methinks proceeded of overmuch ambition, the which in many things made him too much forget the part of an honest man, and only because he would be commended for his eloquence.

25    When he had on a time pleaded Munatius' cause before the judges, who shortly after accused Sabinus a friend of his, it is reported that he was so angry with him, that he told him, 'What, Munatius, hast thou forgotten that thou wert discharged the last day of thine accusation, not for thine innocency, but for a mist I cast before the judges' eyes, that made them they could not discern the fault?' Another time also, having openly praised Marcus Crassus in the pulpit, with good audience of the people, shortly after he spoke to the contrary, all the evil he could of him, in the same place. 'Why, how now,' said Crassus, 'diddest thou not thyself highly praise me in this place, the last day?' 'I cannot deny it,' said Cicero, 'but indeed I took an ill matter in hand to show mine eloquence.' Another time Crassus chanced to say in an open assembly, that none of all the Crassi of his house that ever lived

above lx. years: and afterwards again repenting himself, he called it in again, and said, 'Sure I knew not what I did, when I said so.' Cicero answered him again: 'Thou knewest well enough the people were glad to hear it, and therefore spakest it to please them.' Another time Crassus liking the opinion of the Stoic philosophers, that said the wise man was ever rich, Cicero answered him, and bade him consider whether they meant not thereby, that the wise man had all things. Crassus' covetousness was defamed of every man. Of Crassus' sons, one of them did much resemble Actius, and therefore his mother had an ill name by him: one day this son of Crassus made an oration before the senate, which divers of them commended very much. So, Cicero being asked how he liked it: 'Methinks,' said he, 'it is Actius* of Crassus.'

26    About this time, Crassus being ready to take his journey into Syria, he desired to have Cicero his friend, rather than his enemy. Therefore one night making much of him, he told Cicero that he would come and sup with him. Cicero said he should be welcome. Shortly after some of his friends told him of Vatinius, how he was desirous to be made friends with him, for he was his enemy. 'What,' quoth Cicero, 'and will he come to supper too?' Thus he used Crassus. Now this Vitinius having a swollen neck, one day pleading before Cicero, he called him the swollen orator. Another time when he heard say that he was dead, and then that he was alive again: 'A vengeance on him,' said he, 'that hath lied so shamefully.' Another time when Caesar had made a law for the dividing of the lands of Campania unto the soldiers, divers of the senate were angry with him for it, and among other, Lucius Gellius (a very old man) said, he would never grant it while he lived. Cicero pleasantly answered again, 'Alas, tarry a little, the good old man will not trouble you long.' Another time there was one Octavius, supposed to be an African† born. He when Cicero on a time pleaded a matter, said that he heard him not: Cicero presently answered him again, 'And yet hast thou a hole bored through thine

---

* Ἄξιος Κράσσου. Actius is a proper name of a Roman, and ἄξιος in Greek signifieth, worthy: so the grace of the equivocation cannot be expresseed in any other language.

† Because the Africans have commonly the ears bored through.

ear.' Another time Metellus Nepos told him, that he had over-thrown more men by his witness, than he had saved by his eloquence. 'I grant,' said Cicero, 'for indeed I have more faith, than eloquence in me.' So was there also a young man that was suspected to have poisoned his father with a tart, that boasted he would revile Cicero: 'I had rather have that of thee,' quoth Cicero, 'than thy tart.' Publius Sextius also having a matter before the judges, entertained Cicero, with other of his counsellors: but yet he would speak all himself, and give none of the orators leave to say anything. In the end, when they saw plainly that the judges would discharge him, being ready to give sentence, Cicero said unto him, 'Bestir thee hardily today, for tomorrow, Sextius, thou shalt be a private man.' Another, one Publius Scotta, who would fain have been thought a wise lawyer, and yet had little wit and understanding, Cicero appealed to him as a witness in a matter, and being examined, he answered he knew nothing of it. Cicero replied to him again: 'Thou thinkest peradventure they ask thee touching the law.' Again, Metellus Nepos, in a certain disputation he had with Cicero, did many times repeat, 'Who is thy father?' Cicero answered him again: 'Thy mother hath made this question harder for thee to answer.' This Nepos' mother was reported to be a light housewife, and he as subtle-witted and unconstant. For he being tribune, left in a gear the exercise of his office, and went into Syria to Pompey, upon no occasion: and as fondly again he returned thence, upon a sudden. His schoolmaster Philager also being dead, he buried him very honestly, and set a crow of stone upon the top of his tomb. Cicero finding it, told him, 'Thou hast done very wisely: for thy master hath taught thee rather to fly, than to speak.' Another time Appius Clodius pleading a matter, said in his preamble that his friend had earnestly requested him to employ all his knowledge, diligence, and faith upon this matter. 'O gods,' said Cicero, 'and hast thou showed thyself so hard-hearted to thy friend, that thou hast performed none of all these he requested thee?'

27    Now to use these fine taunts and girds to his enemies, it was a part of a good orator: but so commonly to gird every man to make the people laugh, that won him great ill will of many, as shall appear by some examples I will tell you. Marcus Aquinius had two

sons-in-law, who were both banished: Cicero therefore called him
Adrastus. Lucius Cotta by chance also was censor at that time, when
Cicero sued to be consul: and being there at the day of the election,
he was athirst, and was driven to drink. But while he drank, all his
friends stood about him, and after he had drunk, he said unto them:
'It is well done of ye,' said he, ' to be afraid lest the censor should
be angry with me, because I drink water:' for it was reported
the censor loved wine well. Another time Cicero meeting one
Voconius, with three foul daughters of his with him, he cried out
aloud:

> This man hath gotten children in despite of Phoebus.

It was thought in Rome that Marcus Gellius was not born of free
parents by father and mother: who reading certain letters one day
in the senate very loud, Cicero said unto them that were about
him, 'Wonder not at it,' quoth he, 'for this man hath been a crier
in his days.' Faustus, the son of Sylla dictator at Rome, which set up
bills outlawing divers Romans, making it lawful for any man to kill
them without danger where they found them, this man after he
had spent the most part of his father's goods, was so sore in debt,
that he was driven to sell his household stuff, by bills set up on
every post. Cicero when he saw them, 'Yea marry,' said he, 'these
bills please me better, than those which his father set up.'

28 These taunts and common quips without purpose, made
divers men to malice him. The great ill will that Clodius bore him,
began upon this occasion. Clodius was of a noble house, a young
man, and very wild and insolent. He being in love with Pompeia
Caesar's wife, found the means secretly to get into Caesar's house,
apparelled like a young singing wench, because on that day the
ladies of Rome did solemnly celebrate a secret sacrifice in Caesar's
house, which is not lawful for men to be present at. So there was no
man there but Clodius, who thought he should not have been
known, because he was but a young man without any hair on his
face, and that by this means he might come to Pompeia amongst the
other women. He being got into this great house by night, not
knowing the rooms and chambers in it, there was one of Caesar's
mother's maids of her chamber called Aurelia, who seeing him
wandering up and down the house in this sort, asked him what he
was, and how they called him. So being forced to answer, he said he

sought for Aura, one of Pompeia's maids. The maid perceived straight it was no woman's voice, and therewithal gave a great shriek, and called the other women: the which did see the gates fast shut, and then sought every corner up and down, so that at length they found him in the maid's chamber, with whom he came in. His offence was straight blown abroad in the city, whereupon Caesar put his wife away: and one of the tribunes also accused Clodius, and burdened him that he had profaned the holy ceremonies of the sacrifices.

29    Cicero at that time was yet his friend, being one that had very friendly done for him at all times, and had ever accompanied him to guard him, if any man would have offered him injury in the busy time of the conspiracy of Catiline. Clodius stoutly denied the matter he was burdened with, and said that he was not in Rome at that time, but far from thence. Howbeit Cicero gave evidence against him, and deposed, that the selfsame day he came home to his house unto him, to speak with him about certain matters. This indeed was true, though it seemeth Cicero gave not this evidence so much for the truth's sake, as to please his wife Terentia: for she hated Clodius to the death, because of his sister Clodia that would have married Cicero, and did secretly practise the marriage by one Tullius, who was Cicero's very friend, and because he repaired very often to this Clodia that dwelt hard by Cicero, Terentia began to suspect him. Terentia being a cruel woman, and wearing her husband's breeches, allured Cicero to set upon Clodius in his adversity, and to witness against him, as many other honest men of the city also did: some that he was perjured, others that he committed a thousand lewd parts, that he bribed the people with money, that he had enticed and deflowered many women. Lucullus also brought forth certain maidens which deposed that Clodius had deflowered the youngest of his own sisters, she being in house with him, and married. And there went out a great rumour also, that he knew his two other sisters, of the which the one was called Terentia,* and married unto King Martius: and the other Clodia, whom Metellus Celer had married, and whom they commonly called Quadrantaria: because one of her paramours sent

* Some old books do read Tertia.

her a purse full of quadrins (which are little pieces of copper
money) instead of silver. Clodius was slandered more by her, than
with any of the other two. Notwithstanding, the people were very
much offended with them, that gave evidence against him, and
accused him. The judges being afraid of it, got a great number of
armed men about them, at the day of his judgment, for the safety of
their persons: and in the tables where they wrote their sentences,
their letters for the most part were confusedly set down. This
notwithstanding, it was found that he was quit by the greatest
number: and it was reported also that some of them were close-
fisted. Catulus therefore meeting with some of them going home,
after they had given their sentence, told them: 'Surely ye had good
reason to be well guarded for your safety, for you were afraid your
money should have been taken from you, which you took for
bribes.' And Cicero said unto Clodius, who reproved him that his
witness was not true he gave against him: 'Clean contrary,' quoth
Cicero, 'for five and twenty of the judges have believed me, being
so many that have condemned thee, and the thirty would not
believe thee, for they would not quit thee before they had fingered
money.' Notwithstanding, in this judgment Caesar never gave
evidence against Clodius: and said moreover, that he did not think
his wife had committed any adultery, howbeit that he had put her
away, because he would that Caesar's wife should not only be clean
from any dishonesty, but also void of all suspicion.

30 Clodius being quit of this accusation and trouble, and having
also found means to be chosen tribune, he began straight to
persecute Cicero, changing all things, and stirring up all manner of
people against him. First he won the goodwill of the common
people by devising of new laws which he preferred, for their
benefit and commodity: to both the consuls he granted great and
large provinces: unto Piso, Macedon, and to Gabinius, Syria. He
made also many poor men free citizens, and had always about him
a great number of slaves armed. At that present time there were
three notable men in Rome, which carried all the sway: Crassus,
that showed himself an open enemy unto Cicero: Pompey the
other, made much both of the one and the other: the third was
Caesar, who was prepared for his journey into Gaul with an army.
Cicero did lean unto him (though he knew him no fast friend of

his, and that he mistrusted him for matters past in Catiline's conspiracy) and prayed him that he might go to the wars with him, as one of his lieutenants. Caesar granted him. Thereupon Clodius perceiving that by this means he got him out of the danger of his office of tribuneship for that year, he made fair weather with him (as though he meant to reconcile himself unto him) and told him that he had cause rather to think ill of Terentia, for that he had done against him, than of himself, and always spoke very courteously of him as occasion fell out, and said he did think nothing in him, neither had any malice to him, howbeit it did a little grieve him, that being a friend, he was offered unkindness by his friend. These sweet words made Cicero no more afraid, so that he gave up his lieutenancy unto Caesar, and began again to plead as he did before. Caesar took this in such disdain, that he hardened Clodius the more against him, and besides, made Pompey his enemy. And Caesar himself also said before all the people, that he thought Cicero had put Lentulus, Cethegus and the rest, unjustly to death, and contrary to law, without lawful trial and condemnation. And this was the fault for the which Cicero was openly accused. Thereupon Cicero seeing himself accused for this fact, he changed the usual gown he ware, and put a on a mourning gown: and so suffering his beard and hair of his head to grow without any combing, he went in this humble manner, and sued to the people. But Clodius was ever about him in every place and street he went, having a sight of rascals and knaves with him that shamefully mocked him for that he had changed his gown and countenance in that sort, and oftentimes they cast dirt and stones at him, breaking his talk and requests he made unto the people.

31    This notwithstanding, all the knights of Rome did in manner change their gowns with him for company, and of them there were commonly twenty thousand young gentlemen of noble house which followed him with their hair about their ears, and were suitors to the people for him. Furthermore, the senate assembled to decree that the people should mourn in blacks, as in a common calamity: but the consuls were against it. And Clodius on the other side was with a band of armed men about the senate, so that many of the senators ran out of the senate, crying, and tearing their clothes for sorrow. Howbeit these men seeing all that, were

nothing the more moved with pity and shame: but either Cicero must needs absent himself, or else determine to fight with Clodius. Then went Cicero to entreat Pompey to aid him: but he absented himself of purpose out of the city, because he would not be entreated, and lay at one of his houses in the country, near unto the city of Alba. So he first of all sent Piso his son-in-law unto him to entreat him, and afterwards went himself in person to him. But Pompey being told that he was come, had not the heart to suffer him to come to him, to look him in the face: for he had been past all shame to have refused the request of so worthy a man, who had before showed him such pleasure, and also done and said so many things in his favour. Howbeit Pompey being the son-in-law of Caesar, did unfortunately (at his request) forsake him at his need, unto whom he was bound for so many infinite pleasures, as he had received of him afore: and therefore when he heard say he came to him, he went out at his back gate and would not speak with him. So Cicero seeing himself bewrayed of him, and now having no other refuge to whom he might repair unto, he put himself into the hands of the two consuls. Of them two, Gabinius was ever cruel, and churlish unto him. But Piso on the other side spoke always very courteously unto him, and prayed him to absent himself for a time, and to give place a little to Clodius' fury, and patiently to bear the change of the time: for in so doing, he might come again another time to be the preserver of his country, which was now for his sake in tumult and sedition. Cicero upon this answer of the consul, consulted with his friends: among the which Lucullus gave him advice to tarry, and said that he should be the stronger. But all the rest were of contrary opinion, and would have him to get him away with speed: for the people would shortly wish for him again, when they had once been beaten with Clodius' fury and folly. Cicero liked best to follow this counsel. Whereupon having had a statue of Minerva a long time in his house, the which he greatly reverenced, he carried her himself, and gave her to the Capitol with this inscription: 'Unto Minerva, Protector of Rome'. So, his friends having given him safe conduct, he went out of Rome about midnight, and took his way through the country of Luke by land, meaning to go into Sicily.

32  When it was known in Rome that he was fled, Clodius did presently banish him by decree of the people, and caused bills of inhibition to be set up, that no man should secretly receive him within five hundred miles' compass of Italy. Howbeit divers men reverencing Cicero, made no reckoning of that inhibition: but when they had used him with all manner of courtesy possible, they did conduct him besides at his departure, saving one city only in Luke, called at that time Hipponium, and now Vibone: where a Sicilian called Vibius (unto whom Cicero before had done many pleasures, and specially among others, had made him master of the works in the year that he was consul) would not once receive him into his house, but promised him he would appoint him a place in the country that he might go unto. And Caius Virgilius also, at that time praetor and governor of Sicily, who before had showed himself his very great friend, wrote then unto him, that he should not come near unto Sicily. This grieved him to the heart. Thereupon he went directly unto the city of Brundusium, and there embarked to pass over the sea unto Dyrrachium, and at the first had wind at will: but when he was in the main sea, the wind turned, and brought him back again to the place from whence he came. But after that, he hoist sail again, and the report went, that at his arrival at Dyrrachium when he took land, the earth shook under him, and the sea gave back together: whereby the soothsayers interpreted, that his exile should not be long, because both the one and the other was a token of change. Yet Cicero, notwithstanding that many men came to see him for the goodwill they bore him, and that the cities of Greece contended who should most honour him, he was always sad, and could not be merry, but cast his eyes still towards Italy, as passioned lovers do towards the women they love: showing himself faint-hearted, and took this adversity more basely, than was looked for of one so well studied and learned as he. And yet he oftentimes prayed his friends, not to call him orator, but rather philosopher: saying, that philosophy was his chiefest profession, and that for his eloquence he did not use it, but as a necessary instrument to one that pleadeth in the commonwealth. But glory, and opinion, hath great power to take man's reason from him, even like a colour, from the minds of them that are common pleaders in matters of state, and to make them feel the selfsame passions that common people do, by daily frequenting

their company: unless they take great heed of them, and that they come to practise in the commonwealth with this resolute mind, to have to do with the like matters that the common people have, but not to entangle themselves with the like passions and moods, by the which their matters do rise.

33   Now Clodius was not contented that he had banished Cicero out of Italy, but further he burnt all his houses in the country and his house also in Rome standing in the market-place, of the which he built a temple of liberty, and caused his goods to be sold by the crier: so that the crier was occupied all day long crying the goods to be sold, and no man offered to buy any of them. The chiefest men of the city beginning to be afraid of these violent parts, and having the common people at his commandment, whom he had made very bold and insolent, he began to inveigh against Pompey and spoke ill of his doings in the time of his wars, the which every man else but himself did commend. Pompey then was very angry with himself that he had so forsaken Cicero, and repented him of it, and by his friends procured all the means he could to call him home again from his banishment. Clodius was against it all he could. The senate notwithstanding with one full consent ordained, that nothing should be established for the commonwealth, before Cicero's banishment were first repealed. Lentulus was at that time consul, and there grew such an uproar and stir upon it, that some of the tribunes were hurt in the market-place, and Quintus Cicero (the brother of Cicero) was slain and hidden under the dead bodies. Then the people began to change their minds. And Annius Milo, one of the tribunes, was the first man that durst venture upon Clodius, and bring him by force to be tried before the judges. Pompey himself also having got a great number of men about him, as well of the city of Rome as of other towns adjoining to it, being strongly guarded with them, he came out of his house, and compelled Clodius to get him out of the market-place, and then called the people to give their voices, for the calling home again of Cicero. It is reported that the people never passed thing with so great goodwill, nor so wholly together, as the return of Cicero. And the senate for their parts also, in the behalf of Cicero, ordained that the cities which had honoured and received Cicero in his exile, should be greatly commended: and that his houses which

Clodius had overthrown and razed, should be re-edified at the charge of the commonwealth. So Cicero returned the sixteenth month after his banishment, and the towns and cities he came by, showed themselves so joyful of his return, that all manner of men went to meet and honour him, with so great love and affection, that Cicero's report thereof afterwards came indeed short of the very truth as it was. For he said, that Italy brought him into Rome upon their shoulders. Insomuch as Crassus himself, who before his banishment was his enemy, went then with very goodwill unto him, and became his friend, saying: that he did it for the love of his son, who loved Cicero with all his heart.

34   Now Cicero being returned, he found a time when Clodius was out of the city, and went with a good company of his friends unto the Capitol, and there took away the tables, and broke them, in the which Clodius had written all his acts that he had passed and done in the time of his tribuneship. Clodius would afterwards have accused Cicero for it: but Cicero answered him, that he was not lawfully created tribune, because he was of the patricians, and therefore all that he had done in his tribuneship was void, and of none effect. Therewith Cato was offended, and spoke against him, not for that he liked any of Clodius' doings (but to the contrary, utterly misliked all that he did), but because he thought it out of all reason, that the senate should cancel all those things which he had done and passed in his tribuneship, and specially, because amongst the rest that was there which he himself had done in the Isle of Cyprus, and in the city of Byzantium. Hereupon there grew some strangeness betwixt Cicero and Cato, the which notwithstanding broke not out to open enmity, but only to an abstinence of their wonted familiarity, and access one to another.

35   Shortly after, Milo slew Clodius. Milo being accused of murder, prayed Cicero to plead his cause. The senate fearing that this accusation of Milo (who was a hardy man, and of quality besides) would move some sedition and uproar in the city, they gave commission to Pompey to see justice executed as well in this cause, as in other offences, that the city might be quiet, and judgment also executed with safety. Thereupon Pompey the night before took the highest places of the market-place, by his soldiers that were armed, whom he placed thereabout. Milo fearing that

Cicero would be afraid to see such a number of harnessed men about him, being no usual matter, and that it might peradventure hinder him to plead his cause well, he prayed him he would come betimes in the morning in his litter into the market-place, and there to stay the coming of the judges, till the place were full. For Cicero was not only fearful in wars, but timorous also in pleading. For indeed he never began to speak, but it was in fear: and when his eloquence was come to the best proof and perfection, he never left his trembling and timorousness. Insomuch that pleading a case for Mutius Muraena (accused by Cato), striving to excel Hortensius, whose pleading was very well thought of, he took no rest all night, and what through watching and the trouble of his mind, he was not very well, so that he was not so well liked for his pleading, as Hortensius. So, going to defend Milo's cause, when he came out of his litter, and saw Pompey set aloft as if he had been in a camp, and the market-place compassed about with armed men, glistering in every corner, it so amated him, that he could scant fashion himself to speak, all the parts of him did so quake and tremble, and his voice could not come to him. But Milo on the other side stood boldly by himself, without any fear at all of the judgment of his cause, neither did he let his hair grow, as other men accused did: neither did he wear any mourning gown, the which was (as it seemed) one of the chiefest causes that condemned him. Yet many held opinion that this timorousness of Cicero came rather of the goodwill he bore unto his friends, than of any cowardly mind of himself.

36   He was also chosen one of the priests of the soothsayers, which they call Augures, in the room of P. Crassus the younger, who was slain in the realm of Parthia. Afterwards, the province of Cilicia being appointed to him, with an army of twelve thousand footmen, and two thousand five hundred horsemen, he took the sea to go thither. So when he was arrived there, he brought Cappadocia again into the subjection and obedience of King Ariobarzanes according to his commission and commandment given by the senate: moreover, both there and elsewhere he took as excellent good order as could be devised, in reducing of things to quietness, without wars. Furthermore, finding that the Cilicians were grown somewhat stout and unruly, by the overthrow the

Romans had of the Parthians, and by reason of the rising and rebellion in Syria, he brought them unto reason by gentle persuasions, and never received gifts that were sent him, no, not from kings and princes. Furthermore, he did disburden the provinces of the feasts and banquets they were wont to make other governors before him. On the other side also, he would ever have the company of good and learned men at his table, and would use them well, without curiosity and excess. He had never porter to his gate, nor was seen by any man in his bed: for he would always rise at the break of day, and would walk or stand before his door. He would courteously receive all them that came to salute and visit him. Further they report of him, that he never caused man to be beaten with rods, nor to tear his own garments. In his anger he never reviled any man, neither did despitefully set fine upon any man's head. Finding many things also belonging to the commonwealth, which private men had stolen and embezzled to their own use, he restored them again unto the cities, whereby they grew very rich and wealthy: and yet did he save their honour and credit that had taken them away, and did them no other hurt, but only constrained them to restore that which was the commonwealth's. He made a little war also, and drove away the thieves that kept about the mountain Amanus, for the which exploit his soldiers called him Imperator, to say, chief captain. About that time there was an orator called Caecilius, who wrote unto him from Rome, to pray him to send him some leopards or panthers out of Cilicia, because he would show the people some pastime with them. Cicero boasting of his doings wrote to him again, that there were no more leopards in Cilicia, but that they were all fled into Caria for anger that seeing all things quiet in Cilicia, they had leisure now to hunt them. So when he returned towards Rome, from the charge of his government, he came by Rhodes: and stayed a few days at Athens, with great delight, to remember how pleasantly he lived there before, at what time he studied there. Thither came to him the chiefest learned men of the city, and his friends also, with whom he was acquainted at his first being there. In fine, having received all the honourable entertainment in Greece that could be, he returned unto Rome, where at his arrival he found great factions kindled, the which men saw plainly would grow in the end to civil war.

37   Thereupon the senate having decreed that he should enter in triumph into the city, he answered, that he would rather (all parties agreed) follow Caesar's coach in triumph. So he travelled very earnestly between Pompey and Caesar, eftsoons writing unto Caesar and also speaking unto Pompey that was present, seeking all the means he could, to take up the quarrel and misliking betwixt them two. But it was so impossible a matter, that there was no speech of agreement would take place. So Pompey hearing that Caesar was not far from Rome, he durst no longer abide in Rome, but fled with divers of the greatest men in Rome. Cicero would not follow him when he fled, and therefore men thought he would take part with Caesar: but this is certain, that he was in a marvellous perplexity, and could not easily determine what way to take. Whereupon he wrote in his epistles: 'What way should I take? Pompey hath the juster and honester cause of war, but Caesar can better execute, and provide for himself and his friends with better safety: so that I have means enough to fly, but none to whom I might repair.' In all this stir, there was one of Caesar's friends called Trebatius, which wrote a letter unto Cicero, and told him that Caesar wished him in any case to come to him, and to run with him the hope and fortune he undertook: but if he excused himself by his age, that then he should get him into Greece, and there to be quiet from them both. Cicero marvelling that Caesar wrote not to him himself, answered in anger, that he would do nothing unworthy of his acts all the days of his life thitherto: and to this effect he wrote in his letters.

38   Now Caesar being gone into Spain, Cicero embarked immediately to go to Pompey. So when he came unto him, every man was very glad of his coming, but Cato. Howbeit Cato secretly reproved him for coming unto Pompey, saying: that for himself he had been without all honesty at that time to have forsaken that part, the which he had always taken and followed from the beginning of his first practice in the commonwealth: but for him on the other side, that it had been better for the safety of his country, and chiefly for all his friends, that he had been a neuter to both, and so to have taken things as they had fallen out: and that he had no manner of reason nor instant cause to make him to become Caesar's enemy, and by coming thither to put himself into so great

peril. These persuasions of Cato overthrew all Cicero's purpose
and determination, besides that Pompey himself did not employ
him in any matter of service or importance. But hereof himself
was more in fault than Pompey, because he confessed openly that
he did repent him he was come thither. Furthermore, he scorned
and disdained all Pompey's preparations and counsels, the which
indeed made him to be had in jealousy and suspicion. Also he
would ever be fleering and jibing at those that took Pompey's part,
though he had no list himself to be merry. He would also go up
and down the camp very sad and heavy, but yet he would ever
have one jest or other to make men laugh, although they had as
little lust to be merry as he: and surely, it shall do no hurt to call
some of them to mind in this place. Domitius being very desirous
to prefer a gentleman to have charge of men, to recommend him,
he said he was an honest, wise, and sober man. Whereto Cicero
presently answered: 'Why doest thou not keep him then to bring
up thy children?' Another time when they commended Theo-
phanes Lesbian (that was master of all the artificers of the camp)
because he had notably comforted the Rhodians when they had
received a great loss of their navy: 'See,' said Cicero, 'what a
goodly thing it is to have a Grecian master of artificers in the
camp!' When both battles came to join together, and that Caesar
had in manner all the advantage, and kept them as good as
besieged, Lentulus told him on a time, that he heard say all
Caesar's friends were mad, and melancholy men. 'Why,' quoth
Cicero to him again, 'doest thou say that they do envy Caesar?'
Another called Martius, coming lately out of Italy, said that there
ran a rumour in Rome, that Pompey was besieged. 'What,' quoth
Cicero to him again, 'and diddest thou take ship to come and see
him thyself, because thou mightest believe it, when thou haddest
seen it?' Pompey being overthrown, one Nonius said there was
yet good hope left, because they had taken seven eagles within
Pompey's camp. 'Thy persuasion were not ill,' quoth Cicero, 'so
we were to fight but with pies or daws.' Labienus reposed all his
trust in certain oracles, that Pompey of necessity must have the
upper hand. 'Yea,' said Cicero, 'but for all this goodly stratagem of
war, we have not long since lost our whole camp.'

39   After the battle of Pharsalia, where Cicero was not by reason
of his sickness, Pompey being fled, and Cato at that time at
Dyrrachium, where he had gathered a great number of men of war,
and had also prepared a great navy, he prayed Cicero to take charge
of all this army, as it pertained unto him, having been consul.
Cicero did not only refuse it, but also told them he would meddle
no more with this war. But this was enough to have made him been
slain: for the younger Pompey and his friends called him traitor, and
drew their swords upon him to kill him, which they had done, had
not Cato stepped between them and him: and yet had he much ado
to save him, and to convey him safely out of the camp. When
Cicero came to Brundusium, he stayed there a certain time for
Caesar's coming, who came but slowly, by reason of his troubles he
had in Asia, as also in Egypt. Howbeit news being brought at length
that Caesar was arrived at Tarentum, and that he came by land unto
Brundusium, Cicero departed thence to go meet him, not mistrusting that Caesar would not pardon him, but rather being ashamed to
come to his enemy being a conqueror, before such a number of
men as he had about him. Yet he was not forced to do or speak
anything unseemly to his calling. For Caesar seeing him coming
towards him far before the rest that came with him, he lighted from
his horse and embraced him, and walked a great way a-foot with
him, still talking with him only, and ever after he did him great
honour and made much of him. Insomuch as Cicero having written
a book in praise of Cato, Caesar on the other side wrote another,
and praised the eloquence and life of Cicero, matching it with the
life of Pericles, and Theramenes. Cicero's book was intituled *Cato*,
and Caesar's book called *Anticato*, as much to say, as against Cato.
They say further, that Quintus Ligarius being accused to have been
in the field against Caesar, Cicero took upon him to defend his
cause: and that Caesar said unto his friends about him, 'What hurt is
it for us to hear Cicero speak, whom we have not heard of long
time? For otherwise Ligarius (in my opinion) standeth already a
condemned man, for I know him to be a vile man, and mine
enemy.' But when Cicero had begun his oration, he moved Caesar
marvellously, he had so sweet a grace, and such force in his words,
that it is reported Caesar changed divers colours, and showed
plainly by his countenance, that there was a marvellous alteration in
all the parts of him. For, in the end when the orator came to touch

the battle of Pharsalia, then was Caesar so troubled, that his body shook withal, and besides, certain books he had, fell out of his hands, and he was driven against his will to set Ligarius at liberty.

40   Afterwards, when the commonwealth of Rome came to be a kingdom, Cicero leaving to practise any more in the state, he gave himself to read philosophy to the young men that came to hear him: by whose access unto him (because they were the chiefest of the nobility in Rome) he came again to bear as great sway and authority in Rome, as ever he had done before. His study and endeavour was, to write matters of philosophy dialogue-wise, and to translate out of Greek into Latin, taking pains to bring all the Greek words which are proper unto logic and natural causes, unto Latin. For he was the first man by report that gave Latin names unto these Greek words, which are proper unto philosophers, as, φαντασία, he termed, *visio*; κατάθεσις ἐποχή, *assensus cohibitio*; κατα-λήψις, *comprehensio*; τὸ ἄτομον, *corpus individuum*; τὸ ἄμερες, *corpus simplex*; τὸ κένον, *assensus vacuum*, and many other suchlike words. But though he were not the first, yet was it he that most did devise and use them, and turned some of them by translation, others into proper terms: so that at length they came to be well taken, known, and understood of every man. And of his readiness in writing of verses, he would use them many times for his recreation: for it is reported, that whensoever he took in hand to make any, he would dispatch five hundred of them in a night. Now, all that time of his recreation and pleasure, he would commonly be at some of his houses in the country, which he had near unto Thusculum, from whence he would write unto his friends, that he led Laertes' life: either spoken merrily as his manner was, or else pricked forward with ambition, desiring to return again to be a practiser in the commonwealth, being weary with the present time and state thereof. Howsoever it was, he came oftentimes to Rome, only to see Caesar to keep him his friend, and would ever be the first man to confirm any honours decreed unto him, and was always studious to utter some new matter to praise him and his doings. As that was he said touching the statues of Pompey, the which being over-thrown, Caesar commanded them to be set up again, and so they were. For Cicero said that by that courtesy in setting up of Pompey's statues again, he did establish his own.

41 So, Cicero being determined to write all the Roman history, and to mingle with them many of the Grecians' doings, adding thereunto all the fables and devises which they do write and report, he was hindered of his purpose against his will, by many open and private troubles that came upon him at once: whereof notwithstanding he himself was cause of the most of them. For first of all, he did put away his wife Terentia, because she had made but small account of him in all the wars: so that he departed from Rome having no necessary thing with him to entertain him out of his country, and yet when he came back again into Italy, she never showed any spark of love or goodwill towards him. For she never came to Brundusium to him, where he remained a long time: and worse than that, his daughter having the heart to take so long a journey in hand to go to him, she neither gave her company to conduct her, nor money or other furniture convenient for her, but so handled the matter, that Cicero at his return to Rome found bare walls in his house and nothing in it, and yet greatly brought in debt besides. And these were the honestest causes alleged for their divorce. But besides that Terentia denied all these, Cicero himself gave her a good occasion to clear herself, because he shortly after married a young maiden, being fallen in fancy with her (as Terentia said) for her beauty: or, as Tyro his servant wrote, for her riches, to the end that with her goods he might pay his debts. For she was very rich, and Cicero also was appointed her guardian, she being left sole heir. Now, because he owed a marvellous sum of money, his parents and friends did counsel him to marry this young maiden, notwithstanding he was too old for her, because that with her goods he might satisfy his creditors. But Antonius speaking of this marriage of Cicero, in his answers and orations he made against the Philippians, he doth reprove him for that he put away his wife, with whom he was grown old, being merry with him by the way for that he had been an idle man, and never went from the smoke of his chimney, nor had been abroad in the wars in any service of his country or commonwealth. Shortly after that he had married his second wife, his daughter died in labour of child, in Lentulus' house, whose second wife she was, being before married unto Piso, who was her first husband. So the philosophers and learned men came of all sides to comfort him: but he took her death so sorrowfully, that he put away his second wife, because he thought she did rejoice at the death of his daughter.

42    And thus much touching the state and troubles of his house. Now touching the conspiracy against Caesar, he was not made privy to it, although he was one of Brutus' greatest friends, and that it grieved him to see things in that state they were brought unto, and albeit also he wished for the time past, as much as any other man did. But indeed the conspirators were afraid of his nature, that lacked hardiness: and of his age, the which oftentimes makes the stoutest and most hardiest natures, faint-hearted and cowardly. Notwithstanding, the conspiracy being executed by Brutus and Cassius, Caesar's friends being gathered together, every man was afraid that the city would again fall into civil wars. And Antonius also, who was consul at that time, did assemble the senate, and made some speech and motion then to draw things again unto quietness. But Cicero having used divers persuasions fit for the time, in the end he moved the senate to decree (following the example of the Athenians) a general oblivion of things done against Caesar, and to assign unto Brutus and Cassius some governments of provinces. Howbeit nothing was concluded: for the people of themselves were sorry, when they saw Caesar's body brought through the market-place. And when Antonius also did show them his gown all bebloodied, cut, and thrust through with swords, then they were like madmen for anger, and sought up and down the market-place if they could meet with any of them that had slain him: and taking firebrands in their hands, they ran to their houses to set them afire. But the conspirators having prevented this danger, saved themselves: and fearing that if they tarried at Rome, they should have many such alarms, they forsook the city.

43    Then Antonius began to look aloft, and became fearful to all men, as though he meant to make himself king: but yet most of all unto Cicero, above all others. For Antonius perceiving that Cicero began again to increase in credit and authority, and knowing that he was Brutus' very friend, he did mislike to see him come near him: and besides, there was at that time some jealousy betwixt them, for the diversity and difference of their manners and dispositions. Cicero being afraid of this, was first of all in mind to go with Dolabella to his province of Syria, as one of his lieutenants. But they that were appointed to be consuls the next year following after Antonius, two noble citizens, and Cicero's great friends, Hircius

and Pansa: they entreated him not to forsake them, undertaking
that they would pluck down this overgreat power of Antonius,
so he would remain with them. But Cicero, neither believing
nor altogether mistrusting them, forsook Dolabella, and promised
Hircius and Pansa, that he would spend the summer at Athens, and
that he would return again to Rome so soon as they were entered
into their consulship. With this determination Cicero took sea
alone, to go into Greece. But as it chanceth oftentimes, there was
some let that kept him he could not sail, and news came to him
daily from Rome, as the manner is, that Antonius was wonderfully
changed, and that now he did nothing any more without the
authority and consent of the senate, and that there lacked nothing
but his person, to make all things well. Then Cicero condemning
his dastardly fear, returned forthwith to Rome, not being deceived
in his first hope. For there came such a number of people out to
meet him, that he could do nothing all day long, but take them by
the hands, and embrace them: who to honour him, came to meet
him at the gate of the city, as also by the way to bring him to
his house. The next morning Antonius assembled the senate, and
called for Cicero by name. Cicero refused to go, and kept his bed,
feigning that he was weary with his journey and pains he had
taken the day before: but indeed, the cause why he went not, was
for fear and suspicion of an ambush that was laid for him by the
way, if he had gone, as he was informed by one of his very good
friends. Antonius was marvellously offended that they did wrongfully accuse him, for laying of any ambush for him: and therefore
sent soldiers to his house, and commanded them to bring him by
force, or else to set his house afire. After that time, Cicero and he
were always at jar, but yet coldly enough, one of them taking heed
of another: until that the young Caesar returning from the city of
Apollonia, came as lawful heir unto Julius Caesar dictator, and had
contention with Antonius for the sum of two thousand five
hundred myriads, the which Antonius kept in his hands of his
father's goods.

44    Thereupon, Philip who had married the mother of this young
Caesar, and Marcellus, who had also married his sister, went with
young Caesar unto Cicero, and there agreed together, that Cicero
should help young Caesar with the favour of his authority and

eloquence, as well towards the senate, as also to the people: and
that Caesar in recompense of his goodwill should stand by Cicero
with his money and soldiers. For this young Caesar had many of his
father's old soldiers about him, that had served under him. Now
there was another cause that made Cicero glad to embrace the
friendship of this young Caesar and that was this. Whilst Pompey
and Julius Caesar were alive, and in good case, Cicero dreamed
one night that the senators' sons were called into the Capitol,
because Jupiter had appointed to show them him, that one day
should come to be lord and king of Rome, and that the Romans
being desirous to see who it should be, ran all unto the temple: and
that all the children likewise were waiting there in their goodly
garded gowns of purple, until that suddenly the doors of the temple
were open, and then that all the children rose one after another,
and went and passed by the image of Jupiter, who looked upon
them all, and sent them discontented, saving this young Caesar,
unto whom he put forth his hand as he passed by, and said: 'My
lords of Rome, this child is he that shall end all your civil wars,
when he cometh to be lord of Rome.' Some say, that Cicero had
this vision in his dream, and that he carried in good memory the
look of this child, howbeit that he knew him not: and that the next
morning he went of purpose into the field of Mars, where these
young boys did exercise themselves: who, when he came thither,
had broken up from playing, and were going home, and that
amongst them he first saw him whom he had dreamed of, and
knew him very well, and musing at him the more, asked him
whose son he was. The boy answered, that he was the son of one
Octavius (a man otherwise of no great calling) and of Accia, the
sister of Julius Caesar: who having no child, made him his heir by
his last will and testament, and left him all his lands and goods.
After that time, it is reported that Cicero was very glad to speak to
him when he met with him, and that the boy also liked Cicero's
friendship, and making of him: for by good hap the boy was born
the same year that Cicero was consul. And these be the reasons
alleged, why Cicero did favour this young Caesar.

45  But in truth, first of all the great malice he bore unto
Antonius, and secondly his nature that was ambitious of honour,
were (in my opinion) the chiefest causes why he became young

Caesar's friend: knowing that the force and power of his soldiers would greatly strengthen his authority and countenance in managing the affairs of the state, besides that the young man could flatter him so well, that he called him father. But Brutus being offended with him for it, in his epistles he wrote unto Atticus, he sharply reproveth Cicero, saying, that for fear of Antonius he flattered this young Caesar: whereby it appeared, he did not so much seek for the liberty of Rome, as he did procure himself a loving and gentle master. This notwithstanding, Brutus brought with him Cicero's son that studied philosophy at Athens, and gave him charge of men under him, and employed him in great affairs, wherein he showed himself very forward, and valiant. Now Cicero's authority and power grew again to be so great in Rome, as ever it was before. For he did what he thought good, and so vexed Antonius, that he drove him out of the city, and sent the two consuls Hircius and Pansa against him, to fight with him: and caused the senate also to decree, that young Caesar should have sergeants to carry rods and axes before him, and all other furniture for a praetor, as a man that fighteth for his country. After that Antonius had lost the battle, and that both the consuls were slain, both the armies came unto Caesar. The senate then being afraid of this young man, that had so great good fortune, they practised by honours and gifts to call the armies from him, which he had about him, and so to diminish the greatness of his power: saying, that their country now stood in no need of force, nor fear of defence, if her enemy Antonius was fled and gone. Caesar fearing this, sent men secretly unto Cicero, to pray him to procure that they two together might be chosen consuls, and that when they should be in office, he should do and appoint what he thought good, having the young man at his commandment, who desired no more but the honour only of the name. Caesar himself confessed afterwards, that being afraid he should have been utterly cast away, to have been left alone, he finely served his turn by Cicero's ambition, having persuaded him to require the consulship, through the help and assistance that he would give him.

46 But there was Cicero finely colted, as old as he was, by a young man, when he was contented to sue for the consulship in his behalf, and to make the senate agreeable to it: wherefore his friends

608 THE LIVES OF THE NOBLE GRECIANS AND ROMANS

presently reproved him for it, and shortly after he perceived he had undone himself, and together also lost the liberty of his country. For this young man Octavius Caesar being grown to be very great by his means and procurement, when he saw that he had the consulship upon him, he forsook Cicero, and agreed with Antonius and Lepidus. Then joining his army with theirs, he divided the empire of Rome with them, as if it had been lands left in common between them: and besides that, there was a bill made of two hundred men and upwards, whom they had appointed to be slain. But the greatest difficulty and difference that fell out between them, was about the outlawing of Cicero. For Antonius would hearken to no peace between them, unless Cicero were slain first of all: Lepidus was also in the same mind with Antonius: but Caesar was against them both. Their meeting was by the city of Bolonia, where they continued three days together, they three only secretly consulting in a place environed about with a little river. Some say that Caesar stuck hard with Cicero the two first days, but at the third, that he yielded and forsook him. The exchange they agreed upon between them, was this. Caesar forsook Cicero: Lepidus, his own brother Paulus: and Antonius, Lucius Caesar, his uncle by the mother's side. Such place took wrath in them, as they regarded no kindred nor blood, and to speak more properly, they showed that no brute or savage beast is so cruel as man, if with his licentiousness he have liberty to execute his will.

47  While these matters were a-brewing, Cicero was at a house of his in the country, by the city of Thusculum, having at home with him also his brother Quintus Cicero. News being brought them thither of these proscriptions or outlawries, appointing men to be slain, they determined to go to Astyra, a place by the sea side where Cicero had another house, there to take sea, and from thence to go into Macedon unto Brutus. For there ran a rumour that Brutus was very strong, and had a great power. So, they caused themselves to be conveyed thither in two litters, both of them being so weak with sorrow and grief, that they could not otherwise have gone their ways. As they were on their way, both their litters going as near to each other as they could, they bewailed their miserable estate: but Quintus chiefly, who took it most grievously. For, remembering that he took no money with

him when he came from his house, and that Cicero his brother also had very little for himself, he thought it best that Cicero should hold on his journey, whilst he himself made an errand home to fetch such things as he lacked, and so to make haste again to overtake his brother. They both thought it best so, and then tenderly embracing one another, the tears falling from their eyes, they took leave of each other. Within few days after, Quintus Cicero being bewrayed by his own servants, unto them that made search for him, he was cruelly slain, and his son with him. But Marcus Tullius Cicero being carried unto Astyra, and there finding a ship ready, embarked immediately, and sailed along the coast unto Mount Circe, having a good gale of wind. There the mariners determining forthwith to make sail again, he came ashore, either for fear of the sea, or for that he had some hope that Caesar had not altogether forsaken him: and therewithal returning towards Rome by land, he had gone about a hundred furlong thence. But then being at a strait how to resolve, and suddenly changing his mind, he would needs be carried back again to the sea, where he continued all night marvellous sorrowful, and full of thoughts. For one while he was in mind to go secretly unto Octavius Caesar's house, and to kill himself by the hearth of his chimney, to make the furies of hell to revenge his blood: but being afraid to be intercepted by the way, and cruelly handled, he turned from that determination. Then falling into other unadvised determinations, being perplexed as he was, he put himself again into his servants' hands, to be conveyed by sea to another place called Capites.* There he had a very proper pleasant summer house, where the North winds, called Etesiae, do give a trim fresh air in the summer season. In that place also there is a little temple dedicated unto Apollo, not far from the sea side. From thence there came a great shoal of crows, making a marvellous noise, that came flying towards Cicero's ship, which rowed upon the shore side. This shoal of crows came and lighted upon the yard of their sail, some crying, and some pecking the cords with their bills: so that every man judged straight, that this was a sign of ill luck at hand. Cicero notwithstanding this, came ashore, and went into his house, and laid him down to see if he could sleep. But the most

* Some do read Caiete.

part of these crows came and lighted upon the chamber window where he lay, making a wonderful great noise: and some of them got unto Cicero's bed where he lay, the clothes being cast over his head, and they never left him, till by little and little they had with their bills plucked off the clothes that covered his face. His men seeing that, and saying to themselves that they were too vile beasts, if they would tarry to see their master slain before their eyes, considering that brute beasts had care to save his life, seeing him so unworthily entreated, and that they should not do the best they could to save his life, partly by entreaty, and partly by force, they put him again into his litter to carry him to the sea.

48    But in the meantime came the murderers appointed to kill him, Herennius a centurion, and Popilius Laena, tribune of the soldiers (to wit, colonel of a thousand men, whose cause Cicero had once pleaded before the judges, when he was accused for the murder of his own father), having soldiers attending upon them. So Cicero's gate being shut, they entered the house by force, and missing him, they asked them of the house what was become of him. They answered, they could not tell. Howbeit there was a young boy in the house called Philologus, a slave enfranchised by Quintus Cicero, whom Tullius Cicero had brought up in the Latin tongue, and had taught him the liberal sciences: he told this Herennius, that his servants carried him in a litter towards the sea, through dark narrow lanes, shadowed with wood on either side. Popilius the colonel taking some soldiers with him, ran about on the outside of the lanes to take him at his coming out of them: and Herennius on the other side entered the lanes. Cicero hearing him coming, commanded his men to set down his litter, and taking his beard in his left hand, as his manner was, he stoutly looked the murderers in the faces, his head and beard being all white, and his face lean and wrinkled, for the extreme sorrows he had taken: divers of them that were by, held their hands before their eyes, whilst Herennius did cruelly murder him. So Cicero being three score and four years of age, thrust his neck out of the litter, and had his head cut off by Antonius' commandment, and his hands also, which wrote the orations (called the Philippians) against him. For so did Cicero call the orations he wrote against him, for the malice he bore him: and do yet continue the same name until this present time.

49 When these poor dismembered members were brought to Rome, Antonius by chance was busily occupied at that time about the election of certain officers: who when he heard of them and saw them, he cried out aloud that now all his outlawries and proscriptions were executed: and thereupon commanded his head and his hands should straight be set up over the pulpit for orations, in the place called Rostra. This was a fearful and horrible sight unto the Romans, who thought they saw not Cicero's face, but an image of Antonius' life and disposition: who among so many wicked deeds as he committed, yet he did one act only that had some show of goodness, which was this. He delivered Philologus into the hands of Pomponia, the wife of Quintus Cicero: and when she had him, besides other cruel torments she made him abide, she compelled him to cut his own flesh off by little morsels, and to broil them, and then to eat them. Some historiographers do thus report it. But Tyro who was a slave enfranchised by Cicero, made no mention of the treason of this Philologus. Howbeit I understood that Caesar Augustus, long time after that, went one day to see one of his nephews, who had a book in his hand of Cicero's: and he fearing lest his uncle would be angry to find that book in his hands, thought to hide it under his gown. Caesar saw it, and took it from him, and read the most part of it standing, and then delivered it to the young boy, and said unto him: 'He was a wise man indeed, my child, and loved his country well.' After he had slain Antonius, being consul, he made Cicero's son his colleague and fellow consul with him, in whose time the senate ordained, that the images of Antonius should be thrown down, and deprived his memory of all other honours: adding further unto his decree, that from thenceforth none of the house and family of the Antony should ever after bear the christen name of Marcus. So, God's justice made the extreme revenge and punishment of Antonius, to fall into the house of Cicero.

## Comparison of Cicero with Demosthenes

This is as much as we could gather by our knowledge touching the notable acts and deeds worthy of memory, written of Cicero and Demosthenes. Furthermore, leaving the comparison aside of the difference of their eloquence in their orations, methinks I may say thus much of them. That Demosthenes did wholly employ all his wit and learning (natural or artificial) unto the art of rhetoric, and that in force, and virtue of eloquence, he did excel all the orators in his time: and for gravity and magnificent style, all those also that only write for show or ostentation: and for sharpness and art, all the sophisters and masters of rhetoric. And that Cicero was a man generally learned in all sciences, and that had studied divers books, as appeareth plainly by the sundry books of philosophy of his own making, written after the manner of the Academic philosophers. Furthermore, they may see in his orations he wrote in certain causes to serve him when he pleaded, that he sought occasions in his by-talk to show men that he was excellently well learned. Furthermore, by their phrases a man may discern some spark of their manners and conditions. For Demosthenes' phrase hath no manner of fineness, jests, nor grace in it, but is altogether grave and harsh, and smelleth not of the lamp, as Pytheas said when he mocked him: but showeth a great drinker of water, extreme pains, and therewith also a sharp and sour nature. But Cicero oftentimes fell from pleasant taunts, unto plain scurrility: and turning all his pleadings of matters of importance, to sport and laughter, having a grace in it, many times he did forget the comeliness that became a man of his calling. As in his oration for Caelius, where he sayeth, it is no marvel if in so great abundance of wealth and fineness he give himself a little to take his pleasure: and that it was a folly not to use pleasures lawful and tolerable, if the famousest philosophers that ever were, did place the chief felicity of man, to be in pleasure. And it is reported also, that Marcus Cato having accused Muraena,

Cicero being consul, defended his cause, and in his oration pleasantly girded all the sect of the Stoic philosophers for Cato's sake, for the strange opinions they hold, which they call paradoxes: insomuch as he made all the people and judges also fall a-laughing a-good. And Cato himself also smiling a little, said unto them that sat by him: 'What a laughing and mocking consul have we, my lords?' But letting that pass, it seemeth that Cicero was of a pleasant and merry nature; for his face showed ever great life and mirth in it. Whereas in Demosthenes' countenance on the other side, they might discern a marvellous diligence and care, and a pensive man, never weary with pain: insomuch that his enemies (as he reporteth himself) called him a perverse and froward man.

2    Furthermore, in their writings is discerned, that the one speaks modestly in his own praise, so as no man can justly be offended with him: and yet not always, but when necessity enforceth him for some matter of great importance, but otherwise very discreet and modest to speak of himself. Cicero in contrary manner, using too often repetition of one self thing in all his orations, showed an extreme ambition of glory, when incessantly he cried out:

> Let spear and shield give place to gown,
> And give the tongue the laurel crown.

Yea furthermore, he did not only praise his own acts and deeds, but the orations also which he had written or pleaded: as if he should have contended against Isocrates, or Anaximenes, a master that taught rhetoric, and not to go about to reform the people of Rome:

> Which were both fierce and stout in arms,
> And fit to work their enemies harms.

For, as it is requisite for a governor of a commonwealth to seek authority by his eloquence, so, to covet the praise of his own glorious tongue, or as it were to beg it, that showeth a base mind. And therefore in this point we must confess that Demosthenes is far graver, and of a nobler mind: who declared himself, that all his eloquence came only but by practice, the which also required the favour of his auditory: and further, he thought them fools and madmen (as indeed they be no less) that therefore would make any boast of themselves.

3    In this they were both alike, that both of them had great credit
and authority in their orations to the people, and for obtaining that
they would propound: insomuch as captains, and they that had
armies in their hands, stood in need of their eloquence. As Chares,
Diopithes, and Leosthenes, they all were helped of Demosthenes:
and Pompey, and Octavius Caesar the young man, of Cicero:
as Caesar himself confesseth in his *Commentaries* he wrote unto
Agrippa and Maecenas. But nothing showeth a man's nature and
condition more (as it is reported, and so is it true) than when one is
in authority: for that bewrayeth his humour, and the affections
of his mind, and layeth open also all his secret vices in him.
Demosthenes could never deliver any such proof of himself,
because he never bore any office, nor was called forward. For he
was not general of the army, which he himself had prepared against
King Philip. Cicero on the other side being sent Treasurer into
Sicily, and proconsul into Cilicia and Cappadocia, in such a time as
covetousness reigned most (insomuch that the captains and governors whom they sent to govern their provinces, thinking it villainy
and dastardliness to rob, did violently take things by force, at what
time also to take bribes was reckoned no shame, but to handle it
discreetly, he was the better thought of, and beloved for it), he
showed plainly that he regarded not money, and gave forth many
proofs of his courtesy and goodness. Furthermore, Cicero being
created consul by name, but dictator in deed, having absolute
power and authority over all things to suppress the rebellion and
conspirators of Catiline, he proved Plato's prophecy true, which
was: that the cities are safe from danger, when the chief magistrates
and governors (by some good divine fortune) do govern with
wisdom and justice. Demosthenes was reproved for his corruption,
and selling of his eloquence, because secretly he wrote one oration
for Phormio, and another in the selfsame matter for Apollodorus,
they being both adversaries. Further, he was defamed also for
receiving money of the king of Persia, and therewithal condemned
for the money which he had taken of Harpalus. And though some
peradventure would object, that the reporters thereof (which are
many) do lie, yet they cannot possibly deny this, that Demosthenes
had no power to refrain from looking of the presents which divers
kings did offer him, praying him to accept them in good part for
their sakes: neither was that the part of a man that did take usury by

traffic on the sea, the extremest yet of all other. In contrary manner (as we have said before) it is certain that Cicero being treasurer, refused the gifts which the Sicilians offered him, there: and the presents also which the king of the Cappadocians offered him whilst he was proconsul in Cilicia, and those especially which his friends pressed upon him to take of them, being a great sum of money, when he went as a banished man out of Rome.

4   Furthermore, the banishment of the one was infamous to him, because by judgment he was banished as a thief. The banishment of the other was for as honourable an act as ever he did, being banished for ridding his country of wicked men. And therefore of Demosthenes, there was no speech after he was gone: but for Cicero, all the senate changed their apparel into black, and determined that they would pass no decree by their authority, before Cicero's banishment was revoked by the people. Indeed Cicero idly passed his time of banishment, and did nothing all the while he was in Macedon: and one of the chiefest acts that Demosthenes did, in all the time that he dealt in the affairs of the commonwealth, was in his banishment. For he went unto every city, and did assist the ambassadors of the Grecians, and refused the ambassadors of the Macedonians. In the which he showed himself a better citizen, than either Themistocles or Alcibiades, in their like fortune and exile. So when he was called home, and returned, he fell again to his old trade which he practised before, and was ever against Antipater, and the Macedonians. Where Laelius in open senate sharply took up Cicero, for that he sat still and said nothing, when that Octavius Caesar the young man made petition against the law, that he might sue for the consulships, and being so young that he had never a hair on his face. And Brutus self also doth greatly reprove Cicero in his letters, for that he had maintained and nourished a more grievous and greater tyranny, than that which they had put down.

5   And last of all, methinks the death of Cicero most pitiful, to see an old man carried up and down (with tender love of his servants), seeking all the ways that might be to fly death, which did not long prevent his natural course: and in the end, old as he was, to see his head so pitifully cut off. Whereas Demosthenes, though he yielded a little, entreating him that came to take him, yet for that he had

prepared the poison long before, that he had kept it long, and also used it as he did, he cannot but be marvellously commended for it. For if the god Neptune denied him the benefit of his sanctuary, he betook him to a greater, and that was death: whereby he saved himself out of the soldiers' hands of the tyrant, and also scorned the bloody cruelty of Antipater.

# DEMETRIUS
# MARCUS ANTONIUS

# Life of Demetrius

Who first likened arts to our senses, seemeth to have respected especially that one property of them both, in receiving objects of contrary quality: for, in the use and end of their operation, there is great difference. The senses receive indifferently, without discretion and judgment, white and black, sweet and sour, soft and hard: for their office is only to admit their several objects, and to carry and refer the judgment thereof to the common sense. But arts being the perfection of reason, receive and allow those things only which make for their operation, regarding and eschewing the contraries. The one chiefly, and for use: the other by the way, and with intent to avoid them. So Physic dealeth with diseases, Music with discords, to the end to remove them, and work their contraries: and the great ladies of all other arts, temperance, justice and wisdom, do not only consider honesty, uprightness and profit, but examine withal, the nature and effects of lewdness, corruption and damage. And innocence, which vaunteth her want of experience in undue practices, men call simplicity, and ignorance of things that be necessary and good to be known. And therefore the ancient Lacedaemonians in their solemn feasts forced their Ilotes the bondmen, to overcharge themselves with wine: and such they showed them unto their youth, by the apparent beastliness of drunken men, to work in them an abhorring of so loathsome vice. Wherein, although I cannot much praise them for humanity or wisdom, that corrupt and spoil one man, by example of him to correct and reclaim another, yet (as I hope) it shall not be reprehended in me, if amongst the rest I put in one or two pair of such, as living in great place and account, have increased their fame with infamy. Which in truth I do, not to please and draw on the reader with variety of report, but as Ismenias thè Theban musician showed his scholars, both those that struck a clean stroke, with 'Do so', and such as bungled it, with 'Do not so': and

Antigenidas thought men should like better, and with greater desire
contend for skill, if they heard and discerned untunable notes: so
think I, we shall be the forwarder in reading and following the
good, if we know the lives, and see the deformity of the wicked.
This treaty containeth the lives of Demetrius, surnamed the Fortgainer, and M. Antony the Triumvir, and great examples to
confirm the saying of Plato: that from great minds, both great
virtues and great vices do proceed. They were both given over to
women and wine, both valiant and liberal, both sumptuous and
high-minded; fortune served them both alike, not only in the
course of their lives, in attempting great matters, sometimes with
good, sometimes with ill success, in getting and losing things of
great consequence, overthrowing both when they feared not,
restoring both when they hoped not. But also in their end there was
no great difference, the one brought to his death by his mortal
enemies, and the other's fortune not much unlike. But now to our
history.

2    Antigonus had two sons by his wife Stratonice, the daughter of
Corraeus: the one of them he named Demetrius, and the other
Philip, after his father's name. Thus far the most writers do agree:
howbeit some hold opinion, that Demetrius was not the son of
Antigonus, but his nephew. But because his father died leaving
him a child, and that his mother was straight married again unto
Antigonus, thereupon came the report that he was Antigonus' son.
Howsoever it was, Philip, that was not much younger than
Demetrius, died. Now for Demetrius, though he was a very big
man, he was nothing so high as his father, but yet so passing and
wonderful fair, that no painter could possibly draw his picture and
counterfeit to his likeness. For they saw a sweet countenance,
mixed with a kind of gravity in his face, a fear with courtesy, and an
incomparable princely majesty accompanied with a lively spirit and
youth; and his wit and manners were such, that they were both
fearful and pleasant unto men that frequented him. For as he was
most pleasant in company having leisure, and most given to
banqueting, pleasant life, and more wantonly given to follow any
lust and pleasure, than any king that ever was, yet was he always
very careful and diligent in dispatching matters of importance. And
therefore he marvellously commended, and also endeavoured to

follow Dionysus (as much to say, as Bacchus) above all the other
gods, as he that had been a wise and valiant captain in war, and that
in peace invented and used all the pleasure that might be.

3    He marvellously loved and reverenced his father, and it seemeth
that the dutifulness he showed unto his mother, was more to
discharge the due obedience and duty of a son, than otherwise to
entertain his father, for fear of his power, or hope to be his heir.
And for proof hereof we read, that one day as he came home from
hunting, he went unto his father Antigonus, giving audience to
certain ambassadors, and after he had done his duty to him, and
kissed him, he sat down by him even as he came from hunting
having his darts in his hand, which he carried out a-hunting with
him. Then Antigonus calling the ambassadors aloud as they went
their way, having received their answer: 'My lords,' said he, 'you
shall carry home this report of my son and me: be witnesses I pray
you, how we live one with another.' As meaning to show thereby,
that the agreement betwixt the father and the son together, is a great
safety to the affairs of a king, as also a manifest proof of his greatness:
so jealous is a king to have a companion, besides the hate and
mistrust it should breed. So that the greatest prince and most
ancientest of all the successors of Alexander, boasted that he stood
not in fear of his son but did suffer him to sit by him, having a dart
in his hand. So was this house only of all other the Macedonian
kings, least defiled with such villainy, many successions after: and to
confess a truth, in all Antigonus' race there was not one, but Philip
only, that slew his own son. But we have many examples of divers
other houses of kings that have put their sons, wives, and mothers
to death: and for their brethren, it was an ordinary thing with them
to kill them, and never stick at it. For like as geometricians would
have men grant them certain propositions which they suppose
without proof, even so was this held for a general rule, to kill their
brethren, for the safety of their estate.

4    But further, to show you more plainly that Demetrius was of a
noble and courteous nature, and that he dearly loved his friends,
we may allege this example. Mithridates, the son of Ariobarzanes,
was his familiar friend and companion (for they were both in
manner of an age), and he commonly followed Antigonus' court,
and never practised any villainy or treason to him, neither was he

thought such a man: yet Antigonus did somewhat suspect him, because of a dream he had. He thought that being in a goodly great field, he sowed of these scrapings of gold, and that of that seed, first of all came up goodly wheat which had ears of gold: howbeit that shortly after returning that way again, he found nothing but the straw, and the ears of the wheat cut off, and that he being angry and very sorry for it, some told him that Mithridates had cut off these golden ears of wheat, and had carried them with him into the realm of Pont. Antigonus being marvellously troubled with this dream, after he had made his son swear unto him that he would make no man alive privy to that he would tell him, he told him all his dream what he had dreamed, and therewith that he was determined to put this young man Mithridates to death. Demetrius was marvellous sorry for it, and therefore the next morning, this young noble prince going as he was wont to pass the time away with Mithridates, he durst not by word of mouth utter that he knew, because of his oath: howbeit, taking him aside from his other familiars, when they were both together by themselves, he wrote on the ground with the end of his dart, Mithridates looking on him: 'Fly, Mithridates.' Mithridates found straight what he meant, and fled the very same night into Cappadocia: and shortly after it was his destiny to fulfil Antigonus' dream. For he conquered many goodly countries, and it was he only that established the house of the kingdom of Pont, the which the Romans afterwards overthrew, about the eight succession. By these examples we may easily conjecture the good nature and courtesy of Demetrius.

5   For like as the elements (according to Empedocles' opinion) are ever at strife together, but specially those that are nearest each to other: even so, though all the successors of Alexander were at continual wars together, yet was it soonest kindled, and most cruel between them which bordered nearest unto each other, and that by being near neighbours, had always occasion of brawl together, as fell out at that time between Antigonus and Ptolomy. This Antigonus lay most commonly in the country of Phrygia: who having intelligence that Ptolomy was gone into Cyprus, and that he overran all Syria, winning by force or fair means all the towns and cities subject unto them, he sent his son Demetrius thither, being at that time but two and twenty years of age, and it was the

first time that ever he took charge as general to his father, in matters of great importance. But he being a young man, and that had no skill of wars, fighting a battle with an old soldier (trained up in the discipline of wars under Alexander the Great, and that through him and in his name had fought many great battles) was soon overthrown, and his army put to flight, by the city of Gaza. At which overthrow were slain five thousand men, and almost eight thousand taken: and besides, Demetrius lost his tents and pavilions, his gold and silver, and to be short, all his whole carriage. But Ptolomy sent him all his things again, and his friends also that were taken after the battle, with great courteous words: that he would not fight with them for all things together, but only for honour and empire. Demetrius receiving them at his hands, besought the gods that he might not long live a debtor unto Ptolomy for this great courtesy, but that he might quickly requite it with the like again. Now Demetrius took not this overthrow like a young man, though it was his first soldierfare: but like an old and wise captain, that had abidden many overthrows, he used great diligence to gather men again, to make new armours, and to keep the cities and countries in his hands under obedience, and did train and exercise his soldiers-in-arms, whom he had gathered together.

6    Antigonus having news of the overthrow of his son Demetrius, said no more, but that Ptolomy had overcome beardless men: and that afterwards he should fight with bearded men. But now, because he would not discourage his son altogether, who craved leave once again to fight a battle with Ptolomy, he granted him. So, shortly after came Cilles, Ptolomy's general, with a great puissant army, to drive him altogether out of Syria. For they made no great account of Demetrius, because he had been once overthrown before. Howbeit Demetrius stole upon him, gave him charge on the sudden, and made him so afraid, that he took both the camp and the general, with seven thousand prisoners besides, and won a marvellous treasure of money: which made him a glad man, not so much for the gain he should have by it, as for the opportunity he had thereby to come out of Ptolomy's debt, nothing regarding the treasure nor the honour he had got by this victory, but only the benefit of his requital of Ptolomy's courtesy towards him. But yet he did nothing of his own head, before he had written to his father:

and then receiving full grant and commission from him to dispose of all things as he thought good, he sent back Cilles unto Ptolomy, and all his other friends besides, with great and rich gifts which he bountifully bestowed on them. This misfortune and overthrow did utterly put Ptolomy out of all Syria, and brought Antigonus also from the city of Celaenes, for the exceeding joy he had of this victory, as also for the great desire he had to see his son.

7    After that, he sent Demetrius into Arabia, against a people called the Nabathaeians, to conquer them: but there he was in great danger and distress in the deserts for lack of water, howbeit he never showed any sign that he was afraid. Thereby he so astonished the barbarous people, that he had leisure enough to retire with safety, and with a great booty of a thousand camels, which he brought away with him. About that time Seleucus (whom Antigonus had driven from Babylon) returning thither again, he came and conquered it without other aid than of himself: and went with a great army against the people and nations confining upon the Indians, and the provinces adjoining unto mount Caucasus, to conquer them. Thereupon Demetrius hoping to find Mesopotamia without any guard or defence, suddenly passed over the river of Euphrates, and came unlooked for unto Babylon, and there distressed the garrison of Seleucus, that kept one of the castles or citadels of the city, being two of them: and then putting in seven thousand soldiers to keep them, he commanded the rest of his men to get what they could, and to bring it away with them. After that, he marched towards the sea to return home, leaving thereby the realm and kingdom of Seleucus in better state and safety, than it was when he invaded it. For it appeared that he had taken all the country from Seleucus, leaving him nothing in it, by spoiling and foraging all that was there. At his return home, news were brought him that Ptolomy lay at the siege of the city of Halycarnassus: whereupon he drew thither with speed to make him raise the siege, and thereby saved the city from him.

8    Now, because by this exploit they won great fame, both of them (Antigonus and Demetrius) fell into a marvellous desire to set all Greece at liberty, the which Ptolomy and Cassander kept in servitude and bondage. Never king took in hand a more honourable nor juster war and enterprise, than that was. For, what power

or riches he could gather together, in oppressing of the barbarous people, he bestowed it all in restoring the Grecians to their liberty, and only to win fame and honour by it. So, they being in consultation what way to take, to bring their purpose and desire to pass, and having taken order to begin first at Athens, one of Antigonus' chiefest friends about him, told him that he should take the city, and place a good garrison there for themselves, if they could once win it: 'For,' said he, 'it will be a good bridge to pass further into all Greece.' Antigonus would not hearken to that, but said, that the love and goodwill of men was a surer bridge, and that the city of Athens was as a beacon to all the land, the which would immediately make his doings shine through the world, as a cresset light upon the top of a keep or watch tower. Thus Demetrius hoist sail, having five thousand silver talents, and a fleet of two hundred and fifty sail, and sailed towards the city of Athens: in the which Demetrius Phalerian was governor in the behalf of Cassander, and kept a great strong garrison there within the haven and castle of Munichea. He had an excellent good wind to further his journey, so that with his good foresight and speed he made, he arrived in the haven of Piraea, the five and twenty day of the month Thargelion (now called May), before any man knew of his coming. Now when this fleet was within a kenning of the city, and less, that they might easily see them from thence, every man prepared himself to receive them, taking them to be Ptolomy's ships. But in fine, the captains and governors understanding too late who they were, did what they could to help themselves: but they were all in hurly burly, as men compelled to fight out of order, to keep their enemies from landing, and to repulse them, coming so suddenly upon them. Demetrius having found the bar of the haven open, launched in presently. Then being come to the view of them all, and standing upon the hatches of his galley, he made signs with his hand that he prayed silence. The tumult being pacified, he proclaimed aloud by one of his heralds, that his father had sent him in happy hour to deliver the Athenians from all their garrisons, and to restore them again to their ancient liberty and freedom, to enjoy their laws and ancient government of their forefathers.

9    After the proclamation made, all the common people straight
threw down their weapons and targets at their feet, to clap their
hands with great shouts of joy, praying him to land, and calling
him aloud their saviour and benefactor. Now for them that
were with Demetrius Phalerian, they all thought good to let the
stronger in, although he performed not that he promised, and also
sent ambassadors unto him to treat of peace. Demetrius received
them very courteously, and sent with them for pledge, one of the
dearest friends his father had, Aristodemus Milesian. Furthermore,
he was not careless of the health and safety of Demetrius Phalerian,
who by reason of the change and alteration of the government of
the commonwealth at Athens, stood more in fear of the people of
Athens, than of his enemies. Therefore Demetrius regarding the
fame and virtue of the man, caused him to be conveyed (according
to his desire) unto Thebes, with good and sufficient safe conduct.
And for Demetrius himself, although he was very desirous to see
the city, he said he would not come into it, before he had first
restored it unto her ancient liberty and freedom, and also driven
away the garrison thence: and thereupon he cast trenches round
about the castle of Munychia. In the mean season because he
would not be idle, he hoist sail, and coasted towards the city of
Megara, within the which Cassander also kept a strong garrison.
Demetrius busily following these matters, was advertised that
Cratesipolis, surnamed Polyperchon (who had been Alexander's
wife), a lady of passing fame and beauty, and lay at that time in the
city of Patras, would be glad to see him: he leaving his army within
the territory of the Megarians, took his journey presently unto
her, with a few of his lightest armed men, and yet he stole from
them, and made his tent to be set up a good way from them,
because this lady might not be seen when she came unto him.
Some of his enemies having present intelligence thereof, came and
set upon him before he knew it. Demetrius was so scared, that he
had no further leisure, but to cast an ill favoured cloak about him,
the first that came to hand, and disguising himself to fly for life,
and escaped very hardly, that he was not shamefully taken of his
enemies for his incontinency. But though they missed him, they
took his tent, and all his money in it. After that, the city of Megara
was taken and won from Cassander's men, where Demetrius'
soldiers would have sacked all: howbeit the Athenians made

humble intercession for them, that they might not be spoiled. Demetrius thereupon, after he had driven out Cassander's garrison, he restored it again to her former liberty. In doing that, he called to mind the philosopher Stilpo, a famous man in Megara, though he lived a quiet and contemplative life. He sent for him, and asked him if any of his men had taken anything of his. Stilpo answered him, they had not: 'For,' quoth he, 'I saw no man that took my learning from me.' This notwithstanding, all the slaves of the city were in manner carried away. Another time, Demetrius making much of him, as he was going his way said unto him: 'Well, Stilpo, I leave you your city free.' 'It is true, O king,' quoth he, 'for thou hast left us never a slave.'

10 Shortly after, he returned again unto Athens, and laid siege to the castle of Munichia, the which he took, and drove out the garrison, and afterwards razed it to the ground. After that, through the entreaty and earnest desire of the Athenians, who prayed him to come and refresh himself in their city, he made his entry into it, and caused all the people to assemble, and then restored unto them their ancient laws and liberty of their country, promising them besides, that he would procure his father to send them a hundred and fifty thousand bushels of wheat, and as much wood and timber as should serve to make them a hundred and fifty galleys. Thus, the Athenians through Demetrius' means, recovered the *democratia* again (to wit, their popular government) fifteen years after they had lost it, and lived all the time between their loss and restitution from the war called Lamiacus' war, and the battle that was fought by the city of Cranon, in the state of *oligarchia*, to wit, under the government of a few governors in sight, but in truth a monarchy or kingdom, because they were under the government of one man Demetrius Phalerian, that had absolute authority over them. But by this means they made their saviour and preserver of their country, Demetrius (who seemed to have obtained such honour and glory through his goodness and liberality) hateful and odious to all men, for the overgreat and immeasurable honours which they gave him. For first of all, they called Antigonus and Demetrius kings, who before that time had always refused the name, and the which (among all other princely honours and prerogatives granted) they that had divided between them the empire of Philip and Alexander, durst never

once presume to challenge, nor to take upon them. So unto them only they gave the style and names of the gods' saviours, and took away their yearly mayor, whom they called eponymous, because they did show the years of old time, by the names of them that had been mayors. Furthermore, instead thereof they ordained in the council of the city, that there should yearly be chosen one by voices of the people, whom they should name the Priest of their Saviours, whose name they should write and subscribe in all public grants and covenants, to show the year: and besides all this, that they should cause their pictures to be drawn in the veil or holy banner, in the which were set out the images of their gods, the patrons and protectors of their city. And furthermore they did consecrate the place, where Demetrius first came out of his coach, and there did set up an altar, and called it Demetrius' altar coming out of his coach: and unto their tribes they added two other, the Antigonides and the Demetriades. Their great council at large which they created yearly of five hundred men, was then first of all brought into six hundred, because every tribe must needs furnish of themselves, fifty councillors.

11    But yet the strangest act, and most new found invention of flattery, was that of Stratocles (being the common flatterer and people pleaser), who put forth this decree, by the which it was ordained: that those whom the commonwealth should send unto Antigonus and Demetrius, should instead of ambassadors be called Theori, as much to say, as ministers of the sacrifices. For so were they called, whom they sent to Delphes to Apollo Pytheas, or unto Elide, to Jupiter Olympias, at the common and solemn feasts of all Greece, to do the ordinary sacrifices and oblations for the health and preservation of the cities. This Stratocles in all things else was a desperate man, and one that had always led a wicked and dissolute life: and for his shameless boldness, he seemed wholly to follow the steps of Cleon's foolhardiness, and old insolence, which (when he lived) he showed unto the people. He openly kept a harlot in his house called Phylacion. One day she having bought for his supper, beast's heads and necks commonly eaten, he said unto her: 'Why, how now? Thou hast bought me acates which we toss like balls, that have to do in the commonwealth.' Another time when the army of the Athenians was overthrown by sea, by the Isle of

Amorgos, he would needs prevent the news of this overthrow, and came through the street of Ceramicus, crowned with garlands of flowers, as if the Athenians had won the battle: and was also the author of a decree, whereby they did sacrifice unto the gods, to give them thanks for the victory: and meat was given amongst every tribe, in token of common joy. But shortly after the messengers arrived, which brought report of the shipwreck and overthrow. The people were in an uproar withal, and sent for Stratocles in a marvellous rage. But he with a face of brass came unto them, and arrogantly defended the people's ill will, and angrily told them: 'Well, and what hurt have I done you, if I have made you merry these two days?' Such was Stratocles' impudence and rashness.

12   But, as the poet Aristophanes saith:

> But hotter matters were that time in hand
> Than fire that wasteth both by sea and land.

For there was another that passed Stratocles in knavery. Who procured a decree, that as often as Demetrius came into the city of Athens, he should be received with all ceremonies and like solemnity, as they use in the feasts of Ceres and Bacchus: and further that they should give unto him that did excel all the rest in sumptuousness and riches, at such time as Demetrius made his entry into the city, so much money out of the common treasure, as should serve to make an image or other offering, which should be consecrated to the temples in memory of his liberality. And last of all, they changed the name of the month Munichion (to wit the month of January) and called it Demetrion: and the last day of the month which they called before the new and old moon, they then called it the Demetriade: and the feasts of Bacchus also called then Dionysia, they presently named Demetria. But the gods by divers signs and tokens showed plainly, that they were offended with these changes and alterations. For the holy banner in the which (according to the order set down) they had painted the images of Antigonus and Demetrius, with the pictures of Jupiter and Minerva, as they carried it a procession through the street Ceramicus, it was torn asunder in the midst by a tempest of wind. And furthermore, about the altars which were set up in the honour of Demetrius and Antigonus, there grew a great deal of hemlock, the which otherwise was impossible to grow there. On the feast day also of Bacchus, they were compelled to leave the pomp or procession for that day, it was such an extreme hard frost out of all season: and besides, there fell such a milldew and great frost upon it, that not only their vines and olives were killed with it, but also the most part of the wheat blades which were newly sprung up. And therefore the poet Philippides (an enemy of the aforesaid Stratocles) in one of his comedies writeth certain verses against him to this effect:

> The party for whose wickedness the veil was rent in twain,
> Which with the honour due to God did worship men most vain,
> Is he for whom our budding vines were blasted with the frost.
> Those things and not our comedies have us so dearly cost.

This Philippides was very well beloved of King Lysimachus, insomuch that for his sake the king had done many pleasures to the commonwealth of Athens. For he loved him so dearly, that as often as he saw him, or met with him at the beginning of any war, or matter of great importance, he was of opinion that he brought him good luck. For indeed he did not so much esteem him for the excellency of his art, but he was much more to be beloved and esteemed for his virtuous and honest conditions. He was no troublesome man, neither was he infected with the fineness of court, as he showed one day when the king made much of him, and giving him good countenance said unto him: 'What wilt thou have me give thee of my things, Philippides?' 'Even what it shall please thee, O king, so it be none of thy secrets.' Thus much we thought good to speak of him in bytalk, because an honest player of comedies should match with a shameless and impudent orator of the people.

13   But yet there was another Democlides, of the village of Sphettus, that dreamed out a more stranger kind of honour, touching the consecration of their targets, which they dedicated to the temple of Apollo in Delphes: that is to say, that they should go and ask the oracle of Demetrius. But I will show you the very effect and form of the law as it was set down. 'In good hour: the people ordain that he should be chosen one of the citizens of Athens, which shall go unto our saviour: and after that he hath done due sacrifice unto him, he shall ask Demetrius our saviour, after what sort the people shall with greatest holiness and devotion, without

delay, make consecration of the holiest gifts and offerings: and according to the oracle it shall please him to give them, the people shall duly execute it.' Thus, laying upon Demetrius all these foolish mockeries, who besides was no great wise man, they made him a very fool.

14 Demetrius being at that time at leisure in Athens, he married a widow called Eurydice, which came of that noble and ancient house of Miltiades, and had been married before unto one Opheltas prince of the Cyrenians, and that after his death returned again to Athens. The Athenians were very glad of this marriage, and thought it the greatest honour that came to their city, supposing he had done it for their sakes. Howbeit he was soon won to be married, for he had many wives, but amongst them all, he loved Phila best, and gave her most honour and pre-eminence above them all: partly for the respect of her father Antipater, and partly also for that she had been first married unto Craterus, whom the Macedonians loved best when he lived, and most lamented after his death, above all the other successors of Alexander. His father I suppose made him to marry her by force, although indeed her years was not meet for him: for he was marvellous young, and she very old. And when Demetrius seemed not to be contented withal, his father round him softly in the ear with this saying:

> Refuse no woman ne'er so old,
> Whose marriage bringeth store of gold.

Wherein he alluded cunningly to these verses of Euripides:

> Refuse not to become a thrall,
> Where lucre may ensue withal.

But so much did Demetrius honour his wife Phila, and all his other wives he married, that he was not ashamed to keep a number of courtesans, and other men's wives besides: so that he only of all other kings in his time, was most detected with this vice of lechery.

15 While these things passed on in this sort, he was commanded by his father, to fight with Ptolomy for the realm of Cyprus. So there was no remedy but he must needs obey him, although otherwise he was very sorry to leave the war he had begun, to set the Grecians at liberty, the which had been far more honourable

and famous. Howbeit, before he departed from Athens, he sent unto Cleonides Ptolomy's general, that kept the cities of Corinth and Sicyone, to offer him money if he would set those cities at liberty. But Cleonides would not be dealt withal that way. There-upon Demetrius straightway took sea, and sailed with all his army towards Cyprus, where at his first coming he overcame Menelaus Ptolomy's brother. But shortly after, Ptolomy went thither in person with a great army both by sea and land, and there passed betwixt them fierce threatenings and proud words to each other. For Ptolomy sent to Demetrius to bid him to depart if he were wise, before all his army came together: which would tread him under their feet, and march upon his belly, if he tarried their coming. Demetrius on the other side sent him word, that he would do him this favour to let him escape, if he would swear and promise unto him to withdraw his garrisons which he had in the cities of Corinth and Sycione. So the expectation of this battle made these two princes not only very pensive to fight one with the other, but also all the other lords, princes, and kings: because the success thereof was uncertain, which of them two should prevail. But every man judged this, that which of them obtained the victory, he should not only be lord of the realm of Cyprus and Syria, but therewith also of greater power than all the rest.

16    Ptolomy in person with fifty sail began to row against his enemy Demetrius, and commanded his brother Menelaus that when he saw them fast grappled in fight together, he should launch out of the haven of Salamina, and give charge upon the rearward of Demetrius' ships, to break their order, with the three score galleys he had in charge. Demetrius on the other side prepared ten galleys against these three score, thinking them enough to choke up the haven mouth being but narrow, so that none of the galleys that were within could come out: and further-more, he dispersed his army by land upon the foreland points which reach into the sea, and went himself into the main sea with nine score galleys, and gave such a fierce charge upon Ptolomy, that he valiantly made him fly. Who when he saw his army broken, fled as speedily as he could with eight galleys only: for all the rest were either broken or sunk in fight, and those eight only escaped, besides three score and ten which were taken, and all

their soldiers in them. And as for his carriage, his train, his friends, his officers and household servants, his wives, his gold and silver, his armour, engines of battery, and all such other warlike furniture and munition as was conveyed aboard his carects and great ships riding at anchor: of all these things nothing escaped Demetrius' hands, but all was brought into his camp. Among those spoils also was taken that famous courtesan Lamia, who at the first had her name only, for her passing playing upon the flute: but after she fell to courtesan trade, her countenance and credit increased the more. So that even then when her beauty through years fell to decay, and that she found Demetrius much younger than herself, yet she so won him with her sweet conversation and good grace, that he only liked her, and all the other women liked him. After this victory by sea, Menelaus made no more resistance, but yielded up Salamina and his ships unto Demetrius, and put into his hands also twelve hundred horsemen, and twelve thousand footmen well armed.

17    This so famous and triumphant victory was yet much more beautified, by Demetrius' great bounty and goodness which he showed in giving his enemies slain in battle honourable funerals, setting the prisoners at liberty without ransom paying, and giving moreover twelve hundred complete armours unto the Athenians. After this, Demetrius sent Aristodemus Milesian unto his father Antigonus, to tell him by word of mouth the news of this victory. Aristodemus was the greatest flatterer in all Antigonus' court, who devised then, as it seems to me, to add unto this exploit the greatest flattery possible. For when he had taken land after he was come out of the Isle of Cyprus, he would in no wise have the ship he came in to come near the shore, but commanded them to ride at anchor and no man so hardy to leave the ship: but he himself got into a little boat, and went unto Antigonus, who all this while was in marvellous fear and perplexity for the success of this battle, as men may easily judge they are, which hope after so great uncertainties. Now when word was brought him that Aristodemus was coming to him all alone, then was he worse troubled than afore, insomuch that he could scant keep within doors himself, but sent his servants and friends one after another to meet Aristodemus, to ask him what news, and to bring him word presently again how the world went.

But not one of them could get anything out of him, for he went on still fair and softly with a sad countenance, and very demurely, speaking never a word. Wherefore Antigonus' heart being cold in his belly, he could stay no longer, but would himself go and meet with Aristodemus at the gate, who had a marvellous press of people following on him, besides those of the court which ran out to hear his answer. At length when he came near unto Antigonus, holding out his right hand unto him, he cried out aloud, 'God save thee, O King Antigonus: we have overcome King Ptolomy in battle by sea, and have won the realm of Cyprus, with sixteen thousand and eight hundred prisoners.' Then answered Antigonus, 'And God save thee too: truly Aristodemus thou hast kept us in a trance a good while, but to punish thee for the pain thou hast put us to, thou shalt the later receive the reward of thy good news.'

18    Then was the first time that the people with a loud voice called Antigonus and Demetrius kings. Now for Antigonus, his friends and familiars did at that present instant put on the royal band or diadem upon his head: but for Demetrius, his father sent it unto him, and by his letters called him king. They also that were in Egypt with Ptolomy, understanding that, did also call and salute him by the name of king: because it should not seem that for one overthrow received, their hearts were dead. Thus this ambition by jealousy and emulation, went from man to man to all Alexander's successors. For Lysimachus then also began legally to wear the diadem, and likewise Seleucus, as often as he spoke with the Grecians: for before that time, he dealt in matters with the barbarous people as a king. But Cassander, though others wrote themselves kings, he only subscribed after his wonted manner. Now this was not only an increase of a new name, or changing of apparel, but it was such an honour, as it lift up their hearts, and made them stand upon themselves: and besides it so framed their manner of life and conversation with men, that they grew more proud and stately, than ever they were before: like unto common players of tragedies, who apparelling themselves to play their parts upon the stage, do change their gait, their countenance, their voice, their manner of sitting at the table, and their talk also. So that afterwards they grew more cruel in commanding their subjects, when they had once taken away the vizor and dissimulation of their absolute power, which before made

them far more lowly and gentle in many matters unto them. And all this came through one vile flatterer, that brought such a wonderful change in the world.

19    Antigonus therefore puffed up with the glory of the victory of his son Demetrius, for the conquest of Cyprus, he determined forthwith to set upon Ptolomy. Himself led the army by land, having his son Demetrius still rowing by the shore side with a great fleet of ships. But one of his familiars called Medius, being asleep had a vision one night that told him, what should be the end and success of this journey. He thought he saw Antigonus run with all his army, who should have the upper hand; and that at the first he ran with great force and swiftness, but that afterwards his strength and breath failed him so much, that when he should return, he had scant any pulse or breath, and with much ado retired again. And even so it chanced unto him. For Antigonus by land was eftsoons in great danger: and Demetrius also by sea was often in hazard to leave the coast, and by storm and weather to be cast into places, where was neither haven, creeks, nor harbourer for his ships. And at length having lost a great number of his ships, he was driven to return without any attempt given. Now Antigonus was at that time little less than four score year old, but yet his fat and corpulent body was more cumbersome to him than his years: therefore being grown unmeet for wars, he used his son in his place. Who for that he was fortunate, as also skilful through the experience he had got, did wisely govern the weightiest matters. His father besides did not pass for his youthful parts, lavish expenses, and common drunkenness he gave himself unto. For in time of peace, he was given over to all those vices: but in time of war, he was as sober and continent, as any man so born by nature. And therefore it is reported, that Lamia being manifestly known to be mistress over him, one day when he was come from hunting, he came (as his manner was) to kiss his father: and that Antigonus smiling upon him said, 'What, how now son, doest thou think thou art kissing of Lamia?' Another time Demetrius was many days together drinking and rioting, and saw not his father: and then to excuse himself unto him, he told him he had got a rheum that made him keep his chamber, that he could not come to him. 'So I heard,' said Antigonus, 'but was it of Thasos or Chios, that rheum?' He spoke it, because that in either of those two

islands, there were excellent good wines. Another time Demetrius sent his father word that he was not well. Thereupon Antigonus went to see him, and coming thither, he met a fair young boy at his door. So he went up to his chamber, and sitting down by his bed's side, he took him by the hand to feel his pulse. Demetrius told him that his fever had left him but a little before. 'I know it well,' said Antigonus, 'for I met the young boy even at the door as I came in.' So Antigonus did gently bear with his son's faults, in respect of his many other virtues he had. The voice goeth that the Scythians, when they are disposed to drink drunk together, do divers times twang the strings of their bows, as though that would serve to keep the strength of their courage and hardiness, which otherwise the pleasantness of the wine would take from them. But Demetrius gave himself to one thing at one self time. Sometime to take his pleasure, sometime to deal in matters of weight, and in all extremity he ever used but one of them, and would never mingle the one with the other: and yet this notwithstanding, he was no less politic and circumspect to prepare all manner of munition for wars.

20    For as he was a wise captain to lead an army, so was he also very careful to provide all things meet for their furniture, and would rather have too much, than too little. But above all, he exceeded in sumptuous building of ships, and framing of all sorts of engines of battery, and specially for the delight he took to invent and devise them. For he had an excellent natural wit to devise such works, as are made by wit and hand, and did not bestow his wit and invention in handicrafts, in trifling toys and baubles: as many other kings that have given themselves to play on flutes, others to paint and draw, and others also to turner's craft. As Aeropus king of Macedon, who delighted to make fine tables and pretty lamps. And Attalus, surnamed Philometor (to say, as lover of his mother) that would plant and set physical herbs, as helleborum, lingwort or bearsfoot: hyoscynamum, henbane, cicuta, hemlock, aconitum, libardbane or wolfbane, and dorycinum, for the which we have no English word: all these would he set himself with his own hands in the gardens of his palace, and also gather them in time of the year, to know the virtue and power of them. As Arsaces, the kings of Parthia, that boasted they could themselves make their arrowheads, and sharpen them. But the artificer's works which Demetrius

practised, showed that they came from a king. For his manner of workmanship had a certain greatness in it, the which even with the subtlety and fineness of his works, showed the trim handling of the workman: so that they appeared not only worthy the understanding and riches of a king, but also the forging and making by the hands of a great king. For his friends did not only wonder at their greatness, but his very enemies also were delighted with the beauty of them. And this is more true, than meet to be spoken: the enemies could but marvel when they saw his galleys rowing along the coast, with fifteen or sixteen banks of oars: and his engines of battery which they called Elepolis (to say, engines to take cities) were a spectacle of great admiration unto those whom he besieged, as the events following did thoroughly witness. For Lysimachus, who of all other kings did malice Demetrius most, coming to raise the siege from the city of Soli in Cilicia, the which Demetrius besieged, he sent unto him to pray him to let him see his engines of battery, and his galleys rowing upon the sea. Demetrius granting him, Lysimachus returned with wonderful admiration. The Rhodians also having long time defended his siege, at the last made peace with him, and prayed him to leave some one of his engines with them, for a perpetual testimony and remembrance both of his power and also of their courage and valiantness.

21  The cause why Demetrius made war with the Rhodians was, because they were confederates with King Ptolomy: he brought against their walls the greatest engine he had, the foot whereof was like a tile, more long then broad, and at the base on either side it was eight and forty cubits long, and three score and six high, rising still narrow even to the very top: so that the upper parts were narrower then the nether, and within it were many pretty rooms and places conveyed for soldiers. The forepart of it was open towards the enemy, and every room or partition had windows, out of the which they bestowed all kind of shot, because they were full of armed men, fighting with all sorts of weapons. But now, because it was so well framed and counterpealed, that it gave no way, nor reeled of either side, which way soever they removed it, but that it stood fast and upright upon her foundation, making a terrible noise and sound: that made the work as wonderful to behold, as it was a marvellous pleasure for men to see it. In this war were brought

unto Demetrius two notable armours weighing forty pound apiece, and made by one Zoilus an armourer, who to show the hardness and goodness of the temper, suffered them to be proved and shot at at six score paces, with the engines of their battery: and albeit the armours were shot at, and hit, yet were they never pierced, and but only a little rase or scratch seen, as it were of a bodkin or penknife, and had no more hurt. Demetrius always ware one of them in these wars, and Alcimus Albanian the other, the strongest and valiantest man he had in all his host, and that only carried a complete armour weighing six score pound, where all other soldiers ware none above three score. This Alcimus was slain at Rhodes valiantly fighting by the theatre.

22    In this siege the Rhodians did valiantly defend themselves, that Demetrius could do no act worthy memory. This notwithstanding, although he saw he could not prevail, but lose his time, yet was he the more obstinately bent against them, to be even with them, because they had taken a ship of his, in the which his wife Phila had sent unto him certain hangings of tapestry, linen, apparel, and letters, and because they had sent them all unto Ptolomy, as soon as they had taken them. But therein they did not follow the honest courtesy of the Athenians: who having intercepted certain couriers of King Philip's that made war against them, they opened all the letters they carried, and read them, saving only his wife Olympias' letters she sent him, the which they sent unto King Philip sealed, as they were when they received them. Now though this part did much grieve and offend him, yet he could not find in his heart to serve them in that sort, when he might have done it not long after. For by chance at that time, Protogenes an excellent painter, born in the city of Caunus, did paint them the draft of the city of Ialysus. Demetrius found this table in a house in the suburbs of the city, being almost ended. The Rhodians thereupon sending a herald unto him, to beseech him to spare the defacing of so goodly a work, he returned them answer, that he would rather suffer his father's images to be burnt, than so excellent and passing a work as that to be lost, and brought to nothing. For it is reported, that Protogenes was seven years drawing of the same: and it is also said, that Apelles himself when he saw it did so wonder at it, that his speech failed him, and he stood mute a long time, and at last said: 'Surely there is

a wonderful piece of work, and of great labour, yet they want those graces and ornaments whereby those that I paint do reach unto heaven.' This table afterwards being brought to Rome, and hanged up with others, was in the end burnt by fire. Now as the Rhodians were desirous to be rid of this war, and that Demetrius also was willing to take any honest occasion to do it, the ambassadors of the Athenians came happily to serve both their desires, who made peace between them with these conditions: that the Rhodians should be confederates with Antigonus and Demetrius, against all men but Ptolomy only.

23   The Athenians sent for Demetrius, upon Cassander's coming to lay siege to their city. Whereupon Demetrius immediately hoist sail towards Athens, with three hundred and thirty galleys, and a great number of men of war besides: so that he did not only drive Cassander out of the province of Attica, but followed him even to the strait of Thermopyles, and there overthrew him in set battle, and received the city of Heraclea, which willingly yielded unto him, and six thousand Macedonians that came unto him to take his part. So in his return back, he set all the Grecians at liberty on this side the strait: he made league with the Boeotians, and took the city of Cenchrees, and the castles of Phyle and Panactos, in the fronters and confines of Attica, in the which Cassander had left garrisons to keep the country in subjection: and after he had driven them out of the country, he rendered the forts again unto the Athenians. Therefore though it seemed the Athenians had before bestowed to their uttermost power all kinds of honours that could be offered him, every man striving for life to prefer the same, yet they found out new devises to flatter and please him. For they ordained that the place behind the temple of Minerva called Parthenon (as who would say, the temple of the virgin) should be prepared for his house to lie in: and they said, that the goddess Minerva did lodge him with her. But to say truly, he was too unchaste a guest, to think that a maiden goddess would be content he should lie with her. And yet his father Antigonus perceiving that they had lodged his son Philip on a time in a house, where there were three young women, he said nothing to Philip himself, but before him he sent for the harbinger, and said unto him: 'Wilt thou not remove my son out of this strait lodging, and provide him of a better?

24    And Demetrius, that should have reverenced the goddess Minerva, though for no other respect but because he called her his eldest sister (for so he would she should be called), he defiled all the castle where was the temple of these holy virgins, with horrible and abominable insolencies, both towards young boys of honest houses, as also unto young women of the city. So that this place seemed to be most pure and holy, at such time as he lay with his common courtesans, Chrysis, Lamia, Demo, and Anticyra. It shall not be greatly for the honour of the city of Athens, to tell particularly all the abominable parts he committed there. But Democles' virtue and honesty deserveth worthy and condign remembrance. This Democles was a young boy that had no hair on his face, of whose beauty Demetrius being informed by the surname he had, as commonly called through the city, Democles the fair, he sought divers ways to entice him, both by fair means, large promises and gifts, and also with threats besides. But when he saw no man could bring him to the bent of his bow, and that the young boy in the end seeing him so importunate upon him, came no more to the common places of exercise where other children used to recreate themselves, and that to avoid the common stoves, he went to wash himself in another secret stove, Demetrius watching his time and hour of going thither, followed him, and got in to him being alone. The boy seeing himself alone and that he could not resist Demetrius, took off the cover of the kettle or chawdron where the water was boiling, and leaping into it, drowned himself. Truly he was unworthy of so lamentable an end, but yet he showed a noble heart, worthy of his beauty and country. But he did not as another called Cleaenetus, the son of Cleomedon, who brought letters from Demetrius directed to the people, whereby, through Demetrius' intercession and request, his father's fine of fifty talents in the which he was condemned (and for non-payment remained prisoner) was clearly remitted and forgiven. But by this act, he not only shamed and dishonoured himself, but also troubled all the city. For the people thereupon released Cleomedon of his fine, but therewith they made a decree that no citizen should thenceforth bring any more letters from Demetrius. But afterwards, understanding that Demetrius was marvellously offended with this decree, they did not only revoke their first decree, but they did also put some of them to death, which were the procurers and authors of the decree, and

others also they banished. And further they made a law, that the people of Athens should account all religious to the gods, and just unto men, whatsoever it pleased Demetrius to order and appoint. At that time there was one of the chiefest men of the city, that said Stratocles was a madman to prefer such matters. 'Indeed,' quoth Demochares surnamed Laconian, 'he were a mad man if he were otherwise:' and he spoke it, because this Stratocles had many great pleasures at Demetrius' hands for this flattery. Howbeit Demochares being accused and condemned upon these words, he was banished Athens. See after what sort the Athenians used themselves, who seemed to be delivered from the garrison they had before, and to be restored unto their former liberty and freedom.

25    From thence Demetrius went into Peloponnesus, and never an enemy of his durst tarry his coming, but all fled before him, and left him their castles and towns. Thus Demetrius won unto himself all the country called Acte, and all Archadia, saving the city of Mantinea: and for the sum of an hundred talents given amongst them, he delivered the cities of Argos, Sicyone, and of Corinth, from the garrisons that lay amongst them. About that time fell out the great feast of Iuno in Argos, called Heraea. Therefore Demetrius, to honour this feast with the Grecians, married Deidamia (the daughter of Aeacides, king of the Molossians, and sister of Pyrrhus) and persuaded the Sicyonians to leave their city, and to come and build in another goodly place near unto it, where they now do dwell: and so with the place and situation, he changed also the name of the city. For instead of Sicyone, he made it to be called Demetriade. Then at a general assembly of the states of Greece, which was kept in the strait of Peloponnesus, called Isthmos, Demetrius was chosen lieutenant general of all the Grecians, as Philip and Alexander (both kings of Macedon) had been before him, unto whom he did not only compare himself, but thought himself greater than they, because fortune smiled on him, and for that he had so good success in all his affairs. Whereas Alexander did never take away the title and name of king from any other kings, neither did ever call himself king of kings, although he had given unto divers of them the name and power of a king. And in contrary manner also, Demetrius laughed them to scorn which they called any other princes kings, but his father and himself.

Moreover he took great pleasure to hear his flatterers, who being at banquets called for wine to drink to King Demetrius, and then to Seleucus Master of the Elephants, to Ptolomy Admiral, to Lysimachus Keeper of the Treasure, and to Agathocles Sicilian, Governor of the Isles. All the kings but Lysimachus laughed at these toys when they were reported to them: but Lysimachus was very angry, and thought great scorn that Demetrius should reckon him a gelding, for that it was an old custom commonly to give an eunuch the charge of keeping the treasure. So Lysimachus of all other princes did bear him most malice, and because he would finely taunt him for that he ever kept Lamia his courtesan with him: 'Until this present time,' said he, 'I never saw harlot play in a tragedy before.' Demetrius answered him again, that his harlot was chaster, than Penelope his wife.

26   So Demetrius departing for that time out of Peloponnesus, took his journey towards Athens, and wrote before to the Athenians, that when he came thither he would be received into the fraternity of the holy mysteries, and that he meant they should show him at one self time, all that was to be seen, even from the least to the highest secrets of their ceremonies, called Epoptices, because they made the brethren of the fraternity see them long time after they had been first received into the lesser ceremonies: the which was not lawful then, neither was ever heard of before. For these smaller mysteries in old time were celebrated in the month of November, and the greater in the month of August: and beside it was not lawful to celebrate or use these ceremonies within the space of a year one of the other. When these letters were openly read, no man durst speak against them but Pythodorus the priest, who carried the torch lighted when they showed these mysteries. Howbeit his words prevailed not, for by the device of Stratocles it was enacted at an assembly of the city, that the month of March in the which they were at that time, should be called and reputed November. And so, as they could best help it by their ordinances of the city, they did receive Demetrius into the fraternity of the mysteries: and afterwards again, this self month of March which they had translated into November, became suddenly August: and in the selfsame year was celebrated the other ceremony of these great mysteries, whereby Demetrius was admitted to see the most

straitest and secretest ceremonies. Therefore Philippides the poet inveighing against the sacrilege and impiety of religion profaned by Stratocles, made these verses of him:

> Into one month his coming hither
> Hath thrust up all the year together.

And afterwards because Stratocles was the procurer that Demetrius was lodged in the temple of Minerva within the castle:

> Of chaste Minerva's holy church he makes a filthy stews,
> And in that Virgin's very sight his harlots doth abuse.

27 But yet of all the insolent parts done at that time in Athens (although many were committed), none of all the rest grieved the Athenians more, than this did: that Demetrius commanded them they should presently furnish him with two hundred and fifty talents. The taxation of this payment was very hard unto them, both for the shortness of the time appointed them, as also for the impossibility of abating any part of it. When he had seen all this mass of money laid on a heap before him, he commanded it should be given to Lamia, and among his other courtesans, to buy them soap. The shame the Athenians received by this gift, grieved them more, than the loss of their money: and the words he spoke to the great contempt of them and their city, did more trouble them, than the payment they made. Some say notwithstanding, that Demetrius did not alone use the Athenians thus shamefully, but the Thessalians also in the same manner. But passing this over, Lamia of herself, and through her own countenance, did get a great sum of money together of divers persons for one supper she made unto Demetrius, the preparation whereof was of such exceeding charge, that Lycaeus born in the Isle of Samos, did set down the order thereof in writing. And therefore a certain poet no less pleasantly, than truly, called this Lamia, Elepolis: to wit, an engine to take cities. And Demochares also born in the city of Soli, called Demetrius a fable, because he had Lamia ever with him: as in the fables which old women tell little children, there is ever lightly a Lamia, as much to say, as a witch or sorceress. So that the great credit and authority this Lamia had, and the love which Demetrius bore her, did not only cause his wives suspect and envy him, but made him hated also of all his friends and familiars. And therefore certain gentlemen whom

Demetrius sent in ambassade unto King Lysimachus, he talking familiarly with them, and passing the time away, showed them great wounds of the claws of a lion upon his arms and legs, telling them also how he was forced to fight with the lion, when through King Alexander's fury he was shut up in his den with him: they smiling to hear him, told him that the king their master had also certain marks and bitings on his neck, of a vile beast called Lamia. And to say truly, it was a wonderful thing, that marrying (as he did) his wife Phila so much against his will, because she was too old for him: how he was so ravished with Lamia, and did so constantly love her so long together, considering that she was also very old, and past the best. Therefore Demo, surnamed Mania (as much to say, the mad woman), pleasantly answered Demetrius, asking her one night when Lamia had played on the flute all supper time, what she thought of Lamia: 'An old woman, O king,' quoth she. Another time when fruit was served in, after the board was taken up: 'Do you see,' said Demetrius, 'how many pretty fine knacks Lamia sendeth me?' 'My mother,' answered Demo again, 'will send you more than these, if you please to lie with her.' It is reported of this Lamia, that she overthrew Bocchoris' judgment in a matter. In Egypt there was a young man that had a marvellous fancy unto a famous courtesan, called Thonis: who did ask him such a great sum of money to lie with her, that it was impossible for him to give it her. At length, this amorous youth being so deep in love with her, dreamed one night he lay with her, and enjoyed her: so that for the pleasure he took by his conceit and imagination, when he awaked, his earnest love was satisfied. This courtesan whom he had cast fancy to, hearing of his dream, did put him in suit before the judges, to be paid her hire for the pleasure the young man had taken of her by imagination. Bocchoris hearing the sum of her complaint, commanded the young man to bring before him in some vessel, at a day appointed, as much money as she did ask him to lie with her. Then he bade him toss it to and fro in his hand before the courtesan, that she should but only have the shadow and sight of it: 'For,' quoth he, 'imagination and opinion is but a shadow of truth.' Lamia said this was no equal judgment: 'For,' says she, 'the shadow only, or the sight of the money, did not satisfy the covetousness of the courtesan, as the young man's lust was quenched by his dream.' Thus enough spoken of Lamia.

28   But now, the misfortunes and jests of him we presently write of: they do transport our history, as from a comical into a tragical theatre, that is to say, from pleasant and light matter, into lamentable and bitter tears. For all the princes and kings conspired generally against Antigonus, and joined all their force and armies together. Therefore Demetrius departed forthwith out of Greece, and came to join with his father, whose courage he found more lively and better given to this war, than his years required: besides that Demetrius' coming made him the bolder, and did lift up his heart the more. And yet it seems to me, that if Antigonus would but have yielded up a few trifling things, and that he could or would have bridled his over-immoderate covetous desire to reign, he had both kept for himself all the time of his life, and also left after his death unto his son, the supremest dignity and power, above all the other kings and successors of Alexander. But he was so cruel and rash of nature, and as insolent and brave in his doings, as in his words, that thereby he stirred up, and brought upon him as his enemies, many great and mighty princes. For even at that present time he said, that he would as easily disperse and scatter asunder that conspiracy against him, as choughs or other little birds coming to peck up the corn newly sown, are easily scared away with a stone, or making any little noise. So he carried to the field with him, above three score and ten thousand footmen, ten thousand horsemen, and three score and fifteen elephants. His enemies had three score and four thousand footmen, and five hundred horsemen more than he, with four hundred elephants, and six score carts of war. When the two armies were one near unto the other, methinks he had some imagination in his head that changed his hope, but not his courage. For in all other battles and conflicts, having commonly used to look big of the matter, to have a loud high voice, and to use brave words, and sometime also even in the chiefest of all the battle to give some pleasant mock or other, showing a certain trust he had in himself, and a contempt of his enemy, then they saw him oftentimes alone, and very pensive, without ever a word to any man. One day he called all his army together, and presented his son unto the soldiers, recommending him unto them, as his heir and successor, and talked with him alone in his tent. Whereat men marvelled the more, because that he never used before to impart to any man the secrets of his counsel

and determination, no not to his own son, but did all things of himself and then commanded that thing openly to be done, which he had secretly purposed. For proof hereof it is said, Demetrius being but a young man, asked him on a time when the camp should remove: and that Antigonus in anger answered him, 'Art thou afraid thou shalt not hear the sound of the trumpet?'

29    Furthermore, there fell out many ill signs and tokens that killed their hearts. For Demetrius dreamed that Alexander the Great appeared armed unto him at all pieces, and that he asked him what word or signal of battle they were determined to give at the day of the battle. He answered, that they were determined to give 'Jupiter' and 'Victory'. Then said Alexander, 'I will go to thine enemies that shall receive me.' And afterwards, at the very day of the overthrow, when all their army were set in battle ray, Antigonus coming out of his tent, had such a great fall, that he fell flat on his face on the ground, and hurt himself very sorely. So when he was taken up, then lifting up his hands to heaven, he made his prayers unto the gods, that it would please them to grant him victory, or sudden death without great pain, before he should see himself vanquished, and his army overthrown. When both battles came to join, and that they fought hand to hand, Demetrius that had the most part of the horsemen with him, went and gave charge upon Antiochus the son of Seleucus, and fought it out so valiantly on his side, that he overthrew his enemies, and put them to flight. But too fondly following the chase of them that fled, and out of time, he marred all, and was the occasion of the loss of his victory. For when he returned from the chase, he could not join again with their footmen, because the elephants were between both. Then Seleucus perceiving Antigonus' battle was naked of horsemen, he did not presently set upon them, but turned at one side as though he would environ them behind, and made them afraid: yet making head as he would charge them, only to give them leisure to come on their side, as they did. For the most part of Antigonus' host did forsake him, and yielded unto his enemies: and the rest of them fled every man. And when a great troop of men together went with great fury to give charge on that side where Antigonus was, one of them that were about him, said unto him: 'Your grace had need take heed, for these men come to charge us.'

He answered again: 'But how should they know me? And if they did, my son Demetrius will come and help me.' This was his last hope, and still he looked every way if he could see his son coming towards him: until at length he was slain with arrows, darts, and pikes. For of all his friends and soldiers there tarried not one man by his body, but Thorax of the city of Larissa in Thessalie.

30		Now the battle having such success as you have heard, the kings and princes that had won so glorious a victory, as if they had cut a great body in sundry pieces, they divided Antigonus' kingdom among them, and every man had his part of all the provinces and countries which Antigonus kept, adding that unto their other dominions which they possessed afore. Now Demetrius flying with all possible speed that might be, with five thousand footmen and four thousand horsemen, he got to the city of Ephesus: where every man mistrusted, that being needy of money as he was, he would not spare the temple of Diana in Ephesus, but would rifle all the gold and silver in it. And in contrary manner also, Demetrius being afraid of his soldiers, lest they would spoil it against his will, he suddenly departed thence, and sailed towards Greece, putting his greatest confidence and affiance in the Athenians, because he had left his wife Deidamia at Athens, with ships and some money, supposing he could go no whither with better safety in his adversity, than to Athens, of whose goodwills he thought himself assured. Wherefore when ambassadors of the Athenians came unto him, and found him not far from the isles Cyclades, as he sailed with great speed towards Attica, and that they had declared unto him, he should forbear to come into their city, because the people had made an ordinance to suffer no more kings to come into Athens, and that they had sent Deidamia his wife honourably accompanied unto the city of Megara, then was Demetrius for very anger and passion of mind, clean out of countenance, although until that time he had patiently borne his adversity, and his heart had never failed him. But this nipped him to the heart, when he saw that (contrary to expectation) the Athenians had deceived and failed him in his greatest need, and that in his adversity he found their former friendship counterfeit, and altogether dissembled. Whereby most plainly appeareth, that the most uncertain and deceivable proof of people's goodwills and cities' towards kings and princes, are the immeasurable and extreme

honours they do unto them. For if it is so, that the truth and
certainty of honour proceeds from the goodwill of those that give
it, the fear which the common people commonly stand in of the
power of kings, is sufficient cause for them to mistrust that the
people do it not with goodwill and from their hearts, considering
that for fear they do the selfsame things, which they will also do
for love. Therefore grave and wise princes should not pass so
much for the images and statues they set up for them, or the tables
or divine honours they do decree unto them, as to regard their
own works and deeds, and weighing them truly, so to believe and
receive their honours for true, or otherwise to reject and mistrust
them, as things done by compulsion. For commonly it is that
which maketh the people to hate kings the more, when they do
accept these immeasurable and extreme honours done unto them,
but those sorts chiefly hate them most, that against their wills are
forced to do them those honours.

31    Demetrius seeing then how injuriously the Athenians had used
him, and at that time not knowing how to be revenged of them, he
modestly sent unto them only to make his complaints, and to
demand his ships, among the which was that galley of sixteen banks
of oars. The which when he had received, he hoist sail immediately
towards the strait of Peloponnesus, and there found all things to go
against him. For in every place where he had left any garrison, the
captains that had the charge of them, either yielded them up, or else
revolted, and kept them against him. Therefore leaving Pyrrhus
his lieutenant in Greece, he took sea again, and sailed towards
Cherronesus, and there with the mischiefs he did, and with the
spoils he got in King Lysimachus' land, he paid his men, and
enriched his army, the which began again to increase, and to be
dreadful to his enemies. But now for Lysimachus, the other kings
made no great account of him, neither did they stir to give him aid,
because he was nothing inferior unto Demetrius: and for that he
was of greater power and possessions than themselves, they therefore were the more afraid of him. Shortly after, Seleucus sent unto
Demetrius, to require his daughter Stratonice in marriage, notwithstanding that he had a son already called Antiochus, by his wife
Apama a Persian. Howbeit he thought that his affairs and greatness
of his estate and kingdom, was able enough to maintain many

successors after him. And furthermore, he considered with himself that he should have need of Demetrius' alliance, because he saw Lysimachus himself match with one of Ptolomy's daughters, and his son Agathocles with his other daughter. Demetrius seeing this good fortune offered him beyond all hope, presently took his daughter with him, and sailed with all his ships directly towards Syria. In the which voyage he was constrained of necessity to land sometimes, and specially in Cilicia, the which Plistarchus the brother of Cassander kept at that time, being given him by the other kings for his part and portion of the spoil of Antigonus, after he was overthrown. This Plistarchus thinking that Demetrius landed not to refresh himself, but to forage and spoil, because he would complain of Seleucus for the alliance he made with their common enemy, without the consent and privity of all the other kings and princes confederates, he went purposely unto his brother Cassander.

32 Demetrius having intelligence thereof, suddenly invaded the land, and spoiled as far as the city of Cyndes, and carried away (which he had levied) twelve hundred talents, which he found yet left of his father's treasure: and then with all the speed he could possible he returned to his ships, and hoist sail. Shortly after, his wife Phila also came unto him. So Seleucus received them all near unto the city of Orossus, and there their meeting was princely, without sorrow or suspicion one of the other. First of all Seleucus did feast Demetrius in his tent, in the midst of his camp: and afterwards Demetrius feasted him again in his galley with thirteen banks of oars. Thus they passed many days together, feasting and rejoicing each with other, being unarmed, and having no soldiers to wait upon them: until at length Seleucus with his wife Stratonice departed, and took his way with great pomp towards the city of Antioche. Now for Demetrius, he kept the province of Cilicia, and sent his wife Phila unto her brother Cassander, to answer the complaints and accusations of Plistarchus against him. In the meantime Deidamia his wife departed out of Greece to come unto him: who after she had remained with him a few days, died of a sickness. Afterwards Demetrius coming again in favour with Ptolomy, by Seleucus his son-in-law's means, he married his daughter Ptolemaeide. Hitherunto Seleucus used Demetrius very courteously: but afterwards he prayed him to deliver him Cilicia

again, for a sum of money that he offered him: but Demetrius plainly denied him. Then did Seleucus show a cruel and tyrannical covetousness: for in anger, and with fierce threats and countenance, he asked him the cities of Tyr and Sidon. But therein methinks he lacked honesty and civility: as though he that had under his obedience and subjection all that which lay betwixt the Indians and the sea of Syria, was in such need and poverty, that for two cities only, he should drive his father-in-law from him, who had sustained so hard and bitter change. But thereby he rightly confirmed Plato's saying: that he that will be rich indeed, must endeavour himself not to increase his riches, but rather to diminish his covetousness. For he shall never be but a beggar, and needy, whose covetous desire hath no end.

33 This notwithstanding, Demetrius yielded not for fear, but provided to replenish the cities with good garrisons to keep them against him: saying, that though he had been overcome ten thousand times more in battle, yet it should never sink into his head that he should be contented, and think himself happy to buy Seleucus' alliance so dear. On the other side, being advertised that one Lachares having spied oportunity when the Athenians were in civil wars one against the other, and that he had overcome them, and did tyrannically usurp the government, he then persuaded himself that he might easily win it again, if he came thither upon the sudden. Thereupon he crossed the seas with a great fleet of ships, without any danger: but he had such a great storm and tempest upon the coast of Attica, that he lost the most part of his ships, and a great number of his men besides. But for himself he escaped, and began to make a little war with the Athenians. Yet perceiving that he did no good there, but lost his time, he sent some of his men to gather a number of ships again together, and he himself in the meantime went into Peloponnesus, to lay siege to the city of Messena, where his person was in great danger. For fighting hard by the wall, he had such a blow with a dart, that it hit him full in the mouth, and ran through his cheek. Notwithstanding this, after he was healed of that wound, he brought into his subjection again, certain towns that had rebelled against him. After that, he returned again into Attica, and took the cities of Eleusin, and of Rhamnus: and then spoiled all the country, and

took a ship straight with corn, and hung up the merchant that ought it, and the master of the ship that brought it, thereby to terrify all other merchants, that they should be afraid to bring any more corn thither, and so to famish the city, by keeping them from all things necessary for their sustenance: and so it happened. For a bushel of salt was sold at Athens for forty silver drachmas, and the bushel of wheat for three hundred drachmas. In this extreme necessity, the Athenians had but a short joy for the hundred and fifty galleys they saw near unto Aegina, the which Ptolomy sent to aid them. For when the soldiers that were in them saw that they brought unto Demetrius a great number of ships out of Peloponnesus, out of Cyprus, and divers other parts, which amounted in the whole to the number of three hundred sail, they weighed their anchors, and fled presently. Then Lachares forsook the city, and secretly saved himself.

34  Now the Athenians, who before had commanded upon pain of death, that no man should make any motion to the council, to treat of any peace with Demetrius, they did then upon Lachares flying, pleasantly open the gates next unto Demetrius' camp, and sent ambassadors unto him, not looking for any grace or peace, but because necessity drove them to it. During this so hard and strait siege, there fell out many wonderful and strange things: but among others, this one is of special note. It is reported that the father and the son sitting in their house, void of all hope of life, there fell a dead rat before them from the top of the house, and that the father and son fought who should have it to eat. Moreover, that at the selfsame siege the philosopher Epicurus maintained himself and his scholars, by giving them a proportion of beans every day, by the which they lived. Thus the city of Athens being brought unto this extremity, Demetrius made his entry into it, and gave commandment to all the citizens, that they should assemble every man within the theatre: where he made them to be compassed in with armed soldiers, and then placed all his guard armed about the stage. Afterwards he came down himself into the theatre, through high galleries and entries by the which the common players used to come to play their parts in tragedies, insomuch as the Athenians were then worse afraid than before: howbeit Demetrius presently pacified their fear, as soon as

he began to speak unto them. For he did not fashion his oration with a hasty angry voice, neither did he use any sharp or bitter words: but only after he had courteously told them their faults and discourtesy towards him, he said he forgave them, and that he would be their friend again: and furthermore, he caused ten millions of bushels of wheat to be given unto them, and established such governors there, as the people misliked not of. Then Democles the orator, seeing that the people gave out great shouts of joy in the praise of Demetrius, and that the orators daily contended in the pulpit for orations, who should exceed others in preferring new honours for Demetrius, he caused an order to be made, that the havens of Piraeus and Munychia should be put into Demetrius' hands, to use at his pleasure. This being stablished by voices of the people, Demetrius of his own private authority did place a great garrison within the fort called Musaeum, because the people should rebel no more against him, nor divert him from his other enterprises.

35    Thus when he had taken Athens, he went to set upon the Lacedaemonians. But Archidamus king of Lacedaemon, came against him with a puissant army, whom he discomfited in battle, and put to flight, by the city of Mantinea. After that he invaded Laconia with all his army, and made an inroad to the city of Sparta, where he once again overthrew the Lacedaemonians in set battle, took five hundred of them prisoners, and slew two hundred: insomuch that every man thought he might even then go to Sparta without any danger to take it, the which had never yet been taken afore by any. But there was never king that had so often and sudden changes of fortune as Demetrius, nor that in other affairs was ever so often little, and then great: so suddenly down, and up again: so weak, and straight so strong. And therefore it is reported, that in his great adversities when fortune turned so contrary against him, he was wont to cry out upon fortune, that which Aeschylus speaketh in a place:

> Thou seemest to have begotten me, of purpose for to show
> Thy force in lifting of me up, me down again to throw.

Now again when his affairs prospered so well, and that he was likely to recover a great force and kingdom, news were brought him, first that Lysimachus had taken all his towns from him, which he held in Asia: and on the other side, that Ptolomy had won from him all the realm of Cyprus, the city of Salamina only excepted, in the which he kept his mother and children very straitly besieged. This notwithstanding, fortune played with him, as the wicked woman Archilochus speaketh of, who

> Did in the one hand water show,
> And in the other fire bestow.

For taking him away, and (as it were) the city of Sparta also out of his hands by these dreadful news, even when he was certain to have won it, she presently offered him hopes of other great and new things, by this occasion following.

36 After the death of Cassander, Philip who was the eldest of all his other sons, and left his heir and successor in the kingdom of Macedon, he reigned no long time over the Macedonians, but deceased soon after his father was dead. The two other brethren also fell at great variance, and wars together: so that the one called Antipater slew his own mother Thessalonica: and the other being Alexander, called in to aid him Demetrius and Pyrrhus, the one out of the realm of Epirus, and the other out of Peloponnesus. Pyrrhus came first before Demetrius, and kept a great part of Macedon for recompense of his pains, coming to aid him at his desire: so that he became a dreadful neighbour unto Alexander himself, that had sent for him into his country. Furthermore, when he was advertised that Demetrius did presently upon the receipt of his letters, set forward with all his army to come to aid him, the young Prince Alexander was twice as much more amazed and afraid, for the great estate and estimation of Demetrius. So he went to him notwithstanding, and received him at a place called Deion, and there embraced and welcomed him. But immediately after, he told him that his affairs were now in so good state, that praised be the gods he should not now need his presence to aid him. After these words the one began to mistrust the other. So it chanced one day, that as Demetrius went to Alexander's lodging where the feast was prepared, there came one to him to tell him of an ambush that was laid for him, and how they had determined to kill him when he should think to be merry at the banquet. But Demetrius was nothing abashed at the news, and only went a little softlier, not making such haste as he did before, and in the meantime sent to

command his captains to arm their men, and to have them in readiness: and willed his gentlemen and all the rest of his officers that were about him (which were a greater number by many than those of Alexander's side), every man of them to go in with him into the hall, and to tarry there till he rose from the table. By this means the men whom Alexander had appointed to assault him, they durst not, being afraid of the great train he had brought with him. Furthermore, Demetrius feigning that he was not well at ease at that time to make merry, he went immediately out of the hall, and the next morning determined to depart, making him believe that he had certain news brought him of great importance: and prayed Alexander to pardon him, that he could no longer keep him company, for that he was driven of necessity to depart from him, and that another time they would meet together, with better leisure and liberty. Alexander was very glad to see that Demetrius went his way out of Macedon not offended, but of his own goodwill: whereupon he brought him into Thessaly, and when they were come to the city of Larissa, they began again to feast one another, to entrap each other: the which offered Demetrius occasion to have Alexander in his hand, as he would wish himself. For Alexander of purpose would not have his guard about him, fearing lest thereby he should teach Demetrius also to stand upon his guard. Thus Alexander turned his practice for another, upon himself: for he was determined not to suffer Demetrius to escape his hands, if he once again came within danger. So Alexander being bidden to supper to Demetrius, he came accordingly. Demetrius rising from the board in the midst of supper, Alexander rose also, being afraid of that strange manner, and followed him foot by foot to the very door. Then Demetrius said but to his warders at the gate, 'Kill him that followeth me.' With those words he went out of the doors, and Alexander that followed him was slain in the place, and certain of his gentlemen with him which came to rescue him: of the which, one of them as they killed him said, that Demetrius had prevented them but one day.

37  All that night (as it is no other likely) was full of uproar and tumult. Howbeit, the next morning the Macedonians being marvellously troubled and afraid of Demetrius' great power, when they saw that no man came to assail them, but that Demetrius in

contrary manner sent unto them to tell them that he would speak with them, and deliver them reason for that he had done, then they all began to be bold again, and willingly gave him audience. Now Demetrius need not to use many words, nor to make any long orations, to win them unto him: for, because they hated Antipater as a horrible man-queller and murderer of his mother, and because they had no better man to prefer, they easily chose Demetrius king of Macedon, and thereupon brought him back into Macedon, to take possession of the kingdom. This change was not misliked of the other Macedonians that remained at home in their country, for that they yet remembered the traitorous and wicked fact of Cassander, against Alexander the Great: for which cause they utterly hated and detested all his issue and posterity. And furthermore, if there were any spark of remembrance in their hearts of the bounty and goodness of their grandfather Antipater, Demetrius received the fruit and benefit, for his wife Phila's sake, by whom he had a son that should succeed him in the kingdom, and was a proper youth, in camp with his father.

38 Demetrius having this great good hap and fortune come unto him, he received news also that Ptolomy had not only raised his siege from the city of Salamina, where he kept his mother and children straitly besieged: but further, that he had done them great honour, and bestowed great gifts upon them. On the other side also he was advertised, that his daughter Stratonice, who had before been married unto Seleucus, was now married again unto Antiochus, the son of the said Seleucus, and how that she was crowned queen of all the barbarous nations inhabiting in the high provinces of Asia: and that came to pass in this manner. It chanced that this young prince Antiochus (as love overcometh all men) became in love with his mother-in-law Stratonice, who already had a son by Seleucus his father. She being young, and passing fair, he was so ravished with her, that though he proved all the ways possible to master his fury and passion that way, yet he was still the weaker. So that in the end, condemning himself to death because he found his desire abominable, his passion incurable, and his reason utterly overcome, he resolved to kill himself by little and little, with abstinence from meat and drink, and made no other reckoning to remedy his grief, feigning to have some secret inward

disease in his body. Yet could he not so finely cloak it, but that Erasistratus the physician easily found his grief, that love, not sickness, was his infirmity: howbeit it was hard for him to imagine with whom he was in love. Erasistratus being earnestly bent to find out the party he loved, he sat by this young prince all day long in his chamber, and when any fair young boy or wife came to see him, he earnestly looked Antiochus in the face, and carefully observed all the parts of the body, and outward movings, which do commonly bewray the secret passions and affections of the mind. So having marked him divers times, that when others came to see him, whatsoever they were, he still remained in one self state, and that when Stratonice his mother-in-law came alone or in company of her husband Seleucus to visit him, he commonly perceived those signs in him, which Sappho writeth to be in lovers (to wit, that his words and speech did fail him, his colour became red, his eyes still rolled to and fro, and then a sudden sweat would take him, his pulse would beat fast and rise high, and in the end, that after the force and power of his heart had failed him, and showed all these signs, he became like a man in an ecstasy and trance, and white as a kercher), he then gathering a true conjecture by these so manifest signs and declarations, that it was only Stratonice whom this young prince fancied, and the which he forced himself to keep secret to the death: thought that to bewray it to the king it would offend him much, but yet trusting to his great affection and fatherly love he bore to his son, he ventured one day to tell him, that his son's sickness was no other but love, and withal, that his love was impossible to be enjoyed, and therefore that he must of necessity die, for it was incurable. Seleucus was cold at the heart to hear these news: so he asked him, 'What, is he incurable?' 'Yea, Sir,' answered the physician, 'because he is in love with my wife.' Then replied Seleucus again, 'Alas Erasistratus, I have always loved thee as one of my dearest friends, and wouldst thou not now do me this pleasure, to let my son marry thy wife, if thou knowest it well that I have no more sons but he, and that I see he is but cast away, if thou help me not?' 'But your grace would not do it yourself,' said Erasistratus, 'if he were in love with Stratonice.' 'O,' said Seleucus to him again, 'that it were the will of the gods, some god or man could turn his love that way: for mine own part, I would not only leave him the thing he loved, but I would give my kingdom also to save his life.' Then Erasistratus seeing that the king spoke these words from his heart, and with abundance of tears: he took him by the right hand, and told him plainly, 'Your grace needeth not Erasistratus' help in this. For being father, husband, and king, yourself also may only be the physician, to cure your son's disease.' When Seleucus heard that, he called an assembly of the people, and declared before them all that he was determined to crown his son Antiochus king of the high provinces of Asia, and Stratonice queen, to marry them together: and that he was persuaded that his son (who had always showed himself obedient to his father's will) would not disobey him in this marriage. And as for Stratonice, if she misliked this marriage, and would not consent unto it because it was no common matter, then he prayed that his friends would persuade her she should think all good and comely that should please the king, and withal that concerned the general benefit of the realm and commonwealth. Hereupon Antiochus and Stratonice were married together.

39 But now to return again to the history of Demetrius. Demetrius came by the kingdom of Macedon and Thessalie, by this means as you have heard, and did moreover possess the best part of Peloponnesus, and on this side the strait, the cities of Megara and Athens. Furthermore he led his army against the Boeotians, who were at the first willing to make peace with him. But after that Cleonymus king of Sparta was come into the city of Thebes with his army, the Boeotians encouraged by the fair words and allurement of one Pisis, born in the city of Thespis, who at that time bore all the sway and chief authority amongst them, they gave up their treaty of peace they had begun with Demetrius, and determined to make war. Thereupon Demetrius went to besiege the city of Thebes, and laid his engines of battery unto it: insomuch as Cleonymus for fear, stole secretly out of the city. Thereupon the Thebans being also afraid, yielded themselves unto Demetrius' mercy: who putting great garrisons into the cities, and having levied a great sum of money of the province, left them Hieronymus the historiographer, his lieutenant and governor there. So it appeared that he used them very courteously, and did them many pleasures, and specially unto Pisis. For when he had taken him prisoner, he did him no hurt, but received him very courteously,

and used him well: and furthermore, he made him Polemarchus (to wit, camp master) in the city of Thespis. Shortly after these things were thus brought to pass, King Lysimachus by chance was taken by another barbarous prince called Dromichetes. Thereupon Demetrius, to take such a noble occasion offered him, went with a great army to invade the country of Thracia, supposing he should find no man to withstand him, but that he might conquer it at his pleasure. Howbeit, so soon as Demetrius' back was turned, the Boeotians revolted again from him, and therewithal news was brought him, that Lysimachus was delivered out of prison. Then he returned back with all speed, marvellously offended with the Boeotians, whom he found already discomfited in battle by his son Antigonus, and went again to lay siege to the city of Thebes, being the chief city of all that province of Boeotia.

40   But at that present time, Pyrrhus came and foraged all Thessaly, and entered even to the strait of Thermopyles. Therefore Demetrius was constrained to leave his son to continue the siege at Thebes, whilst he himself went against Pyrrhus, who suddenly returned again into his realm. So Demetrius left ten thousand footmen and a thousand horsemen in Thessaly to defend the country, and returned with the rest of his army to win Thebes. Thereupon he brought his great engine of battery called Elepolis, against the wall, as you have heard before, the which was thrust forward by little and little, with great labour, by reason of the weight and heaviness of it: so that it could scant be driven forward two furlongs in two months. But the Boeotians and the Thebans did valiantly defend themselves: and Demetrius of a malicious mind and desire of revenge (more oftener than needful, or to any purpose) compelled his men to go to the assault, and to hazard themselves: so that there were daily a great number of them slain. Antigonus his son perceiving it: 'Alas,' said he, 'why do we thus suffer our men to be slain and cast away to no purpose?' Wherefore Demetrius angrily answered him again: 'What needest thou to care? Is there any corn to be distributed to those that are dead?' But notwithstanding, because men should not think he still meant to put others in danger, and durst not venture himself, he fought with them, till at length he was shot through the neck with a sharp arrow head, that was shot at him from the wall. Wherewithal he

fell very sick, but yet raised not his siege, nor removed his camp, but took the city of Thebes again by assault: the which being not long before again replenished with people, was in ten years' space twice won and taken. Now he put the Thebans in a marvellous fear, by his cruel threats he gave them at his coming into Thebes: so that they looked to have received the extremest punishment the vanquished could have, through the just wrath and anger of the conqueror. Howbeit after Demetrius had put thirteen of them to death, and banished some, he pardoned all the rest. About that time fell out the celebration of the feast called Pythia, in the honour of Apollo: and because the Aetolians kept all the highways to bring them unto the city of Delphes, in the which of old time they did use to celebrate those sports aforesaid, he caused them to be kept and solemnised at Athens, as in a place where this god in reason should be best honoured and reverenced, because he was patron of the city, and for that the Athenians maintained that he was their progenitor.

41 From thence he returned into Macedon, and knowing that it was against his nature to live idly and in peace, and seeing on the other side also that the Macedonians did him more service, and were more obedient to him in wars, and that in time of peace they grew seditious, full of vanity and quarrel, he went to make war with the Aetolians, and after he had spoiled and destroyed their country, he left Pantauchus his lieutenant there, with a great part of his army. Demetrius himself went in the meantime with the rest of his army against Pyrrhus: and Pyrrhus also against him, but they missed of meeting each with other. Whereupon Demetrius passed further unto the realm of Epirus, the which he spoiled and foraged. Pyrrhus on the other side went on so far that he met with Pantauchus, Demetrius' lieutenant, with whom he fought a battle, and came to the sword with him: so that he did both hurt him, and was also hurt by him. But in the end Pyrrhus had the upper hand: he put Pantauchus to flight, and slew a great number of his men, and took five thousand prisoners: the which was the chief over-throw of Demetrius. For Pyrrhus won not the Macedonians' ill will so much for the mischiefs and hurts he had done unto them, as he got himself great fame and renown with them, because himself alone had with his own hands done all the noble exploits of war in

that journey: for the which, he was afterwards had in great estimation among the Macedonians. Now many of them began to say, that he was the only king of all others, in whom the lively image of the hardiness and valiantness of Alexander the Great was to be seen: and that all the rest (but specially Demetrius) did but counterfeit his gravity and princely countenance, like players upon a stage that would counterfeit his countenance and gesture. And to say truly, there was much fineness and curiosity about Demetrius, to make him a playing stock in common plays. For some say, that he did not only wear a great hat with his diadem upon his head, and was apparelled in purple gowns embroidered with gold: but also that he did use to wear certain woollen shoes on his feet dyed in purple colour, not woven, but fashioned together like a felt, and gilt upon it. And furthermore, he had long before caused a cloak to be made of a marvellous rich and sumptuous piece of work. For upon it was drawn the figure of the world, with stars and circles of heaven, the which was not thoroughly finished by the change of his fortune. So, there was never king of Macedon after him that durst wear it, albeit there were many proud and arrogant kings that succeeded him.

42   Now the Macedonians were not only sorry, and offended to see such things, as they were not wont to be acquainted withal, but they much more misliked this curious manner of life, and specially because he was ill to come to, and worse to be spoken with. For he gave no audience, or if he did, he was very rough, and would sharply take them up that had to do with him. As, he kept the ambassadors of the Athenians two years, and would give them no answer: and yet made as though he loved them better, than any other people of Greece. Another time also he was offended, because the Lacedaemonians had sent but one man only ambassador unto him, taking it that they had done it in despite of him. And so did the ambassador of the Lacedaemonians answer him very gallantly, after the Laconian manner. For when Demetrius asked him, 'How chanceth it that the Lacedaemonians do send but one man unto me?' 'No more but one,' said he, 'O king, unto one.' On a time he came abroad more plainly and popularlike, than he was wont to do: whereby he put the people in good hope that they might the easelier speak with him, and that

he would more courteously hear their complaints. Thereupon many came, and put up their humble supplications and bills of petition unto him. He received them, and put them up in the lap of his cloak. The poor suitors were glad of that, and waited upon him at his heels, hoping they should quickly be dispatched: but when he was upon the bridge of the river of Axius, he opened his cloak, and cast them all into the river. This went to the hearts of the Macedonians, who then thought they were no more governed by a king, but oppressed by a tyrant: and it grieved them so much more, because they did yet remember (either for that they had seen themselves, or otherwise heard their forefathers say) how courteous King Philip was in all such matters, and how that one day as he passed through the street, a poor old woman plucked him by the gown, and eftsoons humbly besought him to hear her, but he answered her he was not then at leisure. Whereupon the poor woman plainly cried out to him, 'Leave then to be king.' This word so nettled him, and he took such a conceit of it, that he returned presently to his palace, and setting all other matters apart, did nothing else many days but gave himself to hear all suits, and began with this poor old woman. For truly nothing becometh a prince better, than to minister justice: for Mars (as Timotheus saith) signifieth force, and is a tyrant: but justice and law, according to Pindarus, is queen of all the world. Moreover, the wise poet Homer saith not that princes and kings have received the custody of engines, and of munition, neither also strong and mighty ships of Jupiter, to keep them to destroy towns withal, but with them to maintain law and justice. And therefore he calleth not the cruel and bloody king, but the just and merciful prince, Jupiter's friend and scholar. And Demetrius boasted that he had a name and title contrary unto Jupiter, whom they called Polieus, or Poliouchos, signifying protector and preserver of cities: and that he was called Poliorcetes, a Fortgainer. Thus the ill was taken for the good, and vice preferred for virtue: because he could not discern the truth from falsehood, which turned his injustice to glory, and iniquity to honour.

43 But now to return where we left: Demetrius fell into a great and dangerous sickness in the city of Pella, during which time he almost lost all Macedon, by a sudden invasion Pyrrhus made, who

in manner rode it all over, and came as far as the city of Edessa. Howbeit so soon as he recovered health again, he easily drove him out, and afterwards made peace with him, because he would not fighting with him (whom he should have daily at his doors still skirmishing sometime here, sometime there) lose the opportunity, and weaken himself to bring that to pass which he had determined. For he had no small matters in his head, but thought to recover all the realms his father had: and besides, the preparation he made was no less sufficient, than the purpose of such an imagination required. For he had levied and assembled an army of a hundred thousand footmen, lacking but two thousand: and unto them he had also well near twelve thousand horsemen, and had besides got above five hundred ships together, which were built part in the haven of Piraeus, part at Corinth, part in the city of Chalcis, and part about Pella. He himself in person went through their work-houses, and showed the artificers how they should make them, and did help to devise them: so that every man wondered not only at his infinite preparation, but at the greatness and sumptuousness of his works. For at that time there was no man living that ever saw a galley of fifteen or sixteen banks of oars. But this is true, that afterwards Ptolomy, surnamed Philopator, built a galley of forty banks of oars, the which was two hundred fourscore cubits long, and from the keel in height to the top of the poop, eight and forty cubits: and to look to the tackle and guide her, required four hundred mariners, and four thousand watermen to row her, and besides all that she could yet carry above the hatches, well near three thousand fighting men. Howbeit this galley never served to other purpose but for show, and was like to a house that never stirred: and it was never removed out of the place where it was built but with marvellous ado, and great danger, more to make men wonder at it, than for any service or commodity it could be employed unto. But now, the beauty of Demetrius' ships did nothing hinder their swiftness and goodness for fight, neither did the hugeness of their building take away the use of them, but their swiftness and nimbleness deserved more commendation, than their sumptuousness and stateliness.

44   Thus as this great power and preparation was in hand, being such as never king before (since the time of Alexander the Great)

had assembled a greater to invade Asia, these three kings, Ptolomy, Seleucus, and Lysimachus, did all join together against him. And afterwards also, they sent ambassadors unto Pyrrhus in the name of them all, to draw him to their side, alluring him to come into Macedon, persuading him not to repose any trust in the peace Demetrius had made with him, to make account of it as a good and sure peace: for, they said that Demetrius did not give him pledge that he would never make war with him, but rather first took opportunity himself to make war with whom he thought good. Pyrrhus considering so much, and finding their words true, there rose a sharp and cruel war on every side against Demetrius, who tracted time, and stayed yet to begin. For at one self time, Ptolomy with a great fleet of ships came down into Greece, and made all Greece revolt from him: and Lysimachus also on Thracia's side, and Pyrrhus upon the borders of Epirus, confining with the realm of Macedon, they entered with a great army, and spoiled and sacked all as they went. Thereupon Demetrius leaving his son Antigonus in Greece, he returned with all possible speed into Macedon, to go first against Lysimachus. But as he was preparing to go against him, news were brought him that Pyrrhus had already taken the city of Berrhoea. This news being blown abroad amongst the Macedonians, all Demetrius' doings were turned topsy turvy. For all his camp was straight full of tears and complaints, and his men began openly to show their anger against him, speaking all the ill they could of him: so that they would tarry no longer, but everyone prayed leave to depart, pretending to look to their business at home, but in truth to go and yield themselves unto Lysimachus. Wherefore Demetrius thought it best for him to get him as far from Lysimachus as he could, and to bend all his army against Pyrrhus: because the other was their countryman, and familiarly known among the most of them, for that they had served together under Alexander the Great, and that as he thought, the Macedonians would not prefer Pyrrhus a stranger, before him. But there his judgment failed him. For as soon as Pyrrhus had pitched his camp hard by him, the Macedonians that had ever loved valiantness, and had of ancient time esteemed him worthier to be king, that was the best soldier and valiantest in the field, and furthermore had heard the report of his great clemency and courtesy he had showed to the prisoners he had taken, they having had goodwill of long time sought but good occasion to forsake Demetrius, and to yield themselves unto Pyrrhus, or to any other prince; whatsoever he were. Then they secretly began to steal away one after another, by small companies at the first: but afterwards there rose such a general tumult against him throughout all the camp, that some of them were so desperate to go into his tent to bid him fly, and save himself, because the Macedonians were too weary with fighting for his curiosity. And yet Demetrius found these words more gentle and modest, in respect of the vile and cruel words which others gave him. So he went into his tent, and cast a black cloak about his face, instead of his rich and stately cloak he was wont to wear: not like unto a king, but like a common player when the play is done, and then secretly stole away. When this was known in the camp, many of his soldiers ran to his tent to rifle it, and every man took such hold of it to have his part, that they tare it in pieces, and drew their swords to fight for it. But Pyrrhus coming in the midst of the tumult, pacified this stir, and presently without blow given, won all Demetrius' camp: and afterwards he divided the realm of Macedon with Lysimachus, in the which Demetrius had quietly reigned the space of seven years.

45  Now Demetrius being thus miserably overthrown, and turned out of all his realm, he fled unto the city of Cassandria. There he found his wife Phila, who took it marvellous heavily, and could not abide to see him again a private man, driven out of his kingdom, and the most miserable king that ever was of all other. Wherefore intending no more to follow vain hope, and detesting the fortune of her husband, she being more constant in calamity than in prosperity, killed herself with poison she took. Demetrius went from thence into Greece, purposing to gather together the rest of his shipwrecks, and there assembled all his captains and friends that he had. So it seemeth to me, the comparison Menelaus maketh of his fortune, in one of the tragedies of Sophocles, in these verses:

> My state doth turn continually about on fortune's wheel,
> Whose double dealing divers times enforced I am to feel:
> Resembling right the moon whose face abideth at no stay
> Two nights together, but doth change in shape from day to day:

At first she riseth small with horns. And as in age she grows,
With fuller cheeks and brighter light a greater face she shows.
And when she cometh to the full, and shineth fair and bright,
Among the goodly glistering stars the goodliest in the night,
She fades and falls away again, and runs a counterpace,
Until she have forgone the light and figure of her face.

The comparison might, I say, much better be applied unto
Demetrius' fortune, to his rising and falling, and to his overthrow
and relief again. For when every man thought his force and power
utterly overthrown, then began he to rise again by repair of
soldiers, which by little and little came unto him, and straight
revived him with good hope. This was the first time that he was
ever seen meanly apparelled, like a private man up and down the
country, without some show or tokens of a king. And there was
one that seeing him in this estate at Thebes, pleasantly applied these
verses of Euripides unto him:

Of god immortal now become a mortal wight:
Ismenus' banks and Dirce's streams he haunteth in our sight.

46    Now when he began to have some hope again, and was (as it
were) entered into the great high way of kings, and had gotten
soldiers about him, which made a body and show of royal power,
he restored the Thebans their liberty and government again. But
the Athenians once more revolted from him, and did revoke the
dignity and priesthood of Diphilus, who had been that year created
priest of the Saviours, instead of the governor, which they called in
old time Eponymous, as we have told you before: and made a law,
that from thenceforth the ancient and common governors of their
city should be restored again to their ancient manner: and they sent
also into Macedon unto King Pyrrhus, rather to terrify Demetrius
(whom they saw begin to rise again) than for any hope they had he
would come and help them. Howbeit Demetrius came against
them with great fury, and did straitly besiege the city of Athens.
Then the Athenians sent Crates the philosopher to him, a man of
great estimation and authority, who so handled him, partly by
entreaty, and partly also through his wise persuasions and counsels
he gave him for his profit, that Demetrius presently raised the siege.
Wherefore, after he had gathered together so many ships as were
left him, and had embarked twelve thousand footmen, and a small

number of horsemen, he presently took sea, and sailed towards Asia, meaning to take the provinces of Caria and Lydia from Lysimachus, and to make them to rebel against him. There Eurydice, sister to his wife Phila, received him by the city of Miletum, having with her one of Ptolomy's daughters and hers, called Ptolemaeide, the which had been afore affianced to him by Seleucus' means. So he married Ptolemaeide there, with the goodwill and consent of her mother Eurydice. After his marriage he presently went into the field again, and did set forwards to win some cities, whereof many willingly received him, and others he took by force. Amongst them he took the city of Sardis, whither came divers captains unto him of King Lysimachus, who yielded themselves, and brought him a great number of men, and much money besides. But Demetrius receiving advertisement that Agathocles, Lysimachus' son, followed him with a great army, he went thence into Phrygia, making account, and also hoping, that if he could win Armenia, he might easily make Media rebel, and then that he would see if he could conquer the high provinces of Asia, where he might have many places of refuge, if fortune turned against him. Agathocles followed him very near, and yet skirmishing divers times with him, Demetrius always had the better: howbeit Agathocles did cut off his victuals from him every way and kept him at such a strait, that his men durst no more stray from the camp to forage: wherefore, they sustained great want of victuals, and then began his men to be afraid, and to mistrust that he would make them follow him into Armenia and Media. The famine daily increased more and more in his army, and it chanced besides, that missing his way, and failing to gauge the ford well as he passed over the river of Lycus, the fury and force of the river carried his men down the stream, and drowned a great number of them: and yet notwithstanding these great troubles, they mocked him besides. For one wrote at the entry and coming in to his tent, the first verse of the tragedy of *Oedipus Colonian*, written by Sophocles, changing only some word:

> Thou imp of old and blind Antigonus,
> To what a point hast thou now carried us?

47    But in the end, the plague began also in the midst of this famine (a common thing, and almost a matter of necessity, it

should so be) because that men being driven to need and necessity, do frame themselves to eat all that comes to hand: whereupon he was driven to bring back those few men that remained, having lost of all sorts (good and bad) not so few as eight thousand fully told. When he came into the province of Tarsus, he commanded his men in no case to meddle with anything, because the country was subject unto King Seleucus, whom he would in no wise displease. But when he saw it was impossible to stay his men being now brought to such extremity and need, and that Agathocles had barred up the straits and passages of Mount Taurus against him, he wrote a letter unto Seleucus, first declaring his miserable state and hard fortune, and then presenting his humble petition and request unto him, praying him to take pity upon his friend, whom spiteful fortune had thrown into such misery and calamity, that could not but move his greatest enemies to have compassion of him. These letters somewhat softened Seleucus' heart, insomuch that he wrote to his governors and lieutenants of those parts, to furnish Demetrius' person with all things needful for a prince's house, and victuals sufficient to maintain his men. But one Patrocles, a grave wise man accounted, and Seleucus' faithful friend also, came to tell him, that the charge to entertain Demetrius' soldiers, was not the greatest fault he made therein, and most to be accounted of, but that he did not wisely look into his affairs, to suffer Demetrius to remain in his country, considering that he had always been a more fierce and venturous prince than any other, to enterprise any matters of great importance; and now he was brought to such despair and extremity, that he had framed his men which were but rank cowards (contrary to their nature) to be most desperate and hardy in greatest dangers. Seleucus being moved with these persuasions, presently took his journey into Cilicia with a great army. Demetrius being astonished with this sudden change, and dreading so great an army, got him to the strongest places of Mount Taurus. Then he sent unto Seleucus, first of all to pray him to suffer him to conquer certain barbarous people thereabouts, who lived according to their own laws, and never had king: to the end that he might yet there with safety end the rest of his life and exile, staying at length in some place where he might be safe. Secondly if that liked him not, then that it would yet please him to victual his men for the winter time only, in the same place where they were, and not to be so hard-hearted unto him as to drive him thence, lacking all needful things, and so to put him into the mouth of his most cruel and mortal enemies.

48 But Seleucus mistrusting his demands, sent unto him that he should winter if he thought good, two months, but no more, in the country of Cataonia, so he gave him the chiefest of his friends for hostages: howbeit in the meantime he stopped up all the ways and passages going from thence into Syria. Demetrius now seeing himself kept in of all sides, like a beast to be taken in the toil, he was driven to trust to his own strength. Thereupon he overran the country thereabouts, and as often as it was his chance to have any skirmish or conflict with Seleucus, he had ever the better of him: and sometime also when they drove the armed carts with scythes against him, he overcame them, and put the rest to flight. Then he drove them away that kept the top of the mountains, and had barred the passages to keep him that he should not go into Syria, and so kept them himself. In fine, finding his men's hearts lift up again, and prettily encouraged, his heart also grew so big, that he determined to fight a battle with Seleucus, and to set all at six and seven. So that Seleucus was at a strait with himself, and wist not what to do. For he had returned back the aid which Lysimachus sent unto him, because he was afraid of him, and mistrusted him. On the other side also he durst not fight with Demetrius alone, being afraid to venture himself with a desperate man: and also mistrusting much his unconstant fortune, the which having brought him to great extremity, raised him up again to great prosperity. But in the mean space Demetrius fell into a great sickness, the which brought his body very weak and low, and had almost utterly overthrown his affairs. For his soldiers, some of them yielded themselves to his enemies, and others stole away without leave, and went where they listed. Afterwards when he had hardly recovered his health, and within forty days' space was prettily grown to strength again, with those few soldiers that remained with him, he seemed to his enemies that he would go and invade Cilicia. But then suddenly in the night without sounding any trumpet, he removed his camp, and went another way: and having passed over Mount Amanus, he spoiled all the country under it, as far as the region of Cyrrestica.

49   But Seleucus followed him, and camped hard by him. Thereupon Demetrius suddenly armed his men, and went out by night
to assault Seleucus, and to take him sleeping when he mistrusted
nothing. So that Seleucus knew nothing of his stealing on him but
late enough, until that certain traitors of Demetrius' camp that fled
before, went quickly to advertise him finding him asleep, and
brought him news of the danger he was in. Then Seleucus in
amaze and fear withal, got up, and sounded the alarm: and as he
was putting on his hose and making him ready he cried out
(speaking to his friends and familiars about him), 'We have now a
cruel and dangerous beast to deal with.' Demetrius on the other
side perceiving by the great stir and noise he heard in the enemies'
camp, that his enterprise was discovered, he retired again with
speed, and the next morning by break of day, Seleucus went and
offered him battle. Demetrius prepared himself to join with him,
and having given one of his faithful friends the leading of one of
the wings of his army, himself led the other, and overthrew some
of his enemies on his side. But Seleucus in the midst of the battle
lighted from his horse, and taking his helmet from his head, he
took a target on his arm, and went to the first ranks of his army, to
make himself known unto Demetrius' men: persuading them to
yield themselves unto him, and to acknowledge in the end, that he
had so long time deferred to give them battle, rather to save them,
than to spare Demetrius. Demetrius' soldiers hearing him say so,
they did him humble reverence, and acknowledging him for their
king, they all yielded unto him. Demetrius having sundry times
before proved so many changes and overthrows of fortune, thinking yet to escape this last also, and to pass it over, he fled unto the
gates Amanides, which are certain straits of the Mount Amanus.
There he found certain little thick groves, where he determined to
stay all night with certain gentlemen of his house, and a few other
of his household servants and officers which had followed him:
meaning, if he could possible, to take his way towards the city of
Caunus, to go to that sea coast, hoping to hear of his ships there.
But when it was told him he had no victuals nor provision left
only to serve him that day, he began then to devise some other
way. At length, one of his familiar friends Sosigenes came unto
him, that had four hundred pieces of gold about him in his girdle.
So hoping that with the same money he might flee to the sea, they

took their way by night directly, to the top of the mountain. But
when they perceived that the enemies kept watch there, and that
there were great store of fires hard by them, they then despaired to
pass any further, lest they should be seen. So they returned to the
selfsame place from whence they came, not all of them, for some
of them fled: neither had they that remained also any life in them
as before. So, one among the rest took upon him to say, that there
was no other way to scape, but to put Demetrius into Seleucus'
hands. Demetrius therewithal drew out his sword, and would
have slain himself: but his friends about him would not suffer him,
but persuaded him to yield himself unto Seleucus. Thereupon he
sent unto Seleucus, to tell him that he yielded himself unto him.

50    Seleucus was so joyful of the news, that he said it was not
Demetrius' good fortune that saved him, but his own: who besides
many other happy good turns she had done him, gave him yet so
honourable occasion and good hap, as to make the world to know
his clemency and courtesy. Thereupon immediately he called for
his officers of household, and commanded them to set up his
richest pavilion, and to prepare all things meet to receive him
honourably. There was one Appolonides a gentleman in Seleucus'
court, who sometime had been very familiar with Demetrius: him
Seleucus sent immediately unto Demetrius, to will him to be of
good cheer, and not to be afraid to come to the king his master, for
he should find him his very good friend. So soon as the king's
pleasure was known, a few of his courtiers went at the first to meet
him: but afterwards, every man strived who should go meet him
first, because they were all in hope that he should presently be
much made of, and grow in credit with Seleucus. But hereby
they turned Seleucus' pity into envy, and gave occasion also to
Demetrius' enemies and spiteful men, to turn the king's bountiful
good nature from him. For they put into his head many doubts and
dangers, saying, that certainly so soon as the soldiers saw him, there
would grow great stir and change in their camp. And therefore,
shortly after that Apollonides was come unto Demetrius, being
glad to bring him these good news, and as others also followed him
one after another, bringing him some good words from Seleucus,
and that Demetrius himself after so great an overthrow (although
that before he thought it a shameful part of him to have yielded his

body into his enemies' hands) changed his mind at that time, and began then to grow bold, and to have good hope to recover his state again: behold, there came one of Seleucus' captains called Pausanias, accompanied with a thousand footmen and horsemen in all, who compassed in Demetrius with them, and made the rest depart that were come unto him before, having charge given him not to bring him to the court, but to convey him into Cherronesus of Syria, whither he was brought, and ever after had a strong garrison about him to keep him. But otherwise, Seleucus sent him officers, money, and all things else meet for a prince's house: and his ordinary fare was so delicate, that he could wish for no more than he had. And furthermore, he had places of liberty and pleasure appointed him, both to ride his horse in, and also pleasant walks, and goodly arbors to walk or sit in, and fine parks full of beasts where he might hunt: moreover, the king suffered his own household servants that followed him when he fled, to remain with him if they would. And furthermore, there daily came someone or other unto him from Seleucus, to comfort him, and to put him in hope, that so soon as Antiochus and Stratonice were come, they would make some good agreement and peace between them.

51 Demetrius remaining in this estate, wrote unto his son Antigonus, and to his friends and lieutenants which he had at Corinth and Athens, that they should give no credit to any letters written in his name, though his seal were to them: but that they should keep the towns they had in charge for his son Antigonus, and all the rest of his forces, as if he himself were dead. When Antigonus heard the pitiful captivity of his father, he marvellous grievously took his hard fortune, wearing blacks for sorrow, and wrote unto all the other kings, but unto Seleucus specially, beseeching him to take him as a pledge for his father, and that he was ready to yield up all that he kept, to have his father's liberty. The like request did many cities make unto him, and in manner all princes, but Lysimachus: who promised Seleucus a great sum of money to put Demetrius to death. But Seleucus, who of long time had no great fancy to Lysimachus, but rather utterly despised him, did then think him the more cruel and barbarous, for this vile and wicked request he made unto him. Wherefore he still delayed time, because he would have Demetrius delivered by his son

Antiochus and Stratonice's means, for that Demetrius should be bound to them for his delivery, and forever should acknowledge it to them.

52 Now for Demetrius, as he from the beginning patiently took his hard fortune, so did he daily more and more forget the misery he was in. For first of all, he gave himself to riding and hunting, as far as the place gave him liberty. Then by little and little he grew to be very gross, and to give over such pastimes, and therewithal he fell into drunkenness and dicing: so that in that sort he passed away the most part of his time, as it should seem, either to avoid the grievous thoughts of his hard fortune, which came into his mind when he was sober: or else under colour of drunkenness and eating, to shadow the thoughts he had: or else finding in himself that it was that manner of life he had long desired, and that through his vain ambition and folly till that time he could never attain unto, greatly turmoiling and troubling himself and others, supposing to find in wars, by sea and land, the felicity and delight which he had found in ease and idleness, when he neither thought of it, nor looked for it. For what better end can evil and unadvised kings and princes look for, of all their troubles, dangers, and wars? Who indeed deceive themselves greatly, not only for that they follow their pleasure and delights as their chiefest felicity, instead of virtue and honest life, but also, because that in truth they cannot be merry, and take their pleasure as they would. So, Demetrius after he had been shut up in Cherronesus three years together, by ease, grossness, and drunkenness, fell sick of a disease whereof he died, when he was four and fifty year old. Therefore was Seleucus greatly blamed, and he himself also did much repent him that he so suspected him as he did, and that he followed not Dromichetes' courtesy, a barbarous man born in Thracia, who had so royally and courteously entreated Lysimachus, whom he had taken prisoner in the wars.

53 But yet there was some tragical pomp in the order of his funeral. For his son Antigonus understanding that they brought him the ashes of his body, he took sea with all his ships, and went to meet them, to receive them in the isles: and when he had received them, he set up the funeral pot of gold (in the which were his embers) upon the poop of his admiral galley. So, all the cities and

towns whereby they passed, or harboured, some of them did put garlands of flowers about the pot, others also sent a number of men thither in mourning apparel, to accompany and honour the convoy, to the very solemnity of his funerals. In this sort sailed all the whole fleet towards the city of Corinth, the pot being plainly seen far off, standing on the top of the admiral galley: all the place about it being hanged about with purple, and over it, the diadem or royal band, and about it also were goodly young men armed, which were as pensioners to Demetrius. Furthermore, Xenophantus the famousest musician in that time, being set hard by it, played a sweet and lamentable song on the flute, wherewithal the oars keeping stroke and measure, the sound did meet with a gallant grace, as in a convoy where the mourners do knock their breasts, at the foot of every verse. But that which most made the people of Corinth to weep and lament, which ran to the pier, and all along the shore side to see it, was Antigonus, whom they saw all beblubbered with tears, apparelled as a mourner in blacks. Now, after they had brought a wonderful number of garlands and nosegays, and cast them upon the funeral pot, and had solemnised all the honours possible for the funerals at Corinth, Antigonus carried away the pot to bury it in the city of Demetriade, the which bore the name of Demetrius that was dead, and was a new city, that had been replenished with people, and built of little towns which are about Iolcos. Demetrius left two children by his first wife Phila, to wit, Antigonus and Stratonice, and two other sons, both of them named Demetrius, the one surnamed the Lean, of a woman of Illyria, and the other king of the Cyrenians, of his wife Ptolemaeide: and another by Deidamia called Alexander, who lived in Egypt. And it is reported also, that he had another son called Corrhaebus, by his wife Eurydice, and that his posterity reigned by succession from the father to the son, until the time of Perseus: who was the last king of Macedon, whom the Romans overcame by Paulus Aemylius, and won all the realm of Macedon unto the empire of Rome. Now that the Macedonian hath played his part, give the Roman also leave to come upon the stage.

## Life of Marcus Antonius

Antonius' grandfather was that famous orator whom Marius slew, because he took Sylla's part. His father was another Antonius surnamed Cretan, who was not so famous, nor bore any great sway in the commonwealth: howbeit otherwise he was an honest man, and of a very good nature, and specially very liberal in giving, as appeareth by an act he did. He was not very wealthy, and therefore his wife would not let him use his liberality and frank nature. One day a friend of his coming to him to pray him to help him to some money, having great need, Antonius by chance had no money to give him, but he commanded one of his men to bring him some water in a silver basin, and after he had brought it him, he washed his beard as though he meant to have shaven it, and then found an errand for his man to send him out, and gave his friend the silver basin, and bade him get him money with that. Shortly after, there was a great stir in the house among the servants, seeking out this silver basin. Insomuch as Antonius seeing his wife marvellously offended for it, and that she would examine all her servants, one after another about it, to know what was become of it, at length he confessed he had given it away, and prayed her to be contented.

2   His wife was Julia, of the noble house and family of Julius Caesar: who for her virtue and chastity, was to be compared with the noblest lady of her time. M. Antonius was brought up under her, being married after her first husband's death, unto Cornelius Lentulus, whom Cicero put to death with Cethegus, and others, for that he was of Catiline's conspiracy against the commonwealth. And this seemeth to be the original cause and beginning of the cruel and mortal hate Antonius bore unto Cicero. For Antonius self saith, that he would never give him the body of his father-in-law to bury him, before his mother went first to entreat Cicero's wife: the which undoubtedly was a flat lie. For Cicero denied

burial to none of them, whom he executed by law. Now Antonius being a fair young man, and in the prime of his youth, he fell acquainted with Curio, whose friendship and acquaintance (as it is reported) was a plague unto him. For he was a dissolute man, given over to all lust and insolence, who to have Antonius the better at his commandment, trained him on into great follies, and vain expenses upon women, in rioting and banqueting. So that in short time, he brought Antonius into a marvellous great debt, and too great for one of his years, to wit: of two hundred and fifty talents, for all which sum Curio was his surety. His father hearing of it, did put his son from him, and forbade him his house. Then he fell in with Clodius, one of the desperatest and most wicked tribunes at that time in Rome. Him he followed for a time in his desperate attempts, who bred great stir and mischief in Rome: but at length he forsook him, being weary of his rashness and folly, or else for that he was afraid of them that were bent against Clodius. Thereupon he left Italy, and went into Greece, and there bestowed the most part of his time, sometime in wars, and otherwhile in the study of eloquence. He used a manner of phrase in his speech, called Asiatic, which carried the best grace and estimation at that time, and was much like to his manners and life: for it was full of ostentation, foolish bravery, and vain ambition.

3 After he had remained there some time, Gabinius proconsul going into Syria, persuaded him to go with him. Antonius told him he would not go as a private man: wherefore Gabinius gave him charge of his horsemen, and so took him with him. So, first of all he sent him against Aristobulus, who had made the Jews to rebel, and was the first man himself that got up to the wall of a castle of his, and so drove Aristobulus out of all his holds: and with those few men he had with him he overcame all the Jews in set battle, which were many against one, and put all of them almost to the sword, and furthermore, took Aristobulus himself prisoner with his son. Afterwards Ptolomy king of Egypt, that had been driven out of his country, went unto Gabinius to entreat him to go with his army with him into Egypt, to put him again into his kingdom: and promised him if he would go with him, ten thousand talents. The most part of the captains thought it not best to go thither, and Gabinius himself made it dainty to enter into this war, although the

covetousness of these ten thousand talents stuck sorely with him. But Antonius that sought but for opportunity and good occasion to attempt great enterprises, and that desired also to gratify Ptolomy's request, he went about to persuade Gabinius to go this voyage. Now they were more afraid of the way they should go, to come to the city of Pelusium, than they feared any danger of the war besides: because they were to pass through deep sands and desert places, where was no fresh water to be had all the marshes thorough, which are called the marshes Serbonides, which the Egyptians call the exhalations or fume, by the which the giant Typhon breathed. But in truth it appeareth to be the overflowing of the red sea, which breaketh out under the ground in that place, where it is divided in the narrowest place from the sea on this side. So Antonius was sent before into Egypt with his horsemen, who did not only win that passage, but also took the city of Pelusium (which is a great city), with all the soldiers in it: and thereby he cleared the way, and made it safe for all the rest of the army, and the hope of the victory also certain for his captain. Now did the enemies themselves feel the fruits of Antonius' courtesy, and the desire he had to win honour. For when Ptolomy (after he had entered into the city of Pelusium) for the malice he bore unto the city, would have put all the Egyptians in it to the sword, Antonius withstood him, and by no means would suffer him to do it. And in all other great battles and skirmishes which they fought, and were many in number, Antonius did many noble acts of a valiant and wise captain: but specially in one battle, where he compassed in the enemies behind, giving them the victory that fought against them, whereby he afterwards had such honourable reward, as his valiantness deserved. So was his great courtesy also much commended of all, the which he showed unto Archelaus. For having been his very friend, he made war with him against his will while he lived: but after his death he sought for his body, and gave it honourable burial. For these respects he won himself great fame of them of Alexandria, and he was also thought a worthy man of all the soldiers in the Romans' camp.

4   But besides all this, he had a noble presence, and showed a countenance of one of a noble house: he had a goodly thick beard, a broad forehead, crook nosed, and there appeared such a manly look in his countenance, as is commonly seen in Hercules' pictures,

stamped or graven in metal. Now it had been a speech of old time, that the family of the Antonii were descended from one Anton, the son of Hercules, whereof the family took name. This opinion did Antonius seek to confirm in all his doings: not only resembling him in the likeness of his body, as we have said before, but also in the wearing of his garments. For when he would openly show himself abroad before many people, he would always wear his cassock girt down low upon his hips, with a great sword hanging by his side, and upon that, some ill-favoured cloak. Furthermore, things that seem intolerable in other men, as to boast commonly, to jest with one or other, to drink like a good fellow with everybody, to sit with the soldiers when they dine, and to eat and drink with them soldierlike: it is incredible what wonderful love it won him amongst them. And furthermore, being given to love, that made him the more desired, and by that means he brought many to love him. For he would further every man's love, and also would not be angry that men should merrily tell him of those he loved. But besides all this, that which most procured his rising and advancement, was his liberality, who gave all to the soldiers, and kept nothing for himself; and when he was grown to great credit, then was his authority and power also very great, the which notwithstanding himself did overthrow by a thousand other faults he had. In this place I will show you one example only of his wonderful liberality. He commanded one day his cofferer that kept his money, to give a friend of his twenty-five myriads: which the Romans call in their tongue, *decies*. His cofferer marvelling at it, and being angry withal in his mind, brought him all this money in a heap together, to show him what a marvellous mass of money it was. Antonius seeing it as he went by, asked what it was: his cofferer answered him, it was the money he willed him to give unto his friend. Then Antonius perceiving the spite of his man, 'I thought,' said he, 'that *decies* had been a greater sum of money than it is, for this is but a trifle,' and therefore he gave his friend as much more another time, but that was afterwards.

5    Now the Romans maintaining two factions at Rome at that time, one against the other, of the which, they that took part with the senate, did join with Pompey being then in Rome, and the contrary side taking part with the people, sent for Caesar to aid

them, who made wars in Gaul: then Curio, Antonius' friend, that had changed his garments, and at that time took part with Caesar, whose enemy he had been before, he won Antonius, and so handled the matter, partly through the great credit and sway he bore amongst the people, by reason of his eloquent tongue, and partly also by his exceeding expense of money he made which Caesar gave him, that Antonius was chosen tribune, and afterwards made Augur. But this was a great help and furtherance to Caesar's practices. For so soon as Antonius became tribune he did oppose himself against those things which the consul Marcellus preferred (who ordained that certain legions which had been already levied and billed, should be given unto Cneus Pompey, with further commission and authority to levy others unto them), and set down an order, that the soldiers which were already levied and assembled, should be sent into Syria, for a new supply unto Marcus Bibulus, who made war at that time against the Parthians. And furthermore, prohibition that Pompey should levy no more men, and also that the soldiers should not obey him. Secondly, where Pompey's friends and followers would not suffer Caesar's letters to be received, and openly read in the senate, Antonius having power and warrant by his person, through the holiness of his tribuneship, did read them openly, and made divers men change their minds: for it appeared to them that Caesar by his letters required no unreasonable matters. At length, when they preferred two matters of consideration unto the senate, whether they thought good that Pompey, or Caesar, should leave their army, there were few of the senators that thought it meet Pompey should leave his army, but they all in manner commanded Caesar to do it. Then Antonius rising up, asked whether they thought it good that Pompey and Caesar both, should leave their armies. Thereunto all the senators jointly together gave their whole consent, and with a great cry commending Antonius, they prayed him to refer it to the judgment of the senate. But the consuls would not allow of that. Therefore Caesar's friends preferred other reasonable demands and requests again, but Cato spoke against them: and Lentulus, one of the consuls, drove Antonius by force out of the senate, who at his going out made grievous curses against him. After that, he took a slave's gown, and speedily fled to Caesar, with Quintus Cassius, in a hired coach. When they came to Caesar, they cried out with open mouth, that all went hand over head at Rome:

for the tribunes of the people might not speak their minds, and were driven away in great danger of their lives, as many as stood with law and justice.

6    Hereupon Caesar incontinently went into Italy with his army, which made Cicero say in his *Philippides*, that as Helen was cause of the war of Troy, so was Antonius the author of the civil wars, which indeed was a stark lie. For Caesar was not so fickle-headed, nor so easily carried away with anger, that he would so suddenly have gone and made war with his country, upon the sight only of Antonius and Cassius, being fled unto him in miserable apparel, and in a hired coach, had he not long before determined it with himself. But if indeed Caesar looked of long time but for some colour, this came as he wished, and gave him just occasion of war. But to say truly, nothing else moved him to make war with all the world as he did, but one self cause, which first procured Alexander and Cyrus also before him: to wit, an insatiable desire to reign, with a senseless covetousness to be the best man in the world, the which he could not come unto, before he had first put down Pompey, and utterly overthrown him. Now, after that Caesar had gotten Rome at his commandment, and had driven Pompey out of Italy, he purposed first to go into Spain, against the legions Pompey had there: and in the meantime to make provision for ships and marine preparation, to follow Pompey. In his absence, he left Lepidus that was praetor, governor of Rome: and Antonius that was tribune, he gave him charge of all the soldiers, and of Italy. Then was Antonius straight marvellously commended and beloved of the soldiers, because he commonly exercised himself among them, and would oftentimes eat and drink with them, and also be liberal unto them, according to his ability. But then in contrary manner, he purchased divers other men's evil wills, because that through negligence he would not do them justice that were injured, and dealt very churlishly with them that had any suit unto him: and besides all this, he had an ill name to entice men's wives. To conclude, Caesar's friends that governed under him, were cause why they hated Caesar's government (which indeed in respect of himself was no less than a tyranny), by reason of the great insolencies and outrageous parts that were committed: amongst whom Antonius, that was of greatest power, and that also committed greatest faults, deserved most blame.

7   But Caesar notwithstanding, when he returned from the wars of Spain, made no reckoning of the complaints that were put up against him: but contrarily, because he found him a hardy man, and a valiant captain, he employed him in his chiefest affairs, and was no whit deceived in his opinion of him. So he passed over the Ionian sea unto Brundusium, being but slenderly accompanied: and sent unto Antonius and Gabinius, that they should embark their men as soon as they could, and pass them over into Macedon. Gabinius was afraid to take the sea, because it was very rough, and in the winter time: and therefore fetched a great compass about by land. But Antonius fearing some danger might come unto Caesar, because he was compassed in with a great number of enemies, first of all he drove away Libo, who rode at anchor with a great army, before the haven of Brundusium. For he manned out such a number of pinnaces, barks, and other small boats about every one of his galleys, that he drove him thence. After that, he embarked into ships twenty thousand footmen, and eight hundred horsemen, and with this army he hoist sail. When the enemies saw him, they made out to follow him: but the sea rose so high, that the billows put back their galleys that they could not come near him, and so he escaped that danger. But withal he fell upon the rocks with his whole fleet, where the sea wrought very high: so that he was out of all hope to save himself. Yet by good fortune, suddenly the wind turned southwest, and blew from the gulf, driving the waves of the river into the main sea. Thus Antonius loosing from the land, and sailing with safety at his pleasure, soon after he saw all the coasts full of shipwrecks. For the force and boisterousness of the wind did cast away the galleys that followed him: of the which, many of them were broken and splitted, and divers also cast away, and Antonius took a great number of them prisoners, with a great sum of money also. Besides all these, he took the city of Lyssus, and brought Caesar a great supply of men, and made him courageous, coming at a pinch with so great a power to him.

8   Now there were divers hot skirmishes and encounters, in the which Antonius fought so valiantly, that he carried the praise from them all: but specially at two several times, when Caesar's men turned their backs, and fled for life. For he stepped before them, and compelled them to return again to fight, so that the victory fell

on Caesar's side. For this cause he had the second place in the camp among the soldiers, and they spoke of no other man unto Caesar, but of him: who showed plainly what opinion he had of him, when at the last battle of Pharsalia (which indeed was the last trial of all, to give the conqueror the whole empire of the world) he himself did lead the right wing of his army, and gave Antonius the leading of the left wing, as the valiantest man, and skilfullest soldier of all those he had about him. After Caesar had won the victory, and that he was created dictator, he followed Pompey step by step: howbeit before, he named Antonius general of the horsemen, and sent him to Rome. The general of the horsemen is the second office of dignity, when the dictator is in the city: but when he is abroad, he is the chiefest man, and almost the only man that remaineth, and all the other officers and magistrates are put down, after there is a dictator chosen.

9    Notwithstanding, Dolabella being at that time tribune, and a young man desirous of change and innovation, he preferred a law which the Romans call *novas tabulas* (as much to say, as a cutting off and cancelling of all obligations and specialities, and were called the new tables, because they were driven then to make books of daily receipt and expense) and persuaded Antonius his friend (who also gaped for a good occasion to please and gratify the common people) to aid him to pass this law. But Trebellius and Asinius dissuaded from it all they could possible. So by good hap it chanced that Antonius mistrusted Dolabella for keeping of his wife, and took such a conceit of it, that he thrust his wife out of his house being his cousin germane, and the daughter of C. Antonius, who was consul with Cicero: and joining with Asinius, he resisted Dolabella, and fought with him. Dolabella had gotten the market-place where the people do assemble in council, and had filled it full of armed men, intending to have this law of the new tables to pass by force. Antonius by commandment of the senate, who had given him authority to levy men, to use force against Dolabella, he went against him, and fought so valiantly, that men were slain on both sides. But by this means, he got the ill will of the common people, and on the other side, the noblemen (as Cicero saith) did not only mislike him, but also hate him for his naughty life: for they did abhor his banquets and drunken feasts he made at unseasonable

times, and his extreme wasteful expenses upon vain light house-
wives, and then in the day time he would sleep or walk out his
drunkenness, thinking to wear away the fume of the abundance of
wine which he had taken overnight. In his house they did nothing
but feast, dance, and masque: and himself passed away the time in
hearing of foolish plays, or in marrying these players, tumblers,
jesters, and such sort of people. As for proof hereof it is reported,
that at Hippias' marriage, one of his jesters, he drank wine so lustily
all night, that the next morning when he came to plead before the
people assembled in council, who had sent for him, he being
queasy-stomached with his surfeit he had taken, was compelled to
lay all before them, and one of his friends held him his gown
instead of a basin. He had another pleasant player called Sergius,
that was one of the chiefest men about him, and a woman also
called Cytheride, of the same profession, whom he loved dearly:
he carried her up and down in a litter unto all the towns he went,
and had as many men waiting upon her litter, she being but a
player, as were attending upon his own mother. It grieved honest
men also very much, to see that when he went into the country, he
carried with him a great number of cupboards full of silver and gold
plate, openly in the face of the world, as it had been the pomp or
show of some triumph: and that eftsoons in the midst of his
journey he would set up his hales and tents hard by some green
grove or pleasant river, and there his cooks should prepare him a
sumptuous dinner. And furthermore, lions were harnessed in traces
to draw his carts: and besides also, in honest men's houses in the
cities where he came, he would have common harlots, courtesans,
and these tumbling gillots lodged. Now it grieved men much, to
see that Caesar should be out of Italy following of his enemies to
end this great war, with such great peril and danger: and that others
in the meantime abusing his name and authority, should commit
such insolent and outrageous parts unto their citizens.

10    This methinks was the cause that made the conspiracy against
Caesar increase more and more, and laid the reins of the bridle
upon the soldiers' necks, whereby they durst boldlier commit
many extortions, cruelties and robberies. And therefore Caesar
after his return pardoned Dolabella, and being created consul the
third time, he took not Antonius, but chose Lepidus his colleague

and fellow consul. Afterwards when Pompey's house was put to
open sale, Antonius bought it: but when they asked him money for
it, he made it very strong, and was offended with them, and writeth
himself that he would not go with Caesar into the wars of Africa,
because he was not well recompensed for the service he had done
him before. Yet Caesar did somewhat bridle his madness and
insolence, not suffering him to pass his fault so lightly away,
making as though he saw them not. And therefore he left his
dissolute manner of life, and married Fulvia that was Clodius'
widow, a woman not so basely minded to spend her time in
spinning and housewifery, and was not contented to master her
husband at home, but would also rule him in his office abroad,
and command him, that commanded legions and great armies: so
that Cleopatra was to give Fulvia thanks for that she had taught
Antonius this obedience to women, that learned so well to be at
their commandment. Now, because Fulvia was somewhat sour,
and crooked of condition, Antonius devised to make her pleasanter, and somewhat better disposed: and therefore he would play
her many pretty youthful parts to make her merry. As he did once,
when Caesar returned the last time of all conqueror out of Spain,
every man went out to meet him: and so did Antonius with the
rest. But on the sudden there ran a rumour through Italy, that
Caesar was dead, and that his enemies came again with a great
army. Thereupon he returned with speed to Rome, and took one
of his men's gowns, and so apparelled came home to his house in a
dark night, saying that he had brought Fulvia letters from
Antonius. So he was let in, and brought to her muffled as he was,
for being known: but she taking the matter heavily, asked him if
Antonius were well. Antonius gave her the letters, and said never a
word. So when she had opened the letters, and began to read them:
Antonius ramped of her neck, and kissed her. We have told you
this tale for example's sake only, and so could we also tell you of
many suchlike as these.

11    Now when Caesar was returned from his last war in Spain, all
the chiefest nobility of the city rode many days journey from Rome
to meet him, where Caesar made marvellous much of Antonius,
above all the men that came unto him. For he always took him into
his coach with him, throughout all Italy: and behind him, Brutus

Albinus and Octavius, the son of his niece, who afterwards was called Caesar, and became emperor of Rome long time after. So Caesar being afterwards chosen consul the fifth time, he immediately chose Antonius his colleague and companion: and desired by deposing himself of his consulship, to make Dolabella consul in his room, and had already moved it to the senate. But Antonius did stoutly withstand it, and openly reviled Dolabella in the senate: and Dolabella also spared him as little. Thereupon Caesar being ashamed of the matter, he let it alone. Another time also when Caesar attempted again to substitute Dolabella consul in his place, Antonius cried out, that the signs of the birds were against it: so that at length Caesar was compelled to give him place, and to let Dolabella alone, who was marvellously offended with him. Now in truth, Caesar made no great reckoning of either of them both. For it is reported that Caesar answered one that did accuse Antonius and Dolabella unto him for some matter of conspiracy: 'Tush,' said he, 'they be not those fat fellows and fine combed men that I fear, but I mistrust rather these pale and lean men,' meaning by Brutus and Cassius, who afterwards conspired his death, and slew him.

12 Antonius unawares afterwards, gave Caesar's enemies just occasion and colour to do as they did: as you shall hear. The Romans by chance celebrated the feast called Lupercalia, and Caesar being apparelled in his triumphing robe, was set in the tribune where they use to make their orations to the people, and from thence did behold the sport of the runners. The manner of this running was this. On that day there are many young men of noble house, and those specially that be chief officers for that year, who running naked up and down the city anointed with the oil of olive, for pleasure do strike them they meet in their way, with white leather thongs they have in their hands. Antonius being one among the rest that was to run, leaving the ancient ceremonies and old customs of that solemnity, he ran to the tribune where Caesar was set, and carried a laurel crown in his hand, having a royal band or diadem wreathed about it, which in old time was the ancient mark and token of a king. When he was come to Caesar, he made his fellow runners with him lift him up, and so he did put this laurel crown upon his head, signifying thereby that he had deserved to be king. But Caesar making as though he refused it, turned away his

head. The people were so rejoiced at it, that they all clapped their
hands for joy. Antonius again did put it on his head: Caesar again
refused it, and thus they were striving off and on a great while
together. As oft as Antonius did put this laurel crown unto him, a
few of his followers rejoiced at it: and as oft also as Caesar refused
it, all the people together clapped their hands. And this was a
wonderful thing, that they suffered all things subjects should do by
commandment of their kings: and yet they could not abide the
name of a king, detesting it as the utter destruction of their liberty.
Caesar in a rage rose out of his seat, and plucking down the collar
of his gown from his neck, he showed it naked, bidding any man
strike off his head that would. This laurel crown was afterwards put
upon the head of one of Caesar's statues or images, the which one
of the tribunes plucked off. The people liked his doing therein so
well, that they waited on him home to his house, with great
clapping of hands. Howbeit Caesar did turn them out of their
offices for it.

13    This was a good encouragement for Brutus and Cassius to
conspire his death, who fell into a consort with their trustiest
friends, to execute their enterprise: but yet stood doubtful whether
they should make Antonius privy to it or not. All the rest liked of
it, saving Trebonius only. He told them, that when they rode to
meet Caesar at his return out of Spain, Antonius and he always
keeping company, and lying together by the way, he felt his mind
afar off: but Antonius finding his meaning, would hearken no more
unto it, and yet notwithstanding never made Caesar acquainted
with this talk, but had faithfully kept it to himself. After that they
consulted whether they should kill Antonius with Caesar. But
Brutus would in no wise consent to it, saying, that venturing on
such an enterprise as that, for the maintenance of law and justice, it
ought to be clear from all villainy. Yet they fearing Antonius'
power, and the authority of his office, appointed certain of the
conspiracy, that when Caesar were gone into the senate, and while
others should execute their enterprise, they should keep Antonius
in a talk out of the senate house.

14    Even as they had devised these matters, so were they executed:
and Caesar was slain in the midst of the senate. Antonius being put
in a fear withal, cast a slave's gown upon him, and hid himself. But

afterwards when it was told him that the murderers slew no man else, and that they went only into the Capitol, he sent his son unto them for a pledge, and bade them boldly come down upon his word. The selfsame day he did bid Cassius to supper, and Lepidus also bade Brutus. The next morning the senate was assembled, and Antonius himself preferred a law that all things past should be forgotten, and that they should appoint provinces unto Cassius and Brutus: the which the senate confirmed, and further ordained, that they should cancel none of Caesar's laws. Thus went Antonius out of the senate more praised, and better esteemed, than ever man was: because it seemed to every man that he had cut off all occasion of civil wars, and that he had showed himself a marvellous wise governor of the commonwealth, for the appeasing of these matters of so great weight and importance. But now, the opinion he conceived of himself after he had a little felt the goodwill of the people towards him, hoping thereby to make himself the chiefest man if he might overcome Brutus, did easily make him alter his first mind. And therefore when Caesar's body was brought to the place where it should be buried, he made a funeral oration in commendation of Caesar, according to the ancient custom of praising noblemen at their funerals. When he saw that the people were very glad and desirous also to hear Caesar spoken of, and his praises uttered, he mingled his oration with lamentable words, and by amplifying of matters did greatly move their hearts and affections unto pity and compassion. In fine, to conclude his oration, he unfold before the whole assembly the bloody garments of the dead, thrust through in many places with their swords, and called the malefactors, cruel and cursed murderers. With these words he put the people into such a fury, that they presently took Caesar's body, and burnt it in the market-place, with such tables and forms as they could get together. Then when the fire was kindled, they took firebrands, and ran to the murderers' houses to set them afire, and to make them come out to fight.

15 Brutus therefore and his accomplices, for safety of their persons, were driven to fly the city. Then came all Caesar's friends unto Antonius, and specially his wife Calpurnia putting her trust in him, she brought the most part of her money into his house, which amounted to the sum of four thousand talents, and furthermore

brought him all Caesar's books and writings, in the which were his memorials of all that he had done and ordained. Antonius did daily mingle with them such as he thought good, and by that means he created new officers, made new senators, called home some that were banished, and delivered those that were prisoners, and then he said that all those things were so appointed and ordained by Caesar. Therefore the Romans mocking them that were so moved, they called them Charonites, because that when they were over-come, they had no other help but to say, that thus they were found in Caesar's memorials, who had sailed in Charon's boat, and was departed. Thus Antonius ruled absolutely also in all other matters, because he was consul, and Caius one of his brethren praetor, and Lucius the other, tribune.

16   Now things remaining in this state at Rome, Octavius Caesar the younger came to Rome, who was the son of Julius Caesar's niece, as you have heard before, and was left his lawful heir by will, remaining at the time of the death of his great-uncle that was slain, in the city of Apollonia. This young man at his first arrival went to salute Antonius, as one of his late dead father Caesar's friends, who by his last will and testament had made him his heir: and withal, he was presently in hand with him for money and other things which were left of trust in his hands, because Caesar had by will bequeathed unto the people of Rome, three score and fifteen silver drachmas to be given to every man, the which he as heir stood charged withal. Antonius at the first made no reckoning of him, because he was very young: and said he lacked wit, and good friends to advise him, if he looked to take such a charge in hand, as to undertake to be Caesar's heir. But when Antonius saw that he could not shake him off with those words, and that he was still in hand with him for his father's goods, but specially for the ready money, then he spoke and did what he could against him. And first of all, it was he that did keep him from being tribune of the people: and also when Octavius Caesar began to meddle with the dedicating of the chair of gold, which was prepared by the senate to honour Caesar with, he threatened to send him to prison, and moreover desisted not to put the people in an uproar. This young Caesar seeing his doings, went unto Cicero and others, which were Antonius' enemies, and by them crept into

favour with the senate: and he himself sought the people's good-will every manner of way, gathering together the old soldiers of the late deceased Caesar, which were dispersed in divers cities and colonies. Antonius being afraid of it, talked with Octavius in the capitol, and became his friend. But the very same night Antonius had a strange dream, who thought that lightning fell upon him, and burnt his right hand. Shortly after word was brought him, that Caesar lay in wait to kill him. Caesar cleared himself unto him, and told him there was no such matter: but he could not make Antonius believe the contrary. Whereupon they became further enemies than ever they were: insomuch that both of them made friends of either side to gather together all the old soldiers through Italy, that were dispersed in divers towns: and made them large promises, and sought also to win the legions of their side, which were already in arms.

17   Cicero on the other side being at that time the chiefest man of authority and estimation in the city, he stirred up all men against Antonius: so that in the end he made the senate pronounce him an enemy to his country, and appointed young Caesar sergeants to carry axes before him, and such other signs as were incident to the dignity of a consul or praetor: and moreover sent Hircius and Pansa, then consuls, to drive Antonius out of Italy. These two consuls together with Caesar, who also had an army, went against Antonius that besieged the city of Modena, and there overthrew him in battle: but both the consuls were slain there. Antonius flying upon this overthrow, fell into great misery all at once: but the chiefest want of all other, and that pinched him most, was famine. Howbeit he was of such a strong nature, that by patience he would overcome any adversity, and the heavier fortune lay upon him, the more constant showed he himself. Every man that feeleth want or adversity, knoweth by virtue and discretion what he should do: but when indeed they are overlaid with extremity, and be sore oppressed, few have the hearts to follow that which they praise and commend, and much less to avoid that they reprove and mislike. But rather to the contrary, they yield to their accustomed easy life: and through faint heart, and lack of courage, do change their first mind and purpose. And therefore it was a wonderful example to the soldiers, to see Antonius that was

brought up in all fineness and superfluity, so easily to drink puddle water, and to eat wild fruits and roots: and moreover it is reported, that even as they passed the Alps, they did eat the barks of trees, and such beasts, as never man tasted of their flesh before.

18 Now their intent was to join with the legions that were on the other side of the mountains, under Lepidus' charge: whom Antonius took to be his friend, because he had helped him to many things at Caesar's hand, through his means. When he was come to the place where Lepidus was, he camped hard by him: and when he saw that no man came to him to put him in any hope, he determined to venture himself, and to go unto Lepidus. Since the overthrow he had at Modena, he suffered his beard to grow at length and never clipped it, that it was marvellous long, and the hair of his head also without combing: and besides all this, he went in a mourning gown, and after this sort came hard to the trenches of Lepidus' camp. Then he began to speak unto the soldiers, and many of them, their hearts yearned for pity to see him so poorly arrayed, and some also through his words began to pity him: insomuch that Lepidus began to be afraid, and therefore commanded all the trumpets to sound together to stop the soldiers' ears, that they should not hearken to Antonius. This notwithstanding, the soldiers took the more pity of him, and spoke secretly with him by Clodius' and Laelius' means, whom they sent unto him disguised in women's apparel, and gave him counsel that he should not be afraid to enter into their camp, for there were a great number of soldiers that would receive him, and kill Lepidus, if he would say the word. Antonius would not suffer them to hurt him, but the next morning he went with his army to wade a ford, at a little river that ran between them: and himself was the foremost man that took the river to get over, seeing a number of Lepidus' camp that gave him their hands, plucked up the stakes, and laid flat the bank of their trench to let him in to their camp. When he was come into their camp, and that he had all the army at his commandment, he used Lepidus very courteously, embraced him, and called him father: and though indeed Antonius did all, and ruled the whole army, yet he always gave Lepidus the name and honour of the captain. Munatius Plancus, lying also in camp hard by with an army, understanding the report of Antonius' courtesy,

he also came and joined with him. Thus Antonius being afoot again, and grown of great power, repassed over the Alps, leading into Italy with him seventeen legions, and ten thousand horsemen, besides six legions he left in garrison among the Gauls, under the charge of one Varius, a companion of his that would drink lustily with him, and therefore in mockery was surnamed Cotylon: to wit, a bibber.

19 So Octavius Caesar would not lean to Cicero, when he saw that his whole travail and endeavour was only to restore the commonwealth to her former liberty. Therefore he sent certain of his friends to Antonius, to make them friends again: and thereupon all three met together, (to wit, Caesar, Antonius, and Lepidus) in an island environed round about with a little river, and there remained three days together. Now as touching all other matters, they were easily agreed, and did divide all the empire of Rome between them, as if it had been their own inheritance. But yet they could hardly agree whom they would put to death: for every one of them would kill their enemies, and save their kinsmen and friends. Yet at length, giving place to their greedy desire to be revenged of their enemies, they spurned all reverence of blood and holiness of friendship at their feet. For Caesar left Cicero to Antonius' will, Antonius also forsook Lucius Caesar, who was his uncle by his mother: and both of them together suffered Lepidus to kill his own brother Paulus. Yet some writers affirm, that Caesar and Antonius requested Paulus might be slain, and that Lepidus was contented with it. In my opinion there was never a more horrible, unnatural, and crueller change than this was. For thus changing murder for murder, they did as well kill those whom they did forsake and leave unto others, as those also which others left unto them to kill: but so much more was their wickedness and cruelty great unto their friends, for that they put them to death being innocents, and having no cause to hate them.

20 After this plot was agreed upon between them, the soldiers that were thereabouts, would have this friendship and league betwixt them confirmed by marriage, and that Caesar should marry Claudia, the daughter of Fulvia, and Antonius' wife. This marriage also being agreed upon, they condemned three hundred of the chiefest citizens of Rome, to be put to death by proscription.

And Antonius also commanded them to whom he had given commission to kill Cicero, that they should strike off his head and right hand, with the which he had written the invective orations (called *Philippides*) against Antonius. So when the murderers brought him Cicero's head and hand cut off, he beheld them a long time with great joy, and laughed heartily, and that oftentimes for the great joy he felt. Then when he had taken his pleasure of the sight of them, he caused them to be set up in an open place, over the pulpit for orations (where when he was alive, he had often spoken to the people), as if he had done the dead man hurt, and not blemished his own fortune, showing himself (to his great shame and infamy) a cruel man, and unworthy the office and authority he bore. His uncle Lucius Caesar also, as they sought for him to kill him, and followed him hard, fled unto his sister. The murderers coming thither, forcing to break into her chamber, she stood at her chamber door with her arms abroad, crying out still: 'You shall not kill Lucius Caesar, before you first kill me, that bore your captain in my womb.' By this means she saved her brother's life.

21   Now the government of these Triumviri grew odious and hateful to the Romans, for divers respects: but they most blamed Antonius, because he being elder than Caesar, and of more power and force than Lepidus, gave himself again to his former riot and excess, when he left to deal in the affairs of the commonwealth. But setting aside the ill name he had for his insolence, he was yet much more hated in respect of the house he dwelt in, the which was the house of Pompey the Great: a man as famous for his temperance, modesty, and civil life, as for his three triumphs. For it grieved them to see the gates commonly shut against the captains, magistrates of the city, and also ambassadors of strange nations, which were sometimes thrust from the gate with violence: and that the house within was full of tumblers, antic dancers, jugglers, players, jesters, and drunkards, quaffing and guzzling, and that on them he spent and bestowed the most part of his money he got by all kind of possible extortions, bribery and policy. For they did not only sell by the crier the goods of those whom they had outlawed and appointed to murder, slanderously deceived the poor widows and young orphans, and also raised all kind of imposts, subsidies, and taxes: but understanding also that the holy vestal nuns had

certain goods and money put in their custody to keep, both of men's in the city, and those also that were abroad, they went thither, and took them away by force. Octavius Caesar perceiving that no money would serve Antonius' turn, he prayed that they might divide the money between them, and so did they also divide the army, for them both to go into Macedon to make war against Brutus and Cassius: and in the meantime they left the government of the city of Rome unto Lepidus.

22 When they had passed over the seas, and that they began to make war, they being both camped by their enemies, to wit, Antonius against Cassius, and Caesar against Brutus, Caesar did no great matter, but Antonius had always the upper hand, and did all. For at the first battle Caesar was overthrown by Brutus, and lost his camp, and very hardly saved himself by flying from them that followed him. Howbeit he writeth himself in his *Commentaries*, that he fled before the charge was given, because of a dream one of his friends had. Antonius on the other side overthrew Cassius in battle, though some write that he was not there himself at the battle, but that he came after the overthrow, whilst his men had the enemies in chase. So Cassius at his earnest request was slain by a faithful servant of his own called Pindarus, whom he had enfranchised, because he knew not in time that Brutus had overcome Caesar. Shortly after they fought another battle again, in the which Brutus was overthrown, who afterwards also slew himself. Thus Antonius had the chiefest glory of all this victory, specially because Caesar was sick at that time. Antonius having found Brutus' body after this battle, blaming him much for the murder of his brother Caius, whom he had put to death in Macedon for revenge of Cicero's cruel death, and yet laying the fault more in Hortensius than in him, he made Hortensius to be slain on his brother's tomb. Furthermore, he cast his coat armour (which was wonderful rich and sumptuous) upon Brutus' body, and gave commandment to one of his slaves enfranchised, to defray the charge of his burial. But afterwards, Antonius hearing that his enfranchised bondman had not burnt his coat armour with his body, because it was very rich, and worth a great sum of money, and that he had also kept back much of the ready money appointed for his funeral and tomb, he also put him to death.

23   After that Caesar was conveyed to Rome, and it was thought
he would not live long, nor scape the sickness he had. Antonius on
the other side went towards the East provinces and regions, to levy
money: and first of all he went into Greece, and carried an infinite
number of soldiers with him. Now, because every soldier was
promised five thousand silver drachmas, he was driven of necessity
to impose extreme tallages and taxations. At his first coming into
Greece, he was not hard nor bitter unto the Grecians, but gave
himself only to hear wise men dispute, to see plays, and also to
note the ceremonies and sacrifices of Greece, ministering justice to
every man: and it pleased him marvellously to hear them call him
Philellen (as much to say, a lover of the Grecians), and specially the
Athenians, to whom he did many great pleasures. Wherefore the
Megarians, to exceed the Athenians, thinking to show Antonius a
goodly sight, they prayed him to come and see their senate house,
and council hall. Antonius went thither to see it: so when he had
seen it at his pleasure, they asked him, 'My lord, how like you our
hall?' 'Methinks,' quoth he, ' it is little, old, and ready to fall down.'
Furthermore, he took measure of the temple of Apollo Pythias,
and promised the senate to finish it.

24   But when he was once come into Asia, having left Lucius
Censorinus governor in Greece, and that he had felt the riches and
pleasures of the east parts, and that princes, great lords and kings,
came to wait at his gate for his coming out, and that queens and
princesses to excel one another, gave him very rich presents, and
came to see him, curiously setting forth themselves, and using all
art that might be to show their beauty, to win his favour the more
(Caesar in the mean space turmoiling his wit and body in civil wars
at home, Antonius living merrily and quietly abroad), he easily fell
again to his old licentious life. For straight one Anaxenor a player
of the citherne, Xoutus a player of the flutes, Metrodorus a
tumbler, and such a rabble of minstrels and fit ministers for the
pleasures of Asia (who in fineness and flattery passed all the other
plagues he brought with him out of Italy), all these flocked in his
court, and bore the whole sway: and after that, all went awry. For
everyone gave themselves to riot and excess, when they saw he
delighted in it: and all Asia was like to the city Sophocles speaketh
of in one of his tragedies:

Was full of sweet perfumes, and pleasant songs,
With woeful weeping mingled thereamongs.

For in the city of Ephesus, women attired as they go in the feasts
and sacrifice of Bacchus, came out to meet him with such solemn-
ities and ceremonies, as are then used, with men and children
disguised like fauns and satyrs. Moreover, the city was full of ivy,
and darts wreathed about with ivy, psalterions, flutes and hautboys, and in their songs they called him Bacchus, father of mirth,
courteous and gentle: and so was he unto some, but to the most
part of men, cruel and extreme. For he robbed noblemen and
gentlemen of their goods, to give it unto vile flatterers: who
oftentimes begged men's goods living, as though they had been
dead, and would enter their houses by force. As he gave a citizen's
house of Magnesia unto a cook, because (as it is reported) he
dressed him a fine supper. In the end he doubled the taxation, and
imposed a second upon Asia. But then Hybraeas the orator, sent
from the estates of Asia to tell him the state of their country, boldly
said unto him: 'If thou wilt have power to lay two tributes in one
year upon us, thou shouldest also have power to give us two
summers, two autumns, and two harvests.' This was gallantly and
pleasantly spoken unto Antonius by the orator, and it pleased him
well to hear it: but afterwards amplifying his speech, he spoke
more boldly, and to better purpose: 'Asia hath paid the two
hundred thousand talents. If all this money be not come to thy
coffers, then ask account of them that levied it: but if thou have
received it, and nothing be left of it, then are we utterly undone.'
Hybraeas' words nettled Antonius roundly. For he understood not
many of the thefts and robberies his officers committed by his
authority, in his treasure and affairs: not so much because he was
careless, as for that he oversimply trusted his men in all things. For
he was a plain man, without subtlety, and therefore overlate found
out the foul faults they committed against him: but when he heard
of them, he was much offended, and would plainly confess it unto
them whom his officers had done injury unto, by countenance of
his authority. He had a noble mind, as well to punish offenders,
as to reward well doers: and yet he did exceed more in giving,
than in punishing. Now for his outrageous manner of railing he
commonly used, mocking and flouting of every man, that was
remedied by itself. For a man might as boldly exchange a mock

with him, and he was as well contented to be mocked, as to mock others. But yet it oftentimes marred all. For he thought that those which told him so plainly and truly in mirth, would never flatter him in good earnest, in any matter of weight. But thus he was easily abused by the praises they gave him, not finding how these flatterers mingled their flattery, under this familiar and plain manner of speech unto him, as a fine devise to make difference of meats with sharp and tart sauce, and also to keep him by this frank jesting and bourding with him at the table, that their common flattery should not be troublesome unto him, as men do easily mislike to have too much of one thing: and that they handled him finely thereby, when they would give him place in any matter of weight, and follow his counsel, that it might not appear to him they did it so much to please him, but because they were ignorant, and understood not so much as he did.

25    Antonius being thus inclined, the last and extremest mischief of all other (to wit, the love of Cleopatra) lighted on him, who did waken and stir up many vices yet hidden in him, and were never seen to any: and if any spark of goodness or hope of rising were left him, Cleopatra quenched it straight, and made it worse than before. The manner how he fell in love with her was this. Antonius going to make war with the Parthians, sent to command Cleopatra to appear personally before him, when he came into Cilicia, to answer unto such accusations as were laid against her, being this: that she had aided Cassius and Brutus in their war against him. The messenger sent unto Cleopatra to make this summons unto her, was called Dellius: who when he had thoroughly considered her beauty, the excellent grace and sweetness of her tongue, he nothing mistrusted that Antonius would do any hurt to so noble a lady, but rather assured himself, that within few days she should be in great favour with him. Thereupon he did her great honour, and persuaded her to come into Cilicia, as honourably furnished as she could possible, and bade her not to be afraid at all of Antonius, for he was a more courteous lord, than any that she had ever seen. Cleopatra on the other side believing Dellius' words, and guessing by the former access and credit she had with Julius Caesar and Cneus Pompey (the son of Pompey the Great), only for her beauty, she began to have good hope that she might more easily

win Antonius. For Caesar and Pompey knew her when she was but a young thing, and knew not then what the world meant: but now she went to Antonius at the age when a woman's beauty is at the prime, and she also of best judgment. So, she furnished herself with a world of gifts, store of gold and silver, and of riches and other sumptuous ornaments, as is credible enough she might bring from so great a house, and from so wealthy and rich a realm as Egypt was. But yet she carried nothing with her wherein she trusted more than in herself, and in the charms and enchantment of her passing beauty and grace.

26   Therefore when she was sent unto by divers letters, both from Antonius himself, and also from his friends, she made so light of it, and mocked Antonius so much, that she disdained to set forward otherwise, but to take her barge in the river of Cydnus, the poop whereof was of gold, the sails of purple, and the oars of silver, which kept stroke in rowing after the sound of the music of flutes, hautboys, citherns, viols, and such other instruments as they played upon in the barge. And now for the person of her self: she was laid under a pavilion of cloth of gold of tissue, apparelled and attired like the goddess Venus, commonly drawn in picture: and hard by her, on either hand of her, pretty fair boys, apparelled as painters do set forth god Cupid, with little fans in their hands, with the which they fanned wind upon her. Her ladies and gentlewomen also, the fairest of them were apparelled like the nymphs Nereides (which are the mermaids of the waters) and like the Graces, some steering the helm, others tending the tackle and ropes of the barge, out of the which there came a wonderful passing sweet savour of perfumes, that perfumed the wharf's side, pestered with innumerable multitudes of people. Some of them followed the barge all along the river's side: others also ran out of the city to see her coming in. So that in the end, there ran such multitudes of people one after another to see her, that Antonius was left post alone in the marketplace, in his imperial seat to give audience: and there went a rumour in the people's mouths, that the goddess Venus was come to play with the god Bacchus, for the general good of all Asia. When Cleopatra landed, Antonius sent to invite her to supper to him. But she sent him word again, he should do better rather to come and sup with her. Antonius therefore to show himself courteous unto

her at her arrival, was contented to obey her, and went to supper to her: where he found such passing sumptuous fare, that no tongue can express it. But amongst all other things, he most wondered at the infinite number of lights and torches hanged on the top of the house, giving light in every place, so artificially set and ordered by devises, some round, some square, that it was the rarest thing to behold that eye could discern, or that ever books could mention.

27    The next night, Antonius feasting her, contended to pass her in magnificence and fineness: but she overcame him in both. So that he himself began to scorn the gross service of his house, in respect of Cleopatra's sumptuousness and fineness. And when Cleopatra found Antonius' jests and slants to be but gross, and soldierlike, in plain manner, she gave it him finely, and without fear taunted him thoroughly. Now her beauty (as it is reported) was not so passing, as unmatchable of other women, nor yet such, as upon present view did enamour men with her: but so sweet was her company and conversation, that a man could not possibly but be taken. And besides her beauty, the good grace she had to talk and discourse, her courteous nature that tempered her words and deeds, was a spur that pricked to the quick. Furthermore, besides all these, her voice and words were marvellous pleasant: for her tongue was an instrument of music to divers sports and pastimes, the which she easily turned to any language that pleased her. She spoke unto few barbarous people by interpreter, but made them answer herself, or at the least the most part of them: as the Ethiopians, the Arabians, the Troglodytes, the Hebrews, the Syrians, the Medes, and the Parthians, and to many others also, whose languages she had learned. Whereas divers of her progenitors, the kings of Egypt, could scarce learn the Egyptian tongue only, and many of them forgot to speak the Macedonian.

28    Now, Antonius was so ravished with the love of Cleopatra, that though his wife Fulvia had great wars, and much ado with Caesar for his affairs, and that the army of the Parthians (the which the king's lieutenants had given to the only leading of Labienus) was now assembled in Mesopotamia ready to invade Syria: yet, as though all this had nothing touched him, he yielded himself to go with Cleopatra into Alexandria, where he spent and lost in childish sports (as a man might say) and idle pastimes, the most precious

thing a man can spend, as Antiphon saith: and that is, time. For they made an order between them, which they called *amimetobion* (as much to say, no life comparable and matchable with it), one feasting each other by turns, and in cost, exceeding all measure and reason. And for proof hereof, I have heard my grandfather Lampryas report, that one Philotas a physician, born in the city of Amphissa, told him that he was at that present time in Alexandria, and studied physic: and that having acquaintance with one of Antonius' cooks, he took him with him to Antonius' house (being a young man desirous to see things), to show him the wonderful sumptuous charge and preparation of one only supper. When he was in the kitchen, and saw a world of diversities of meats, and amongst others, eight wild boars roasted whole, he began to wonder at it, and said, 'Sure you have a great number of guests to supper.' The cook fell a-laughing, and answered him, 'No,' quoth he, 'not many guests, nor above twelve in all: but yet all that is boiled or roasted must be served in whole, or else it would be marred straight. For Antonius peradventure will sup presently, or it may be a pretty while hence, or likely enough he will defer it longer, for that he hath drunk well today, or else hath had some other great matters in hand: and therefore we do not dress one supper only, but many suppers, because we are uncertain of the hour he will sup in.' Philotas the physician told my grandfather this tale, and said moreover, that it was his chance shortly after to serve the eldest son of the said Antonius, whom he had by his wife Fulvia: and that he sat commonly at his table with his other friends, when he did not dine nor sup with his father. It chanced one day there came a physician that was so full of words, that he made every man weary of him at the board: but Philotas to stop his mouth, put out a subtle proposition to him: 'It is good in some sort to let a man drink cold water that hath an ague: every man that hath an ague hath it in some sort, ergo it is good for a man that hath an ague to drink cold water.' The physician was so gravelled and amated withal, that he had not a word more to say. Young Antonius burst out in such a laughing at him, and was so glad of it, that he said unto him: 'Philotas, take all that, I give it thee,' showing him his cupboard full of plate, with great pots of gold and silver. Philotas thanked him, and told him he thought himself greatly bound to him for this liberality, but he would never have thought that he had had power to have given so many things, and of so great value. But much more he marvelled, when shortly after one of young Antonius' men brought him home all the pots in a basket, bidding him set his mark and stamp upon them, and to lock them up. Philotas returned the bringer of them, fearing to be reproved if he took them. Then the young gentleman Antonius said unto him: 'Alas poor man, why doest thou make it nice to take them? Knowest thou not that it is the son of Antonius that gives them thee, and is able to do it? If thou wilt not believe me, take rather the ready money they come to, because my father peradventure may ask for some of the plate, for the antique and excellent workmanship of them.' This I have heard my grandfather tell oftentimes.

29    But now again to Cleopatra. Plato writeth that there are four kinds of flattery: but Cleopatra divided it into many kinds. For she, were it in sport, or in matter of earnest, still devised sundry new delights to have Antonius at commandment, never leaving him night nor day, nor once letting him go out of her sight. For she would play at dice with him, drink with him, and hunt commonly with him, and also be with him when he went to any exercise or activity of body. And sometime also, when he would go up and down the city disguised like a slave in the night, and would peer into poor men's windows and their shops, and scold and brawl with them within the house, Cleopatra would be also in a chambermaid's array, and amble up and down the streets with him, so that oftentimes Antonius bore away both mocks and blows. Now, though most men misliked this manner, yet the Alexandrians were commonly glad of this jollity, and liked it well, saying very gallantly and wisely: that Antonius showed them a comical face, to wit, a merry countenance; and the Romans a tragical face, to say, a grim look. But to reckon up all the foolish sports they made, revelling in this sort; it were too fond a part of me, and therefore I will only tell you one among the rest. On a time he went to angle for fish, and when he could take none, he was as angry as could be, because Cleopatra stood by. Wherefore he secretly commanded the fishermen, that when he cast in his line, they should straight dive under the water, and put a fish on his hook which they had taken before: and so snatched up his angling rod, and brought up fish twice or

thrice. Cleopatra found it straight, yet she seemed not to see it, but wondered at his excellent fishing: but when she was alone by herself among her own people, she told them how it was, and bade them the next morning to be on the water to see the fishing. A number of people came to the haven, and got into the fisher boats to see this fishing. Antonius then threw in his line, and Cleopatra straight commanded one of her men to dive under water before Antonius' men, and to put some old salt fish upon his bait, like unto those that are brought out of the country of Pont. When he had hung the fish on his hook, Antonius thinking he had taken a fish indeed, snatched up his line presently. Then they all fell a-laughing. Cleopatra laughing also, said unto him: 'Leave us, my lord, Egyptians, which dwell in the country of Pharus and Canobus, your angling rod: this is not thy profession: thou must hunt after conquering of realms and countries.'

30 Now Antonius delighting in these fond and childish pastimes, very ill news were brought him from two places. The first from Rome, that his brother Lucius, and Fulvia his wife, fell out first between themselves, and afterwards fell to open war with Caesar, and had brought all to nought, that they were both driven to flee out of Italy. The second news, as bad as the first: that Labienus conquered all Asia with the army of the Parthians, from the river of Euphrates, and from Syria, unto the countries of Lydia and Ionia. Then began Antonius with much ado, a little to rouse himself as if he had been wakened out of a deep sleep, and as a man may say, coming out of a great drunkenness. So, first of all he bent himself against the Parthians, and went as far as the country of Phoenicia: but there he received lamentable letters from his wife Fulvia. Whereupon he straight returned towards Italy, with two hundred sail: and as he went, took up his friends by the way that fled out of Italy, to come to him. By them he was informed, that his wife Fulvia was the only cause of this war: who being of a peevish, crooked, and troublesome nature, had purposely raised this uproar in Italy, in hope thereby to withdraw him from Cleopatra. But by good fortune, his wife Fulvia going to meet with Antonius, sickened by the way, and died in the city of Sicyone: and therefore Octavius Caesar and he were the easier made friends together. For when Antonius landed in Italy, and that men saw Caesar asked

nothing of him, and that Antonius on the other side laid all the fault and burden on his wife Fulvia, the friends of both parties would not suffer them to unrip any old matters, and to prove or defend who had the wrong or right, and who was the first procurer of this war, fearing to make matters worse between them: but they made them friends together, and divided the empire of Rome between them, making the sea Ionium the bounds of their division. For they gave all the provinces eastward, unto Antonius: and the countries westward, unto Caesar: and left Africa unto Lepidus: and made a law, that they three one after another should make their friends consuls, when they would not be themselves.

31    This seemed to be a sound counsel, but yet it was to be confirmed with a straiter bond, which fortune offered thus. There was Octavia the eldest sister of Caesar, not by one mother, for she came of Ancharia, and Caesar himself afterwards of Accia. It is reported, that he dearly loved his sister Octavia, for indeed she was a noble lady, and left the widow of her first husband Caius Marcellus, who died not long before: and it seemed also that Antonius had been widower ever since the death of his wife Fulvia. For he denied not that he kept Cleopatra, but so did he not confess that he had her as his wife: and so with reason he did defend the love he bore unto this Egyptian Cleopatra. Thereupon every man did set forward this marriage, hoping thereby that this Lady Octavia, having an excellent grace, wisdom, and honesty, joined unto so rare a beauty, that when she were with Antonius (he loving her as so worthy a lady deserveth) she should be a good mean to keep good love and amity betwixt her brother and him. So when Caesar and he had made the match between them, they both went to Rome about this marriage, although it was against the law, that a widow should be married within ten months after her husband's death. Howbeit the senate dispensed with the law, and so the marriage proceeded accordingly.

32    Sextus Pompeius at that time kept in Sicilia, and so made many an inroad into Italy with a great number of pinnaces and other pirates' ships, of the which were captains two notable pirates, Menas and Menecrates, who so scoured all the sea thereabouts, that none durst peep out with a sail. Furthermore, Sextus Pompeius had

dealt very friendly with Antonius, for he had courteously received his mother, when she fled out of Italy with Fulvia: and therefore they thought good to make peace with him. So they met all three together by the mount of Misena, upon a hill that runneth far into the sea: Pompey having his ships riding hard by at anchor, and Antonius and Caesar their armies upon the shore side, directly over against him. Now, after they had agreed that Sextus Pompeius should have Sicily and Sardinia, with this condition, that he should rid the sea of all thieves and pirates, and make it safe for passengers, and withal that he should send a certain [quantity] of wheat to Rome, one of them did feast another, and drew cuts who should begin. It was Pompeius' chance to invite them first. Whereupon Antonius asked him: 'And where shall we sup?' 'There,' said Pompey, and showed him his admiral galley which had six banks of oars: 'That,' said he, 'is my father's house they have left me.' He spoke it to taunt Antonius, because he had his father's house, that was Pompey the Great. So he cast anchors enough into the sea, to make his galley fast, and then built a bridge of wood to convey them to his galley, from the head of Mount Misena: and there he welcomed them, and made them great cheer. Now in the midst of the feast, when they fell to be merry with Antonius' love unto Cleopatra, Menas the pirate came to Pompey, and whispering in his ear, said unto him: 'Shall I cut the cables of the anchors, and make thee lord not only of Sicily and Sardinia, but of the whole empire of Rome besides?' Pompey having paused a while upon it, at length answered him: 'Thou shouldest have done it, and never have told it me, but now we must content us with that we have. As for myself, I was never taught to break my faith, nor to be counted a traitor.' The other two also did likewise feast him in their camp, and then he returned into Sicily.

33 Antonius after this agreement made, sent Ventidius before into Asia to stay the Parthians, and to keep them they should come no further: and he himself in the meantime, to gratify Caesar, was contented to be chosen Julius Caesar's priest and sacrificer, and so they jointly together dispatched all great matters, concerning the state of the empire. But in all other manner of sports and exercises, wherein they passed the time away the one with the other, Antonius was ever inferior unto Caesar, and always lost, which

grieved him much. With Antonius there was a soothsayer or astronomer of Egypt, that could cast a figure, and judge of men's nativities, to tell them what should happen to them. He, either to please Cleopatra, or else for that he found it so by his art, told Antonius plainly, that his fortune (which of itself was excellent good, and very great) was altogether blemished and obscured by Caesar's fortune: and therefore he counselled him utterly to leave his company, and to get him as far from him as he could. 'For thy daemon,' said he (that is to say, the good angel and spirit that keepeth thee) 'is afraid of his: and being courageous and high when he is alone, becometh fearful and timorous when he cometh near unto the other.' Howsoever it was, the events ensuing proved the Egyptian's words true. For it is said, that as often as they two drew cuts for pastime, who should have anything, or whether they played at dice, Antonius always lost. Oftentimes when they were disposed to see cockfight, or quails that were taught to fight one with another, Caesar's cocks or quails did ever overcome: the which spited Antonius in his mind, although he made no outward show of it: and therefore he believed the Egyptian the better. In fine, he recommended the affairs of his house unto Caesar, and went out of Italy with Octavia his wife, whom he carried into Greece, after he had had a daughter by her. So Antonius lying all the winter at Athens, news came unto him of the victories of Ventidius, who had overcome the Parthians in battle, in the which also were slain Labienus and Pharnabates, the chiefest captain King Orodes had. For these good news he feasted all Athens, and kept open house for all the Grecians, and many games of prize were played at Athens, of the which he himself would be judge. Wherefore leaving his guard, his axes, and tokens of his empire at his house, he came into the show place (or lists) where these games were played, in a long gown and slippers after the Grecian fashion, and they carried tipstaffs before him, as marshal's men do carry before the judges to make place: and he himself in person was a stickler to part the young men, when they had fought enough.

34    After that, preparing to go to the wars, he made him a garland of the holy olive, and carried a vessel with him of the water of the fountain Clepsydra, because of an oracle he had received that so commanded him. In the meantime, Ventidius once again overcame

Pacorus (Orodes' son king of Parthia) in a battle fought in the country of Cyrrestica, he being come again with a great army to invade Syria: at which battle was slain a great number of the Parthians, and among them Pacorus, the king's own son slain. This noble exploit, as famous as ever any was, was a full revenge to the Romans, of the shame and loss they had received before by the death of Marcus Crassus: and he made the Parthians fly, and glad to keep themselves within the confines and territories of Mesopotamia and Media, after they had thrice together been overcome in several battles. Howbeit Ventidius durst not undertake to follow them any further, fearing lest he should have gotten Antonius' displeasure by it. Notwithstanding, he led his army against them that had rebelled, and conquered them again: amongst whom he besieged Antiochus, king of Commagena, who offered him to give a thousand talents to be pardoned his rebellion, and promised ever after to be at Antonius' commandment. But Ventidius made him answer, that he should send unto Antonius, who was not far off, and would not suffer Ventidius to make any peace with Antiochus, to the end that yet this little exploit should pass in his name, and that they should not think he did anything but by his lieutenant Ventidius. The siege grew very long, because they that were in the town, seeing they could not be received upon no reasonable composition, determined valiantly to defend themselves to the last man. Thus Antonius did nothing, and yet received great shame, repenting him much that he took not their first offer. And yet at last he was glad to make truce with Antiochus, and to take three hundred talents for composition. Thus after he had set order for the state and affairs of Syria, he returned again to Athens: and having given Ventidius such honours as he deserved, he sent him to Rome, to triumph for the Parthians. Ventidius was the only man that ever triumphed of the Parthians until this present day, a mean man born, and of no noble house nor family: who only came to that he attained unto, through Antonius' friendship, the which delivered him happy occasion to achieve to great matters. And yet to say truly, he did so well quit himself in all his enterprises, that he confirmed that which was spoken of Antonius and Caesar: to wit, that they were always more fortunate when they made war by their lieutenants, than by themselves. For Sossius, one of Antonius' lieutenants in Syria, did notable good service: and Canidius, whom he had also left his lieutenant in the borders of Armenia, did conquer it all. So did he also overcome the kings of the Iberians and Albanians, and went on with his conquests unto Mount Caucasus. By these conquests, the fame of Antonius' power increased more and more, and grew dreadful unto all the barbarous nations.

35   But Antonius notwithstanding, grew to be marvellously offended with Caesar, upon certain reports that had been brought unto him: and so took sea to go towards Italy with three hundred sail. And because those of Brundusium would not receive his army into their haven, he went further unto Tarentum. There his wife Octavia that came out of Greece with him, besought him to send her unto her brother: the which he did. Octavia at that time was great with child, and moreover had a second daughter by him, and yet she put herself in journey, and met with her brother Octavius Caesar by the way, who brought his two chief friends, Maecenas and Agrippa, with him. She took them aside, and with all the instance she could possible, entreated them they would not suffer her that was the happiest woman of the world, to become now the most wretched and unfortunatest creature of all other. 'For now,' said she, 'every man's eyes do gaze on me, that am the sister of one of the emperors and wife of the other. And if the worst counsel take place (which the gods forbid), and that they grow to wars: for yourselves, it is uncertain to which of them two the gods have assigned the victory, or overthrow. But for me, on which side soever victory fall, my state can be but most miserable still.' These words of Octavia so softened Caesar's heart, that he went quickly unto Tarentum. But it was a noble sight for them that were present, to see so great an army by land not to stir, and so many ships afloat in the road, quietly and safe: and furthermore, the meeting and kindness of friends, lovingly embracing one another. First, Antonius feasted Caesar, which he granted unto for his sister's sake. Afterwards they agreed together, that Caesar should give Antonius two legions to go against the Parthians: and that Antonius should let Caesar have a hundred galleys armed with brazen spurs at the prows. Besides all this, Octavia obtained of her husband, twenty brigantines for her brother: and of her brother for her husband, a thousand armed men. After they had taken leave of each other, Caesar went immediately to make war with Sextus

Pompeius, to get Sicilia into his hands. Antonius also leaving his wife Octavia and little children begotten of her, with Caesar, and his other children which he had by Fulvia, he went directly into Asia.

36 Then began this pestilent plague and mischief of Cleopatra's love (which had slept a long time, and seemed to have been utterly forgotten, and that Antonius had given place to better counsel) again to kindle, and to be in force, so soon as Antonius came near unto Syria. And in the end, the horse of the mind as Plato terms it, that is so hard of rein (I mean the unreined lust of concupiscence) did put out of Antonius' head, all honest and commendable thoughts: for he sent Fonteius Capito to bring Cleopatra into Syria. Unto whom, to welcome her, he gave no trifling things: but unto that she had already, he added the provinces of Phoenicia, those of the nethermost Syria, the Isle of Cyprus, and a great part of Cilicia, and that country of Jewry where the true balm is, and that part of Arabia where the Nabatheians do dwell, which stretcheth out towards the Ocean. These great gifts much misliked the Romans. But now, though Antonius did easily give away great seigniories, realms, and mighty nations unto some private men, and that also he took from other kings their lawful realms (as from Antigonus king of the Jews, whom he openly beheaded, where never king before had suffered like death), yet all this did not so much offend the Romans, as the unmeasurable honours which he did unto Cleopatra. But yet he did much more aggravate their malice and ill will towards him, because that Cleopatra having brought him two twins, a son and a daughter, he named his son Alexander, and his daughter Cleopatra, and gave them to their surnames, the Sun to the one, and the Moon to the other. This notwithstanding, he that could finely cloak his shameful deeds with fine words, said that the greatness and magnificence of the empire of Rome appeared most, not where the Romans took, but where they gave much: and nobility was multiplied amongst men, by the posterity of kings, when they left of their seed in divers places: and that by this means his first ancestor was begotten of Hercules, who had not left the hope and continuance of his line and posterity, in the womb of one only woman, fearing Solon's laws, or regarding the ordinances of men touching the procreation

of children: but that he gave it unto nature, and established the foundation of many noble races and families in divers places.

37   Now when Phraortes had slain his father Orodes, and possessed the kingdom, many gentlemen of Parthia forsook him, and fled from him. Amongst them was Monaeses, a nobleman, and of great authority among his countrymen, who came unto Antonius, that received him, and compared his fortune unto Themistocles, and his own riches and magnificence unto the kings of Persia. For he gave Monaeses three cities, Larissa, Arethusa, and Hierapolis, which was called before Bombyce. Howbeit the king of Parthia shortly after called him home again, upon his faith and word. Antonius was glad to let him go, hoping thereby to steal upon Phraortes unprovided. For he sent unto him, and told him that they would remain good friends, and have peace together, so he would but only redeliver the standards and ensigns of the Romans, which the Parthians had won in the battle where Marcus Crassus was slain, and the men also that remained yet prisoners of this overthrow. In the meantime he sent Cleopatra back into Egypt, and took his way towards Arabia and Armenia, and there took a general muster of all his army he had together, and of the kings his confederates, that were come by his commandment to aid him, being a marvellous number: of the which, the chiefest was Artavasdes, king of Armenia, who did furnish him with six thousand horsemen, and seven thousand footmen. There were also of the Romans about three score thousand footmen, and of horsemen (Spaniards and Gauls reckoned for Romans) to the number of ten thousand, and of other nations thirty thousand men, reckoning together the horsemen and light-armed footmen. This so great and puissant army, which made the Indians quake for fear, dwelling about the country of the Bactrians, and all Asia also to tremble, served him to no purpose, and all for the love he bore to Cleopatra. For the earnest great desire he had to lie all winter with her, made him begin his war out of due time, and for haste, to put all in hazard, being so ravished and enchanted with the sweet poison of her love, that he had no other thought but of her, and how he might quickly return again, more than how he might overcome his enemies.

38   For first of all, where he should have wintered in Armenia to refresh his men, wearied with the long journey they had made,

having come eight thousand furlongs, and then at the beginning of the spring to go and invade Media, before the Parthians should stir out of their houses and garrisons, he could tarry no longer, but led them forthwith unto the province of Atropatene, leaving Armenia on the left hand, and foraged all the country. Furthermore, making all the haste he could, he left behind him engines of battery which were carried with him in three hundred carts (among the which also there was a ram four score foot long), being things most necessary for him, and the which he could not get again for money if they were once lost or marred. For the high provinces of Asia have no trees growing of such height and length, neither strong nor straight enough to make suchlike engines of battery. This notwithstanding, he left them all behind him, as a hindrance to bring his matters and intent speedily to pass: and left a certain number of men to keep them, and gave them in charge unto one Tatianus. Then he went to besiege the city of Phraata, being the chiefest and greatest city the king of Media had, where his wife and children were. Then he straight found his own fault, and the want of his artillery he left behind him, by the work he had in hand: for he was fain for lack of a breach (where his men might come to the sword with their enemies that defended the wall) to force a mount of earth hard to the walls of the city, the which by little and little with great labour, rose to some height. In the meantime King Phraortes came down with a great army: who understanding that Antonius had left his engines of battery behind him, he sent a great number of horsemen before, which environed Tatianus with all his carriage, and slew him, and ten thousand men he had with him. After this, the barbarous people took these engines of battery and burnt them, and got many prisoners, amongst whom they took also King Polemon.

39 This discomfiture marvellously troubled all Antonius' army, to receive so great an overthrow (beyond their expectation) at the beginning of their journey: insomuch that Artabazus, king of the Armenians, despairing of the good success of the Romans, departed with his men, notwithstanding that he was himself the first procurer of this war and journey. On the other side, the Parthians came courageously unto Antonius' camp, who lay at the siege of their chiefest city, and cruelly reviled and threatened him. Antonius

therefore fearing that if he lay still and did nothing, his men's hearts would fail them, he took ten legions, with three cohorts or ensigns of the praetors (which are companies appointed for the guard of the general), and all his horsemen, and carried them out to forage, hoping thereby he should easily allure the Parthians to fight a battle. But when he had marched about a day's journey from his camp, he saw the Parthians wheeling round about him to give him the onset, and to skirmish with him, when he would think to march his way. Therefore he set out his signal of battle, and yet caused his tents and fardels to be trussed up, as though he meant not to fight, but only to lead his men back again. Then he marched before the army of the barbarous people, the which was marshalled like a crescent or half-moon: and commanded his horsemen, that as soon as they thought the legions were near enough unto their enemies to set upon the forward, that then they should set spurs to their horses, and begin the charge. The Parthians standing in battle ray, beholding the countenance of the Romans as they marched, they appeared to be soldiers indeed, to see them march in so good array as was possible. For in their march, they kept the ranks a like space one from another, not straggling out of order, and shaking their pikes, speaking never a word. But so soon as the alarm was given, the horsemen suddenly turned head upon the Parthians, and with great cries gave charge on them: who at the first received their charge courageously, for they were joined nearer than within an arrow's shoot. But when the legions also came to join with them, shouting out aloud, and rattling of their armours, the Parthians' horses and themselves were so afraid and amazed withal, that they all turned tail and fled, before the Romans could come to the sword with them. Then Antonius followed them hard in chase, being in great good hope by this conflict to have brought to end all, or the most part, of this war. But after that his footmen had chased them fifty furlongs off, and the horsemen also thrice as far, they found in all but thirty prisoners taken, and about four score men only slain. But this did much discourage them, when they considered with themselves, that obtaining the victory, they had slain so few of their enemies: and where they were overcome, they lost as many of their men as they had done at the overthrow when the carriage was taken. The next morning, Antonius' army trussed up their carriage, and marched back towards their camp: and by the way in their return they met at the first a few of the Parthians: then going further, they met a few more. So at length when they all came together, they reviled them, and troubled them on every side, as freshly and courageously, as if they had not been overthrown: so that the Romans very hardly got to their camp with safety. The Medes on the other side, that were besieged in their chief city of Phraata, made a sally out upon them that kept the mount, which they had forced and cast against the wall of the city, and drove them for fear from the mount they kept. Antonius was so offended withal, that he executed the decimation. For he divided his men by ten legions, and then of them he put the tenth legion to death on whom the lot fell: and to the other nine, he caused them to have barley given them instead of wheat.

40   Thus this war fell out troublesome unto both parties, and the end thereof much more fearful. For Antonius could look for no other of his side, but famine: because he could forage no more, nor fetch in any victuals, without great loss of his men. Phraortes on the other side, he knew well enough that he could bring the Parthians to anything else, but to lie in camp abroad in the winter. Therefore he was afraid, that if the Romans continued their siege all winter long, and made war with him still, that his men would forsake him, and specially because the time of the year went away apace, and the air waxed cloudy and cold in the equinoctial autumn. Thereupon he called to mind this devise. He gave the chiefest of his gentlemen of the Parthians charge, that when they met the Romans out of their camp, going to forage, or to water their horse, or for some other provision, that they should not distress them too much, but should suffer them to carry somewhat away, and greatly commend their valiantness and hardiness, for the which their king did esteem them the more, and not without cause. After these first baits and allurements, they began by little and little to come near unto them, and to talk with them a-horseback, greatly blaming Antonius' self-will that did not give their King Phraortes to make a good peace, who desired nothing more, than to save the lives of so goodly a company of valiant men: but that he was too fondly bent to abide two of the greatest and most dreadful enemies he could have: to wit, winter, and famine, the which they should hardly away withal, though the Parthians

did the best they could to aid and accompany them. These words being oftentimes brought to Antonius, they made him a little pliant, for the good hope he had of his return: but yet he would not send unto the king of Parthia, before they had first asked these barbarous people that spoke so courteously unto his men, whether they spoke it of themselves, or that they were their master's words. When they told them the king himself said so, and did persuade them further not to fear or mistrust them, then Antonius sent some of his friends unto the king, to make demand for the delivery of the ensigns and prisoners he had of the Romans, since the overthrow of Crassus: to the end it should not appear, that if he asked nothing, they should think he were glad that he might only escape with safety out of the danger he was in. The king of Parthia answered him, that for the ensigns and prisoners he demanded, he should not break his head about it: notwithstanding, that if he would presently depart without delay, he might depart in peaceable manner, and without danger. Wherefore Antonius after he had given his men some time to truss up their carriage, he raised his camp, and took his way to depart. But though he had an excellent tongue at will, and very gallant to entertain his soldiers and men of war, and that he could passingly well do it, as well or better than any captain in his time, yet being ashamed for respects, he would not speak unto them at his removing, but willed Domitius Aenobarbus to do it. Many of them took this in very ill part, and thought that he did it in disdain of them: but the most part of them presently understood the truth of it, and were also ashamed. Therefore they thought it their duties to carry the like respect unto their captain, that their captain did unto them: and so they became the more obedient unto him.

41    So Antonius was minded to return the same way he came, being a plain barren country without wood. But there came a soldier to him, born in the country of the Mardians, who by oft frequenting the Parthians of long time, knew their fashions very well, and had also showed himself very true and faithful to the Romans, in the battle where Antonius' engines of battery and carriage were taken away. This man came unto Antonius, to counsel him to beware how he went that way, and to make his army a prey, being heavily armed, unto so great a number of

horsemen, all archers, in the open field, where they should have nothing to let them to compass him round about: and that this was Phraortes' fetch, to offer him so friendly conditions and courteous words to make him raise his siege, that he might afterwards meet him as he would, in the plains: howbeit, that he would guide him, if he thought good, another way on the right hand, through woods and mountains, a far nearer way, and where he should find great plenty of all things needful for his army. Antonius hearing what he said, called his council together, to consult upon it. For after he had made peace with the Parthians, he was loth to give them cause to think he mistrusted them: and on the other side also he would gladly shorten his way, and pass by places well inhabited, where he might be provided of all things necessary: therefore he asked the Mardian what pledge he would put in, to perform that he promised. The Mardian gave himself to be bound hand and foot, till he had brought his army into the country of Armenia. So he guided the army thus bound, two days together, without any trouble or sight of enemy. But the third day Antonius thinking the Parthians would no more follow him, and trusting therein, suffered the soldiers to march in disorder as every man listed. The Mardian perceiving that the dams of a river were newly broken up, which they should have passed over, and that the river had overflown the banks and drowned all the way they should have gone, he guessed straight that the Parthians had done it, and had thus broken it open, to stay the Romans for getting too far before them. Thereupon he bade Antonius look to himself, and told him that his enemies were not far from thence. Antonius having set his men in order, as he was placing of his archers and sling men to resist the enemies, and to drive them back, they descried the Parthians that wheeled round about the army to compass them in on every side, and to break their ranks, and their light-armed men gave charge upon them. So after they had hurt many of the Romans with their arrows, and that they themselves were also hurt by them with their darts and plummets of lead, they retired a little, and then came again and gave charge, until that the horsemen of the Gauls turned their horses, and fiercely galloped towards them, that they dispersed them so, as all that day they gathered no more together.

42   Thereby Antonius knew what to do, and did not only strengthen the rearward of his army, but both the flanks also, with darters and sling men, and made his army march in a square battle: commanding the horsemen, that when the enemies should come to assail them, they should drive them back, but not follow them too far. Thus the Parthians four days after, seeing they did no more hurt to the Romans, than they also received of them, they were not so hot upon them as they were commanded, but excusing themselves by the winter that troubled them, they determined to return back again. The fifth day, Flavius Gallus, a valiant man of his hands, that had charge in the army, came unto Antonius to pray him to let him have some more of his light-armed men than were already in the rearward, and some of the horsemen that were in the forward, hoping thereby to do some notable exploit. Antonius granting them unto him, when the enemies came according to their manner to set upon the tail of the army, and to skirmish with them, Flavius courageously made them retire, but not as they were wont to do before, to retire and join presently with their army, for he overrashly thrust in among them to fight it out at the sword. The captains that had the leading of the rearward, seeing Flavius stray too far from the army, they sent unto him to will him to retire, but he would not hearken to it. And it is reported also, that Titius himself the Treasurer, took the ensigns, and did what he could to make the ensign bearers return back, reviling Flavius Gallus, because that through his folly and desperateness he caused many honest and valiant men to be both hurt and slain to no purpose. Gallus also fell out with him, and commanded his men to stay. Wherefore Titius returned again into the army, and Gallus still overthrowing and driving the enemies back whom he met in the forward, he was not ware that he was compassed in. Then seeing himself environed of all sides, he sent unto the army, that they should come and aid him: but there the captains that led the legions (among the which Canidius, a man of great estimation about Antonius, made one) committed many faults. For where they should have made head with the whole army upon the Parthians, they sent him aid by small companies: and when they were slain, they sent him others also. So that by their beastliness and lack of consideration, they had like to have made all the army flee, if Antonius himself had not come from the front of the battle with

the third legion, the which came through the midst of them that fled, until they came to front of the enemies, and that they stayed them from chasing any further.

43 Howbeit at this last conflict there were slain no less than three thousand men, and five thousand besides brought sore hurt into the camp, and amongst them also Flavius Gallus, whose body was shot through in four places, whereof he died. Antonius went to the tents to visit and comfort the sick and wounded, and for pity's sake he could not refrain from weeping: and they also showing him the best countenance they could, took him by the hand, and prayed him to go and be dressed, and not to trouble himself for them, most reverently calling him their emperor and captain: and that for themselves, they were whole and safe, so that he had his health. For indeed to say truly, there was not at that time any emperor or captain that had so great and puissant an army as his together, both for lusty youths and courage of the soldiers, as also for their patience to away with so great pains and trouble. Furthermore, the obedience and reverence they showed unto their captain, with a marvellous earnest love and goodwill, was so great, and all were indifferently (as well great as small, the noblemen as mean men, the captains and soldiers) so earnestly bent to esteem Antonius' goodwill and favour above their own life and safety, that in this point of martial discipline, the ancient Romans could not have done any more. But divers things were cause thereof, as we have told you before: Antonius' nobility and ancient house, his eloquence, his plain nature, his liberality and magnificence, and his familiarity to sport and to be merry in company: but specially the care he took at that time to help, visit, and lament those that were sick and wounded, seeing every man to have that which was meet for him: that was of such force and effect, as it made them that were sick and wounded to love him better, and were more desirous to do him service, than those that were whole and sound.

44 This victory so encouraged the enemies (who otherwise were weary to follow Antonius any further) that all night long they kept the fields, and hovered about the Romans' camp, thinking that they would presently flee, and then that they should take the spoil of their camp. So the next morning by break of day, there were gathered together a far greater number of the Parthians, than they

were before. For the rumour was, that there were not much fewer than forty thousand horse, because their king sent thither even the very guard about his person, as unto a most certain and assured victory, that they might be partners of the spoil and booty they hoped to have had: for as touching the king himself, he was never in any conflict or battle. Then Antonius desirous to speak to his soldiers, called for a black gown, to appear the more pitiful to them: but his friends did dissuade him from it. Therefore he put on his coat armour, and being so apparelled, made an oration to his army: in the which he highly commended them that had over-come and driven back their enemies, and greatly rebuked them that had cowardly turned their backs. So that those which had overcome, prayed him to be of good cheer: the other also to clear themselves, willingly offered to take the lots of decimation if he thought good, or otherwise to receive what kind of punishment it should please him to lay upon them, so that he would forget any more to mislike, or to be offended with them. Antonius seeing that, did lift up his hands to heaven, and made his prayer to the gods, that if in exchange of his former victories, they would now send him some bitter adversity, then that all might light on himself alone, and that they would give the victory to the rest of his army.

45    The next morning, they gave better order on every side of the army, and so marched forward: so that when the Parthians thought to return again to assail them, they came far short of the reckoning. For where they thought to come not to fight, but to spoil and make havoc of all, when they came near them, they were sore hurt with their slings and darts, and such other javelins as the Romans darted at them, and the Parthians found them as rough and desperate in fight, as if they had been fresh men they had dealt withal. Whereupon their hearts began again to fail them. But yet when the Romans came to go down any steep hills or mountains, then they would set on them with their arrows, because the Romans could go down but fair and softly. But then again, the soldiers of the legion that carried great shields, returned back, and enclosed them that were naked or light-armed, in the midst amongst them, and did kneel of one knee on the ground, and so set down their shields before them: and they of the second rank also covered them of the first rank, and the third also covered the

second, and so from rank to rank all were covered. Insomuch that this manner of covering and sheathing themselves with shields, was devised after the fashion of laying tiles upon houses, and to sight, was like the degrees of a theatre, and is a most strong defence and bulwark against all arrows and shot that falleth upon it. When the Parthians saw this countenance of the Roman soldiers of the legion, which kneeled on the ground in that sort upon one knee, supposing that they had been wearied with travail: they laid down their bows, and took their spears and lances, and came to fight with them man for man. Then the Romans suddenly rose upon their feet, and with the darts that they threw from them, they slew the foremost, and put the rest to flight, and so did they the next days that followed. But by means of these dangers and lets, Antonius' army could win no way in a day, by reason whereof they suffered great famine: for they could have but little corn, and yet were they driven daily to fight for it, and besides that, they had no instruments to grind it, to make bread of it. For the most part of them had been left behind, because the beasts that carried them were either dead, or else employed to carry them that were sore and wounded. For the famine was so extreme great, that the eight part of a bushel of wheat was sold for fifty drachmas, and they sold barley bread by the weight of silver. In the end, they were compelled to live off herbs and roots, but they found few of them that men do commonly eat of, and were enforced to taste of them that were never eaten before: among the which there was one that killed them, and made them out of their wits. For he that had once eaten of it, his memory was gone from him, and he knew no manner of thing, but only busied himself in digging and hurling of stones from one place to another, as though it had been a matter of great weight, and to be done with all possible speed. All the camp over, men were busily stooping to the ground, digging and carrying of stones from one place to another: but at the last, they cast up a great deal of choler, and died suddenly, because they lacked wine, which was the only sovereign remedy to cure that disease. It is reported that Antonius seeing such a number of his men die daily, and that the Parthians left them not, neither would suffer them to be at rest, he oftentimes cried out sighing, and said: 'O, ten thousand.' He had the valiantness of ten thousand Grecians, in such admiration, whom Xenophon brought away after the overthrow of Cyrus: because they had come a farther journey from Babylon, and had also fought against much more enemies many times told, than themselves, and yet came home with safety.

46    The Parthians therefore seeing that they could not break the good order of the army of the Romans, and contrarily that they themselves were oftentimes put to flight, and well-favouredly beaten, they fell again to their old crafty subtleties. For when they found any of the Romans scattered from the army to go forage, to seek some corn, or other victuals: they would come to them as if they had been their friends, and showed them their bows unbent, saying, that themselves also did return home to their country as they did, and that they would follow them no further, howbeit that they should yet have certain Medes that would follow them a day's journey or two, to keep them that they should do no hurt to the villages from the highways: and so holding them with this talk, they gently took their leave of them, and bade them farewell, so that the Romans began again to think themselves safe. Antonius also understanding this, being very glad of it, determined to take his way through the plain country, because also they should find no water in the mountains, as it was reported unto him. So as he was determined to take this course, there came into his host one Mithridates, a gentleman from the enemies' camp, who was cousin unto Monaezes that fled unto Antonius, and unto whom he had given three cities. When he came to Antonius' camp, he prayed them to bring him one that could speak the Parthian, or Syrian tongue. So one Alexander Antiochian, a familiar of Antonius, was brought unto him. Then the gentleman told him what he was, and said, that Monaezes had sent him to Antonius, to requite the honour and courtesy he had showed unto him. After he had used this ceremonious speech, he asked Alexander if he saw those high mountains afar off, which he pointed unto him with his finger. Alexander answered he did. 'The Parthians,' said he, 'do lie in ambush at the foot of those mountains, under the which lieth a goodly plain champaign country: and they think that you being deceived with their crafty subtle words, will leave the way of the mountains, and turn into the plain. For the other way, it is very hard and painful, and you shall abide great thirst, the which you are

well acquainted withal: but if Antonius take the lower way, let him assure himself to run the same fortune that Marcus Crassus did'.

47   So Mithridates having said, he departed. Antonius was marvellously troubled in his mind when he heard thus much, and therefore called for his friends, to hear what they would say to it. The Mardian also that was their guide, being asked his opinion, answered: that he thought as much as the gentleman Mithridates had said. 'For,' said he, 'admit that there were no ambush of enemies in the valley, yet is it a long crooked way, and ill to hit: where taking the mountain way, though it be stony and painful, yet there is no other danger, but a whole day's travelling without any water.' So Antonius changing his first mind and determination, removed that night, and took the mountain way, commanding every man to provide himself of water. But the most part of them lacking vessels to carry water in, some were driven to fill their salletts and murrians with water, and others also filled goatskins to carry water in. Now they marching forward, word was brought unto the Parthians that they were removed: whereupon, contrary to their manner, they presently followed them the selfsame night, so that by break of day they overtook the rearward of the Romans, who were so lame and wearied with going, and lack of sleep, that they were even done. For, beyond expectation, they had gone that night two hundred and forty furlong, and further, to see their enemies so suddenly at their backs, that made them utterly despair: but most of all, the fighting with them increased their thirst, because they were forced to fight as they marched, to drive their enemies back, yet creeping on still. The forward of the army by chance met with a river that was very clear, and cold water, but it was salt and venomous to drink: for straight it did gnaw the guts of those that had drunk it, and made them marvellous dry, and put them into a terrible ache and pricking. And notwithstanding that the Mardian had told them of it before, yet they would not be ruled, but violently thrust them back that would have kept them from drinking, and so drank. But Antonius going up and down amongst them, prayed them to take a little patience for a while, for hard by there was another river that the water was excellent good to drink, and that from thenceforth the way was so stony and ill for horsemen, that the enemies could follow them no further. So he

caused the retreat to be sounded to call them back that fought, and commanded the tents to be set up, that the soldiers might yet have shadow to refresh them with.

48    So when the tents were set up, and the Parthians also retired according to their manner, the gentleman Mithridates before named, returned again as before, and Alexander in like manner again brought unto him for interpreter. Then Mithridates advised him, that after the army had reposed a little, the Romans should remove forthwith, and with all possible speed get to the river: because the Parthians would go no further, but yet were cruelly bent to follow them thither. Alexander carried the report thereof unto Antonius, who gave him a great deal of gold plate to bestow upon Mithridates. Mithridates took as much of him as he could well carry away in his gown, and so departed with speed. So Antonius raised his camp being yet daylight, and caused all his army to march, and the Parthians never troubled any of them by the way: but amongst themselves it was as ill and dreadful a night as ever they had. For there were villains of their own company, who cut their fellows' throats for the money they had, and besides that, robbed the sumpters and carriage of such money as they carried: and at length, they set upon Antonius' slaves that drove his own sumpters and carriage, they broke goodly tables and rich plate in pieces, and divided it among themselves. Thereupon all the camp was straight in tumult and uproar: for the residue of them were afraid it had been the Parthians that had given them this alarm, and had put all the army out of order. Insomuch that Antonius called for one Rhamnus, one of his slaves enfranchised that was of his guard, and made him give him his faith that he would thrust his sword through him when he would bid him, and cut off his head: because he might not be taken alive of his enemies, nor known when he were dead. This grieved his friends to the heart, that they burst out a-weeping for sorrow. The Mardian also did comfort him, and assured him that the river he sought for was hard by, and that he did guess it by a sweet moist wind that breathed upon them, and by the air which they found fresher than they were wont, and also, for that they fetched their wind more at liberty: and moreover, because that since they did set forward, he thought they were near their journey's end, not lacking much of day. On the other

side also, Antonius was informed, that this great tumult and trouble came not through the enemies, but through the vile covetousness and villainy of certain of his soldiers. Therefore Antonius to set his army again in order, and to pacify this uproar, sounded the trumpet that every man should lodge.

49 Now day began to break, and the army to fall again into good order, and all the hurly burly to cease, when the Parthians drew near, and that their arrows lighted among them of the rearward of his army. Thereupon the signal of battle was given to the light-armed men, and the legioners did cover themselves as they had done before with their shields, with the which they received and defended the force of the Parthians' arrows, who never durst any more come to hand strokes with them: and thus they that were in the forward, went down by little and little, till at length they spied the river. There Antonius placed his armed men upon the sands to receive and drive back the enemies, and first of all, got over his men that were sick and hurt, and afterwards all the rest. And those also that were left to resist the enemies, had leisure enough to drink safely, and at their pleasure. For when the Parthians saw the river, they unbent their bows, and bade the Romans pass over without any fear, and greatly commended their valiantness. When they had all passed over the river at their ease, they took a little breath, and so marched forward again, not greatly trusting the Parthians. The sixth day after this last battle, they came to the river of Araxes, which divideth the country of Armenia from Media: the which appeared unto them very dangerous to pass, for the depth and swiftness of the stream. And furthermore, there ran a rumour through the camp, that the Parthians lay in ambush thereabouts, and that they would come and set upon them whilst they were troubled in passing over the river. But now, after they were all come safely over without any danger, and that they had gotten to the other side, into the province of Armenia, then they wor-shipped that land, as if it had been the first land they had seen after a long and dangerous voyage by sea, being now arrived in a safe and happy haven: and the tears ran down their cheeks, and every man embraced each other for the great joy they had. But now, keeping the fields in this fruitful country so plentiful of all things, after so great a famine and want of all things, they so crammed

themselves with such plenty of victuals, that many of them were cast into fluxes and dropsies.

50   There Antonius mustering his whole army, found that he had lost twenty thousand footmen, and four thousand horsemen, which had not all been slain by their enemies: for the most part of them died of sickness, making seven and twenty days' journey, coming from the city of Phraata into Armenia, and having overcome the Parthians in eighteen several battles. But these victories were not thoroughly performed nor accomplished, because they followed no long chase: and thereby it easily appeared, that Artabazus king of Armenia had reserved Antonius to end this war. For if the sixteen thousand horsemen which he brought with him out of Media, had been at these battles, considering that they were armed and apparelled much after the Parthians' manner, and acquainted also with their fight, when the Romans had put them to flight that fought a battle with them, and that these Armenians had followed the chase of them that fled, they had not gathered themselves again in force, neither durst they also have returned to fight with them so often, after they had been so many times overthrown. Therefore, all those that were of any credit and countenance in the army, did persuade and egg Antonius to be revenged of this Armenian king. But Antonius wisely dissembling his anger, he told him not of his treachery, nor gave him the worse countenance, nor did him less honour than he did before: because he knew his army was weak, and lacked things necessary. Howbeit afterwards he returned again into Armenia with a great army, and so with fair words, and sweet promises of messengers, he allured Artabazus to come unto him: whom he then kept prisoner, and led in triumph in the city of Alexandria. This greatly offended the Romans, and made them much to mislike it, when they saw that for Cleopatra's sake he deprived his country of her due honour and glory, only to gratify the Egyptians. But this was a pretty while after.

51   Howbeit then, the great haste he made to return unto Cleopatra, caused him to put his men to so great pains, forcing them to lie in the field all winter long when it snowed unreasonably, that by the way he lost eight thousand of his men, and so came down to the sea side with a small company, to a certain place called Blancbourg, which standeth betwixt the cities of Berytus

and Sidon, and there tarried for Cleopatra. And because she tarried longer than he would have had her, he pined away for love and sorrow. So that he was at such a strait, that he wist not what to do, and therefore to wear it out, he gave himself to quaffing and feasting. But he was so drowned with the love of her, that he could not abide to sit at the table till the feast were ended: but many times while others banqueted, he ran to the sea side to see if she were coming. At length she came, and brought with her a world of apparel and money to give unto the soldiers. But some say notwithstanding, that she brought apparel, but no money, and that she took of Antonius' money, and caused it to be given among the soldiers in her own name, as if she had given it them.

52 In the meantime it chanced, that the king of the Medes, and Phraortes king of the Parthians, fell at great wars together, the which began (as it is reported) for the spoils of the Romans: and grew to be so hot between them, that the king of Medes was no less afraid, than also in danger to lose his whole realm. Thereupon he sent unto Antonius to pray him to come and make war with the Parthians, promising him that he would aid him to his uttermost power. This put Antonius again in good comfort, considering that unlooked for, the only thing he lacked (which made him he could not overcome the Parthians, meaning that he had not brought horsemen, and men with darts and slings enough), was offered him in that sort, that he did him more pleasure to accept it, than it was pleasure to the other to offer it. Hereupon, after he had spoken with the king of Medes at the river of Araxes, he prepared himself once more to go through Armenia, and to make more cruel war with the Parthians, than he had done before.

53 Now whilst Antonius was busy in this preparation, Octavia his wife, whom he had left at Rome, would needs take sea to come unto him. Her brother Octavius Caesar was willing unto it, not for his respect at all (as most authors do report) as for that he might have an honest colour to make war with Antonius if he did misuse her, and not esteem of her as she ought to be. But when she was come to Athens, she received letters from Antonius, willing her to stay there until his coming, and did advertise her of his journey and determination. The which though it grieved her much, and that she knew it was but an excuse, yet by her letters to him of answer,

she asked him whether he would have those things sent unto him which she had brought him, being great store of apparel for soldiers, a great number of horse, sum of money, and gifts to bestow on his friends and captains he had about him: and besides all those, she had two thousand soldiers, chosen men, all well armed, like unto the praetors' bands. When Niger, one of Antonius' friends whom he had sent unto Athens, had brought these news from his wife Octavia, and withal did greatly praise her, as she was worthy, and well deserved, Cleopatra knowing that Octavia would have Antonius from her, and fearing also that if with her virtue and honest behaviour,(besides the great power of her brother Caesar), she did add thereunto her modest kind love to please her husband, that she would then be too strong for her, and in the end win him away, she subtly seemed to languish for the love of Antonius, pining her body for lack of meat. Furthermore, she every way so framed her countenance, that when Antonius came to see her, she cast her eyes upon him like a woman ravished for joy. Straight again when he went from her, she fell a-weeping and blubbering, looked ruefully of the matter, and still found the means that Antonius should oftentimes find her weeping: and then when he came suddenly upon her, she made as though she dried her eyes, and turned her face away, as if she were unwilling that he should see her weep. All these tricks she used, Antonius being in readiness to go into Syria, to speak with the king of Medes. Then the flatterers that furthered Cleopatra's mind, blamed Antonius, and told him that he was a hard-natured man, and that he had small love in him, that would see a poor lady in such torment for his sake, whose life depended only upon him alone. For Octavia, said they, that was married unto him as it were of necessity, because her brother Caesar's affairs so required it, hath the honour to be called Antonius' lawful spouse and wife: and Cleopatra, being born a queen of so many thousands of men, is only named Antonius' leman, and yet that she disdained not so to be called, if it might please him she might enjoy his company, and live with him: but if he once leave her, that then it is impossible she should live. To be short, by these their flatteries and enticements, they so wrought Antonius' effeminate mind, that fearing lest she would make herself away, he returned again unto Alexandria, and referred the king of Medes to the next year following, although he received news that the Parthians at that time were at civil wars among themselves. This notwithstanding, he went afterwards and made peace with him. For he married his daughter which was very young, unto one of the sons that Cleopatra had by him: and then returned, being fully bent to make war with Caesar.

54 When Octavia was returned to Rome from Athens, Caesar commanded her to go out of Antonius' house, and to dwell by herself, because he had abused her. Octavia answered him again, that she would not forsake her husband's house, and that if he had no other occasion to make war with him, she prayed him then to take no thought for her: 'For,' said she, 'it were too shameful a thing, that two so famous captains should bring in civil wars among the Romans, the one for the love of a woman, and the other for the jealousy betwixt one another.' Now as she spoke the word, so did she also perform the deed. For she kept still in Antonius' house, as if he had been there, and very honestly and honourably kept his children, not those only she had by him, but the other which her husband had by Fulvia. Furthermore, when Antonius sent any of his men to Rome, to sue for any office in the commonwealth, she received him very courteously, and so used herself unto her brother, that she obtained the thing she requested. Howbeit thereby, thinking no hurt, she did Antonius great hurt. For her honest love and regard to her husband, made every man hate him, when they saw he did so unkindly use so noble a lady: but yet the greatest cause of their malice unto him, was for the division of lands he made amongst his children in the city of Alexandria. And to confess a truth, it was too arrogant and insolent a part, and done (as a man would say) in derision and contempt of the Romans. For he assembled all the people in the show place, where young men do exercise themselves, and there upon a high tribunal silvered, he set two chairs of gold, the one for himself, and the other for Cleopatra, and lower chairs for his children: then he openly published before the assembly, that first of all he did establish Cleopatra queen of Egypt, of Cyprus, of Lydia, and of the lower Syria, and at that time also, Caesarion king of the same realms. This Caesarion was supposed to be the son of Julius Caesar, who had left Cleopatra great with child. Secondly he called the sons he had by her, the kings of kings, and gave Alexander for his portion,

Armenia, Media and Parthia, when he had conquered the country: and unto Ptolomy for his portion, Phenicia, Syria and Cilicia. And therewithal he brought out Alexander in a long gown after the fashion of the Medes, with a high coptanct hat on his head, narrow in the top, as the kings of the Medes and Armenians do use to wear them: and Ptolomy apparelled in a cloak after the Macedonian manner, with slippers on his feet, and a broad hat, with a royal band or diadem. Such was the apparel and old attire of the ancient kings and successors of Alexander the Great. So after his sons had done their humble duties, and kissed their father and mother, presently a company of Armenian soldiers set there of purpose, compassed the one about, and a like company of the Macedonians the other. Now for Cleopatra, she did not only wear at that time, but at all other times else when she came abroad, the apparel of the goddess Isis, and so gave audience unto all her subjects, as a new Isis.

55    Octavius Caesar reporting all these things unto the senate, and oftentimes accusing him to the whole people and assembly in Rome, he thereby stirred up all the Romans against him. Antonius on the other side sent to Rome likewise to accuse him, and the chiefest points of his accusations he charged him with, were these: first, that having spoiled Sextus Pompeius in Sicily, he did not give him his part of the isle. Secondly, that he did detain in his hands the ships he lent him to make that war. Thirdly, that having put Lepidus their companion and triumvirate out of his part of the empire, and having deprived him of all honours, he retained for himself the lands and revenues thereof, which had been assigned unto him for his part. And last of all, that he had in manner divided all Italy amongst his own soldiers, and had left no part of it for his soldiers. Octavius Caesar answered him again: that for Lepidus, he had indeed deposed him, and taken his part of the empire from him, because he did overcruelly use his authority. And secondly, for the conquests he had made by force of arms, he was contented Antonius should have his part of them, so that he would likewise let him have his part of Armenia. And thirdly, that for his soldiers, they should seek for nothing in Italy, because they possessed Media and Parthia, the which provinces they had added to the empire of Rome, valiantly fighting with their emperor and captain.

56 Antonius hearing these news, being yet in Armenia, commanded Canidius to go presently to the sea side with his sixteen legions he had: and he himself with Cleopatra went unto the city of Ephesus, and there gathered together his galleys and ships out of all parts, which came to the number of eight hundred, reckoning the great ships of burden: and of those, Cleopatra furnished him with two hundred, and twenty thousand talents besides, and provision of victuals also to maintain all the whole army in this war. So Antonius, through the persuasions of Domitius, commanded Cleopatra to return again into Egypt, and there to understand the success of this war. But Cleopatra, fearing lest Antonius should again be made friends with Octavius Caesar, by the means of his wife Octavia, she so plied Canidius with money, and filled his purse, that he became her spokesman unto Antonius, and told him there was no reason to send her from this war, who defrayed so great a charge: neither that it was for his profit, because that thereby the Egyptians would then be utterly discouraged, which were the chiefest strength of the army by sea, considering that he could see no king of all the kings their confederates that Cleopatra was inferior unto, either for wisdom or judgment, seeing that long before she had wisely governed so great a realm as Egypt, and besides that she had been so long acquainted with him, by whom she had learned to manage great affairs. These fair persuasions won him: for it was predestined that the government of all the world should fall into Octavius Caesar's hands. Thus, all their forces being joined together, they hoist sail towards the Isle of Samos, and there gave themselves to feasts and solace. For as all the kings, princes, and commonalties, peoples and cities from Syria unto the marshes Maeotides, and from the Armenians to the Illyrians, were sent unto, to send and bring all munition and warlike preparation they could, even so all players, minstrels, tumblers, fools, and jesters, were commanded to assemble in the Isle of Samos. So that, where in manner all the world in every place was full of lamentations, sighs and tears, only in this Isle of Samos there was nothing for many days' space, but singing and piping, and all the theatre full of these common players, minstrels, and singing men. Besides all this, every city sent an ox thither to sacrifice, and kings did strive one with another who should make the noblest feasts, and give the richest gifts. So that every man said, 'What can they do more for

joy of victory, if they win the battle, when they make already such sumptuous feasts at the beginning of the war?'

57    When this was done, he gave the whole rabble of these minstrels, and such kind of people, the city of Priene to keep them withal, during this war. Then he went unto the city of Athens, and there gave himself again to see plays and pastimes, and to keep the theatres. Cleopatra on the other side, being jealous of the honours which Octavia had received in this city, where indeed she was marvellously honoured and beloved of the Athenians: to win the people's goodwill also at Athens, she gave them great gifts: and they likewise gave her many great honours, and appointed certain ambassadors to carry the decree to her house, among the which Antonius was one, who as a citizen of Athens reported the matter unto her, and made an oration in the behalf of the city. Afterwards he sent to Rome to put his wife Octavia out of his house, who (as it is reported) went out of his house with all Antonius' children, saving the eldest of them he had by Fulvia, who was with her father, bewailing and lamenting her cursed hap that had brought her to this, that she was accounted one of the chiefest causes of this civil war. The Romans did pity her, but much more Antonius, and those specially that had seen Cleopatra: who neither excelled Octavia in beauty, nor yet in young years.

58    Octavius Caesar understanding the sudden and wonderful great preparation of Antonius, he was not a little astonished at it (fearing he should be driven to fight that summer), because he wanted many things, and the great and grievous exactions of money did sorely oppress the people. For all manner of men else, were driven to pay the fourth part of their goods and revenue: but the Libertines (to wit, those whose fathers or other predecessors had some time been bondmen), they were sessed to pay the eight part of all their goods at one payment. Hereupon, there rose a wonderful exclamation and great uproar all Italy over: so that among the greatest faults that ever Antonius committed, they blamed him most, for that he delayed to give Caesar battle. For he gave Caesar leisure to make his preparations, and also to appease the complaints of the people. When such a great sum of money was demanded of them, they grudged at it, and grew to mutiny upon it: but when they had once paid it, they remembered it no more.

Furthermore, Titius and Plancus (two of Antonius' chiefest friends and that had been both of them consuls) for the great injuries Cleopatra did them, because they hindered all they could, that she should not come to this war, they went and yielded themselves unto Caesar, and told him where the testament was that Antonius had made, knowing perfectly what was in it. The will was in the custody of the Vestal nuns: of whom Caesar demanded for it. They answered him, that they would not give it him: but if he would go and take it, they would not hinder him. Thereupon Caesar went thither, and having read it first to himself, he noted certain places worthy of reproach: so assembling all the senate, he read it before them all. Whereupon divers were marvellously offended, and thought it a strange matter that he being alive, should be punished for that he had appointed by his will to be done after his death. Caesar chiefly took hold of this that he ordained touching his burial: for he willed that his body, though he died at Rome, should be brought in funeral pomp through the midst of the market-place, and that it should be sent into Alexandria unto Cleopatra. Furthermore, among divers other faults wherewith Antonius was to be charged, for Cleopatra's sake, Calvisius, one of Caesar's friends reproved him, because he had frankly given Cleopatra all the libraries of the royal city of Pergamum, in the which she had above two hundred thousand books. Again also, that being on a time set at the table, he suddenly rose from the board, and trod upon Cleopatra's foot, which was a sign given between them, that they were agreed of. That he had also suffered the Ephesians in his presence to call Cleopatra, their sovereign lady. That divers times sitting in his tribunal and chair of state, giving audience to all kings and princes, he had received love letters from Cleopatra, written in tables of onyx or crystal, and that he had read them, sitting in his imperial seat. That one day when Furnius, a man of great account, and the eloquentest man of all the Romans, pleaded a matter before him, Cleopatra by chance coming through the market-place in her litter where Furnius was pleading, Antonius straight rose out of his seat, and left his audience to follow her litter.

59 This notwithstanding, it was thought Calvisius devised the most part of all these accusations of his own head. Nevertheless they that loved Antonius, were intercessors to the people for him, and

amongst them they sent one Geminius unto Antonius, to pray him
he would take heed, that through his negligence his empire were
not taken from him, and that he should be counted an enemy to the
people of Rome. This Geminius being arrived in Greece, made
Cleopatra jealous straight of his coming, because she surmised that
he came not but to speak for Octavia. Therefore she spared not to
taunt him all suppertime, and moreover to spite him the more,
she made him be set lowest of all at the board, the which he
took patiently, expecting occasion to speak with Antonius. Now
Antonius commanding him at the table to tell him what wind
brought him thither, he answered him, that it was no table talk, and
that he would tell him tomorrow morning fasting: but drunk or
fasting, howsoever it were, he was sure of one thing, that all would
not go well on his side, unless Cleopatra were sent back into Egypt.
Antonius took these words in very ill part. Cleopatra on the other
side answered him, 'Thou doest well Geminius,' said she, 'to tell
the truth before thou be compelled by torments': but within few
days after, Geminius stole away, and fled to Rome. The flatterers
also to please Cleopatra, did make her drive many other of
Antonius' faithful servants and friends from him, who could not
abide the injuries done unto them: among the which these two
were chief, Marcus Syllanus, and Dellius the historiographer: who
wrote that he fled, because her physician Glaucus told him, that
Cleopatra had set some secretly to kill him. Furthermore he had
Cleopatra's displeasure, because he said one night at supper, that
they made them drink sour wine, where Sarmentus at Rome drank
good wine of Falerna. This Sarmentus was a pleasant young boy,
such as the lords of Rome are wont to have about them to make
them pastime, which they call their joys, and he was Octavius
Caesar's boy.

60   Now, after Caesar had made sufficient preparation, he proclaimed open war against Cleopatra, and made the people to
abolish the power and empire of Antonius, because he had before
given it up unto a woman. And Caesar said furthermore, that
Antonius was not master of himself, but that Cleopatra had
brought him beside himself, by her charms and amorous poisons:
and that they that should make war with them should be Mardian the eunuch, Photinus, and Iras, a woman of Cleopatra's

bedchamber, that frizzled her hair and dressed her head, and Charmion, the which were those that ruled all the affairs of Antonius' empire. Before this war, as it is reported, many signs and wonders fell out. First of all, the city of Pisaurum which was made a colony to Rome, and replenished with people by Antonius, standing upon the shore side of the sea Adriatic, was by a terrible earthquake sunk into the ground. One of the images of stone which was set up in the honour of Antonius, in the city of Alba, did sweat many days together: and though some wiped it away, yet it left not sweating still. In the city of Patras, whilst Antonius was there, the temple of Hercules was burnt with lightning. And at the city of Athens also, in a place where the war of the giants against the gods is set out in imagery, the statue of Bacchus with a terrible wind was thrown down in the theatre. It was said that Antonius came of the race of Hercules, as you have heard before, and in the manner of his life he followed Bacchus: and therefore he was called the new Bacchus. Furthermore, the same blustering storm of wind overthrew the great monstrous images at Athens, that were made in the honour of Eumenes and Attalus, the which men had named and intituled, the Antonians, and yet they did hurt none of the other images, which were many besides. The admiral galley of Cleopatra was called Antoniade, in the which there chanced a marvellous ill sign. Swallows had bred under the poop of her ship, and there came others after them that drove away the first, and plucked down their nests.

61 Now when all things were ready, and that they drew near to fight: it was found that Antonius had no less than five hundred good ships of war, among the which there were many galleys that had eight and ten banks of oars, the which were sumptuously furnished, not so meet for fight, as for triumph: a hundred thousand footmen, and twelve thousand horsemen, and had with him to aid him these kings and subjects following: Bocchus king of Lybia, Tarcondemus king of high Cilicia, Archelaus king of Cappadocia, Philadelphus king of Paphlagonia, Mithridates king of Comagena, and Adallas king of Thracia. All the which were there every man in person. The residue that were absent sent their armies, as Polemon king of Pont, Manchus king of Arabia, Herodes king of Jewry and furthermore, Amyntas king of Lycaonia, and of the Galatians: and besides all

these, he had all the aid the king of Medes sent unto him. Now for Caesar, he had two hundred and fifty ships of war, four score thousand footmen, and well near as many horsemen as his enemy Antonius. Antonius for his part, had all under his dominion from Armenia and the river of Euphrates unto the sea Ionium and Illyricum. Octavius Caesar had also for his part, all that which was in our hemisphere, or half part of the world, from Illyria unto the Ocean sea upon the west: then all from the Ocean unto Mare Siculum: and from Africa, all that which is against Italy, as Gaul, and Spain. Furthermore, all from the province of Cyrenia unto Ethiopia, was subject unto Antonius.

62  Now Antonius was made so subject to a woman's will, that though he was a great deal the stronger by land, yet for Cleopatra's sake, he would needs have this battle tried by sea: though he saw before his eyes, that for lack of watermen, his captains did press by force all sorts of men out of Greece that they could take up in the field, as travellers, muleteers, reapers, harvest men, and young boys, and yet could they not sufficiently furnish his galleys: so that the most part of them were empty, and could scant row, because they lacked watermen enough. But on the contrary side, Caesar's ships were not built for pomp, high and great, only for a sight and bravery, but they were light of yarage, armed and furnished with watermen as many as they needed, and had them all in readiness, in the havens of Tarentum and Brundusium. So Octavius Caesar sent unto Antonius, to will him to delay no more time, but to come on with his army into Italy: and that for his own part he would give him safe harbour, to land without any trouble, and that he would withdraw his army from the sea, as far as one horse could run, until he had put his army ashore, and had lodged his men. Antonius on the other side bravely sent him word again, and challenged the combat of him man to man, though he were the elder: and that if he refused him so, he would then fight a battle with him in the fields of Pharsalia, as Julius Caesar and Pompey had done before. Now whilst Antonius rode at anchor, lying idly in harbour at the head of Actium, in the place where the city of Nicopolis standeth at this present, Caesar had quickly passed the sea Ionium, and taken a place called Toryne, before Antonius understood that he had taken ship. Then began his men to be afraid, because his army by

land was left behind. But Cleopatra making light of it 'And what danger, I pray you,' said she, 'if Caesar keep at Toryne?'*

63   The next morning by break of day, his enemies coming with full force of oars in battle against him, Antonius was afraid that if they came to join, they would take and carry away his ships that had no men of war in them. So he armed all his watermen, and set them in order of battle upon the forecastle of their ships, and then lift up all his ranks of oars towards the element, as well of the one side, as the other, with the prows against the enemies, at the entry and mouth of the gulf, which beginneth at the point of Actium, and so kept them in order of battle, as if they had been armed and furnished with watermen and soldiers. Thus Octavius Caesar being finely deceived by this stratagem, retired presently, and therewithal Antonius very wisely and suddenly did cut him off from fresh water. For, understanding that the places where Octavius Caesar landed, had very little store of water, and yet very bad, he shut them in with strong ditches and trenches he cast, to keep them from sallying out at their pleasure, and so to go seek water further off. Furthermore, he dealt very friendly and courteously with Domitius, and against Cleopatra's mind. For, he being sick of an ague when he went and took a little boat to go to Caesar's camp, Antonius was very sorry for it, but yet he sent after him all his carriage, train, and men: and the same Domitius, as though he gave him to understand that he repented his open treason, he died immediately after. There were certain kings also that forsook him, and turned on Caesar's side: as Amyntas, and Deiotarus. Furthermore, his fleet and navy that was unfortunate in all things, and unready for service, compelled him to change his mind, and to hazard battle by land. And Canidius also, who had charge of his army by land, when time came to follow Antonius' determination, he turned him clean contrary, and counselled him to send Cleopatra back again, and himself to retire into Macedon, to fight there on the mainland. And furthermore told him, that

* The grace of this taunt cannot properly be expressed in any other tongue, because of the equivocation of this word Toryne, which signifieth a city in Albania, and also a ladle to scum the pot with: as if she meant, Caesar sat by the fireside, scumming of the pot.

Dicomes king of the Getes promised him to aid him with a great power: and that it should be no shame nor dishonour to him to let Caesar have the sea (because himself and his men both had been well practised and exercised in battles by sea, in the war of Sicilia against Sextus Pompeius), but rather that he should do against all reason, he having so great skill and experience of battles by land as he had, if he should not employ the force and valiantness of so many lusty armed footmen as he had ready, but would weaken his army by dividing them into ships. But now, notwithstanding all these good persuasions, Cleopatra forced him to put all to the hazard of battle by sea: considering with herself how she might fly, and provide for her safety, not to help him to win the victory, but to fly more easily after the battle lost. Betwixt Antonius' camp and his fleet of ships, there was a great high point of firm land that ran a good way into the sea, the which Antonius often used for a walk, without mistrust of fear or danger. One of Caesar's men perceived it, and told his master that he would laugh an they could take up Antonius in the midst of his walk. Thereupon Caesar sent some of his men to lay in ambush for him, and they missed not much of taking of him: for they took him that came before him, because they discovered too soon, and so Antonius scaped very hardly.

64    So when Antonius had determined to fight by sea, he set all the other ships afire, but three score ships of Egypt, and reserved only but the best and greatest galleys, from three banks unto ten banks of oars. Into them he put two and twenty thousand fighting men, with two thousand darters and slingers. Now, as he was setting his men in order of battle, there was a captain, and a valiant man, that had served Antonius in many battles and conflicts, and had all his body hacked and cut: who as Antonius passed by him, cried out unto him, and said: 'O noble emperor, how cometh it to pass that you trust to these vile brittle ships? What, do you mistrust these wounds of mine, and this sword? Let the Egyptians and Phaenicians fight by sea, and set us on the mainland, where we use to conquer, or to be slain on our feet.' Antonius passed by him, and said never a word, but only beckoned to him with his hand and head, as though he willed him to be of good courage, although indeed he had no great courage himself. For when the masters of the galleys and pilots would have let their sails alone, he made them

clap them on, saying to colour the matter withal, that not one of his enemies should escape.

65 All that day, and the three days following, the sea rose so high, and was so boisterous, that the battle was put off. The fifth day the storm ceased, and the sea calmed again, and then they rowed with force of oars in battle one against the other: Antonius leading the right wing with Publicola, and Caelius the left, and Marcus Octavius and Marcus Iusteius the midst. Octavius Caesar on the other side, had placed Agrippa in the left wing of his army, and had kept the right wing for himself. For the armies by land, Canidius was general of Antonius' side, and Taurus of Caesar's side: who kept their men in battle ray the one before the other, upon the sea side, without stirring one against the other. Further, touching both the chieftains: Antonius being in a swift pinnace, was carried up and down by force of oars through his army, and spoke to his people to encourage them to fight valiantly, as if they were on main land, because of the steadiness and heaviness of their ships: and commanded the pilots and masters of the galleys, that they should not stir, none otherwise than if they were at anchor, and so to receive the first charge of their enemies, and that they should not go out of the strait of the gulf. Caesar betimes in the morning going out of his tent, to see his ships thorough out, met a man by chance that drove an ass before him. Caesar asked the man what his name was. The poor man told him, his name was Eutychus, to say, Fortunate: and his ass's name Nicon, to say, Conqueror. Therefore Caesar after he had won the battle, setting out the market-place with the spurs of the galleys he had taken, for a sign of his victory, he caused also the man and his ass to be set up in brass. When he had visited the order of his army thorough out, he took a little pinnace, and went to the right wing, and wondered when he saw his enemies lie still in the strait, and stirred not. For, discerning them afar off, men would have thought they had been ships riding at anchor, and a good while he was so persuaded: so he kept his galleys eight furlong from his enemies. About noon there rose a little gale of wind from the sea, and then Antonius' men waxing angry with tarrying so long, and trusting to the greatness and height of their ships, as if they had been invincible, they began to march forward with their left wing. Caesar seeing that, was a glad man, and began a little to give back

from the right wing, to allure them to come further out of the strait and gulf: to the end that he might with his light ships well manned with watermen, turn and environ the galleys of the enemies, the which were heavy of yarage, both for their bigness, as also for lack of watermen to row them.

66   When the skirmish began, and that they came to join, there was no great hurt at the first meeting, neither did the ships vehemently hit one against the other, as they do commonly in fight by sea. For on the one side, Antonius' ships for their heaviness, could not have the strength and swiftness to make their blows of any force: and Caesar's ships on the other side took great heed, not to rush and shock with the forecastles of Antonius' ships, whose prows were armed with great brazen spurs. Furthermore they durst not flank them, because their points were easily broken, which way soever they came to set upon his ships, that were made of great main square pieces of timber, bound together with great iron pins: so that the battle was much like to a battle by land, or to speak more properly, to the assault of a city. For there were always three or four of Caesar's ships about one of Antonius' ships, and the soldiers fought with their pikes, halberds, and darts, and threw pots and darts with fire. Antonius' ships on the other side bestowed among them, with their crossbows and engines of battery, great store of shot from their high towers of wood, that were upon their ships. Now Publicola seeing Agrippa put forth his left wing of Caesar's army, to compass in Antonius' ships that fought, he was driven also to loose off to have more room, and going a little at one side, to put those further off that were affrayed, and in the midst of the battle. For they were sore distressed by Aruntius. Howbeit the battle was yet of even hand, and the victory doubtful, being indifferent to both, when suddenly they saw the three score ships of Cleopatra busy about their yard masts, and hoisting sail to flee. So they fled through the midst of them that were in fight, for they had been placed behind the great ships, and did marvellously disorder the other ships. For the enemies themselves wondered much to see them sail in that sort, with full sail towards Peloponnesus. There Antonius showed plainly, that he had not only lost the courage and heart of an emperor, but also of a valiant man, and that he was not his own man (proving that true which an old man spoke in mirth,

that the soul of a lover lived in another body, and not in his own):
he was so carried away with the vain love of this woman, as if he
had been glued unto her, and that she could not have removed
without moving of him also. For when he saw Cleopatra's ship
under sail, he forgot, forsook, and bewrayed them that fought for
him, and embarked upon a galley with five banks of oars, to follow
her that had already begun to overthrow him, and would in the end
be his utter destruction.

67   When she knew this galley afar off, she lift up a sign in the
poop of her ship, and so Antonius coming to it, was plucked up
where Cleopatra was, howbeit he saw her not at his first coming,
nor she him, but went and sat down alone in the prow of his ship,
and said never a word, clapping his head between both his hands.
In the meantime came certain light brigantines of Caesar's that
followed him hard. So Antonius straight turned the prow of his
ship, and presently put the rest to flight, saving one Eurycles
Lacedaemonian, that followed him near, and pressed upon him
with great courage, shaking a dart in his hand over the prow, as
though he would have thrown it unto Antonius. Antonius seeing
him, came to the forecastle of his ship, and asked him what he was
that durst follow Antonius so near? 'I am,' answered he, 'Eurycles,
the son of Lachares, who through Caesar's good fortune seeketh to
revenge the death of my father.' This Lachares was condemned of
felony, and beheaded by Antonius. But yet Eurycles durst not
venture on Antonius' ship, but set upon the other admiral galley
(for there were two), and fell with him with such a blow of his
brazen spur, that was so heavy and big, that he turned her round,
and took her, with another that was laden with very rich stuff and
carriage. After Eurycles had left Antonius, he returned again to his
place, and sat down, speaking never a word as he did before: and so
lived three days alone, without speaking to any man. But when he
arrived at the head of Taenarus, there Cleopatra's women first
brought Antonius and Cleopatra to speak together, and afterwards,
to sup and lie together. Then began there again a great number of
merchants' ships to gather about them, and some of their friends
that had escaped from this overthrow: who brought news, that his
army by sea was overthrown, but that they thought the army by
land was yet whole. Then Antonius sent unto Canidius, to return

with his army into Asia, by Macedon. Now for himself, he determined to cross over into Africa, and took one of his carects or hulks laden with gold and silver, and other rich carriage, and gave it unto his friends: commanding them to depart, and to seek to save themselves. They answered him weeping, that they would neither do it, nor yet forsake him. Then Antonius very courteously and lovingly did comfort them, and prayed them to depart: and wrote unto Theophilus governor of Corinth, that he would see them safe, and help to hide them in some secret place, until they had made their way and peace with Caesar. This Theophilus was the father of Hipparchus, who was had in great estimation about Antonius. He was the first of all his enfranchised bondmen that revolted from him, and yielded unto Caesar, and afterwards went and dwelt at Corinth.

68    And thus it stood with Antonius. Now for his army by sea, that fought before the head or foreland of Actium: they held out a long time, and nothing troubled them more than a great boisterous wind that rose full in the prows of their ships, and yet with much ado, his navy was at length overthrown, five hours within night. There were not slain above five thousand men: but yet there were three hundred ships taken, as Octavius Caesar writeth himself in his *Commentaries*. Many plainly saw Antonius flee, and yet could hardly believe it, that he that had nineteen legions whole by land, and twelve thousand horsemen upon the sea side, would so have forsaken them, and have fled so cowardly as if he had not oftentimes proved both the one and the other fortune, and that he had not been thoroughly acquainted with the divers changes and fortunes of battles. And yet his soldiers still wished for him, and ever hoped that he would come by some means or other unto them. Furthermore, they showed themselves so valiant and faithful unto him, that after they certainly knew he was fled, they kept themselves whole together seven days. In the end Canidius, Antonius' lieutenant, flying by night, and forsaking his camp, when they saw themselves thus destitute of their heads and leaders, they yielded themselves unto the stronger. This done, Caesar sailed towards Athens, and there made peace with the Grecians, and divided the rest of the corn that was taken up for Antonius' army, unto the towns and cities of Greece, the which had been brought

to extreme misery and poverty, clean without money, slaves, horse, and other beasts of carriage. So that my grandfather Nicarchus told, that all the citizens of our city of Chaeronea (not one excepted) were driven themselves to carry a certain measure of corn on their shoulders to the sea side, that lieth directly over against the Isle of Anticyra, and yet were they driven thither with whips. They carried it thus but once: for, the second time that they were charged again to make the like carriage, all the corn being ready to be carried, news came that Antonius had lost the battle, and so scaped our poor city. For Antonius' soldiers and deputies fled immediately, and the citizens divided the corn amongst them.

69 Antonius being arrived in Libya, he sent Cleopatra before into Egypt from the city of Paraetonium: and he himself remained very solitary, having only two of his friends with him, with whom he wandered up and down, both of them orators, the one Aristocrates a Grecian, and the other Lucilius a Roman. Of whom we have written in another place, that at the battle where Brutus was overthrown, by the city of Philippes, he came and willingly put himself into the hands of those that followed Brutus, saying that it was he: because Brutus in the meantime might have liberty to save himself. And afterwards because Antonius saved his life, he still remained with him: and was very faithful and friendly unto him till his death. But when Antonius heard, that he whom he had trusted with the government of Libya, and unto whom he had given the charge of his army there, had yielded unto Caesar, he was so mad withal, that he would have slain himself for anger, had not his friends about him withstood him, and kept him from it. So he went unto Alexandria, and there found Cleopatra about a wonderful enterprise, and of great attempt. Betwixt the red sea, and the sea between the lands that point upon the coast of Egypt, there is a little piece of land that divideth both the seas, and separateth Africa from Asia: the which strait is so narrow at the end where the two seas are narrowest, that it is not above three hundred furlongs over. Cleopatra went about to lift her ships out of the one sea, and to hale them over the strait into the other sea: that when her ships were come into this gulf of Arabia, she might then carry all her gold and silver away, and so with a great company of men go and dwell in some place about the Ocean sea, far from the sea Medi-

terranean, to escape the danger and bondage of this war. But now, because the Arabians dwelling about the city of Petra, did burn the first ships that were brought a-land, and that Antonius thought that his army by land, which he left at Actium, was yet whole, she left off her enterprise, and determined to keep all the ports and passages of her realm. Antonius, he forsook the city and company of his friends, and built him a house in the sea, by the Isle of Pharos, upon certain forced mounts which he caused to be cast into the sea, and dwelt there, as a man that banished himself from all men's company: saying that he would lead Timon's life, because he had the like wrong offered him, that was afore offered unto Timon: and that for the unthankfulness of those he had done good unto, and whom he took to be his friends, he was angry with all men, and would trust no man.

70    This Timon was a citizen of Athens, that lived about the war of Peloponnesus, as appeareth by Plato, and Aristophanes' comedies: in the which they mocked him, calling him a viper, and malicious man unto mankind, to shun all other men's companies, but the company of young Alcibiades, a bold and insolent youth, whom he would greatly feast, and make much of, and kissed him very gladly. Apemantus wondering at it, asked him the cause what he meant to make so much of that young man alone, and to hate all others: Timon answered him, 'I do it,' said he, 'because I know that one day he shall do great mischief unto the Athenians.' This Timon sometimes would have Apemantus in his company, because he was much like to his nature and conditions, and also followed him in manner of life. On a time when they solemnly celebrated the feasts called Choae at Athens (to wit, the feasts of the dead, where they make sprinklings and sacrifices for the dead), and that they two then feasted together by themselves, Apemantus said unto the other: 'O, here is a trim banquet, Timon.' Timon answered again, 'Yea,' said he, 'so thou wert not here.' It is reported of him also, that this Timon on a time (the people being assembled in the market-place about dispatch of some affairs) got up into the pulpit for orations, where the orators commonly use to speak unto the people: and silence being made, every man listening to hear what he would say, because it was a wonder to see him in that place, at length he began to speak in this manner: 'My lords of Athens, I have a little yard

in my house where there groweth a fig tree, on the which many
citizens have hanged themselves: and because I mean to make some
building upon the place, I thought good to let you all understand it,
that before the fig tree be cut down, if any of you be desperate, you
may there in time go hang yourselves.' He died in the city of Hales,
and was buried upon the sea side. Now it chanced so, that the sea
getting in, it compassed his tomb round about, that no man could
come to it: and upon the same was written this epitaph:

> Here lies a wretched corse, of wretched soul bereft,
> Seek not my name: a plague consume you wicked wretches left.

It is reported, that Timon himself when he lived made this epitaph:
for that which is commonly rehearsed was not his, but made by the
poet Callimachus:

> Here lie I Timon, who alive all living men did hate:
> Pass by, and curse thy fill: but pass, and stay not here thy gait.

71   Many other things could we tell you of this Timon, but this
little shall suffice at this present. But now to return to Antonius
again. Canidius himself came to bring him news, that he had lost all
his army by land at Actium. On the other side he was advertised
also, that Herodes king of Jewry, who had also certain legions and
bands with him, was revolted unto Caesar, and all the other kings
in like manner: so that, saving those that were about him, he had
none left him. All this notwithstanding did nothing trouble him,
and it seemed that he was contented to forgo all his hope, and so to
be rid of all his care and troubles. Thereupon he left his solitary
house he had built in the sea, which he called Timoneon, and
Cleopatra received him into her royal palace. He was no sooner
come thither, but he straight set all the city off rioting and banqueting again, and himself to liberality and gifts. He caused the son
of Julius Caesar and Cleopatra, to be enrolled (according to the
manner of the Romans) amongst the number of young men: and
gave Antyllus, his eldest son he had by Fulvia, the man's gown, the
which was a plain gown without gard or embroidery of purple. For
these things, there was kept great feasting, banqueting, and dancing
in Alexandria many days together. Indeed they did break their first
order they had set down, which they called *amimetobion* (as much
to say, no life comparable) and did set up another which they called

*synapothanumenon* (signifying the order and agreement of those that will die together), the which in exceeding sumptuousness and cost was not inferior to the first. For their friends made themselves to be enrolled in this order of those that would die together, and so made great feasts one to another: for every man when it came to his turn, feasted their whole company and fraternity. Cleopatra in the meantime was very careful in gathering all sorts of poisons together to destroy men. Now to make proof of those poisons which made men die with least pain, she tried it upon condemned men in prison. For when she saw the poisons that were sudden and vehement, and brought speedy death with grievous torments: and in contrary manner, that such as were more mild and gentle, had not that quick speed and force to make one die suddenly: she afterwards went about to prove the stinging of snakes and adders, and made some to be applied unto men in her sight, some in one sort, and some in another. So when she had daily made divers and sundry proofs, she found none of all them she had proved so fit, as the biting of an aspic, the which only causeth a heaviness of the head, without swooning or complaining, and bringeth a great desire also to sleep, with a little sweat in the face, and so by little and little taketh away the senses and vital powers, no living creature perceiving that the patients feel any pain. For they are so sorry when anybody waketh them, and taketh them up: as those that being taken out of a sound sleep, are very heavy and desirous to sleep.

72    This notwithstanding, they sent ambassadors unto Octavius Caesar in Asia, Cleopatra requesting the realm of Egypt for her children, and Antonius praying that he might be suffered to live at Athens like a private man, if Caesar would not let him remain in Egypt. And because they had no other men of estimation about them, for that some were fled, and those that remained, they did not greatly trust them, they were enforced to send Euphronius the schoolmaster of their children. For Alexas Laodician, who was brought into Antonius' house and favour by means of Timagenes, and afterwards was in greater credit with him, than any other Grecian (for that he had always been one of Cleopatra's ministers to win Antonius, and to overthrow all his good determinations to use his wife Octavia well): him Antonius had sent unto Herodes

king of Jewry, hoping still to keep him his friend, that he should not revolt from him. But he remained there, and bewrayed Antonius. For where he should have kept Herodes from revolting from him, he persuaded him to turn to Caesar: and trusting King Herodes, he presumed to come in Caesar's presence. Howbeit Herodes did him no pleasure: for he was presently taken prisoner, and sent in chains to his own country, and there by Caesar's commandment put to death. Thus was Alexas in Antonius' lifetime put to death, for bewraying of him.

73    Furthermore, Caesar would not grant unto Antonius' requests: but for Cleopatra, he made her answer, that he would deny her nothing reasonable, so that she would either put Antonius to death, or drive him out of her country. Therewithal he sent Thyreus one of his men unto her, a very wise and discreet man, who bringing letters of credit from a young lord unto a noble lady, and that besides greatly liked her beauty, might easily by his eloquence have persuaded her. He was longer in talk with her than any man else was, and the queen herself also did him great honour: insomuch as he made Antonius jealous of him. Whereupon Antonius caused him to be taken and well-favouredly whipped, and so sent him unto Caesar: and bade him tell him that he made him angry with him, because he showed himself proud and disdainful towards him, and now specially when he was easy to be angered, by reason of his present misery. To be short, 'If this mislike thee,' said he, 'thou hast Hipparchus one of my enfranchised bondmen with thee: hang him if thou wilt, or whip him at thy pleasure, that we may cry quittance.' From thenceforth, Cleopatra to clear herself of the suspicion he had of her, she made more of him than ever she did. For first of all, where she did solemnise the day of her birth very meanly and sparingly, fit for her present misfortune, she now in contrary manner did keep it with such solemnity, that she exceeded all measure of sumptuousness and magnificence: so that the guests that were bidden to the feasts, and came poor, went away rich. Now things passing thus, Agrippa by divers letters sent one after another unto Caesar, prayed him to return to Rome, because the affairs there did of necessity require his person and presence.

74    Thereupon he did defer the war till the next year following: but when winter was done, he returned again through Syria by

the coast of Africa, to make wars against Antonius, and his other captains. When the city of Pelusium was taken, there ran a rumour in the city, that Seleucus, by Cleopatra's consent, had surrendered the same. But to clear herself that she did not, Cleopatra brought Seleucus' wife and children unto Antonius, to be revenged of them at his pleasure. Furthermore, Cleopatra had long before made many sumptuous tombs and monuments, as well for excellency of work-manship, as for height and greatness of building, joining hard to the temple of Isis. Thither she caused to be brought all the treasure and precious things she had of the ancient kings her predecessors: as gold, silver, emeralds, pearls, ebony, ivory, and cinnamon, and besides all that, a marvellous number of torches, faggots, and flax. So Octavius Caesar being afraid to lose such a treasure and mass of riches, and that this woman for spite would set it afire, and burn it every whit, he always sent someone or other unto her from him, to put her in good comfort, whilst he in the meantime drew near the city with his army. So Caesar came, and pitched his camp hard by the city, in the place where they run and manage their horses. Antonius made a sally upon him, and fought very valiantly, so that he drove Caesar's horsemen back, fighting with his men even into their camp. Then he came again to the palace, greatly boasting of this victory, and sweetly kissed Cleopatra, armed as he was, when he came from the fight, recommending one of his men of arms unto her, that had valiantly fought in this skirmish. Cleopatra to reward his manliness, gave him an armour and headpiece of clean gold: howbeit the man at arms when he had received this rich gift, stole away by night, and went to Caesar.

75 Antonius sent again to challenge Caesar, to fight with him hand to hand. Caesar answered him, that he had many other ways to die than so. Then Antonius seeing there was no way more honourable for him to die, than fighting valiantly, he determined to set up his rest, both by sea and land. So being at supper (as it is reported), he commanded his officers and household servants that waited on him at his board, that they should fill his cups full, and make as much of him as they could: 'For,' said he, 'you know not whether you shall do so much for me tomorrow or not, or whether you shall serve another master: and it may be you shall see me no more, but a dead body.' This notwithstanding, perceiving that his

friends and men fell a-weeping to hear him say so, to salve that he had spoken, he added this more unto it, that he would not lead them to battle, where he thought not rather safely to return with victory, than valiantly to die with honour. Furthermore, the self-same night within little of midnight, when all the city was quiet, full of fear and sorrow, thinking what would be the issue and end of this war, it is said that suddenly they heard a marvellous sweet harmony of sundry sorts of instruments of music, with the cry of a multitude of people, as they had been dancing, and had sung as they use in Bacchus' feasts, with movings and turnings after the manner of the satyrs: and it seemed that this dance went through the city unto the gate that opened to the enemies, and that all the troop that made this noise they heard, went out of the city at that gate. Now, such as in reason sought the depth of the interpretation of this wonder, thought that it was the god unto whom Antonius bore singular devotion to counterfeit and resemble him, that did forsake them.

76    The next morning by break of day, he went to set those few footmen he had in order upon the hills adjoining unto the city: and there he stood to behold his galleys which departed from the haven, and rowed against the galleys of his enemies, and so stood still, looking what exploit his soldiers in them would do. But when by force of rowing they were come near unto them, they first saluted Caesar's men: and then Caesar's men resaluted them also, and of two armies made but one, and then did all together row toward the city. When Antonius saw that his men did forsake him, and yielded unto Caesar, and that his footmen were broken and overthrown, he then fled into the city, crying out that Cleopatra had bewrayed him unto them, with whom he had made war for her sake. Then she being afraid of his fury, fled into the tomb which she had caused to be made, and there locked the doors unto her, and shut all the springs of the locks with great bolts, and in the meantime sent unto Antonius to tell him that she was dead. Antonius believing it, said unto himself: 'What doest thou look for further, Antonius, if spiteful fortune hath taken from thee the only joy thou haddest, for whom thou yet reservedst thy life?' When he had said these words, he went into a chamber and unarmed himself, and being naked said thus: 'O Cleopatra, it grieveth me

not that I have lost thy company, for I will not be long from thee:
but I am sorry, that having been so great a captain and emperor, I
am indeed condemned to be judged of less courage and noble
mind, than a woman.' Now he had a man of his called Eros, whom
he loved and trusted much, and whom he had long before caused
to swear unto him, that he should kill him when he did command
him: and then he willed him to keep his promise. His man drawing
his sword, lift it up as though he had meant to have stricken
his master: but turning his head at one side, he thrust his sword
into himself, and fell down dead at his master's foot. Then said
Antonius, 'O noble Eros, I thank thee for this, and it is valiantly
done of thee, to show me what I should do to myself, which thou
couldest not do for me.' Therewithal he took his sword, and thrust
it into his belly, and so fell down upon a little bed. The wound he
had killed him not presently, for the blood stinted a little when he
was laid: and when he came somewhat to himself again, he prayed
them that were about him to dispatch him. But they all fled out of
the chamber, and left him crying out and tormenting himself: until
at last there came a secretary unto him called Diomedes, who was
commanded to bring him into the tomb or monument where
Cleopatra was.

77 When he heard that she was alive, he very earnestly prayed his
men to carry his body thither, and so he was carried in his men's
arms into the entry of the monument. Notwithstanding, Cleopatra
would not open the gates, but came to the high windows, and cast
out certain chains and ropes, in the which Antonius was trussed:
and Cleopatra her own self, with two women only, which she had
suffered to come with her into these monuments, trised Antonius
up. They that were present to behold it, said they never saw so
pitiful a sight. For, they plucked up poor Antonius all bloody as he
was, and drawing on with pangs of death, who holding up his hands
to Cleopatra, raised up himself as well as he could. It was a hard
thing for these women to do, to lift him up: but Cleopatra stooping
down with her head, putting to all her strength to her uttermost
power, did lift him up with much ado, and never let go her hold,
with the help of the women beneath that bade her be of good
courage, and were as sorry to see her labour so, as she herself. So
when she had got him in after that sort, and laid him on a bed: she

rent her garments upon him, clapping her breast, and scratching her face and stomach. Then she dried up his blood that had berayed his face, and called him her lord, her husband, and emperor, forgetting her own misery and calamity, for the pity and compassion she took of him. Antonius made her cease her lamenting, and called for wine, either because he was athirst, or else for that he thought thereby to hasten his death. When he had drunk, he earnestly prayed her, and persuaded her, that she would seek to save her life, if she could possible, without reproach and dishonour: and that chiefly she should trust Proculeius above any man else about Caesar. And as for himself, that she should not lament nor sorrow for the miserable change of his fortune at the end of his days: but rather that she should think him the more fortunate, for the former triumphs and honours he had received, considering that while he lived he was the noblest and greatest prince of the world, and that now he was overcome, not cowardly but valiantly, a Roman by another Roman.

78   As Antonius gave the last gasp, Proculeius came that was sent from Caesar. For after Antonius had thrust his sword in himself, as they carried him into the tombs and monuments of Cleopatra, one of his guard called Dercetaeus, took his sword with the which he had stricken himself, and hid it: then he secretly stole away, and brought Octavius Caesar the first news of his death, and showed him his sword that was bloodied. Caesar hearing these news, straight withdrew himself into a secret place of his tent, and there burst out with tears, lamenting his hard and miserable fortune, that had been his friend and brother-in-law, his equal in the empire, and companion with him in sundry great exploits and battles. Then he called for all his friends, and showed them the letters Antonius had written to him, and his answers also sent him again, during their quarrel and strife: and how fiercely and proudly the other answered him, to all just and reasonable matters he wrote unto him. After this, he sent Proculeius, and commanded him to do what he could possible to get Cleopatra alive, fearing lest otherwise all the treasure would be lost: and furthermore, he thought that if he could take Cleopatra, and bring her alive to Rome, she would marvellously beautify and set out his triumph. But Cleopatra would never put herself into Proculeius' hands, although they

spoke together. For Proculeius came to the gates that were very thick and strong, and surely barred, but yet there were some crannies through the which her voice might be heard, and so they without understood, that Cleopatra demanded the kingdom of Egypt for her sons: and that Proculeius answered her, that she should be of good cheer, and not be afraid to refer all unto Caesar.

79   After he had viewed the place very well, he came and reported her answer unto Caesar. Who immediately sent Gallus to speak once again with her, and bade him purposely hold her with talk, whilst Proculeius did set up a ladder against that high window, by the which Antonius was trised up, and came down into the monument with two of his men hard by the gate, where Cleopatra stood to hear what Gallus said unto her. One of her women which was shut in her monuments with her, saw Proculeius by chance as he came down, and shrieked out: 'O, poor Cleopatra, thou art taken.' Then when she saw Proculeius behind her as she came from the gate, she thought to have stabbed herself in with a short dagger she ware of purpose by her side. But Proculeius came suddenly upon her, and taking her by both the hands, said unto her: 'Cleopatra, first thou shalt do thyself great wrong, and secondly unto Caesar, to deprive him of the occasion and opportunity, openly to show his bounty and mercy, and to give his enemies cause to accuse the most courteous and noble prince that ever was, and to appeach him, as though he were a cruel and merciless man, that were not to be trusted.' So even as he spoke the word, he took her dagger from her, and shook her clothes for fear of any poison hidden about her. Afterwards Caesar sent one of his enfranchised men called Epaphroditus, whom he straitly charged to look well unto her, and to beware in any case that she made not herself away: and for the rest, to use her with all the courtesy possible.

80   And for himself, he in the meantime entered the city of Alexandria, and as he went, talked with the philosopher Arrius, and held him by the hand, to the end that his countrymen should reverence him the more, because they saw Caesar so highly esteem and honour him. Then he went into the show place of exercises and so up to his chair of state which was prepared for him of a great height: and there according to his commandment, all the people of Alexandria were assembled, who quaking for fear, fell down on

their knees before him, and craved mercy. Caesar bade them all stand up, and told them openly that he forgave the people, and pardoned the felonies and offences they had committed against him in this war. First, for the founders' sake of the same city, which was Alexander the Great: secondly, for the beauty of the city, which he much esteemed and wondered at: thirdly, for the love he bore unto his very friend Arrius. Thus did Caesar honour Arrius, who craved pardon for himself and many others, and specially for Philostratus, the eloquentest man of all the sophisters and orators of his time, for present and sudden speech: howbeit he falsely named himself an Academic philosopher. Therefore, Caesar that hated his nature and conditions, would not hear his suit. Thereupon he let his grey beard grow long, and followed Arrius step by step in a long mourning gown, still buzzing in his ears this Greek verse:

> A wise man if that he be wise indeed,
> May by a wise man have the better speed.

Caesar understanding this, not for the desire he had to deliver Philostratus of his fear, as to rid Arrius of malice and envy that might have fallen out against him, he pardoned him.

81 Now touching Antonius' sons, Antyllus, his eldest son by Fulvia, was slain, because his schoolmaster Theodorus did bewray him unto the soldiers, who struck off his head. And the villain took a precious stone of great value from his neck, the which he did sew in his girdle, and afterwards denied that he had it: but it was found about him, and so Caesar trussed him up for it. For Cleopatra's children, they were very honourably kept, with their governors and train that waited on them. But for Caesarion, who was said to be Julius Caesar's son, his mother Cleopatra had sent him unto the Indians through Ethiopia, with a great sum of money. But one of his governors also called Rhodon, even such another as Theodorus, persuaded him to return into his country, and told him that Caesar sent for him to give him his mother's kingdom. So, as Caesar was determining with himself what he should do, Arrius said unto him:

> Too many Caesars is not good:

alluding unto a certain verse of Homer that saith:

> Too many lords doth not well.

82 Therefore Caesar did put Caesarion to death, after the death of his mother Cleopatra. Many princes, great kings and captains did crave Antonius' body of Octavius Caesar, to give him honourable burial: but Caesar would never take it from Cleopatra, who did sumptuously and royally bury him with her own hands, whom Caesar suffered to take as much as she would to bestow upon his funerals. Now was she altogether overcome with sorrow and passion of mind, for she had knocked her breast so pitifully, that she had martyred it, and in divers places had raised ulcers and inflammations, so that she fell into a fever withal: whereof she was very glad, hoping thereby to have good colour to abstain from meat, and that so she might have died easily without any trouble. She had a physician called Olympus, whom she made privy of her intent, to the end he should help her to rid her out of her life: as Olympus writeth himself, who wrote a book of all these things. But Caesar mistrusted the matter, by many conjectures he had, and therefore did put her in fear, and threatened her to put her children to shameful death. With these threats, Cleopatra for fear yielded straight, as she would have yielded unto strokes: and afterwards suffered herself to be cured and dieted as they listed.

83 Shortly after, Caesar came himself in person to see her, and to comfort her. Cleopatra being laid upon a little low bed in poor estate, when she saw Caesar come in to her chamber, she suddenly rose up, naked in her smock, and fell down at his feet marvellously disfigured: both for that she had plucked her hair from her head, as also for that she had martyred all her face with her nails, and besides, her voice was small and trembling, her eyes sunk into her head with continual blubbering: and moreover, they might see the most part of her stomach torn in sunder. To be short, her body was not much better than her mind: yet her good grace and comeliness, and the force of her beauty was not altogether defaced. But notwithstanding this ugly and pitiful state of hers, yet she showed herself within, by her outward looks and countenance. When Caesar had made her lie down again, and sat by her bed's side, Cleopatra began to clear and excuse herself for that she had done, laying all to the fear she had of Antonius. Caesar, in contrary manner, reproved her in every point. Then she suddenly altered her speech, and prayed him to pardon her, as though she were afraid to die, and desirous to live. At

length, she gave him a brief and memorial of all the ready money and treasure she had. But by chance there stood Seleucus by, one of her treasurers, who to seem a good servant, came straight to Caesar to disprove Cleopatra, that she had not set in all, but kept many things back of purpose. Cleopatra was in such a rage with him, that she flew upon him, and took him by the hair of the head, and boxed him well-favouredly. Caesar fell a-laughing, and parted the fray. 'Alas,' said she, 'O Caesar: is not this a great shame and reproach, that thou having vouchsafed to take the pains to come unto me, and have done me this honour, poor wretch and caitiff creature, brought into this pitiful and miserable estate: and that mine own servants should come now to accuse me, though it may be I have reserved some jewels and trifles meet for women, but not for me (poor soul) to set out myself withal, but meaning to give some pretty presents and gifts unto Octavia and Livia, that they making means and intercession for me to thee, thou mightest yet extend thy favour and mercy upon me?' Caesar was glad to hear her say so, persuading himself thereby that she had yet a desire to save her life. So he made her answer, that he did not only give her that to dispose of at her pleasure, which she had kept back, but further promised to use her more honourably and bountifully than she would think for: and so he took his leave of her, supposing he had deceived her, but indeed he was deceived himself.

84   There was a young gentleman Cornelius Dolabella, that was one of Caesar's very great familiars, and besides did bear no evil will unto Cleopatra. He sent her word secretly as she had requested him, that Caesar determined to take his journey through Syria, and that within three days he would send her away before with her children. When this was told Cleopatra, she requested Caesar that it would please him to suffer her to offer the last oblations of the dead, unto the soul of Antonius. This being granted her, she was carried to the place where his tomb was, and there falling down on her knees, embracing the tomb with her women, the tears running down her cheeks, she began to speak in this sort: 'O my dear lord Antonius, not long since I buried thee here, being a free woman: and now I offer unto thee the funeral sprinklings and oblations, being a captive and prisoner, and yet I am forbidden and kept from tearing and murdering this captive body of mine with blows,

which they carefully guard and keep, only to triumph of thee: look therefore henceforth for no other honours, offerings, nor sacrifices from me, for these are the last which Cleopatra can give thee, if now they carry her away. Whilst we lived together, nothing could sever our companies: but now at our death, I fear me they will make us change our countries. For as thou being a Roman, hast been buried in Egypt, even so wretched creature I, an Egyptian, shall be buried in Italy, which shall be all the good that I have received by thy country. If therefore the gods where thou art now have any power and authority, if our gods here have forsaken us, suffer not thy true friend and lover to be carried away alive, that in me, they triumph of thee: but receive me with thee, and let me be buried in one self tomb with thee. For though my griefs and miseries be infinite, yet none hath grieved me more, nor that I could less bear withal, than this small time, which I have been driven to live alone without thee.'

85    Then having ended these doleful plaints, and crowned the tomb with garlands and sundry nosegays, and marvellous lovingly embraced the same, she commanded they should prepare her bath, and when she had bathed and washed herself, she fell to her meat, and was sumptuously served. Now whilst she was at dinner, there came a countryman, and brought her a basket. The soldiers that warded at the gates, asked him straight what he had in his basket. He opened the basket, and took out the leaves that covered the figs, and showed them that they were figs he brought. They all of them marvelled to see so goodly figs. The countryman laughed to hear them, and bade them take some if they would. They believed he told them truly, and so bade him carry them in. After Cleopatra had dined, she sent a certain table written and sealed unto Caesar, and commanded them all to go out of the tombs where she was, but the two women: then she shut the doors to her. Caesar when he received this table, and began to read her lamentation and petition, requesting him that he would let her be buried with Antonius, found straight what she meant, and thought to have gone thither himself: howbeit he sent one before in all haste that might be, to see what it was. Her death was very sudden. For those whom Caesar sent unto her ran thither in all haste possible, and found the soldiers standing at the gate, mistrusting nothing, nor

understanding of her death. But when they had opened the doors, they found Cleopatra stark dead, laid upon a bed of gold, attired and arrayed in her royal robes, and one of her two women, which was called Iras, dead at her feet: and her other woman called Charmion half dead, and trembling, trimming the diadem which Cleopatra ware upon her head. One of the soldiers seeing her, angrily said unto her: 'Is that well done Charmion?' 'Very well,' said she again, 'and meet for a princess descended from the race of so many noble kings.' She said no more, but fell down dead hard by the bed.

86   Some report that this aspic was brought unto her in the basket with figs, and that she had commanded them to hide it under the fig leaves, that when she should think to take out the figs, the aspic should bite her before she should see her: howbeit, that when she would have taken away the leaves for the figs, she perceived it, and said, 'Art thou here then?' And so, her arm being naked, she put it to the aspic to be bitten. Other say again, she kept it in a box, and that she did prick and thrust it with a spindle of gold, so that the aspic being angered withal, leapt out with great fury, and bit her in the arm. Howbeit few can tell the truth. For they report also, that she had hidden poison in a hollow razor which she carried in the hair of her head: and yet was there no mark seen of her body, or any sign discerned that she was poisoned, neither also did they find this serpent in her tomb. But it was reported only, that there were seen certain fresh steps or tracks where it had gone, on the tomb side toward the sea, and specially by the door's side. Some say also, that they found two little pretty bitings in her arm, scant to be discerned: the which it seemeth Caesar himself gave credit unto, because in his triumph he carried Cleopatra's image, with an aspic biting of her arm. And thus goeth the report of her death. Now Caesar, though he was marvellous sorry for the death of Cleopatra, yet he wondered at her noble mind and courage, and therefore commanded she should be nobly buried, and laid by Antonius: and willed also that her two women should have honourable burial. Cleopatra died being eight and thirty year old, after she had reigned two and twenty years, and governed above fourteen of them with Antonius. And for Antonius, some say that he lived three and fifty years: and others say, six and fifty. All his statues,

images, and metals, were plucked down and overthrown, saving those of Cleopatra which stood still in their places, by means of Archibius one of her friends, who gave Caesar a thousand talents that they should not be handled as those of Antonius were.

87    Antonius left seven children by three wives, of the which, Caesar did put Antyllus, the eldest son he had by Fulvia, to death. Octavia his wife took all the rest and brought them up with hers, and married Cleopatra, Antonius' daughter, unto Iuba, a marvellous courteous and goodly prince. And Antonius the son of Fulvia came to be so great, that next unto Agrippa, who was in greatest estimation about Caesar, and next unto the children of Livia, which were the second in estimation, he had the third place. Furthermore, Octavia having had two daughters by her first husband Marcellus, and a son also called Marcellus, Caesar married his daughter unto that Marcellus, and so did adopt him for his son. And Octavia also married one of her daughters unto Agrippa. But when Marcellus was dead, after he had been married a while, Octavia perceiving that her brother Caesar was very busy to choose someone among his friends, whom he trusted best to make his son-in-law, she persuaded him, that Agrippa should marry his daughter (Marcellus' widow) and leave her own daughter. Caesar first was contented withal, and then Agrippa: and so she afterwards took away her daughter and married her unto Antonius, and Agrippa married Julia, Caesar's daughter. Now there remained two daughters more of Octavia and Antonius. Domitius Aenobarbus married the one: and the other, which was Antonia, so fair and virtuous a young lady, was married unto Drusus the son of Livia, and son-in-law of Caesar. Of this marriage came Germanicus and Claudius: of the which, Claudius afterwards came to be emperor. And of the sons of Germanicus, the one whose name was Caius, came also to be emperor: who, after he had licentiously reigned a time, was slain, with his wife and daughter. Agrippina also, having a son by her first husband Aenobarbus called Lucius Domitius, was afterwards married unto Claudius, who adopted her son, and called him Nero Germanicus. This Nero was emperor in our time, and slew his own mother, and had almost destroyed the empire of Rome, through his madness and wicked life, being the fifth emperor of Rome after Antonius.

## Comparison of Demetrius with Antonius

Now, since it falleth out, that Demetrius and Antonius were one of them much like to the other, having fortune alike divers and variable unto them, let us therefore come to consider their power and authority, and how they came to be so great. First of all, it is certain that Demetrius' power and greatness fell unto him by inheritance from his father Antigonus: who became the greatest and mightiest prince of all the successors of Alexander, and had won the most part of Asia, before Demetrius came of full age. Antonius in contrary manner, born of an honest man, who otherwise was no man of war, and had not left him any mean to arise to such greatness, durst take upon him to contend for the empire with Caesar that had no right unto it by inheritance, but yet made himself successor of the power, the which the other by great pain and travail had obtained, and by his own industry became so great, without the help of any other: that the empire of the whole world being divided into two parts, he had the one half, and took that of the greatest countenance and power. Antonius being absent, oftentimes overcame the Parthians in battle by his lieutenants, and chased away the barbarous people dwelling about Mount Caucasus, unto the sea Hyrcanium: insomuch as the thing they most reprove him for, did most witness his greatness. For Demetrius' father made him gladly marry Phila, Antipater's daughter, although she was too old for him, because she was of a nobler house than himself. Antonius on the other side was blamed for marrying of Cleopatra, a queen that for power and nobility of blood, excelled all other kings in her time, but Arsaces: and moreover made himself so great, that others thought him worthy of greater things, than he himself required.

2   Now for the desire that moved the one and the other to conquer realms: the desire of Demetrius was unblameable and

just, desiring to reign over people, which had been governed at all times, and desired to be governed by kings. But Antonius' desire was altogether wicked and tyrannical: who sought to keep the people of Rome in bondage and subjection, but lately before rid of Caesar's reign and government. For the greatest and most famous exploit Antonius ever did in wars (to wit, the war in the which he overthrew Cassius and Brutus) was begun to no other end, but to deprive his countrymen of their liberty and freedom. Demetrius in contrary manner, before fortune had overthrown him, never left to set Greece at liberty, and to drive the garrisons away, which kept the cities in bondage: and not like Antonius, that boasted he had slain them that had set Rome at liberty. The chiefest thing they commended in Antonius, was his liberality and bounty: in the which Demetrius excelled him so far, that he gave more to his enemies, than Antonius did to his friends: although he was marvellously well thought of, for the honourable and sumptuous funeral he gave unto Brutus' body. Howbeit Demetrius caused all his enemies be buried that were slain in battle, and returned unto Ptolomy all the prisoners he had taken, with great gifts and presents he gave them.

3   They were both in their prosperity, very riotously and licentiously given: but yet no man can ever say, that Demetrius did at any time let slip any opportunity or occasion to follow great matters, but only gave himself indeed to pleasure, when he had nothing else to do. And further, to say truly, he took pleasure of Lamia, as a man would have a delight to hear one tell tales, when he hath nothing else to do, or is desirous to sleep: but indeed when he was to make any preparation for war, he had not then ivy at his dart's end, nor had his helmet perfumed, nor came not out of ladies' closets, picked and prinked to go to battle: but he let all dancing and sporting alone, and became as the poet Euripides saith,

> The soldier of Mars, cruel, and bloody.

But to conclude, he never had overthrow or misfortune through negligence, nor by delaying time to follow his own pleasure: as we see in painted tables, where Omphale secretly stealeth away Hercules' club, and took his lion's skin from him. Even so Cleopatra oftentimes unarmed Antonius, and enticed him to her, making him lose matters of great importance, and very needful journeys, to come and be dandled with her, about the rivers of Canobus and Taphosiris. In the end, as Paris fled from the battle, and went to hide himself in Helen's arms, even so did he in Cleopatra's arms, or to speak more properly, Paris hid himself in Helen's closet, but Antonius to follow Cleopatra, fled and lost the victory.

4  Furthermore, Demetrius had many wives that he had married, and all at one time: the which was not disallowable or not forbidden by the kings of Macedon, but had been used from Philip and Alexander's time, as also King Lysimachus and Ptolomy had, and did honour all them that he married. But Antonius first of all married two wives together, the which never Roman durst do before, but himself. Secondly, he put away his first Roman wife, which he had lawfully married, for the love of a strange woman he fondly fell in fancy withal, and contrary to the laws and ordinances of Rome. And therefore Demetrius' marriages never hurt him, for any wrong he had done to his wives: but Antonius contrarily was undone by his wives. Of all the lascivious parts Antonius played, none were so abhominable, as this only fact of Demetrius. For the historiographers write, that they would not suffer dogs to come into the castle of Athens, because of all beasts he is too busy with bitchery: and Demetrius in Minerva's temple itself lay with court-esans, and there defiled many citizens' wives. And besides all this, the horrible vice of cruelty, which a man would think were least mingled with these wanton delights, is joined with Demetrius' concupiscence: who suffered (or more properly compelled) the goodliest young boy of Athens to die a most pitiful death, to save himself from violence, being taken. And to conclude, Antonius by his incontinency, did no hurt but to himself: and Demetrius did hurt unto all others.

5  Demetrius never hurt any of his friends: and Antonius suffered his uncle by his mother's side to be slain, that he might have his will of Cicero to kill him: a thing so damnable, wicked, and cruel of itself, that he hardly deserved to have been pardoned, though he had killed Cicero, to have saved his uncle's life. Now where they falsified and broke their oaths, the one making Artabazus prisoner, and the other killing of Alexander, Antonius out of doubt had best cause, and justest colour. For Artabazus had betrayed him, and

forsaken him in Media. But Demetrius (as divers do report) devised a false matter to accuse Alexander, to cloak the murder he had committed: and some think he did accuse him, to whom he himself had done injury unto, and was not revenged of him, that would do him injury. Furthermore, Demetrius himself did many noble feats in war, as we have recited of him before: and contrarily Antonius, when he was not there in person, won many famous and great victories by his lieutenants: and they were both overthrown being personally in battle, but yet not both after one sort.

6   For the one was forsaken of his men being Macedonians, and the other contrarily forsook his that were Romans: for he fled, and left them that ventured their lives for his honour. So that the fault the one did was, that he made them his enemies that fought for him: and the fault in the other, that he so beastly left them that loved him best, and were most faithful to him. And for their deaths, a man cannot praise the one nor the other, but yet Demetrius' death the more reproachful. For he suffered himself to be taken prisoner, and when he was sent away to be kept in a strange place, he had the heart to live yet three year longer, to serve his mouth and belly, as brute beasts do. Antonius on the other side slew himself (to confess a truth) cowardly, and miserably, to his great pain and grief: and yet was it before his body came into his enemies' hands.

# DION
## BRUTUS

## Life of Dion

Like as Simonides, O Sossius Senecio, saith that the city of Ilium was not offended with the Corinthians, for that they came to make war with them with other Grecians, because Glaucus (whose first ancestors came from Corinth) had taken arms, and lovingly fought for the same: even so methinks, that neither the Grecians nor Romans have cause to complain of the Academy, since they be both alike praised of the same in this present book, in the which are contained the lives of Dion and Brutus. Of the which, the one of them having been very familiar with Plato himself, and the other from his childhood brought up in Plato's doctrine, they both (as it were) came out of one self schoolhouse, to attempt the greatest enterprises amongst men. And it is no marvel if they two were much like in many of their doings, proving that true which their schoolmaster Plato wrote of virtue: that to do any noble act in the government of a commonwealth, which should be famous and of credit, authority and good fortune must both meet in one self person, joined with justice and wisdom. For, as a certain fencer called Hippomachus said, that he knew his scholars far off, if he did but see them coming from the market with meat in their hands, so it must needs follow, that men having been virtuously brought up, must needs be wise in all their doings, and beside that it bringeth them to civility and honesty, even so it frameth their conditions much like one unto another.

2    Furthermore, their fortunes having also fallen out both alike, more by chance than by any reason, do make their lives very like to each other. For, they were both of them slain, before they could bring their enterprises to pass which they had determined. But the greatest wonder of all is this: that their deaths were foreshowed unto them both, by a wicked spirit that visibly appeared unto either of them: albeit there be some that cannot abide those

opinions, and do maintain that these sights and evil spirits do never appear to any man that hath his right wits, but that they are fancies of little children, or old women, or of some men that their wits are weakened by sickness, and so have a certain imagination of such strange sights, being of this superstitious mind, that they have a wicked spirit, and an evil angel in them. But if Dion and Brutus, both of them grave and learned philosophers, and very constant men, not overcome by any sudden passion or imagination of mind, have been moved by such sights and spirits, and have also told it unto their friends, I cannot tell whether we shall be enforced to grant the most strangest and oldest opinion of this, which saith: that there be evil spirits which envying the virtue of good men, to withdraw them from their godly minds, do make them afraid with these fearful sights, enticing them to forsake their godliness, lest that persisting therein, they should be rewarded with better life in the world to come, than theirs is. But let us refer this disputation to some other book, and now in this twelfth couple of these famous men's lives compared, let us first begin to write the life of him that is the elder of these two men we speak of.

3   Dionysius the elder, after he had the government of Sicilia in his hands, he married the daughter of Hermocrates, a citizen of Syracusa. But yet not being thoroughly settled in his tyranny, the Syracusans did rebel against him, and did so cruelly and abominably handle the body of his wife, that she willingly poisoned herself. So after he had established himself in his government with more surety than before, he married again two other wives together, the one a stranger of the city of Locres, called Doride: and the other of the country itself, called Aristomache, the daughter of Hipparinus the chiefest man of all Syracusa, and that had been companion with Dionysius, the first time he was chosen general. It was said that Dionysius married them both in one day, and that they could never tell which of them he knew first: but otherwise, that he made as much of the one, as he did of the other. For they commonly sat together with him at his table, and did either of them lie with him by turns: though the Syracusans would have their own country-woman preferred before the stranger. Howbeit the strange woman had this good hap, to bring forth Dionysius his eldest son, which was a good countenance to defend her, being a foreigner. Aristo-

mache in contrary manner, continued a long time with Dionysius, without fruit of her womb, although he was very desirous to have children by her: so that he put the Locrian woman's mother to death, accusing her that she had with sorceries and witchcraft kept Aristomache from being with child.

4    Dion being the brother of Aristomache, was had in great estimation at the first, for his sister's sake: but afterwards the tyrant finding him to be a wise man, he loved him then for his own sake. Insomuch, that among many sundry things and pleasures he did for him, he commanded his treasurers to let him have what money he asked of them, so they made him acquainted withal the selfsame day they gave him any. Now though Dion had ever before a noble mind in him by nature, yet much more did that magnanimity increase, when Plato by good fortune arrived in Sicily. For his coming thither surely was no man's devise, as I take it, but the very providence of some god: who (bringing far off the first beginning and foundation of the liberty of the Syracusans, and to overthrow the tyrannical state) sent Plato out of Italy unto the city of Syracusa, and brought him acquainted with Dion, who was but a young man at that time, but yet had an apter wit to learn, and readier goodwill to follow virtue, than any young man else that followed Plato: as Plato himself writeth, and his own doings also do witness. For Dion having from a child been brought up with humble conditions under a tyrant, and acquainted with a servile timorous life, with a proud and insolent reign, with all vanity and curiosity, as placing chief felicity in covetousness, nevertheless, after he had felt the sweet reasons of philosophy, teaching the broad way to virtue, his heart was inflamed straight with earnest desire to follow the same. And because he found that he was so easily persuaded to love virtue and honesty, he simply thinking (being of an honest plain nature) that the selfsame persuasions would move a like affection in Dionysius, obtained of Dionysius, that being at leisure, he was contented to see Plato, and to speak with him.

5    When Plato came to Dionysius, all their talk in manner was of virtue, and they chiefly reasoned what was fortitude: where Plato proved that tyrants were no valiant men. From thence passing further into justice, he told him that the life of just men was happy, and contrarily the life of unjust men unfortunate. Thus the tyrant

Dionysius perceiving he was overcome, durst no more abide him, and was angry to see the bystanders to make such estimation of Plato, and that they had such delight to hear him speak. At length he angrily asked him, what business he had to do there? Plato answered him, he came to seek a good man. Dionysius then replied again: 'What, in God's name, by thy speech then it seemeth thou hast found none yet.' Now Dion thought that Dionysius' anger would proceed no further, and therefore at Plato's earnest request, he sent him away in a galley with three banks of oars, the which Pollis a Lacedaemonian captain carried back again into Greece. Howbeit, Dionysius secretly requested Pollis to kill Plato by the way, as ever he would do him pleasure: if not, yet that he would sell him for a slave, howsoever he did. 'For,' said he, 'he shall be nothing the worse for that: because if he be a just man, he shall be as happy to be a slave, as a freeman.' Thus, as it is reported, this Pollis carried Plato into the Isle of Aegina, and there sold him. For the Aeginetes having war at that time with the Athenians, made a decree, that all the Athenians that were taken in their isle, should be sold. This notwithstanding, Dionysius refused not to honour and trust Dion, as much as ever he did before, and did also send him ambassador in matters of great weight. As when he sent him unto the Carthaginians, where he behaved himself so well, that he won great reputation by his journey: and the tyrant could well away with his plain speech. For no man but he durst say their minds so boldly unto him, to speak what he thought good: as on a time he reproved him for Gelon. One day when they mocked Gelon's government before the tyrant's face, and that Dionysius himself said (finely descanting of his name, which signifieth laughter) that he was even the very laughing stock himself of Sicily, the courtiers made as though they liked this encounter and interpretation of laughter passingly well. But Dion not being well pleased withal, said unto him: 'For his sake, men trusted thee, whereby thou camest to be tyrant: but for thine own sake they will never trust any man.' For, to say truly, Gelon showed by his government, that it was as goodly a thing as could be, to see a city governed by an absolute prince: but Dionysius by his government on the other side, made it appear as detestable a thing.

6    This Dionysius had by his Locrian wife three children, and by Aristomache four: of the which two were daughters, the one called Sophrosyne, and the other Arete. Of them, Dionysius' eldest son married Sophrosyne, and Arete was married unto his brother Thearides, after whose death Dion married her, being his niece. Now when Dionysius her father fell sick, not likely to escape, Dion would have spoken with him for his children he had by his sister Aristomache. Howbeit the physicians about him, to curry favour with the next heir and successor of the tyranny, would never let him have any time or opportunity to speak with him. For, as Timaeus writeth, they gave Dionysius the elder (as he had commanded them) a strong opiate drink to cast him in a sleep, and so thereby they took from him all his senses and joined death with his sleep. Notwithstanding, in the first council and assembly held by his friends, to consult about the state and affairs of the younger Dionysius, Dion moved matter so necessary and profitable for that present time, that by his wisdom he showed they were all but children, and by his bold and frank speech, made them know that they were but slaves of the tyranny: because they beastly and cowardly gave such counsel and advice, as might best please and feed the young tyrant's humour. But he made them most to wonder at him, when they fearing above all other things, the danger Dionysius' state was in, by reason of Carthage, he did promise them, that if Dionysius would have peace, he would then go forthwith into Africa, and find the means honourably to quench the wars: or if otherwise he better liked of war, that he would furnish him at his own proper costs and charges, fifty galleys ready to row.

7    Dionysius wondered greatly at the noble mind of Dion, and thanked him much for the goodwill he bore unto him, touching his estate. But all men else taking Dion's noble offer to be a reproach of their avarice, and his credit and authority an impair unto theirs, they presently upon this liberal offer took occasion to accuse him, not sparing any reproachful words against him, to move Dionysius to be offended with him. For they complained of him, and said that he cunningly practised to possess the tyranny, making himself strong by sea, going about by his galleys to make the tyranny fall into the hands of the children of Aristomache his

sister. But the chiefest cause of all why they did malice and hate him, was his strange manner of life: that he neither would keep company with them, nor live after their manner. For they that from the beginning were crept in favour and friendship with this young evil brought up tyrant, by flattering of him, and feeding him with vain pleasures, studied for no other thing, but to entertain him in love matters, and other vain exercises, as to riot and banquet, to keep light women company, and all such other vile vicious pastimes and recreations, by the which the tyranny became like iron softened by fire, and seemed to be very pleasant unto the subjects, because the overgreat majesty and severity thereof was somewhat milder, not so much by the bounty and goodness, as by the folly and recklessness, of the lord. Thus, this little care and regard increasing more and more, still winning way with the young tyrant, did at length melt and break asunder those strong diamond chains, with the which Dionysius the elder made his boast that he left his monarchy and tyranny chained to his son. For sometime he would be three days together without inter-mission, still banqueting and drunk: and all that time his court gates were kept shut unto grave and wise men, and for all honest matters, and was then full of drunkards, of common plays, dancings, masques, and mummeries, and full of all such trumpery and dissolute pastimes.

8    And therefore Dion undoubtedly was much envied of them, because he gave himself to no sport nor pleasure: whereupon they accused him, and misnamed his virtues vices, being somewhat to be resembled unto them. As in calling his gravity, pride: his plainness and boldness in his oration, obstinacy: if he did persuade them, that he accused them: and because he would not make one in their fond pastimes, that therefore he despised them. For to say truly, his manners by nature had a certain haughtiness of mind and severity, and he was a sour man to be acquainted with: whereby his company was not only troublesome, but also unpleasant to this younger Dionysius, whose ears were so fine, that they could not away to hear any other thing but flattery. And furthermore, divers of his very friends and familiars, that did like and commend his plain manner of speech and noble mind, they did yet reprove his sternness, and austere conversation with men. For it seemed unto

them, that he spoke too roughly, and dealt overhardly with them that had to do with him, and more than became a civil or courteous man. And for proof hereof, Plato himself sometime wrote unto him (as if he had prophesied what should happen) that he should beware of obstinacy, the companion of solitariness, that bringeth a man in the end to be forsaken of everyone. This notwithstanding, they did more reverence him at that time, than any man else, because of the state and government, and for that they thought him the only man that could best provide for the safety and quietness of the tyranny, the which stood then in tickle state. Now Dion knew well enough, that he was not so well taken and esteemed through the goodwill of the tyrant, as against his will, and for the necessity of the state and time.

9 So Dion supposing that ignorance and want of knowledge in Dionysius was the cause, he devised to put him into some honest trade or exercise, and teach him the liberal sciences, to frame him to a civil life, that thenceforth he should no more be afraid of virtue, and should also take pleasure and delight in honest things. For Dionysius of his own nature, was none of the worst sort of tyrants, but his father fearing that if he came once to have a feeling and conceit of himself, or that he companied with wise and learned men, he would go near to enter into practice, and put him out of his seat, he ever kept him locked up in a chamber, and would suffer no man to speak with him. Then the younger Dionysius having nothing else to do, gave himself to make little chariots, candlesticks, chairs, stools, and tables of wood. For his father Dionysius was so fearful and mistrustful of everybody, that he would suffer no man with a pair of barber's scissors to pull the hairs off his head, but caused an image maker of earth to come unto him, and with a hot burning coal to burn his goodly bush of hair round about. No man came into his chamber where he was, with a gown on his back, no not his own brother nor son, but he was driven before he could come in, to put off his gown, and the guard of his chamber to strip him naked whatsoever he was: and then they gave him another gown to cast upon him, but not his own. One day his brother Leptines, going about to describe unto him the situation of some place, he took a halberd from one of the guard, and with the point thereof began to draw out a plot of the same upon the ground.

Dionysius was terribly offended with him, and did put the soldier
to death that gave him his halberd. He said he was afraid of his
friends, yea and of the wisest of them: because he knew that they
desired rather to rule, than to be ruled, and to command, than to
obey. He slew one of his captains called Marsyas, whom he had
preferred, and had given him charge of men, because he dreamed
that he killed him: saying that he dreamed of this in the night,
because that waking in the day he had determined to kill him.
Now Dionysius that was so timorous, and whose mind through
fearfulness was still miserably occupied, he was notwithstanding
marvellously offended with Plato, because he did not judge him to
be the noblest and valiantest man alive.

10    Dion therefore seeing (as we have said) the younger Dionysius clean marred, and in manner cast away for lack of good
education, persuaded him the best he could to give himself unto
study, and by the greatest entreaty he could possibly make, to pray
the prince of all philosophers to come into Sicily. And then when
through his entreaty he were come, that he would refer himself
wholly unto him, to the end that reforming his life by virtue and
learning, and knowing God thereby (the best example that can be
possible, and by whom all the whole world is ruled and governed,
which otherwise were out of all order and confused), he should
first obtain great happiness to himself, and consequently unto
all his citizens also, who ever after through the temperance and
justice of a father, would with goodwill do those things, which
they presently unwillingly did for the fear of a lord, and in doing
this, from a tyrant he should come to be a king. For, the chains of
a diamond to keep a realm in safety, were not force and fear, as his
father Dionysius held opinion, neither the great multitude of
young soldiers, nor the guard of ten thousand barbarous people:
but in contrary manner, that they were the love and goodwill
of their subjects, which the prince obtaineth through virtue and
justice: the which chains though they be slacker than the other
that are so hard and stiff, yet are they stronger, and will last longer
time, to keep a realm and kingdom in safety. 'And furthermore,
the prince,' said he, 'is not desirous of honour, neither is a man
that deserveth greatly to be praised and commended, that only
studieth to wear sumptuous apparel, and that glorieth to see his

court richly furnished, and himself curiously served: and in the meantime doth not frame himself to speak better, to be wiser, and to carry a greater majesty than any other mean or common person, not esteeming to adorn and beautify the princely palace of his mind, as becometh the royal majesty of a king.'

11    Dion oftentimes rehearsing these exhortations unto Dionysius, and otherwhile interlacing between, some reasons he had learned of Plato, he graft in him a wonderful, and as it were a vehement desire to have Plato in his company, and to learn of him. So sundry letters came from Dionysius unto Athens, divers requests from Dion, and great entreaty made by certain Pythagorean philosophers, that prayed and persuaded Plato to come into Sicily, to bridle the light disposition of this young man, by his grave and wise instructions: who without regard of reason, led a dissolute and licentious life. Therefore Plato, as himself reporteth, blushing to himself, and fearing lest he should give men cause to think that it was but the opinion men had of him, and that of himself he was unwilling to do any worthy act: and further, hoping that doing good but unto one man alone, who was the only guide of all the rest, he should as it were recover all Sicilia from her corruption and sickness, he performed their requests that sent unto him. But Dion's enemies fearing the change and alteration of Dionysius, they persuaded him to call Philistus the historiographer home again from banishment, who was a learned man, and had been brought up and acquainted with the tyrant's fashions: to the end he should serve as a counterpiece, to withstand Plato and his philosophy. For this Philistus, from the first time that the tyranny began to be established, did show himself very willing and conformable to the establishment thereof, and had of long time kept the castle: and the voice went, that he kept the mother of Dionysius the elder, and as it was supposed, not altogether without the tyrant's knowledge. But afterwards, Leptines having had two daughters by one woman, whom he enticed to folly being another man's wife, he married one of these his daughters unto Philistus, and made not Dionysius privy to it before. The tyrant therewith was so offended, that he put Leptines' woman in prison fast locked up, and drove Philistus out of Sicilia. He being banished thus, repaired unto some of his friends that dwelt about the Adriatic sea, where it seemeth he

wrote the most part of all his history, being then at good leisure.
For he was not called home again during the life of Dionysius the
elder: but after his death, the malice the courtiers bore unto Dion,
caused them to procure Philistus' calling home again, as we have
told you, as the man they thought would stick stoutly in defence of
the tyranny.

12   So Philistus no sooner returned, but he stoutly began to defend
the tyranny: and others in contrary manner, devised accusations to
the tyrant against Dion, accusing him that he had practised with
Theodotes and Heraclides, to overthrow the tyranny of Dionysius.
For Dion, in my opinion, hoped by Plato's coming to bridle and
lessen a little the overlicentious and imperious tyranny of
Dionysius, and thereby to frame Dionysius a wise and righteous
governor. But on the other side, if he saw he would not follow his
counsel, and that he yielded not to his wise instructions, he then
determined to put him down, and to bring the government of
the commonwealth into the hands of the Syracusans: not that he
allowed of *democratia* (to wit, where the people govern) but yet
certainly thinking that *democratia* was much better than the tyranny,
when they could not come unto *aristocratia*, to wit, the government
of a few of the nobility.

13   Now things being in this state, Plato arrived in Sicily, where
he was marvellously received and honoured by Dionysius. For
when he landed on the shore, leaving his galley that brought him:
there was ready for him one of the king's rich and sumptuous
chariots to convey him to the castle: and the tyrant made sacrifice
to give the gods thanks for his coming, as for some wonderful great
good hap chanced unto his seigniory. Furthermore, the wonderful
modesty and temperance that was begun to be observed in feasts
and banquets, the court clean changed, and the great goodness and
clemency of the tyrant in all things, in ministering justice to every
man, did put the Syracusans in great good hope of change, and
every man in the court was very desirous to give himself to
learning and philosophy. So that, as men reported, the tyrant's
palace was full of sand and dust, with the numbers of students
that drew plates and figures of geometry. Shortly after Plato was
arrived, by chance the time was come about to do a solemn
sacrifice within the castle, at which sacrifice the herald (as the

manner was) proclaimed aloud the solemn prayer accustomed to be done, that it would please the gods long to preserve the state of the tyranny: and that Dionysius being hard by him, said unto him, 'What, wilt thou not leave to curse me?' This word grieved Philistus and his companions to the heart, thinking that with time, by little and little, Plato would win such estimation and great authority with Dionysius, that afterwards they should not be able to resist him: considering that in so short a time as he had been with Dionysius, he had so altered his mind and courage.

14 And therefore they now began, not one by one, nor in hugger mugger, but all of them with open mouth together to accuse Dion: and said, that it was easy to be seen, how he charmed and enchanted Dionysius through Plato's eloquence, to make him willing to resign his government, because he would transfer it to the hands of the children of his sister Aristomache. Others seemed to be offended, for that the Athenians having come before into Sicilia with a great army, both by sea and land, they were all lost and cast away, and could not win the city of Syracusa: and that now by one only sophister, they utterly destroyed and overthrew the empire of Dionysius, persuading him to discharge the ten thousand soldiers he had about him for his guard, to forsake the four hundred galleys, the ten thousand horsemen, and as many more footmen, to go to the Academy to seek an unknown happiness never heard of before, and to make him happy by geometry, resigning his present happiness and felicity to be a great lord, to have money at will, and to live pleasantly, unto Dion and his nephews. By suchlike accusations and wicked tongues, Dionysius began first to mistrust Dion, and afterwards to be openly offended with him, and to frown upon him. In the meantime they brought letters Dion wrote secretly unto the governors of the city of Carthage, willing them that when they would make peace with Dionysius, they should not talk with him unless he stood by: assuring them that he would help them to set things in quietness, and that all should be well again. When Dionysius had read these letters with Philistus, and had taken his advice and counsel what he should do, as Timaeus said, he deceived Dion under pretence of reconciliation, making as though he meant him no hurt, and saying that he would become friends again with him. So he brought Dion one day to the sea side under his castle,

and showed him these letters, burdening him to have practised with
the Carthaginians against him. And as Dion went about to make
him answer, to clear himself, Dionysius would not hear him, but
caused him to be taken up as he was, and put into a pinnace, and
commanded the mariners to set him a-land upon the coast of Italy.

15    After this was done, and that it was known abroad in the city,
every man thought it a cruel part of Dionysius: insomuch that the
tyrant's palace was in a marvellous peck of troubles, for the great
sorrow the women made for the departure of Dion. Moreover, the
city self of Syracusa began to look about them, looking for some
sudden great change and innovation, for the tumult and uproar
that would happen by means of Dion's banishment, and for the
mistrust also that all men would have of Dionysius. Dionysius
considering this, and being afraid of some misfortune, he gave his
friends and the women of his palace comfortable words, telling
them that he had not banished him, but was contented that he
should absent himself for a time: being afraid, that in his sudden
angry mood he might peradventure be compelled to do him some
worse turn if he remained, because of his obstinacy and self-will.
Furthermore, he gave unto Dion's friends two ships, to carry as
much goods, money, and as many of Dion's servants as they
would, and to convey them unto him unto Peloponnesus. Dion
was a marvellous rich man, and for the pomp of his service, and
sumptuous moveables of his house, they were like unto the person
of a tyrant. All these riches Dion's friends brought aboard upon
those ships, and carried them unto him: besides many other rich
gifts, which the women and his friends sent unto him. So that by
means of his great riches, Dion was marvellously esteemed among
the Grecians: who by the riches of a banished citizen, conjectured
what the power of a tyrant might be.

16    But now concerning Plato: when Dion was exiled, Dionysius
caused him to be lodged in his castle, and by this means craftily
placed, under cloak of friendship, an honourable guard about him,
because he should not return into Greece to seek Dion, to tell him
of the injury he had done unto him. Howbeit Dionysius often
frequenting his company (as a wild beast is made tame by company
of man), he liked his talk so well, that he became in love with him,
but it was a tyrannical love. For he would have Plato to love none

but him, and that he should esteem him above all men living, being ready to put the whole realm into his hands, and all his forces, so that he would think better of him, than of Dion. Thus was this passionate affection of Dionysius grievous unto Plato. For he was so drowned with the love of him, as men extremely jealous of the women they love, that in a moment he would suddenly fall out with him, and straight again become friends, and pray him to pardon him. And to say truly, he had a marvellous desire to hear Plato's philosophy: but on the other side, he reverenced them that did dissuade him from it, and told him that he would spoil himself, if he entered overdeeply into it. In the meantime fell out war, and thereupon he sent Plato again away, promising him that the next spring he would send for Dion home. But he broke promise therein, and yet sent him his revenues: and prayed Plato to pardon him, though he had not kept promise at his time appointed. For he alleged the war was the cause, and that so soon as he had ended his war, he would send for Dion: whom in the meantime he prayed to have patience and not to attempt any stir or alteration against him, nor to speak evil of him among the Grecians.

17   This Plato sought to bring to pass, and brought Dion to study philosophy, and kept him in the Academy at Athens. Dion lay in the city of Athens with one Callippus, whom he had known of long time, howbeit he bought him a house in the country, to lie there sometime for his pleasure, the which he gave afterwards (at his return into Sicilia) unto Speusippus that kept him company, and was continually with him, more than with any other friend he had in Athens, through Plato's counsel: who to soften and recreate Dion's manners, gave him the company of some pleasant conceited man, knowing that this Speusippus could modestly observe time and place to be pleasant and merry: for which respect, Timon in his satirical jests, calleth Speusippus a good jester. Now Plato himself having undertaken to defray the charges of common plays in the dancings of young children, Dion took the pains to teach and exercise them, and moreover was himself at the whole charge of these plays, Plato suffering him to bestow that liberality and courtesy upon the Athenians: the which won Dion a great deal more goodwill, than Plato honour. Dion kept not still at Athens, but went also to see the other good cities of Greece, passing his

time away. He being at common feasts and assemblies with the chiefest men, and best learned in matters of state and government, and never showing any light parts, nor sign of tyrannical pride in his manner of life, nor of a man that had been brought up with all pomp and pleasure, but like a grave virtuous man, and well studied in philosophy, whereby he grew to be generally beloved and esteemed of all men: the cities granted him public honours, and sent him decrees of his glory, made in their councils and assemblies. Furthermore, the Lacedaemonians made him a Spartan and burgess of the city, not passing for Dionysius' displeasure, though at that time he had given them great aid, in the war they made against the Thebans. Some report, that Dion on a time was entreated by Ptaeodorus Megarian, to come and see him at his house: and Dion went thither. This Ptaeodorus was a marvellous great rich man, and therefore Dion seeing a great number of people standing at his gates, and that it was a hard thing to come and speak with him, he had such great business, he turned unto his friends that did accompany him, who were angry they made him tarry so long at the gate, and said unto them: 'What cause have we to think evil of him, if we did the like when we were at Syracusa?'

18 But Dionysius being incensed with envy against him, and fearing the goodwill the Grecians bore him: he kept back his revenue, and would no more send it him, and ceased all his goods, the which he gave to his receivers to keep. Furthermore, because he would clear himself of the infamy he had got amongst the philosophers for Plato's sake, he sent for divers wise and learned men, and vainly coveting to excel them all in wisdom, he was driven improperly, and out of time, to allege many wise sayings he had learned of Plato. Thereupon he began again to wish for him, and to condemn himself, for that he had no wit to use him well when he had him at his commandment, and that he had not heard so much as he should have done of him: and like a tyrant as he was, madly carried away with light desires, and easily changing mind from time to time, a sudden vehement desire took him in the head, to have Plato again. So he sought all the means and ways he could devise, to pray Archytas the Pythagorean philosopher to tell him, that he might boldly come, and to be his surety unto him for that he would promise him: for first of all, they were acquainted

together by his means. Therefore Archytas sent thither Archidamus the philosopher. Dionysius also sent certain galleys, and some of his friends thither, to pray Plato to come to him: and he himself wrote specially, and plainly, that it should not go well with Dion, if Plato came not into Sicilia: but if he would be persuaded to come, that then he would do what he would have him. Many letters and requests came unto Dion from his wife and sister, insomuch as Dion so used the matter, that Plato obeyed Dionysius, without making any excuse at all. So Plato writeth himself, that he was driven to come again the third time into the strait of Sicilia:

> To try if once again he could Charibdis' dangers pass.

19    Now Plato being arrived in Sicilia, he made Dionysius a great joyful man, and filled all Sicilia again with great good hope: for they were all very desirous, and did what they could, to make Plato overcome Philistus and the tyranny, with his philosophy. The women of Dionysius' court did entertain Plato the best they could: but above all, Dionysius seemed to have a marvellous trust and affiance in him, and more than in any other of all his friends. For he suffered Plato to come to him without searching of him, and oftentimes offered to give him a great sum of money: but Plato would take none of it. Therefore Aristippus Cyrenian being at that time in the tyrant's court in Sicilia, said that Dionysius bestowed his liberality surely. 'For, to us that ask much he giveth little, and much unto Plato that requireth nothing.' After Dionysius had given Plato his welcome, he began to move him again of Dion. Dionysius on the other side, at the first did use him with fine delays, but afterwards he showed himself angry indeed: and at length fell out with Plato, but yet so covertly, that others saw it not. For Dionysius dissembled that, and otherwise in all other things he did him as much honour as he could devise, practising thereby to make him to forsake Dion's friendship. Now Plato found him at the first, that there was no trust to be given to his words, and that all were but lies and devises he either said or did: howbeit he kept it to himself, and ever patiently bore all things, hoping for the best, and made as though he believed him. They too thus finely dissembling with each other, thinking to deceive all men, and that none should understand their secrets: Helycon Cyzicenian, one of Plato's

friends, did prognosticate the eclipse of the sun. The same falling out as he had prognosticated, the tyrant esteemed marvellously of him, and gave him a silver talent for his labour. Then Aristippus sporting with other philosophers, said he could tell them of a stranger thing to happen than that. So when they prayed him to tell them what it was: 'I do prognosticate,' said he, 'that Plato and Dionysius will be enemies ere it be long.' In the end it came to pass, that Dionysius made port sale of all Dion's goods, and kept the money to himself, and lodged Plato that before lay the next court to his palace, among the soldiers of his guard, whom he knew maliced him of long time, and sought to kill him, because he did persuade Dionysius to leave his tyranny and to live without his guard.

20    Plato being in this instant danger, Archytas sent ambassadors forthwith unto Dionysius, in a galley of thirty oars, to demand Plato again: declaring that Plato came again to Syracusa, upon his word and caution. Dionysius to excuse himself, and to show that he was not angry with him at his departure from him, he made him all the great cheer and feasts he could, and so sent him home with great shows of goodwill. One day among the rest, he said unto Plato: 'I am afraid, Plato,' said he, 'that thou wilt speak evil of me, when thou art among thy friends and companions in the Academy.' Then Plato smiling, answered him again: 'The gods forbid that they should have such scarcity of matter in the Academy, as that they must needs talk of thee.' Thus was Plato's return, as it is reported, although that which he himself writeth agreeth not much with this report.

21These things went to Dion's heart, so that shortly after he showed himself an open enemy unto Dionysius, but specially when he heard how he had handled his wife. Plato under covert words, sent Dionysius word of it by his letters. And thus it was. After Dion was exiled, Dionysius returning Plato back again, he willed him secretly to feel Dion's mind, whether he would not be angry that his wife should be married to another man: because there ran a rumour abroad (whether it were true, or invented by Dion's enemies) that he liked not his marriage, and could not live quietly with his wife. Therefore when Plato was at Athens, and had told Dion of all things, he wrote a letter unto Dionysius the tyrant, and did set all other things down so plainly, that every man might understand him, but this one thing only so darkly, that he alone and none other could understand him, but him to whom he had written: declaring unto him, that he had spoken with Dion about the matter he wrote of, and that he did let him understand he would be marvellous angry, if Dionysius did it. So at that time, because there was great hope of reconciliation between them, the tyrant did nothing lately touching his sister, but suffered her still to remain with Dion's son. But when they were so far out, that there was no more hope to return in favour again, and that he had also sent home Plato in disgrace and displeasure, then he married his sister Arete (Dion's wife) against her will, unto one of his friends called Timocrates, not following therein his father's justice and lenity. For Polyxenus that had married his father's sister Thesta, being also become his enemy, he fled out of Sicilia. Dionysius the elder sent for his sister Thesta, and took her up very sharply, for that she knowing her husband would fly, she did not come and tell him of it. Thesta nobly answered him again, and never was afraid nor abashed: 'Why, Dionysius, doest thou think me a woman so faint-hearted and beastly, that if I had known my husband would have gone his way, and left me, that I would not have taken the sea with him, and both have run one fortune together? Truly I knew not of his departure till he was gone: for it had been more for mine honour to have been called the wife of the banished Polyxenus, than the sister of thee a tyrant.' Dionysius marvelled to hear his sister speak thus boldly, and the Syracusans wondered at her noble courage: insomuch that when the tyranny was utterly destroyed, they did not refuse to do her all the honour they could devise, as unto a queen. And when she was dead also, all the citizens of Syracusa by a common decree, did accompany her body at her burial. This little digression from our history, is not altogether unprofitable.

22   But now again to our matter. Dion from thenceforth disposed himself altogether unto war, against Plato's counsel and advice: who did his best endeavour to dissuade him from it, both for the respect of Dionysius' good entertainment he had given him, as also for that Dion was of great years. Howbeit on the other side, Speusippus, and his other friends did provoke him unto it, and did persuade him to deliver Sicilia from the slavery and bondage of the

tyrant, the which held up her hands unto him, and would receive him with great love and goodwill. For whilst Plato lay at Syracusa, Speusippus keeping the citizens company more than Plato did, he knew their minds better than he. For at the first they were afraid to open themselves unto him, and frankly to speak what they thought, mistrusting he was a spy unto the tyrant, sent amongst them to feel their minds: but within a short time they began to trust him, and were all of one mind, for they prayed and persuaded Dion to come, and not to care otherwise for bringing of ships, soldiers nor horses with him, but only to hire a ship, and to lend the Sicilians his body and name against Dionysius. Speusippus reporting these news unto Dion, did put him in good heart again: whereupon he began secretly to levy men by other men's means, to hide his purpose and intent. The philosophers do set forward Dion's wars. Many citizens dealing in the affairs of the commonwealth did aid him, and divers of them also that only gave their minds to the study of philosophy: and among them, Eudemus Cyprian (on whose death Aristotle wrote his dialogue of the soul) and Timonides Leucadian went with him. Furthermore, there joined also with him Miltas Thessalian, a soothsayer, and that had been his companion in study in the Academy. Now of all them whom the tyrant had banished (which were no less than a thousand persons), there were but only five and twenty that durst accompany him in this war. For all the other were such dastards, that they forsook him, and durst not go with him. The place where they appointed to meet, was the Isle of Zacynthe, where they levied all their soldiers, that were not above eight hundred in all, but all of them brave soldiers, and valiant men, and excellently well trained in wars: and to conclude, such lusty men, as would encourage all the army Dion hoped of at his arrival in Sicily, to fight like valiant men with them.

23    These hired soldiers, the first time that they understood it was to go into Sicilia, to make war with Dionysius, they were amazed at the first, and misliked the journey, because it was undertaken rather of malice and spite that Dion had to be revenged, than otherwise of any good cause or quarrel, who having no better hope, took upon him desperate and impossible enterprises. Therefore the soldiers were offended with their captains that had pressed them, because they had not told them of this war before. But after

that Dion by a notable oration had told them, how tyrannies have
evil foundations, and are subject unto ruin, and that he led them
not into Sicilia so much for soldiers, as he did to make them
captains of the Syracusans, and the other Sicilians, who of long
time desired nothing more than occasion to rise. And when after
him also Alcimenes (a companion with him in this war, and the
chiefest man of all the Achaians, both for nobility and estimation)
did speak unto them in like manner, then they were all contented
to go whither they would lead them. It was then in the heart of
summer, and the wind blew called the Grecian wind, the moon
being at the full, and Dion having prepared to make a sumptuous
sacrifice unto the god Apollo, he led all his men armed with white
corselets in procession into the temple: and after the sacrifice done,
he made them a feast in the park or show place of the Zacynthians.
There the tables were laid, and the soldiers wondered to see the
great state and magnificence of the great number of pots of gold
and silver, and such other furniture and preparation as passed a
private man's wealth, then they thought with themselves, that a
man being so old, and lord of so great a good, would not attempt
things of such danger, without good ground, and great assurance of
his friends' aid and help.

24   But after his oblations of wine, and common prayers made to
the gods at feasts, suddenly the moon eclipsed. Dion thought it not
strange to see an eclipse, considering the revolutions of the eclipses,
and knowing very well it is a shadow that falleth upon the body of
the moon, because of the direct interposition of the earth betwixt
her and the sun. But because the soldiers that were afraid and
astonished withal, stood in need of some comfort and encouragement, Miltas the soothsayer standing up in the midst amongst
them, said unto them: 'My fellow soldiers, be of good cheer, and
assure yourselves that we shall prosper: for God doth foreshow us
by this sight we see, that some one of the chiefest things now in
highest place and dignity shall be eclipsed. And at this present time
what thing carrieth greater glory and fame, than the tyranny of
Dionysius? Therefore you must think, that so soon as you arrive in
Sicilia, yourselves shall put out his light and glory.' This interpretation of the eclipse of the moon, did Miltas the soothsayer
make, before all the whole company. But touching the swarm of

bees that lighted on the poop of Dion's ship, he told him and his friends privately, that he was afraid his acts which should fall out famous and glorious, should last but a while, and flourishing a few days, would straight consume away. It is reported also, that Dionysius in like manner had many strange signs and wonderful tokens from above. Among others, there came an eagle that snatched the partisan out of the soldiers' hands, and carried it quite away with her, and then let it fall into the sea. The sea also beating against the walls of the castle, was as sweet to drink a whole day together, as any conduit or running water: as those that tasted of it, found it true. Furthermore, a sow farrowed pigs that lacked no parts of the body, but only their ears. This the soothsayers said did signify rebellion, and disobedience of his subjects: and that the citizens would no more hear him, nor obey his tyranny. Furthermore, they told also, that the sweetness of the salt water prognosticated to the Syracusans, change of cruel and evil time unto good and civil government: and that the eagle, Jupiter's minister, and the partisan, the mark and token of the kingdom and empire, did betoken that Jupiter the chief of all gods had determined to destroy and put down the tyranny. Theopompus reporteth this matter thus.

25   So Dion's soldiers were embarked into two great ships of burden, and another third ship that was not very great, and two pinnaces with thirty oars followed them. For their armour and weapon, beside those the soldiers had, he carried two thousand targets, a great number of bows and arrows, of darts, of pikes, and plenty of victuals: that they should lack nothing all the time they were upon the sea, considering that their journey stood altogether at the courtesy of the winds and sea, and for that they were afraid to land, understanding that Philistus rode at anchor in the coast of Apulglia, with a fleet of ships that lay in wait for their coming. So having a pleasant gale of wind, they sailed the space of twelve days together, and the thirteen day they came to the foreland of Sicilia called Pachynus. There the pilot thought it best they should land presently: for if they willingly luffed into the sea, and lost that point, they were sure they should lose also many nights and days in vain in the midst of the sea, being then summer time, and the wind at the south. But Dion being afraid to land so near his enemies,

he was desirous to go further, and so passed by the foreland of
Pachynus. Then the north wind rose so big and great, that with
great violence it drove back their ships from the coast of Sicilia.
Furthermore, lightning and thunder mingled withal (because it
was at that time when the star Arcturus beginneth to show) it made
so terrible a tempest, and poured down such a sore shower of rain
upon them, that all the mariners were amazed withal, and knew
not whither the wind would drive them: till that suddenly they saw
the storm had cast them upon the Isle of Cercina (which is on the
coast of Libya), and specially where it is most dangerous to arrive
for the rocks, for their ships were like to have run upon them, and
to have made shipwreck. But with much ado they bore off the
ships with the great long poles, and wandered up and down the sea,
not knowing whither they went, until the storm ceased. Then they
met a ship, whereby they knew that they were in the flat, which
the mariners call the heads of the great Syrte. Thus they wandering
up and down, being marvellous angry that the sea was calm, there
rose a little South wind from the land, although they least looked
for any such wind at that time, and little thinking it would so have
changed: but seeing the wind rise bigger and bigger, they packed
on all the sails they had, and making their prayers unto the gods
they crossed the sea, and sailed from the coast of Libya directly
unto Sicily, and had the wind so lucky, that at the fifth day they
were near unto a little village of Sicilia, called Minoa, the which
was subject to the Carthaginians. Synalus Carthaginian, being at
that time captain and governor of the town of Minoa, and Dion's
friend, was there by chance at that present, who being ignorant of
his enterprise and coming, did what he could to keep Dion's
soldiers from landing. But they notwithstanding suddenly leapt a-
land armed, but slew no man. For Dion had commanded them the
contrary, for the friendship he bore the captain: and they following
the townsmen hard that fled before them, entered the town, hand
over head amongst them, and so won the market-place. When
both the captains met, and that they had spoken together, Dion
redelivered the town into Synalus' hands again, without any hurt
or violence offered him. Synalus on the other side did endeavour
himself all he could to make much of the soldiers, and help Dion to
provide him of all things necessary.

26 But this did most of all encourage the soldiers, because Dionysius at their arrival, was not then in Sicilia: for it chanced so, that not many days before he went into Italy, with four score sail. Therefore when Dion willed them to remain there a few days to refresh themselves, because they had been so sore seabeaten a long time together, they themselves would not, they were so glad to embrace the occasion offered them, and prayed Dion to lead them forthwith to Syracusa. Dion leaving all his superfluous armour and provision in the hands of Synalus, and praying him to send them to him when time served, he took his way towards Syracusa. So by the way, two hundred horsemen of the Agrigentines, which dwell in that part called Ecnomus, came first to join with him, and after them, the Geloians. The rumour of their coming ran straight to Syracusa. Thereupon Timocrates that had married Arete, Dion's wife and Dionysius the father's sister, and unto whom Dionysius the younger had left the charge and government of all his men and friends in the city, he presently dispatched a post with letters, to advertise Dionysius of Dion's coming. He himself also in the meantime had taken such order, that there rose no tumult nor mutiny in the city, though they all of them lacked no goodwill to rebel: but because they were uncertain whether this rumour was true or false, being afraid, every man was quiet. Now there chanced a strange misfortune unto the messenger, that carried the letters unto Dionysius. For after he had passed the strait, and that he was arrived in the city of Rheggio of Italy's side, making haste to come to the city of Caulonia, where Dionysius was, he met by the way one of his acquaintance that carried a mutton but newly sacrificed. This good fellow gave him a piece of it, and the messenger spurred away with all the speed he could possible. But when he had ridden the most part of the night, he was so weary and drowsy for lack of sleep, that he was driven to lie down. So he lay down upon the ground, in a wood hard by the highway. The savour of this flesh brought a wolf to him, that carried away the flesh and the portmanteau it was wrapped in, and in the which also were his letters of advertisement, which he carried unto Dionysius. When he awoke out of his sleep, and saw that his portmanteau was gone, he enquired for it, and went wandering up and down a long time to seek it: howbeit all in vain, for he could never find it. Therefore he thought it was not good for him to go to the tyrant

without his letters, but rather to flee into some unknown place where nobody knew him.

27 Thus overlate received Dionysius advertisement by others of this war, which Dion made in Sicilia. In the meantime, the Camarinians came and joined with Dion's army, in the highway towards Syracusa: and still there came unto him also a great number of the Syracusans that were up in arms, which were got into the field. On the other side, certain Campanians and Leontines, which were got into the castle of Epipoles with Timocrates, of purpose to keep it, upon a false rumour Dion gave out (and which came unto them) that he would first go against their towns, they forsook Timocrates, and went to take order to defend their own goods. Dion understanding that, being lodged with his army in a place called Macrae, he presently removed his camp being dark night, and marched forward till he came unto the river of Anapus, which is not from the city above ten furlongs off: and there staying a while, he sacrificed unto the river, and made his prayer, and worshipped the rising of the sun. At the selfsame instant also, the soothsayers came and told him, that the gods did promise him assured victory. And the soldiers also seeing Dion wear a garland of flowers on his head, which he had taken for the ceremony of the sacrifice: all of them with one self goodwill, took every man one of them (being no less than five thousand men that were gathered together by the way, and but slenderly armed with such things as came first to hand, howbeit supplying with goodwill their want of better furniture and armour), and when Dion commanded them to march, for joy they ran, and encouraged one another with great cries, to show themselves valiant for recovery of their liberty.

28 Now for them that were within the city self of Syracusa, the noblemen and chief citizens went to receive them at the gates in their best gowns. The common people on the other side ran and set upon them that took part with the tyrant, and spoiled them that were called the *prosagogides* (as much to say, the common promoters of men), the detestablest villains, hateful to the gods and men. For they like sycophants and busy tale bearers, would jet up and down the city, and mingle among the citizens, having an ear in every man's matter, being full of prittle prattle, and busy-headed, to know

what every man said and did, and then to go carry it to the tyrant. These men were they that had their payment first of all, for they killed them with dry blows, beating them to death with staves. When Timocrates could not enter into the castle with them that kept it, he took his horseback, and fled out of the city, and flying made all men afraid and amazed where he came, enlarging Dion's power by his report, because it should not seem that for fear of a trifle, he had forsaken the city. In the meantime, Dion came on towards the city with his men, and was come so near, that they might see him plainly from the city, marching foremost of all, armed with a fair bright white corselet, having his brother Megacles on his right hand of him, and Callippus Athenian on the left hand, crowned with garlands of flowers: and after him also there followed a hundred soldiers that were strangers, chosen for his guard about him, and the rest came marching after in good order of battle, being led by their captains. The Syracusans saw him coming, and went out and received him as a holy and blessed procession, that brought them their liberty and popular state again, the which they had lost the space of eight and forty years.

29   When Dion was come into the city by the gate called Menitide, he caused his trumpeter sound to appease the rumour and tumult of the people. Then he commanded a herald to proclaim aloud, that Dion and Megacles, who were come to put down the tyranny, did set all the Syracusans at liberty, and all the other Sicilians also, from the bondage and subjection of the tyrant: and because Dion himself was desirous to speak unto the people, he went to the upper part of the town called Acradina. The Syracusans all the streets thorough as he passed by, had on either hand of him prepared sacrifices, and set up tables, and cups upon them: and as he passed by their houses, they cast flowers and fruits on him, and made prayers unto him, as if he had been a god. Now under the castle there was a place called Pentapyla, a clock to know by the sun how the day went, the which Dionysius had caused to be made, and it was of a good pretty height. Dion got up upon it, and from thence made his oration to the people that were gathered round about him, exhorting and persuading his countrymen to do their endeavour to recover their liberty again, and to maintain it. They being in a marvellous joy withal, and desirous to please Dion,

did choose him and his brother Megacles their lieutenants general, with absolute power and authority. Afterwards also, by the consent of Dion himself and his brother, and at their requests in like manner, they chose twenty other captains, of the which the most part of them had been banished by the tyrant, and were returned again with Dion. The soothsayers and prognosticators liked it well, and said it was a good sign for Dion, that he trod that sumptuous building and workmanship of the tyrant under his feet, when he made his oration: but because the hand of the dial did show the course of the sun, which never leaveth going, upon the which he got up when he was chosen lieutenant general with absolute power and authority, they were afraid again, that it was a sign Dion's affairs should have a sudden change of fortune. After this, Dion having taken the castle of Epipoles, he set all the citizens at liberty which were kept there as prisoners in captivity by the tyrant, and environed the castle round about with a wall. Within seven days after, Dionysius returned by sea to the castle of Syracusa, and therewithal also came the carts laden with armour and weapon to Syracusa, the which Dion had left with Synalus: the which Dion caused to be distributed among the citizens of Syracusa that had none. Others did furnish themselves as well as they could, and showed that they had courage and goodwill to fight for the maintenance and defence of their liberty.

30 In the meantime, Dionysius sent ambassadors, first unto Dion privately, to see if he would yield to any composition. But Dion would not hear them, but bade them tell the Syracusans openly what they had to say, being men that were free, and enjoyed liberty. Then the ambassadors spoke in the behalf of the tyrant, unto the people of Syracusa, promising them with mild and gentle words, that they should pay no more subsidies and taxes, but very little, and should be no more troubled with wars, other than such as they themselves should like of. The Syracusans made a mockery at those offers, and Dion also answered the ambassadors, and willed Dionysius to send no more to the Syracusans, before he had dispossessed himself of his tyranny: and so that he would leave it, he would be his mean to obtain all things just and reasonable of the people. Dionysius liked very well of this good offer, and therefore sent his ambassadors again to pray the Syracusans that they would

appoint some amongst them to come to the castle, to talk with him for the benefit and commodity of the commonwealth, that he might hear what they would allege, and they also what answer he would make. Dion chose certain whom he sent unto him. Now there ran a rumour in the city among the Syracusans, which came from the castle: that Dionysius would willingly of himself, rather than by reason of Dion's coming, depose himself of the tyranny. But this was but a false alarm, and crafty fetch of Dionysius, to entrap the Syracusans by. For those that were sent him from the city, he kept them prisoners every man of them: and one morning having made his soldiers drink wine lustily, which he kept in pay to guard his person, he sent them with great fury to assault the wall the Syracusans had built against the castle. Now, because the Syracusans looked for nothing less than for the sudden assault, and for that these barbarous people with a wonderful courage and great tumult overthrew the wall, and others of them also did set upon the Syracusans, there was not a man of them that durst make head to fight with them, saving the soldiers that were strangers, whom Dion had brought with him. Who, when they heard the noise, ran straight to repulse them, and yet they themselves could not well tell what they should do upon that sudden. For they could hear nothing, for the great noise and hurly burly of the Syracusans which fled with great disorder, and came and mingled themselves amongst them. Till at length, Dion perceiving he could not be heard, to show them by deed what they should do, he went first himself against these barbarous people, and about him there was a cruel and bloody fight. For his enemies knew him as well as his own men, and they all ran upon him with great cries. Now for Dion himself, indeed because of his age, he was heavier than was requisite for one that should away with the pains of such battles: but he had such a valiant courage in him, that he went thorough withal lustily, and slew them that did assail him. Yet he had his hand also thrust thorough with a pike, and very hardly did his cuirasses hold out the blows of the darts and thrusts by hand which he received on them, they were so mangled and hacked with such a number of darts and pikes passed thorough his shield and broken on him, that in the end he was beaten down: howbeit his soldiers rescued him straight. Then he made Timonides their captain, and he himself took his horseback, and went up and down the city,

staying and quieting the flying of the Syracusans. Then he sent
for his soldiers the strangers, which he had put in garrison in that
part of the city called the Acradine to keep it, and brought them
being fresh, against the barbarous people of the castle that were
wearied, and almost all of them discouraged to attempt any further
enterprise. For they had made this sally out, in hope to have taken
all the city at the first onset, only running up and down: but when
contrary to their expectation, they met these valiant soldiers and
fresh supply, they then began to retire again unto the castle. And
the Grecian soldiers on the other side, perceiving they gave back,
they came the faster upon them, so that they were compelled to
turn their backs, and were driven within their walls, after they had
slain three score and fourteen of Dion's men, and lost a great
number of their own.

31 This was a noble victory, and therefore the Syracusans gave
the soldiers that were strangers, an hundred silver minas, in reward
for their good service: and they gave Dion their general, a crown of
gold. After this, there came letters to Dion by a trumpet from the
castle, written from the women of his house: and among the packet
of letters, there was one of them directed 'To my father': the which
Hipparinus wrote unto him. For that was Dion's son's name,
though Timaeus writeth he was called Areteus, after his mother's
name Areta. But in such matters, methinks Timonides is better to
be credited, because he was his friend and companion in arms.
All the other letters that were sent, were openly read before the
assembly of the Syracusans, and did only concern requests of these
women unto Dion. The Syracusans would not have the supposed
letter of his son to be openly read: but Dion against their minds
opened it, and found that it was Dionysius' letter, who by words
made the direction of it unto Dion, but in effect he spoke unto
the Syracusans. For in sight, it seemed a manner of request and
justification of himself: but in truth, it was written of purpose to
accuse Dion. First of all he remembered him of the things he had
done before, for the establishing and preservation of the tyranny:
and afterwards of cruel threats against those whom he should love
best, as his wife, his son and sister: and last of all, full of most
humble requests and entreaties with sorrow and lamentation. But
that which most moved Dion of all other was, that he required him

not to destroy the tyranny, but rather to take it for himself, and not to set them at liberty that hated him, and would always remember the mischief he had done unto them: and that he would himself take upon him to be lord, saving by that means the lives of his parents and friends.

32 When these letters had been read before the whole assembly of the people, the Syracusans thought not how to reverence (as they ought) with admiration, the inflexible constancy and magnanimity of Dion, that stood firm and fast for justice and virtue, against such vehement entreaty and persuasion of his kinsfolk and friends: but they contrarily began to be afraid, and to mistrust him, as he that of necessity should be forced to pardon the tyrant, for the great pledges and hostages he had of him. Wherefore, they began to choose them new governors, and the rather, because they heard that Heraclides was coming unto them, whom they loved singularly well. This Heraclides was one of them that had been banished, a good soldier and captain, and well esteemed of for the charge and office he bore under the tyrants: howbeit a very inconstant man in everything, and would not continue long in a mind, and least constant in wars, where he had great charge of honour in hand. He had fallen out with Dion in Peloponnesus, wherefore he determined to come with a power by himself, and with his own fleet against the tyrant. So he arrived at length at Syracusa, with seven galleys, and three other ships, where he found Dionysius again shut up into his castle with a wall, and the Syracusans also to have the better hand of him. Then he began to curry favour with the common people all the ways he could possibly devise, having by nature a certain pleasing manner to win the common people, which seek nothing else but to be flattered. Furthermore, he found it the easier for him to win them, because the people did already mislike Dion's severity, as a man too severe and cruel to govern a commonwealth. For they had now their will so much, and were grown so strong-headed, because they saw themselves the stronger, that they would be flattered (as commonly the people be in free cities, where they only be lords, and do rule) before they were fully set at liberty.

33 Therefore first of all, not being called together by the authority of the governors, they all ran in a fury, of their own light heads, unto the place of common assemblies, and there chose Heraclides

admiral. Then Dion understanding this, came to complain of the injury they had done him, declaring unto them, that to give this power now unto Heraclides, was to take that away which they had first given unto him: because he should no more be general, if they chose any other admiral by sea than himself. The Syracusans then, as it were against their wills, did revoke the power they had given unto Heraclides: but afterwards Dion sent for Heraclides, to pray him to come home to him. When he came, he rebuked him a little, and told him that it was not honestly nor profitably done of him, to sue to the people, and to contend for honour against him in so dangerous a time, when the least occasion in the world was enough to have marred all. Afterwards Dion himself called an assembly again of the city, and established Heraclides admiral: and persuaded the citizens to give him soldiers, as he had indeed. Heraclides outwardly seemed to honour Dion, and confessed openly that he was greatly bound unto him, and was always at his heels very lowly, being ready at his commandment: but in the meantime, secretly he enticed the common people to rebel, and to stir up those whom he knew meet men to like of change. Whereby he procured Dion such trouble, and brought him into such perplexity, that he knew not well what way to take. For if he gave them advice to let Dionysius quietly come out of the castle, then they accused him, and said he did it to save his life. If on the other side, because he would not trouble them, he continued siege still, and did establish nothing, then they thought he did it of purpose to draw out the wars in length, because he might the longer time remain their chieftain general, and so to keep the citizens longer in fear.

34 At that time there was one Sosis in Syracusa, a man of no name, but noted among the Syracusans for his villainy and wickedness, esteeming that full and ample liberty, when he might unchecked licentiously speak what he would, as indeed he did. For he seeking to do Dion a displeasure, first of all one day at a common council he stood up on his feet, and called the Syracusans beasts (amongst many other vile words he gave them) if they did not perceive, that being come from a fond and drunken tyranny, they had now received a sober master, and a wise and ware tyrant. So when he had thus openly showed himself an enemy unto Dion, he came no more that day into the market-place: but the next morning he was seen

running up and down the city naked, his head and face all of agore blood, as if he had been followed by men to have slain him. Thus Sosis coming in this manner into the midst of the market-place, cried out, that Dion's strangers had lain in wait for him, and had handled him in this sort, showing his wound on his head. Many of the people took this matter very grievously, and cried out upon Dion, and said it was vilely and tyrannically done of him, by fear of murder and danger, to take away the liberty from the citizens to speak. Now though the whole assembly hereupon fell into an uproar withal, Dion notwithstanding came thither to clear himself of these accusations, and made them presently see, that this Sosis was brother to one of Dionysius' guard: who had put into his head, in this sort to put the city of Syracusa in an uproar, because Dionysius had no other hope nor means to escape, but by stirring up faction and sedition among them, to make one of them fall out with another. The surgeons were sent for forthwith to search the wound of this Sosis: who found that it was rather a little scratch, than any violent wound given him. For the wounds or cuts of a sword, are ever deepest in the midst: and Sosis' cut was but very little, and not deep, having had many beginnings, and given him (as it seemed) at sundry times, that for very pain the party that cut him was driven to leave off, and so came to cut him at divers times. Furthermore, there came certain of his friends in the meantime, that brought a razor before the assembly, and reported that as they came, they met Sosis by the way all bloodied: who said, that he fled from Dion's soldiers, which had but newly hurt him. Whereupon they presently followed them, but found no man, and only they saw a razor, which somebody had cast upon a hollow stone thereabout, where they first saw him coming unto them.

35 Thus Sosis' devise had but evil success. For beside all these proofs and tokens, Dion's household servants came to be a witness against him that very early in the morning he went abroad alone with a razor in his hand. Then they that before did burden and accuse Dion, knew not what to say to the matter, but shrunk away: whereupon the people condemning Sosis to death, they were quiet again with Dion. Yet were they always afraid of these soldiers that were strangers, specially when they saw the greatest conflicts they had with the tyrant, was by sea, after that Philistus was come from

the coast of Apuglia with a great number of galleys to aid the tyrant. For then they thought, that these soldiers the strangers being armed at all parts to fight by land, they would do them no more service by sea, because the citizens themselves were they that kept them in safety, for that they were men practised to fight by sea, and were also the stronger by means of their ships. But beside all this, the only thing that made them to be courageous again, was the good fortune they had at the battle by sea, in the which when they had overcome Philistus, they cruelly and barbarously used him. Truly Ephorus saith, that Philistus slew himself, when he saw his galley taken. Howbeit Timonides (who was always with Dion from the first beginning of this war) writing unto Speusippus the philosopher, saith that Philistus was taken alive, because his galley ran a-land: and that the Syracusans first took off his cuirasses, and stripped him naked, and after they had done him all the villainy and spite they could, they cut off his head, and gave his body unto boys, commanding them to drag it into that part of the city called Acradine, and then to cast it into the common privy. Timaeus also to spite him the more, saith that the boys tied the dead body by his lame leg, and so dragged him up and down the city, where all the Syracusans did what villainy to it they could, being glad to see him dragged by the leg, that had said Dionysius should not flee from the tyranny upon a light horse, but that they should pull him out by the leg against his will. Now Philistus reporteth this matter thus, not as spoken to Dionysius by himself, but by some other.

36 But Timaeus taking a just occasion and colour to speak evil of the goodwill, fidelity, and care that Philistus had always seemed to show in the confirmation and defence of the tyranny, doth liberally bestow injurious words on him in this place. Now for them whom he had indeed offended, if they of malice and spite to be revenged, did offer him cruelty, peradventure they were not much to be blamed: but for them that since his death have written the jests, who were never offended by him in his lifetime, and who ought to show themselves discreet in their writing, methinks that if they had regarded their own credit and estimation, they should not so fondly and outrageously have reproved the adversities and misfortunes, which by fortune may as well chance to the honestest man, as unto him. Thus fondly doth Ephorus praise Philistus, who though he

have an excellent fine wit to counterfeit goodly excuses, and cunningly to hide wicked and dishonest parts, and eloquently to devise by honest words to defend an evil cause, yet cannot he with all the five wits he hath excuse himself, that he hath not been the only man of the world that hath most favoured tyrants, and that hath ever loved and specially desired power, wealth, and alliance with tyrants. But he in my opinion taketh the right course of an historiographer, that neither doth commend Philistus' doings, nor yet casteth his adversities in his teeth to his reproach.

37    After Philistus' death, Dionysius sent unto Dion, to make him an offer to deliver him the castle, armour, munition, and soldiers that were in it, with money also to pay them for five months' space. For himself, he prayed that he might be suffered to go safely into Italy, and to lie there, to take the pleasure of the fruits of the country called Gyarta, which was within the territory of Syracusa, and lieth out from the sea towards the mainland. Dion refused this offer, and answered the ambassadors that they must move the Syracusans in it. They supposing they should easily take Dionysius alive, would not hear the ambassadors speak, but turned them away. Dionysius seeing no other remedy, left the castle in the hands of his eldest son Apollocrates, and having a lusty gale of wind, he secretly embarked certain of his men he loved best, with the richest things he had, and so hoist sail, unawares to Heraclides, the admiral of Syracusa. The people were marvellously offended with Heraclides for it, and began to mutiny against him. But Heraclides, to pacify this tumult of the people suborned one Hippon an orator, who preferred the law *agraria* unto the people, for the division of all the island amongst them: and that the beginning of liberty was equality, and of bondage poverty, unto them that had no lands. Heraclides giving his consent to this decree, and stirring the common people to sedition against Dion, that withstood it, persuaded the Syracusans not only to confirm the law Hippon had propounded, but also to discharge the hired strangers, to choose other captains and governors, and to rid themselves of Dion's severe government. But they supposing straight to have been rid from the tyranny, as from a long and grievous sickness, overrashly taking upon them like people that of long time had been at liberty, they utterly undid themselves, and

overthrew Dion's purpose: who like a good physician was careful to see the city well ordered and governed.

38 So when they were assembled to choose new officers in the midst of summer, there fell such horrible thunders, and other terrible storms and unfortunate signs in the element, that for the space of fifteen days together, the people were still scattered and dispersed when they were assembled: insomuch, that being afraid of these signs above, they durst not at that time create any new captains. Certain days after, as the orators had chosen a fair time to proceed to the election of officers, an ox drawing in a cart (being daily acquainted with every sight and noise) suddenly without any occasion offered, fell into a madness against the carter that drove him, and breaking his yoke asunder, ran straight to the theatre, and there made the people run into every corner, to fly and save themselves: and then flinging and bearing all down before him that stood in his way, he ran through as much of the city as the enemies afterwards won of them. This notwithstanding, the Syracusans making light account of all these signs, they chose five and twenty captains, of the which Heraclides was one: and secretly they sent to feel the hired soldiers, to see if they could entice them from Dion, to cause them to take their part, and made them large promises to make them free men, as themselves, of Syracusa. The soldiers would not be enticed from him, but faithfully and lovingly took Dion amongst them with their armour and weapon, and putting him in the midst of them, led him in this manner out of the city, and did no man hurt, but reproving their unthankfulness and villainy unto all those they met by the way. Then the Syracusans despising them for their small number, and because they did not first set upon them, but trusting on the other side to themselves for that they were the greater number, they came to assail them, supposing they should easily overcome them in the city, and kill every man of them.

39 Dion being thus at a strait, that of necessity he must fight against his own countrymen, or else be slain himself with his soldiers, he held up his hands to the Syracusans and very earnestly prayed them to be content, pointing them with his finger to the castle that was full of their enemies, which showed themselves upon the walls, and saw what they did. In the end, when he saw

that he could not pacify their fury and tumult, and that all the city
was in an uproar with the prittle prattle of these seditious people,
who like the sea were carried with the wind, he did yet forbid his
soldiers to give any charge upon them, who notwithstanding made
a countenance with great cries, and rattling of their harness, as if
they had meant to run on them. Then the Syracusans durst not
abide by it, but ran away like sheep through the streets, and no man
chased them. So Dion called back his men again, and led them
directly into the country of the Leontines. Then the new officers
and governors of Syracusa, perceiving that the women laughed
them to scorn, because they would recover the shame they had
lost, they armed their men anew again, and did march after Dion to
fight with him, whom they overtook at a river, as he was ready to
pass over. Then began their horsemen a little to skirmish with
Dion's company. But when they saw he did no more bear with
their faults for country's sake, but frowned indeed upon them, and
did set his men in battle ray against them, then they turned their
backs again, with more shame and reproach than before, and so
fled unto the city of Syracusa, and had not many of their men slain.

40    The Leontines received Dion very honourably, took the
strangers his soldiers, and gave them pay, and made them free
citizens with them: and sent ambassadors also unto the Syracusans,
to will them to let the strangers have their pay. The Syracusans on
their side also, sent ambassadors unto the Leontines to accuse Dion.
So all their confederates were assembled in the city of the Leontines, and in that assembly, after both parties had been heard,
to hear what they would say, it was judged that the Syracusans
were to blame. Howbeit they would not stand to the judgment of
their confederates, for they were now grown proud and careless,
because they were governed by no man, but had captains that
studied to please them, and were afraid also to displease them.

41    After that, there arrived certain galleys of Dionysius at Syracusa, of the which Nypsius Neapolitan was captain: which brought
victuals and money, to help them that were besieged within the
castle. These galleys were fought with, and the Syracusans obtained
victory, and took four of the tyrant's galleys with three banks of
oars apiece: howbeit they fondly abused their victory. For they
having nobody to command nor rule them, employed all their joy

in rioting and banqueting, and in fond and dissolute meetings, taking so little care and regard to their business, that now when they thought the castle was sure their own, they almost lost their city. For Nypsius perceiving that every part of the city was out of order, and that the common people did nothing all day long unto dark night, but bib and drink drunk, dancing after their pipes and hautboys, and that the governors themselves were very glad also to see such feasting, or else for that they dissembled it, and durst not command and compel them that were drunk, he wisely took the occasion offered him, and scaled the wall which had shut up the castle, and won it, and overthrew it. Then he sent the barbarous soldiers into the city, and commanded them to do with them they met, what they would or could. The Syracusans then too late found their fault, and hardly gave present remedy, they were so amazed and suddenly set on: for indeed they made a right sack of the city. Here men were killed, there they overthrew the wall, in another place they carried away women and little children prisoners into the castle, weeping and crying out: and lastly, they made the captains at their wits' end, who could give no present order, nor have their men to serve them against their enemies, that came hand over head on every side amongst them.

42    The city being thus miserably in garboyle, and the Acradine also in great hazard of taking, in the which they put all their hope and confidence to rise again, every man thought then with himself that Dion must be sent for, but yet no man moved it notwithstanding, being ashamed of their unthankfulness and overgreat folly they had committed, in driving him away. Yet necessity enforcing them unto it, there were certain of the horsemen and of their confederates that cried, they must send for Dion, and the Peloponnesians his soldiers, which were with him in the territory of the Leontines. As soon as the first word was heard, and that one had the heart to tell it to the people, all the Syracusans cried out, there was the point: and they were so glad of it, that the water stood in their eyes for joy, and besought the gods it would please them to bring him unto them, they were so desirous to have him again. For they called to mind how valiant and resolute he was in danger, and how that he was never afraid, but did encourage them with his manhood in such sort, that being led by him, they were

not afraid to set upon their enemies. So the confederates for them sent presently Archonides and Telesides unto him: and the noblemen that served on horseback, they sent him also five amongst them, beside Hellanicus. Who took their horses, and posted for life, so that they came to the city of the Leontines about sunset, and lighting from their horses, they went first of all and kneeled down at Dion's feet, and weeping, told him the miserable state of the Syracusans. Straight there came divers of the Leontines, and many of the Peloponnesian soldiers unto Dion, mistrusting then that there was some news in hand, to see the earnest and humble suit the ambassadors of Syracusa made unto him. Wherefore Dion took them presently with him, and brought them himself unto the theatre, where the common councils and assemblies of the city were held. Thither ran every man to hear what the matter was. Then Archonides and Hellanicus brought in by Dion, told openly before the whole assembly, the greatness of their misery, and requested the hired soldiers to come and aid the Syracusans, forgetting the injury they had received: considering that they had more dearly paid for their folly, than they themselves whom they had so injured, would have made them to have suffered.

43    When they had said their minds, there was a great silence through all the theatre: and then Dion rose up, and began to speak. But the great tears that fell from his eyes would not suffer him to speak: wherefore the hired soldiers being sorry to see him weep, prayed him not to trouble himself, but to be of good courage. Then Dion letting go the sorrow and grief he had conceived, he began to speak unto them in this manner: 'My lords of Peloponnesus, and you also the confederates, I have called you together to consult with you, what you should do. For myself, it were no honesty for me to consult what I should do now, when the city of Syracusa standeth in peril of destruction: and therefore if I cannot save it from destruction, yet at the least I will bury myself in the fire and ruin of my country. But for you, if it please you once more to help us, unadvised and more unfortunate people, you shall by your means set the poor distressed city of Syracusa again afoot, which is your deed. Or if it be so, that remembering the injuries the Syracusans have offered you, you will suffer it to be destroyed: yet I beseech the gods that at the least they will requite your valiantness, fidelity,

and good love you have borne me until this present, beseeching you to remember Dion, who neither forsook you at any time when you have been injured, nor his countrymen, when they were in trouble.' So, going on still with his tale, the mercenary strangers stepped forth with great noise, and prayed him to lead them to aid Syracusa. Then the ambassadors also that were sent from the Syracusans, saluted and embraced them, and prayed the gods to bless Dion and them, with all the good hap that might be. So when all was whisht and quiet, Dion willed them forthwith to go and prepare themselves, and that they should be there ready armed after supper, determining the very same night to go to aid Syracusa.

44 But now at Syracusa, while daylight lasted, Dionysius' soldier and captains did all the mischief and villainy they could in the city: and when night came, they retired again into their castle, having lost very few of their men. Then the seditious governors of the Syracusans took heart again unto them, hoping that the enemies would be contented with that they had done: and therefore began anew to persuade the citizens to let Dion alone, and not to receive him with his mercenary soldiers if they came to aid him, saying, that they themselves were honester men than the strangers, to save their city, and to defend their liberty without help of any other. So other ambassadors were sent again unto Dion, some from the captains and governors of the city, to stay them that they should not come: and others also from the horsemen, and noble citizens his friends, to hasten his journey. Whereupon by reason of this variance, Dion marched very softly at his ease. Now by night, Dion's enemies within the city got to the gates, and kept them that Dion should not come in. Nypsius on the other side made a sally out of the castle with his mercenary soldiers, being better appointed, and a greater number of them than before: and with them he straight plucked down all the wall which they had built before the castle, and ran and sacked the city. At this sally out of the castle they did not only kill the men they met, but women and little children also, and stayed no more to spoil, but to destroy and put all to havoc. For, because Dionysius saw that he was brought to a strait and desperate case, he bore such mortal malice against the Syracusans, that if there was no remedy but that he must needs forgo his tyranny, he determined to bury it with the utter destruction and desolation of their city. And

therefore, to prevent Dion's aid, and to make a quick dispatch to destroy all, they came with burning torches in their hands, and did set fire of all things they could come to: and further off, they fired their darts and arrows, and bestowed them in every place of the city. So, they that fled for the fire, were met withal, and slain in the streets by the soldiers, and others also that ran into their houses, were driven out again by force of fire. For there were a number of houses that were afire, and fell down upon them that went and came.

45   This misery was the chiefest cause why all the Syracusans agreed together, to set open the gates unto Dion. For when Dion heard by the way, that Dionysius' soldiers were gone again into the castle, he made no great haste to march forward: but when day was broken, there came certain horsemen from Syracusa unto Dion, who brought him news that the enemies had once again taken the city. Then also came other of his enemies unto him, and prayed him to make haste. Now their misery increasing still, and they being brought into hard state, Heraclides first sent his brother unto Dion, and then Theodotes his uncle, to pray him to come quickly, and help them. For now there was no man left to resist the enemies, because he himself was hurt, and the city also was in manner clean burnt and destroyed. When these news came to Dion, he was yet about three score furlong from the town. So he told his mercenary soldiers the danger the town was in, and having encouraged them, he led them no more fair and softly, but running towards the city, and meeting messengers one of another's neck as he went, that prayed him to make all the possible speed he could. By this means, the soldiers marching with wonderful speed and goodwill together, he entered the gates of the city at a place called Hecatompedon. First of all, he sent the lightest armed he had against the enemies, to the end that the Syracusans seeing them, they might take a good heart again to them: whilst he himself in the meantime did set all the other heavy-armed soldiers and citizens that came to join with him, in battle ray, and did cast them into divers squadrons, of greater length than breadth, and appointed them that should have the leading of them, to the end that setting upon the enemies in divers places together, they should put them in the greater fear and terror.

46   When he had set all things in this order, and had made his
prayers unto the gods, and that they saw him marching through the
city against their enemies, then there rose such a common noise
and rejoicing, and great shout of the soldiers, mingled with vows,
prayers, and persuasions of all the Syracusans, that they called Dion
their god and saviour, and the mercenary soldiers their brethren
and fellow citizens. Furthermore, there was not a Syracusan that so
much regarded his own life and person, but he seemed to be more
afraid of the loss of Dion only, than of all the rest. For they saw him
the foremost man running through the danger of the fire, treading
in blood, and upon dead bodies that lay slain in the midst of the
streets. Now indeed to charge the enemies, it was a marvellous
dangerous enterprise: for they were like mad beasts, and stood
beside in battle ray along the wall which they had overthrown, in
a very dangerous place, and hard to win. Howbeit the danger of
the fire did most of all trouble and amaze the strangers, and did stop
their way. For, on which side soever they turned them, the houses
round about them were all of a fire, and they were driven to march
over the burnt timber of the houses, and to run in great danger of
the walls of the house sides that fell on them, and to pass through
the thick smoke mingled with dust, and beside, to keep their ranks
with great difficulty. And when they came to assail the enemies,
they could not come to fight hand to hand, but a few of them
in number, because of the straitness of the place: howbeit the
Syracusans with force of cries and shouts did so animate and
encourage their men, that at length they drove Nypsius and his
men to forsake the place. The most part of them got into the castle,
being very near unto them: the other that could not get in in time,
fled straggling up and down, whom the Grecian soldiers slew,
chasing of them. The extremity of the time did not presently suffer
the conquerors to reap the fruit of their victory, neither the joys
and embracings meet for so great an exploit. For the Syracusans
went every man home to his own house, to quench the fire, the
which could scarcely be put out all the night.

47   When day broke, there was none of these seditious flatterers
of the people that durst tarry in the city, but condemning themselves, they fled to take their fortune. Heraclides and Theodotes
came together of their own goodwills to yield themselves unto

Dion, confessing that they had done him wrong, and humbly praying him to show himself better unto them, than they had showed themselves unto him: and that it was more honourable for him, being every way unmatchable for his virtues, to show himself more noble to conquer his anger, than his unthankful enemies had done: who contending with him before in virtue, did now confess themselves to be far inferior unto him. This was the sum and effect of Heraclides' and Theodotes' submission unto Dion. But his friends did persuade him not to pardon two such wicked men, who did malice and envy his honour: and as he would do the strangers his soldiers any pleasure, that he should put Heraclides into their hands, to root out of the commonwealth of Syracusa his vile manner to flatter and curry favour with the people, the which was as dangerous and great a plague to a city, as the tyranny. Dion pacifying them, answered: 'Other generals of armies,' said he, 'do employ all their wits in martial exercise and wars': but for himself, that he had of long time studied, and learned in the school of the Academy, to overcome anger, envy, and all malice and contention. The noble proof whereof is most seen, not in using honest men and his friends moderately, but showing mercy also unto his enemies, and forgetting his anger against them that have offended him: and that for his part, he had rather overcome Heraclides, not in riches and wisdom, but in clemency and justice, for therein chiefly consisted excellency, since no man else in wars can challenge power and government, but fortune, that ruleth most. 'And though Heraclides,' said he, 'through envy hath done like a wicked man, must Dion therefore through anger blemish his virtue? Indeed by man's law it is thought meeter, to revenge an injury offered, than to do an injury: but nature showeth, that they both proceed of one self imperfection. Now, though it be a hard thing to change and alter the evil disposition of a man, after he is once nuseled in villainy, yet is not man of so wild and brutish a nature, that his wickedness may not be overcome with often pleasures, when he seeth that they are continually showed him.'

48   Dion answering his friends thus, he forgave Heraclides, and beginning again to shut up the castle with a wall round about, he commanded the Syracusans every man of them to cut down a stake, and to bring it thither. So, when night was come, setting his

soldiers the strangers in hand withal, whilst the Syracusans slept and took their ease, by morning he had compassed the castle round about with a pale. The next day, they that saw the greatness and sudden expedition of this work, wondered much at it, as well the enemies as also the citizens: and when he had buried the dead bodies, and redeemed them that were taken prisoners (which were not much less then two thousand persons), he called a common council of the city, in the which Heraclides made a motion, that Dion should be chosen general of Syracusa, with absolute power and authority, both by sea and land. The chiefest men of the city liked very well of it, and would have had the people to have passed it. But the rabble of these mariners, and other mechanical people living by their labour, would not suffer Heraclides to be put from his admiralship, but fell to mutiny, thinking that though Heraclides did them no pleasure else, yet he would ever be a more popular man than Dion, and please the common people better. Dion granted their desire, and made Heraclides admiral again of the sea: howbeit he did anger them as much another way, when he did not only reject the earnest suit they made to have the law *agraria* pass for division of lands in equality amongst them, but did also cancel and revoke all that had been done before. Wherefore Heraclides remaining at Messina, began thenceforth to enter into new practices again, and to flatter the soldiers and seafaring men he had brought thither with him, and to stir them up to rebel against Dion, saying, that he would make himself tyrant: and himself in the meantime secretly practised with Dionysius, by means of a Spartan called Pharax. The noblest men of the Syracusans mistrusted it, and thereupon there fell out great mutiny in their camp, whereby also followed great famine in Syracusa: so that Dion was at such a strait, that he could not tell what to say to it, and was reproved of all his friends for that he had again preferred to great authority against himself, so intractable a man, and so malicious and wicked a person as Heraclides was.

49  Now, when Pharax lay in camp with an army near unto the city of Naples, in the marches of the Agrigentines, Dion did bring the army of the Syracusans into the field, being yet determined not to fight with him till another time. But through Heraclides' and the seamen's crying out, that said he would not try this war by

battle, but would draw it out in length because he would be still general, he was forced to give battle, and lost it. Howbeit the overthrow was not great, and happened rather because his men were at a jar among themselves, by reason of their faction and division, than otherwise. Dion therefore prepared to fight another battle, and gathered his men together again, encouraging them, when even at twilight word was brought him that Heraclides with all his fleet was under sail towards Syracusa, meaning to take the city, and to shut Dion and his army out of it. Wherefore he presently took with him the chiefest men of authority in the city, and the most willingest men, and rode all night with them in such haste, that they were at the gates of Syracusa the next morning by nine of the clock, having ridden seven hundred furlong. Heraclides that had sailed with all the possible speed he could to prevent him with his ships, perceiving that he came short, he turned sail, and taking seas at all adventure, by chance he met with Gaesylus Lacedaemonian, who told him he was sent from Lacedaemon, to be general to the Sicilians in this war, as Gylippus was sent at other times before. He was glad he had met with him, to have such a remedy and defence against Dion, and boasted of it unto the friends and confederates of Syracusa, and sent a herald before unto the Syracusans, summoning them to receive Gaesylus Lacedaemonian, who was sent to be their general. Dion made answer: that the Syracusans had governors enough, and though that their affairs did of necessity require a Lacedaemonian captain, yet that himself was he, for that he was made free in Sparta. Then Gaesylus perceiving he could not obtain to be general, he went unto Syracusa, and came to Dion, and there made Heraclides and him friends again, by the great and solemn oaths he made, and because Gaesylus also swore, that he himself would be revenged of him for Dion's sake, and punish Heraclides, if ever after he did once more conspire against him.

50    After that, the Syracusans broke up their army by sea, because it did them then no service, and was beside chargeable keeping of it, and further did also breed sedition and trouble amongst their governors: and so went to lay straiter siege to the castle than ever they did, and built up the wall again, which the enemies had overthrown. Then Dionysius' son seeing no aid to come to him

from any part, and that victuals failed them, and further, that the soldiers began to mutiny, being unable to keep them, he fell to a composition with Dion, and delivered up the castle into his hands, with all the armour and munition in it: and so took his mother and his sisters of Dion, and put them aboard upon five galleys, with the which he went unto his father, through the safe conduit of Dion. There was not a man at that time in all Syracusa, but was there to see this sight, or if by chance there were any absent, the other that were there called them thither as loud as they could cry, saying, that they did not see the goodliest day and sunshine, which the city of Syracusa might see then at her rising, the same being now restored again to her former liberty. If until this present day they do reckon the flying of Dionysius, for one of the rarest examples of fortune's change, as one of the greatest and notablest thing that ever was, what joy think we had they that drove him out, and what pleasure had they with themselves, that with the least mean that could be possible, did destroy the greatest tyranny in the world?

51   So when Apollocrates Dionysius' son was embarked, and that Dion was entered into the castle, the women within the castle would not tarry till he came into the house, but went to meet him at the gates, Aristomache leading Dion's son in her hand, and Areta following her weeping, being very fearful how she should call and salute her husband, having lain with another man. Dion first spoke to his sister, and afterwards to his son: and then Aristomache offering him Areta, said unto him: 'Since thy banishment, O Dion, we have led a miserable and captive life: but now that thou art returned home with victory, thou hast rid us out of care and thraldom, and hast also made us again bold to lift up our heads, saving her here, whom I wretched creature have by force (thyself alive) seen married unto another man. Now then, since fortune hath made thee lord of us all, what judgment givest thou of this compulsion? How wilt thou have her to salute thee, as her uncle, or husband?' As Aristomache spoke these words, the water stood in Dion's eyes: so he gently and lovingly taking his wife Areta by the hand, he gave her his son, and willed her to go home to his house where he then remained, and so delivered the castle to the Syracusans.

52 He having this prosperous success and victory, would not reap any present benefit or pleasure thereby, before he had showed himself thankful to his friends, given great gifts also unto the confederates of Syracusa, and specially, before he had given every one of his friends in the city, and his mercenary soldiers the strangers, some honourable reward according to their deserts, exceeding his ability with magnanimity of mind, when he himself lived soberly, and kept a moderate diet, contenting him with anything that came first to hand. Every man that heard of it, wondered at him, considering that not only all Sicilia and Carthage, but generally all Greece, looked upon his great prosperity and good fortune, thinking no man living greater than himself, nor that any captain ever attained to such fame and wonderful fortune, as he was come unto. This notwithstanding, Dion lived as temperately and modestly in his apparel, and also in his number of servants and service at his board, as if he had lived with Plato in the Academy at Athens, and had not been conversant amongst soldiers and captains, which have no other comfort nor pleasure for all the pains and dangers they suffer continually, but to eat and drink their fill, and to take their pleasure all day long. Plato wrote unto him, that all the world had him in admiration. But Dion, in my opinion, had no respect but to one place, and to one city (to wit, the Academy) and would have no other judges nor lookers into his doings, but the scholars of the same: who neither wondered at his great exploits, valiantness, nor victory, but only considered if he did wisely and modestly use this fortune he had, and could so keep himself within modest bounds, having done so great things. Furthermore, touching the gravity he had when he spoke to anybody, and his inflexible severity which he used towards the people, he determined never to alter or change it: notwithstanding that his affairs required him to show courtesy and lenity, and that Plato also reproved him for it, and wrote, that severity and obstinacy (as we said before) was the companion of solitariness. But it seemeth to me that Dion did use it for two respects. The first, because nature had not framed him courteous and affable to win men: secondly, he did what he could to draw the Syracusans to the contrary, who were over-licentious, and spoiled with too much flattery: for Heraclides began again to be busy with him.

53    First of all, Dion sending for him to come to council, he sent him word he would not come: and that being a private citizen, he would be at the common council amongst others when any was kept. Afterwards he accused him, for that he had not overthrown and razed the castle: and also because he would not suffer the people to break open the tomb of Dionysius the elder, to cast out his body: and because he sent for counsellors to Corinth, and disdained to make the citizens his companions in the government of the commonwealth. Indeed to confess a truth, Dion had sent for certain Corinthians, hoping the better to stablish the form of a commonwealth, which he had in his mind, when they were come. For his mind was utterly to break the government of *democratia* (to wit, the absolute government and authority of the people in a city, not being as it were a commonwealth, but rather a fair and market where things are sold, as Plato saith) and to establish the Laconian or Cretan commonwealth, mingled with a princely and popular government: and that should be, *aristocratia*, to wit, the number of a few noblemen that should govern and direct the chiefest and weightiest matters of state. And for that purpose, he thought the Corinthians the meetest men for him to frame this common-wealth, considering that they governed their affairs more by choosing a few number of the nobility, than otherwise, and that they did not refer many things to the voice of the people. And because he was assured that Heraclides would be against him in it all that he could, and that otherwise he knew he was a seditious, a troublesome, and light-headed fellow, he then suffered them to kill him who had long before done it, if he had not kept them from it: and so they went home to his house, and slew him there. The murder of Heraclides was much misliked of the Syracusans: how-beit Dion caused him to be honourably buried, and brought his body to the ground, followed with all his army. Then he made an oration himself to the people, and told them, that it was impossible to avoid sedition and trouble in the city, so long as Dion and Heraclides did both govern together.

54    At that time there was one Callippus an Athenian, a familiar of Dion's, who (as Plato saith) came not acquainted with Dion through the occasion of his study in philosophy, but because he had been his guide to bring him to see the secret mysteries and

ceremonies of the sacrifices, and for such other like common talk and company. This notwithstanding, Callippus did accompany him in all this war, and was very much honoured of him, and was one of the first of all his friends that entered into Syracusa with him, and did valiantly behave himself in all the battles and conflicts that were fought. This Callippus seeing that Dion's best and chiefest friends were all slain in this war, and that Heraclides also was dead, that the people of Syracusa had no more any head, and besides, that the soldiers which were with Dion did love him better than any other man, he became the unfaithfullest man and the veriest villain of all other, hoping that for reward to kill his friend Dion, he should undoubtedly come to have the whole government of all Sicilia, and as some do report, for that he had taken a bribe of his enemies of twenty talents for his labour to commit this murder. So he began the practice, to bribe, and to suborn certain of the mercenary soldiers against Dion, and that by a marvellous crafty and subtle fetch. For, using commonly to report unto Dion certain seditious words, spoken peradventure by the soldiers indeed, or else devised of his own head: he won such a liberty and boldness by the trust Dion had in him, that he might safely say what he would to any of the soldiers, and boldly speak evil of Dion by his own commandment: to the end he might thereby understand the better whether any of the soldiers were angry with him, or wished his death. By this policy, Callippus straight found out those that bore Dion grudge, and that were already corrupted, whom he drew to his conspiracy. And if any man unwilling to give ear unto him, went and told Dion, that Callippus would have enticed him to conspire against him: Dion was not angry with him for it, thinking that he did but as he had commanded him to do.

55    Now as this treason was practising against Dion, there appeared a great and monstrous ghost or spirit unto him. By chance sitting late one evening all alone, in a gallery he had, and being in a deep thought with himself, suddenly he heard a noise: and therewith casting his eye to the end of his gallery, (being yet daylight) he saw a monstrous great woman, like unto one of the furies showed in plays, and saw her sweeping of the house with a broom. This vision so amazed and affrighted him, that he sent for his friends, and told them what a sight he had seen: and prayed them to tarry with him

all night, being as it were a man beside himself, fearing lest the spirit would come to him again if they left him alone, of the which notwithstanding he never heard more afterwards. Howbeit shortly after, his son being grown to man's state, for a certain light anger he had taken when he was but a boy, he cast himself headlong down from the top of the house, and so was slain.

56   Dion being in this state, Callippus went on still with his treason, and spread a rumour abroad among the Syracusans, that Dion seeing himself now destitute of children, was determined to send for Apollocrates, Dionysius' son, to make him his heir and successor, being cousin germane to his wife, and his sister's daughter's son. Then began Dion, his wife, and sister to mistrust Callippus' practices, and they were told of it by divers sundry and manifest proofs. But Dion being sorry (as I suppose) for Heraclides' death, and inwardly taking that murder in very evil part, as a foul blot to his life and doings, he said he had rather die a thousand deaths, and to offer his throat to be cut to any that would, rather than he would live in that misery, to be compelled to take heed as well of his friends, as of his enemies. Callippus then seeing the women so busy and inquisitive of his doings, and fearing lest he should be bewrayed, he came weeping unto them, and told them it was nothing, and that he was ready to assure them of it by any manner of way they would devise. The women then willed him to swear by the great oath, which was in this manner. He that must take this oath, cometh into the temple of the goddesses Thesmophores, which are, Ceres and Proserpina. And after certain sacrifices done, he putteth on the purple chaplet of the goddess Proserpina, holding a burning torch in his hand, and sweareth in this manner. Callippus having done all these ceremonies, and made the oath in form as I have told you, he made so light account of the goddesses, that he tarried no longer to do the murder he had determined, but till the very feast day of the goddess should come, by whom he had sworn: and slew him on the day of the feast of Proserpina. Now, I do not think that he chose that day of set purpose, knowing right well that he did always sin against her, what time soever he had killed his brother, being by his means specially admitted to the society and brotherhood with him, of the fraternity and mysteries of Ceres and Proserpina.

57    Of this conspiracy there were divers. For, as Dion was set in
his chamber talking with his friends, where there were many beds
to sit on, some compassed the house round about, others came to
the doors and windows of his chamber, and they that should do the
deed to dispatch him, which were the Zacynthian soldiers, came
into his chamber in their coats without any sword. But when they
were come in, they that were without did shut the doors after
them, and locked them in, lest any man should come out: and they
that were within, fell upon Dion, and thought to have strangled
him. But when they saw they could not, they called for a sword.
Never a man that was within, durst open the doors, though there
were many with Dion. For they thought every man to save their
own lives, by suffering him to be killed, and therefore durst not
come to help him. So the murderers tarried a long time within, and
did nothing. At length there was one Lycon a Syracusan, that gave
one of these Zacynthian soldiers a dagger in at the window, with
the which they cut Dion's throat, as a wether they had holden a
long time in their hands, even dead for fear. The murder being
executed, they cast his sister and wife, great with child, into prison,
and there the poor lady was pitifully brought to bed of a goodly
boy: the which they rather determined to bring up, than otherwise
to do anything with the child. Their keepers that had the charge of
them, were contented to let them do it, because Callippus began
then a little to grow to some trouble.

58    For at the first, after he had slain Dion, he bore all the whole
sway for a time, and kept the city of Syracusa in his hands: and
wrote unto Athens, the which next unto the immortal gods he was
most afraid of, having defiled his hands in so damnable a treason.
And therefore, in my opinion, it was not evil spoken, that Athens
is a city of all other that bringeth forth the best men when they give
themselves to goodness, and the wickedest people also, when they
do dispose themselves to evil: as their country also bringeth forth
the best honey that is, and hemlock in like manner that quickly
dispatcheth a man of his life. Howbeit the gods, and fortune, did
not suffer this treason and wicked man to reign long, having come
to the government of a realm by so damnable a murder: but shortly
after they gave him his payment he had deserved. For Callippus
going to take a little town called Catana, he lost the city of

Syracusa: whereupon he said that he had lost a city, and got a cheese-knife.* Afterwards he went to assail the Messenians, and there he lost a great number of his men, and amongst them were slain those that killed Dion. Now Callippus finding no city in all Sicilia, that would receive him, but that they all did hate and abhor him, he went to take the city of Rhegio in Italy. There being in great distress and need of all things, and not able to maintain his soldiers, he was slain by Leptines and Polyperchon, with the selfsame dagger wherewith Dion before was slain: the which was known by the fashion, being short after the Laconian daggers, and also by the workmanship upon it, that was very excellently wrought. And thus was the end and death of Callippus. Now for Aristomache and Areta, they were taken out of prison: and Icetes Syracusan, that sometimes had been one of Dion's friends, took them home to his own house, and used them very well and faithfully for a certain time, but afterwards was won and corrupted by Dion's enemies. So he caused a ship to be provided for them, and bore them in hand that he would send them into Peloponnesus: but he gave them charge that carried them away, to kill them as they went, and to throw them overboard into the sea. Some say, that the two women, and the little young boy, were cast alive into the sea. But this reward of the sinful act that he committed, returned again upon himself, as it had done before unto others. For he was taken by Timoleon that put him to death: and besides, the Syracusans did also kill two of his daughters in revenge of the unfaithfulness he had showed unto Dion.

---

* Κατάνη in corrupt speech signifieth a knife to scrape or cut cheese, which is trulier called πατάνη.

## Life of Marcus Brutus

Marcus Brutus came of that Junius Brutus, for whom the ancient Romans made his statue of brass to be set up in the Capitol, with the images of the kings, holding a naked sword in his hand: because he had valiantly put down the Tarquins from their kingdom of Rome. But that Junius Brutus being of a sour stern nature, not softened by reason, being like unto sword blades of too hard a temper, was so subject to his choler and malice he bore unto the tyrants, that for their sakes he caused his own sons to be executed. But this Marcus Brutus in contrary manner, whose life we presently write, having framed his manners of life by the rules of virtue and study of philosophy, and having employed his wit, which was gentle and constant, in attempting of great things, methinks he was rightly made and framed unto virtue. So that his very enemies which wish him most hurt, because of his conspiracy against Julius Caesar, if there were any noble attempt done in all this conspiracy, they refer it wholly unto Brutus, and all the cruel and violent acts unto Cassius, who was Brutus' familiar friend, but not so well given and conditioned as he. His mother Servilia, it is thought came of the blood of Servilius Hala, who, when Spurius Melius went about to make himself king, and to bring it to pass had enticed the common people to rebel, took a dagger and hid it close under his arm, and went into the market-place. When he was come thither, he made as though he had somewhat to say unto him, and pressed as near him as he could: wherefore Melius stooping down with his head, to hear what he would say, Servilius stabbed him in with his dagger, and slew him. Thus much all writers agree for his mother. Now touching his father, some for the evil will and malice they bore unto Brutus, because of the death of Julius Caesar, do maintain that he came not of Junius Brutus that drove out the Tarquins, for there were none left of his race, considering that his two sons were executed for conspiracy with the Tarquins: and that Marcus Brutus

came of a mean house, the which was raised to honour and office in
the commonwealth, but of late time. Posidonius the philosopher
writeth the contrary, that Junius Brutus indeed slew two of his sons
which were men grown, as the histories do declare: howbeit that
there was a third son, being but a little child at that time, from
whom the house and family afterwards was derived: and furthermore, that there were in his time certain famous men of that family,
whose stature and countenance resembled much the image of
Junius Brutus. And thus much for this matter.

2   Marcus Cato the philosopher was brother unto Servilia, M.
Brutus' mother: whom Brutus studied most to follow of all
the other Romans, because he was his uncle, and afterwards he
married his daughter. Now touching the Grecian philosophers,
there was no sect nor philosopher of them, but he heard and liked
it: but above all the rest, he loved Plato's sect best, and did not
much give himself to the new nor mean Academy as they call it,
but altogether to the old Academy. Therefore he did ever greatly
esteem the philosopher Antiochus, of the city of Ascalon: but
he was more familiar with his brother Ariston, who for learning
and knowledge was inferior to many other philosophers, but for
wisdom and courtesy, equal with the best and chiefest. Touching
Empylus, whom Marcus Brutus himself doth mention in his
*Epistles*, and his friends also in many places: he was an orator, and
left an excellent book he wrote of the death of Julius Caesar, and
tituled it *Brutus*. He was properly learned in the Latin tongue, and
was able to make long discourse in it, beside that he could also
plead very well in Latin. But for the Greek tongue, they do note in
some of his Epistles, that he counterfeited that brief compendious
manner of speech of the Lacedaemonians. As when the war was
begun, he wrote unto the Pargamenians in this sort: 'I understand
you have given Dolobella money: if you have done it willingly,
you confess you have offended me: if against your wills, show
it then by giving me willingly.' Another time again unto the
Samians: 'Your counsels be long, your doings be slow, consider
the end.' And in another Epistle he wrote unto the Patareians:
'The Xanthians despising my goodwill, have made their country a
grave of despair: and the Patareians that put themselves into my
protection, have lost no jot of their liberty. And therefore whilst

you have liberty, either choose the judgment of the Patareians, or the fortune of the Xanthians.' These were Brutus' manner of letters which were honoured for their briefness.

3    So Brutus being but a young stripling went into Cyprus with his uncle Cato, who was sent against Ptolomy king of Egypt: who having slain himself, Cato staying for certain necessary business he had in the Isle of Rhodes, had already sent Caninius,* one of his friends before, to keep his treasure and goods. But Cato fearing he would be light-fingered, wrote unto Brutus forthwith to come out of Pamphylia (where he was but newly recovered of a sickness) into Cyprus, the which he did. The which journey he was sorry to take upon him, both for respect of Caninius' shame, whom Cato as he thought wrongfully slandered, as also because he thought this office too mean and unmeet for him, being a young man, and given to his book. This notwithstanding, he behaved himself so honestly and carefully, that Cato did greatly commend him: and after all the goods were sold and converted into ready money, he took the most part of it, and returned withal to Rome.

4    Afterwards when the empire of Rome was divided into factions, and that Caesar and Pompey both were in arms one against the other, and that all the empire of Rome was in garboyle and uproar, it was thought then that Brutus would take part with Caesar, because Pompey not long before had put his father unto death. But Brutus preferring the respect of his country and commonwealth, before private affection, and persuading himself that Pompey had juster cause to enter into arms than Caesar, he then took part with Pompey, though oftentimes meeting him before, he thought scorn to speak to him, thinking it a great sin and offence in him, to speak to the murderer of his father. But then submitting himself unto Pompey, as unto the head of the commonwealth, he sailed into Sicilia, lieutenant under Sestius that was governor of that province. But when he saw that there was no way to rise, nor to do any noble exploits, and that Caesar and Pompey were both camped together, and fought for victory, he went of himself unsent for into Macedon, to be partaker of the danger. It is reported that Pompey being glad, and wondering at his coming when he saw him come to him, he

* Or Canidius.

rose out of his chair, and went and embraced him before them all, and used him as honourably as he could have done the noblest man that took his part. Brutus being in Pompey's camp, did nothing but study all day long, except he were with Pompey, and not only the days before, but the selfsame day also before the great battle was fought in the fields of Pharsalia, where Pompey was overthrown. It was in the midst of summer, and the sun was very hot, besides that the camp was lodged near unto marshes, and they that carried his tent, tarried long before they came: whereupon, being very weary with travel, scant any meat came into his mouth at dinner time. Furthermore, when others slept, or thought what would happen the morrow after, he fell to his book, and wrote all day long till night, writing a breviary of Polybius.

5    It is reported that Caesar did not forget him, and that he gave his captains charge before the battle, that they should beware they killed not Brutus in fight, and if he yielded willingly unto them, that then they should bring him unto him: but if he resisted, and would not be taken, then that they should let him go, and do him no hurt. Some say he did this for Servilia's sake, Brutus' mother. For when he was a young man, he had been acquainted with Servilia, who was extremely in love with him. And because Brutus was born in that time when their love was hottest, he persuaded himself that he begat him. For proof hereof the report goeth, that when the weightiest matters were in hand in the senate, about the conspiracy of Catiline, which was likely to have undone the city of Rome, Caesar and Cato sat near together, and were both of contrary minds to each other: and then, that in the meantime one delivered Caesar a letter. Caesar took it, and read it softly to himself: but Cato cried out upon Caesar, and said he did not well to receive advertisements from enemies. Whereupon the whole senate began to murmur at it. Then Caesar gave Cato the letter as it was sent him, who read it, and found that it was a love letter sent from his sister Servilia: thereupon he cast it again to Caesar, and said unto him, 'Hold, drunken sop.' When he had done so, he went on with his tale, and maintained his opinion as he did before: so commonly was the love of Servilia known which she bore unto Caesar.

6    So, after Pompey's overthrow at the battle of Pharsalia, and that he fled to the sea, when Caesar came to besiege his camp, Brutus

went out of the camp gates unseen of any man, and leapt into a marsh full of water and reeds. Then when night was come, he crept out, and went unto the city of Larissa: from whence he wrote unto Caesar, who was very glad that he had escaped, and sent for him to come unto him. When Brutus was come, he did not only pardon him, but also kept him always about him, and did as much honour and esteem him, as any man he had in his company. Now no man could tell whither Pompey was fled, and all were marvellous desirous to know it: wherefore Caesar walking a good way alone with Brutus, he did ask him which way he thought Pompey took. Caesar perceiving by his talk that Brutus guessed certainly whither Pompey should be fled, he left all other ways, and took his journey directly towards Egypt. Pompey, as Brutus had conjectured, was indeed fled into Egypt, but there he was villainously slain. Furthermore, Brutus obtained pardon of Caesar for Cassius: and defending also the king of Lybia's cause,* he was overlaid with a world of accusations against him, howbeit entreating for him, he saved him the best part of his realm and kingdom. They say also that Caesar said, when he heard Brutus plead: 'I know not,' said he, 'what this young man would, but what he would, he willeth it vehemently.' For as Brutus' gravity and constant mind would not grant all men their requests that sued unto him, but being moved with reason and discretion, did always incline to that which was good and honest: even so when it was moved to follow any matter, he used a kind of forcible and vehement persuasion that calmed not, till he had obtained his desire. For by flattering of him, a man could never obtain anything at his hands, nor make him to do that which was unjust. Further, he thought it not meet for a man of calling and estimation, to yield unto the requests and entreaties of a shameless and importunate suitor, requesting things unmeet: the which notwithstanding, some men do for shame, because they dare deny nothing. And therefore he was wont to say, that he thought them evil brought up in their youth, that could deny nothing. Now when Caesar took sea to go into Africa, against Cato and Scipio, he

---

* This king was Juba: howbeit it is true also, that Brutus made intercession for Deiotarus king of Galatia, who was deprived notwithstanding of the most part of his country by Caesar: and therefore this place were best to be understanded by Deiotarus.

left Brutus governor of Gaul in Italy, on this side of the Alps, which was a great good hap for that province. For where others were spoiled and polled by the insolency and covetousness of the governors, as if it had been a country conquered, Brutus was a comfort and rest unto their former troubles and miseries they sustained. But he referred it wholly unto Caesar's grace and goodness. For, when Caesar returned out of Africa, and progressed up and down Italy, the things that pleased him best to see, were the cities under Brutus' charge and government, and Brutus himself, who honoured Caesar in person, and whose company also Caesar greatly esteemed.

7    Now there were divers sorts of praetorships at Rome, and it was looked for that Brutus or Cassius would make suit for the chiefest praetorship, which they called the praetorship of the city, because he that had that office, was as a judge to minister justice unto the citizens. Therefore they strove one against the other, though some say that there was some little grudge betwixt them for other matters before, and that this contention did set them further out, though they were allied together. For Cassius had married Junia, Brutus' sister. Others say, that this contention betwixt them came by Caesar himself, who secretly gave either of them both hope of his favour. So their suit for the praetorship was so followed and laboured of either party, that one of them put another in suit of law. Brutus with his virtue and good name contended against many noble exploits in arms, which Cassius had done against the Parthians. So Caesar after he had heard both their objections, he told his friends with whom he consulted about this matter: 'Cassius' cause is the juster,' said he, 'but Brutus must be first preferred.' Thus Brutus had the first praetorship, and Cassius the second: who thanked not Caesar so much for the praetorship he had, as he was angry with him for that he had lost. But Brutus in many other things tasted of the benefit of Caesar's favour in anything he requested. For if he had listed, he might have been one of Caesar's chiefest friends, and of greatest authority and credit about him. Howbeit Cassius' friends did dissuade him from it (for Cassius and he were not yet reconciled together since their first contention and strife for the praetorship) and prayed him to beware of Caesar's sweet enticements, and to fly his tyrannical

favours: the which they said Caesar gave him, not to honour his virtue, but to weaken his constant mind, framing it to the bent of his bow.

8   Now Caesar on the other side did not trust him overmuch, nor was not without tales brought unto him against him: howbeit he feared his great mind, authority, and friends. Yet on the other side also, he trusted his good nature, and fair conditions. For, intelligence being brought him one day, that Antonius and Dolabella did conspire against him, he answered, that these fat long-haired men made him not afraid, but the lean and whitely-faced fellows, meaning by that, Brutus and Cassius. At another time also when one accused Brutus unto him, and bade him beware of him: 'What,' said he again, clapping his hand on his breast: 'think ye that Brutus will not tarry till this body die?' Meaning that none but Brutus after him was meet to have such power as he had. And surely, in my opinion, I am persuaded that Brutus might indeed have come to have been the chiefest man of Rome, if he could have contented himself for a time and have been next unto Caesar, and to have suffered his glory and authority, which he had got by his great victories, to consume with time. But Cassius being a choleric man, and hating Caesar privately, more than he did the tyranny openly, he incensed Brutus against him. It is also reported, that Brutus could evil away with the tyranny, and that Cassius hated the tyrant, making many complaints for the injuries he had done him, and amongst others, for that he had taken away his lions from him. Cassius had provided them for his sports, when he should be Aedilis, and they were found in the city of Megara, when it was won by Calenus, and Caesar kept them. The rumour went, that these lions did marvellous great hurt to the Megarians. For when the city was taken, they broke their cages where they were tied up, and turned them loose, thinking they would have done great mischief to the enemies, and have kept them from setting upon them: but the lions contrary to expectation, turned upon themselves that fled unarmed, and did so cruelly tear some in pieces, that it pitied their enemies to see them.

9   And this was the cause, as some do report, that made Cassius conspire against Caesar. But this holdeth no water. For Cassius even from his cradle could not abide any manner of tyrants, as it appeared

when he was but a boy, and went unto the same school that Faustus, the son of Sylla did. And Faustus bragging among other boys, highly boasted of his father's kingdom: Cassius rose up on his feet, and gave him two good whirts on the ear. Faustus' governors would have put this matter in suit against Cassius: but Pompey would not suffer them, but caused the two boys to be brought before him, and asked them how the matter came to pass. Then Cassius, as it is written of him, said unto the other: 'Go to, Faustus, speak again and thou darest, before this nobleman here, the same words that made me angry with thee, that my fists may walk once again about thine ears.' Such was Cassius' hot stirring nature. But for Brutus, his friends and countrymen, both by divers procurements, and sundry rumours of the city, and by many bills also, did openly call and procure him to do that he did. For, under the image of his ancestor Junius Brutus, that drave the kings out of Rome, they wrote: 'O, that it pleased the gods thou wert now alive, Brutus': and again, 'That thou wert here among us now'. His tribunal (or chair) where he gave audience during the time he was praetor, was full of such bills: 'Brutus, thou art asleep, and art not Brutus indeed'. And of all this, Caesar's flatterers were the cause: who beside many other exceeding and unspeakable honours they daily devised for him, in the night time they did put diadems upon the heads of his images, supposing thereby to allure the common people to call him king, instead of dictator. Howbeit it turned to the contrary, as we have written more at large in Julius Caesar's life.

10   Now when Cassius felt his friends, and did stir them up against Caesar, they all agreed and promised to take part with him, so Brutus were the chief of their conspiracy. For they told him, that so high an enterprise and attempt as that, did not so much require men of manhood and courage to draw their swords, as it stood them upon to have a man of such estimation as Brutus, to make every man boldly think, that by his only presence the fact were holy, and just. If he took not this course, then that they should go to it with fainter hearts, and when they had done it, they should be more fearful: because every man would think that Brutus would not have refused to have made one with them, if the cause had been good and honest. Therefore Cassius considering this matter with himself, did first of all speak to Brutus, since they grew strange together for

MARCUS BRUTUS                    821

the suit they had for the praetorship. So when he was reconciled to him again, and that they had embraced one another, Cassius asked him if he were determined to be in the senate house, the first day of the month of March, because he heard say that Caesar's friends should move the counsel that day that Caesar should be called king by the senate. Brutus answered him he would not be there. 'But if we be sent for,' said Cassius, 'how then?' 'For myself then,' said Brutus, 'I mean not to hold my peace, but to withstand it, and rather die than lose my liberty.' Cassius being bold, and taking hold of this word: 'Why,' quoth he, 'what Roman is he alive that will suffer thee to die for thy liberty? What, knowest thou not that thou art Brutus? Thinkest thou that they be cobblers, tapsters, or suchlike base mechanical people, that write these bills and scrolls which are found daily in thy praetor's chair, and not the noblest men and best citizens that do it? No, be thou well assured, that of other praetors they look for gifts, common distributions amongst the people, and for common plays, and to see fencers fight at the sharp, to show the people pastime: but at thy hands, they specially require (as a due debt unto them) the taking away of the tyranny, being fully bent to suffer any extremity for thy sake, so that thou wilt show thyself to be the man thou art taken for, and that they hope thou art.' Thereupon he kissed Brutus, and embraced him: and so each taking leave of other, they went both to speak with their friends about it.

11    Now amongst Pompey's friends, there was one called Caius Ligarius,* who had been accused unto Caesar for taking part with Pompey, and Caesar discharged him. But Ligarius thanked not Caesar so much for his discharge, as he was offended with him for that he was brought in danger by his tyrannical power. And therefore in his heart he was always his mortal enemy, and was besides very familiar with Brutus, who went to see him being sick in his bed, and said unto him: 'O Ligarius, in what a time art thou sick!' Ligarius rising up in his bed, and taking him by the right hand, said unto him: 'Brutus,' said he, 'if thou hast any great enterprise in hand worthy of thyself, I am whole.'

12    After that time they began to feel all their acquaintance whom they trusted, and laid their heads together consulting upon it, and

---

* In another place they call him Quintus.

did not only pick out their friends, but all those also whom they thought stout enough to attempt any desperate matter, and that were not afraid to lose their lives. For this cause they durst not acquaint Cicero with their conspiracy, although he was a man whom they loved dearly, and trusted best: for they were afraid that he being a coward by nature, and age also having increased his fear, he would quite turn and alter all their purpose, and quench the heat of their enterprise, the which specially required hot and earnest execution, seeking by persuasion to bring all things to such safety, as there should be no peril. Brutus also did let other of his friends alone, as Statilius Epicurian, and Faonius, that made profession to follow Marcus Cato. Because that having cast out words afar off, disputing together in philosophy to feel their minds, Faonius answered, that civil war was worse than tyrannical government usurped against the law. And Statilius told him also, that it were an unwise part of him, to put his life in danger for a sight of ignorant fools and asses. Labeo was present at this talk, and maintained the contrary against them both. But Brutus held his peace, as though it had been a doubtful matter, and a hard thing to have decided. But afterwards, being out of their company, he made Labeo privy to his intent: who very readily offered himself to make one. And they thought good also to bring in another Brutus to join with him, surnamed Albinus: who was no man of his hands himself, but because he was able to bring good force of a great number of slaves, and fencers at the sharp, whom he kept to show the people pastime with their fighting, besides also that Caesar had some trust in him. Cassius and Labeo told Brutus Albinus of it at the first, but he made them no answer. But when he had spoken with Brutus himself alone, and that Brutus had told him he was the chief ringleader of all this conspiracy, then he willingly promised him the best aid he could. Furthermore, the only name and great calling of Brutus did bring on the most of them to give consent to this conspiracy. Who having never taken oaths together, nor taken or given any caution or assurance, nor binding themselves one to another by any religious oaths, they all kept the matter so secret to themselves, and could so cunningly handle it, that notwithstanding the gods did reveal it by manifest signs and tokens from above, and by predictions of sacrifices, yet all this would not be believed.

13   Now Brutus, who knew very well that for his sake all the noblest, valiantest, and most courageous men of Rome did venture their lives, weighing with himself the greatness of the danger, when he was out of his house, he did so frame and fashion his countenance and looks, that no man could discern he had anything to trouble his mind. But when night came that he was in his own house, then he was clean changed. For, either care did wake him against his will when he would have slept, or else oftentimes of himself he fell into such deep thoughts of this enterprise, casting in his mind all the dangers that might happen, that his wife lying by him, found that there was some marvellous great matter that troubled his mind, not being wont to be in that taking, and that he could not well determine with himself. His wife Porcia (as we have told you before) was the daughter of Cato, whom Brutus married being his cousin, not a maiden, but a young widow after the death of her first husband Bibulus, by whom she had also a young son called Bibulus, who afterwards wrote a book of the acts and gestes of Brutus, extant at this present day. This young lady being excellently well seen in philosophy, loving her husband well, and being of a noble courage, as she was also wise, because she would not ask her husband what he ailed before she had made some proof by herself, she took a little razor such as barbers occupy to pare men's nails, and causing all her maids and women to go out of her chamber, gave herself a great gash withal in her thigh, that she was straight all of a gore blood: and incontinently after, a vehement fever took her, by reason of the pain of her wound. Then perceiving her husband was marvellously out of quiet, and that he could take no rest, even in her greatest pain of all, she spoke in this sort unto him: 'I being, O Brutus,' said she, 'the daughter of Cato, was married unto thee, not to be thy bedfellow and companion in bed and at board only, like a harlot: but to be partaker also with thee, of thy good and evil fortune. Now for thyself, I can find no cause of fault in thee touching our match: but for my part, how may I show my duty towards thee, and how much I would do for thy sake, if I cannot constantly bear a secret mischance or grief with thee, which requireth secrecy and fidelity? I confess, that a woman's wit commonly is too weak to keep a secret safely: but yet, Brutus, good education, and the company of virtuous men, have some power to reform the defect

of nature. And for myself, I have this benefit moreover: that I am the daughter of Cato, and wife of Brutus. This notwithstanding, I did not trust to any of these things before, until that now I have found by experience, that no pain nor grief whatsoever can overcome me.' With those words she showed him her wound on her thigh, and told him what she had done to prove herself. Brutus was amazed to hear what she said unto him, and lifting up his hands to heaven, he besought the gods to give him the grace he might bring his enterprise to so good pass, that he might be found a husband worthy of so noble a wife as Porcia: so he then did comfort her the best he could.

4    Now a day being appointed for the meeting of the senate, at what time they hoped Caesar would not fail to come, the conspirators determined then to put their enterprise in execution, because they might meet safely at that time without suspicion, and the rather, for that all the noblest and chiefest men of the city would be there. Who when they should see such a great matter executed, would every man then set to their hands, for the defence of their liberty. Furthermore, they thought also that the appointment of the place where the council should be kept, was chosen of purpose by divine providence, and made all for them. For it was one of the porches about the theatre, in the which there was a certain place full of seats for men to sit in, where also was set up the image of Pompey, which the city had made and consecrated in honour of him, when he did beautify that part of the city with the theatre he built, with divers porches about it. In this place was the assembly of the senate appointed to be, just on the fifteenth day of the month of March, which the Romans call, *Idus Martias*: so that it seemed some god of purpose had brought Caesar thither to be slain, for revenge of Pompey's death. So when the day was come, Brutus went out of his house with a dagger by his side under his long gown, that nobody saw nor knew, but his wife only. The other conspirators were all assembled at Cassius' house, to bring his son into the market-place, who on that day did put on the man's gown, called *toga virilis*: and from thence they came all in a troop together unto Pompey's porch, looking that Caesar would straight come thither. But here is to be noted, the wonderful assured constancy of these conspirators, in so dangerous and weighty

an enterprise as they had undertaken. For many of them being praetors, by reason of their office, whose duty is to minister justice to everybody, they did not only with great quietness and courtesy hear them that spoke unto them, or that pleaded matters before them, and gave them attentive ear, as if they had had no other matter in their heads: but moreover, they gave just sentence, and carefully dispatched the causes before them. So there was one among them, who being condemned in a certain sum of money, refused to pay it, and cried out that he did appeal unto Caesar. Then Brutus casting his eyes upon the conspirators, said, 'Caesar shall not let me to see the law executed.'

15 Notwithstanding this, by chance there fell out many misfortunes unto them, which was enough to have marred the enterprise. The first and chiefest was, Caesar's long tarrying, who came very late to the senate: for because the signs of the sacrifices appeared unlucky, his wife Calpurnia kept him at home, and the soothsayers bade him beware he went not abroad. The second cause was, when one came unto Casca being a conspirator, and taking him by the hand, said unto him: 'O Casca, thou keptest it close from me, but Brutus hath told me all.' Casca being amazed at it, the other went on with his tale, and said: 'Why, how now, how cometh it to pass thou art thus rich, that thou doest sue to be Aedilis?' Thus Casca being deceived by the other's doubtful words, he told them it was a thousand to one, he blabbed not out all the conspiracy. Another senator called Popilius Laena, after he had saluted Brutus and Cassius more friendly than he was wont to do, he rounded softly in their ears, and told them, I pray the gods you may go through with that you have taken in hand, but withal, dispatch I rede you, for your enterprise is bewrayed.' When he had said, he presently departed from them, and left them both afraid that their conspiracy would out. Now in the meantime, there came one of Brutus' men post haste unto him, and told him his wife was a-dying. For Porcia being very careful and pensive for that which was to come, and being too weak to away with so great and inward grief of mind, she could hardly keep within, but was frighted with every little noise and cry she heard, as those that are taken and possessed with the fury of the Bacchantes, asking every man that came from the market-place, what Brutus did, and still sent

messenger after messenger, to know what news. At length, Caesar's coming being prolonged as you have heard, Porcia's weakness was not able to hold out any longer, and thereupon she suddenly swounded, that she had no leisure to go to her chamber, but was taken in the midst of her house, where her speech and senses failed her. Howbeit she soon came to herself again, and so was laid in her bed, and tended by her women. When Brutus heard these news, it grieved him, as it is to be presupposed: yet he left not off the care of his country and commonwealth, neither went home to his house for any news he heard.

16 Now, it was reported that Caesar was coming in his litter: for he determined not to stay in the senate all that day (because he was afraid of the unlucky signs of the sacrifices) but to adjourn matters of importance unto the next session and council held, feigning himself not to be well at ease. When Caesar came out of his litter, Popilius Laena, that had talked before with Brutus and Cassius, and had prayed the gods they might bring this enterprise to pass, went unto Caesar, and kept him a long time with a talk. Caesar gave good ear unto him. Wherefore the conspirators (if so they should be called) not hearing what he said to Caesar, but conjecturing by that he had told them a little before that his talk was none other but the very discovery of their conspiracy, they were afraid every man of them, and one looking in another's face, it was easy to see that they all were of a mind, that it was no tarrying for them till they were apprehended, but rather that they should kill themselves with their own hands. And when Cassius and certain other clapped their hands on their swords under their gowns to draw them, Brutus marking the countenance and gesture of Laena, and considering that he did use himself rather like an humble and earnest suitor, than like an accuser, he said nothing to his companion (because there were many amongst them that were not of the conspiracy) but with a pleasant countenance encouraged Cassius. And immediately after, Laena went from Caesar, and kissed his hand: which showed plainly that it was for some matter concerning himself, that he had held him so long in talk.

17 Now all the senators being entered first into this place or chapter house where the council should be kept, all the other conspirators straight stood about Caesar's chair, as if they had had

something to have said unto him. And some say, that Cassius casting his eyes upon Pompey's image, made his prayer unto it, as if it had been alive. Trebonius* on the other side, drew Antonius outside, as he came into the house where the senate sat, and held him with a long talk without. When Caesar was come into the house, all the senate rose to honour him at his coming in. So when he was set, the conspirators flocked about him, and amongst them they presented one Tullius Cimber,† who made humble suit for the calling home again of his brother that was banished. They all made as though they were intercessors for him, and took him by the hands, and kissed his head and breast. Caesar at the first, simply refused their kindness and entreaties: but afterwards, perceiving they still pressed on him, he violently thrust them from him. Then Cimber with both his hands plucked Caesar's gown over his shoulders, and Casca that stood behind him, drew his dagger first, and struck Caesar upon the shoulder, but gave him no great wound. Caesar feeling himself hurt, took him straight by the hand he held his dagger in, and cried out in Latin: 'O traitor, Casca, what doest thou?' Casca on the other side cried in Greek, and called his brother to help him. So divers running on a heap together to fly upon Caesar, he looking about him to have fled, saw Brutus with a sword drawn in his hand ready to strike at him: then he let Casca's hand go, and casting his gown over his face, suffered every man to strike at him that would. Then the conspirators thronging one upon another because every man was desirous to have a cut at him, so many swords and daggers lighting upon one body, one of them hurt another, and among them Brutus caught a blow on his hand, because he would make one in murdering of him, and all the rest also were every man of them bloodied.

18    Caesar being slain in this manner, Brutus standing in the midst of the house, would have spoken, and stayed the other senators that were not of the conspiracy, to have told them the reason why they had done this fact. But they as men both afraid and amazed, fled one upon another's neck in haste to get out at the door, and no man

* In Caesar's life it is said, it was Decius Brutus Albinus that kept Antonius with a talk without.

† In Caesar's life he is called Metellus Cimber.

followed them. For it was set down and agreed between them, that they should kill no man but Caesar only, and should entreat all the rest to look to defend their liberty. All the conspirators but Brutus, determining upon this matter, thought it good also to kill Antonius, because he was a wicked man, and that in nature favoured tyranny: besides also, for that he was in great estimation with soldiers, having been conversant of long time amongst them: and specially, having a mind bent to great enterprises, he was also of great authority at that time, being consul with Caesar. But Brutus would not agree to it. First, for that he said it was not honest: secondly, because he told them there was hope of change in him. For he did not mistrust, but that Antonius being a noble-minded and courageous man, when he should know that Caesar was dead, would willingly help his country to recover her liberty, having them an example unto him, to follow their courage and virtue. So Brutus by this means saved Antonius' life, who at that present time disguised himself, and stole away. But Brutus and his consorts, having their swords bloody in their hands, went straight to the Capitol, persuading the Romans as they went, to take their liberty again. Now, at the first time when the murder was newly done, there were sudden outcries of people that ran up and down the city, the which indeed did the more increase the fear and tumult. But when they saw they slew no man, neither did spoil or make havoc of anything, then certain of the senators, and many of the people emboldening themselves, went to the Capitol unto them. There a great number of men being assembled together one after another, Brutus made an oration unto them to win the favour of the people, and to justify that they had done. All those that were by, said they had done well, and cried unto them that they should boldly come down from the Capitol. Whereupon, Brutus and his companions came boldly down into the market-place. The rest followed in troop, but Brutus went foremost, very honourably compassed in round about with the noblest men of the city, which brought him from the Capitol, thorough the market-place, to the pulpit for orations. When the people saw him in the pulpit, although they were a multitude of rakehells of all sorts, and had a goodwill to make some stir, yet being ashamed to do it for the reverence they bore unto Brutus, they kept silence, to hear what he would say. When Brutus began to speak, they gave him quiet audience: howbeit immediately after, they

showed that they were not all contented with the murder. For
when another called Cinna would have spoken, and began to
accuse Caesar, they fell into a great uproar among them, and
marvellously reviled him. Insomuch that the conspirators returned
again into the Capitol. There Brutus being afraid to be besieged,
sent back again the noblemen that came thither with him, thinking
it no reason, that they which were no partakers of the murder,
should be partakers of the danger.

19   Then the next morning the senate being assembled, and held
within the temple of the goddess Tellus, to wit the earth, and
Antonius, Plancus and Cicero having made a motion to the senate
in that assembly, that they should take an order to pardon and
forget all that was past, and to establish friendship and peace again,
it was decreed, that they should not only be pardoned, but also that
the consuls should refer it to the senate what honours should be
appointed unto them. This being agreed upon, the senate broke
up, and Antonius the consul, to put them in heart that were in
the Capitol, sent them his son for a pledge. Upon this assurance,
Brutus and his companions came down from the Capitol, where
every man saluted and embraced each other, among the which,
Antonius himself did bid Cassius to supper to him: and Lepidus also
bade Brutus, and so one bade another, as they had friendship and
acquaintance together. The next day following, the senate being
called again to council, did first of all commend Antonius, for that
he had wisely stayed and quenched the beginning of a civil war:
then they also gave Brutus and his consorts great praises, and lastly
they appointed them several governments of provinces. For unto
Brutus, they appointed Crete: Africa, unto Cassius: Asia, unto
Trebonius: Bithynia, unto Cimber: and unto the other Decius
Brutus Albinus, Gaul on this side the Alps.

20   When this was done, they came to talk of Caesar's will and
testament, and of his funerals and tomb. Then Antonius thinking
good his testament should be read openly, and also that his body
should be honourably buried, and not in hugger mugger, lest the
people might thereby take occasion to be worse offended if they did
otherwise, Cassius stoutly spoke against it. But Brutus went with
the motion, and agreed unto it: wherein it seemeth he committed a
second fault. For the first fault he did was, when he would not

consent to his fellow conspirators, that Antonius should be slain: and therefore he was justly accused, that thereby he had saved and strengthened a strong and grievous enemy of their conspiracy. The second fault was, when he agreed that Caesar's funerals should be as Antonius would have them: the which indeed marred all. For first of all, when Caesar's testament was openly read among them, whereby it appeared that he bequeathed unto every citizen of Rome, 75 drachmas a man, and that he left his gardens and arbours unto the people, which he had on this side of the river of Tyber, in the place where now the temple of Fortune is built, the people then loved him, and were marvellous sorry for him. Afterwards when Caesar's body was brought into the market-place, Antonius making his funeral oration in praise of the dead, according to the ancient custom of Rome, and perceiving that his words moved the common people to compassion, he framed his eloquence to make their hearts yearn the more, and taking Caesar's gown all bloody in his hand, he laid it open to the sight of them all, showing what a number of cuts and holes it had upon it. Therewithal the people fell presently into such a rage and mutiny, that there was no more order kept amongst the common people. For some of them cried out, 'Kill the murderers!' Others plucked up forms, tables, and stalls about the market-place, as they had done before at the funerals of Clodius, and having laid them all on a heap together, they set them on fire, and thereupon did put the body of Caesar, and burnt it in the midst of the most holy places. And furthermore, when the fire was thoroughly kindled, some here, some there, took burning firebrands, and ran with them to the murderers' houses that had killed him, to set them afire. Howbeit the conspirators foreseeing the danger before, had wisely provided for themselves, and fled. But there was a poet called Cinna, who had been no partaker of the conspiracy, but was always one of Caesar's chiefest friends: he dreamed the night before, that Caesar bade him to supper with him, and that he refusing to go, Caesar was very importunate with him, and compelled him, so, that at length he led him by the hand into a great dark place, where being marvellously afraid, he was driven to follow him in spite of his heart. This dream put him all night into a fever, and yet notwithstanding, the next morning when he heard that they carried Caesar's body to burial, being ashamed not to accompany his funerals, he went out of his house, and thrust himself into the press of the common people that were in a great uproar. And because someone called him by his name, Cinna, the people thinking he had been that Cinna, who in an oration he made had spoken very evil of Caesar, they falling upon him in their rage, slew him outright in the market-place.

21   This made Brutus and his companions more afraid, than any other thing, next unto the change of Antonius. Wherefore they got them out of Rome, and kept at the first in the city of Antium, hoping to return again to Rome, when the fury of the people were a little assuaged. The which they hoped would be quickly, considering that they had to deal with a fickle and inconstant multitude, easy to be carried, and that the senate stood for them: who notwithstanding made no enquiry of them that had torn poor Cinna the poet in pieces, but caused them to be sought for and apprehended, that went with firebrands to set fire of the conspirators' houses. The people growing weary now of Antonius' pride and insolency, who ruled all things in manner with absolute power, they desired that Brutus might return again: and it was also looked for, that Brutus would come himself in person to play the plays which were due to the people, by reason of his office of praetorship. But Brutus understanding that many of Caesar's soldiers which served under him in the wars, and that also had lands and houses given them in the cities where they lay, did lie in wait for him to kill him, and that they daily by small companies came by one and by one into Rome, he durst no more return thither, but yet the people had the pleasure and pastime in his absence, to see the games and sports he made them, which were sumptuously set forth and furnished with all things necessary, sparing for no cost. For he had bought a great number of strange beasts, of the which he would not give one of them to any friend he had, but that they should all be employed in his games: and went himself as far as Byzantium, to speak to some players of comedies and musicians that were there. And further he wrote unto his friends for one Canutius an excellent player, that whatsoever they did, they should entreat him to play in these plays: 'For,' said he, 'it is no reason to compel any Grecian, unless he will come of his own goodwill.' Moreover, he wrote also unto Cicero, and earnestly prayed him in any case to be at these plays.

22    Now the state of Rome standing in these terms, there fell out another change and alteration, when the young man Octavius Caesar came to Rome. He was the son of Julius Caesar's niece, whom he had adopted for his son, and made his heir, by his last will and testament. But when Julius Caesar his adopted father was slain, he was in the city of Apollonia, where he studied tarrying for him, because he was determined to make war with the Parthians: but when he heard the news of his death, he returned again to Rome, where to begin to curry favour with the common people, he first of all took upon him his adopted father's name, and made distribution among them of the money which his father had bequeathed unto them. By this means he troubled Antonius sorely, and by force of money, got a great number of his father's soldiers together, that had served in the wars with him. And Cicero himself, for the great malice he bore Antonius, did favour his proceedings. But Brutus marvellously reproved him for it, and wrote unto him, that he seemed by his doings not to be sorry to have a master, but only to be afraid to have one that should hate him: and that all his doings in the commonwealth did witness, that he chose to be subject to a mild and courteous bondage, if by his words and writings he did commend this young man Octavius Caesar, to be a good and gentle lord. 'For our predecessors,' said he, 'would never abide to be subject to any masters, how gentle or mild soever they were': and for his own part, that he had never resolutely determined with himself to make war or peace, but otherwise, that he was certainly minded never to be slave nor subject. And therefore he wondered much at him, how Cicero could be afraid of the danger of civil wars, and would not be afraid of a shameful peace: and that to thrust Antonius out of the usurped tyranny, in recompense he went about to stablish young Octavius Caesar tyrant.

23    These were the contents of Brutus' first letters he wrote unto Cicero. Now, the city of Rome being divided in two factions, some taking part with Antonius, other also leaning unto Octavius Caesar, and the soldiers making port sale of their service to him that would give most, Brutus seeing the state of Rome would be utterly overthrown, he determined to go out of Italy, and went afoot through the country of Luke, unto the city of Elea, standing by the sea. There Porcia being ready to depart from her husband Brutus,

and to return to Rome, did what she could to dissemble the grief and sorrow she felt at her heart: but a certain painted table bewrayed her in the end, although until that time she always showed a constant and patient mind. The device of the table was taken out of the Greek stories, how Andromachè accompanied her husband Hector, when he went out of the city of Troy, to go to the wars, and how Hector delivered her his little son, and how her eyes were never off him. Porcia seeing this picture, and likening herself to be in the same case, she fell a-weeping: and coming thither oftentimes in a day to see it, she wept still. Acilius one of Brutus' friends perceiving that, rehearsed the verses Andromache speaketh to this purpose in Homer:

> Thou Hector art my father, and my mother, and my brother,
> And husband eke, and all in all: I mind not any other.

Then Brutus smiling answered again:' But yet,' said he, 'I cannot for my part say unto Porcia, as Hector answered Andromache in the same place of the poet:

> Tush, meddle thou with weighing duly out
> Thy maids their task, and pricking on a clout.

For indeed, the weak constitution of her body doth not suffer her to perform in show, the valiant acts that we are able to do: but for courage and constant mind, she showed herself as stout in the defence of her country, as any of us.' Bibulus, the son of Porcia, reporteth this story thus.

24 Now Brutus embarking at Elea in Luke, he sailed directly towards Athens. When he arrived there, the people of Athens received him with common joys of rejoicing, and honourable decrees made for him. He lay with a friend of his, with whom he went daily to hear the lectures of Theomnestus Academic philosopher, and of Cratippus the Peripatetic, and so would talk with them in philosophy, that it seemed he left all other matters, and gave himself only unto study: howbeit secretly notwithstanding, he made preparation for war. For he sent Herostratus into Macedon, to win the captains and soldiers that were upon those marches, and he did also entertain all the young gentlemen of the Romans, whom he found in Athens studying philosophy: amongst them he found Cicero's son, whom he highly praised and

834 THE LIVES OF THE NOBLE GRECIANS AND ROMANS

commended, saying that whether he waked or slept, he found him of a noble mind and disposition, he did in nature so much hate tyrants. Shortly after, he began to enter openly into arms: and being advertised that there came out of Asia a certain fleet of Roman ships that had good store of money in them, and that the captain of those ships (who was an honest man, and his familiar friend) came towards Athens, he went to meet him as far as the Isle of Carystos, and having spoken with him there, he handled him so, that he was contented to leave his ships in his hands. Whereupon he made him a notable banquet at his house because it was on his birthday. When the feast day came, and that they began to drink lustily one to another, the guests drank to the victory of Brutus, and the liberty of the Romans. Brutus therefore to encourage them further, called for a bigger cup, and holding it in his hand, before he drank spoke this aloud:

> My destiny and Phoebus are agreed,
> To bring me to my final end with speed.

And for proof hereof, it is reported, that the same day he fought his last battle by the city of Philippes, as he came out of his tent, he gave his men for the word and signal of battle, 'Phoebus': so that it was thought ever since, that this his sudden crying out at the feast, was a prognostication of his misfortune that should happen.

25   After this, Antistius gave him of the money he carried into Italy, 50 myriads. Furthermore, all Pompey's soldiers that straggled up and down Thessaly, came with very goodwill unto him. He took from Cinna also, five hundred horsemen, which he carried into Asia, unto Dolabella. After that, he went by sea unto the city of Demetriade, and there took a great deal of armour and munition which was going to Antonius, and the which had been made and forged there by Julius Caesar's commandment, for the wars against the Parthians. Furthermore, Hortensius governor of Macedon, did resign the government thereof unto him. Besides, all the princes, kings and noblemen thereabouts came and joined with him, when it was told him that Caius, (Antonius' brother) coming out of Italy, had passed the sea, and came with great speed towards the city of Dyrrachium, and Apollonia, to get the soldiers into his hands, which Gabinius had there. Brutus therefore to prevent him, went presently with a few of his men in the midst of winter when it

snowed hard, and took his way thorough hard and foul countries, and made such speed indeed, that he was there long before Antonius' sumpters, that carried the victuals. So that when he came near unto Dyrrachium, a disease took him which the physicians call Βουλιμία, to say, a cormorant and unsatiable appetite to eat, by reason of the cold and pains he had taken. This sickness chanceth often, both to men and beasts, that travail when it hath snowed: either because the natural heat being retired into the inward parts of the body, by the coldness of the air hardening the skin, doth straight digest and consume the meat: or else because a sharp subtle wind coming by reason of the snow when it is molten, doth pierce into the body, and driveth out the natural heat which was cast outward. For it seemeth, that the heat being quenched with the cold, which it meeteth withal coming out of the skin of the body, causeth the sweats that follow the disease. But hereof we have spoken at large in other places.

26  Brutus being very faint, and having nothing in his camp to eat, his soldiers were compelled to go to their enemies; and coming to the gates of the city, they prayed the warders to help them to bread. When they heard in what case Brutus was, they brought him both meat and drink: in requital whereof, afterwards when he won the city, he did not only entreat and use the citizens thereof courteously, but all the inhabitants of the city also for their sakes. Now, when Caius Antonius was arrived in the city of Apollonia, he sent unto the soldiers thereabouts to come unto him. But when he understood that they went all to Brutus, and furthermore, that the citizens of Apollonia did favour him much, he then forsook that city, and went unto the city of Buthrotus, but yet he lost three of his ensigns by the way, that were slain every man of them. Then he sought by force to win certain places of strength about Byllis, and to drive Brutus' men from thence, that had taken it before: and therefore to obtain his purpose, he fought a battle with Cicero, the son of Marcus Tullius Cicero, by whom he was overcome. For Brutus made the younger Cicero a captain, and did many notable exploits by his service. Shortly after, having stolen upon Caius Antonius in certain marshes far from the place from whence he fled, he would not set on him with fury, but only rode round about him, commanding his soldiers to spare him and his men, as reckoning

them all his own without stroke striking: and so indeed it happened. For they yielded themselves, and their captain Antonius, unto Brutus: so that Brutus had now a great army about him. Now Brutus kept this Caius Antonius long time in his office, and never took from him the marks and signs of his consulship, although many of his friends, and Cicero among others, wrote unto him to put him to death. But when he saw Antonius secretly practised with his captains to make some alteration, then he sent him into a ship, and made him to be kept there. When the soldiers whom C. Antonius had corrupted, were got into the city of Apollonia, and sent from thence unto Brutus to come unto them, he made them answer, that it was not the manner of Roman captains to come to the soldiers, but the soldiers to come to the captain, and to crave pardon for their offences committed. Thereupon they came to him, and he pardoned them.

27    So Brutus preparing to go into Asia, news came unto him of the great change at Rome. For Octavius Caesar was in arms, by commandment and authority from the senate, against Marcus Antonius. But after that he had driven Antonius out of Italy, the senate then began to be afraid of him, because he sued to be consul, which was contrary to the law, and kept a great army about him, when the empire of Rome had no need of them. On the other side, Octavius Caesar perceiving the senate stayed not there, but turned unto Brutus that was out of Italy, and that they appointed him the government of certain provinces, then he began to be afraid for his part, and sent unto Antonius to offer him his friendship. Then coming on with his army near to Rome, he made himself to be chosen consul, whether the senate would or not, when he was yet but a stripling or springal of twenty year old, as himself reporteth in his own *Commentaries*. So when he was consul, he presently appointed judges to accuse Brutus and his companions, for killing of the noblest person in Rome, and chiefest magistrate, without law or judgment: and made L. Cornificius accuse Brutus, and M. Agrippa, Cassius. So, the parties accused were condemned, because the judges were compelled to give such sentence. The voice went, that when the herald (according to the custom after sentence given) went up to the chair or pulpit for orations, and proclaimed Brutus with a loud voice, summoning him to appear in person before the

judges, the people that stood by sighed openly, and the noblemen that were present hung down their heads, and durst not speak a word. Among them, the tears fell from Publius Silicius' eyes: who shortly after, was one of the proscripts or outlaws appointed to be slain. After that, these three, Octavius Caesar, Antonius and Lepidus, made an agreement between themselves, and by those articles divided the provinces belonging to the empire of Rome among themselves, and did set up bills of proscription and outlawry, condemning two hundred of the noblest men of Rome to suffer death, and among that number, Cicero was one.

28 News being brought thereof into Macedon, Brutus being then enforced to it, wrote unto Hortensius, that he should put Caius Antonius to death, to be revenged of the death of Cicero and of the other Brutus, of the which the one was his friend, and the other his kinsman. For this cause therefore, Antonius afterwards taking Hortensius at the battle of Philippes, he made him to be slain upon his brother's tomb. But then Brutus said, that he was more ashamed of the cause for the which Cicero was slain, than he was otherwise sorry for his death: and that he could not but greatly reprove his friends he had at Rome, who were slaves more through their own fault, than through their valiantness or manhood which usurped the tyranny: considering that they were so cowardly and faint-hearted, as to suffer the sight of those things before their eyes, the report whereof should only have grieved them to the heart. Now when Brutus had passed over his army (that was very great) into Asia, he gave order for the gathering of a great number of ships together, as well in the coast of Bithynia, as also in the city of Cyzicum, because he would have an army by sea: and himself in the meantime went unto the cities, taking order for all things, and giving audience unto princes and noblemen of the country that had to do with him. Afterwards, he sent unto Cassius in Syria, to turn him from his journey into Egypt, telling him that it was not for the conquest of any kingdom for themselves, that they wandered up and down in that sort, but contrarily, that it was to restore their country again to their liberty: and that the multitude of soldiers they gathered together, was to subdue the tyrannies that would keep them in slavery and subjection. Wherefore regarding their chief purpose and intent, they should not be far from Italy, as

near as they could possible, but should rather make all the haste
they could, to help their countrymen. Cassius believed him, and
returned. Brutus went to meet him, and they both met at the city
of Smyrna, which was the first time that they saw together, since
they took leave each of other, at the haven of Piraea in Athens: the
one going into Syria, and the other into Macedon. So they were
marvellous joyful, and no less courageous, when they saw the great
armies together which they had both levied: considering that they
departing out of Italy like naked and poor banished men, without
armour and money, nor having any ship ready, nor soldier about
them, nor any one town at their commandment: yet notwithstanding, in a short time after they were now met together, having
ships, money and soldiers enough, both footmen and horsemen, to
fight for the empire of Rome.

29   Now Cassius would have done Brutus as much honour, as
Brutus did unto him: but Brutus most commonly prevented him,
and went first unto him, both because he was the elder man, as also
for that he was sickly of body. And men reputed him commonly to
be very skilful in wars, but otherwise marvellous choleric and
cruel, who sought to rule men by fear, rather than with lenity: and
on the other side he was too familiar with his friends, and would
jest too broadly with them. But Brutus in contrary manner, for his
virtue and valiantness, was well-beloved of the people and his own,
esteemed of noble men, and hated of no man, not so much as of his
enemies, because he was a marvellous lowly and gentle person,
noble minded, and would never be in any rage, nor carried away
with pleasure and covetousness, but had ever an upright mind with
him, and would never yield to any wrong or injustice, the which
was the chiefest cause of his fame, of his rising, and of the goodwill
that every man bore him: for they were all persuaded that his intent
was good. For they did not certainly believe, that if Pompey
himself had overcome Caesar, he would have resigned his authority to the law: but rather they were of opinion, that he would still
keep the sovereignty and absolute government in his hands, taking
only, to please the people, the title of consul or dictator, or of some
other more civil office. And as for Cassius, a hot, choleric, and
cruel man, that would oftentimes be carried away from justice for
gain, it was certainly thought that he made war, and put himself

into sundry dangers, more to have absolute power and authority, than to defend the liberty of his country. For, they that will also consider others, that were elder men than they, as Cinna, Marius and Carbo, it is out of doubt that the end and hope of their victory, was to be lords of their country: and in manner they did all confess that they fought for the tyranny, and to be lords of the empire of Rome. And in contrary manner, his enemies themselves did never reprove Brutus, for any such change or desire. For, it was said that Antonius spoke it openly divers times, that he thought, that of all them that had slain Caesar, there was none but Brutus only that was moved to do it, as thinking the act commendable of itself: but that all the other conspirators did conspire his death, for some private malice or envy, that they otherwise did bear unto him. Hereby it appeareth, that Brutus did not trust so much to the power of his army, as he did to his own virtue: as is to be seen by his writings. For approaching near to the instant danger, he wrote unto Pomponious Atticus, that his affairs had the best hap that could be. 'For,' said he, 'either I will set my country at liberty by battle, or by honourable death rid me of this bondage.' And furthermore, that they being certain and assured of all things else, this one thing only was doubtful to them: whether they should live or die with liberty. He wrote also that Antonius had his due payment for his folly. For where he might have been a partner equally of the glory of Brutus, Cassius, and Cato, and have made one with them, he liked better to choose to be joined with Octavius Caesar alone: 'With whom, though now he be not overcome by us, yet shall he shortly after also have war with him.' And truly he proved a true prophet, for so came it indeed to pass.

30  Now whilst Brutus and Cassius were together in the city of Smyrna, Brutus prayed Cassius to let him have some part of his money whereof he had great store, because all that he could rap and rend of his side, he had bestowed it in making so great a number of ships, that by means of them they should keep all the sea at their commandment. Cassius' friends hindered this request, and earnestly dissuaded him from it, persuading him, that it was no reason that Brutus should have the money which Cassius had got together by sparing, and levied with great evil will of the people their subjects, for him to bestow liberally upon his soldiers, and

by this means to win their goodwills, by Cassius' charge. This notwithstanding, Cassius gave him the third part of his total sum. So Cassius and Brutus then departing from each other, Cassius took the city of Rhodes, where he too dishonestly and cruelly used himself: although when he came into the city, he answered some of the inhabitants, who called him lord and king, that he was neither lord nor king, but he only that had slain him, that would have been lord and king. Brutus departing from thence, sent unto the Lycians, to require money and men of war. But there was a certain orator called Naucrates, that made the cities to rebel against him, insomuch that the countrymen of that country kept the straits and little mountains, thinking by that means to stop Brutus' passage. Wherefore Brutus sent his horsemen against them, who stole upon them as they were at dinner, and slew six hundred of them: and taking all the small towns and villages, he did let all the prisoners he took go without payment of ransom, hoping by this his great courtesy to win them, to draw all the rest of the country unto him. But they were so fierce and obstinate, that they would mutiny for every small hurt they received as they passed by their country, and did despise his courtesy and good nature, until that at length he went to besiege the city of the Xanthians, within the which were shut up the cruellest and most warlikest men of Lycia. There was a river that ran by the walls of the city, in the which many men saved themselves, swimming between two waters, and fled: howbeit they laid nets overthwart the river, and tied little bells on the top of them, to sound when any man was taken in the nets. The Xanthians made a sally out by night, and came to fire certain engines of battery that beat down their walls: but they were presently driven in again by the Romans, so soon as they were discovered. The wind by chance was marvellous big, and increased the flame so sore, that it violently carried it into the crannies of the wall of the city, so that the next houses unto them were straight set afire thereby. Wherefore Brutus being afraid that all the city would take of a fire, he presently commanded his men to quench the fire, and to save the town if it might be.

31    But the Lycians at that instant fell into such a frenzy, and strange and horrible despair, that no man can well express it: and

a man cannot more rightly compare or liken it, than to a frantic and most desperate desire to die. For all of them together, with their wives and children, masters and servants, and of all sorts of age whatsoever, fought upon the rampart of their walls, and did cast down stones and fireworks on the Romans, which were very busy in quenching the flame of the fire, to save the city. And in contrary manner also, they brought faggots, dry wood, and reeds, to bring the fire further into the city as much as might be, increasing it by such things as they brought. Now when the fire had got into all the parts of the city, and that the flame burnt bright in every place, Brutus being sorry to see it, got upon his horse, and rode round about the walls of the city, to see if it were possible to save it, and held up his hands to the inhabitants, praying them to pardon their city, and to save themselves. Howbeit they would not be persuaded, but did all that they could possible to cast themselves away, not only men and women, but also little children. For some of them weeping and crying out, did cast themselves into the fire: others headlong throwing themselves down from the walls, broke their necks: others also made their necks bare, to the naked swords of their fathers, and undid their clothes, praying them to kill them with their own hands. After the city was burnt, they found a woman hanged up by the neck, holding one of her children in her hand dead by her, hanged up also: and in the other hand a burning torch setting fire on her house. Some would have had Brutus to have seen her, but he would not see so horrible and tragical a sight: but when he heard it, he fell a-weeping, and caused a herald to make proclamation by sound of trumpet, that he would give a certain sum of money, to every soldier that could save a Xanthian. So there were not (as it is reported) above fifty of them saved, and yet they were saved against their wills. Thus the Xanthians having ended the revolution of their fatal destiny, after a long continuance of time, they did through their desperation, renew the memory of the lamentable calamities of their ancestors. Who in like manner, in the wars of the Persians, did burn their city, and destroyed themselves.

32    Therefore Brutus likewise besieging the city of the Patareians, perceiving that they stoutly resisted him, he was also afraid of that, and could not well tell whether he should give assault to it, or

not, lest they would fall into the despair and desperation of the Xanthians. Howbeit having taken certain of their women prisoners, he sent them back again, without payment of ransom. Now they that were the wives and daughters of the noblest men of the city, reporting unto their parents, that they had found Brutus a merciful, just and courteous man, they persuaded them to yield themselves and their city unto him, the which they did. So after they had thus yielded themselves, divers other cities also followed them, and did the like: and found Brutus more merciful and courteous, than they thought they should have done, but specially far above Cassius. For Cassius, about the selfsame time, after he had compelled the Rhodians every man to deliver all the ready money they had in gold and silver in their houses, the which being brought together, amounted to the sum of eight thousand talents, yet he condemned the city besides, to pay the sum of five hundred talents more. Where Brutus in contrary manner, after he had levied of all the country of Lycia but a hundred and fifty talents only, he departed thence into the country of Ionia, and did them no more hurt.

33   Now Brutus in all this journey, did many notable acts and worthy of memory, both for rewarding, as also in punishing those that had deserved it: wherefore among the rest, I will tell you of one thing, of the which he himself, and all the noblemen of the Romans, were marvellous glad. When Pompey the Great (having lost the battle against Julius Caesar, in the fields of Pharsalia) came and fell upon the coast of Egypt, hard by the city of Pelusium, those that were protectors to the young King Ptolomy, being then but a child, sat in council with his servants and friends, what they should determine in that case. They were not all of one mind in this consultation: for some thought it good to receive Pompey, others also, that they should drive him out of Egypt. But there was a certain rhetorician called Theodotus, that was born in the Isle of Chio, who was the king's schoolmaster to teach him rhetoric. He being called to this council for lack of sufficienter men, said, that both the one and the other side went awry, as well those that were of opinion to receive Pompey, as the other that would have had him driven away: and that the best way was (considering the present time) that they should lay hold on him, and kill him, adding withal this sentence, that a dead man biteth not. The whole council stuck

to this opinion. So, for a notable example of incredible misfortune, and unlooked for unto Pompey, Pompey the Great was slain, by the motion and counsel of this wicked rhetorician Theodotus, as Theodotus afterwards did himself boast of it. But when Julius Caesar came afterwards into Egypt, the wicked men that consented to this counsel, had their payment according to their deserts: for they died every man of them a wicked death, saving this Theodotus, whom fortune respited a little while longer, and yet in that time he lived a poor and miserable life, never tarrying long in any one place. So Brutus going up and down Asia, Theodotus could hide himself no longer, but was brought unto Brutus, where he suffered pains of death: so that he won more fame by his death, than ever he did in his life.

34    About that time, Brutus sent to pray Cassius to come to the city of Sardis, and so he did. Brutus understanding of his coming, went to meet him with all his friends. There, both their armies being armed, they called them both emperors. Now, as it commonly happeneth in great affairs between two persons, both of them having many friends, and so many captains under them, there ran tales and complaints betwixt them. Therefore, before they fell in hand with any other matter, they went into a little chamber together, and bade every man avoid, and did shut the doors to them. Then they began to pour out their complaints one to the other, and grew hot and loud, earnestly accusing one another, and at length fell both a-weeping. Their friends that were without the chamber hearing them loud within, and angry between themselves, they were both amazed, and afraid also lest it would grow to further matter: but yet they were commanded, that no man should come to them. Notwithstanding, one Marcus Phaonius, that had been a friend and follower of Cato while he lived, and took upon him to counterfeit a philosopher, not with wisdom and discretion, but with a certain bedlam and frantic motion: he would needs come into the chamber, though the men offered to keep him out. But it was no boot to let Phaonius, when a mad mood or toy took him in the head: for he was a hot hasty man, and sudden in all his doings, and cared for never a senator of them all. Now, though he used this bold manner of speech after the profession of the Cynic philosophers (as who would say, dogs), yet this boldness did no

hurt many times, because they did but laugh at him to see him so mad. This Phaonius at that time, in despite of the doorkeepers, came into the chamber, and with a certain scoffing and mocking gesture which he counterfeited of purpose, he rehearsed the verses which old Nestor said in Homer:

> My lords, I pray you hearken both to me,
> For I have seen more years than suchye three.

Cassius fell a-laughing at him: but Brutus thrust him out of the chamber, and called him dog, and counterfeit Cynic. Howbeit his coming in broke their strife at that time, and so they left each other. The selfsame night Cassius prepared his supper in his chamber, and Brutus brought his friends with him. So when they were set at supper, Phaonius came to sit down after he had washed. Brutus told him aloud, no man sent for him, and bade them set him at the upper end: meaning indeed at the lower end of the bed. Phaonius made no ceremony, but thrust in amongst the midst of them, and made all the company laugh at him: so they were merry all supper time, and full of their philosophy.

35    The next day after, Brutus, upon complaint of the Sardians, did condemn and noted Lucius Pella for a defamed person, that had been a praetor of the Romans, and whom Brutus had given charge unto, for that he was accused and convicted of robbery and pilfery in his office. This judgment much misliked Cassius, because he himself had secretly (not many days before) warned two of his friends, attainted and convicted of the like offences, and openly had cleared them: but yet he did not therefore leave to employ them in any manner of service as he did before. And therefore he greatly reproved Brutus, for that he would show himself so strait and severe in such a time as was meeter to bear a little, than to take things at the worst. Brutus in contrary manner answered, that he should remember the Ides of March, at which time they slew Julius Caesar: who neither pilled nor polled the country, but only was a favourer and suborner of all them that did rob and spoil, by his countenance and authority. And if there were any occasion whereby they might honestly set aside justice and equity, they should have had more reason to have suffered Caesar's friends to have robbed and done what wrong and injury they had would, than to bear with their own men. For then said he, they could but

have said they had been cowards: 'And now they may accuse us of injustice, beside the pains we take, and the danger we put ourselves into.' And thus may we see what Brutus' intent and purpose was.

36  But as they both prepared to pass over again, out of Asia into Europe, there went a rumour that there appeared a wonderful sign unto him. Brutus was a careful man, and slept very little, both for that his diet was moderate, as also because he was continually occupied. He never slept in the day time, and in the night no longer, than the time he was driven to be alone, and when everybody else took their rest. But now whilst he was in war, and his head ever busily occupied to think of his affairs, and what would happen, after he had slumbered a little after supper, he spent all the rest of the night in dispatching of his weightiest causes, and after he had taken order for them, if he had any leisure left him, he would read some book till the third watch of the night, at what time the captains, petty captains and colonels did use to come unto him. So, being ready to go into Europe, one night very late (when all the camp took quiet rest) as he was in his tent with a little light, thinking of weighty matters, he thought he heard one come in to him, and casting his eye towards the door of his tent, that he saw a wonderful strange and monstrous shape of a body coming towards him, and said never a word. So Brutus boldly asked what he was, a god, or a man, and what cause brought him thither. The spirit answered him,' I am thy evil spirit, Brutus: and thou shalt see me by the city of Philippes.' Brutus being no otherwise afraid, replied again unto it: 'Well, then I shall see thee again.'

37  The spirit presently vanished away, and Brutus called his men unto him, who told him that they heard no noise, nor saw anything at all. Thereupon Brutus returned again to think on his matters as he did before: and when the day broke, he went unto Cassius, to tell him what vision had appeared unto him in the night. Cassius being in opinion an Epicurian, and reasoning thereon with Brutus, spoke to him touching the vision thus. 'In our sect, Brutus, we have an opinion, that we do not always feel or see, that which we suppose we do both see and feel: but that our senses being credulous, and therefore easily abused (when they are idle and unoccupied in their own objects), are induced to imagine they see and conjecture that which they in truth do not. For,

our mind is quick and cunning to work (without either cause or matter) anything in the imagination whatsoever. And therefore the imagination is resembled to clay, and the mind to the potter: who without any other cause than his fancy and pleasure, changeth it into what fashion and form he will. And this doth the diversity of our dreams show unto us. For our imagination doth upon a small fancy grow from conceit to conceit, altering both in passions and forms of things imagined. For the mind of man is ever occupied, and that continual moving is nothing but an imagination. But yet there is a further cause of this in you. For you being by nature given to melancholic discoursing, and of late continually occupied, your wits and senses having been overlaboured, do easier yield to such imaginations. For, to say that there are spirits or angels, and if there were, that they had the shape of men, or such voices, or any power at all to come unto us, it is a mockery. And for mine own part, I would there were such, because that we should not only have soldiers, horses, and ships, but also the aid of the gods, to guide and further our honest and honourable attempts.' With these words Cassius did somewhat comfort and quiet Brutus. When they raised their camp, there came two eagles that flying with a marvellous force, lighted upon two of the foremost ensigns, and always followed the soldiers, which gave them meat, and fed them, until they came near to the city of Philippes: and there one day only before the battle, they both flew away.

38 Now Brutus had conquered the most part of all the people and nations of that country: but if there were any other city or captain to overcome, then they made all clear before them, and so drew towards the coasts of Thassos. There Norbanus lying in camp in a certain place called the straits, by another place called Symbolon (which is a port of the sea), Cassius and Brutus compassed him in in such sort, that he was driven to forsake the place which was of great strength for him, and he was also in danger beside to have lost all his army. For, Octavius Caesar could not follow him because of his sickness, and therefore stayed behind: whereupon they had taken his army, had not Antonius' aid been, which made such wonderful speed, that Brutus could scant believe it. So Caesar came not thither of ten days after: and Antonius camped against Cassius, and Brutus on the other side against Caesar. The Romans called the valley

between both camps, the Philippian fields: and there were never seen two so great armies of the Romans, one before the other, ready to fight. In truth, Brutus' army was inferior to Octavius Caesar's in number of men: but for bravery and rich furniture, Brutus' army far excelled Caesar's. For the most part of their armours were silver and gilt, which Brutus had bountifully given them, although in all other things he taught his captains to live in order without excess. But for the bravery of armour and weapon, which soldiers should carry in their hands, or otherwise wear upon their backs, he thought that it was an encouragement unto them that by nature are greedy of honour, and that it maketh them also fight like devils that love to get, and be afraid to lose: because they fight to keep their armour and weapon, as also their goods and lands.

39 Now when they came to muster their armies, Octavius Caesar took the muster of his army within the trenches of his camp, and gave his men only a little corn, and five silver drachmas to every man to sacrifice to the gods, and to pray for victory. But Brutus scorning this misery and niggardliness, first of all mustered his army, and did purify it in the fields, according to the manner of the Romans: and then he gave unto every band a number of wethers to sacrifice, and fifty silver drachmas to every soldier. So that Brutus' and Cassius' soldiers were better pleased, and more courageously bent to fight at the day of the battle, than their enemies' soldiers were. Notwithstanding, being busily occupied about the ceremonies of this purification, it is reported that there chanced certain unlucky signs unto Cassius. For one of his sergeants that carried the rods before him, brought him the garland of flowers turned backwards, the which he should have worn on his head in the time of sacrificing. Moreover it is reported also, that at another time before, in certain sports and triumph where they carried an image of Cassius' victory of clean gold, it fell by chance, the man stumbling that carried it. And yet further, there were soon a marvellous number of fowls of prey, that feed upon dead carcasses: and beehives also were found, where bees were gathered together in a certain place within the trenches of the camp: the which place the soothsayers thought good to shut out of the precinct of the camp, for to take away the superstitious fear and mistrust men would have of it. The which began somewhat to alter

Cassius' mind from Epicurus' opinions, and had put the soldiers also in a marvellous fear. Thereupon Cassius was of opinion not to try this war at one battle, but rather to delay time, and to draw it out in length, considering that they were the stronger in money, and the weaker in men and armours. But Brutus in contrary manner, did always before, and at that time also, desire nothing more, than to put all to the hazard of battle, as soon as might be possible: to the end he might either quickly restore his country to her former liberty, or rid him forthwith of this miserable world, being still troubled in following and maintaining of such great armies together. But perceiving that in the daily skirmishes and bickerings they made, his men were always the stronger, and ever had the better, that yet quickened his spirits again, and did put him in better heart. And furthermore, because that some of their own men had already yielded themselves to their enemies, and that it was suspected moreover divers others would do the like, that made many of Cassius' friends, which were of his mind before (when it came to be debated in council whether the battle should be fought or not), that they were then of Brutus' mind. But yet was there one of Brutus' friends called Atellius, that was against it, and was of opinion that they should tarry the next winter. Brutus asked him what he should get by tarrying a year longer? 'If I get nought else,' quoth Attellius again, 'yet have I lived so much longer.' Cassius was very angry with this answer: and Atellius was maliced and esteemed the worse for it of all men. Thereupon it was presently determined they should fight battle the next day.

40    So Brutus all supper time looked with a cheerful countenance, like a man that had good hope, and talked very wisely of philosophy, and after supper went to bed. But touching Cassius, Messala reporteth that he supped by himself in his tent with a few of his friends, and that all supper time he looked very sadly, and was full of thoughts, although it was against his nature: and that after supper he took him by the hand, and holding him fast (in token of kindness as his manner was) told him in Greek: 'Messala, I protest unto thee, and make thee my witness, that I am compelled against my mind and will (as Pompey the Great was) to jeopardy the liberty of our country, to the hazard of a battle. And yet we must be lively, and of good courage, considering our good fortune, whom we should

wrong too much to mistrust her, although we follow evil counsel.'
Messala writeth, that Cassius having spoken these last words unto
him, he bade him farewell, and willed him to come to supper to
him the next night following, because it was his birthday. The next
morning by break of day, the signal of battle was set out in Brutus'
and Cassius' camp, which was an arming scarlet coat: and both the
chieftains spoke together in the midst of their armies. There Cassius
began to speak first, and said: 'The gods grant us, O Brutus, that this
day we may win the field, and ever after to live all the rest of our
life quietly, one with another. But since the gods have so ordained
it, that the greatest and chiefest things amongst men are most
uncertain, and that if the battle fall out otherwise today than we
wish or look for, we shall hardly meet again: what art thou then
determined to do: to fly, or die?' Brutus answered him, 'Being yet
but a young man, and not overgreatly experienced in the world, I
trust (I know not how) a certain rule of philosophy, by the which I
did greatly blame and reprove Cato for killing of himself, as being
no lawful nor godly act, touching the gods, nor concerning men
valiant, not to give place and yield to divine providence, and not
constantly and patiently to take whatsoever it pleaseth him to send
us, but to draw back, and fly: but being now in the midst of the
danger, I am of a contrary mind. For if it be not the will of God, that
this battle fall out fortunate for us, I will look no more for hope,
neither seek to make any new supply for war again, but will rid me
of this miserable world, and content me with my fortune. For, I
gave up my life for my country in the Ides of March, for the which
I shall live in another more glorious world.' Cassius fell a-laughing
to hear what he said, and embracing him, 'Come on then,' said he,
'let us go and charge our enemies with this mind. For either we shall
conquer, or we shall not need to fear the conquerors.' After this talk,
they fell to consultation among their friends for the ordering of the
battle. Then Brutus prayed Cassius he might have the leading of the
right wing, the which men thought was far meeter for Cassius, both
because he was the elder man, and also for that he had the better
experience. But yet Cassius gave it him, and willed that Messala
(who had charge of one of the warlikest legions they had) should be
also in that wing with Brutus. So Brutus presently sent out his
horsemen, who were excellently well appointed, and his footmen
also were as willing and ready to give charge.

41    Now Antonius' men did cast a trench from the marsh by the which they lay, to cut off Cassius' way to come to the sea: and Caesar, at the least his army, stirred not. As for Octavius Caesar himself, he was not in his camp, because he was sick. And for his people, they little thought the enemies would have given them battle, but only have made some light skirmishes to hinder them that wrought in the trench, and with their darts and slings to have kept them from finishing of their work: but they taking no heed to them that came full upon them to give them battle, marvelled much at the great noise they heard, that came from the place where they were casting their trench. In the meantime Brutus that led the right wing, sent little bills to the colonels and captains of private bands, in the which he wrote the word of the battle: and he himself riding a-horseback by all the troops, did speak to them, and encouraged them to stick to it like men. So by this means very few of them understood what was the word of the battle, and besides, the most part of them never tarried to have it told them, but ran with great fury to assail the enemies: whereby through this disorder, the legions were marvellously scattered and dispersed one from the other. For first of all Messala's legion, and then the next unto them, went beyond the left wing of the enemies, and did nothing, but glancing by them, overthrew some as they went, and so going on further, fell right upon Caesar's camp, out of the which (as himself writeth in his *Commentaries*) he had been conveyed away a little before, thorough the counsel and advice of one of his friends called Marcus Artorius: who dreaming in the night, had a vision appeared unto him, that commanded Octavius Caesar should be carried out of his camp. Insomuch as it was thought he was slain, because his litter (which had nothing in it) was thrust through and through with pikes and darts. There was great slaughter in this camp. For amongst others, there were slain two thousand Lacedaemonians, who were arrived but even a little before, coming to aid Caesar.

42    The other also that had not glanced by, but had given a charge full upon Caesar's battle, they easily made them flee, because they were greatly troubled for the loss of their camp, and of them there were slain by hand, three legions. Then being very earnest to follow the chase of them that fled, they ran in amongst them hand over

head into their camp, and Brutus among them. But that which the
conquerors thought not of, occasion showed it unto them that were
overcome: and that was, the left wing of their enemies left naked,
and unguarded of them of the right wing, who were strayed too far
off, in following of them that were overthrown. So they gave a hot
charge upon them. But notwithstanding all the force they made,
they could not break into the midst of their battle, where they
found men that received them, and valiantly made head against
them. Howbeit they broke and overthrew the left wing where
Cassius was, by reason of the great disorder among them, and also
because they had no intelligence how the right wing had sped. So
they chased them beating them into their camp, the which they
spoiled, none of both the chieftains being present there. For
Antonius, as it is reported, to fly the fury of the first charge, was
got into the next marsh: and no man could tell what became of
Octavius Caesar, after he was carried out of his camp. Insomuch
that there were certain soldiers that showed their swords bloodied,
and said that they had slain him, and did describe his face, and
showed what age he was of. Furthermore the forward and the midst
of Brutus' battle, had already put all their enemies to flight that
withstood them, with great slaughter: so that Brutus had conquered
all of his side, and Cassius had lost all on the other side. For nothing
undid them, but that Brutus went not to help Cassius, thinking he
had overcome them, as himself had done: and Cassius on the other
side tarried not for Brutus, thinking he had been overthrown, as
himself was. And to prove that the victory fell on Brutus' side,
Messala confirmeth it: that they won three eagles, and divers other
ensigns of their enemies, and their enemies won never a one of
theirs. Now Brutus returning from the chase, after he had slain and
sacked Caesar's men, he wondered much that he could not see
Cassius' tent standing up high as it was wont, neither the other tents
of his camp standing as they were before, because all the whole
camp had been spoiled, and the tents thrown down, at the first
coming in of the enemies. But they that were about Brutus, whose
sight served them better, told him that they saw a great glistering of
harness, and a number of silvered targets, that went and came into
Cassius' camp, and were not (as they took it) the armours, nor the
number of men, that they had left there to guard the camp: and
yet that they saw not such a number of dead bodies, and great

overthrow, as there should have been, if so many legions had
been slain. This made Brutus at the first mistrust that which had
happened. So he appointed a number of men to keep the camp of
his enemy which he had taken, and caused his men to be sent for
that yet followed the chase, and gathered them together, thinking
to lead them to aid Cassius, who was in this state as you shall hear.

43    First of all he was marvellous angry, to see how Brutus' men
ran to give charge upon their enemies, and tarried not for the word
of the battle, nor commandment to give charge: and it grieved him
beside, that after he had overcome them, his men fell straight to
spoil, and were not careful to compass in the rest of the enemies
behind. But with tarrying too long also, more than through the
valiantness or foresight of the captains his enemies, Cassius found
himself compassed in with the right wing of his enemies' army.
Whereupon his horsemen broke immediately, and fled for life
towards the sea. Furthermore, perceiving his footmen to give
ground, he did what he could to keep them from flying, and took
an ensign from one of the ensign bearers that fled, and stuck it fast
at his feet, although with much ado he could scant keep his own
guard together. So Cassius himself was at length compelled to fly,
with a few about him, unto a little hill, from whence they might
easily see what was done in all the plain: howbeit Cassius himself
saw nothing, for his sight was very bad, saving that he saw (and yet
with much ado) how the enemies spoiled his camp before his eyes.
He saw also a great troop of horsemen, whom Brutus sent to aid
him, and thought that they were his enemies that followed him:
but yet he sent Titinnius, one of them that was with him, to go and
know what they were. Brutus' horsemen saw him coming afar off,
whom when they knew that he was one of Cassius' chiefest friends,
they shouted out for joy: and they that were familiarly acquainted
with him, lighted from their horses, and went and embraced him.
The rest compassed him in round about a-horseback, with songs of
victory and great rushing of their harness, so that they made all the
field ring again for joy. But this marred all. For Cassius thinking
indeed that Titinnius was taken of the enemies, he then spoke
these words: 'Desiring too much to live, I have lived to see one of
my best friends taken, for my sake, before my face.' After that, he
got into a tent where nobody was, and took Pyndarus with him,

one of his freed bondmen, whom he reserved ever for such a
pinch, since the cursed battle of the Parthians, where Crassus was
slain, though he notwithstanding escaped from that overthrow: but
then casting his cloak over his head, and holding out his bare neck
unto Pindarus, he gave him his head to be stricken off. So the head
was found severed from the body: but after that time Pindarus was
never seen more. Whereupon some took occasion to say, that he
had slain his master without his commandment. By and by they
knew the horsemen that came towards them, and might see
Titinnius crowned with a garland of triumph, who came before
with great speed unto Cassius. But when he perceived by the cries
and tears of his friends which tormented themselves, the misfortune that had chanced to his captain Cassius, by mistaking, he
drew out his sword, cursing himself a thousand times that he had
tarried so long, and so slew himself presently in the field.

44   Brutus in the meantime came forward still, and understood
also that Cassius had been overthrown: but he knew nothing of his
death, till he came very near to his camp. So when he was come
thither, after he had lamented the death of Cassius, calling him the
last of all the Romans, being unpossible that Rome should ever
breed again so noble and valiant a man as he, he caused his body to
be buried, and sent it to the city of Thassos, fearing lest his funerals
within the camp should cause great disorder. Then he called his
soldiers together, and did encourage them again. And when
he saw that they had lost all their carriage, which they could
not brook well, he promised every man of them two thousand
drachmas in recompense. After his soldiers had heard his oration,
they were all of them prettily cheered again, wondering much at
his great liberality, and waited upon him with great cries when he
went his way, praising him, for that he only of the four chieftains,
was not overcome in battle. And to speak the truth, his deeds
showed that he hoped not in vain to be conqueror. For with few
legions, he had slain and driven all them away, that made head
against him: and yet if all his people had fought, and that the most
of them had not outgone their enemies to run to spoil their goods,
surely it was like enough he had slain them all, and had left never
a man of them alive.

45   There were slain of Brutus' side, about eight thousand men, counting the soldiers' slaves, whom Brutus called Brigas: and of the enemies' side, as Messala writeth, there were slain as he supposeth, more than twice as many more. Wherefore they were more discouraged than Brutus, until that very late at night, there was one of Cassius' men called Demetrius, who went unto Antonius, and carried his master's clothes, whereof he was stripped not long before, and his sword also. This encouraged Brutus' enemies, and made them so brave, that the next morning betimes they stood in battle ray again before Brutus. But on Brutus' side, both his camps stood wavering, and that in great danger. For his own camp being full of prisoners, required a good guard to look unto them: and Cassius' camp on the other side took the death of their captain very heavily, and beside, there was some vile grudge between them that were overcome, and those that did overcome. For this cause therefore Brutus did set them in battle ray, but yet kept himself from giving battle. Now for the slaves that were prisoners, which were a great number of them, and went and came to and fro amongst the armed men, not without suspicion, he commanded they should kill them. But for the freemen, he sent them freely home, and said, that they were better prisoners with his enemies, than with him. For with them, they were slaves and servants: and with him, they were free men and citizens. So when he saw that divers captains and his friends did so cruelly hate some, that they would by no means save their lives, Brutus himself hid them, and secretly sent them away. Among these prisoners, there was one Volumnius a jester, and Sacculio a common player, of whom Brutus made no account at all. Howbeit his friends brought them unto him, and did accuse them, that though they were prisoners, they did not let to laugh them to scorn, and to jest broadly with them. Brutus made no answer to it, because his head was occupied otherwise. Whereupon, Messala Corvinus said, that it were good to whip them on a scaffold, and then to send them naked, well whipped, unto the captains of their enemies, to show them their shame, to keep such mates as those in their camp, to play the fools, to make them sport. Some that stood by, laughed at his devise. But Publius Casca, that gave Julius Caesar the first wound when he was slain, said then: 'It doth not become us to be thus merry at Cassius' funerals: and for thee,

Brutus, thou shalt show what estimation thou madest of such a captain thy compeer, by putting to death, or saving the lives of these bloods, who hereafter will mock him, and defame his memory.' Brutus answered again in choler: 'Why then do you come to tell me of it, Casca, and do not yourselves what you think good?' When they heard him say so, they took his answer for a consent against these poor unfortunate men, to suffer them to do what they thought good: and therefore they carried them away, and slew them.

46   Afterwards Brutus performed the promise he had made to the soldiers, and gave them the two thousand drachmas  piece, but yet he first reproved them, because they went and gave charge upon the enemies at the first battle, before they had the word of battle given them: and made them a new promise also, that if in the second battle they fought like men, he would give them the sack and spoil of two cities, to wit, Thessalonica and Lacedaemon. In all Brutus' life there is but this only fault to be found, and that is not to be gainsaid: though Antonius and Octavius Caesar did reward their soldiers far worse for their victory. For when they had driven all the natural Italians out of Italy, they gave their soldiers their lands and towns, to the which they had no right: and moreover, the only mark they shot at in all this war they made, was but to overcome, and reign. Where in contrary manner they had so great an opinion of Brutus' virtue, that the common voice and opinion of the world would not suffer him, neither to overcome, nor to save himself, otherwise than justly and honestly, and specially after Cassius' death: whom men burdened, that oftentimes he moved Brutus to great cruelty. But now, like as the mariners on the sea after the rudder of their ship is broken by tempest, do seek to nail on some other piece of wood in lieu thereof, and do help themselves to keep them from hurt, as much as may be upon that instant danger, even so Brutus, having such a great army to govern, and his affairs standing very tickle, and having no other captain coequal with him in dignity and authority, he was forced to employ them he had, and likewise to be ruled by them in many things, and was of mind himself also to grant them anything, that he thought might make them serve like noble soldiers at time of need. For Cassius' soldiers were very evil to be ruled, and did show themselves very stubborn

and lusty in the camp, because they had no chieftain that did command them: but yet rank cowards to their enemies, because they had once overcome them.

47   On the other side Octavius Caesar and Antonius were not in much better state: for first of all, they lacked victuals. And because they were lodged in low places, they looked to abide a hard and sharp winter, being camped as they were by the marsh side, and also for that after the battle there had fallen plenty of rain about the autumn, where through, all their tents were full of mire and dirt, the which by reason of the cold did freeze incontinently. But beside all these discommodities, there came news unto them of the great loss they had of their men by sea. For Brutus' ships met with a great aid and supply of men, which were sent them out of Italy, and they overthrew them in such sort, that there escaped but few of them: and yet they were so famished, that they were compelled to eat the tackle and sails of their ships. Thereupon they were very desirous to fight a battle again, before Brutus should have intelligence of this good news for him: for it chanced so, that the battle was fought by sea, on the selfsame day it was fought by land. But by ill fortune, rather than through the malice or negligence of the captains, this victory came not to Brutus' ear till twenty days after. For had he known of it before, he would not have been brought to have fought a second battle, considering that he had excellent good provision for his army for a long time, and besides, lay in a place of great strength, so as his camp could not be greatly hurt by the winter, nor also distressed by his enemies: and further, he had been a quiet lord, being a conqueror by sea, as he was also by land. This would have marvellously encouraged him. Howbeit the state of Rome (in my opinion) being now brought to that pass, that it could no more abide to be governed by many lords, but required one only absolute governor, God, to prevent Brutus that it should not come to his government, kept this victory from his knowledge, though indeed it came but a little too late. For the day before the last battle was given, very late in the night, came Clodius, one of his enemies, into his camp, who told that Caesar hearing of the overthrow of his army by sea, desired nothing more than to fight a battle before Brutus understood it. Howbeit they gave no credit to his words, but despised him so much, that they would not vouchsafe to bring

him unto Brutus, because they thought it was but a lie devised, to be the better welcome for this good news.

48 The selfsame night, it is reported that the monstrous spirit which had appeared before unto Brutus in the city of Sardis, did now appear again unto him in the selfsame shape and form, and so vanished away, and said never a word. Now Publius Volumnius, a grave and wise philosopher, that had been with Brutus from the beginning of this war, he doth make mention of this spirit, but saith: that the greatest eagle and ensign was covered over with a swarm of bees, and that there was one of the captains, whose arm suddenly fell a-sweating, that it dropped oil of roses from him, and that they oftentimes went about to dry him, but all would do no good. And that before the battle was fought, there were two eagles fought between both armies, and all the time they fought, there was a marvellous great silence all the valley over, both the armies being one before the other, marking this fight between them: and that in the end, the eagle towards Brutus gave over, and flew away. But this is certain, and a true tale: that when the gate of the camp was open, the first man the standard bearer met that carried the eagle, was an Ethiopian, whom the soldiers for ill luck mangled with their swords.

49 Now, after that Brutus had brought his army into the field, and had set them in battle ray, directly against the forward of his enemy, he paused a long time, before he gave the signal of battle. For Brutus riding up and down to view the bands and companies, it came in his head to mistrust some of them, besides that some came to tell him so much as he thought. Moreover, he saw his horsemen set forward but faintly, and did not go lustily to give charge, but still stayed to see what the footmen would do. Then suddenly, one of the chiefest knights he had in all his army, called Camulatius, and that was always marvellously esteemed of for his valiantness, until that time, he came hard by Brutus a-horseback, and rode before his face to yield himself unto his enemies. Brutus was marvellous sorry for it, wherefore partly for anger, and partly for fear of greater treason and rebellion, he suddenly caused his army to march, being past three of the clock in the afternoon. So in that place where he himself fought in person, he had the better: and broke into the left wing of his enemies, which gave him way, through the help of his

horsemen that gave charge with his footmen, when they saw the
enemies in amaze, and afraid. Howbeit the other also on the right
wing, when the captains would have had them to have marched,
they were afraid to have been compassed in behind, because they
were fewer in number than their enemies, and therefore did spread
themselves, and leave the midst of their battle. Whereby they
having weakened themselves, they could not withstand the force of
their enemies, but turned tail straight, and fled. And those that had
put them to flight, came in straight upon it to compass Brutus
behind, who in the midst of the conflict, did all that was possible for
a skilful captain and valiant soldier, both for his wisdom as also for
his hardiness, for the obtaining of victory. But that which won him
the victory at the first battle, did now lose it him at the second. For
at the first time, the enemies that were broken and fled, were
straight cut in pieces: but at the second battle, of Cassius' men that
were put to flight, there were few slain: and they that saved
themselves by speed, being afraid because they had been overcome,
did discourage the rest of the army when they came to join with
them, and filled all the army with fear and disorder. There was the
son of M. Cato slain, valiantly fighting amongst the lusty youths.
For, notwithstanding that he was very weary, and overharried, yet
would he not therefore flee, but manfully fighting and laying about
him, telling aloud his name, and also his father's name, at length he
was beaten down amongst many other dead bodies of his enemies,
which he had slain round about him. So there were slain in the
field, all the chiefest gentlemen and nobility that were in his army:
who valiantly ran into any danger, to save Brutus' life.

50    Amongst them there was one of Brutus' friends called Lucilius,
who seeing a troop of barbarous men making no reckoning of all
men else they met in their way, but going all together right against
Brutus, he determined to stay them with the hazard of his life, and
being left behind, told them that he was Brutus: and because they
should believe him, he prayed them to bring him to Antonius, for
he said he was afraid of Caesar, and that he did trust Antonius
better. These barbarous men being very glad of this good hap, and
thinking themselves happy men, they carried him in the night, and
sent some before unto Antonius, to tell him of their coming. He
was marvellous glad of it, and went out to meet them that brought

him. Others also understanding of it, that they had brought Brutus prisoner, they came out of all parts of the camp to see him, some pitying his hard fortune, and others saying that it was not done like himself so cowardly to be taken alive of the barbarous people, for fear of death. When they came near together, Antonius stayed a while, bethinking himself how he should use Brutus. In the meantime Lucilius was brought to him, who stoutly with a bold countenance said: 'Antonius, I dare assure thee, that no enemy hath taken, nor shall take Marcus Brutus alive: and I beseech God keep him from that fortune. For wheresoever he be found, alive or dead, he will be found like himself. And now for myself, I am come unto thee, having deceived these men of arms here, bearing them down that I was Brutus: and do not refuse to suffer any torment thou wilt put me to.' Lucilius' words made them all amazed that heard him. Antonius on the other side, looking upon all them that had brought him, said unto them: 'My companions, I think ye are sorry you have failed of your purpose, and that you think this man hath done you great wrong: but I do assure you, you have taken a better booty, than that you followed. For, instead of an enemy, you have brought me a friend: and for my part, if you had brought me Brutus alive, truly I cannot tell what I should have done to him. For, I had rather have such men my friends, as this man here, than enemies.' Then he embraced Lucilius, and at that time delivered him to one of his friends in custody, and Lucilius ever after served him faithfully, even to his death.

51 Now Brutus having passed a little river, walled in on either side with high rocks, and shadowed with great trees, being then dark night, he went no further, but stayed at the foot of a rock with certain of his captains and friends that followed him: and looking up to the firmament that was full of stars, sighing he rehearsed two verses, of the which Volumnius wrote the one, to this effect:

> Let not the wight from whom this mischief went
> (O Jove) escape without due punishment.

And saith that he had forgotten the other. Within a little while after, naming his friends that he had seen slain in battle before his eyes, he fetched a greater sigh than before: specially, when he came to name Labio and Flavius, of the which the one was his lieutenant, and the other, captain of the pioneers of his camp. In the meantime, one of

the company being athirst, and seeing Brutus athirst also, he ran to
the river for water, and brought it in his sallet. At the selfsame time
they heard a noise on the other side of the river. Whereupon
Volumnius took Dardanus, Brutus' servant with him, to see what it
was: and returning straight again, asked if there were any water left.
Brutus smiling, gently told them all was drunk, 'But they shall bring
you some more.' Thereupon he sent him again that went for water
before, who was in great danger of being taken by the enemies, and
hardly scaped, being sore hurt. Furthermore, Brutus thought that
there was no great number of men slain in battle, and to know the
truth of it, there was one called Statilius, that promised to go
through his enemies (for otherwise it was impossible to go see their
camp) and from thence if all were well, that he would lift up a
torchlight in the air, and then return again with speed to him. The
torchlight was lift up as he had promised, for Statilius went thither.
Now Brutus seeing Statilius tarry long after that, and that he came
not again, he said: 'If Statilius be alive, he will come again.' But his
evil fortune was such, that as he came back, he lighted in his
enemies' hands, and was slain.

52   Now, the night being far spent, Brutus as he sat bowed
towards Clitus one of his men, and told him somewhat in his ear:
the other answered him not, but fell a-weeping. Thereupon he
proved Dardanus, and said somewhat also to him: at length he came
to Volumnius himself, and speaking to him in Greek, prayed him
for the studies' sake which brought them acquainted together, that
he would help him to put his hand to his sword, to thrust it in him
to kill him. Volumnius denied his request, and so did many others:
and amongst the rest, one of them said, there was no tarrying for
them there, but that they must needs fly. Then Brutus rising up,
'We must fly indeed,' said he, 'but it must be with our hands, not
with our feet.' Then taking every man by the hand, he said these
words unto them with a cheerful countenance: 'It rejoiceth my
heart that not one of my friends has failed me at my need, and I do
not complain of my fortune, but only for my country's sake: for, as
for me, I think myself happier than they that have overcome,
considering that I leave a perpetual fame of our courage and
manhood, the which our enemies the conquerors shall never attain
unto by force nor money, neither can let their posterity to say, that

they being naughty and unjust men, have slain good men, to usurp tyrannical power not pertaining to them.' Having said so, he prayed every man to shift for themselves, and then he went a little aside with two or three only, among the which Strato was one, with whom he came first acquainted by the study of rhetoric. He came as near to him as he could, and taking his sword by the hilts with both his hands, and falling down upon the point of it, ran himself through. Others say, that not he, but Strato (at his request) held the sword in his hand, and turned his head aside, and that Brutus fell down upon it: and so ran himself through, and died presently.

53 Messala, that had been Brutus' great friend, became afterwards Octavius Caesar's friend. So, shortly after, Caesar being at good leisure, he brought Strato, Brutus' friend, unto him, and weeping said: 'Caesar, behold, here is he that did the last service to my Brutus.' Caesar welcomed him at that time, and afterwards he did him as faithful service in all his affairs, as any Grecian else he had about him, until the battle of Actium. It is reported also, that this Messala himself answered Caesar one day, when he gave him great praise before his face, that he had fought valiantly, and with great affection for him, at the battle of Actium (notwithstanding that he had been his cruel enemy before, at the battle of Philippes, for Brutus' sake): 'I ever loved,' said he, 'to take the best and justest part.' Now, Antonius having found Brutus' body, he caused it to be wrapped up in one of the richest coat armours he had. Afterwards also, Antonius understanding that this coat armour was stolen, he put the thief to death that had stolen it, and sent the ashes of his body unto Servilia his mother. And for Porcia, Brutus' wife, Nicolaus the philosopher and Valerius Maximus do write, that she determining to kill herself (her parents and friends carefully looking to her to keep her from it) took hot burning coals, and cast them into her mouth, and kept her mouth so close, that she choked herself. There was a letter of Brutus found written to his friends, complaining of their negligence, that his wife being sick, they would not help her, but suffered her to kill herself, choosing to die, rather than to languish in pain. Thus it appeareth, that Nicolaus knew not well that time, since the letter (at the least if it were Brutus' letter) doth plainly declare the disease and love of this lady, and also the manner of her death.

## Comparison of Dion with Brutus

To come now to compare these two noble personages together, it is certain that both of them having had great gifts in them (and specially Dion), of small occasions they made themselves great men: and therefore Dion of both deserveth chiefest praise. For, he had no co-helper to bring him unto that greatness, as Brutus had of Cassius: who doubtless was not comparable unto Brutus, for virtue and respect of honour, though otherwise in matters of war, he was no less wise and valiant than he. For many do impute unto Cassius, the first beginning and original of all the war and enterprise: and said it was he that did encourage Brutus, to conspire Caesar's death: where Dion furnished himself with armour, ships and soldiers, and won those friends and companions also that did help him, to prosecute his war. Nor he did not as Brutus, who rose to greatness by his enterprises, and by war got all his strength and riches. But he in contrary manner, spent of his own goods to make war for the liberty of his country, and disbursed of his own money, that should have kept him in his banishment. Furthermore, Brutus and Cassius were compelled of necessity to make wars, because they could not have lived safely in peace, when they were driven out of Rome, for that they were condemned to death, and pursued by their enemies. And for this cause therefore they were driven to hazard themselves in war, more for their own safety, than for the liberty of their countrymen. Whereas Dion on the other side, living more merrily and safely in his banishment, than the tyrant Dionysius himself that had banished him, did put himself to that danger, to deliver Sicily from bondage.

2    Now the matter was not alike unto the Romans, to be delivered from the government of Caesar, as it was for the Syracusans, to be rid of Dionysius' tyranny. For Dionysius denied not, that he was not a tyrant, having filled Sicily with such misery and calamity.

Howbeit Caesar's power and government when it came to be established, did indeed much hurt at his first entry and beginning unto those that did resist him: but afterwards, unto them that being overcome had received his government, it seemed he rather had the name and opinion only of a tyrant, than otherwise that he was so indeed. For there never followed any tyrannical nor cruel act, but contrarily, it seemed that he was a merciful physician, whom God had ordained of special grace to be governor of the empire of Rome, and to set all things again at quiet stay, the which required the counsel and authority of an absolute prince. And therefore the Romans were marvellous sorry for Caesar after he was slain, and afterwards would never pardon them that had slain him. On the other side, the cause why the Syracusans did most accuse Dion, was because he did let Dionysius escape out of the castle of Syracusa, and because he did not overthrow and deface the tomb of his father.

3    Furthermore, touching the wars: Dion always showed himself a captain unreprovable, having wisely and skilfully taken order for those things which he had enterprised of his own head and counsel: and did amend the faults others committed, and brought things to better state than he found them. Where it seemeth, that Brutus did not wisely to receive the second battle, considering his rest stood upon it. For, after he had lost the battle, it was impossible for him ever to rise again: and therefore his heart failed him, and so gave up all, and never durst strive with his evil fortune as Pompey did, considering that he had present cause enough in the field to hope of his soldiers, and being beside a dreadful lord of all the sea over. Furthermore, the greatest reproach they could object against Brutus, was that Julius Caesar having saved his life, and pardoned all the prisoners also taken in battle, as many as he had made request for, taking him for his friend, and honouring him above all his other friends, Brutus notwithstanding had imbrued his hands in his blood, wherewith they could never reprove Dion. For on the contrary side, so long as Dion was Dionysius' friend and kinsman, he did always help him to order and govern his affairs. But after he was banished his country, and that his wife was forcibly married to another man, and his goods also taken from him, then he entered into just and open wars against Dionysius the tyrant. But in this point, they were contrary together. For wherein their chiefest

praise consisted, to wit, in hating of tyrants and wicked men, it is most true that Brutus' desire was most sincere of both. For having no private cause of complaint or grudge against Caesar, he ventured to kill him, only to set his country again at liberty. Where if Dion had not received private cause of quarrel against Dionysius, he would never have made war with him. The which Plato proveth in his *Epistles*, where is plainly seen, that Dion being driven out of the tyrant's court against his will, and not putting himself to voluntary banishment, he drove out Dionysius. Furthermore, the respect of the commonwealth caused Brutus, that before was Pompey's enemy, to become his friend, and enemy unto Caesar, that before was his friend, only referring his friendship and enmity unto the consideration of justice and equity. And Dion did many things for Dionysius' sake and benefit, all the while he trusted him: and when he began to mistrust him, then for anger he made war with him. Wherefore all his friends did not believe, but after he had driven out Dionysius, he would stablish the government to himself, flattering the people with a more courteous and gentle title than the name of a tyrant. But for Brutus, his very enemies themselves confessed, that of all those that conspired Caesar's death, he only had no other end and intent to attempt his enterprise, but to restore the empire of Rome again, to her former state and government.

4 And furthermore, it was not all one thing to deal with Dionysius, as it was to have to do with Julius Caesar. For no man that knew Dionysius, but would have despised him, considering that he spent the most part of his time in drinking, dicing, and in haunting lewd women's company. But to have undertaken to destroy Julius Caesar, and not to have shrunk back for fear of his great wisdom, power, and fortune, considering that his name only was dreadful unto every man, and also not to suffer the kings of Parthia and India to be in rest for him, this could not come but of a marvellous noble mind of him, that for fear never fainted, nor let fall any part of his courage. And therefore, so soon as Dion came into Sicilia, many thousands of men came and joined with him, against Dionysius. But the fame of Julius Caesar did set up his friends again after his death, and was of such force, that it raised a young stripling, Octavius Caesar (that had no means nor power of himself), to be one of the greatest men of Rome: and they used him

as a remedy to encounter Antonius' malice and power. And if men will say, that Dion drove out the tyrant Dionysius with force of arms, and sundry battles: and that in contrary manner Brutus slew Caesar, being a naked man, and without guard, then do I answer again, that it was a noble part, and of a wise captain, to choose so apt a time and place, to come upon a man of so great power, and to find him naked without his guard. For he went not suddenly in a rage, and alone, or with a small company, to assail him: but his enterprise was long time before determined of, and that with divers men, of all the which, not a man of them once failed him: but it is rather to be thought, that from the beginning he chose them honest men, or else that by his choice of them, he made them good men. Whereas Dion, either from the beginning made no wise choice in trusting of evil men, or else because he could not tell how to use them he had chosen, of good men he made them become evil, so that neither the one nor the other could be the part of a wise man. For Plato himself reproveth him, for that he had chosen such men for his friends, that he was slain by them, and after he was slain, no man would then revenge his death.

5   And in contrary manner, of the enemies of Brutus, the one (who was Antonius) gave his body honourable burial: and Octavius Caesar the other, reserved his honours and memories of him. For at Millayne (a city of Gaul on Italy side) there was an image of his in brass, very like unto him: the which Caesar afterwards passing that way, beheld very advisedly, for that it was made by an excellent workman, and was very like him, and so went his way. Then he stayed suddenly again, and called for the governors of the city, and before them all told them, that the citizens were his enemies, and traitors unto him, because they kept an enemy of his among them. The governors of the city at the first were astonished at it, and stoutly denied it: and none of them knowing what enemy he meant, one of them looked on another. Octavius Caesar then turning him unto Brutus' statue, bending his brows, said unto them: 'This man you see standing up here, is he not our enemy?' Then the governors of the city were worse afraid than before, and could not tell what answer to make him. But Caesar laughing, and commending the Gauls for their faithfulness to their friends, even in their adversities, he was contented Brutus' image should stand still as it did.

# GLOSSARY OF PROPER NAMES

Abulites – Abouletes
Acradina, Acradine – Achradina
Adallas – Sadalas
Adimantus – Adeimantus
Aeges – Aegae
Aegestaeans – Egestaeans
Aegines – Aegina
Aemylius – Aemilius
Aemylius Paulus – Aemilius
  Paullus
Aenobarbus – Ahenobarbus
Aeques – Aequi
Aeschilus – Aeschylus
Aeschynes – Aeschines
Agartharchus – Agatharchus
Agnon – Hagnon
Aigles – Aigle
Alesandropolis – Alexandropolis
Alexia – Alesia
Amathunta – Amathus
Ambrons – Ambrones
Aminias – Ameinias
Amphisse – Amphissa
Andramettin – Adramyttium
Anienes – Anienus
Anius – Aous
Antheus – Antaeus
Antigona – Antigone
Antigones – Antigonus
Antiliban – Antilibanus
Antiopa – Antiope

Antoniade – Antonias
Aphidnes – Aphidnae
Apollonide – Apollonis
Appolonides – Apollonides
Appolonius – Apollonius
Apuglia, Apulglia – Apulia
Arbeles – Arbela
Archadia – Arcadia
Archilocus – Archilochus
Argus – Argo
Aridaeus – Arrhidaeus
Ariston – Aristus
Arpos – Arpinum
Arrius – Areius
Aruntius – Arruntius
Arymbas – Arybas
Ascalona – Ascalon
Aspende – Aspendos
Astiochus – Astyochus
Atellius – Atillius
Athesis – Atiso
Atho – Athos
Atrius – Atreus
Atteius – Ateius

Baies – Baiae
Balinus – Cebalinus
Bardiaeians – Bardyaeans
Bardillis – Bardyllis
Batabaces – Bataces
Battes – Battiadae

Bellaeus – Belaeus
Benevento – Beneventum
Berrhoea, Berroea – Beroea
Bizatines – Byzantines
Blancbourg – *a French translation
of* leuce kome *(white village)*
Boles – Bola
Bolonia – Bononia
Bottieians – Bottiaeans
Brigas – Briges
Brundusium – Brundisium
Bucephal – Bucephalus
Buthrotus – Buthrotum
Bythinia – Bithynia

Cabrias – Chabrias
Cadmia – Cadmeia
Caiete – Caieta
Calcide – Chalcis
Calistratus – Callistratus
Calphurnius, Calphurnia –
Calpurnius, Calpurnia
Camarine – Camerina
Camulatius – Camulatus
Carres – Carrhae
Cassandra, Cassandria –
Cassandreia
Catilin, Catline – Catiline
Catulus Luctatius – Lutatius
Catulus
Celaenes – Celaenae
Cenchrees – Cenchreae
Ceo – Ceos
Chalcidonians – Chalcidians
Chalcodus – Chalcodon
Charibdis – Charybdis
Charmion – Charmian
Chelidonida – Chilonis
Cherronesus – Chersonnesus
Cholchide – Colchis
Chio – Chios
Cimbres – Cimbri
Circe – Circaeum

Circees – Circeii
Cizicum, Cizycum – Cyzicus
Clazomenes – Clazomenae
Cleones – Cleonae
Cneus Pompey – Cnaeus
Pompey
Comagena – Commagene
Corcyriaeians – Corcyraeans
Corioles – Corioli
Cossaeians – Cossaeans
Cranon – Crannon
Creta – Crete
Crotona – Croton
Cyndes – Quinda
Cyrrestica – Cyrrhestica
Cytheride – Cytheris
Cytheron – Cithaeron

Danubie, Danuby – Danube
Dason – Daesius
Deion – Dion
Delphes – Delphi
Demarathus, Demartus –
Demaratus
Demetriade – Demetrias
Dexius – Dexous
Dicaearcus, Dicearchus –
Dicaearchus
Diddius – Didius
Diopithes – Diopeithes
Dino – Deinon
Doride – Doris
Dromichetes – Dromichaetes
Dyrrachium – Dyrrhachium

Eleusin – Eleusis
Eleutheres – Eleutherae
Elide – Elis
Epicurian – Epicurean
Epidaurum – Epidaurus
Epipoles, Epipolis – Epipolae
Erichtheus, Erichtheides –
Erechtheus, Erechtheides

Erix – Eryx
Euritus – Eurytus

Faonius – Favonius
Fidena – Fidenae
Formio – Phormio

Gabinius – Vatinius
Gausameles – Gaugamela
Genuoa – Genoa
Gnidos, Gnidians – Cnidos,
  Cnidians
Gnosus – Knossos
Gomphes – Gomphi
Grotonians – Crotonians

Hales – Halae
Halonesus – Halonnesus
Halycarnassus – Halicarnassus
Hellicon, Helycon – Helicon
Heraclides – Heraclidae
Herodes – Herod
Hephestion – Hephaestion
Hesiodus – Hesiod
Hillus – Hyllus
Hipsus – Ipsus
Hircius – Hirtius
Hister – Ister
Hybraeas – Hybreas
Hyppolita – Hippolyta

Ianiculum – Janiculum
Iliades – Iliad
Ilotes – Helots
Ioppa – Iope
Ipes – Usipes
Ischnes – Ichnae
Iuba – Juba
Iugurthe – Jugurtha
Iulide – Iulis
Iuno – Juno
Iusteius – Insteius

Labio – Labeo
Laciades – Laciadae
Lamea – Lamia
Lamiacus – Lamian
Lampryas – Lamprias
Lebethres – Leibethra
Lemachus – Lamachus
Leonatus – Leonnatus
Leotychides – Leotychidas
Leuctres – Leuctra
Levinus – Laevinus
Licymmias – Licymnius
Ligdamis – Lygdamis
Locres – Locri
Lucium – Lyceum
Luke – Lucca, Lucania
Lybia – Libya
Lycaeians – Lycaeans
Lyssus – Lissus

Magarians – Megarians
Manchus – Malchus
Manius Acilius – Manius
  Aquillius
Mantinians – Mantineans
Mardian – Mardion
Marselles – Marseilles
Marssilians – Massalians
Mazeus – Mazaeus
Megabizus – Megabyzus
Megalipolis – Megalopolis
Megares – Megara
Melia – Melos
Menda – Mende
Menitide – Temenitid
Menynge – Meninx
Meotia – Maeotis
Messena – Messene
Miletum – Miletus
Milesius – Milesias
Millayne – Milan (Mediolanum)
Minturnes – Minturnae
Misena, Misene – Misenum

Molosside – Molossia
Monaezes – Monaeses
Munichea, Munichya,
  Munychea – Munichia
Munichion – Mounychion
Muraena – Murena

Nabathaeians, Nabatheians –
  Nabataeans
Nicea – Nicaea
Nisea – Nisaea
Noe – Noah
Nylus – Nile

Oplacus – Oplax
Oraesus – Oryssus
Orossus – Rhosus

Pamphilia – Pamphylia
Pargamenians – Pergamenes
Peribaea – Periboea
Perinthe – Perinthus
Petelie – Petelia
Pexodorus – Pixodarus
Pitheus – Pittheus
Phaenicians – Phoenicians
Phalerus – Phalerum
Phaonius – Favonius
Phar – Pharos
Pharsalia – Pharsalus
Phenicia, Phenicians –
  Phoenicia, Phoenicians
Pherebaea – Phereboea
Pherecides – Pherecydes
Philager – Philagros
Philarchus – Phylarchus
Phillina – Philinna
Philippes – Philippi
Phillius – Phyllius
Phocide – Phocis
Photinus – Potheinus
Phraortes – Phraates
Phrynicus – Phrynichus
Phyladelphus – Philadelphus

Pidna – Pydna
Piraea – Piraeus
Piraica – of Piraeus
Pisa – Piso
Pithia – Pythia
Plataeians, Plateians – Plataeans
Plistarchus – Pleistarchus
Pnyce – Pnyx
Polyzelios – Polyzelus
Pomponious Atticus –
  Pomponius Atticus
Pont, Ponte – Pontus
Popilius – Popillius
Popilius Laena – Popilius
  Laenus
Posideon – Poseideon
Pothinus – Potheinus
Prescque – *an error: from
  presque-isle, peninsula*
Proconesus – Proconnesus
Ptaeodorus – Ptoeodorus
Ptolemaeide – Ptolemais
Ptolome, Ptolomie, Ptolomy –
  Ptolemy
Pyle – Pylos
Pyndarus – Pindarus
Pynepsion – Pyanepsion
Pyrra – Pyrrha
Pyrrides – Pyrrhides
Pyrrus – Pyrrhus

Radamanthus – Rhadamanthus
Rheggio, Rhegio – Rhegium
Roesaces – Rhoesaces
Rubico – Rubicon

Sabynes – Sabines
Sacculio – Saculio
Salamina – Salamis
Sardianians – Sardians
Scotusa – Scotussa
Selybrea, Selybrianians –
  Selymbria, Selymbrians

Sequanes – Sequani
Servilius Hala – Servilius Ahala
Sicinius – Sicinnius
Sicyone – Sicyon
Sinnaces – Sinnaca
Sinnis – Sinis
Sisimethres – Sisimithres
Soles – Soli
Sossius Senecio – Sosius
    Senecio
Spacteria – Sphacteria
Sperchius – Spercheius
Spurius Melius – Spurius
    Maelius
Stagyra – Stageira
Statilius – Statyllius
Statira – Stateira
Stira – Steiris
Straebus – Stroebus
Sulpitius Galba – Sulpicius
    Galba
Suse – Susa
Swevians – Suevians
Sycione – Sicyon
Sylla – Sulla
Syllanus – Silanus
Syracusa – Syracuse

Talassius – Talasius
Tarquine – Tarquin
Terracine – Terracina
Tesmophoria – Thesmophoria
Tharrytas – Tharrypas
Tharsis – Tarsus
Thassos – Thasos
Theorides – Theoris
Thermopiles, Thermopyles –
    Thermopylae

Thesmophores – Thesmophoria
Thespis – Thespiae
Thessalie – Thessaly
Thesta – Theste
Thrasibulus – Thrasybulus
Thuries – Thurii
Thuscan, Thuscane – Tuscan,
    Tuscany
Thusculum – Tusculum
Thyreatide – Thyreatis
Thyreus – Thyrsus
Tinnius – Titinnius
Tireus – Teireus
Tisaphernes – Tissaphernes
Titinnius – Titinius
Trachina – Trachis
Troia, Troie, Troya – Troy
Troiade – Troas
Tyber – Tiber
Tyndarus – Tyndareus
Tyr – Tyre
Tyro – Tiro

Veies – Veii
Velitres – Velitrae
Vercingentorix – Vercingetorix
Verselles – Vercellae
Vibius Piciacus – Vibius
    Paciacus
Volsces – Volsci

Xanthum – Xanthus
Xoutus – Xanthus

Zacynthe – Zacynthus